IDG BOOKS

PC World Excel 4 for W...

Overview

You issue commands to Excel via the menu bar, by clicking a toolbar icon, or by pressing a shortcut key combination. If the command operates on a range, select the range before issuing the command. If a range or graphic object is selected, you can press the right mouse button to access a shortcut menu. To access the menu bar without a mouse, press F10 or Alt and then press the key that corresponds to the underlined letter in a command (or use the arrow keys to traverse the menus and press Enter to issue a command).

Tip: Lotus 1-2-3 users can find the equivalent Excel command by selecting the Help ⇨ Lotus 1-2-3 command. Enter the 1-2-3 keystrokes and Excel demonstrates the equivalent commands and performs the action for you.

Note: This card is by no means a comprehensive listing of Excel's features. For more information and additional shortcuts, consult the on-line help system.

Basic Operations

Create a new file	File ⇨ New, specify type of document
Open an existing file	File ⇨ Open (or Ctrl+F12), type or select document name
Import a file from another application	File ⇨ Open, type or select document name
Save a file	File ⇨ Save, or Shift+F12
Save a file with new name	File ⇨ Save As (or F12), enter new name
Close a file	File ⇨ Close
Print a worksheet or chart	File ⇨ Print, or Ctrl+Shift+F12
Undo last action	Edit ⇨ Undo, or Alt+Backspace
Access on-line help	Help, or press F1 or Shift+F1
Quit Excel	File ⇨ Exit, or Alt+F4

Getting Around

Move to a specific cell	Click on the cell. Or Formula ⇨ Goto (or F5), then enter cell reference
Move one screen vertically	PgUp, PgDn, or click on vertical scroll bar
Move one screen horizontally	Tab, Shift+Tab, or click on horizontal scroll bars
Move an amount relative to size of worksheet	Drag scroll bar button
Go to end of range vertically	Ctrl+up arrow or Ctrl+down arrow (or End, followed by arrow key)
Go to end of range horizontally	Ctrl+right arrow or Ctrl+left arrow (or End, followed by arrow key)
Go to cell A1	Ctrl+Home
Go to last active cell	Ctrl+End
Switch to another open Excel document	Window, then click document
Switch to the next open document	Ctrl+F6

Note: Excel analyzes what you enter into a cell and makes it a value, label, date, or formula based on the contents. When entering or editing a cell, use Del and Backspace to erase.

Enter a numeric value	Type the number, with or without dollar signs, comma, percent sign, and so on
Enter a label	Type the text; for a label that looks like a value, start with = and use quotes; for example, ="1992" is a label
Enter a formula	Start with = and enter cell references, values and functions
Edit a cell	Select cell and then click in formula bar or press F2; make changes, then press Enter or click check mark icon
Cancel cell editing	Esc, or click X icon
Erase a cell or range	Make selection, then Edit ⇨ Delete (or Del key); choose All to erase everything
Move a cell or range	Make selection, then Edit ⇨ Cut (or Ctrl+X); move to new location, then Edit ⇨ Paste (or Ctrl+V)
Toggle between insert to overwrite mode	Ins
Define a range name	Select range, then Formula ⇨ Define Name
Copy cell to adjacent cells	Select the cell and range to copy it to; then Edit ⇨ Fill Right or Edit ⇨ Fill Down. Or drag the lower-right corner of the source cell to the target range

Making Selections

Select a contiguous range	Drag over range with mouse; or hold down Shift and use arrow keys
Select a noncontiguous range	Hold Ctrl while you drag over multiple ranges; or press Shift F8 and make selections
Select a graphic object	Click on the object; hold down Ctrl to make a multiple selection

Formatting Data

Note: The following commands apply to the current selection (either a cell or range). Many formatting commands are also available on toolbars.

Numeric formatting	Format ⇨ Number
Change font or size	Format ⇨ Font
Change alignment within a cell	Format ⇨ Alignment
Change color of cell contents	Format ⇨ Font
Change background color or pattern in cell	Format ⇨ Patterns
Add border around cell or range	Format ⇨ Border

MW01490477

IDG BOOKS

PC World Excel 4 for Windows Handbook

Adjusting Windows

Fill the screen with one document	Click the title bar maximize button (upward arrow)
Make a window an icon	Click the title bar minimize button (downward arrow)
Return a window to its previous size	Click the title bar restore button (two arrows)
See multiple windows on-screen	Window ⇨ Arrange
Zoom window larger or smaller	Window ⇨ Zoom
Move a nonmaximized window	Click on title bar and drag windows
Resize a nonmaximized window	Click window border and drag to desired size

Adjusting the Worksheet

Insert one or more new columns	Click column letter(s), Edit ⇨ Insert.
Insert one or more new rows	Click row number(s), Edit ⇨ Insert
Delete one or more columns	Click column letter(s), Edit ⇨ Delete
Delete one or more rows	Click row number(s), Edit ⇨ Delete
Change column width	Format ⇨ Column Width, or drag column border in column heading
Change row height	Format ⇨ Row Height, or drag row border in row heading.
Remove grid from screen display	Options ⇨ Display, uncheck Gridlines.

Toolbars

Note: The Standard toolbar is one of seven included with Excel. In addition, you can create custom toolbars that contain the icons you use most frequently or that you use with certain tasks.

Find out what a tool does	Click on the icon, but drag the mouse pointer away before releasing
Execute a tool	Click the appropriate icon
Customize a toolbar	Options ⇨ Toolbars and then Customize option (or right-click on any toolbar).

Databases

Define a range as a database	Select data and then Data ⇨ Set Database
Enter new data in a database	Data ⇨ Form (after defining database)
Search for data	Data ⇨ Form (after defining database), enter criteria in fields; or use Formula ⇨ Find without defining a database
Sort data	Select range and then Data ⇨ Sort

Printing

Note: Changes made using File ⇨ Page Setup are stored with the worksheet and revert to their default values when you create a new worksheet.

Print/remove cell gridlines	File ⇨ Page Setup
Print/remove worksheet frame	File ⇨ Page Setup
Add page numbers	File ⇨ Page Setup. Click Header or Footer button and then click the # icon.
Change scaling of printed output	File ⇨ Page Setup
Ignore colors when printing	File ⇨ Page Setup
Change paper orientation	File ⇨ Page Setup
Preview output before printing	File ⇨ Print Preview
Change margins	File ⇨ Page Setup. Or File ⇨ Print Preview, click Margins button and adjust margins dynamically by dragging

Charting

Note: Typically, you can modify any aspect of a chart by right-clicking on it to bring up a shortcut menu specific to the chart component.

Create a chart	Select data, then File ⇨ New (with Chart option); or press F11; or use ChartWizard tool
Change a chart's type	Gallery command; or use Chart toolbar
Print a chart	File ⇨ Print (from a chart window)
Add a chart to a worksheet	In chart window, Chart ⇨ Select Chart and then Edit ⇨ Copy; move to worksheet and then Edit ⇨ Paste; adjust size and location by dragging
Rotate a 3-D chart	Format ⇨ 3-D View, or right-click on axis and use mouse to drag a corner

Macros

Note: Macros are stored in macro sheets, not worksheets. You can store general-purpose macros on the "global" macro sheet that Excel manages. For macros not stored on the global macro sheet, the macro sheet must be loaded before you can execute the macro. Macros in 1-2-3 worksheets can be executed by pressing Ctrl+ the macro name (for example, Ctrl+Z to execute \Z macro).

Record a macro	Macro ⇨ Record; stop recording with Macro ⇨ Stop Recorder
Execute a macro	Macro ⇨ Run, or use Ctrl+ a defined macro shortcut key
Edit a macro	Activate the macro sheet and use normal worksheet editing commands
Name a macro	In a macro sheet, Formula ⇨ Define Name
Stop a macro in progress	Esc or Ctrl+Break.

IDG Expert Authors in Action

Expert authors who are both specialists in their technology field and writers of proven ability allow IDG Books to be consistently rated the best books in their category. John Walkenbach led the InfoWorld Test Center review team for *InfoWorld* magazine's benchmark review of Excel 4 for Windows. Already an acknowledged spreadsheet guru, Walkenbach brings to this all-new PC World Handbook both inside information and enthusiasm, making this book the perfect companion for mastering Excel 4 for Windows.

REPORT CARD **INFO WORLD**

Report Card

WINDOWS
SPREADSHEET

Microsoft Excel

VERSION 4.0

Criterion	(Weighting)	Score
Performance		
Formulas/analysis	(100)	Excellent
Compatibility	(50)	Excellent
Speed	(75)	Very Good
Database	(75)	Excellent
Graphics	(100)	Excellent
Output	(75)	Excellent
Macros	(50)	Excellent
Consolidation/linking	(50)	Excellent
Capacity	(50)	Excellent
Networkability	(50)	Very Good
Documentation	(50)	Very Good
Ease of learning	(50)	Excellent
Ease of use	(75)	Excellent
Support		
Support policies	(25)	Very Good
Technical support	(25)	Satisfactory
Value	(100)	Excellent
Final score		**9.3**

PC World Handbooks
Expert Information at Your Fingertips

PC World Handbooks are authorized by PC World, the magazine trusted by over a million readers each month as their most authoritative guide to DOS and Windows desktop computing. The Handbooks are perfect for readers who need a complete tutorial of features as well as a reference to software applications and operating systems.

Get the inside scoop on the world of computers with IDG Books Authorized Editions. Behind every Authorized Edition from IDG Books stands the expertise and authority of the world's largest publisher of information on computers and electronic technology. In addition to over 180 computer magazines worldwide, IDG Books has assets including the InfoWorld Test Center, a $5 million product performance, quality, and compatibility laboratory; and IDC, the world's largest market research company dedicated to information technology. These resources give IDG Books and its expert authors hands-on expertise about the latest hardware and software products and sophisticated insight into future technology trends.

IDG BOOKS

Authorized Editions from IDG Books

Whether you are looking for an introductory users guide
that emphasizes productivity or an expert's advice on maximizing performance,
look to the Authorized Editions from IDG Books.

PC WORLD

Excel 4
FOR Windows

Handbook

By
John Walkenbach and
David Maguiness

IDG BOOKS

IDG Books Worldwide, Inc.
An International Data Group Company
San Mateo, California 94402

PC World Excel 4 for Windows Handbook
Published by
IDG Books Worldwide, Inc.
An International Data Group Company
155 Bovet Road, Suite 610
San Mateo, CA 94402
415-312-0650

Library of Congress Catalog Card No.: 92-71237

ISBN 1-878058-46-0

Printed in the United States of America

10 9 8 7 6 5 4 3 2

Distributed in the United States by IDG Books Worldwide, Inc.

Distributed in Canada by Macmillan of Canada, a Division of Canada Publishing Corporation; by Woodslane Pty. Ltd. in Australia; and by Computer Bookshops in the U.K.

For information on translations and availability in other countries, contact Marc Jeffrey Mikulich, Foreign Rights Manager, at IDG Books Worldwide. Fax: 415-358-1260.

For sales inquiries and special prices for bulk quantities, write to the address above or call IDG Books Worldwide at 415-312-0650.

Dedication

DM — To Karen and Kyle

Acknowledgments

We wrote the bulk of this book over a 12-week period. During that time, this project pretty much dominated my life. Since I also have a full-time job, I did my writing on evenings, weekends, holidays, and even used up quite a bit of my vacation time to meet the aggressive deadlines. Special thanks to Joice for holding down the fort during my intensive three-month affair with my EPS 486/33. Now I finally understand what the term "get a life" means. Dave Maguiness was an excellent coauthor, and I hope we'll work together again (and maybe even meet each other some day). Sincere thanks to the folks at Microsoft — specifically Mark Kroese and Joan Morse in Product Management — and all the members of the Excel 4 development team (none of whom I've met). I've never seen cleaner and more stable beta versions of any software, and I truly believe this is the best spreadsheet product that's ever seen the light of day. And thanks to Sandra Pace at Waggener Edstrom for her help throughout the process. I'd also like to thank Dan Fylstra from Frontline Systems for the information he provided me on Excel's Solver add-in. And I'm indebted to IDG Books for choosing me to work on this book. As usual, Janna Custer was a joy to work with, and I appreciated her encouraging words throughout the project. The IDG Books staff and University Graphics did their typical superb job in whipping this book into shape. Thanks also go to Steve Rath, who did a great job indexing and to Ray Valdés, who provided the thorough and accurate technical review (but I take responsibility for any errors that may have slipped through the cracks — unless they're Dave's fault). And here's to Mark Crowley, a coworker and pal who has always wanted to be mentioned in a book's acknowledgment section. Mark's the only person I know who still gets excited about Excel 2.1.

John Walkenbach

Many thanks to Janna Custer, Shirley Coe, and the entire IDG Production crew for making this book happen, and to my comrade-in-arms John Walkenbach for orchestrating the project and providing numerous disks and state-of-the-art technical advice. Special thanks to Karen, recent convert and now Windows expert, for minding the store while I blasted away at the computer. And a special note of gratitude to Terrie Solomon, for a once-in-a-lifetime opportunity and friendship through thick and thin.

David Maguiness

(The publisher would like to give special thanks to Patrick J. McGovern, without whom this book would not have been possible.)

About the Authors

John Walkenbach is a contributing editor for both *PC World* and *InfoWorld*, two of the country's leading personal computer publications. He has written more than 200 articles and software reviews for a variety of magazines and technical journals. He earned a Ph.D. in experimental psychology from the University of Montana, and has worked as an instructor, consultant, programmer, and most recently as market research manager for a large West Coast bank. Besides spreadsheets, John's interests include MIDI music, CD-ROM technology, multimedia, digital photography, and anything else that expands the functionality of his computer systems.

John's first exposure to electronic spreadsheets was VisiCalc, running on a 64K Apple II. He was fascinated by the concept and eventually saved enough from his meager graduate student earnings to buy one of the original model IBM PCs and a copy of Lotus 1-2-3. Since then, he has used virtually every spreadsheet product ever marketed for DOS and OS/2, including all versions of Excel. This is John's second book, which he wrote while living in San Diego. His first book, coauthored with Phillip Robinson, was the *PC World 1-2-3 for Windows Complete Handbook,* also available from IDG Books.

David Maguiness is a freelance writer who has written or co-written more than a dozen books about spreadsheets, including the *Macworld Guide to Excel.* He also contributes to *Lotus Magazine,* and was editor-in-chief of *Absolute Reference: The Journal for 1-2-3 and Symphony Users.* He earned B.S. and M.B.A. degrees in finance from Purdue and Miami (Ohio) universities, respectively. His financial analyst experience includes several Fortune 500 companies.

Dave's love affair with computers and spreadsheets began in 1981 while he was using MicroPlan running under CP/M on an Applied Digital Systems microcomputer. He was enjoying the demise of erasers, white-out, and adding machines to cross-foot totals and enthusiastically tackled SuperCalc, MultiPlan, 1-2-3 (all flavors), Symphony, Quattro Pro, and last but not least, Excel, while using just about every computer system ever conceived.

Production notes

John and Dave both used Microsoft Word for Windows (version 2.0, running under Windows 3.0) to write this book, making extensive use of the product's outlining and style features. The multitasking nature of Windows proved ideal, since the authors were able to run Excel and Word for Windows simultaneously and could copy actual formulas and examples from Excel directly into the document. After copy editing, the chapter files were imported into Microsoft Word for the Macintosh for formatting, and eventually the pages were laid out using Aldus PageMaker running on a Mac. The screen images were captured to TIFF files using Tiffany Plus.

Comments are welcome

We are interested in your comments about this book — good, bad, or otherwise. Did any sections, chapters, or subjects not get enough coverage? Did we dwell too long on certain topics? What did you find particularly valuable? Did you learn anything that you've been struggling with for years? We'd like to hear from you. Write to us in care of IDG Books Worldwide, 155 Bovet Road, Suite 610, San Mateo, CA 94402, or you can fill out the Reader Response questionnaire in the back of this book.

Credits

President and Publisher
John J. Kilcullen

Publishing Director
David Solomon

Project Editor
Janna Custer

Production Director
Lana J. Olson

Acquisitions Editor
Terrie Lynn Solomon

Contributing Editor
Sandra Blackthorn

Technical Reviewer
Ray Valdés, Sapphire Software

Copy Editor
Michael D. Welch

Editorial Assistant
Megg Bonar

Text Preparation
Shirley E. Coe
Dana Bryant Sadoff

Proofreading
Mary Ann Cordova

Indexer
Steve Rath

Book Design and Production
Peppy White
Francette Ytsma
(University Graphics, Palo Alto, California)

About IDG Books Worldwide

Welcome to the world of IDG Books Worldwide.

IDG Books Worldwide, Inc., is a division of International Data Group (IDG), the world's leading publisher of computer-related information and the leading global provider of information services on information technology. IDG publishes over 178 computer publications in more than 55 countries. Thirty million people read one or more IDG publications each month.

If you use personal computers, IDG Books is committed to publishing quality books that meet your needs. We rely on our extensive network of publications — including such leading periodicals as *PC World, InfoWorld, Computerworld, Macworld, Lotus, Publish, Network World,* and *SunWorld* — to help us make informed and timely decisions in creating useful computer books that meet your needs.

Every IDG book strives to bring extra value and skill-building instruction to the reader. Our books are written by experts, with the backing of IDG periodicals, and with careful thought devoted to issues such as audience, interior design, use of icons, and illustrations. Our editorial staff is a careful mix of high-tech journalists and experienced book people. Our close contact with the makers of computer products helps ensure accuracy and thorough coverage. Our heavy use of personal computers at every step in production means we can deliver books in the most timely manner.

We are delivering books of high quality at competitive prices on topics customers want. At IDG, we believe in quality and we have been delivering quality for 25 years. You'll find no better book on a subject than an IDG book.

John Kilcullen
President and Publisher
IDG Books Worldwide, Inc.

International Data Group's publications include: **ARGENTINA'S** Computerworld Argentina; **ASIA'S** Computerworld Hong Kong, Computerworld Southeast Asia, Computerworld Malaysia; **AUSTRALIA'S** Computerworld Australia, Australian PC World, Australian Macworld, Profit, Information Decisions, Reseller; **AUSTRIA'S** Computerwelt Oesterreich; **BRAZIL'S** DataNews, PC Mundo, Mundo IBM, Mundo Unix, Publish; **BULGARIA'S** Computerworld Bulgaria, Ediworld, PC World Express; **CANADA'S** ComputerData, Direct Access, Graduate Computerworld, InfoCanada, Network World Canada; **CHILE'S** Computerworld, Informatica; **COLUMBIA'S** Computerworld Columbia; **CZECHOSLOVAKIA'S** Computerworld Czechoslovakia, PC World Czechoslovakia; **DENMARK'S** CAD/CAM WORLD, Communications World, Computerworld Danmark, Computerworld Focus, Computerworld Uddannelse, LAN World, Lotus World, Macintosh Produktkatalog, Macworld Danmark, PC World Danmark, PC World Produktguide, Windows World; **EQUADOR'S** PC World; **EGYPT'S** PC World Middle East; **FINLAND'S** Mikro PC, Tietoviikko, Tietoverkko; **FRANCE'S** Computer Direct, Distributique, GOLDEN MAC, InfoPC, Languages & Systems, Le Guide du Monde Informatique, Le Monde Informatique, Telecoms & Reseaux International; **GERMANY'S** Computerwoche, Computerwoche Focus, Computerwoche Extra, Computerwoche Karriere, edv aspekte, Information Management, Lotus Welt, Macwelt, Netzwelt, PC Welt, PC Woche, Publish, Unit, Unix Welt; **GREECE'S** Infoworld, PC Games, PC World Greece; **HUNGARY'S** Computerworld SZT, Mikrovilag Magazin, PC World; **INDIA'S** Computers & Communications; **ISRAEL'S** Computerworld Israel, PC World Israel; **ITALY'S** Computerworld Italia, Macworld Italia, Networking Italia, PC World Italia; **JAPAN'S** Computerworld Japan, Macworld Japan, SunWorld Japan; **KOREA'S** Computerworld Korea, Macworld Korea, PC World Korea; **MEXICO'S** Compu Edicion, Compu Manufactura, Computacion/Punto de Venta, Computerworld Mexico, MacWorld, Mundo Unix, PC Journal, Windows; **THE NETHERLAND'S** Computer! Totaal, Computerworld Netherlands, LAN Magazine, MacWorld Magazine; **NEW ZEALAND'S** Computer Listings, Computerworld New Zealand, New Zealand PC World; **NIGERIA'S** PC World Africa; **NORWAY'S** Computerworld Norge, C/world, Lotusworld Norge, Macworld Norge, Networld, PC World Ekspress, PC World Norge, PC World's Product Guide, Publish World, Student Guiden, Unix World, Windowsworld, IDG Direct Response; **PERU'S** PC World; **PEOPLE'S REPUBLIC OF CHINA'S** China Computerworld, PC World China, Electronics International; **IDG HIGH TECH** Newproductworld; **PHILLIPPINE'S** Computerworld, PC World; **POLAND'S** Computerworld Poland, Komputer; **ROMANIA'S** InfoClub Magazine; **RUSSIA'S** Computerworld-Moscow, Networks, PC World; **SPAIN'S** Amiga World, Autoedicion, CIM World, Communicaciones World, Computerworld Espana, Macworld Espana, PC World Espana, Publish; **SWEDEN'S** Affarsekonomi Management, Attack, CAD/CAM World, ComputerSweden, Digital/Varlden, Lokala Natverk/LAN, Mikrodatorn, Lotus World, MAC&PC, Macworld, Mikrodatorn, PC World, Publish & Design (CAP), Unix/Oppna system, Datalngenjoren, Maxi Data, Windows; **SWITZERLAND'S** Computerworld Schweiz, Macworld Schweiz, PC & Workstation; **TAIWAN'S** Computerworld Taiwan, PC World Taiwan; **THAILAND'S** Thai Computerworld; **TURKEY'S** Computerworld Monitor, Macworld Turkiye, PC World Turkiye; **UNITED KINGDOM'S** Lotus Magazine, Macworld; **UNITED STATES'** AmigaWorld, Cable in the Classroom, CIO, Computer Buying World, Computerworld, Digital News, DOS Resource Guide, Electronic News, Federal Computer Week, GamePro, inCider/A+, IDG Books, InfoWorld, Lotus, Macworld, Momentum, MPC World, Network World, NeXTWORLD, PC Games, PC World, PC Letter, Publish, RUN, SunWorld, SWATPro; **VENEZUELA'S** Computerworld Venezuela, Micro-Computerworld Venezuela; **YUGOSLAVIA'S** Moj Mikro.

x

Contents at a Glance

Table of Contents

PART I

First Things First 9

PART II

The Basic Concepts 63

PART

III The Advanced Features 361

Chapter 19: Customizing Toolbars 363

Chapter 20: The Excel Add-Ins 383

PART

IV

Tables

Introduction

Welcome to the *PC World Excel 4 for Windows Handbook* — your personal guide to a powerful and easy-to-use spreadsheet.

This book is about Microsoft Excel 4. We think this is the best spreadsheet program on the market — bar none. The product has been around since 1985, and each subsequent release keeps getting better. Our goal is to share with you what we know about Excel and to make your job (and maybe even your life) easier.

The book contains everything you need to know to learn the basics of Excel and then move on to more advanced topics at your own pace. You'll find many useful examples, as well as some of the tips and techniques that we've accumulated over the years. The book can easily substitute for the printed material that's included with Excel 4, or augment it for those who are looking for more.

Is this book for you?

We wrote this book for beginning to intermediate users of Excel 4. We cover all of the essential components of Excel and provide clear examples that you can adapt to your own needs. Excel can be used at many levels — from the simple to the extremely complex. We think we've drawn a pretty good balance here, focusing on the topics that are most useful to the majority of users.

Yes — If you have no spreadsheet experience

If you're new to the world of spreadsheets, this book has everything you need to get started with Excel and then advance to other topics as the need arises.

Yes — If you've used previous versions of Excel

If you've used a previous version of Excel, you'll find many new features in version 4. If you're moving up from version 3, the differences won't be quite as drastic as they would be if you're upgrading from version 2.1. In either case, this book can get you up to speed quickly.

Yes — If you've used Excel for the Macintosh

The Macintosh version of Excel is very similar to the Windows version. If you're moving over from the Mac platform, you'll find some good background information and specific details to make your transition as smooth as possible.

 Yes — If you've used 1-2-3 or Quattro Pro

If you're abandoning a text-based spreadsheet such as Lotus 1-2-3 or Borland's Quattro Pro in favor of a more modern graphical product, this book will serve you well. You'll have a head start, since you already know what spreadsheets are all about, and you'll discover some great new ways of doing things.

No — If you're an Excel expert who wants to learn advanced macro programming

We had to draw the line somewhere. Excel has an extremely powerful macro language that could be the subject for an entire book. Although we cover macros in this book, we don't go into the depth that very advanced users might require. Sorry folks, keep looking. Perhaps that's our next assignment. . . .

What's a spreadsheet? In 250 words or less.

An electronic spreadsheet is a highly interactive computer program that consists of a collection of rows and columns that are displayed on-screen in a scrollable window. The intersection of each row and column is called a *cell*, and a cell can hold a number, a text string, or a formula that performs a calculation using one or more other cells. It's easy to copy cells, move cells, and modify any formulas you create. A spreadsheet can be saved in a file for use later on or discarded after it has served its intended purpose. An entire spreadsheet, or a group of selected cells, can be formatted in any number of ways and printed for hard copy reference. In addition, groups of numerical cells can be used to generate charts.

The most significant advantage of an electronic spreadsheet is that the formulas recalculate their results if you change any of the cells they use. As a result, once you get your spreadsheet set up by defining formulas, you can use this "model" to explore different possibilities with little additional effort on your part. A dozen or so electronic spreadsheet programs are currently available. Lotus 1-2-3 is the biggest-selling spreadsheet, but Excel 4 is the best — and in the pages of this book we hope to explain why.

No — If you want to learn all about Windows

Sorry, you're browsing in the wrong section. Try looking a little to your left — yeah, that's it, right next to the database books and a bit to the right of the DOS section. Although we tell you enough about Windows to get by, this book is not intended to be a Windows manual. Try Brian Livingston's *Windows 3.1 Secrets* (IDG Books, 1992) or *PC World You Can Do It With Windows,* by Chris Van Buren (IDG Books, 1992).

Conventions We Use

Take a minute to scan through this section to learn some of the typographical conventions used in this book.

Keyboard conventions

While it's definitely recommended that you use a mouse with an advanced Windows program such as Excel, you'll obviously have to use the keyboard to input data. In addition, you can invoke commands directly from the keyboard, which is often easier than moving from the keyboard to the mouse.

Excel commands

In Excel, as in all Windows programs, you select commands from the pull-down menu system. In this book, such commands appear in normal typeface, but are distinguishable because the commands have a single letter underlined — just like they appear in the menus. The underlined letter represents the "hotkey" letter. For example, if we mention the File ⇨ Save command, note that F and S are underlined. These correspond to the single letter keys that you can use to access the commands from the keyboard. In this example, you would press Alt+F and then the letter S to issue the File ⇨ Save command.

Filenames, named ranges, and your input

Filenames, named ranges, and input that you make from the keyboard appears in a different font. Lengthy input usually appears on a separate line. For instance, we may instruct you to enter a formula such as this:

```
=IF(ISNUMBER(A1),"Value",IF(ISTEXT(A1),"Text",IF(ISBLANK(A1),"Blank")))
```

Key names

Names of the keys on your keyboard appear in normal type. When two keys should be pressed simultaneously, they will be connected with a plus sign, like this: Press Alt+E to select the Edit menu. Here's a list of the key names, as we refer to them throughout the book:

Alt	End	PgUp	spacebar
Backspace	Home	Pause	Tab
Caps Lock	Ins	Print Screen	up arrow
Ctrl	left arrow	right arrow	
Del	Num Lock	Scroll Lock	
down arrow	PgDn	Shift	

Functions

Built-in functions appear in small capitals, like this: Enter a SUM formula in cell C20. Macro names also appear in small capitals, like this: Execute the SUMMARIZE macro.

Mouse conventions

This book assumes that you are using a mouse or some other pointing device. If, for some reason, you shun such tools, you'll need to mentally convert our mouse-oriented commands into keyboard commands. Here are some terms we'll be using:

Mouse pointer   The small graphic figure that moves on-screen when you move your mouse. The mouse pointer is usually an arrow, but it changes shape when you move to certain areas of the screen or when you are performing some actions.

Point   Move the mouse so the mouse pointer is on a specific item. For example, "point to the text object in the chart."

Press   Press the left mouse button and keep it pressed. This is normally used when dragging (see further). The right mouse button is used in Excel to pop up shortcut menus appropriate for whatever is currently selected (more on this later in the book).

Click   Press the left mouse button once and release it immediately.

Double-click	Press the left mouse button twice in rapid succession. You can adjust the double-click sensitivity using the Windows Control Panel program.
Drag	Press the left mouse button and keep it pressed while you move the mouse. Dragging is often used to select a range of cells or a group of objects.

Icons and Alerts

Throughout the book you'll notice special graphic symbols, or icons, in the left margin. These are provided to call your attention to points that are particularly important or relevant to a specific group of readers. The icons we use are as follows:

Pay particular attention to paragraphs marked with this symbol. It denotes something that is fundamental to understanding subsequent material or imparts information that is particularly important.

A tip, or a more efficient way of doing something that may not be obvious.

We use this symbol when there is a possibility that the operation we're describing could cause problems if you're not careful.

If you're upgrading from a previous release of Excel, pay attention to these symbols. They denote features that are implemented differently in Excel 4.

How This Book Is Organized

This book is divided into four main sections of 32 chapters and two appendixes.

Chapter organization

Part I, *First Things First*, consists of the first four chapters. In Chapter 1 we give you some background on the product and an overview of its features. Chapter 2 covers installation — what you need in terms of hardware and software and how to get Excel running properly. In Chapter 3 you'll learn how to start and stop Excel, plus several techniques for moving between Excel and other applications. Chapter 4 is a hands-on test drive of Excel, provided to give new users a lap around the race track to show what this baby can do.

Part II, called *The Basic Concepts,* is made up of the next 14 chapters. You'll learn how to move through worksheets efficiently in Chapter 5. Chapter 6 discusses the file types Excel uses and how to retrieve and save your work. In Chapter 7, you'll learn how to enter, edit, and format data in a worksheet. Chapter 8 moves on to discuss a variety of operations that are essential to working with Excel — things such as adjusting rows and columns, justifying text, and so on. Chapters 9–11 cover ranges, formulas, and the built-in functions. Chapter 12 discusses how to make your worksheets look good, and this is followed by a chapter on printing your work. In Chapter 14, you'll learn how to control some of the customizable features of Excel. Chapters 15–17 explore the world of charts: how to create them, annotate them, and print them. The section ends with a chapter that summarizes everything an Excel user should know.

Part III consists of the final 14 chapters, and we call it *The Advanced Features*. Chapter 19 discusses Excel's toolbars — how to use them and customize them. Add-ins are covered in Chapter 20, and Chapter 21 tells you how to link worksheets together and consolidate them. We discuss array formulas in Chapter 22 and spreadsheet outlines in Chapter 23. Chapter 24 covers the essentials of spreadsheet databases, including how to work with external databases. Chapter 25 is for more technically oriented users and covers the Analysis ToolPak — a collection of statistical and engineering procedures included with Excel. Chapter 26 jumps into macros, Chapter 27 covers "what-if" analysis, and Chapter 28 extends the discussion into goal seeking and Excel's Solver. In Chapter 29 you'll learn some techniques on how to share data with other applications. Chapter 30 presents some techniques for auditing your work, and Chapter 31 is for those who prepare worksheet applications for others to use. The last chapter provides some tips on how to improve Excel's performance.

Appendixes and reference material

Part IV is the appendixes. Appendix A is included for those who are upgrading from another spreadsheet product — either the previous version of Excel or Lotus 1-2-3. If you fall into one of these categories, this is a good place to start. Appendix B is for reference and includes descriptions of all Excel worksheet functions. And the handy booklet provided in the inside cover of the book lists all the macro functions available in the product.

How to Use This Book

We've attempted to organize this book in such a way that new users are exposed to the concepts in a fairly natural progression, starting with the basics and moving on towards more advanced topics. Nothing prevents you, of course, from skipping chapters and reading them out of order.

Note: The index in this book is particularly thorough, so you can find every context where we discuss a particular topic you're interested in.

■ ■ ■

With that out of the way, let's get busy.

PART

I

First Things First

Chapter 1

What Is Excel?

In this chapter . . .

▶ A perspective on what Microsoft Excel is all about, including a brief historical sketch of its origins.

▶ The advantages of using Microsoft Windows as an operating environment.

▶ A brief overview of the major features available in Excel 4.

Excel Is . . .

First and foremost, Excel is a *spreadsheet* program. Like other products in this genre, it's used for numerical applications that are appropriate for row-and-column-oriented analyses such as budgets, proposals, financial models, and many other applications (see Figure 1-1). You can develop dynamic formulas that work with cells in your worksheet and also use a tremendous assortment of built-in functions that add advanced computing power.

Excel is also a *graphics program*. Its charting capability ranks among the best available in any spreadsheet program, and — except for the most demanding applications — it can take the place of a stand-alone presentation graphics

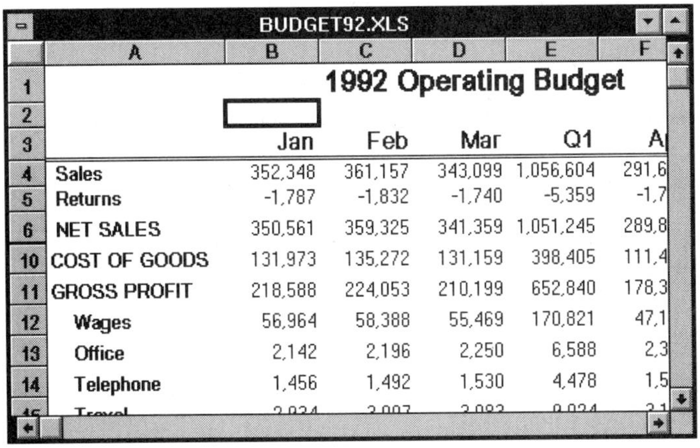

Figure 1-1: Excel gives you state-of-the-art spreadsheet features.

	A	B	C	D	E	F
1			1992 Operating Budget			
2						
3		Jan	Feb	Mar	Q1	A
4	Sales	352,348	361,157	343,099	1,056,604	291,6
5	Returns	-1,787	-1,832	-1,740	-5,359	-1,7
6	NET SALES	350,561	359,325	341,359	1,051,245	289,8
10	COST OF GOODS	131,973	135,272	131,159	398,405	111,4
11	GROSS PROFIT	218,588	224,053	210,199	652,840	178,3
12	Wages	56,964	58,388	55,469	170,821	47,1
13	Office	2,142	2,196	2,250	6,588	2,3
14	Telephone	1,456	1,492	1,530	4,478	1,5
15	Travel	3,034	3,007	3,083	9,024	3,1

BUDGET92.XLS

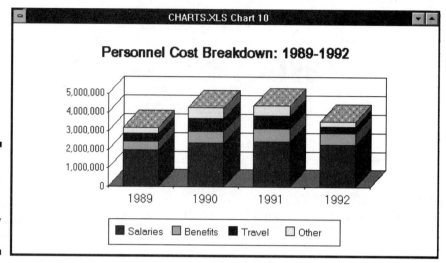

Personnel Cost Breakdown: 1989-1992

■ Salaries ▨ Benefits ■ Travel □ Other

Figure 1-2:
The charting
capability is
both easy to
use and very
extensive.

program (see Figure 1-2). You can even prepare on-screen slide show presentations with Excel, complete with slick transition effects and sound.

The product is also a *database management tool.* You can work with record- and field-oriented data, process queries, and generate reports (see Figure 1-3). The data can be stored in one or more worksheets or reside in files on your disk. Although Excel doesn't offer the full range of features found in stand-alone database products such as Paradox or dBASE, many users find that Excel suits their database needs just fine.

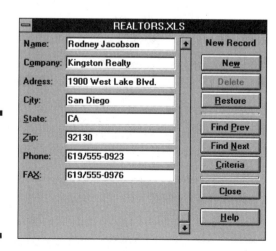

Figure 1-3:
Excel enables
you to work
with databases
using familiar
spreadsheet
tools.

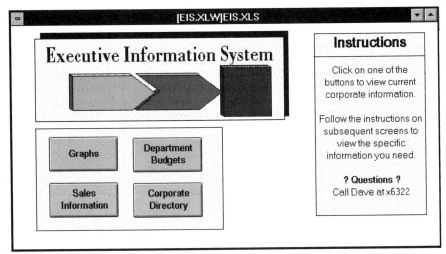

Figure 1-4: With macros, advanced users can create sophisticated applications that resemble stand-alone programs.

Finally, Excel is an *application development environment.* Although it's not a programming language per se (like Basic or C), Excel's built-in macro language provides the power to create user-oriented "applications" that resemble those produced by programming languages — complete with buttons, custom menus, and dialog boxes (see Figure 1-4). Complete coverage of this topic is beyond the scope of this book, but we provide enough information about macros to satisfy the majority of users.

Simply describing what Excel 4 can do doesn't really do it justice. After all, just about every other spreadsheet on the market can boast the same features. The real advantage of Excel is how it does what it does. That's what we're trying to impart to you in the next 600 and some odd pages (and some are odder than others).

The Windows Advantage

Broadly speaking, personal computer applications come in two varieties: text-based and graphics-based. Text-based programs interact with the user through just a single typeface on-screen, which is usually fixed at 80 characters wide by 25 characters tall. In a text-based application, all characters are basically the same size, but some may appear boldfaced, underlined, or in different colors. The printed output may or may not resemble what you see on-screen.

Graphical programs, on the other hand, are WYSIWYG (which stands for "what you see is what you get"). WYSIWYG means that the on-screen display closely approximates what will be printed — including different typefaces, sizes, borders, shading, graphic images, and so on. All applications that run on a Macintosh computer, for example, are WYSIWYG. Programs written for DOS-based PCs can be either text-based or graphical.

In May 1990, Microsoft released Windows 3.0 — an operating environment that improved on previous releases of Windows. Windows 3 took the PC user community by storm and became the fastest-selling software product in history. Now, PC programs can be classified into one of two categories: Windows programs and non-Windows programs. Virtually all the major applications now being developed for PCs are designed for Windows.

Besides providing a more attractive display, Windows has several other key advantages:

- **Windows programs all tend to use the same, or similar, commands.** If you know how to load a file in one Windows program, you basically know how to load a file in *all* Windows programs.

- **Windows itself handles the printing from all Windows programs.** Therefore, you only have to configure your printer one time, and all Windows programs print correctly. If you purchase a new printer, all your Windows applications can use it after you tell Windows what printer it is.

- **Windows also enables you to run more than one program at a time.** In addition, you can instantly switch among the programs in memory (see Figure 1-5).

- **Windows provides several methods by which programs can communicate with each other.** You can copy data more easily, set up permanent links so programs share each other's data, and embed objects created in other applications.

The net effect of using Windows is often an overall increase in productivity. But if you're migrating to Windows from text-based programs, don't expect instant results. Like any other sophisticated system, Windows has a lot of intricacies that you must learn. Getting up to speed with Windows itself and with the applications that run in this environment definitely takes some time. Compared to traditional character-based software programs, however, Windows programs are much easier to learn, more fun to use, and generally more forgiving.

The downside to Windows (there's always a downside) is that more computing power is needed for you to handle graphical displays and to deal with multiple programs running at once. Consequently, you need a fairly fast computer with lots of memory to run Windows programs efficiently. We recommend an 80386 or 80486 processor running at 25 MHz (megahertz) or faster. At minimum, you should have 4MB (megabytes) of RAM — but you'll be happier with 8MB. Also, if your computer doesn't have a hard drive (increasingly rare nowadays), you'd better get one. More likely, you may find that the existing hard drive on your

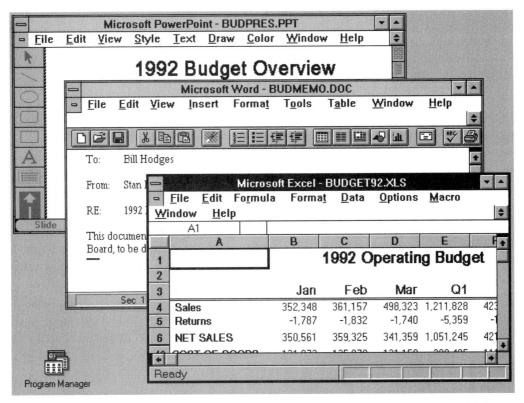

Figure 1-5: Microsoft Windows enables you to work with several different applications at once, each in its own window.

machine doesn't have enough room to hold the megabytes of files that Windows and Excel comprise. So you may have to clear out some room or even add a second drive.

Both Windows and Excel were developed by Microsoft. Consequently, Excel takes advantage of the Windows environment superbly — something you can appreciate fully only if you've worked with Windows programs that fall short in this area. In addition, Excel works particularly well with Microsoft Word for Windows.

The Evolution of Excel

Excel is manufactured by Microsoft Corporation — a company that has more than a decade's worth of experience with electronic spreadsheets. The company's first spreadsheet, MultiPlan, was released in 1982 for computers running the CP/M operating system. The product was subsequently ported to other systems, including Apple II, Apple III, XENIX, and MS-DOS. MultiPlan has gone through many revisions across several different operating systems.

The latest DOS version of MultiPlan is version 3.2, released in late 1989. Although the later versions of MultiPlan had some advanced features that were unavailable in other spreadsheets, the product pretty much ignored any existing software user-interface "standards" and was a real bear to learn and use. Consequently, MultiPlan never really had much of a following in the United States and was far outdistanced by the success of Lotus 1-2-3.

Excel sort of evolved from MultiPlan and first surfaced in 1985 on the Macintosh. Like all Mac applications, Excel was a graphical program (unlike character-based MultiPlan). The first version of Excel for Windows was released in November 1987. Because Windows was not in widespread use at this time, the original version included a run-time version of Windows — a special version that had just enough features to run Excel and nothing else.

The initial Windows version was labeled version 2.0 to correspond with the Macintosh version. This version was followed up in less than a year with version 2.1 for Windows, and in July 1990, Microsoft released a minor upgrade (labeled 2.1d) that was compatible with Windows 3.0. These 2.*x* versions were rather rudimentary by current standards and didn't have the attractive "sculpted" look of later versions. But Excel attracted a strong group of supporters and provided an excellent foundation for future development.

In the meantime, Microsoft developed another version of Excel for OS/2 Presentation Manager and released it in September 1989. This version was numbered 2.20. As you may know, OS/2 never quite caught on the way it was expected (IBM is still trying to make this operating system viable). Nevertheless, the OS/2 version was upgraded to version 2.21 about ten months later.

Version 3 of Excel for Windows was released in December 1990, and the OS/2 version upgrade came out five months later. This upgrade was a significant improvement in both appearance and features. It included a toolbar, drawing

Bill Gates is doing OK

Microsoft must be doing something right. Bill Gates, the company's founder and chairman, is now the richest person in the United States and has a net worth of about $7.4 billion. A few quick calcula- tions in an Excel worksheet shows that this figure works out to more than half a million dollars for every day that Gates has been alive.

capabilities, Solver, support for add-ins, Object Linking and Embedding (OLE) support, the capacity to work with external databases (via Q+E), 3-D charts, macro buttons, simplified file consolidation, workgroup editing, and wrap-around text in a cell.

The latest version of Excel, 4.0, was released in April 1992. It builds even more on the original foundation, and addresses usability for all users and increases power and sophistication for advanced users. Note that Excel's user interface is virtually identical across all the platforms it runs on. Therefore, a user of Excel for Macintosh can move over to Excel for Windows without having to learn new commands and procedures. Perhaps more important is that macros developed in the Mac version also work in the Windows version (and vice versa).

Microsoft's spreadsheets have come a long way since MultiPlan — from barely adequate to the best in the business.

What Excel Offers

The following paragraphs briefly describe some of the key features in Excel 4 and will whet your appetite for things to come in this book.

Context-sensitive help

In the past, users were lucky if the manual that accompanied a software product covered all the features and was accurate. Nowadays, almost all applications' written documentation is augmented with on-line help, and Excel is a good example. While you're working in Excel, you can always get help on the topic you're dealing with. And former 1-2-3 users (and even MultiPlan users) can access a special help system to find out the equivalent Excel procedure for 1-2-3 commands.

Graphical user interface

Excel makes excellent use of the features of Windows, including pull-down menus, dialog boxes, and WYSIWYG formatting. As mentioned earlier, WYSIWYG means that the information you work with on your computer screen closely resembles what it will look like in printed form. Because Excel enables you to work with different type styles and graphic elements, WYSIWYG is an important feature that distinguishes Excel from older-generation spreadsheets that ran exclusively in text mode.

Ease-of-use features

The latest version of Excel is much easier to use than prior versions. In fact, we think that Excel is definitely the easiest to use of any spreadsheet available. The product now includes many new features designed specifically to make commonly used tasks straightforward and fast — for both beginners and experts. For example, several "Wizards" walk you through procedures in a step-by-step manner, and basic editing and formatting commands are just a mouse click away.

Text handling

Excel's forte is crunching numbers, but it's not too shabby at handling text. You can put text into cells and format or orient it in any manner you like. You can also insert movable and resizable text boxes anywhere on your worksheet.

Microsoft's Usability Lab

Although most large software companies conduct market research, none approaches the challenge like Microsoft. Besides having traditional surveys and focus groups, the company has established a laboratory to perform research on the usability of its products. Microsoft's programmers developed a special "instrumented version" of Excel that electronically records every keystroke and mouse click that a user makes. These instrumented versions are given to a representative sample of Excel users who go about their normal spreadsheet business — while data on their usage patterns is collected automatically. Microsoft ends up with a vast quantity of data, which is analyzed and interpreted.

For example, the company knows exactly which tasks users perform most frequently. More specifically, it found that users spend about 95 percent of their time using only 5 percent of Excel's functionality. The results of studies like these have changed the way Microsoft approaches product development and upgrades. The company understands that innovation is re-

quired at the most basic levels. One of the development goals of Excel 4.0 was to focus on the 5 percent of the tasks that are most frequently used and make them as easy as possible.

Microsoft also developed what it calls Activity Based Planning, which focuses product development on solving real-life user problems rather than just adding features per se. Their research people identify what users really do, and they prioritize these activities and develop groups of features to support the most important ones. Then they head for the usability lab to test users' reactions to the new features and make changes before they are incorporated into the final version.

The result is that Excel — unlike most software products — is optimized for real use. For the end user, this optimization means that complex tasks are simplified and shortened. So you can accomplish more in less time. This whole research thing may sound like a bunch of hype, but we think it works. And it clearly shows in Excel 4.

Sound

If you have the Windows 3.0 Multimedia Extensions installed (or use Windows 3.1 with a sound board), you can attach sound notes to cells in a worksheet. If you don't have such sound capabilities, you are limited to plain old text notes.

Customizable toolbars

One of the hottest new features in version 4 is the customizable toolbars — collections of icons that perform common tasks quickly and efficiently. This concept originated in a Lotus word processor called Ami Pro and has subsequently been incorporated into all of Lotus's Windows software (as well as products from several other software companies). The toolbar can be a real time-saver because you can avoid using the menu for most common commands, and you can specify your own shortcut buttons for tasks you do most often.

Multiple files and workbooks

Excel enables you to work with many files at once, which is probably the way you work normally. As a result, you don't need to close down a file if you need to consult another. In practical terms, this feature makes transferring information between worksheets easy. New with this version is the concept of workbooks. A *workbook* is a collection of related worksheets, charts, and possibly macro files that are all stored together in a single file. With Excel, managing and working with such groups is easy.

Built-in functions

In addition to all the standard mathematical and logical operators, Excel includes an enormous collection of built-in functions. The functions can perform sophisticated operations that would be difficult or impossible to do otherwise. For example, the CORREL function automatically calculates the correlation coefficient for two sets of data. Version 4 adds about 100 new functions — many in the area of statistics and engineering.

Graphs and charts

Excel's charting features are among the best available in any spreadsheet. You can select from a wide assortment of graph types, and modify and augment them to your liking. A chart can be inserted anywhere within a worksheet.

Cross-platform consistency

Excel runs on the Macintosh and the PC (under Windows), and — of increasing importance — the two products are virtually identical across these two platforms. If you learn the Windows version, you can move to a Mac and feel right at home. This feature may seem like a given to you, but it's not. For example, Lotus 1-2-3 for Windows is very different from 1-2-3 for Macintosh (and you can't share macros between the two versions).

File compatibility

Excel has its own file format for worksheets, identifiable by the xls file extension. In addition, the program can read files produced by other spreadsheet programs, such as Lotus 1-2-3, Quattro Pro, and MultiPlan. The program can also read text files and dBASE database files.

Printing and print preview

You'll be pleased to see how easily you can put your work on paper. Besides the normal WYSIWYG formatting, Excel provides you with the best print previewer we've seen. You can make last-minute adjustments directly from the preview window — including changing column widths and margins by dragging with the mouse.

Scenario Manager

Spreadsheets are often used for a "what if" analysis that involves changing one or more assumptions and observing the effects on related variables. Excel simplifies this process with its new Scenario Manager. You can provide names for various scenarios and switch among them with a few mouse clicks.

Worksheet outlining

Version 3 of Excel introduced the concept of spreadsheet outlines. This feature enables you to collapse hierarchical information to show any level of detail you want. Those who work with multilevel budgets will find this feature particularly valuable.

Spell checking

An integrated spell checker spots spelling errors in your worksheets and charts and enables you to avoid the embarrassment of displaying a chart in a crowded boardroom that reads "1992 Bugdet Review."

Templates

If your work tends to fall into a few specific categories, you'll want to take time to set up a custom spreadsheet *template* — a preconfigured "shell" that includes text, row and column headings, formats, column widths, macros, and so on. You can use templates to speed the creation of similar spreadsheets.

Database management

The ability to work with spreadsheet data as if it were a database is common in spreadsheets. Excel features all the standard database commands and also enables you to work with external files directly from the Excel environment. It supports dBASE, SQL Server, Oracle, and standard text files. An accompanying program called Q+E enables Excel to gather information from these remote databases.

Macros

Macros enable you to create shortcuts by playing back a predefined series of keystrokes or commands. In addition, you can create sophisticated user-oriented applications with macros. By the way, Excel can also interpret 1-2-3 macros, so you don't have to scrap those old 1-2-3 applications.

Custom dialog boxes

Advanced users who develop worksheet applications can create attractive and professional-looking dialog boxes to solicit input from users and make their worksheets easier to use.

Analytical tools

Number crunchers have a lot to get excited about with Excel. Its unique array feature enables you to do things that are impossible in other spreadsheets. The product also includes goal seeking, a powerful Solver feature, plus several add-ins for specialized analyses.

Add-in capability

Although Microsoft didn't originate the concept of add-ins (Lotus did), the company implemented the feature well. You can "attach" a spreadsheet add-in to Excel to provide new functionality. Excel 4 includes many add-ins that you may or may not need. For example, the Analysis ToolPak provides extensive statistical, financial, engineering, and scientific functions and procedures. An add-in manager enables you to specify which add-ins are loaded automatically.

Data exchange

As a Windows product, Excel can access all the normal Windows features, such as copying and pasting between different applications, as well as the powerful Dynamic Data Exchange (DDE) facility. In addition, Excel incorporates the new Object Linking and Embedding (OLE) technology that makes data sharing easier than ever.

Presentation capabilities

Excel 4 also enables you to create sophisticated on-screen slide shows. These slide shows can consist of worksheet tables, charts, drawings, or other information obtained from other software. The program offers optional sound (if you have the Windows Multimedia extensions and a sound board) and a wide selection of sophisticated transition effects to move from screen to screen.

Summary

▶ Excel 4 is the latest in a line of increasingly sophisticated spreadsheets from Microsoft Corporation, the company that also developed Windows.

▶ Excel is available in versions that run in the Windows environment, with OS/2, and on a Macintosh — making it ideal for offices that use multiple platforms.

▶ Although the worksheet is its central focus, Excel has a much broader appeal. It can work with databases (either in memory or on disk), produces excellent graphics, and has sophisticated macro programming capability.

▶ The key features of Excel 4 include context-sensitive help, a graphical user interface, many new ease-of-use features, sophisticated text handling, sound notes, customizable toolbars, the capacity to work with multiple files and "workbooks," a wide selection of built-in functions, superb charting capability, cross-platform consistency (with the Macintosh version), file compatibility, excellent printing and preview capabilities, a scenario manager for "what if" analyses, worksheet outlining, spell checking, templates, database management features, extensive macro capabilities, custom dialog boxes, a variety of advanced analytical tools, add-in capability, support for DDE and OLE, and on-screen presentation capabilities.

Chapter 2
Installing Excel

In this chapter . . .

▶ What you need in terms of hardware and software before you can run Excel.

▶ How to get Excel up and running on your computer.

▶ Things to check for if the installation doesn't work properly.

Before you can use Excel, you must install it on your computer. This is a straightforward operation that pretty much occurs automatically, with minimal assistance from you. You merely have to feed the requested disks to your floppy disk drive when prompted for them and answer a few simple questions. The entire process takes about 15 to 30 minutes.

 Many companies have a special person or department devoted to installing and troubleshooting software. If this is the case with your company, you may want to let the department take care of the installation so it's standardized with the other systems in your company. On the other hand, Excel 4 may already be installed on your system. If your system is part of a local area network (LAN), you should check with your system administrator before installing Excel.

Examining What You Need

Excel requires specific hardware and software to run. This section provides details on the minimum requirements and our recommended requirements.

Hardware requirements

You need a fairly sophisticated computer to run Excel 4. According to Microsoft, the minimum hardware requirement is an 80286 (in other words, an IBM AT or clone) with 2MB of RAM. Although Excel *will* run on such a system, you'll probably find it to be painfully slow and not much fun. Instead, we strongly recommend an 80386SX, 80386, or 80486 processor with at least 4MB of RAM. You're better off with even more memory; 8MB is ideal for running

Windows comfortably. More memory means that you can run more applications simultaneously, and less disk access occurs (which means faster overall performance).

Your hard disk must have at least 10MB free for the full installation and preferably quite a bit more to hold the files you create. If you don't have enough available hard disk space, you can perform a partial installation or delete some files to free up space.

Excel looks best on a VGA monitor, but an EGA display will do if that's all you have. Depending on your video adapter and display type, you may want to run Windows in Super VGA mode. This setup gives you 800×600 pixels (or maybe even $1,024 \times 768$) on your screen rather than the normal 640×480 pixels with VGA. The net effect is that you can see more information on-screen, and the display may even be sharper. The manual that came with your video card probably describes the process of changing your Windows video driver.

Although a mouse is not required for you to run Excel, we recommend using one (or some other type of pointing device, such as a trackball).

Because mouse use has become so widespread, this book assumes that you have such a device connected.

You can run Excel without a printer, but you can't print without one. (This book is filled with revelations, eh?) Excel works with any printer that's supported by Windows, which includes just about all printers except daisy-wheel printers.

Your computer may have a math coprocessor chip installed. This is a rather expensive computer chip (called an 80287 or 80387) that greatly speeds up numeric calculations in some software. Excel uses a math coprocessor if you have one. Unless you plan to do some serious number crunching, you can definitely get by without a math chip. If your system has an 80486 processor, the math chip is built in.

Software requirements

Excel requires that you have Microsoft Windows, either version 3.0 or 3.1, installed on your system. Windows is an operating environment that runs on top of DOS and provides some of the resources that Excel uses.

You must be using DOS 3.1 or later to install Windows. Any "brand" of DOS works including PC-DOS, MS-DOS, or DR-DOS.

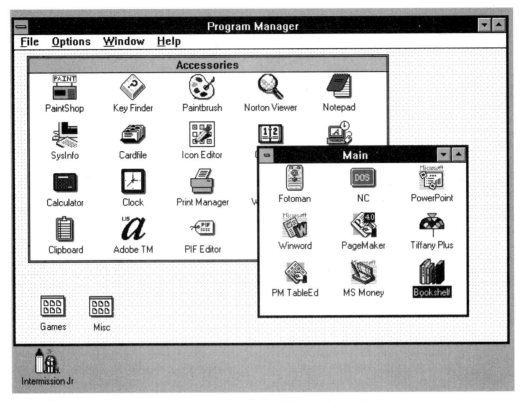

Figure 2-1: The Windows Program Manager is where Excel's installation begins.

 Windows is *not* included with Excel and must be purchased separately. If Windows is not yet installed on your system, follow the instructions in the Windows manual and make sure that it's running properly before you proceed with your Excel installation.

Preparing Your System

At this point, we assume that you have Windows 3.0 or 3.1 properly installed on your system. Before you start the actual installation process, checking a few things is a good idea. If it's not already running, start Windows from the DOS prompt by typing `win`. In a few moments, your screen displays the Program Manager and looks something like Figure 2-1.

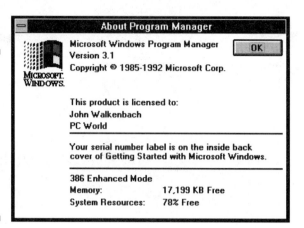

Figure 2-2:
You can find
out which
Windows
mode you're
running in by
selecting
Help ➩ About
from Program
Manager.

The Windows screens shown in this chapter are from Windows 3.1. If you're
using Windows 3.0, your screens will look slightly different.

First, you need to make sure that Windows is running in the proper mode.
Windows automatically checks out your hardware and starts in one of three
different modes: real mode, standard mode, or 386 enhanced mode. Excel
requires either standard or 386 enhanced mode and does not work if Windows
is in real mode. If you're running Windows 3.1, this is moot because this version
of Windows doesn't operate in real mode.

To check which mode your Windows is running in, select Help from the Program Manager menu to pull down the Help menu. From this menu, select About.
The Program Manager displays a box like that shown in Figure 2-2. If the box
tells you that Windows is running in real mode, your system may not be
capable of running Excel. Refer to the Windows manual (good luck!), seek
additional help (a good idea), or buy a new computer (sorry about that).

Assuming that Windows is running in either standard or 386 enhanced mode,
you're now ready to see how much disk space is available. Locate the icon
labeled File Manager and double-click on it. If you can't find such an icon, select
File ➩ Run from the Program Manager menu, enter winfile into the text box,
and select OK. Either method starts the Windows File Manager application.

File Manager displays an icon for each disk drive attached to your system. Click
on the drive letter that corresponds to the drive on which you'll be installing
Excel (not A: or B: because these are floppy drives), and the amount of free
space is displayed at the bottom of the File Manger window. The figure displayed is in bytes, and each byte is roughly equivalent to a single character.
You need at least 10,000,000 bytes free in order to install all of Excel.

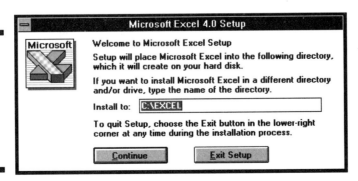

Figure 2-3: The File ⇨ Run command in the Program Manager enables you to run a program that's not associated with an icon.

 If you don't have enough space, you need to erase some files that you no longer need (you can do this task while you're in File Manager). If you're not sure of what you're doing, seek some assistance. Deleting one wrong file can make your entire system inoperable, so be careful.

Installing Excel _____

Now you're ready to install Excel. Make sure that Windows is running and that you're in the Program Manager. Insert the Excel disk labeled Setup into a floppy drive and close the drive door. Select File ⇨ Run from the menu. You see the dialog box shown in Figure 2-3. Enter `a:setup` into the text box (if you're installing from drive B:, enter `b:setup`). Click on the OK button or press Enter, and the installation begins.

The Setup program needs some information from you. If this is the first installation from the disks you're using, you are asked to customize your copy of the program with your name and company (to help prevent software pirating). Enter your name and (optionally) your company name.

Next, you're asked where you want to install Excel (see Figure 2-4). The default directory is `c:\excel`, but you can change this directory if you want. For example, you may want to place all your Windows applications in

Figure 2-4: You can install Excel in the default `c:\excel` directory or choose another directory if you want.

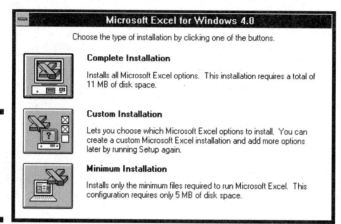

Figure 2-5:
You can
install Excel
in any of
three differ-
ent ways.

subdirectories located within your ~~Win~~dows directory. In this case, you may
enter c:\windows\excel in response to this prompt. If the directory does not
exist, it is created for you.

If you are upgrading from a previous version of Excel, you can safely install the
new version in the directory you used for the prior version. The Setup program
replaces your old program files with the new ones (and leaves all your other files
intact). Next, Setup asks what type of installation you want (see Figure 2-5). Three
options are available:

Complete Installation   This option installs everything in the directory you
specified.

Custom Installation   This option enables you to pick which options you
want to install and also specify a different directory. If
you choose to omit some options, you can rerun Setup
later to add them.

Minimum Installation   This option installs only the bare minimum — enough
to run Excel but without things like the tutorial and
Solver. This option is designed for systems with
minimal hard disk space (such as laptops) or for those
who don't need many features.

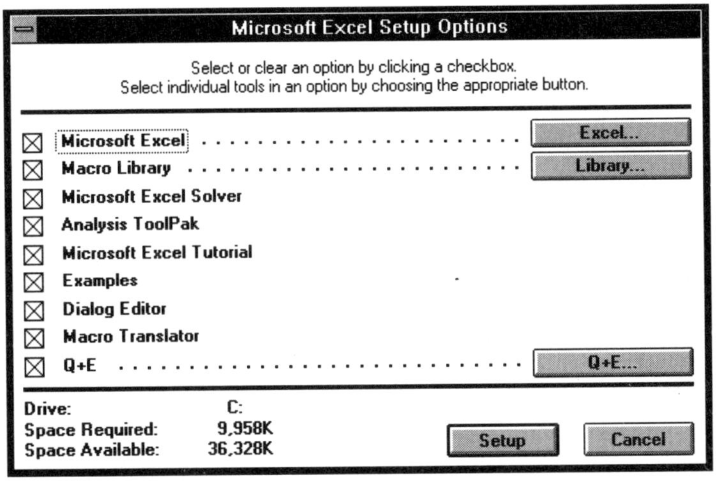

Figure 2-6:
In a custom installation, you can choose which setup options you want to use.

If you have enough disk space, choose the full installation. If you choose the custom installation, Setup presents you with a list of options you can choose to install or not install. Figure 2-6 shows the options. Simply click on the check boxes beside the options you don't want to install; the X disappears, and the option is no longer selected.

The Setup program then asks whether you want to enable certain help features designed for 1-2-3 users who are switching to Excel. If you've used 1-2-3, enabling these options may be a good idea. Otherwise, don't. Setup also asks whether it can update your autoexec.bat file to change your path. Unless you have a good reason not to, let Setup make this modification for you.

Setup proceeds with the installation and prompts you to insert the remaining disks as needed. The process takes awhile because the files on the floppy disks are compressed. Setup expands these files while it copies them to your hard drive.

Figure 2-7:
This screen appears when Excel is successfully installed.

If you see the dialog box shown in Figure 2-7, congratulations. All went well and you're ready to run Excel 4. The Setup program created a new Program Group called Microsoft Excel 4. If you opted for the full installation, this Program Group has five icons with the following names (see Figure 2-8):

Microsoft Excel   This icon starts Excel.

Dialog Editor   This icon starts a program that enables you to create dialog boxes for use in macros. This program is used primarily by advanced users.

Q+E   This icon launches Q+E, which is a database program that works in conjunction with Excel.

readme.txt   This icon displays an information file with the latest information about Excel. After you read this file, you can safely delete the icon (the file remains on your disk).

network.txt   This icon displays an information file with information about how Excel works on LANs. After you read this file, you can safely delete the icon (the file remains on your disk).

Figure 2-8:
The Setup program creates a new Program Group for you.

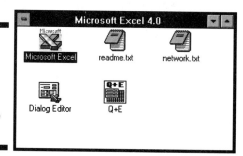

Modifying the Excel icon

If you want, you can change some of the properties of the Excel 4 icon. Make sure that you're in the Windows Program Manager. Click once on the Excel icon to select it and then issue the File ⇨ Properties command (click on File in the main menu and then click on Properties in the menu that drops down). Windows displays the Program Item Properties dialog box, which enables you to change some of the properties of the selected icon.

If you're using Windows 3.0, you'll notice that the icon names overlap. You can easily change this setup in the File Properties dialog box; simply type in a shorter name for the icon and click on OK. If you're using Windows 3.1, this situation doesn't occur because this version of Windows wraps long icon titles to another line.

You can modify the command line so Excel doesn't start with a blank worksheet named `sheet1.xls` by adding /e to the command line.

When you run Excel, it looks for files to load in the \excel directory. You can specify a different default directory by adding /p to the command line, followed by a directory path. For example, you may change the command line to read `c:\excel\excel.exe /p c:\sheets` if you want to use a directory named c:\sheets to store your worksheets. If you're using Windows 3.1, you can simply insert a different directory name in the Working Directory text box.

You can also change the icon displayed by clicking on the Change Icon button. This action brings up the Change Icon dialog box. Click on the horizontal scroll bar to display the icons in the file (five icons are in `excel.exe`). When you find one you like, click on it and select the OK button. This process works a bit differently in Windows 3.0; you need to click on the View Next button to cycle through the icons.

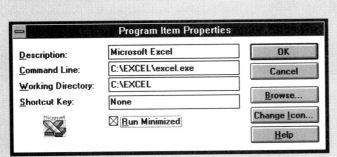

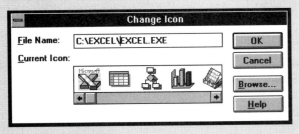

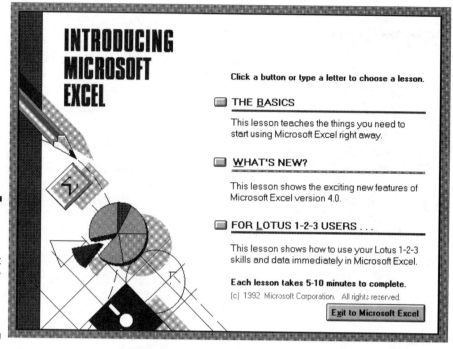

Figure 2-9:
The first time you start Excel, it automatically loads an introductory preview.

You may want to move or copy the Excel 4 icon to another Program Group, such as one called Main or Windows Apps. To move an icon, simply drag the icon to another Program Group. To make a copy, hold down Ctrl while you drag the icon.

Now you're ready to test the installation. Locate the new Excel program icon and double-click it. If all went well, Excel should start running. At this point, you may want to go through the introductory preview that runs automatically (see Figure 2-9). Click on one of the buttons and follow the remaining instructions on-screen. When you've had enough of the preview, follow the instructions to exit and you return to Excel with a blank worksheet displayed. To exit Excel and return to the Program Manager, select File ➪ Exit from the pull-down menu.

The introductory preview is loaded automatically only the first time you run Excel. You can get back to this preview at any time by selecting Help ➪ Introducing Microsoft Excel from the menu.

Troubleshooting

During the installation process, something may go wrong. Usually, the Setup program tells you what it thinks the problem is — for example, your disk is full or an error occurred while the floppy disk was read.

If your hard disk is full, you need to erase some files and start again. You can use the Windows File Manager for this task, or do it directly from DOS or a DOS window.

An error during the reading of a floppy disk can be anything from an operator error (inserting the wrong floppy) to a hardware problem with the drive or a defect on the floppy disk itself. You may try starting the installation process all over again. Or, if your computer has both kinds of floppy drives (3 ½- and 5 ¼-inch), try using the second set of disks included in your Excel package (it includes both formats).

If you have problems reading other floppy disks (all of the same format), you probably have a problem with your floppy drive. You may want to check your hardware warranty records. Or, if someone in your office is knowledgeable about such things, now's the time to call him or her. If all else fails, call Microsoft and see whether it can figure out what's going wrong for you. Microsoft's technical support number is 206-635-7070.

Next steps

OK. Excel is installed and it seems to be working just fine. Now what? As we just mentioned, you may want to go through one or both of the tutorials provided with Excel. You can run these tutorials at any time. Select the Help command from Excel's menu and then click on either Introducing Microsoft Excel or Learning Microsoft Excel.

And don't forget about this book. You have 30 more chapters to explore!

Summary

▶ You need to have Windows 3.0 or 3.1 installed on your system before you can install Excel. Windows is not included with Excel.

▶ Your system must be capable of running Windows in either standard or 386 enhanced mode and have at least 10MB of free space on your hard disk for the full installation.

▶ You can run Excel without a mouse, but you'll probably prefer to have one. This book assumes that you have a mouse or some other pointing device.

▶ When you install Excel, you can omit one or more options to reduce the amount of disk space required. At any time in the future, you can add options not installed initially by rerunning the Setup program.

▶ Excel provides two on-line tutorials, which you can access at any time with Excel's Help menu.

Chapter 3

Starting, Stopping, and Switching

In this chapter . . .

▶ A discussion of the different ways to start Excel.

▶ How to switch out of Excel to work with other applications and return where you left off.

▶ The safe way to exit the program.

This chapter assumes that Excel is properly installed on your system, as described in the preceding chapter. This chapter certainly qualifies as a "basic" chapter, but it contains information that may be new to even some experienced Windows users. You have essentially three different ways to start Excel:

■ From a Program Manager icon (by far, the most common method)

■ From File Manager (along with an Excel file)

■ Directly from DOS (but only if Windows is not running)

Starting from Program Manager

The Program Manager may be considered "control central" for Windows. The Program Manager is the standard Windows "shell" program that enables you to launch applications and perform other housekeeping chores within Windows.

Program Manager isn't the only Windows shell program. Several software companies have developed other Windows shells that improve on many aspects of Program Manager. Perhaps the best of all these programs is Norton Desktop for Windows from Symantec (we recommend it). If your Windows installation is set up with a different shell program, the following instructions won't make much sense.

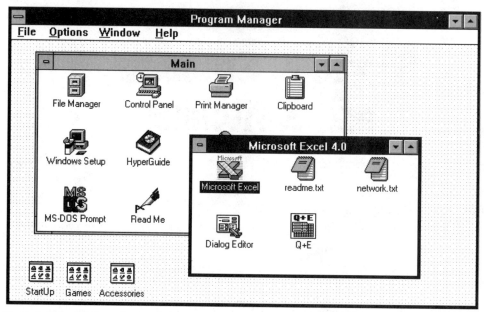

Figure 3-1: The Windows Program Manager is the place where you usually start applications.

The Windows Program Manager is shown in Figure 3-1. Because the Program Manager is highly customizable, your screen will only vaguely resemble this one. Nevertheless, you will have one or more program groups, each of which contains one or more program items.

If you installed Excel properly, one of your program groups contains an icon labeled Microsoft Excel or something to that effect. The most straightforward way to start Excel is to locate the icon and double-click on it. When you install Excel, it creates a new program group for you. The Excel icon, however, can be moved or copied to any program group, which may or may not be visible on your screen because a program group can be minimized (reduced to an icon). You may have to double-click on a program group icon in order to open up the program group and expose the Excel icon.

All this double-clicking sounds more difficult than it actually is. You'll soon learn where your Excel icon is located and be able to get to it without even thinking.

Another less efficient method of starting Excel from Program Manager is to select File ⇨ Run from the Program Manager menu and enter `excel` into the text box. You never really need to use this method because double-clicking an icon is much easier.

When Excel starts, a blank worksheet called `sheet1` is displayed. If you want to retrieve a worksheet, you can use Excel's File ⇨ Open command to load a worksheet from a disk.

You can prevent Excel from creating the blank `sheet1` worksheet by changing the command line that executes Excel. Click the Excel icon once and select File ⇨ Properties from the Program Manager menu. Edit the command line so it includes /e after `excel.exe`. For example, your edited command line may read `c:\excel\excel.exe/e`. Select OK for the change to take effect.

Starting from File Manager

If you want to load a specific worksheet or workbook into Excel, you may prefer to launch Excel from File Manager. The File Manager program is included with Windows and is designed to enable you to manipulate the files on your disks. If you're not familiar with File Manager, consult your Windows manual for instructions on how to use it.

Figure 3-2 shows File Manager, which is displaying the files located in the `Excel \examples` directory. Your File Manager window will look different because you have different files and directories.

Figure 3-2 is the Windows 3.1 File Manager. The version included with Windows 3.0 looks quite a bit different, but the concept is the same.

You can double-click on any filename used by Excel. When you do, Windows starts Excel and loads the file you clicked on. Valid Excel file types are identified by their extension — the three characters following the period in a filename (See Table 3-1).

Table 3-1: Valid Excel file types	
File extension	**Description**
XLS	An Excel worksheet file
XLC	An Excel chart file
XLM	An Excel macro file
XLW	An Excel workbook file
XLA	An Excel add-in file
XLT	An Excel template file

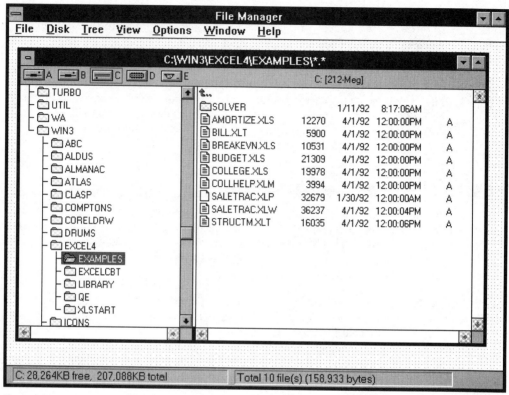

Figure 3-2: You can load Excel and a specific file from the Windows File Manager program.

These file types are discussed in detail in Chapter 6. For now just remember that double-clicking on any of these file types in File Manager launches Excel and loads the file into Excel.

If Excel is already running, double-clicking on an Excel file in File Manager launches another "instance" of Excel, without warning. In most cases, this action is probably not what you want, because it uses up more memory and can be confusing (but it won't cause any harm). As you'll see, Excel enables you to load more than one file at a time, so you don't really need to run more than one instance of Excel.

Starting from DOS

If Windows is not running, you can start Windows and Excel in one fell swoop and even load a worksheet if you want. Make sure that you're at the DOS prompt, which probably looks something like this:

```
c:\>
```

The key to this method is that both Windows and Excel accept *command line parameters* — extra information that you can tag on to the end of a command. To run Windows and automatically launch Excel, enter the following:

```
c:\>win excel
```

To run Windows, launch Excel, and load a worksheet file called `budget.xls` (located in your `c:\sheets` directory), enter:

```
c:\>win excel c:\sheets\budget.xls
```

Of course, you should substitute the appropriate worksheet file and directory name in place of `c:\sheets\budget.xls`. Starting Excel this way bypasses the Program Manager screen and brings you directly to your specified worksheet in Excel.

This technique only works if your Windows and Excel directories are in the DOS path. This should be the case if you followed the instructions when installing Windows and Excel. You may prefer to use this method if Excel is the only Windows program you'll ever run.

 Before attempting to start Excel (and Windows) in this manner, be sure that you aren't running a DOS shell from Windows. To check, type `exit` at the C: prompt then press Enter. If you are returned to Windows, then you were running a DOS shell from Windows and Windows was already running. If you type `exit` at the C: prompt and get a "Bad command" message, then you can proceed with the method of starting Excel as described.

Switching to Another Application

One of the main advantages of Windows is its task-switching capability — the capability to run multiple programs at the same time. For example, you can have Excel running alongside your favorite word processor and switch between them whenever you want. You don't need to exit one program before launching another.

This feature may not seem like such a big deal, but for those of us who have been involved with PCs for the past ten years, it's a *major* step forward. Back in

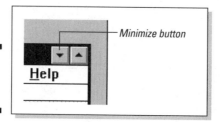

Figure 3-3: The Minimize button reduces Excel to an icon but keeps it available for immediate access.

the old days (about three years ago) personal computing was a linear process; you could run one program at a time. If you were working on a spreadsheet and wanted to write a memo, you had to close your spreadsheet program and start your word processor. To return to the spreadsheet, you had to close down the word processor first. For those of us who have lived through such inefficient times, the Windows task-switching capability is indeed a big deal.

When Excel is running, you can temporarily put it aside and switch to any other program that's running (including the Program Manager, which itself is considered a program). You have several ways to do this procedure:

1. Reduce Excel to an icon by clicking on the downward-pointing triangle button located at the top of the Excel title bar (see Figure 3-3). This action enables you to work with the underlying application — usually the Program Manager. From the Program Manager, you can launch another application.

2. Press Ctrl+Esc to bring up the Windows Task List (see Figure 3-4). The Task List displays the names of all currently running programs. Simply double-click on the program that you want to jump to, and you're there in a flash. If you want to launch a program that's not running, select the Program Manager from the Task List. You can also access the Task List by clicking once on the Control button in the left corner of any program's title bar (see Figure 3-5). This action drops down a menu, from which you can select Switch To to display the Task List. Double-clicking on the Control button is a shortcut way to close an application.

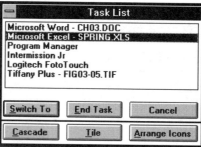

Figure 3-4: The Windows Task List enables you to jump quickly to another application.

Figure 3-5: Every Windows application has a Control button in the left corner or in the title bar. Click on it once to pull down a menu.

File

3. Press Alt+Tab to cycle through all active applications. Hold down the Alt key and press Tab until you see the name of the program you want to work with in the box in the center of the screen (it may be the Program Manager, where you can launch a new application). When you see the program you want, release the Alt key and the selected application is activated. Note that this feature works a little differently in Windows 3.0. The names aren't displayed in a box, but the title bars of the windows are highlighted. The result is the same, however.

This last technique is by far the easiest way to switch among applications. We urge you to practice it until you understand how it works.

To return to Excel where you left off, you can use any of these techniques from the program that's currently active. The Alt+Tab method is the most efficient.

Exiting Excel

When you're finished with the Excel task at hand, you're responsible for exiting properly. Sure, you could just turn off the power, say your good-byes, and leave for the day. Although that's the easiest method, it's not the safest; in fact, it's downright dangerous. Windows uses many different files during the course of its operation, many of which you may not even be aware of. Some of these files are "temporary" files that are deleted when you exit certain applications or when you quit Windows. If you don't exit your applications gracefully, some of these files may not close properly, which can result in hard disk problems that are not immediately apparent (but may come back to haunt you days or even weeks later).

Another possible risk is that unsaved data is in Excel or another program that may be running. Simply turning off the power switch destroys this data. Trust us; use one of these methods to exit from Excel:

■ Select File ➪ Exit from Excel's menu.

■ Press the Alt+F4 shortcut key combination.

■ Double-click on the Control button in Excel's title bar.

Figure 3-6: If you try to exit with any unsaved work, Excel gives you the opportunity to save your files.

■ Bring up the Task List, select Excel from the list, and then click on the End Task button. This method enables you to close Excel while you're in another application.

If you use any of these techniques to exit Excel, it lets you know if you have any unsaved data by displaying a dialog box like that shown in Figure 3-6. This dialog box gives you a chance to save your work or abandon it.

Actually, you're perfectly safe if you simply select File ➪ Exit from the Program Manager to end Windows. The Program Manager lets you know if you have any applications open that have unsaved data and gives you a chance to save your work. Then the Program Manager closes down any open applications for you (including Excel) before it shuts down Windows.

Summary

▶ You have several ways to start Excel. The most common method is to double-click on the Excel program icon from the Windows Program Manager.

▶ You can also launch Excel, along with a selected file, from the Windows File Manager.

▶ If Windows is not running, you can start Windows, run Excel, and even load an Excel file — all from the DOS prompt.

▶ Avoid the temptation to simply turn off the power to your computer when you're finished working. Exit Excel (and Windows) gracefully by selecting File ➪ Exit from the system menu (or by using any of the other techniques mentioned in this chapter). This practice ensures you don't lose any unsaved data and can also prevent damage to files that are not properly closed.

Chapter 4
A Hands-On Tour of Excel

In this chapter . . .

▶ The obligatory tour of the screen — you'll learn the official names for the elements that make up Excel.

▶ A step-by-step introductory example of a simple Excel session, designed to give the newcomer a taste of what this product can do.

▶ A simple Excel session: You'll create a new worksheet, enter data and a formula, create a graph, save your work, and print the results.

If you haven't figured it out yet, you'll soon discover that Excel 4 is a powerful product that can be used at several different levels. Beginners can easily be overwhelmed by the sheer number of features at their disposal. We developed this chapter as a way to get your feet wet and give you some hands-on experience by sampling some of the things this product can do.

This chapter is primarily for those who have never used a spreadsheet before. If you're new to spreadsheets, taking the time to go through this introductory tutorial will make you more comfortable with the rest of your learning. But even if you've used spreadsheets before, you can breeze through this chapter to get a quick look at some of the new features in Excel 4.

A Tour of the Screen

Throughout this book we'll be referring to various parts of the Excel display. It's a good idea to become familiar with these terms, so here goes.

The Excel window

Figure 4-1 shows an Excel 4 screen with some of the key elements pointed out.

Main title bar   This tells you what program is currently active by displaying the name of the program and the currently active file (if applicable). Note that Excel is running in a window, and that Excel itself can also have windows within it.

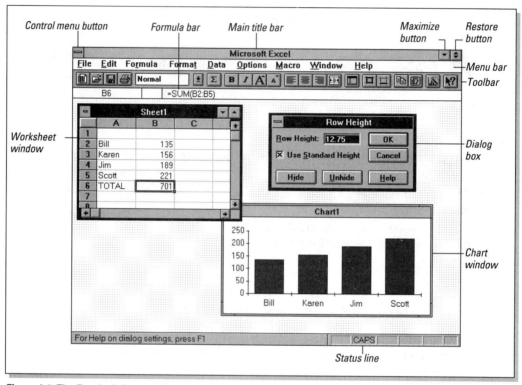

Figure 4-1: The Excel window and the names for some of its parts.

Control menu button	Most windows have this button in their upper-left corner. Clicking it drops down a menu that lets you do certain things with the window (minimize it, maximize it, close it, and so on).
Minimize button	Clicking this button reduces Excel to an icon (it will still be running and can be reactivated by double-clicking the icon).
Restore button	Restores the Excel window to its previous size.
Maximize button	This button does not appear in the figure because Excel is already maximized. If the application were not maximized, the restore button would be replaced with a single triangle pointing up. Clicking that button makes Excel fill the entire screen.

Menu bar	When you click on one of the words in the menu bar, a menu drops down, from which you can make more choices.
Toolbar	This consists of a group of icons that represent shortcut ways to issue commands. Excel provides several different toolbars, appropriate for different tasks, and you can customize the toolbars to include the icons you use most often. In addition, you can move the toolbars to a different location.
Dialog box	This is a sample of one of many dialog boxes used by Excel. They pop up when you issue certain commands from the menu. Dialog boxes make it easy to change settings, specify parameters, and so on.
Formula bar	This line displays the cell coordinates of the current cell, as well as the information in the current cell.
Status line	This line displays a variety of information, depending on what you're doing with the worksheet. The boxes on the right side tell you if certain keyboard settings are active. For example, if you have Num Lock on, NUM will appear on the status line.
Worksheet window	This is a window within Excel that holds a worksheet. The title bar is highlighted, which means it's the currently active window.
Chart window	This is a window within Excel that holds a chart.

A worksheet window

Figure 4-2 shows a worksheet window, with some essential parts pointed out. Since Excel also uses chart windows and macro windows, many of the parts of these windows are identical to worksheet windows. You'll discover the differences in later chapters.

Worksheet title bar	This displays the name of the file you are currently working on.
Row numbers	This border contains numbers from 1 to 16,384 — the number of rows available in a single worksheet. Depending on the size of the window, only a portion of these rows are visible at any one time, typically a few dozen.

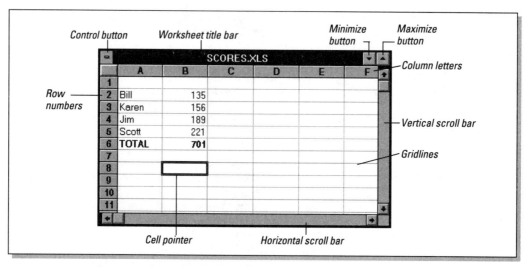

Figure 4-2: An Excel worksheet window and the names for some of its parts.

Just how big is an Excel worksheet?

When you're working with Excel, you can see only a small portion of the entire worksheet area. A single Excel worksheet contains exactly 4,194,304 cells. Memory limitations prevent you from ever using all of these cells, but's it's interesting to ponder how much a worksheet can theoretically hold. A standard VGA monitor can display 198 standard sized cells at once, which represents only 0.00472 percent of the entire worksheet. Put another way, there are 21,183 screenfuls of information in an Excel worksheet.

If you tried to save a completely full worksheet, you'd better have about 60MB of memory free on your hard drive — more if you use formulas. Also, set aside an hour or so while you stare at the hourglass icon, waiting for the file to be saved. If you want to back up this file on high-density floppies, have about 40 disks at your disposal.

If we assume a printed page has 49 rows and 9 columns, printing a completely filled Excel worksheet would use up 9,511 sheets of paper — or about 19 reams. With a relatively fast 8-page per minute laser printer, you'd be able to print the complete worksheet in just under 20 hours (not counting time to change the paper and toner cartridges).

Recalculating such a worksheet would depend on how many formulas you had. We have no way of gauging recalc time, but it might be a good occasion to visit your aunt in Walla Walla after you hit the F9 key.

Column letters	This border contains letters from A through IV (256 columns). After column Z comes column AA, AB, AC, and so on. After column AZ comes BA, BB, BC, etc. and so on up to column IV.
Vertical scroll bar	This provides a quick way of moving up and down through a worksheet (you can access it only with a mouse).
Horizontal scroll bar	This provides a quick way of moving left and right through a worksheet (you can access it only with a mouse).
Control button	All active windows have this button in their upper-left corner. Clicking it displays a drop-down menu offering various commands specific to controlling the size, shape, position, and status of that window.
Minimize button	Clicking this button reduces the worksheet to an icon (it is available and can be reactivated by double-clicking the icon).
Maximize button	This button makes the current worksheet fill the entire Excel workspace. It also removes the worksheet title bar to give you even more space. When a worksheet is maximized, the restore button for the worksheet appears on the Excel menu line.
Restore button	This button restores the Excel window to its previous size. It appears only if the worksheet window is maximized within the Excel window (and therefore does not appear in Figure 4-2).
Gridlines	These help you keep track of cells. If you find them distracting, you can turn gridlines off.
Cell pointer	The heavy border indicates the currently active cell.

A Simple Excel Session _____

Before proceeding, we need to make sure you're ready to follow along on your own computer. Just to make sure we're in sync, do the following steps.

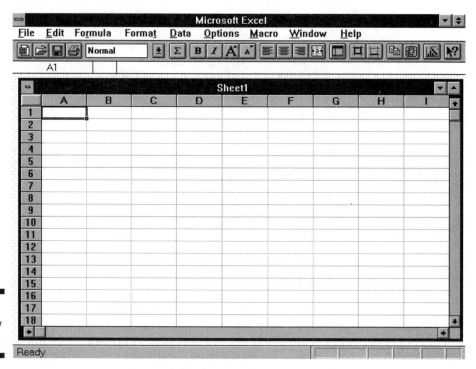

Figure 4-3:
Excel, ready
to go.

Steps: Getting to an active worksheet

Step 1. **Start your computer.** Power up your system and start Windows if it doesn't come up automatically (type `win` at the C:\ prompt, then press Enter).

Step 2. **Run Excel 4.** Click on the Excel 4 icon, or use one of the other methods described in Chapter 3.

Step 3. **Maximize the Excel window.** In the upper-right corner of the Excel window (which is labeled "Microsoft Excel") you'll see two square gray boxes with triangles in them. If the box on the right has two triangles, Excel is already maximized (go on to the next step). If one of the triangles is pointing up, click on that box to maximize the Excel Window. If you're using the standard VGA driver, your screen should now look like Figure 4-3 (but it may show more rows and columns if you're using a higher video resolution).

Step 4. **Set up your workspace.** You'll notice a row of words along the top of your screen (File, Edit, Formula, and so on). This is the Excel menu. We simply need to make sure that your settings correspond to ours. Click on the Options menu item. This drops down a list of additional menu

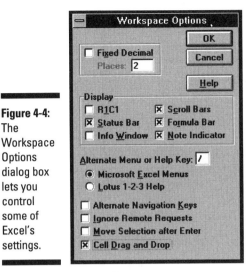

Figure 4-4:
The
Workspace
Options
dialog box
lets you
control
some of
Excel's
settings.

commands. Click on the Workspace item. This displays a dialog box in which you can change some of the settings by clicking various boxes with your mouse. Make sure the dialog box is exactly the same as Figure 4-4 (in particular, make sure the box labeled Cell Drag and Drop is clicked on). When the settings are correct, choose OK.

Now we're ready to move on. The goal of this exercise it to create a simple worksheet, including some formulas. Then we'll format it so it looks nice, save it to disk, create a chart, and finally print the numbers and chart. Figure 4-5 shows the

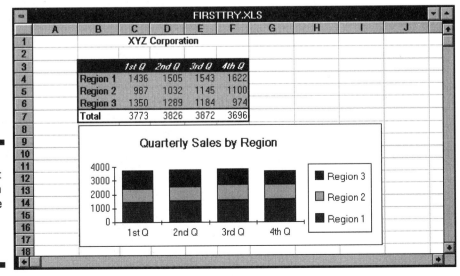

Figure 4-5:
This is what
your screen
will look like
after this
initial
exercise.

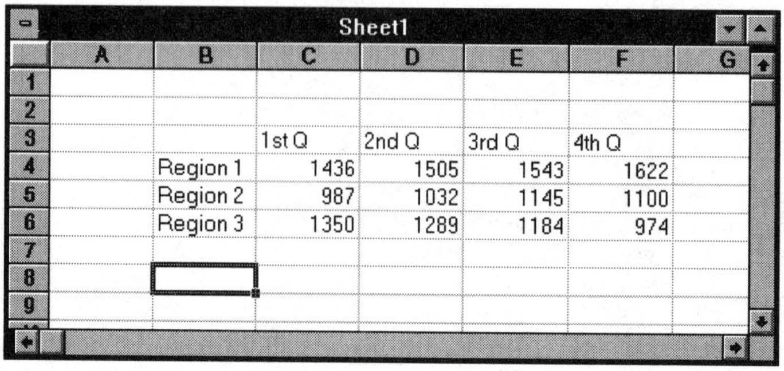

Figure 4-6: The sample table of numbers used in this exercise.

completed worksheet that you'll be developing. You might be surprised to discover how easy it is to get from a blank worksheet to the results in this figure.

Entering some data

First, we'll enter the column and row labels for the data table. Move the cell cursor to cell C3 — the intersection of the column labeled C and the row numbered 3. You can either use the arrow keys on your keyboard or move the cell cursor with the mouse by moving the mouse pointer to the target cell and clicking once. Note that the current cell coordinates appear in the Formula bar.

Make sure cell C3 is selected, and then enter the text 1st Q and press Enter. We could move to the cell to the right and type in 2nd Q, but we'll let Excel do some of the work. Make sure cell C3 is still selected. You'll notice a tiny box in the lower-right corner of the cell outline. Move the mouse directly over this small box until the mouse pointer turns into a small solid cross. When this happens, press the left mouse button and drag the mouse to the right until you've covered three more cells (D3, E3, and F3). Release the mouse button. You'll see that Excel fills in the highlighted range with the next three elements in the series: 2nd Q, 3rd Q, and 4th Q. This is an example of Excel's Autofill feature — a great time-saver that you'll learn more about in Chapter 7.

Next, move the cell cursor to cell B4, enter the text Region 1, and press Enter. We'll use Autofill again to add labels for two more regions. Grab the tiny box with the mouse, and this time drag it down two more cells and release the mouse button. Excel should have filled in the text, Region 2 and Region 3.

Now, we need to enter the values to complete the table. Move the cell cursor to cell C4 and enter 1436 (do not enter a comma) and press the right arrow key. Pressing this key enters the information into the cell and also moves the cell pointer to the cell to the right. Continue filling in the numbers until your worksheet looks like Figure 4-6. When you get to the end of the row, use the arrow keys to move down a row and over three columns to the left (or click on the appropriate cell with the mouse). You can enter the numbers in any order.

Figure 4-7: The summation tool will automatically insert a SUM formula.

Creating a formula

The next step is to create a formula to add the numbers for each quarter.

First, move to cell B7 and enter the text `Total` into the cell. Move the cell cursor to cell C7 — this will hold a formula that adds the values in the range C4:C6. Excel provides a shortcut for adding a series of numbers.

Locate the summation symbol (shown in Figure 4-7) in the toolbar and click it once with the mouse. You'll notice that Excel "proposes" a formula on the Formula bar: =SUM(C4:C6). This formula is comprised of a built-in function (SUM) and an "argument" for the function (C4:C6). This formula can be interpreted as: "*Compute the sum of the values in cells C4 through C6 and insert the result into the current cell.*" Since this is exactly what we want to do, click the summation button again to insert the formula into cell C7. Excel displays the results of the formula — in this case, 3773.

We *could* go through these same steps to add three more formulas into cells D7, E7, and F7. But we'll use Autofill again to copy the existing formula to these other cells. Make sure the cell pointer is on cell C7. Use the mouse to grab the small box and drag the highlighting over to the three adjacent cells (D7:F7). Release the mouse button and take a look at what Excel did.

You'll notice that it created three new formulas, with the appropriate cell references — again, just what we wanted. Note that it didn't make an exact copy of the formula. Rather, it adjusted the cell references for each column of numbers. At this point, your worksheet should look like Figure 4-8. Note, of course, that you see the results of the formula rather than the formulas themselves.

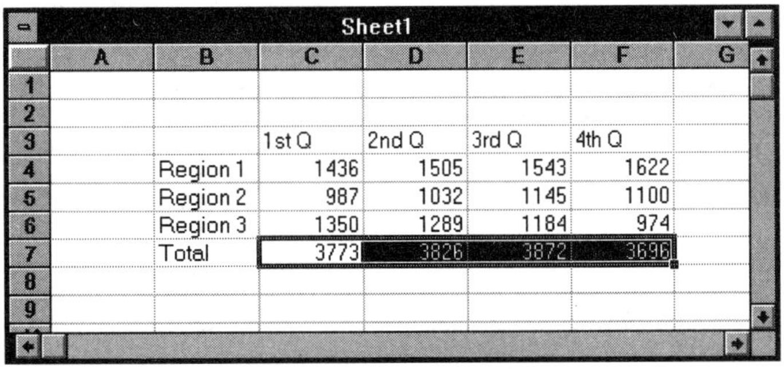

Figure 4-8: The worksheet in our excercise with the formulas inserted.

	A	B	C	D	E	F	G
1							
2							
3			1st Q	2nd Q	3rd Q	4th Q	
4		Region 1	1436	1505	1543	1622	
5		Region 2	987	1032	1145	1100	
6		Region 3	1350	1289	1184	974	
7		Total	3773	3826	3872	3696	
8							
9							

Sheet1

Figure 4-9: The Autoformat tool will format a table of numbers in one of several attractive styles.

Formatting the table

The worksheet, so far, shows the quarterly sales data for each region, plus the total for each quarter. We could quit now, print it, and be on our way. Instead, we'll spend a little more time to make the table look more attractive and easier to read. We could use Excel's extensive formatting capabilities to make the table look exactly how we like. But we'll use the new Autoformat feature to select a preconfigured table layout.

Move the cell cursor anywhere within the table. Examine the toolbar at the top of the screen and locate the icon shown in Figure 4-9 — the Autoformat tool. Click this tool and your table will be instantly transformed with borders, colors, and numeric formats. If you don't care for this format, hold down the Shift key and click the Autoformat tool again. Each time you do this, Excel reformats the table using a different set of formatting options. Repeat this procedure until you find a style that you like (don't forget to hold down Shift while you click the icon). Figure 4-10 shows the table with one of the preset formats applied.

Adding a title

Next, we'll add a descriptive title to this worksheet. You can add text anywhere you like in a worksheet, but we'll put the title in cell B1 and then center it over the table we created. Move the cell cursor to cell B1, type XYZ Corporation, and press Enter.

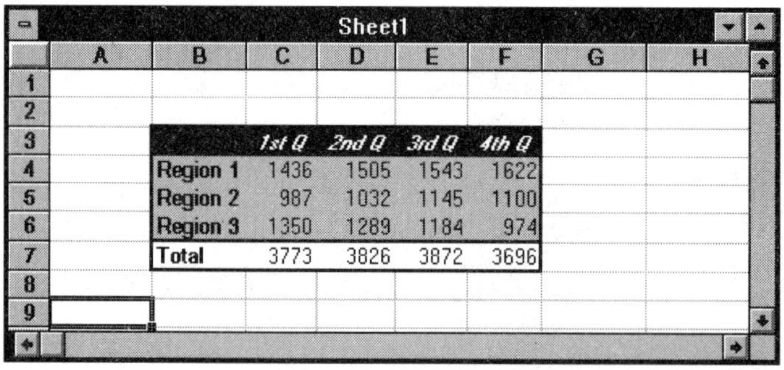

Figure 4-10: The table of numbers in the current example, after clicking the Autoformat tool.

	A	B	C	D	E	F	G	H
1								
2								
3			1st Q	2nd Q	3rd Q	4th Q		
4		Region 1	1436	1505	1543	1622		
5		Region 2	987	1032	1145	1100		
6		Region 3	1350	1289	1184	974		
7		Total	3773	3826	3872	3696		
8								
9								

Sheet1

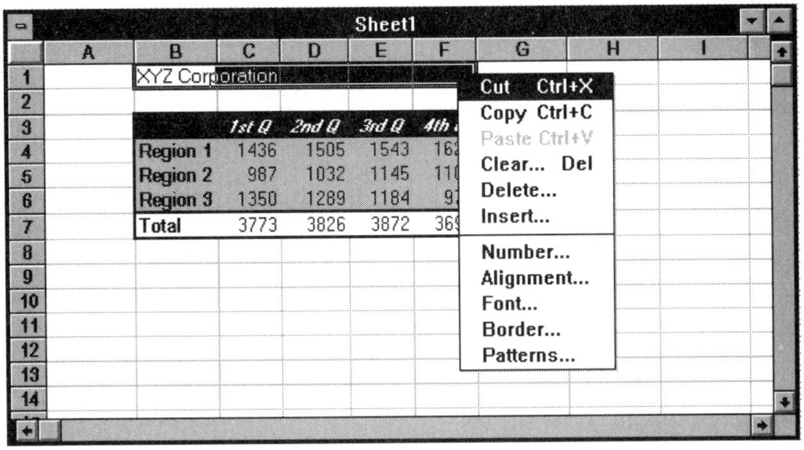

Figure 4-11:
Preparing to
center the
title over a
range of
columns
using the
shortcut
menu
(invoked
with the
right mouse
button).

	A	B	C	D	E	F	G	H	I
1		XYZ Corporation					Cut Ctrl+X		
2							Copy Ctrl+C		
3			1st Q	2nd Q	3rd Q	4th	Paste Ctrl+V		
4		Region 1	1436	1505	1543	162	Clear... Del		
5		Region 2	987	1032	1145	110	Delete...		
6		Region 3	1350	1289	1184	9	Insert...		
7		Total	3773	3826	3872	369			
8							Number...		
9							Alignment...		
10							Font...		
11							Border...		
12							Patterns...		
13									
14									

To center the title over the table, we need to first select the range B1:F1 by dragging the mouse over these cells (don't drag the Autofill handle, or you'll copy the cell). When this range is selected, make sure the mouse pointer is located anywhere within the selected cells and click the *right* mouse button. As you'll see, the right mouse button plays a key role in Excel — it pops up a shortcut menu that's appropriate for whatever information is currently selected. Your screen should look something like Figure 4-11 (the location of the shortcut menu will depend on where the mouse pointer was when you clicked the right button).

Select the menu option labeled Alignment. This brings up a dialog box with many different options for aligning information in a cell or across multiple cells. Select the option labeled Center across selection. This does just what it says: it centers the text in the selected cells across the entire selection. Choose OK to close the dialog box and display the results. Your screen should now look like Figure 4-12.

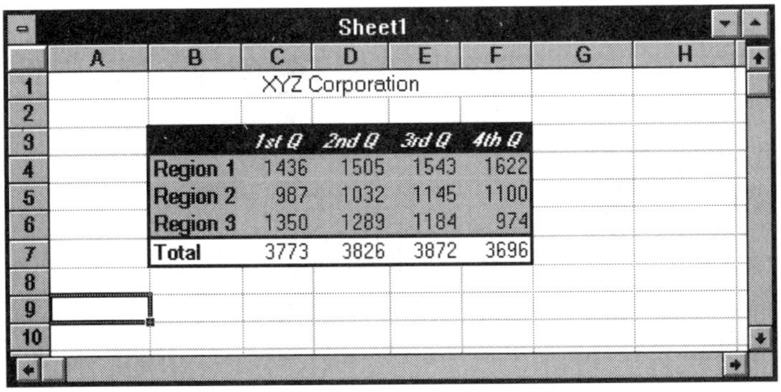

Figure 4-12:
The text in
cell B1 is
centered
across five
columns.

	A	B	C	D	E	F	G	H
1			XYZ Corporation					
2								
3			1st Q	2nd Q	3rd Q	4th Q		
4		Region 1	1436	1505	1543	1622		
5		Region 2	987	1032	1145	1100		
6		Region 3	1350	1289	1184	974		
7		Total	3773	3826	3872	3696		
8								
9								
10								

Figure 4-13: The ChartWizard tool will walk you through the steps necessary to create a chart.

Note that the text we entered is still located in cell B1, although it looks like it might be in column C or D. If you wanted to change this text, you would do so by editing the contents of cell B1. In fact, let's make this title bold. Click on cell B1 to select it, and then click the toolbar icon that has the large "B" on it. The text in cell B1 should now be bold.

Creating a chart

The worksheet is looking better, but we can improve it even more by making a graph of the data. First, select all of the table except the last row that holds the totals (we don't want to plot the total sales on this graph). In other words we'll plot the range B3:F6.

Excel now walks you through the steps required to create a chart with its ChartWizard feature. Examine the toolbar and locate the icon shown in Figure 4-13, the ChartWizard tool. Verify that the range B3:F6 is selected and click the tool. Notice the message at the bottom of the screen: "Drag in document to create a chart." Excel wants you to draw an outline on the worksheet where you want the graph placed. Use the mouse to locate the upper-left corner, press and hold the mouse button and drag the outline until you're satisfied with the size of the graph, and then release the mouse button. You might try locating the chart directly below the table. Don't worry, you can always resize or move the chart later.

The first of five ChartWizard dialog boxes pops up, and is shown in Figure 4-14. We've preselected the chart data, so it already appears in the text box. We can

Figure 4-14: The first of five Chart-Wizard dialog boxes.

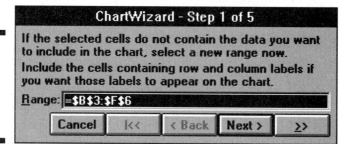

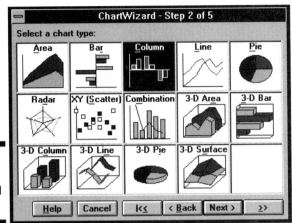

Figure 4-15:
The Second
ChartWizard
dialog box.

now click on the Next button to go to the next step, the second dialog box, which lets you select the general type of chart.

Figure 4-15 shows the second ChartWizard dialog box. The default type is a column chart — which is highlighted and appears in reverse video. Since this is what we want, simply choose Next to move to the next step, which lets you further specify the chart type. For this example, we want a stacked column chart, which is labeled 3. Click this chart type to select it, and then choose Next to move on.

If you change your mind or make a mistake while working in ChartWizard, choose Back to go to the previous step.

The fourth dialog box displays your chart and lets you change some specifications. It just so happens that the chart displayed is what we want, so we'll move on to the last step by choosing Next.

The final dialog box in this series lets us add a few more options. We'll add a title. Click in the text box labeled Chart Title, and enter Quarterly Sales by Region. Choose OK and your chart is displayed in the worksheet in the area you specified. At this point, you can resize the graph by pointing to one of the four corners and stretching or shrinking the chart box.

As you'll see, you can also make many adjustments to your charts. For example, the legend probably appears too large. But we're getting ahead of ourselves. Suffice it to say that the actual charts you produce can look much better than this simple example.

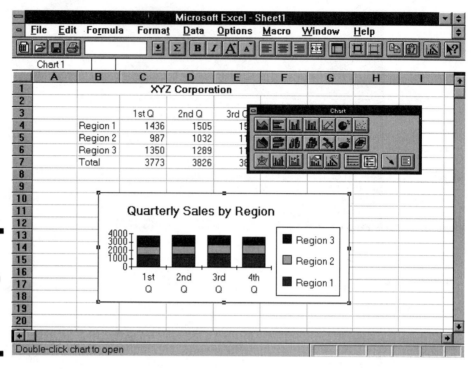

Figure 4-16:
Our sample
project, with
a table,
chart, and
the Chart
toolbar.

When you return to the worksheet from the ChartWizard, you'll notice that the Chart toolbar is displayed on your screen, as shown in Figure 4-16. This lets you change or annotate your chart, and the toolbar is displayed whenever you click on a chart. Click on an area outside of the chart and the Chart toolbar disappears.

Saving your work

Things are starting to look pretty good, and it's time to save your work. Saving your work places a copy of your worksheet into a file that is stored on your hard disk. Once it's stored on disk, you can retrieve it again at any time to work on it more.

Up until this point, everything we've done has taken place in your computer's memory. If you suddenly experienced a power failure or someone kicked the plug out of the wall socket, all of your work would be sent into oblivion — gone for good. You can see why it's a good idea to save your work frequently. It only takes a few seconds and can prevent the loss of hours of work.

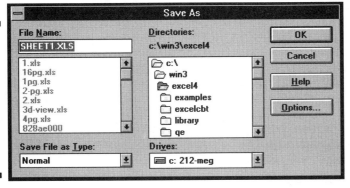

Figure 4-17: The File Save As dialog box gives you various options for saving your work.

Select File from the main menu. This drops down some more menu options. Choose Save. Since this worksheet doesn't have an official name (it's still labeled Sheet1), Excel gives you the opportunity to provide a filename in its Save As dialog box (see Figure 4-17).

Note that sheet1.xls is highlighted in this dialog box. Enter firsttry, and the old name is replaced with your new name. Choose OK or press Enter and the worksheet will be saved with a filename of firsttry.xls. Note that you don't have to enter the xls part of the filename — Excel provides it for you.

Printing your work

Now it's time to get this masterpiece onto paper. We're assuming that you have a printer installed for Windows and the connections are properly made.

Before we print, we'll preview the document on-screen. This is usually a good idea, since you can see exactly how your printed results will look. Select File from the main menu and then choose Print Preview in the drop-down menu. After a few seconds, Excel displays a miniature replica of your worksheet — exactly as it will be printed. You should see something like what is shown in Figure 4-18.

You'll notice that there are outlines around all of the cells. We don't like the way that looks, since it tends to obscure the borders in the table. It's easy enough to get rid of these gridlines. In the Preview window, select the button labeled Setup. This pops up a dialog box that gives you extensive options as to how your printed page is set up. For our purposes, select the box labeled Cell Gridlines to remove the small x. Choose OK to close the dialog box and return to the preview screen.

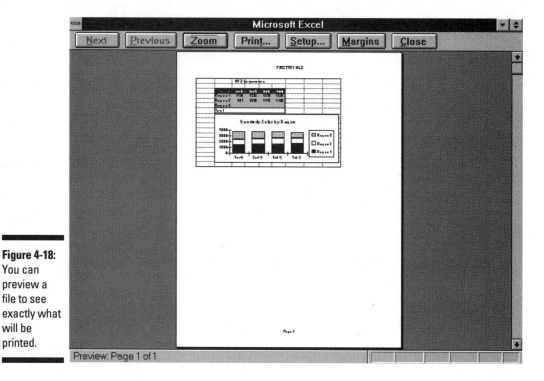

Figure 4-18:
You can
preview a
file to see
exactly what
will be
printed.

Notice that the mouse pointer is in the shape of a magnifying glass. This tells you that you can click anywhere in the previewed output to enlarge what you're seeing. Try it. When you click in an enlarged view, it returns to the small view.

When you're satisfied with the preview, select the Print button to start printing. This returns you to your worksheet and pops up yet another dialog box that gives you one last chance to specify some print options. Just choose OK to start the printing.

Depending on your printer, it may take several minutes before the output comes out of the printer. Printers vary in quality, so you may or may not be happy with the results. Often, you can make some adjustments to improve the quality. We'll cover printing in detail in Chapter 13.

Ready for more?

Congratulations. If you followed these instructions, you should have a better feel for what Excel can do and what you're in for.

If you had problems with this chapter, you might want to try again by starting over from scratch. Make sure you follow the instructions precisely and don't move on to the next step until you understand what you did.

In this simple exercise, you've been exposed to the following concepts:

- Cell selection using the mouse
- Creating a formula
- Dialog boxes
- Autoformat
- Excel's ChartWizard
- Print Preview

- Entering data
- Menus
- Autofill
- Shortcut menus
- File saving
- Printing

Hopefully, this brief exercise will excite you enough to want to tackle the rest of this book — or at least the beginning chapters for now.

One word of advice: Don't be afraid to experiment. There's nothing you can do in Excel that will cause any harm to your computer or software (assuming, of course that you're not using the only copy of your company's budget projections to fiddle around with). Go for it!

Summary

▶ Excel is made up of many parts. We pointed out some of the most important screen elements.

▶ Excel is an application that runs in a window. Excel uses worksheets, charts, and dialog boxes that run in separate windows within the Excel window.

▶ Excel has many shortcut features (this chapter exposed you to a few of them) that greatly simplify spreadsheet work.

PART
II

The Basic Concepts

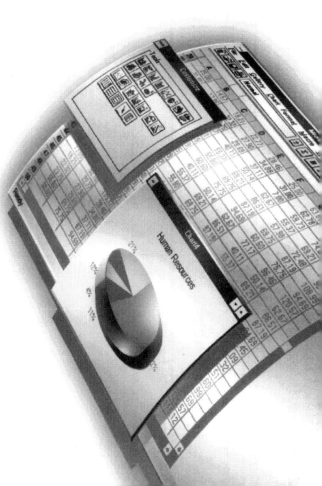

Chapter 5
Getting Around
the Spreadsheet

In this chapter . . .

▶ The pros and cons of using the mouse, the keyboard, or both.

▶ The various forms the mouse pointer can take and what they mean.

▶ How to quickly move and size windows with the keyboard or mouse.

▶ Efficient ways to move the cell pointer around a worksheet.

▶ How to use Excel's pull-down menus, toolbar, and dialog boxes.

▶ How to get the most out of Excel's on-line Help system.

Whether you're a spreadsheet newcomer or an old hand, you need to know how to perform some basic Excel tasks, which can differ quite a bit from other spreadsheet programs. Essential spreadsheet operations include moving the cell pointer around your spreadsheet, choosing commands, and selecting options from dialog boxes. This chapter explains how to accomplish these tasks, using the keyboard, the mouse, or a combination of both. If you've never used a spreadsheet program or mouse, this chapter contains information you'll find essential. If you've abandoned Lotus 1-2-3 and are moving up in life, perusing this chapter will do you good.

If you run into trouble using Excel, or if you have a thirst for more knowledge, this chapter also introduces you to Excel's on-line help system. Help is your silent spreadsheet partner that is just a keystroke (or mouse click) away. No one is an island unto him- or herself; we all need a little help from our friends occasionally. You'll learn how to get the most from Help so your Excel sessions will be as productive as possible.

Using the Keyboard or Mouse: Which Is Best for You?

Every computer comes with a keyboard. The keyboard is an essential tool for using Excel because it enables you to select cells and ranges, issue commands, and enter labels, values, and formulas.

Similarly, you can perform these same functions by using a mouse. A mouse (or other pointing device, such as a trackball) is an optional peripheral. But for some Excel operations, and any Windows programs, a mouse can make your computer sessions much more productive and easier.

If you've used a spreadsheet or another program prior to Excel, you may find using a mouse uncomfortable. Fortunately, you can use Excel successfully with the keyboard only and gradually increase your use of the mouse. We recommend that you play a few games of Windows Solitaire to help you hone your mouse skills. If you've used a previous version of Excel or another graphics-based program, you'll feel right at home with Excel and the mouse.

If you're like most users, however, you'll probably use the keyboard for some operations (such as data entry) and the mouse for others (such as moving and sizing windows).

Examining keyboard pros and cons

Because your computer comes with a keyboard, no additional investment is needed on your part. And if you've used another personal computer program or a typewriter, the keyboard will look familiar to you. In addition, your hands don't need to leave the keyboard to accomplish an Excel task.

On the downside, a keyboard really isn't oriented toward graphics-based programs such as Windows and Excel. You can navigate pull-down menus and dialog boxes much more quickly and efficiently with a mouse. And moving and sizing windows, or an Excel graphics object, is tedious with a keyboard. Also, mouseless users do not have access to Excel's toolbars. Finally, getting used to using a mouse, is a good idea because the trend in computing is toward graphical programs that rely on a mouse.

Using the keyboard

Most of us have at one time or another used a typewriter, so your computer's keyboard should look familiar. Like a typewriter, the keyboard contains keys for entering the letters of the alphabet into a worksheet. Above those keys are the numbers 0 through 9 that you use to enter values.

From there the similarity ends. The keyboard contains other keys that can perform many Excel operations. Depending on your keyboard, you have a set of function keys (or F keys) located along the left side or along the top of the keyboard. These keys are assigned a specific task. You can also use these keys in combination with other special keys (such as Alt and Ctrl) to carry out additional Excel and Windows operations. These key combinations are known as "keyboard shortcuts." To use them, you press and hold down a special key (such as Alt) and then press and release a second key. For example, pressing Ctrl+F12 enables you to quickly open a worksheet you created in a previous Excel session.

On the right side of the keyboard is a numeric keypad, much like you find on an adding machine or a calculator. Depending on whether you have the Num Lock key activated, you can enter values or move the cell pointer. Table 5-1 summarizes the major keys and their purpose.

Table 5-1: Keyboard keys and their functions in Excel	
Key	**Function**
Alphabetic keys	Similar to a typewriter; use these keys to enter text characters into a cell.
Numeric keys	Similar to a typewriter; use these keys to enter values into a cell.
Shift	Enables you to type uppercase letters, certain punctuation marks, and shortcut key combinations.
Caps Lock	Makes all alphabetic keys uppercase.
Tab	Moves the cell pointer on the worksheet and the highlighted item in dialog boxes.
Ctrl	Used in shortcut key combinations.
Alt	Used in shortcut key combinations and for invoking Excel's pull-down menu bar.
Esc	Used in shortcut key combinations and for backing out (escaping) from a command menu or dialog box.
Del	Erases (deletes) selected characters.
Backspace	Deletes characters immediately to the left of the pointer.
F keys	Used for executing commands and in shortcut key combinations. These keys are labeled with an F followed by a number located along the left-hand side or top of the keyboard. They are also known as function keys.
Numeric keypad	Similar to an adding machine; the keys on the right-hand side of the keyboard that have numbers and arithmetic operators. When Num Lock is on, you can enter numbers into your worksheet; when Num Lock is off, you can use the same keys to move the cell pointer.

Continued next page

Table 5-1: Keyboard keys and their functions in Excel (continued)	
Key	Function
Left arrow	Moves the cell pointer one cell to the left.
Right arrow	Moves the cell pointer one cell to the right.
Up arrow	Moves the cell pointer one cell up.
Down arrow	Moves the cell pointer one cell down.
PgUp	Moves the cell pointer one screen up.
PgDn	Moves the cell pointer one screen down.
Home	Moves the cell pointer to column A of the current row.
End	Moves the cell pointer to the end of the current row, stopping at the last column that contains an entry.
Spacebar	The blank bar at the bottom of the alphabetic keys. Creates a blank space between characters.
Enter	Similar to a typewriter's Return key; the key on the right side of the alphabetic keys. Used for entering an entry into a cell, moving the cell pointer down one cell, selecting commands, and completing dialog box requests.

Examining mouse pros and cons

A mouse is clearly the way to go in using Excel or any other graphics-based program. You can perform almost all keyboard equivalents much more easily and quickly, including moving and sizing windows, and selecting ranges and graphics objects. A mouse also provides you with the opportunity to execute operations using Excel's toolbars, making your work that much more faster and efficient. And if you need to get up and running quickly with Excel, you can use a mouse to select commands without having to memorize them.

If you hate meeses to pieces . . .

If the idea of using a mouse is still unfathomable to you, you may want to consider a trackball. A trackball resembles a billiards cue ball and is really a stationary upside-down mouse. Some laptop computers have a trackball built right into the keyboard because trying to balance a laptop and a mouse on an airline seat tray is a bit rough.

Few bad things can be said about a mouse. Because Excel was developed from the ground up as a spreadsheet for the Windows environment, the two go hand in hand. After you get used to it, you'll find a mouse an essential spreadsheet tool. What was once known as a "pesky electronic rodent" is now an integral part of most users' computer systems and is a component included with most new computers.

Using the mouse

The mouse is the small rectangle or oval with at least one button (most have two and some have three). It's connected to the back of your computer with a cord (its "tail" — hence the name "mouse") and has a small rubber ball underneath. When you have the mouse on your desk or table, moving it around causes a ball to move, which in turn moves a "pointer" on the computer screen. You use this pointer to select icons, ranges, commands, and so forth. As you move the mouse around, the pointer's shape may change, depending on the region of the Excel screen where it's located. Table 5-2 shows you the many faces of the mouse pointer in Excel.

The movement of the pointer corresponds to the movement of the mouse. If you move the mouse away from you, the pointer moves up your computer screen; if you move the mouse toward you, the pointer moves downward, and so on. You can always pick up and reposition the mouse if you run out of desk space but need to move the pointer further in the same direction. Make sure that you are holding the mouse in the proper orientation (button side at the tip of your fingers). Otherwise the pointer moves up in a different direction from your hand.

To select an item on-screen, such as a button on Excel's toolbar, you first point at it by moving the mouse. When the pointer is on the item, you press the left mouse button once, which is known as *clicking* on it. If you want to select multiple items, such as a contiguous range of cells, you click and hold down the left mouse button and move the mouse so the range is highlighted. This procedure is known as *clicking and dragging*. You release the mouse button when you're finished, and the range remains selected (highlighted).

Pen computing: The wave of the future?

A software innovation on the horizon is pen computing. Pen computing, as its name implies, offers you another input and selection device — namely, a pen. If you've worked with mainframe computers in another life, you're probably familiar with pens through light pens. Pen computing enables you to enter words and numbers by drawing them on-screen with a pen plugged into your computer.

As of this writing, pen computing for personal computers isn't commercially available, and details are sketchy. But we do know that you'll need a special version of Windows currently in development, Windows for Pen Computing, to use a pen with your computer. A pen-based version of Excel is also being developed. Basically, Excel appears the same, but the Formula bar is larger so you can enter your text and numbers easily. And Excel also displays a Barrel button that enables you to select commands or specify whether you want to copy or move a range of cells.

Further down the road? In the not-too-distant future, we'll probably be saying, "File Open Sales94," and Excel will do just that.

Table 5-2: The mouse pointer's various shapes and functions in Excel	
Pointer shape	Function
White arrow	For selecting commands, making dialog box selections, and selecting items (windows and graphics objects).
White cross	For selecting worksheet cells and ranges.
White left-right arrow	For resizing a window.
Black up-down arrow	For resizing a worksheet row or horizontal window pane.
Black left-right arrow	For resizing a worksheet column or vertical window pane.
Hourglass	Indicates to wait while Excel or Windows completes a task.
I-beam	Displays the location of where new characters will be placed.
Hand with upward-pointing index finger	For selecting a definition or example in a help window.

Learning mouse commands

As discussed earlier, a mouse is your one-stop, all-in-one productivity tool. Depending on what you're doing at any given time, the mouse can help you accomplish a wide variety of Excel (and Windows) tasks. You perform the following with the mouse:

Point   Move the mouse pointer to a specific point on your screen. Use the tip of the point to select items on the screen.

Press   Press and hold the button on the mouse — usually the left one if your mouse has two or more.

Click   Press the mouse button once and then release it.

Double-click   Press and release the mouse button twice in quick succession.

Drag   Point the mouse at an item on the screen, press and hold down the button, and move the mouse.

Moving and Sizing Windows _____

As your proficiency with Excel increases, you will eventually need to move and/or size the windows displayed on the computer screen. For example, you may have a chart that you want to see simultaneously on-screen with the worksheet that contains the data it's based on. You can move and size windows using the keyboard or mouse.

Managing windows with the mouse

You can take full advantage of the mouse to manipulate windows. A mouse provides you with many more options than the keyboard to handle windows efficiently. But first examine some Windows background.

Everything in Windows (application programs, files, and dialog boxes) is displayed in a window. Each window also has a Control button, which is the small box with a bar in the left corner of the title bar. The Control button contains a pull-down menu that enables you to perform specific actions on the active window.

Before you can perform an action on a window, you must make the window you want to modify the *active* window — the window that can receive commands. You can identify the active window by its title bar; it's the one that's highlighted, as shown in Figure 5-1. To make a window the active window, click anywhere in the window. Next, select the Control button to pull down its menu and then choose the command you need. Figure 5-2 displays the commands available to you (remember some windows won't have every command). Note that you can close or move any window, but you can't change the size of certain kinds of windows — specifically, dialog boxes.

You can bypass the Control menu altogether for some operations. To move a window, click on and drag the window's title bar to move it. To size a window, choose one of the following options:

- Click the Minimize button (the downward-pointing triangle) in the upper-right corner of the window, as shown in Figure 5-3, to display the window as an icon.

- Click the Maximize button (the upward-pointing triangle) in the upper-right corner of the window, as shown in Figure 5-3, for a full-screen display of the window.

- Position the mouse pointer at the lower-right corner of the window's border until the pointer changes to a diagonal two-headed arrow. Click on and drag the window until it's the size you want and then move the window if you want.

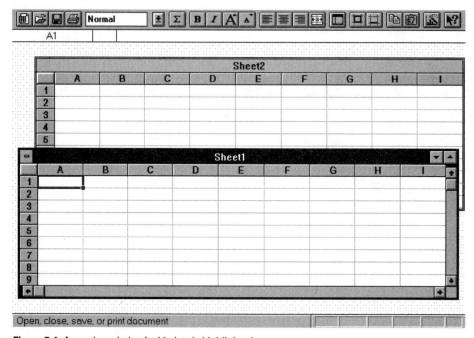

Figure 5-1: An active window's title bar is highlighted.

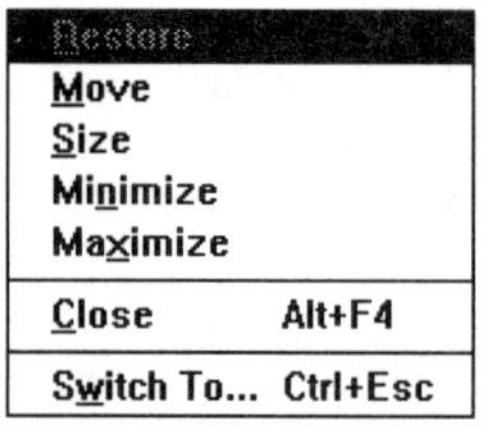

Restore	
Move	
Size	
Mi**n**imize	
Ma**x**imize	
Close	Alt+F4
S**w**itch To...	Ctrl+Esc

Figure 5-2: The window's Control menu enables you to move, size, close, and manage the open windows on your screen.

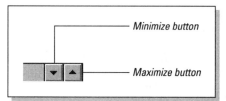

Figure 5-3: You can quickly change a window into an icon (minimize) or zoom it so it fills the computer screen (maximize) by clicking on the Minimize and Maximize buttons, respectively.

You can return the window to its previous size after maximizing it by clicking where the Maximize button used to be. When you maximize a window, that window's Maximize button turns into the Restore button, displayed as two triangles — one pointing up and the other down. When you restore a window, the Restore button again becomes the Maximize button.

Figure 5-4:
Currently open windows are listed on the Window menu. The document name with a check mark is the active window.

Managing windows with the keyboard

You need to jump through a few hoops to manipulate an Excel document (worksheet, chart, macro, etc.) window with the keyboard. First, you must make the window you want to modify the active window. Pull down the Window menu by pressing Alt+W or by pressing F10 and then W. When you do, the menu shown in Figure 5-4 appears.

Notice the check mark next to the document name (Sheet1); this check mark indicates that this window is active. To make another window active, select the appropriate name and that window becomes active. You can also press Ctrl+F6 to cycle through all open windows to make one active.

Moving from Cell to Cell

To enter data in cells and select ranges for operations, you need to move the cell pointer to different locations on the worksheet. Navigating through your spreadsheet is explained next.

Using the mouse

Moving the cell pointer with the mouse is a snap. Simply click on the cell you want the cell pointer on, and Excel makes that cell the active cell. If you need to move the cell pointer to a cell that's not currently on-screen, use the scroll bars to display the area of your worksheet that contains the cell you want to move the cell pointer to. Click on the respective scroll box to scroll the worksheet one row or one column at a time. If you click on a scroll box and hold the mouse button, the worksheet scrolls multiple rows or columns quickly until you release the mouse.

If you're in a hurry, click anywhere on the scroll bar, or click on and drag a scroll box. Excel pages through the worksheet pronto.

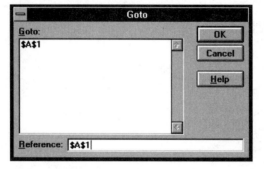

Figure 5-5: To move the cell pointer quickly to a particular cell, you can enter the cell address or name of the cell in the Goto dialog box.

Using the keyboard

Excel provides you with a host of keyboard options for moving the cell pointer around your worksheet. Table 5-3 summarizes these options for you. In addition, if you know which cell you need to go to, you can move the cell pointer there quickly by using the Formula ➭ Goto command (or the F5 shortcut key). In the dialog box that appears, simply enter the cell address or name of the cell you need to move to, as shown in Figure 5-5, and choose OK.

Table 5-3: Keys to move the cell pointer around the Excel worksheet	
Key	**Action**
Right arrow, Tab	Moves the cell pointer one cell to the right.
Left arrow, Shift+Tab	Moves the cell pointer one cell to the left.
Up arrow	Moves the cell pointer up one cell.
Down arrow, Enter	Moves the cell pointer down one cell.
PgUp	Moves the cell pointer up one screen.
PgDn	Moves the cell pointer down one screen.
Home	Moves the cell pointer to column A of the current row.
End	Moves the cell pointer to the end of the current row as far as the last column to the right.
Ctrl+Home	Moves the cell pointer to cell A1.
Ctrl+End	Moves the cell pointer to the last cell in the active worksheet area.
Ctrl+PgUp	Moves the cell pointer left one screen.
Ctrl+PgDn	Moves the cell pointer right one screen.

Using Menus and Commands

Menus are the heart and soul of Excel. The commands contained in Excel's pull-down menus enable you to perform operations on the labels, values, and formulas you've entered into the worksheet. Think of menus as Excel's command center where you're the boss.

Excel veterans may find that this latest version reduces the number of trips you make to the menus — thanks to the toolbars. Microsoft has conveniently located the most commonly used menu commands on the toolbar.

Using the mouse

Menus are another great use for the mouse. To select a command using the mouse, first be sure that the window with the menu you want to access is active. Then move the mouse pointer to the command category you need. Press and hold down the mouse button; then move the mouse toward you (or away if you've gone too far) to highlight the command you want. When you release the mouse button, Excel will be off and running with the selected command.

Choosing some commands (indicated by the three periods following the command on the pull-down menu) causes a dialog box to open, which means Excel needs a little more information from you before executing the command. (Using dialog boxes is discussed in the next section.)

Using the keyboard

As always, make sure that the window with the menu you want to access is active. Then press the Alt or F10 key to activate Excel's menu bar and follow these steps:

- Select the command category (menu) by highlighting it with the left and right arrow keys or by pressing the appropriate underlined letter.

- Select the command by highlighting it with the up and down arrow keys and then pressing Enter or by pressing the appropriate underlined letter.

If you change your mind and want to bail out of the menu, simply press the Esc key.

Figure 5-6: An
Excel shortcut
menu, which
you access by
making a
selection and
clicking the
right mouse
button.

Cut	Ctrl+X
Copy	Ctrl+C
Paste	Ctrl+V
Clear...	Del
Delete...	
Insert...	
Number...	
Alignment...	
Font...	
Border...	
Patterns...	

Using Shortcut Menus

A new feature in version 4.0 is shortcut menus. When you make a selection in a
worksheet or chart, you can press the right mouse button for a "context sensitive" menu that usually contains the command you want. For example, if you
click the right mouse button after you select a range of cells, the shortcut menu
shown in Figure 5-6 appears. Simply make your choice and you're on your way.
You'll find that this method is *much* more efficient than pulling down menus.

Using Dialog Boxes

Dialog boxes are just that — boxes from which Excel can talk with you. Dialog
boxes appear after you select a command that requires you to furnish additional information. Dialog boxes contain all sorts of other boxes (option, check,
text, list, and drop-down menu) that enable you to specify certain actions you
want Excel to take. You can move or close dialog boxes with the mouse or
keyboard, but you can't change their size.

Using the mouse

Dialog boxes offer you another opportunity to make quick work with Excel. In
general, you just point and click on the options you want (or don't want). When
you're finished with the dialog box, click on OK and Excel proceeds with the
command. Here's a brief look at the specifics:

Buttons   Simply point and then click on the button. Some buttons
                        lead you to additional options.

Option buttons   Point and then click on the round button or its name. An option button that is selected contains a black dot.

Check boxes   Point and then click on the box or its name. A check box that is selected contains an X.

Text boxes   Point and then click on the box or its name, and when the pointer changes to an I-beam, enter any values or labels in the box.

List boxes   Point and then click on the box or its name; then click on the choice you want. If you're sure of your selection, double-clicking on it chooses the item and closes the dialog box, side-stepping choosing OK.

Drop-down boxes   Point and then click on the box or its name. A menu appears (similar to Excel's pull-down command menus). Move the mouse toward you to choose the item you want. When it's highlighted, release the mouse to select it.

Using the keyboard

After a dialog box is open, you can select an option with the keyboard by pressing the Alt key and the underlined letter of the option name. You can also cycle forward and backward through the dialog box's options by pressing the Tab and Shift+Tab keys, respectively. Here's a brief look at the specifics:

Buttons   Press Enter for OK or Esc for Cancel. Press Alt and the underlined letter of the option's name or tab to it until it's enclosed in a dashed underline. Press Enter to accept your selection.

Option buttons   Press Alt and the underlined letter of the option's name. An option button that is selected contains a black dot, as shown in Figure 5-7.

Check boxes   Press Alt and the underlined letter of the option's name. A check box that is selected contains an X.

Text boxes   Press Alt and the underlined letter of the option's name, and enter any values or labels in the box.

List boxes   Press Alt and the underlined letter of the option's name, then use the up and down arrow keys to select the item you want from the list.

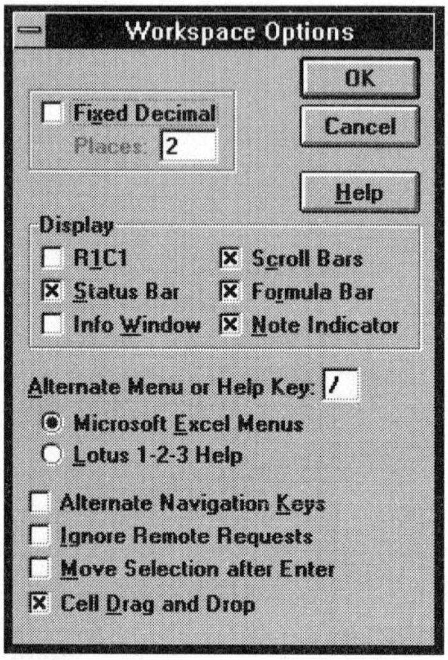

Figure 5-7: A typical dialog box in Excel, which provides you with the opportunity to select the options you need.

Drop-down boxes   Press Alt and the underlined letter of the option's name. Then use the up and down arrow keys to select the item you want. Note that the menu won't drop down (you need a mouse for that); one item appears at a time in the window.

Using the Toolbar

The toolbar provides you with quick access to common Excel operations. Simply make a selection in a worksheet or chart, point and click on the button representing the operation you want to perform, and Excel takes care of the rest. Figure 5-8 displays Excel's Standard toolbar. You need to have a mouse to use the toolbar.

Figure 5-8: Excel's Standard toolbar enables mouse users to quickly access often-used commands which results in more efficient use of Excel. Each tool (button) represents a specific Excel command.

Getting Help

All of us at one time or another have a question about how to accomplish a task using Excel. Several sources of information can help you extricate yourself out of a tough spot, however.

You can ask your coworkers or other Excel experts for help, or if you're fortunate enough, you can give your company's computer information center a call. You also can check the documentation that came with your copy of Excel and turn to books such as this one.

But what if you're working late (at the office or at home), no one's around, and the manuals and books are nowhere to be found? Don't panic — you don't need to feel abandoned. Excel has on-line help waiting for you at the touch of a key (or mouse button).

Where to find your life preserver

Excel provides you with many easy ways to get help. You can do the following:

- Press the F1 key.
- Invoke the Help command from Excel's pull-down menu bar.

Mouse users can also select the button that resembles a question mark on Excel's toolbar or press Shift+F1. A question mark appears next to the mouse pointer. You can then point and click on any item for which you want help.

You can get help from Excel no matter what you're doing at the time — entering data, choosing options from a dialog box, selecting a command, looking at error messages, and even while you're within Help itself. What happens next depends on how you've accessed help and the task you were performing at the time. For some background and a blow-by-blow account of help, read on.

Essentials of on-line Help

You can get help on every aspect of Excel — commands, worksheets, charts, macros, you name it. Help provides you with a detailed explanation of the subject, instructions on how to carry out the task, and suggestions for how to use it.

Help is a program unto itself that appears in its own window. Consequently, you can move, size, and close the Help window like other Windows and Excel windows. Figure 5-9 shows you what Help looks like when you press F1 when no spreadsheet activity is in progress.

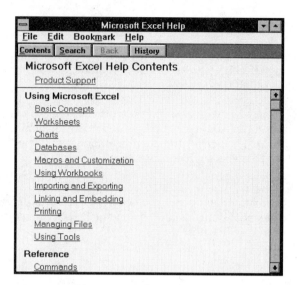

Figure 5-9: The Help window that appears when no commands have been chosen and you press F1. This window is also dis-played when you select Help ➪ Contents.

Which method to use?

You can get help at any time during your Excel session, but some ways to access it will be more beneficial to you than others. For example, if you have a question about your current Excel activity, press the F1 key. Excel presents specific information about that activity, because Help is *context-sensitive*. That is, Help displays appropriate information for the task in progress. In this man-ner, you don't need to go hunting through Help screens for the answer you need. Next, you learn how to find the information you need for a particular task.

Help with commands by using a mouse

You team up the mouse and Excel's toolbar to get help using a command. First, click on the Help tool button (the one that resembles a question mark). This action displays the mouse pointer with a question mark, indicating that you're in help mode. Second, point to the command as you normally do with the mouse pointer. When you release the mouse, Help appears for that command.

Microsoft Excel
Error in formula.
OK
Help

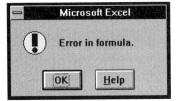

Figure 5-10: Excel displays this box if you make a formula error.

You can also receive help on window elements by clicking on the element with the mouse pointer when the question mark is displayed.

Help with commands by using the keyboard

Highlight, but don't select, the command you need help on. Then press F1. Help appears on-screen for the corresponding command.

Help with dialog and message boxes

Simply choose the Help button that appears in the box, and Excel displays help for that subject. Figure 5-10 displays the screen you see as a result of a formula error. Just select the Help button, and Help displays the help topic "Error in formula value."

Excel's Help menu

You've seen how to get help on the current topic of interest. But suppose that you need help on something not so context-sensitive, such as keyboard shortcuts. Excel provides ways to easily find the information you need.

Remember, Help is another program that is linked to Excel. In addition to its own window (which you can change the size and position of), Help also has its own pull-down menu bar and button commands, as shown in Figure 5-11. Think of the Help command buttons as Help's toolbar.

Figure 5-11: Help also has its own pull-down menu bar and button commands.

Microsoft Excel Help
File
Edit
Bookmark
Help
Contents
Search
Back
History

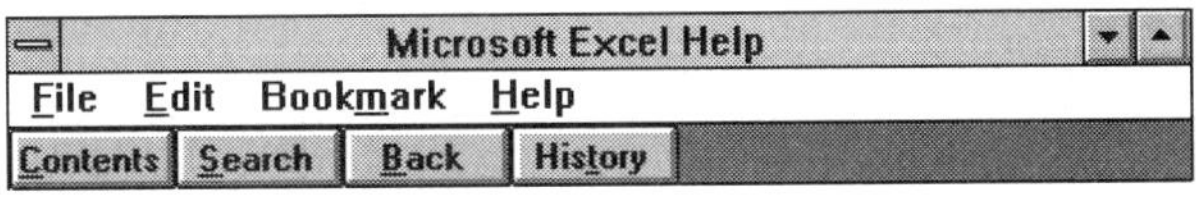

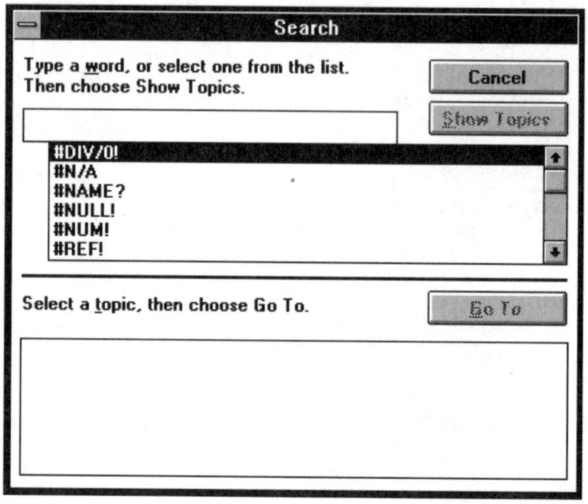

Figure 5-12:
The Search
dialog box
enables you
to find the
help you
need based
on a key-
word that
you enter.

Besides pressing the F1 key, you can access Help through the <u>H</u>elp menu on Excel's menu bar. The menu choices provide you with a number of entry points into Help. Pressing Alt (or F10) and H, or selecting <u>H</u>elp with the mouse, presents you with the following sources of Excel information:

<u>C</u>ontents   This option leads off the <u>H</u>elp menu choices and displays the text you see if you press F1 without highlighting a command. (You learn how to use the Help Contents screen in the following section.) Note that you can also access the Help Contents screen from the Help window's <u>C</u>ontents command button.

<u>S</u>earch   The second choice in the <u>H</u>elp menu is one of the most useful. When you choose <u>S</u>earch, the dialog box in Figure 5-12 appears.

You can use the Search dialog box in two ways to find the help information you need. One way is to type a keyword. As you do, Help begins scrolling the available Help topics in the upper list box. Another way is to scroll the list directly with the scroll bar or by pressing Tab, using the up and down arrow keys, and then selecting Show Topics or pressing Enter. A list of relevant topics is displayed in the lower list box. Select the one you want using the same procedure for the Help topics list and select Go To or press Enter. Help displays the information on that topic.

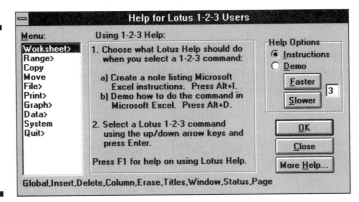

Figure 5-13: The Help for Lotus 1-2-3 Users dialog box shows you how you can use your 1-2-3 skills to accomplish tasks in Excel and assists you in learning Excel quickly.

Product Support The third option tells you how to contact Microsoft and provides you with answers to some of the most common questions Microsoft receives about Excel. You not only find the answer you need, but you also find that you're not alone with some of the challenges Excel users occasionally face.

Introduction to Microsoft Excel This fourth choice on the Help menu offers an excellent hands-on tutorial to help you understand what Excel is all about. If you're new to spreadsheets, this option is definitely worth your while.

Learning Microsoft Excel This Help menu option also offers an excellent hands-on tutorial to help you learn Microsoft Excel.

Lotus 1-2-3 Help The sixth option is indispensable for users of Lotus 1-2-3. Whether you're changing from 1-2-3 to Excel or need to be proficient with both programs, this option assists in making your transition quick and relatively painless.

When you select this command, the dialog box in Figure 5-13 is displayed.

The left-hand side of the dialog box displays 1-2-3's commands. You select the command you need help on, and a step-by-step list of instructions appears in the center of the dialog box. In addition, you have your choice of either seeing Excel step through its 1-2-3 command equivalent (Demo) or having Excel place a small note on your worksheet with the information (Instructions). If you select Demo, you can vary the speed at which Excel walks you

Figure 5-14: An example of a note Excel places on your worksheet. Use the instructions in the note to carry out 1-2-3's counterpart worksheet procedure in Excel.

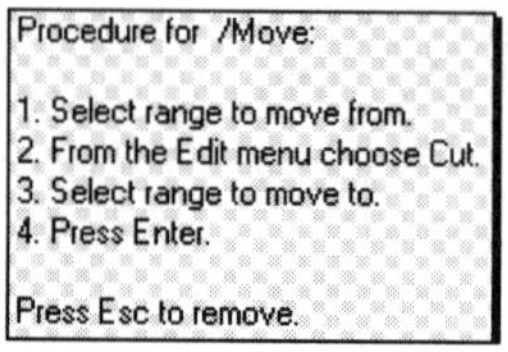

Procedure for /Move:

1. Select range to move from.
2. From the Edit menu choose Cut.
3. Select range to move to.
4. Press Enter.

Press Esc to remove.

through the command, which appears in place of the toolbar. If you choose Instructions, Excel places a temporary note on the worksheet, as shown in Figure 5-14 for 1-2-3's /Move command.

Pressing Esc clears the note from your worksheet; you can't save it along with the worksheet.

The More Help button leads you directly to the Help program.

MultiPlan Help The seventh option assists users of Microsoft's MultiPlan spreadsheet program with Excel. When you select this option, a dialog box appears and enables you to type in a MultiPlan command. After you select OK, Excel displays a Help screen that is appropriate for that command.

About Microsoft Excel The final option provides you with information about your version of Excel and your computer's available RAM.

A tour of Excel's Help system

By now you're probably feeling a little more confident about using help and would like to look around on your own. A good jumping-off place is the main Help window, shown back in Figure 5-9. Recall that you open this window by pressing F1 or selecting Help ⇨ Contents. From this window, Help provides you with several paths and command options to find your way through Help. They are:

■ Selecting an underlined cross-reference (shown in green on color monitors)

■ Selecting a definition or example

■ Choosing a button command

■ Choosing a command from the Help pull-down menu

■ Scrolling through Help

Each option is discussed next.

Cross-references

If a Help entry is underlined (also shown in green for those with color monitors) you can select that item and quickly move to information on that topic. If you use a mouse, the mouse pointer changes to the hand icon when you move the pointer over the entry. Click the mouse to select the entry, and Help appears. If you use the keyboard, press the Tab key to choose the entry you want. The entry is highlighted in purple on color monitors. (Who chose these colors anyway?) Press Enter to see the corresponding Help screen.

Definitions and examples

You can differentiate a definition or example from a cross-reference by its dotted underline. Select these items as before, but click and hold down the mouse button or hold down the Enter key. Instead of taking you to another Help screen, the program displays an information box with a definition or example of the entry. Releasing the mouse button or Enter key removes the box from the screen. If you prefer something more permanent than these temporary displays, choose the Contents button and the appropriate category for the entry from the main Help screen. You can close it when you're ready.

Button commands

Four commands appear directly above the Help window, as displayed in Figure 5-9. They are, from left to right, Contents, Search, Back, and History. You select these commands just like any command in Excel. Point and click on the button, or press the Alt key and the appropriate letter for that command. Remember, too, that if a button is dimmed, it's currently not available (if you've initially opened the Help window, for example, no help is currently available for you to go back to). The functions of the four commands follow:

Contents This button moves you to the initial help window, just as when you press F1 or select Help ⇨ Contents from Excel's menu bar. This button provides an easy way to get back to square one quickly.

Search Similar to the Contents button, Search displays the Search dialog box, the same as choosing Help ⇨ Search from the Excel command menu.

Back The Back button enables you to reverse engines — to step back one screen at a time in reverse order through the Help screens you've chosen.

History Whether you've realized it or not, Help has been keeping tabs on your activity. When you invoke History, the dialog box in Figure 5-15 opens.

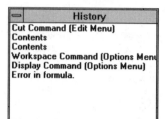

Figure 5-15: The History dialog box enables you to take another look at help topics you've previously seen during your current Excel session.

The History dialog box lists all the help topics you've chosen. To select one you've previously accessed, point and double-click on the topic, or use the up and down arrow keys and then press Enter. Help displays the help information for that topic. Selecting History is a good way to review information you've seen if you can't quite put your finger on where you last saw it.

Help window command menus

Above the command buttons is the Help pull-down menu bar, which contains the comands File, Edit, Bookmark, and Help. These commands enable you to control aspects of the Help program itself rather than provide you with ways to seek information. You select these commands by pointing, clicking, and releasing the mouse, or by pressing Alt or F10 and the corresponding letter for that command.

The File and Edit commands are very similar to their Excel and Windows counterparts. For example, Edit ⇨ Copy enables you to place the current Help window's text on the Windows Clipboard so you can paste it into an Excel or another Windows document.

Bookmark can be a real time-saver, especially if you're new to Excel. Bookmark enables you to attach a name to a Help topic, much like a range name in Excel. In this manner, you can quickly find Help topics that have been particularly useful to you by selecting the name from the Bookmark menu.

Finally, Help provides you with information about how to use Help. How's that for user-friendliness?

How to get the most from Help

Your use of Help depends primarily on what you're doing at the time you invoke it. You may need to perform a task and can't remember the required command. Or you know a keyboard shortcut is available for saving a file with a new name (F12), but you're drawing a blank.

Because Help is in its own window, you can open or close it any time you want. And you can keep it open along with your Excel spreadsheet if you like (as long as Excel isn't maximized to fill the entire screen). The F1 key (or the Help tool) is your gateway to context-sensitive help and saves you many hours of searching.

How to exit Help and return to Excel

When you're ready, you have a full plate of options to close the Help window.

For mouse users, the following options are available:

- Double-click on the Control button.
- Pull down the Control menu and select Close.
- Pull down the File menu and select Exit.

For keyboard users, the following options are available:

- Press Alt (or F10) and choose File ⇨ Exit.
- Press Alt+F4.

Summary

▶ Most Excel users use both their mouse and keyboard, depending on the task and their own level of spreadsheet and Windows experience.

▶ The mouse is a more intuitive tool for making command, dialog box, or cell range selections and for moving and sizing windows, and it is necessary for using the toolbar.

▶ The keyboard is used for entering text and numeric data and for executing shortcut key combinations.

▶ To move and size a window with the mouse, click on and drag any corner of the window; then click on and drag its title bar. To move and size a window with the keyboard, use the Control menu in the active window's left-hand corner.

▶ To select a command with the mouse, point to the menu's title on Excel's menu bar; then click and hold down the mouse button. Move the mouse to the command you want until it's highlighted and then release the mouse button.

▶ To select a command with the keyboard, press the Alt or F10 key. Use the left and right arrow keys to highlight the command menu or press the underlined letter of the menu name. Select the specific command from the menu by highlighting the command with the up and down arrow keys and then pressing Enter, or by pressing the underlined letter of the command name.

▶ To select dialog box options with the mouse, click on the option and then click on the OK button. To select dialog box options with the keyboard, press Alt and the underlined letter of the option you want. Use the arrow keys to select items from a list or to move between options with round buttons. When you're finished, press Tab until a dashed line appears around OK and press Enter.

▶ Press the F1 key at any time during the Excel session for context-sensitive help.

▶ Excel's Help menu provides you with many entry points into Help. From there, you can survey Help by using the pull-down menus or Help buttons and by selecting definitions.

▶ Because Help appears in its own window, you can move and size it and even keep it open along side the worksheet if you want.

Chapter 6
Working with Files

In this chapter . . .

▶ Files — what they are and how computers use them.

▶ A description of the file types that Excel uses.

▶ Specifics on creating new files, opening existing files, and saving files.

▶ Spreadsheet templates — what they are and how they can save you time and make your work more consistent.

▶ The concept of an Excel workbook and how it can simplify your life if you work with several related files at a time.

▶ How to set up files so they load automatically whenever you start Excel.

▶ Tips on working with files.

Everyone who starts using personal computers soon discovers the concept of files. You can't do much on a PC without using files, so the sooner you understand files, the better off you'll be. This chapter examines everything you need to know about files — well, at least the part that's relevant to Excel users.

Understanding How Computers Use Files

All computers store information in files. A file can contain a computer program or data used by programs. Data files may be Excel worksheets, word processing documents, graphics images, databases, and so on. Files can be stored on your hard disk or on floppy disks. Computer programs use files by loading them into memory.

In Excel, you deal with files by first selecting the File command. This action pulls down the menu shown in Figure 6-1. For historical reasons, not all of the commands in this menu are actually relevant to dealing with files. For example, this menu also holds the commands used for printing.

The File commands are discussed later in the chapter. But first, you need some general background information on files.

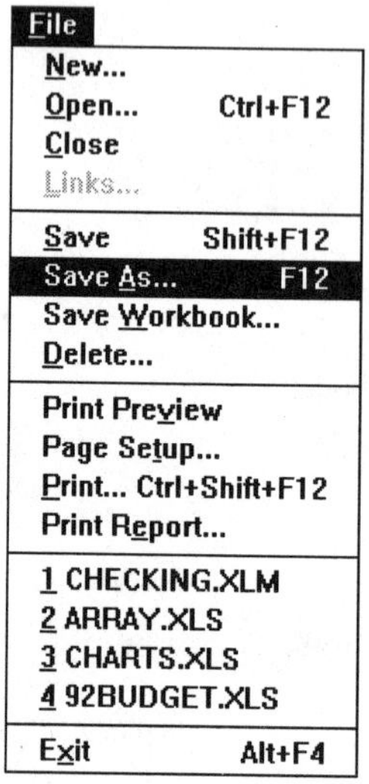

```
File
 New...
 Open...        Ctrl+F12
 Close
 Links...

 Save          Shift+F12
 Save As...         F12
 Save Workbook...
 Delete...

 Print Preview
 Page Setup...
 Print... Ctrl+Shift+F12
 Print Report...

 1 CHECKING.XLM
 2 ARRAY.XLS
 3 CHARTS.XLS
 4 92BUDGET.XLS

 Exit            Alt+F4
```

Figure 6-1:
Clicking Excel's File command leads to the commands you use to manipulate files.

In DOS, files are identified by several components:

■ The disk drive that they are on. Drives are designated by a single letter followed by a colon. For example, C: refers to drive C:.

■ The directory that they reside in (also known as the file's *path*). Directory names are preceded and followed by a backslash, and they are often preceded by the drive letter. For example, c:\excel refers to the excel directory on drive C:. c:\windows\tools refers to the tools directory, which is a subdirectory of the windows directory on drive C:.

■ A two-part name: the filename (consisting of one to eight alphanumeric characters) and an extension (consisting of one to three alphanumeric characters). The filename and extension are separated by a period. For example, budget.xls is a valid filename.

To completely specify a file, you include its drive and directory. Here are some examples:

```
a:checking.dat

c:\autoexec.bat

c:\sheets\budget92.xls

c:\windows\excel\library\analysis\analysis.xla
```

Fortunately, with Excel's dialog boxes, you can easily work with files, regardless of where they are located. You can bet your daily dinner that you'll never have to enter a complex filename like the last example just listed.

Every file also has three other components: the file size (measured in bytes), the time and date it was last written, and a list of attributes (such as read-only, archive, and hidden). In general, you don't need to be concerned with file attributes, but you should be aware of the size of your files. And if you ever discover two files with the same name, you can determine which file was updated more recently by examining the date and time the files were last written. (Although you can't have two files with the same name in one directory, you can have two files with the same name in different directories.)

The Windows File Manager program enables you to manipulate files — copy them, move them, erase them, and check their sizes and dates. Learning to use this program is worthwhile. Alternatively, you may have another file management program such as Norton Desktop for Windows, Norton Commander, or X-Tree. All these programs (and many others) make manipulating the files on your disks easy.

Understanding How Excel Uses Files _____

Excel, the program, requires many files in order to run on your PC. As you work with the program, Excel periodically loads additional files into memory to help perform operations you request. These files are stored in the directory in which you installed Excel — most likely your c:\excel directory. For the most part, you don't need to be concerned about the Excel program files. Just make sure that you don't erase any of them, or the program may not work.

If you accidentally erase a critical file that Excel needs, it usually displays a message to that effect. In such a case, reinstall Excel and it works like new.

The files that you *do* need to be concerned with are the data files that Excel uses. When you are working in Excel, the specifics of your work can be stored in data files. That way, you can come back later and resume your work where you left off.

Most computer applications use what are generically called *data files*. These files are essentially the files you create to do your work. Excel uses several types of data files.

Worksheet files

Most of the files you create in Excel are worksheet files. Worksheet files always have an `xls` extension. Worksheet files hold data, formulas, functions, and even charts and other graphics objects. Normally, each project you work on has its own `xls` file. For example, you may have a worksheet file for your departmental budget, one for your personal checking account, another that analyzes various options for refinancing your home, and so on. For some projects, you may even use more than one `xls` file, which can be the most efficient approach. All of this will become more clear as you gain experience with Excel.

Examining Excel's directories

When you install Excel with the full installation option, the program creates 13 new directories on your hard disk, arranged as follows:

Directory	Contents
`\excel\`	Program files for Excel
`\excel\examples`	Sample files that come with Excel
`\excel\examples\solver`	Sample files for the Solver feature
`\excel\library`	Add-ins and macros that come with Excel
`\excel\library\solver`	Solver add-in and related files
`\excel\library\analysis`	Analysis ToolPak add-in and related files
`\excel\library\slides`	For Slide Presentations
`\excel\library\crosstab`	For the Crosstab Wizard
`\excel\library\color`	Worksheets with color palettes that you can use
`\excel\library\checkup`	System information macro
`\excel\exclecbt`	Computer-based training (accessible from the Help menu)
`\excel\qe`	Q+E database program
`\excel\xlstart`	Files that are opened automatically when Excel starts

By default, the data files you create with Excel are stored in the `excel` directory. You can store your files in any directory on any drive, but don't get carried away. Maintaining some semblance of order in storing your files is important, or your hard disk will be a disaster waiting to happen.

Chart files

Excel can also produce chart files, identifiable by their xlc extension. A chart file holds all the specifications for a particular chart you've created and is usually associated with a worksheet file that supplies the data that makes up the chart. As you'll see, however, you may never need to work with Excel chart files because Excel can also store charts in a regular worksheet file.

Macro files

Advanced users can use Excel to create macro files with an xlm extension. Excel's macro files hold instructions that can perform operations automatically, much like a programming language. You can write macro xlm files to work with a specific worksheet file or more generally to work with all your worksheet files. Excel includes several macro files, which you can open to provide additional functionality to the program. Macros are discussed in Chapter 26.

Workbook files

Some projects that you work on in Excel may require more than one file. For example, your annual budgeting process may use two worksheet files (current year and next year), several chart files, and maybe even a macro file. Excel enables you to organize such related files into a *workbook*. By opening a single workbook file, you have quick access to all the documents you need for a specific task. Better yet, Excel actually stores all the individual documents in a single workbook file, which means that you don't have to remember which files belong to which project. Workbook files have an xlw extension.

Add-in files

When you install Excel, you have access to a variety of analytical features. In addition, Excel includes other features that you can add to its arsenal if you like. These features are made available through add-in files, which you can identify by their xla extension. (Actually, some add-in files are xlm macro files.) You can load specific add-ins as needed or set up Excel so it always loads one or more particular add-ins when it starts up. Add-ins are discussed in Chapter 20.

Template files

Excel also uses template files, which have an xlt extension. A template file is similar to a normal worksheet or chart file, but it's set up with information that you may need repeatedly or contains some specific settings that you like. For example, if you don't want Excel to display gridlines in your worksheets, you can create a template that has this setting disabled. This action merely saves you the trouble of turning the gridlines off manually every time you create a new worksheet. As you might expect, templates can get much more sophisticated. We discuss templates in more detail later in this chapter.

Toolbar files

Excel stores the information about its toolbars in files with an xlb extension. Unless you customize toolbars, you don't need to be concerned with this file type. Chapter 19 is devoted to customizing toolbars.

Foreign files

All the file types we've discussed so far are unique to Excel. However, Excel can also read files produced by other programs — foreign files, if you will. It can also save a worksheet in a format that can be used by other programs. For example, you may want to work on a worksheet that was produced by Lotus 1-2-3. You can read such a file into Excel directly. On the other hand, you may want to save your worksheet data so it can be used in dBASE. Again, Excel can handle this task with ease.

Creating and Opening Files _____

When you launch Excel, you normally start out by doing one of two things:

1. Create a new file.

2. Open an existing file (or group of files).

When Excel starts up, you're greeted with a blank worksheet, called sheet1. This worksheet is not a file because it did not come from a disk. Rather, think of it as a *potential* file. You can put information into this worksheet and then save it as a file by using the File ⇨ Save command.

You can prevent Excel from starting with a blank worksheet by using the /e command line switch. See Chapter 3 for details.

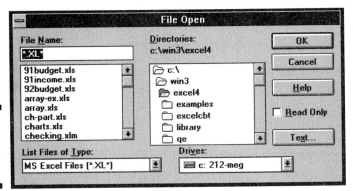

Figure 6-2:
The File
Open dialog
box.

To open a file that's already stored on disk, you use the File ⇨ Open command. Selecting this command brings up the dialog box shown in Figure 6-2. This dialog box consists of several parts:

Drives This pull-down box enables you to select the disk drive where you will be retrieving your file. To change the current drive, click the down arrow to pull down a list of all available disk drives and click on the correct one. This choice affects the contents of the Directories section of the dialog box.

Directories This section of the dialog box displays the current directory Excel is looking at (the example shows the c:\win3\excel4 directory) and provides a list box in which you can quickly change the directory that Excel uses. You can scroll through the list box until you find the proper directory. Move up the directory tree by double-clicking on a directory that's above the current directory. This choice affects the contents of the File Name section. See the sidebar "Navigating through dialog boxes" for tips on working with directories in a dialog box.

File Name The text box at the top displays the current "wildcard" specification, using standard DOS conventions. Wildcard characters are represented by a question mark (?) or an asterisk (*). Use a question mark to represent any one character and an asterisk to represent any two or more characters. The actual filenames displayed in this box are determined by the directory that's currently selected and by the selection in the pull-down text box labeled List Files of Type.

List Files of Type   This pull-down box enables you to display only files of a certain type. When you pull down the list, you can select which type of file or files you are interested in retrieving.

Read Only   Click this option if you just want to look at a file and prevent over-writing it with any changes. When you retrieve a file with this option set, you cannot save the file under the same name (in other words, the original will always remain intact).

Navigating through dialog boxes

Excel 4 uses a new design to enable you to select files in its dialog boxes. This design is the same one used by Windows 3.1. Excel has several dialog boxes in which you select a file, and they all work the same. You can select the three components you need: the disk drive, the directory, and the filename. Selecting the drive is easy enough: Click on the down arrow, and a list of all available drives drops down. Click on the drive letter you want, and the directory box changes to reflect the directory structure on the drive you selected.

Working with the directory list is a bit more challenging, but it's a piece of cake after you understand how it works. The key is to understand that directories on a disk are arranged in a hierarchy. Each disk has a "root" directory (which can hold files), and the root directory can have other directories (which can also hold files). Each of these other directories can also have subdirectories, and so on. As a result, a file may be "nested" several directories deep. You indicate such nested directories with a backslash (\). In this manner, you can specify the complete "path" to any file on your disk. For example, the path to a file named 1992.xls that's located in your budget directory, which is located off your excel directory, which is located off your win3 directory, which is located off your root directory (c:\), is specified as follows:

```
c:\win3\excel\budget\1992.xls
```

With Excel, you never have to actually type out such paths. Rather, Excel's dialog boxes enable you to move up or down through such a directory tree simply by clicking on a directory name. When you click on a directory, the files in that directory are displayed in the File Name box to the left. The accompanying figure shows how you can select this file in an Excel dialog box.

Notice that the directory names listed in the dialog box are indented (much like an outline), and each directory name has a folder icon to the left. If you look carefully, you see that actually three different folder icons exist. Directories in the current path have icons that are open, and the current directory has an open icon that's shaded on the inside. The icons for all other directories are closed folders. Furthermore, the path is written out for you in the line above the directory box.

To move one level up, click the directory name that's indented one level to the left. Note particularly that you have to move "up" a directory tree before you can move to a different branch on the same level that you're on.

Text	This button is relevant only if you're opening a text file. Selecting this button displays some options that describe the type of text file. Dealing with text files is covered in Chapter 29.
Cancel	Select this button if you change your mind about opening a file. The dialog box closes down with no action taken.
Help	Click this button if you want to view the help screen that describes your options.
OK	Selecting this button opens the file displayed in the text box under File Name. If no file is listed, the OK button has no effect.

Use the dialog box controls to locate the file you want to open and then choose OK. You can open several files at once if you hold down the Ctrl key while you click the filenames you want to open. Then choose OK to open all the files you selected (each appears in its own window).

 As a shortcut, you can double-click on a filename displayed in the File Name list box. This action opens the file and saves you the trouble of choosing OK.

If you're new to Windows, the process of opening files takes some getting used to. Nevertheless, you'll find that nearly all other Windows applications you encounter use the same (or nearly the same) procedure.

Besides its own xls worksheet files, Excel can also open files produced by other applications. Actually, Excel can open *any* file, but what shows up on screen may be complete garbage. Table 6-1 lists the file types that Excel can open and use intelligently.

Table 6-1: File types Excel can open	
File type	**Description**
xls	Excel worksheet files. Excel 4 can open files produced by all previous versions of Excel.
wks	Worksheet files produced by 1-2-3 Release 1A.
wk1*	Worksheet files produced by 1-2-3 Release 2.*x.*
wk3*	Worksheet files produced by 1-2-3 Release 3.*x* and by 1-2-3 for Windows.
dbf	Files produced by dBASE (version II, III, or IV).
txt	Text files.
csv	Comma-separated-value files (a type of text file in which values are separated by commas).
slk	Files produced by Microsoft's MultiPlan.
* When you open one of these files, Excel searches for the associated formatting file (either fmt or fm3) and translates it automatically.	

When you select the File command, the drop-down menu displays the four most recently opened files. If the file you want is listed in this menu, you can simply click on it or press the number assigned to it to avoid using the File Open dialog box.

Saving Files

The work you do while you are in Excel is rather ephemeral because it exists only in your computer's memory. If your system crashes or someone trips over the power cord, your work is lost forever — unless it is saved to a file. Saving your work frequently is a good habit that applies not only to Excel, but to all the work you do on your PC.

 When you save a file, Excel takes the information it is working with in memory and converts it so it can be stored in a disk file. An xls file is not a text file and therefore cannot be read like text. For example, if you try to view an xls file from a DOS prompt (with the type command) you see what appears to be garbage. Similarly, if you load an Excel file into a program that doesn't understand its file format, the file shows up as strange characters. You can see the effect by loading an xls file into Windows Write. You see small bits and pieces of text, but the document is pretty much unintelligible.

Two Excel commands are relevant here:

- File ⇨ Save

- File ⇨ Save As

The File ⇨ Save command (or its Shift+F12 shortcut) simply saves the currently active file under its existing name. One exception exists: When you start a new file, you must give it a name before you save it. Consequently, when you select File ⇨ Save with a new file, Excel automatically brings up the File Save As dialog box, as shown in Figure 6-3. Notice that it's similar to the File Open dialog box that was discussed earlier. The File ⇨ Save As command is very versatile. This command enables you to save a file:

- For the first time

- Under a different name

- To a different drive or directory

- In a format that's usable by other programs

- With a password

- With a "reservation" so no one else can overwrite it (relevant only on a multiuser network)

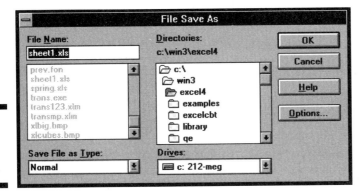

Figure 6-3:
The File
Save As
dialog box.

- As an Excel template
- For use by previous versions of Excel
- And make a backup of the previous version

Although every Excel worksheet consists of 256 columns and 16,384 rows, Excel only saves the part of the worksheet that contains information. As a result, the size of a worksheet file is proportional to the amount of information it contains.

Saving a file for the first time

You can select either File ⇨ Save or File ⇨ Save As to save a file for the first time. In either case, Excel displays the File Save As dialog box. When saving a file for the first time, make sure that the drive is set properly. You generally save your files to your hard disk (usually designated as drive C:), but on occasion you may want to save a file to a floppy disk or to a network drive (if your system is part of a LAN).

Next, make sure that the proper directory is selected. You can use the directory list box to choose the correct directory if it's not already selected.

Finally, enter a filename in the File Name text box. You're limited to eight alphanumeric characters. You don't need to enter a file extension; Excel takes care of that for you.

If you enter a filename that already exists, Excel lets you know and asks whether you want to replace the existing file. Don't replace it unless you are certain you want to do so (replacing it overwrites the old file).

Saving a file under a different format

Most of the time, you'll save your files in the normal Excel format. Sometimes, however, you may need to save the file under a different format — as a text file, for example, or in a format that can be read into Lotus 1-2-3. You use the File ⇨ Save As command to do this procedure. Simply click on the pull-down list (labeled Save File as Type) to display a list of file formats. Table 6-2 lists the various file formats that Excel can save to.

Table 6-2: File types Excel can save to	
File type	**Description**
Normal	The standard Excel 4 xls format. This is the default file type.
Template	As an Excel 4 template file.
Excel 3.0	As a file that can be read into version 3 of Excel.
Excel 2.1	As a file that can be read into either version 2.1 or 3 of Excel.
slk	As a file that can be read into Microsoft's MultiPlan spreadsheet.
Text	As a text (ASCII) file. You lose all formulas and formatting, but the values can be read by just about every word-processing program.
csv	As a comma-separated-value file. Each cell is separated by a comma, and labels are in quotes.
wks	As a file that can be read by 1-2-3 Release 1A.
wk1*	As a file that can be read by 1-2-3 Release 2.x.
wk3*	As a file that can be read by 1-2-3 Release 3.x or by 1-2-3 for Windows.
dif	As a data-interchange-format file. This is a rather out-of-date format but is useful for older programs such as VisiCalc.
dbf2	As a dBASE II database file.
dbf3	As a dBASE III database file.
dbf4	As a dBASE IV database file.
Text (Macintosh)	As a text file suitable for some Macintosh applications.
Text (OS/2 or DOS)	As a text file suitable for some OS/2 and DOS applications.
csv (Macintosh)	As a comma-separated-value file suitable for some Macintosh applications.
csv (OS/2 or DOS)	As a comma-separated-value file suitable for some OS/2 and DOS applications.
* If you select either the wk1 or wk3 format, Excel creates a formatting file for use with 1-2-3. These formatting files have the same filename but use either fmt or fm3 for the extension.	

Using file saving options

The File Save As dialog box offers a few more options when you save a file. Click on the Options button, and you see the dialog box shown in Figure 6-4. The following options are available:

Create Backup File   This option is useful if you don't want to overwrite the existing file with your changed file. Excel renames the existing file to have a bak extension and then saves your changes to the original name. This option remains set for the file, so the backup is changed every time you save the file (until you uncheck the box).

Protection Password   Use this option if you want to keep others from opening or viewing your worksheet. If you click this option, you are asked to enter a password (and verify it) before the file is saved. On subsequent accesses, you need to enter the password before Excel opens the file. This option also encrypts the file so it can't be read by any other programs or file viewing utilities.

Write Reservation Password   Enter a password here if you don't want anyone to overwrite the file. In other words, others can have "read access" only.

Read-Only Recommended   If you click on this option, Excel displays the dialog box shown in Figure 6-5 when someone attempts to open the file. Users can save the changed document with a different name.

Figure 6-5: This dialog box appears if a file has been saved as "Read-only recommended."

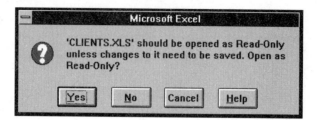

Using Templates

Worksheet templates can save you a great deal of time by not forcing you to "reinvent the wheel" every time you create a new file. In addition, templates can add consistency across your worksheets.

Basically, a template can be any worksheet file (although it can also be a chart or macro file) that is saved as a template (specified as such in the File Save As dialog box). When you open a template file, Excel opens an exact copy of the file but doesn't enable you to save it under the original name. When you use the File ⇨ Save command after opening a template file, Excel displays the File Save As dialog box, forcing you to supply a filename.

To change the characteristics of an existing template file, select the File ⇨ Open command and select the template (xlt extension) file that you want to edit. Hold down the Shift key when you click OK. You can then modify your template and save it with the File ⇨ Save command.

Template files are useful if you tend to create a lot of worksheets that have some features in common: display attributes, custom cell formats, row or column titles, specific column widths, and so on. For example, suppose that you have to create a sales summary report each month. Rather than start with a new worksheet each month, set up a basic worksheet with column headings, column widths, styles, numeric formats, borders, shading, and whatever else is common to all your sales reports. Save this file as a template, and you have a running start on next month's task.

If you copy or move a template file to your excel\xlstart directory, Excel displays the template name in the selection box when you create a new file with the File ⇨ New command. An example is shown in Figure 6-6. This dialog box lists three template files: Nogrid, Budget, and Format.

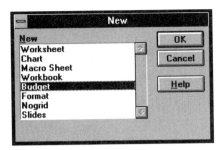

Figure 6-6: Templates placed in the `xlstart` directory are listed when you create a new file.

Using Excel Workbooks

The concept of workbooks is new in Excel 4 and is well worth your acquaintance. A workbook is useful for projects in which you use more than one Excel file, because a workbook makes managing your files and keeping related files together easy. In fact, Excel can even store what would normally be different files in a single workbook file. This feature is especially useful if you share worksheets with others or bring work home from the office. In the past, overlooking one or more files when copying a group of related files for an associate was far too easy. Storing all related files in a single workbook file makes a lot of sense.

Excel 3 users should note that the concept of a workbook is an extension of the previous version's workspace. The main difference is that Excel can now store all the files in a single workbook file. In addition, Excel provides some handy new commands for moving easily among your open files.

Some other advantages of Excel workbooks follow:

- If you use file links, you can be assured that all the necessary files are accessible.

- You can store a group of files in a workbook and set up one password for the entire group.

- A workbook remembers your exact setup — including window sizes and placements. When you open a workbook, your workspace is just like you left it (including settings made via the Options Workspace dialog box).

- You can assign extended names to files stored in a workbook (you aren't limited to the eight-character DOS names).

- If you import a three-dimensional wk3 file (from 1-2-3 Release 3 or 1-2-3 for Windows), Excel automatically converts it into a workbook; each layer of the original worksheet becomes a separate worksheet in the workbook.

- Workbooks provide new and more efficient ways to move among open files. If you ever get into a situation where you have 20 files open at once, you'll see what we're talking about.

You use the File ➩ Save Workbook command to save a group of files as a workbook. Workbooks are discussed in detail in Chapter 14.

Loading Files Automatically

When you install Excel, the Setup program (by default) creates a subdirectory of your `excel` directory called `xlstart`. This directory holds files that you want to load whenever you start Excel. These files can be of the following types:

Worksheet files (`xls`)   Excel loads these files into memory, each in its own window.

Chart files (`xlc`)   Excel loads these files into memory, each in its own window. If the associated worksheet file(s) holding the series is not loaded, Excel asks whether you want to update the references.

Macro files (`xlm`)   Excel loads these files into memory, making the macros available to you.

Workbook files (`xlw`)   Excel loads these files into memory.

Add-in files (`xla`)   Excel loads these add-ins, making them available to you.

Template files (`xlt`)   Excel does not load these files. Rather, it displays them when you issue the File ⇨ New command.

If you find yourself loading the same files or add-ins whenever you start Excel, you probably should be storing these files in your `\excel\xlstart` directory.

You can specify another start-up directory to be used in addition to `xlstart`. Do this procedure by loading the `altstart.xla` add-in (located in the `\excel\library` directory) and then enter the complete path for the alternate start-up directory. This setup is most useful if you're running on a LAN. You have a LAN-wide start-up directory plus your *own* start-up directory.

Tips for Working with Files

■ If you will be sharing your Excel files with someone else who has Excel, make sure that you know which Excel version he or she is using. If you save a file as Normal, it cannot be retrieved with either version 2.1 or 3 of Excel. If you save it in version 3 format, it cannot be read with version 2.1. Unfortunately, Microsoft did not change the file extensions to indicate which version of the product produced the file.

■ Similarly, workbook files cannot be opened by either of the previous Excel versions.

■ Back up your files to another disk frequently. Getting in the habit of making regular backups of the files on your hard drive is a good idea. You may want to buy a program that automates this process for you.

■ Save your worksheet before you make any drastic changes to your worksheet. Although Excel's Edit ⇨ Undo command can usually come to the rescue, Excel must sometimes disable Undo if it runs short of memory.

■ If the information in your worksheet is confidential, you may want to save the file with a password. The password must be entered before it can be loaded into Excel and encrypts the file so it can't be viewed by any file viewing utility. Passwords can be up to 15 characters, including spaces and special symbols. They are also case-sensitive, which makes FRANK a different password from Frank.

■ To close all files that are open, press Shift when you select the File command from the menu. This action displays a command called Close All. Excel prompts you to save any unsaved data.

■ When you save a worksheet under a different name, the original file remains on disk. Using File ⇨ Save As does not erase the old file if you save it under a different name.

■ If you open a 1-2-3 file (a file with a wk1 or wk3 extension), Excel looks for an associated formatting file (for example, a file with the same name but with an fmt or fm3 extension). It then translates the formats so the newly imported file closely resembles the original. Because of different fonts used, the translation is not exact, which is likely to be a problem only when the original worksheet was fine-tuned to precisely fit something such as a preprinted form.

Dealing with files on a LAN

If your system is part of a LAN, you need to be aware of some of the implications of working with files that others have access to. LANs often have one or more central file servers — areas in which files are stored that all people on the LAN can access.

Consider the following scenario: You just landed a new client, and you need to update your company's central client list. So you open a file called clients.xls that's stored on your LAN's file server. As you're working on the file, someone else in your department wants to add a new client to the list, so he or she opens the same file. You save your file, and a few minutes later, your associate saves his or her version of the file — overwriting the changes you made! A way is available to handle situations like this. In this situation, Excel does not enable a user to save a file that is also being used by someone else. In addition, some files may be designated as read-only files so that they can't be changed. In either case, Excel automatically handles LAN situations in which a potential risk exists for data loss.

■ The File ▷ Save command overwrites the previous version of your file on disk. If you retrieve a worksheet and then proceed to totally mess it up, don't save the file! Retrieve the version on disk and start again (Excel asks whether you want to revert to the saved version of the file — choose yes).

■ If you read a foreign file into Excel (such as a 1-2-3 worksheet or a dBASE file), it is saved in the same format. If you continue to work on it in Excel, saving it as a Normal (xls) file with the File ▷ Save As command is more efficient.

■ If you tend to use several different directories, get in the habit of checking the current directory when you issue the File ▷ Save As command. Excel remembers the last directory you accessed, and it is the one selected. This practice prevents the common problem of "losing" a file when it's actually saved in a directory that you didn't intend it to go into.

■ If you find yourself getting short on disk space, you can delete files through Excel with the File ▷ Delete command. This operation works one file at a time, because the multiple file selection keys do not work in this dialog box. Consequently, if you have a lot of files to erase, use the File Manager or some other disk utility. In either case, never erase temporary files (those with a tmp extension) while Windows is running.

 Documents can be either saved in a workbook or saved separately and simply "listed" as being in a workbook. The former method is preferable, since it ensures that the file can always be located.

Summary

▶ Excel, like every other computer program, uses files that are stored on disk. It has files for its own use and works with data files that you create. A computer uses files by loading them into memory.

▶ You can completely locate a file by specifying its drive, directory path, and filename. Windows makes this task easy for you.

▶ Excel enables you to open files, save files, and erase files.

▶ Excel can read and write several "foreign" file formats.

▶ You can attach a password to a file so no one else can open it.

▶ Most files you use with Excel are worksheet files (with an xls extension).

▶ Excel also uses chart files, macro files, workbook files, template files, add-in files, and toolbar files.

▶ By default, Excel starts out with an empty worksheet called sheet1. To open an existing file, use the File ➪ Open command. To save a file, select the File ➪ Save command.

▶ You can create template files that include preestablished settings, headings, formulas, and so on.

▶ Excel uses workbook files to efficiently manage projects that consist of more than one file.

▶ You can instruct Excel to automatically load specific files when it starts by storing the files in the excel\xlstart directory.

Chapter 7
Entering and Editing Worksheet Data

In this chapter . . .

▶ A discussion of the three types of data you enter into Excel: numbers, labels (text), and formulas.

▶ The basic rules for entering data into a worksheet.

▶ How to edit data after it has been entered.

▶ Details on all the editing commands available in Excel.

▶ How to attach a note to a cell.

▶ How to apply formats to numbers to change their appearance.

Many Excel worksheet tasks and procedures are important and critical, but none compares in scope to entering and editing data. Entering labels, values, and formulas into a blank Excel worksheet is similar to shifting an automobile into drive (or shifting into first gear, for those with manual transmissions). You use labels, values, and formulas to create a worksheet that will provide you with the results or answers you need and get you where you need to go.

In this chapter, you learn about the various types of data, how to enter data into an Excel worksheet, and how to change (edit) data if you make a mistake or change your mind. If you're new to spreadsheet programs or Excel, this chapter is a must. If you're an experienced spreadsheet war-horse, you may want to stay tuned because as you're likely to pick up a few tidbits here and there (especially if you're moving over from Lotus 1-2-3 or other character-based spreadsheets).

Examining Types of Data

Recall from previous chapters that an Excel worksheet is a gigantic electronic grid of blank cells. A cell, in turn, is the intersection of one of Excel's rows and columns. Figure 7-1 refreshes your memory of a highlighted cell, also known as the active cell, because it contains your cell pointer. The active cell is your gateway to entering data into your worksheet. A cell can hold one of the following four types of data:

- Labels or text
- Numeric data or values
- Functions
- Formulas (which can include functions, numeric data, and lables)

 Note that labels and values have different purposes but in some cases appear similar or identical on your spreadsheet. Make sure that you enter a label as a label and a value as a value. If you don't, a formula that references the cell may return incorrect or unexpected results.

Numeric data

Numeric data is simply numbers that represent some quantity. Numeric data can be revenues, expenses, test scores, and so on. Excel bases its calculations on the values in your worksheet. Excel also uses these numeric values to generate charts. Figure 7-2 shows several examples of numeric data.

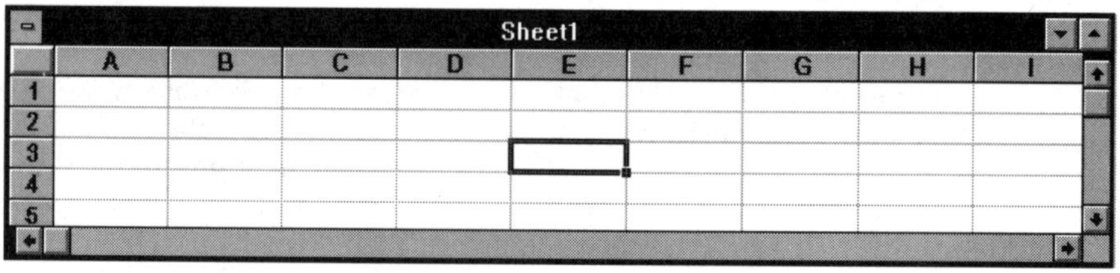

	A	B	C	D	E	F	G	H	I
1									
2									
3									
4									
5									

Sheet1

Figure 7-1: The cell pointer indicates the location of the active cell, which you can enter data into.

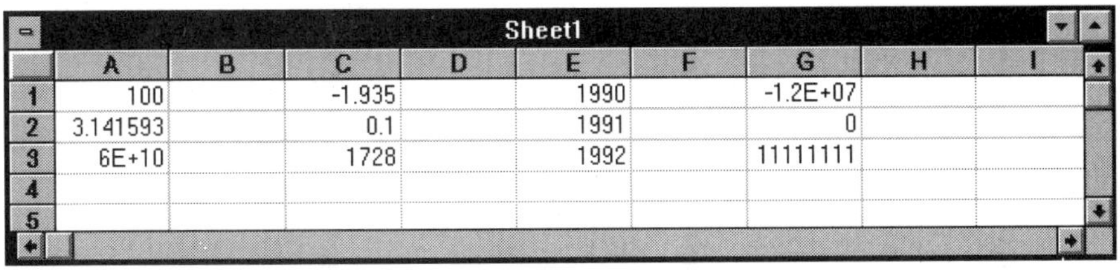

	A	B	C	D	E	F	G	H	I
1	100		-1.935		1990		-1.2E+07		
2	3.141593		0.1		1991		0		
3	6E+10		1728		1992		11111111		
4									
5									

Figure 7-2: Values are one of the basic building blocks of every worksheet. Functions and formulas use values to perform calculations.

Labels and text

Labels (also known as text) are composed of characters you enter by using your alphabetic keys. You use labels to name or describe the data contained in your worksheets, such as the months of the year, expense categories, and so on. Labels are commonly entered in column A and near the top of columns — one label per column. Figure 7-3 displays several examples of labels.

Formulas

Formulas are mathematical relationships, or equations, that you create. Formulas produce a result in the cell that contains them, based on other cells that contain data (labels, values, and functions) and mathematical operators (+, −, *, /, and ^, for example). The result may be another value or label, which another formula in your worksheet can refer to. Figure 7-4 shows a few examples of formulas.

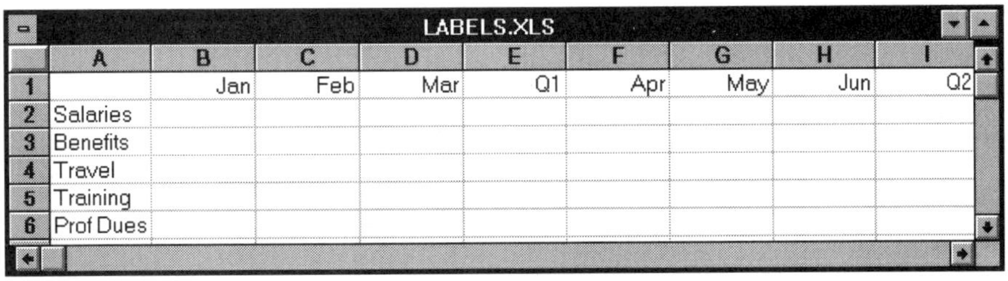

	A	B	C	D	E	F	G	H	I
1		Jan	Feb	Mar	Q1	Apr	May	Jun	Q2
2	Salaries								
3	Benefits								
4	Travel								
5	Training								
6	Prof Dues								

Figure 7-3: Labels are text characters that, like values, are stored in individual cells in a worksheet. Labels help identify the purpose of the values stored in the rows and columns of the worksheet.

	FORMULAS.XLS:1						FORMULAS.XLS:2	
	A	B	C	D	E		A	B
1	3					1	=1+2	
2	3					2	=A1	
3	6					3	=A1+A2	
4	5					4	=A1+2	
5	32					5	=SUM(A1:A3)+20	
6	49					6	=SUM(A1:A3)+SUM(A4:A5)	
7	715					7	=(45+20)*(22/2)	
8	Total					8	="Total"	
9	0					9	=qtr_tot	
10	100					10	=qtr_tot+100	
11						11		
						12		

Figure 7-4:
Examples of
formulas.

Excel normally displays the results (values) of formulas. You can, however, display the formulas in your worksheet as formulas by using the Options ⇨ Display command and then clicking the Formulas box on the Display Options dialog box, as shown in Figure 7-5.

Functions

Excel's worksheet functions can be thought of as built-in formulas. A worksheet function calculates results for common mathematical operations more quickly and accurately than its formula counterpart. For example, =SUM(B1:B5) calculates faster than =B1+B2+B3+B4+B5 and is easier to enter and less prone to errors. Excel has a whole arsenal of worksheet functions at your disposal. Although you probably won't need them all, they're available for a variety of applications. Figure 7-6 shows a sample of functions vis-a-vis the equivalent formula.

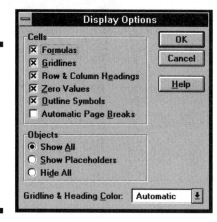

Figure 7-5:
Choosing
Formulas from
the Display
Options dialog
box enables
you to display
the formulas
in your
worksheet.

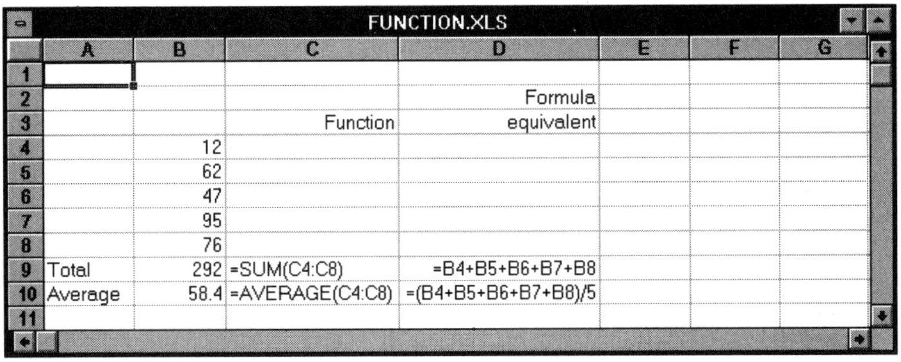

	A	B	C	D	E	F	G
1							
2				Formula			
3			Function	equivalent			
4		12					
5		62					
6		47					
7		95					
8		76					
9	Total	292	=SUM(C4:C8)	=B4+B5+B6+B7+B8			
10	Average	58.4	=AVERAGE(C4:C8)	=(B4+B5+B6+B7+B8)/5			
11							

Figure 7-6: Excel's worksheet functions enable you to perform calculations more quickly and accurately than their formula counterparts.

Entering Data in Excel

Entering data into your worksheet is basically an easy three-step process, with some slight variations depending on the type of data you're entering and whether you've selected a single-cell or multicell range. To enter data, do the following steps.

Steps: Entering data

Step 1. Select the cell or range of cells.

Step 2. Type the data.

Step 3. Enter your data into the cell.

More information about each of these steps is provided next.

Selecting a cell

To select a single cell for data entry using a mouse, simply click on the cell. To select a cell using your keyboard, use the arrow keys to move to the cell. The cell you select is highlighted because it contains the cell pointer, as shown in Figure 7-1.

To select a range of cells, click and drag the mouse to highlight the cells or use the arrow keys to move to the first cell for data entry and then press and hold down one of the Shift keys while pressing an arrow key.

You can select a nonadjacent cell or range by pressing and holding down the Ctrl key and then selecting the cell or range. When you are through entering data in the first cell or range, Excel automatically moves the cell pointer to the nonadjacent cell for data entry.

Typing data

Type the letters or numbers of the data you want to enter from the keyboard. As you type, the characters appear in the Formula bar, as well as in the cell you've selected. A cell can contain up to 255 characters, and the Formula bar expands vertically when you get to the end.

Excel also evaluates whether your entry is a label or a value. Excel regards text and alphanumeric character entries as labels. Numbers and the following symbols indicate to Excel that a value is on the way:

$$+ - ( ) , \$ \% . E e$$

If you want to enter a value as a label, start with an equal sign and put the value in quotation marks. For example, ="2001" inserts the text "2001" into a cell.

If you make a mistake as you type, press the Backspace key to erase the character immediately to the left of the cursor; then type its replacement.

Entering data

The final step in data entry is to say yea or nay about your cell entry to Excel. For mouse users, select the Enter box (check mark) on the Formula bar to confirm your entry. For keyboard users, press the Enter key. If you decide that you don't want the entry in the cell, click the Cancel box (the X), or press the Esc key. The entry is completely removed from the Formula bar and the cell, enabling you to start over.

If you change your mind after you enter data into a cell, select Edit ⇨ Undo Entry immediately. Excel removes the entry from the cell. Conversely, if you want to start typing the entry from the beginning while the Formula bar is still active for the same cell, select Edit ⇨ Undo Typing.

A	B	C	D	E	F	G	H	I
1								
2		Jan	Feb	Mar	Apr	May	Jun	Jul	Au
3 Salaries	100	101	102	103	103	104	104	10
4 Wages	150	152	154	156	156	157	157	15
5 Benefits	30	30	30	30	30	30	30	3
6 Travel & E	25	25	25	25	25	25	25	2
7 Recruiting	5	5	5	7	7	7	7	
8 Prof Dues	2	2	2	2	2	2	2	
9 Subscriptions								
10								

Figure 7-7: Labels longer than the width of the column spill over into adjacent columns to the right until meeting a cell that contains an entry.

Displaying lengthy labels

As you know, a cell can contain a maximum of 255 characters. If you type an exceptionally long label, the characters roll by in the cell, and the Formula bar expands by dropping down so you can view the characters.

You can, of course, enter a label that is longer than the width of the column it's in. What happens next depends on the cells to the immediate right. If the cells are blank, Excel displays the entry in its entirety, spilling the entry over adjacent cells. If a cell contains an entry, Excel displays as much of the long label as possible. Figure 7-7 displays the effect of long labels in cells.

If you need to display the label that is adjacent to a cell with an entry, shorten the long label or increase the width of the column.

You can quickly adjust the width of a column to accommodate the longest label in the column by double-clicking on the line to the right of the column letter.

Displaying voluminous values

Excel displays long values a little differently than long labels. You may have a long value as a result of data entry or a calculation. If the cell doesn't fit in the column, Excel displays the value as a series of number signs (#####), as shown in Figure 7-8. Unlike long labels, long values are displayed in their own cell and do not spill over to adjacent cells to the right. Excel maintains the correct value; it just can't display it in such a narrow column.

Changing the number's format may give you enough space to display the value. If not, widening the column carries the day.

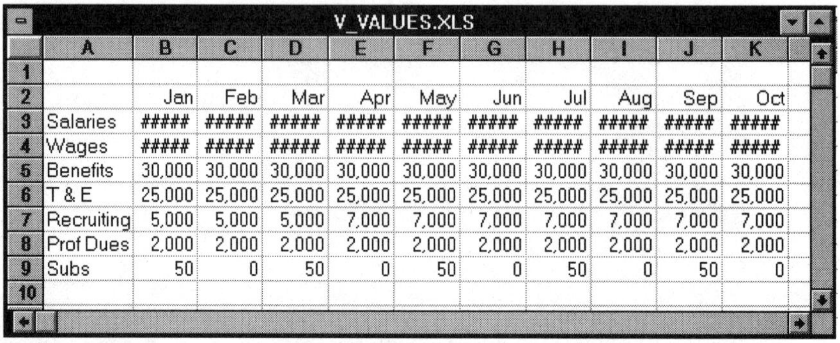

	A	B	C	D	E	F	G	H	I	J	K	
1												
2		Jan	Feb	Mar	Apr	May	Jun	Jul	Aug	Sep	Oct	
3	Salaries	####	####	####	####	####	####	####	####	####	####	
4	Wages	####	####	####	####	####	####	####	####	####	####	
5	Benefits	30,000	30,000	30,000	30,000	30,000	30,000	30,000	30,000	30,000	30,000	
6	T & E	25,000	25,000	25,000	25,000	25,000	25,000	25,000	25,000	25,000	25,000	
7	Recruiting	5,000	5,000	5,000	7,000	7,000	7,000	7,000	7,000	7,000	7,000	
8	Prof Dues	2,000	2,000	2,000	2,000	2,000	2,000	2,000	2,000	2,000	2,000	
9	Subs	50	0	50	0	50	0	50	0	50	0	
10												

V_VALUES.XLS

Figure 7-8: Values longer than the width of the column are displayed as a row of number signs, indicating that a wider column or another number format is needed.

Entering Labels and Text

Entering labels is probably the easiest data entry duty. Simply select the cell, type the entry, and enter it into the cell. For an example, use budgeting, a primary use of Excel where typically the months of the year appear across columns and categories appear down column A. To label columns for the month of the year, follow these steps:

Steps: Labeling rows and columns

Step 1. Create a new worksheet by using File ⇨ New and then select OK.

Step 2. Move to cell B3 by clicking it or using the arrow keys.

Step 3. Type Jan and press Tab or the right arrow key.

Step 4. Type Feb and press Tab or the right arrow key.

Step 5. Continue this process until you have entered all months of the year. Enter Total in the cell to the immediate right of Dec.

In this manner, a value represents a quantity for that month (such as planned telephone expense for April). You can change the alignment of labels (discussed next) and their formatting, which includes fonts, styles, and colors (discussed in Chapter 12).

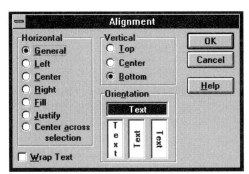

Figure 7-9: Choose Format ➪ Alignment to access this dialog box, which offers a full plate of label alignment options.

By default, Excel aligns values flush right in the cell and aligns labels flush left. Your worksheet will be more attractive if your values and labels have similar alignments. You can easily change the alignment of labels by selecting the cell or range and then choosing the appropriate tool on the Toolbar. You can also use the Format ➪ Alignment command to select an alignment option, as shown in Figure 7-9. Figure 7-10 displays text with the available alignment options.

Use Format ➪ Alignment ➪ Wrap Text to display a long label in a single cell. Excel automatically expands the height of the row to accommodate the label, as shown in Figure 7-10.

Figure 7-10: Use these alignment options to display labels as you want.

	A	B	C	D	E	F	G	H
1	General							
2	Left		Text centered across columns C through G					
3	Center							
4	Right							
5	FillFillFillFillFill							
6	Wrapped text in a cell can be useful in special situations							
7								

L_ALIGN.XLS

Entering Numeric Data _____

Excel recognizes three types of numeric data:

- Numbers
- Worksheet functions
- Formulas

Numbers are numeric values such as –1, 0, 1.25, and so on. *Worksheet functions,* as you know, are built-in Excel formulas. *Formulas,* in turn, are mathematical relationships between the contents of cells that calculate a result using these contents, arithmetic operators, and/or worksheet functions.

Entering a numeric value is similar to entering a label into a worksheet: Select a cell, type the number using the numeric keypad or the numbers across the top of the alphabetic keys, and enter it into the cell by pressing Enter. Numeric values can also be broken down further into these categories:

- Numbers
- Dates
- Times

Using dates in worksheets

You can enter a date either as a label or a value. Enter a date as a label when you want to describe a cell or range in your worksheet, such as Dec-92. Enter a date as a value when you need to use dates in calculations, such as the number of days between two dates.

Date as label: The process is the same as for any kind of label. Select a cell, type the date, and press Enter. If the style of date you want to use as a label begins with one of the dates as values formats listed in the following section, type an equal sign and enclose the date in quotation marks; =`"Dec-92"` is an example.

Date as value: You have several options to enter dates as values. The options, in order of user-friendliness, follow.

Entering dates as formatted values

Type the day, month, and year in one of these formats:

Format	Example
m/d/yy	1/1/92
d-mmm-yy	1-Jan-92
d-mmm	1-Jan
mmm-yy	Jan-92

All these formats return the serial number 33604. Use one of the first two formats when you need to specify the day of the month. Or use a format that displays a date in a manner that appeals to you (remember, you're the boss here).

Entering dates as worksheet functions

Type =DATE(yy,m,d), such as =DATE(92,1,1), for January 1, 1992. Excel returns the serial number equivalent, 33604.

Use this method when you need a date in a serial number format.

Entering dates as numerical values

Type the number that represents the day numbering from January 1, 1900. For example, January 1, 1992, is 33604.

This tedious method isn't used by many Excel users. It requires you to know the number for each day of each month and year. Although Excel stores dates in this format, you're much better off using a date format that is easier to enter and understand.

 To quickly use the current date or time in your worksheet, use the NOW() worksheet function; then format it using a date or time format. For the date only, you can use the TODAY() worksheet function.

If the width of the cell can't accommodate the cell, number signs are displayed, as shown in Figure 7-8. Like with any other value that is too long to fit in a cell, Excel stores the date value and can perform operations with it, and the program displays it as a date if you increase the width of the column.

Using the time in worksheets

Entering the time is similar to entering dates. As before, you can enter a date either as a label or a value. Enter the time as a label when you want to describe a cell or range in a worksheet, as with 12:00 PM. Enter a time as a value when you need to use the time in calculations, such as the number of minutes between two times.

Time as label: As with dates, enter the time as a label by selecting, typing, and pressing Enter. If the style you're using to represent time begins with one of the time formats listed in the following section, type an equal sign and then enclose the time in quotation marks; ="1:00 PM" is an example.

Time as value: You also have similar options to enter the time as a value. Following are the options.

Entering time as a formatted value

Type the hour, minutes, and seconds in one of these formats:

Format	Example
h:mm AM/PM	1:00 PM
h:mm:ss AM/PM	1:00:01 PM
hh:mm	13:00
hh:mm:ss	13:00:01
m/d/yy hh:mm	1/1/92 13:00

Choose a format that best meets your needs. Note that the last three formats show the 24-hour clock (military) style of time. Be sure to type a space between the last number in the time and the AM or PM.

Entering time as a worksheet function

Type =TIME(hh,m,s), such as =TIME(13,0,0), for 1:00:00 PM. As with dates, use this method when you need a time in a serial number format.

Entering time as a numerical value

Type the number that represents the time numbering from 0:00:00 (12:00:00 AM). For example, 0.5 is 12:00:00 PM.

This is again a tough row to hoe and is generally not the preferred method of entering the time. It requires you to know the fractional number for each minute of the day. Excel stores all time values as fractions of a day so that noon is 0.5 (half the day) and 0.25 is 6 o'clock in the morning. Although Excel stores the time in this format, you're much better off using a time that has meaning to you.

Decimal fractions of date numbers are times. Dates and times can therefore be represented by a single value. For example, 33604.75 is 6:00 p.m. on January 1, 1992.

Entering formulas

Excel has three types of formulas: numeric, text, and logical. These types are discussed in the sections that follow.

Numeric formulas

Numeric formulas always begin with an equal sign (=) and operate on values, references to cells containing data, worksheet functions, and other formulas to calculate a result. In addition, numeric formulas use *operators* to arrive at an answer. The numeric formula operators are as follows:

Operator	Purpose
^	Exponentiation
*	Multiplication
/	Division
+	Addition
–	Subtraction

Excel also follows the rules of precedence. That is, Excel calculates expressions in formulas by using these operators in descending order. So, for example, one expression is multiplied before another is added. You can also control precedence by using parentheses. Expressions enclosed in parentheses are calculated first. (In the event of more than one set of parentheses, Excel calculates them from left to right.) Here are a few examples:

Formula	How Excel evaluates	Result
=10+5*2	10+(5*2)	20.0
=(10+5)*2	(10+5)*2	30.0
=10+5*2/4-6	(10+((5*2)/4))-6	6.5
=(10+5)*(2/4)-6	(10+5)*(2/4)-6	1.5

Excel calculates formulas up to 15 decimal places unless you control the amount of precision by using the ROUND function. Excel also displays only the number of decimals you specify with the Forma𝑡 ⇨ Number command.

Text formulas

As their name implies, text formulas operate on text. You must enclose text in quotation marks (" ") for Excel to recognize the entry as text. Besides the quotation marks, the only other text operator is the ampersand (&). The ampersand enables you to concatenate, or combine, two or more text entries into one. Two simple text formulas follow:

Formula	Result
="Net"&"Sales"	NetSales
="Net'&" "&"Sales"	Net Sales

Excel also contains worksheet text functions to use with text formulas. See Chapter 10 for more information about creating text formulas.

Logical formulas

A logical formula enables worksheets to perform conditional tests. If a cell meets the condition, Excel returns 1, for true. If not, Excel returns 0, for false. The logical formula operators are as follows:

Operator	Purpose
=	Equal
>	Greater than
<	Less than
>=	Greater than or equal to
<=	Less than or equal to
<>	Not equal

A few simple logical values follow:

```
=A1=25

=A2<>B2
```

The following steps describe how to enter formulas into a worksheet:

Steps: Entering a formula in a worksheet

Step 1. Select a cell.

Step 2. Type an equal sign (=), which tells Excel to expect a formula.

Step 3. Type a value or cell address. If you just want to reference another cell, press Enter now.

Step 4. Type an operator.

Step 5. Type the next value or cell address.

Step 6. If you want to continue creating the formula, repeat Steps 4 and 5. When finished, complete the formula by pressing Enter.

Editing Data _____

Now that you know how to enter data into a worksheet, you may be wondering how to make changes to it. You may have misspelled a label or want to use a different label or value in a cell. You may even want to move it to another location on the worksheet or remove it entirely. If you're a spreadsheet beginner, you'll definitely want to read this section and learn how to make changes to your data. If you're new to Windows, you'll especially want to find out what all this "Clipboard" business is about. Spreadsheet gurus may want to hang around a bit and check out how to copy and move data around in Excel in comparison with other spreadsheet programs — particularly those that are DOS-based.

Understanding when and why you edit data

When you hear the word "edit," the first thing that may come to mind is the type of editing that occurs with magazines, newspapers, and books — including this one. In the world of bits and bytes, however, editing refers to making a change or modifying a data item (or items) in the current file. You can change the text in a word processing document, data in a spreadsheet, or objects in a chart, for example. When you're satisfied with your changes, you resave the file to disk and go about your business again (say, printing another copy of the document or worksheet).

In Excel, you edit data when it doesn't meet your needs. You may have a label that is misspelled or doesn't accurately describe the values in your worksheet. On the other hand, you may have to rearrange a worksheet to accommodate new assumptions or categories of data. If you need to edit the actual contents of a single cell, you can edit the contents before or after you enter the information into a cell. If you need to edit a range of cells, you can "pick up" the contents of the range and "put them down" in another area of the worksheet, copy the contents, or remove them entirely.

Excel provides you with a variety of editing tools, which are discussed in the sections that follow.

Using the mouse or the keyboard

When selecting commands, a cell, or a range or when choosing dialog box options, you have a choice of whether to use the mouse or keyboard. The method you use depends on the task at hand, your experience with spreadsheets and Windows, and your personal preference.

If you're editing a single cell, you may want to use the keyboard. Single-cell editing is best suited to the keyboard; because you've already selected the cell, you need only to type the characters or numbers you want, without moving your hands from the keyboard. You can then select Enter and move on.

If you're editing a range of cells, however, you may want to use the mouse. Although single-cell editing tends to be more keyboard-oriented, multicell editing is more likely to be a mouse job. Selecting a range of cells with a mouse is much quicker than using the keyboard, and because you use Excel commands to edit ranges, selecting the appropriate editing command is also easier with a mouse.

The bottom line is that you should use the input device you feel more comfortable with. Remember, however, you'll always be more productive using the right tool for the right job.

Editing a single cell

Editing the contents of a single cell is easy. To edit a cell, you use Excel's Formula bar. In this instance, think of the Formula bar as the place where you put the cell's contents for repair. Follow these steps to edit the current contents of a cell:

Steps: Editing the current contents of a cell

Step 1. Select the cell.

Step 2. Press F2 or click on the Formula bar.

Step 3. Edit the cell's contents (as shown in Figure 7-11) using the appropriate editing keys and entering replacement characters (if any).

Step 4. Press Enter or cancel your changes by pressing Esc or selecting the Cancel box.

	B4	X	✓	=PMT(B1/12,B2*12,-B3)			

EDIT.XLS

	A	B	C	D	E	F	G
1	Int rate	9%					
2	No. of yrs.	30					
3	Loan amt.	100,000					
4	Payment	B2*12,-B3)					
5							
6							
7							
8							
9							
10							
11							

Figure 7-11:
Edit a cell's contents by selecting the cell and then making the changes in the Formula bar.

If you've edited and entered the contents of the Formula bar into a cell and then change your mind about the entry, immediately invoke Edit ⇨ Undo to reinstate the original contents to the cell.

As you know, you can select the cell and enter or cancel the edited cell entry with the keyboard or mouse. You can even move the cursor in the Formula bar with the mouse (the pointer is the I-beam) or keyboard. But you can only enter any new characters or numbers from the keyboard. The keys you use to edit are as follows:

Backspace: The Backspace key erases any character to the immediate left of the cursor and then moves the cursor one character left. Recall from Chapter 5 that the Backspace key is the key with the large left-pointing arrow located on the upper-right side of the keyboard's alphabetic keys. It may or may not say "Backspace," depending on your keyboard model.

Del: The Del (Delete) key also erases characters but only the one directly underneath the cursor. The Del key is on the bottom of the numeric keypad and, on some keyboards, between the alphabetic keys and numeric keypad.

Ins: The Ins (Insert) key places Excel in OVR (Overtype) mode when you're editing, which means that instead of adding characters to the cell's contents, you overwrite them with new ones, depending on the position of the cursor. If the cursor is above a character and you type a new one in OVR mode, the character is overwritten with the replacement character. Ins is located on the zero on the numeric keypad and, on some keyboards, between the alphabetic keys and numeric keypad.

Left/right arrow: The left and right arrow keys move the cursor left and right one character, without deleting any characters. The left and right arrows are on the numbers 4 and 6, respectively, on the numeric keypad and, on some keyboards, between the alphabetic keys and numeric keypad. Remember that Num Lock should be off if you want to use the keys on the numeric keypad as cursor keys.

Home/End: The Home and End keys move the cursor to the beginning and end of the cell entry, respectively, and do not delete any characters. Home and End are on the numbers 7 and 1, respectively, on the numeric keypad and, on some keyboards, between the alphabetic keys and numeric keypad.

Enter: In most computer programs, you use Enter to tell your computer "Yes, this is what I want — do it." Pressing Enter after editing tells Excel this is what you want in the cell and to go ahead with the revised entry. Enter is located on the right-hand side of the alphabetic keys — somewhat of a holdover from the typewriter. On some keyboards, you also have an Enter key on the bottom right-hand side of the numeric keypad.

You can also edit the characters before you enter them into a cell by pressing F2. If you don't press F2, only Backspace works as an editing key. The left and right arrows and Home, for example, enter the characters in the Formula bar into the cell and then move the cell pointer according to the direction of the arrow.

Editing a range of cells

Central to making changes to a range of cells is the Windows Clipboard facility. You may have heard a lot about the Clipboard (shown in Figure 7-12). It's an area of every computer's RAM that Windows sets aside for temporary storage. You can place text, values, or a chart on the Clipboard. The item you place on the Clipboard remains there until you place another item on it (thus overwriting it), you end your Windows session, or you turn off your computer.

Another theme of cell range editing is cutting and pasting. Not that long ago, many of us (who are too embarrassed to admit it) had to literally use scissors and glue (or paste) to cut a row and place it elsewhere on a piece of accounting paper. Getting totals to cross-foot again was difficult, and the task was messy and time-consuming. In any event, given that background, you figuratively do the same with an Excel worksheet and the Clipboard, without all the muss and fuss.

For example, to move the contents of a single cell or multiple range of cells, use the Edit ⇨ Cut command to remove it from its current location and then use Edit ⇨ Paste to place it in its new location on a worksheet. To copy the contents of a cell or multiple cells use Edit ⇨ Copy to duplicate the cells and then Edit ⇨ Paste to place them in the second location (or in as many places as you need) on the

❏	EDIT.XLS				—	Clipboard	▼ ▲
					File Edit Display Help		

	A	B	C	D
1	Int rate	9%		
2	No. of yrs.	30		
3	Loan amt.	100,000		
4	Payment	$804.62		
5				
6				
7				
8				
9				
10				
11				

Clipboard panel contents:

Int rate   9%
No. of yrs.   30
Loan amt.   100,000
Payment $804.62

Figure 7-12: The Clipboard stores data you've cut or copied from the worksheet or the Formula bar. You display the Clipboard by selecting it from the Main Windows program group.

worksheet. When you use the commands Edit ⇨ Cut or Copy, as opposed to using Clear or Del from the keyboard, the Clipboard temporarily holds the data until you're ready to paste it onto the worksheet. In short, you cut or copy the data to the Clipboard and then place it back in your worksheet by pasting.

You can use Edit ⇨ Cut with the contents of the Formula bar when Excel is in Edit mode. The contents you select, however, are completely removed from the Formula bar and placed on the Clipboard. If you use Edit ⇨ Cut or Copy again, the contents previously in the Formula bar but now on the Clipboard are overwritten with the new selection.

Next we'll examine some details on how to use Excel's editing commands.

Using commands for editing

Excel's editing commands are found, as you may expect, on the Edit menu. The Edit menu is your gateway to the Clipboard. Edit menu commands are shown in Figure 7-13 (note that Edit ⇨ Insert Paste only appears after you choose the Edit ⇨ Cut or Copy command). Like with many Excel operations, you must select a cell or range of cells before using these commands.

Edit ⇨ Undo

Edit ⇨ Undo enables you to reverse any cut, copy, or paste action, including most worksheet operations (Undo can't help you with saving a file to disk or printing). If you've cut and pasted something, for example, selecting Edit ⇨ Undo returns the cell contents to their original location. For Edit ⇨ Undo to work as expected,

Figure 7-13: Excel's Edit menu enables access to the Windows Clipboard, through cutting, copying, and pasting.

you *must* use it immediately following the action you want to reverse. You can select this command by using any of the following methods:

Mouse   Select the Edit menu and choose Undo.

Shortcut keys   Press Alt+Backspace.

Edit ⇨ Cut

Edit ⇨ Cut's action depends on where you're cutting. If you're cutting data in the Formula bar, the data is removed entirely and placed on the Clipboard. Excel closes up any space among characters in the Formula bar, and any data on the Clipboard is overwritten by data from the Formula bar. If you're cutting data from a worksheet, Excel places a marquee around the cut data and passes the data up to the Clipboard and back down to the worksheet when you choose Edit ⇨ Paste. You can select this command by using any of the following methods:

Mouse   Select the Edit menu and choose Cut.

Shortcut keys   Press Shift+Del or Ctrl+X.

Edit ⇨ Copy

Edit ⇨ Copy enables you to copy the contents of a single cell or range of cells. Edit ⇨ Copy duplicates these contents without moving or deleting them and passes the data up to the Clipboard and back down to the worksheet when you choose Edit ⇨ Paste. You can select this command by using any of the following methods:

Mouse   Select the Edit menu and choose Copy.

Shortcut keys   Press Ctrl+Ins or Ctrl+C.

Edit ⇨ Paste

Edit ⇨ Paste enables you to paste cut or copied data into the Formula bar or a worksheet. Data cut from the Formula bar is on the Clipboard, so you can paste it as many times as you like. You can select this command by using any of the following methods:

Mouse   Select the Edit menu and choose Paste.

Shortcut keys   Press Shift+Ins or Ctrl+V.

Edit ⇨ Insert Paste

Edit ⇨ Insert Paste is a special form of the Paste command that you use following an Edit ⇨ Cut or Copy command. Unlike Edit ⇨ Paste, Edit ⇨ Insert Paste inserts cut or copied data onto a worksheet without overwriting any existing cell contents. Edit ⇨ Insert Paste enables you to shift existing cell contents to the right or down to make room for cut or copied data. You can select this command by using any of the following methods:

Mouse   Select the Edit menu and choose Insert Paste.

Shortcut keys   None.

Edit ⇨ Paste Special

Edit ⇨ Paste Special is another variation of Edit ⇨ Paste. You can only use Edit ⇨ Paste Special following the Edit ⇨ Copy command. Edit ⇨ Paste Special provides you with powerful and convenient copying features. The Edit Paste Special dialog box provides you with the opportunity to paste All cell attributes, or only Formulas, Values, Formats, or Notes from the selected range. In this manner, you can choose only the attributes you want copied to the active worksheet or other open worksheets. This command is further described in Chapter 9. Your options follow:

Add, Subtract, Multiply, or Divide: These options enable you to perform a mathematical operation on the contents of the selected cell range with the cell contents in the paste area. In effect, the cells in the paste area are overwritten with the results of the arithmetic operation.

Transpose: Transpose changes the orientation of the data to be pasted. Specifically, a selected row range is pasted down a column; a selected column range is pasted across a row. To invoke Edit ⇨ Paste Special, you can use any of the following methods:

Mouse   Select the Edit menu and choose Paste Special.

Shortcut keys   None.

Edit ⇨ Clear

Edit ⇨ Clear completely removes the selected data from the Formula bar or the worksheet, bypassing the Clipboard entirely. Using Edit ⇨ Clear gives you the opportunity to remove either everything or selected cell attributes and contents, such as formatting and notes, from worksheet data. You can select this command by using any of the following methods:

Mouse   Select the Edit menu and choose Clear.

Shortcut keys   Press Del.

Adding a note to a cell

Now that you've edited and entered data into your worksheet, you're all set, right? Well, not quite. An optional but highly recommended habit to get into is to add notes to cells in your worksheet — especially those cells that contain complex formulas. It's difficult enough to remember something you did last week, not to mention last year.

In addition, if you create worksheets for others, or leave your position, cell notes become a valuable documentation source for those who will use your Excel applications. Trying to understand an application created by another user is one of the most daunting worksheet tasks. Unfortunately, no add-in or macro (yet) can analyze the thinking that went on when you put your application together. Cell notes, however, go a long way toward refreshing your memory and helping others understand the logic behind your application. (Cell notes also help cut down on those inconvenient telephone calls for help.)

 If you use Windows 3.1 or have the Multimedia Extension for Windows 3.0, you can also add a sound note, which requires a compatible sound card such as a SoundBlaster or Pro Audio Spectrum.

Adding a note to a cell is easy. Simply select the cell you want to add a note to and then invoke the Formula ⇨ Note command. When you do so, the dialog box in Figure 7-14 appears. Type your note and then choose OK. If you want to continue adding notes to other cells, select Add instead. Choose Close when you're finished adding, deleting, or editing cell notes.

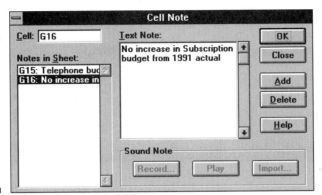

Figure 7-14:
The Cell Note dialog box enables you to attach a descriptive note to one or more cells at a time.

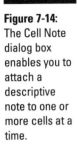

You can identify cells that have a note attached to them by the small red dot that appears in the upper-right corner of the cell.

Formatting Numbers

After you've edited and entered your data, you can begin *formatting* your numbers. Formatting refers to how you want to display your numbers (and text) and is actually a two-step process. First, you should choose the symbols you want to have displayed with the numbers (commas, dollar signs, number of decimal places, and so on) and, second, the type and size of font, with bold-facing, underlining, or italics. This section shows you how to add symbols to the numbers, and Chapter 12 shows you how to apply the fancy typographic stuff to your data to produce professional quality reports, screen displays, and worksheets with pizzazz.

Examining formatting basics

When you initially enter a value into a worksheet, Excel displays the value by using its default format, known as General. General format displays positive values with no symbols and negative values with a minus sign preceding the first digit. You can easily use another format by selecting the cell or range to format and then choosing the Format ⇨ Number command. When you choose Format ⇨ Number, the dialog box in Figure 7-15 appears, showing you Excel's predefined format choices.You can select a general category first and then quickly find the specific format you need.

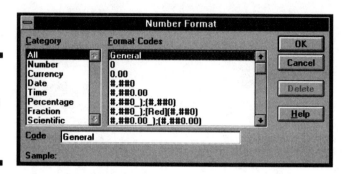

Figure 7-15: The Number Format dialog box provides you with a variety of number formatting options.

You can either use the scroll bar to scroll through the list or use the up and down arrow keys, which simultaneously displays the format in the Code box below the list. When you locate the format you want, choose OK and Excel uses that format on each cell in the selected range. It's as easy as that. Table 7-1 summarizes Excel's predefined formats and how they display the numbers on-screen and on paper.

If the selected range has a cell entry in the upper-left cell, watch the Sample area of the dialog box to see how the format appears before choosing OK.

Some predefined formats can be entered along with the number from the keyboard. For example, if you enter a dollar sign ($) before or a percentage sign (%) after a number, Excel automatically uses the dollar and percentage formats, respectively. You can also enter numbers in the following date and time formats directly:

Date		Time	
Format	**Display**	**Format**	**Display**
m/d/yy	1/1/92	h:mm AM/PM	1:00 PM
d-mmm-yy	1-Jan-92	hh:mm:ss AM/PM	1:00:00 PM
d-mmm	1-Jan	hh:mm	13:00
mmm-yy	Jan-92		
m/d/yy hh:mm	1/1/92 13:00		

m, mmm = month   h, hh = hour
d = day   mm = minute
y, yy = year   ss = second

Table 7-1: Excel's predefined formats		
Format	**Positive**	**Negative**
General	1234.5	-1234.5
0	1235	-1235
0.00	1234.50	-1234.50
"#,##0"	"1,235"	"-1,235"
"#,##0.00"	"1,234.50"	"-1,234.50"
"#,##0_);(#,##0)"	"1,235"	"-1,235"
"#,##0_);[Red](#,##0)"	"1,235"	"-1,235"[1]
"#,##0.00_);(#,##0.00)"	"1,234.50"	"-1,234.50"
"#,##0.00_);[Red](#,##0.00)"	"1,234.50"	"-1,234.50"[1]
"$#,##0_);($#,##0)"	"$1,235"	"-$1,235"
"$#,##0_);[Red]($#,##0)"	"$1,235"	"-$1,235"[1]
"$#,##0.00_);($#,##0.00)"	"$1,234.50"	"-$1,234.50"
"$#,##0.00_);[Red]($#,##0.00)"	"$1,234.50"	"-$1,234.50"[1]
0%	12%	-12%
0.00%	12.35%	-12.35%
0.00E+100	1.23E+03	-1.23E+03
#?/?	1 2/3	-1 2/3
#??/??	1 2/3	-1 2/3 [2]

[1] Displays negative values in red.
[2] Left aligned in cell.

 You can quickly apply a format to a selected cell range by pulling down the Style box menu and choosing the format, or you can use the following shortcut keys:

Format	Key combination
General	Ctrl+Shift+~
#,##0.00	Ctrl+Shift+!
$#,##0.00);($#,##0.00)	Ctrl+Shift+$
0%	Ctrl+Shift+%
0.00E+00	Ctrl+Shift+^
d-mmm-yy	Ctrl+Shift+#
h:mm AM/PM	Ctrl+Shift+@

When a number isn't a number

You need to keep in mind that when you format numbers (values or the results of formulas) in a worksheet, you're only changing the *display* of the numbers and not the underlying numbers Excel uses to perform calculations. In some situations, this setup may cause results of calculations to appear incorrect, such as in totaling numbers with decimal places. Even though Excel calculated a correct answer, it may display an incorrect answer due to formatting, as shown in column D of the following worksheet.

	A	B	C	D	E	F	G	
1								
2		Values		Formatted to 2		Values		
3		as entered		decimal places		rounded		
4		100.096		100.10		100.1		
5		100.096		100.10		100.1		
6		200.192		200.19		200.2		
7								
8								
9								
10								

OCP_01.XLS

What's wrong with this picture? Check your worksheet carefully if you've applied a number format that changes the display of numbers to the right of the decimal point.

You have two solutions to this problem. One is to select Options ⇨ Calculation ⇨ Precision as Displayed, which instructs Excel to use numbers as displayed in calculations. Note, however, that Excel warns you with the message box shown here that the underlying values will be permanently changed to match their appearance. Keep a backup copy of the worksheet on disk if you select this option. You may need it if you have second thoughts later.

This message box offers you a last chance to change your mind before your worksheet uses values as displayed in calculations. Make sure that you have a recent version of your worksheet saved to disk in case you have a change of heart later.

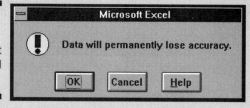

Microsoft Excel

Data will permanently lose accuracy.

OK   Cancel   Help

A second solution is to use the ROUND function on individual values. In this manner, you can specify the number of decimal places to round to. Remember to round the values and not the cells that rely on the values (your formulas, for example).

Don't like what you see? No problem; you can have it your way. Excel enables you to change predefined formats or create your own. To learn how, read on. If you're new to spreadsheets, you may want to skip this section, because it is fairly esoteric. You can always come back to it later.

Creating a format

To master the process of creating your own number formats, as a first step you need to understand the meaning of the symbols Excel uses in its formats, as described in Table 7-2.

Table 7-2: Excel's format symbols		
Symbol	**Meaning**	**Details**
General	Default format	Displays as many digits in the number that the width of the column allows, without symbols.
#	Digit placeholder	Does not display 0 if a number does not exist. Decimal fractions round up to the number of # signs to the right of the decimal point. For example, 1.26 is displayed as 1.3 with a #.# format.
0	Digit placeholder	Displays 0 if no number is entered. Decimal fractions round up to the number of zeroes to the right of the decimal point. For example, 1.2 is displayed as 1.20 with a #.00 format.
?	Digit placeholder	Same as 0, but spaces are inserted in place of insignificant digits so numbers align properly.
. (period)	Decimal point	Use to determine the number of digits to the left and right of the whole and decimal fraction of the number. A 0 as a leading zero to the left of the decimal point eliminates numbers less than one appearing with a decimal point in the beginning of the number.
%	Percentage	Number is multiplied by 100 and appears with a % symbol following the last digit.
, (comma)	Thousands separator	Separates thousands in large numbers. Only one comma is needed in the format to separate thousands.
_ (underline)	Skip the width of the next character	Use to align a positive number with a negative number enclosed in parentheses.
E-E+e-e+	Scientific notation	0s or # signs following one of these characters display the power of the exponent.

continued next page

Table 7-2: Excel's format symbols (continued)		
Symbol	**Meaning**	**Details**
$-+/():space	Displays character	Displays the character at the same position in every selected number.
/ (slash)	Separates numerator and denominator	Displays fractions.
\ (backslash)	Displays next entry	Displays the next character in the format.
* (asterisk)	Displays next entry	Displays the next character so that the cell is filled.
"text"	Displays text	Displays text in double quotation marks.
@	Displays text	Uses any existing text in the cell in the format.
[color]	Displays a color	Displays the color you specify.
[cond_stmt]	Use a conditional statement	Enables you to use a conditional statement in the format to choose which format to use.

The next step is to understand the format structure. For example, the predefined formats have four sections, separated by semicolons. The custom formats contain these parts:

Positive format; Negative format; Zero format; Text format

Each section of the format tells Excel how you want your numbers displayed, depending on the specific number. Note that not every format has to include all four sections.

To create a custom numeric format, choose the Format ⇨ Number command (or Number from the Shortcut menu); then decide how you want positive and negative numbers and zeroes displayed and whether you want any text in your format. See whether an existing format is close to the format you want to create in the Format Code list box. If so, you can save time by selecting and then editing it in the Code box. If you need to create one from scratch, type the appropriate symbols in the Code box. Either way, use the symbols just listed to create the format you need and don't forget to separate each section with a semicolon. Choose OK when you're finished, and you're ready to apply the custom format. Figure 7-16 shows you several examples of useful custom formats you can create.

You can use formats to hide zeros. In your custom format, use a semicolon to tell Excel that you're going to format zeroes but then don't use a symbol. In this manner, Excel doesn't display a zero. For example, the format $#,##0_);($#,##0); displays 1000 as $1,000 or ($1,000), depending on whether it's positive or negative, but zero isn't displayed.

	A	B	C	D	E	F
			C_FORMAT.XLS			
	Type	Format	Entered value	Displayed value		
1						
2						
3	Fractions		0.000	1 5/8	1.625	
4						
5	Currency	#,###0 "US Dollars"	500	500 US Dollars		
6						
7	Data validation	0.00 ,"Positive numbers only"	123	123.00		
8			-123	Positive numbers only		
9						
10	Zero with dashes	#,##0_):(#,##0);-0-	0	-0-		
11						
12	Telephone	(###) ###-####	3175711000	(317) 571-1000		
13						
14	Social Security	"SSN" ###-##-####		SSN 123-45-6789		

Figure 7-16: For specialized applications, you can create unique format codes to fit your particular situation.

Summary

▶ Cells in a worksheet hold your data, which is comprised of labels, values, functions, and formulas.

▶ Labels are text characters that describe and explain a worksheet and its purpose. Enter a label or value into a cell by selecting it, typing the label or value, and pressing Enter.

▶ Values are numeric and represent a quantity. A value can be a number, date, time, or scientific number.

▶ Functions are built-in formulas that Excel provides for you.

▶ Formulas calculate results based on the contents of other cells. Enter a formula into a cell by selecting it, typing an equal (=) sign, typing the formula, and clicking the Enter box or pressing OK.

▶ Use Options ⇨ Display ⇨ Formulas to display the formulas in a worksheet rather than their results.

▶ To edit the contents of a cell, select the cell then press F2 or click on the Formula bar.

▶ Data you cut or copy is placed on the Clipboard so you can paste it back into a worksheet.

▶ Use Edit ⇨ Undo immediately after a command or other worksheet action to reverse the result of that action.

▶ Edit ⇨ Clear removes the contents of cells without placing them on the Clipboard.

▶ You can attach a note to a cell by using the Formula ⇨ Note command.

▶ You can change the appearance of numbers by using the Format ⇨ Numbers command.

▶ You can create your own custom formats by editing a predefined format or starting one from scratch.

Chapter 8
Learning Essential Spreadsheet Operations

In this chapter . . .

▶ How to adjust column widths and row heights and why you need to do so.

▶ How to insert and delete rows and columns.

▶ How to justify text across several columns.

▶ How to find and replace data in your worksheet.

▶ How to add notes to cells as reminders.

Sooner or later, after you've created an Excel worksheet, you'll need to modify it to accommodate your current needs. For example, you may have a new account item to incorporate, a calendar to add to a fiscal-year-basis report, or an analysis that you can perform by making a few changes to an existing worksheet rather than starting one from scratch. Whatever the reason, the topics covered in this chapter address many of the commands and procedures you can use to quickly bring your worksheet up to warp speed.

This chapter is best suited for those who at this point have studied the material in earlier chapters and have gained some hands-on experience with Excel. Spreadsheet gurus may also want to take a peek to compare how Excel performs these spreadsheet operations with how the program you've been using performs the operations.

Adjusting Rows and Columns _____

You're most likely to need to adjust the height of rows or the width of columns as you enter labels into your worksheet, format numbers, or apply different font types and sizes to your cell entries. The need to widen your columns is apparent; if you have a column that displays repeating pound signs or number signs, Excel can't display a value within the column width, so you need to increase its width to display the number.

The need to change the height of a row is a little less obvious, because Excel automatically increases the height of the row if you apply a larger font to a cell in the row. You may want to increase row height to draw attention to important items in your worksheet, such as subtotals or grand totals. Adjusting row heights is also a good way to spread out a table vertically so it fills up a page or compress it so it doesn't take up as much space. In any case, adjusting rows and columns is easy.

Changing row height

Changing the height of one or more rows is a relatively painless procedure. You can change the height of one row at a time or of multiple rows, if you want the rows to have the same height. Basically, changing row height is a four-step procedure:

Steps: Changing row height

Step 1. Select the row(s) for which you want to change the height.

Step 2. Choose the Format ⇨ Row Height command.

Step 3. Specify the height in the Row Height dialog box (see Figure 8-1).

Step 4. Confirm the height by selecting OK.

 To change the height of all rows in your worksheet, select all rows in your worksheet (click any column letter) or the entire worksheet (click the rectangle at the intersection of row 1 and column A).

Figure 8-1: The Format ⇨ Row Height command enables you to specify row heights and hide and unhide rows.

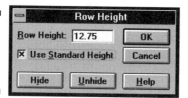

You can also use your mouse to change the height of rows (see the following tip). The only major difference between the two methods is how you select the row or rows for your height adjustment. You select rows as follows:

Selecting rows with a mouse:

Single row	Click any cell in the row for which you want to change the height or click the row number.
Multiple rows	Click on and drag one cell (or row number) from each row you want to change. Select nonadjacent rows by holding down the Ctrl key and clicking a cell in the row or its number.

Selecting rows with the keyboard:

Single row	Use the arrow keys to select any cell in the row for which you want to change the height.
Multiple rows	Select a cell from the first row for which you want to change the height; then press F8 or hold down the Shift key and press the up or down arrow keys.

Menus and mice and shortcut keys, oh my!

You've probably discovered by now that you can accomplish a task with Excel in more than one way. You can change the width of a column, for example, by using the Column Width command from the Edit menu or the shortcut menu. Or you can use your mouse to change the column width by dragging or clicking twice (for Best Fit). Tool icons on various tool bars enable you to quickly accomplish a task by simply clicking the icon (which you learn about in Chapter 19). The question is, which is the best technique to use?

Actually, the choice all boils down to personal preference. If you're a Windows or Excel veteran, you're probably used to sliding a mouse around your desk, so you may find the shortcut menu and tools the most efficient way for you. If you're new to graphical computing (or prefer to keep your hands on the keyboard), stick with your keyboard until you get comfortable with the idea of using a pointing device. If you choose the latter, be sure to keep Excel's shortcut keys in mind. Of course, nothing prohibits you from using a combination of keyboard and mouse options, which you need to do to enter labels and values anyway.

Whichever method you choose, don't let the multiple ways of performing Excel worksheet tasks overwhelm you. Look at it as an opportunity to select what works best for you, and we give you some helpful advice along the way to help you decide.

If you've selected one or more rows by selecting the row number(s), you can access the Row Height command from the shortcut menu. Instead of using the Format ⇨ Row Height command to change row height, you can use the mouse to quickly change the height of one or more selected rows by clicking on and dragging the line separating Excel's row numbers. For example, to change the height of row 10, you click on and drag the line separating row numbers 10 and 11. When you do, the mouse pointer appears as a black up-and-down arrow. If you've selected multiple rows, clicking on and dragging one row number line changes the height for all selected rows.

As you specify a row height, keep in mind that Excel displays row heights in points (as with fonts) and uses integers or decimal fractions to represent those points. For example, a new worksheet has a default row height of 12.75. If you specify a row height that is smaller than the font used in the row, Excel may cut off the display of your cell entries along their top (this varies by the font used). If you do find yourself with clipped characters, use the Standard Height option from the dialog box to have Excel automatically adjust the row height to accommodate the largest font in the row.

You cannot change the height of rows in a protected worksheet.

The Row Height dialog box also provides you with the opportunity to hide or show selected rows by using the Hide and Unhide options. You can also hide and show rows quickly by using the shortcut keys Ctrl+9 and Ctrl+Shift+(, respectively. Specifying a row height of zero also hides a row.

Changing column width

Changing the width of one or more columns is virtually identical to changing row heights. This time, however, you're working with columns rather than rows. You can change the width of one column at a time or multiple columns if you want the columns to have the same width. As with row height, changing column width is a four-step procedure:

Steps: Changing column width

Step 1. Select the column(s) for which you want to change the width.

Step 2. Choose Format ⇨ Column Width.

Step 3. Specify the width in the Column Width text box (see Figure 8-2).

Step 4. Confirm the width by selecting OK.

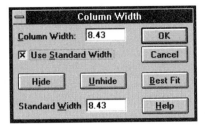

Figure 8-2: Similar to the Row Height dialog box, the Column Width dialog box enables you to change the width of columns and hide and unhide them.

To change the width of all columns in your worksheet, select either all the columns (click any row number) or the entire worksheet (click the rectangle at the intersection of row 1 and column A).

Again, you can use your mouse or the keyboard for column-width changes. The only major difference between the two methods is in the selection process, which is summarized as follows:

Selecting columns with a mouse:

Single column	Click any cell in the column for which you want to change the width or click the column letter.
Multiple columns	Click on and drag one cell (or column letter) from each column you want to change. Select nonadjacent columns by holding down the Ctrl key and clicking a cell in the column or its letter.

Selecting columns with the keyboard:

Single column	Use the arrow keys to select any cell in the column for which you want to change the width.
Multiple columns	Select a cell from the first column for which you want to change the width; then press F8 or hold down the Shift key and press the left or right arrow keys.

If you've selected one or more columns by selecting the column letter(s), the Column Width command appears on the shortcut menu. Rather than use the Format ⇨ Column Width command to change the column width, you can use the mouse to quickly change the width of one or more selected columns by clicking on and dragging the line separating Excel's column letters. For example, to change the width of column A, you click on and drag the line separating column letters A and B. When you do, the mouse pointer appears as a black left-and-right arrow. If you've selected multiple columns, clicking on and dragging one of the selected column's adjacent lines changes the width for all selected columns.

Excel displays column widths as the number of characters for the current font and size and uses integers or decimal fractions to represent this. For example, a new worksheet has a default column width of 8.43. You can quickly adjust the width of a column to accommodate the longest entry in the column by using the Best Fit option.

Here are a few pointers about Best Fit: If you make another cell entry that is even wider, you need to use Best Fit again or widen the column yourself (sorry, Best Fit isn't automatic — yet). And Best Fit bases its calculations on screen fonts (as opposed to printer fonts), so you may need to do a little column-width adjusting during the File ⇨ Print Preview stage.

You can quickly specify the Best Fit option by double-clicking on the line separating column letters. For example, to use the Best Fit column width for column B, double-click on the line separating column letters B and C.

The dialog box displayed by the Format ⇨ Column Width command also provides you with an opportunity to hide or show selected columns by using the Hide and Unhide options. You can also hide and show columns quickly by using the shortcut keys Ctrl+0 and Ctrl+Shift+), respectively. Specifying a column width of zero also creates a hidden column.

You cannot change the width of columns in a protected worksheet.

Justifying Text

Adding some explanatory text to the bottom of a report isn't always easy. Adjusting a long label so that it doesn't extend farther than the columns in your report (not to mention page) can be a tedious and time-consuming task. Excel is a great spreadsheet, but a word processor it's not.

Don't despair, however. Excel is actually pretty adept at dealing with small amounts of text and has just what you need to turn your long labels into attractive-looking paragraphs. The Format ⇨ Justify command rearranges a long label so that the text fits nicely in a range you specify. In short, you shorten or lengthen your label by moving text to cells directly below the cell containing your label, as necessary.

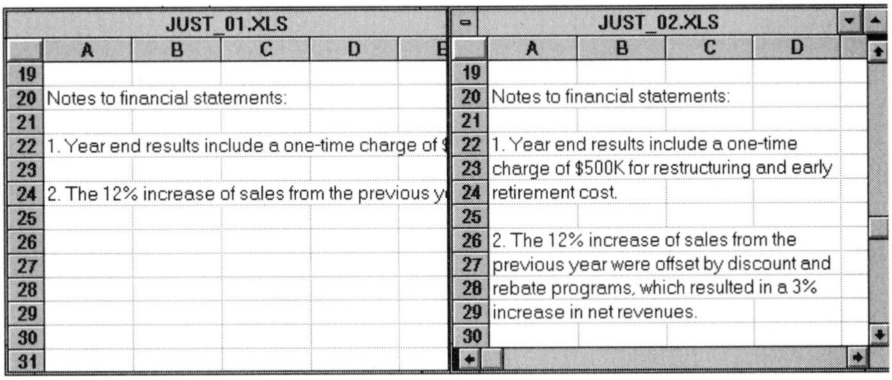

Figure 8-3:
Before and after worksheets showing the results of the Format ⇨ Justify command.

		JUST_01.XLS						JUST_02.XLS			
	A	**B**	**C**	**D**	**E**	**A**	**B**	**C**	**D**	
19						**19**					
20	Notes to financial statements:					**20**	Notes to financial statements:				
21						**21**					
22	1. Year end results include a one-time charge of $					**22**	1. Year end results include a one-time				
23						**23**	charge of $500K for restructuring and early				
24	2. The 12% increase of sales from the previous y					**24**	retirement cost.				
25						**25**					
26						**26**	2. The 12% increase of sales from the				
27						**27**	previous year were offset by discount and				
28						**28**	rebate programs, which resulted in a 3%				
29						**29**	increase in net revenues.				
30						**30**					
31											

Format ⇨ Justify does not adjust the height of rows as does the Format ⇨ Alignment ⇨ Wrap Text command.

You can justify text that contains labels in any column. If you have multiple cells with labels you want to justify, the cells containing the labels should be in the same column for best results. Figure 8-3 shows a result of using the Format ⇨ Justify command.

The actual process of justifying text is simple. First, select the range where you want the justified text to appear. This range should include the cells that contain your label. Also select how far to the right you want the justified text to extend. For example, you may have a report that uses Excel's default column widths, spans columns A through I, and has a tremendously long label in column A. You select the cell containing the label in column A and include the range out to column I. Next you include in the range the cells below the label where you want your text to appear and choose Format ⇨ Justify.

What happens next depends on two things:

■ Whether you've specified an adequate justify range

■ Whether the range contains cell entries

If you haven't specified an adequate range, such as any additional rows in your justify range, Excel displays the warning message "Text will extend below range." If you choose OK, Excel justifies as much text as it can to fit column I using any cells below your label to hold the justified text. Any existing cell entries are overwritten by your justified text.

If you've specified a justify range that includes cell entries, they are overwritten without a warning from Excel (either way, it's a bad day for cell contents). Be sure to move existing cell entries to another area of the current worksheet or insert more rows before you unleash the Format ⇨ Justify command. Increasing the width of the columns in your justify range may also help.

 Format ⇨ Justify is for cells containing text entries only. If you attempt to justify a range of text where one or more cells contain values, Excel displays a warning message to that effect and essentially puts the brakes on the operation. Choose OK to clear the message and edit the offending cell(s).

Finally, note that Excel treats a blank cell to the far left of your justify range as if you pressed Enter in a word processing document; Excel treats such labels as two separate paragraphs. As a result, Excel justifies the first group of labels and then the second group, with a blank row in between the two.

 Format ⇨ Justify does not lead you to a dialog box and proceeds with a justify operation without confirmation. If you do not like the results of a justify operation, invoke Edit ⇨ Undo immediately or revert to the backup copy of your worksheet on disk.

Inserting and Deleting Rows and Columns

One of the most common modifications you're likely to need to make after you create a worksheet is to insert a row or column in between rows or columns that contain data. For example, suppose that you've included a line item called Telephone (in column A) as part of your company's budget. Your supervisor, however, wants to keep an eye on fax-related telephone expenses next year. Instead of re-creating your budget worksheet, you can insert a column directly after Telephone to accommodate the new budget item.

When you insert a row or column in your worksheet, you're *not* creating new Excel rows or columns (they are both fixed and cannot be increased or decreased in number). Rather, you're moving your data around your worksheet, as shown in Table 8-1. Excel provides you with two ways to insert and delete:

■ You can insert or delete partial rows or columns.

■ You can insert or delete rows or columns the entire width or length of the Excel worksheet.

The technique you use depends on your application and needs. Use partial rows and columns when you know the position of adjacent data. Use entire rows and columns when data in nonadjacent ranges won't be effected by your

Table 8-1: Insertions and deletions that move data	
Action	**Result**
Insert a row	Moves data beneath the cell pointer down
Insert a column	Moves data to the right of the cell pointer further to the right
Delete a row	Moves data beneath the cell pointer up
Delete a column	Moves data to the right of the cell pointer over to the left

insert or delete operation. In either case, inserting and deleting are potentially destructive operations, so be sure to use Edit ⇨ Undo or save your worksheet to disk before proceeding, if necessary.

Approach partial insert and delete operations with caution. If you specify a partial insert or delete a range that does not include all the cell entries in the row or column, corresponding cell contents may not line up properly. For example, if you have a worksheet arranged in a database format and want to add a new field, a partial column insert results in record fields to the right of your selected range being shifted and not in the correct column (in this case, field). Remember, if you don't like what you see, use Edit ⇨ Undo immediately after the operation.

To insert and delete *partial* rows and columns, position your cell pointer where you want to begin adding or deleting cells to your worksheet and then select a range. To insert and delete an *entire* row or column, place your cell pointer on any cell in the row or column you want to insert or delete. Then use the commands and options listed in Table 8-2.

You can select an entire row from your keyboard by pressing Shift+spacebar and an entire column by pressing Ctrl+spacebar.

You can also insert and delete entire multiple rows and columns in one step. Position your cell pointer on the cell of the first row or column you want to insert or delete; then select as many adjacent rows or columns as you need. You use the same commands listed in Table 8-2 when working with multiple rows and columns. That way, you'll be ready when your supervisor wants the telephone category separated into voice, facsimile, and data transmission telephone expenses.

Table 8-2: Commands and options for insertions and deletions		
Action	**Command**	**Option**
Insert a partial row	Edit ⇨ Insert	Shift Cells Down
Insert an entire row	Edit ⇨ Insert	Entire Row
Insert a partial column	Edit ⇨ Insert	Shift Cells Right
Insert an entire column	Edit ⇨ Insert	Entire Column
Delete a partial row	Edit ⇨ Delete	Shift Cells Up
Delete an entire row	Edit ⇨ Delete	Entire Row
Delete a partial column	Edit ⇨ Delete	Shift Cells Left
Delete an entire column	Edit ⇨ Delete	Entire Column

Finding and Replacing Cells

Excel includes several tools to help you locate specified cell contents anywhere on your worksheet. You can have Excel search for cells that contain a specific format, text, value, formula, error message, or range name. You have the option of finding the item only, or finding it and replacing it with something else. Finding and replacing the contents of cells is useful, for example, when you want to change from one number format to another or if you're the unlucky recipient of an overly complicated worksheet created by another user and you need to understand it quickly.

Two commands on the Formula menu, Find and Replace, enable you to find and/or replace cell contents easily. The following sections examine how you can put them to work for you.

Finding cell contents

The Formula ⇨ Find command removes the drudgery of having to search cell by cell for something you're interested in or need — a range name or a text entry, for example. To find the item you need, you select the area of the worksheet that you want Excel to search. You can select a range or a single cell. Note, however, that selecting a single cell selects the rest of your entire worksheet from that point.

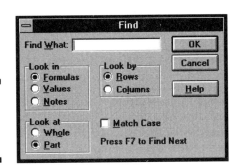

Figure 8-4: The Find dialog box enables you to pinpoint the data you're looking for in your formulas, values, and cell notes.

To have Excel scan your entire worksheet from the beginning, move your cell pointer to cell A1 — or select the entire worksheet — before choosing the Formula ⇨ Find command.

Next, choose the Formula ⇨ Find command. The dialog box shown in Figure 8-4 appears. The Find dialog box helps you tailor your search operation to your needs.

Use the Shift+F5 shortcut keys to display the Find dialog box.

To begin your search, type the data or item you need in the Find What text box. You can use the asterisk (*) and question mark (?) wildcards with other characters, if needed. Next, specify how you want Excel to conduct its search. You can choose from the options listed in Table 8-3.

Table 8-3: Search options in Excel	
Option	**Purpose**
Look in	Specifies where to search: Formulas, Values, or cell Notes. Default is Formulas.
Look at	Specifies amount of cell contents to search: Whole or Part. Default is Part.
Look by	Specifies direction of search: Rows or Columns. Default is Rows.
Match Case	Specifies whether you want search characters to match uppercase and lowercase characters in your worksheet. Default is off (to find regardless of capitalization).

After you make your selections, choose OK. Excel makes the cell with the first occurrence of a match the active cell and closes the Find dialog box. To continue searching, press F7. To return to the previous occurrence, press Shift+F7. If Excel is unable to find your characters, the message "No match" appears. Choose OK or press Esc to clear the message; then check the characters you entered in the Find What text box and try again.

You can make the find operation search backward from the active cell by holding down the Shift key before choosing OK.

Finding and replacing cell contents

Finding and replacing cell contents, as you've probably guessed, is an extension of finding cell contents. Formula ⇨ Replace is a more powerful version of Formula ⇨ Find, as you can see from the dialog box in Figure 8-5, and is similar to the search-and-replace capability in word processing programs. Thus, Formula ⇨ Replace is a quick and convenient way to update your worksheet with new information. Formula ⇨ Replace differs from Find in the following aspects:

- You find and replace the contents of worksheet cells only — not formulas or cell notes.

- You can choose to replace the contents of the active cell or all cells in your worksheet that contain the find characters.

Use the Formula ⇨ Replace command the same way as the Formula ⇨ Find command. Move the cell pointer to the cell or highlight the range where you want Excel to begin finding and replacing. Choose Formula ⇨ Replace and enter the characters you want to find and use as replacements in the Find What and Replace With text boxes, respectively. Next, if you want, make your Look at, Look by, and Match Case selections.

Now you're ready to begin finding and replacing. Choose Find Next, and Excel finds the first occurrence of the characters you entered in the Find What text box. If you want to replace the characters with those in the Replace With text box, choose Replace. Excel makes the replacement and then moves on and finds the next occurrence of the find characters. Repeat this process until you've made all the substitutions in your worksheet. When you're finished, choose Close to exit from the dialog box.

Close does not reverse any substitutions you've made with Replace.

If you want to bypass finding and go right to replacing, press the Ctrl key as you choose Replace. If you're confident of what you want to replace, you can

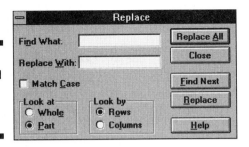

Figure 8-5: The Replace dialog box enables you to find and then replace one set of characters with another in your worksheet cells.

choose Replace All. Excel automatically substitutes all instances of the find characters with the replace characters in your worksheet. Remember to use Edit ➪ Undo immediately after a Formula ➪ Replace ➪ Replace All operation if the results are not what you had in mind.

The Find and Replace dialog boxes may cover up cells that match your find characters. If this situation happens, remember that you can move (but not size) the dialog boxes and, in this manner, view the contents of the cells underneath. You can also watch Excel's Reference area for the cell's address to determine which cell matches your find characters.

You can also use the Formula ➪ Replace command to find without replacing specified cell contents. Simply choose Find Next to locate the next occurrence of your find characters without replacing them. In this manner, you have a dialog box that remains open so you can perform multiple find and/or replace operations.

Using Cell Notes

The final section of this chapter covers a useful feature in Excel — cell notes, which you were introduced to in the preceding chapter. While using a worksheet, you may want to make a note to yourself about a particular cell entry. For example, suppose that the salary increase assumption used in your budget was given to you by the accounting department and is preliminary. Cell notes are also useful as a way to document your work — for yourself or for others. These notes can either be textual or auditory, provided that you have a sound board installed in your PC.

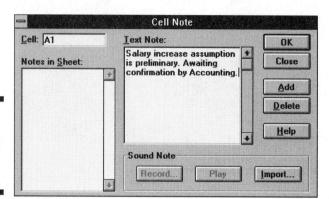

Figure 8-6: You can attach a note to a cell as a reminder to yourself or to document your work.

Text notes

You can attach a note to any cell in the worksheet. Cells with a note attached appear with a small red dot in the upper-right corner of the cell. If you double-click the cell, the note is displayed. You can also view the note from the Cell Note dialog box and the Info window.

To add a note to a cell, select the cell. Then choose the Formula ⇨ Note command to bring up the dialog box shown in Figure 8-6. The box labeled Notes in Sheet displays all the cells that have notes attached, and the text box labeled Cell displays the current cell reference. Enter your note in the box labeled Text Note. This box features word wrap, so don't use the Enter key when you come to the end of a line (this action closes the dialog box). To start a new line, however, you can press Ctrl+Enter. Your note can be fairly long, because it doesn't take up space in the worksheet but is attached as a separate item.

You can scroll through the Notes in Sheet list box to select other cells and view their notes. Or you can enter a cell reference in the Cell box and enter a note for another cell (use the Add button). The Delete button — as you may expect — deletes the note associated with the cell displayed in the Cell box. When you're finished entering, viewing, and deleting notes, choose OK or Close.

As you would expect, moving a cell moves the attached note with it. Similarly, if you copy a cell that has a note, the copy has the same note. If you want to copy only the note and not the cell contents, use the Edit ⇨ Paste Special command and select the Notes option.

By default, cell notes are not printed with the worksheet. To print the cell notes, specify either Notes or Both in the Print dialog box.

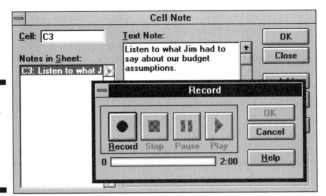

Figure 8-7: If your PC is equipped for multimedia, you can record a sound note to attach to a cell.

Sound notes

If your PC is equipped for multimedia, you can attach a sound note to a cell. If your system is not set up for multimedia, the Record button is grayed and you're out of luck.

Cells with sound notes attached to them appear with an asterisk in the Notes in Sheet box of the Cell Note dialog box. If you're running Windows 3.1, you need a compatible sound card (such as a Sound Blaster Pro or Pro Audio Spectrum) that is properly installed. If you're running Windows 3.0, you need to have a sound card and the Windows Multimedia Extensions installed. To attach a sound note, select the cell and then choose the Formula ⇨ Note command. Select the Record button. This action brings up a dialog box that enables you to start and stop the recording process (see Figure 8-7). The sound note can be up to two minutes long. Keep your sound notes short because they use an incredible amount of disk space.

You can also import a waveform (wav) file and attach it to the cell. For example, you may attach a sound-effects file so you hear applause whenever a cell is clicked. Use the Import button to import a wav file. Windows 3.1 includes four wav files, and you can record your own wave files if you have a microphone attached to your sound card. In addition, your sound card probably came with many other wav files of sound effects, music, and so on.

Summary

▶ You can change the height of a row by selecting any cell in the row and then choosing the Format ⇨ Row Height command.

▶ Excel automatically adjusts the height of a row to accommodate the tallest font in the row.

▶ You can change the width of a column by selecting any cell in the column and then choosing the Format ⇨ Column Width command.

▶ You can arrange long labels into attractive-looking paragraphs by using the Format ⇨ Justify command.

▶ You can insert and delete rows and columns into your worksheet. You can insert or delete a partial or an entire row or column. To insert a row or column, use the Edit ⇨ Insert command. To delete a row or column, use the Edit ⇨ Delete command.

▶ To find specific characters in formulas, values, or cell notes, use the Formula ⇨ Find command. To find and then replace one set of characters with another in the cells in your worksheet, use the Edit ⇨ Replace command.

▶ Excel enables you to attach a text note or a sound note to a particular cell. Double-clicking the cell displays the note.

Chapter 9
Working with Ranges

In this chapter . . .

▶An introduction to the concept of ranges.

▶Why you should name your ranges and how to do it.

▶Common operations performed on ranges of cells — erasing, moving, and copying.

▶Details on the range name commands.

If you've used spreadsheets prior to Excel, you already know the importance of worksheet ranges (they're so important that every version of Lotus 1-2-3 has a menu of Range commands). If you're new to spreadsheets, learning about ranges is fundamental and will help you to use Excel efficiently. On the other hand, if ranges are old hat to you, this chapter examines how to perform range operations Excel-style.

What Is a Range?

A *range* is a group of cells on your worksheet. You use ranges to group blocks of related data together to make it easier to work with. A range can be as small as a single cell or as large as your entire worksheet. Frequently, ranges are a rectangular block of contiguous cells, such as the range A1 through F20. Ranges can also consist of noncontiguous cells.

Contiguous ranges

Contiguous ranges are composed of cells that are adjacent to each other. Figure 9-1 illustrates several examples of contiguous ranges.

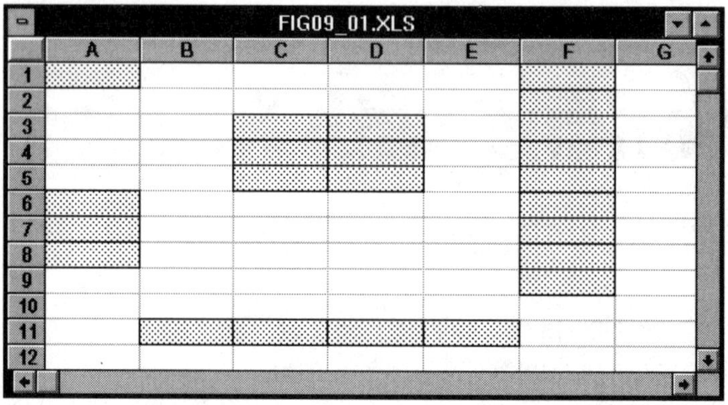

Figure 9-1:
Various
contiguous
cell ranges
(note their
rectangular
orientation).

Ranges have addresses just like the cells in your worksheet. Here are some range types you're likely to encounter and use:

Type of range	Address composition	Example
Single cell	Intersection of row and column	A1
Row	Far left and far right cells	A1:F1
Column	Top and bottom cells	A1:A10
Rectangle	Top left and bottom right cells	A1:F20

Note that multicell ranges have a colon separating the first cell in the range from the last. If you've come to Excel from Lotus 1-2-3, remember not to use two dots to indicate ranges; use the colon instead. Also remember from earlier chapters that to select a range of cells, you make the first cell in the desired range the active cell; then you click on and drag the cells to highlight and thereby select them. Alternatively, with the keyboard, you can press F8 or press and hold down one of the Shift keys; then you use the arrow keys to highlight the desired group of cells.

Noncontiguous ranges

Noncontiguous ranges, as you'd expect, are comprised of ranges of cells that are not adjacent to each other. Even so, you can still use a noncontiguous range similarly to a contiguous one, such as for data entry, erasing cell contents, and so on. Figure 9-2 shows an example of a noncontiguous range.

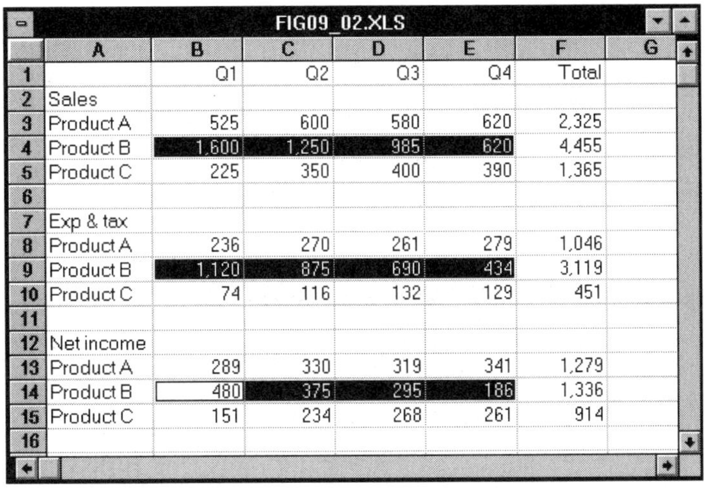

	A	B	C	D	E	F	G
		Q1	Q2	Q3	Q4	Total	
1							
2	Sales						
3	Product A	525	600	580	620	2,325	
4	Product B	1,600	1,250	985	620	4,455	
5	Product C	225	350	400	390	1,365	
6							
7	Exp & tax						
8	Product A	236	270	261	279	1,046	
9	Product B	1,120	875	690	434	3,119	
10	Product C	74	116	132	129	451	
11							
12	Net income						
13	Product A	289	330	319	341	1,279	
14	Product B	480	375	295	186	1,336	
15	Product C	151	234	268	261	914	
16							

FIG09_02.XLS

Figure 9-2: A noncontiguous cell range is used less frequently than its contiguous cell cousin, but in some situations it is just as valuable.

Selecting a noncontiguous range is almost as easy as selecting a contiguous one. Again, first make the first cell in the range the active cell and then perform the following steps:

Steps: Selecting a noncontiguous range

With the mouse

Step 1. Click on and drag the first set of cells.

Step 2. Press the Ctrl key; then click on and drag the second set.

Step 3. Repeat Step 2 for each additional set of cells you want as part of the range.

With the keyboard

Step 1. Press F8 or hold down one of the Shift keys as you press the arrow keys to select the first set of cells.

Step 2. Press Shift+F8; then press F8 or hold down one of the Shift keys as you press the arrow keys to select the second set of cells.

Step 3. Repeat Step 2 for each additional set of cells you want as part of the range.

From earlier chapters, you've learned that after you select cells on your worksheet, you can perform more than one operation on those cells. In the next section, you learn how to give frequently used ranges a descriptive name. A named range helps you use your worksheet more efficiently because a range name that has meaning to you (such as Total_Income) is much easier to remember than its cell address counterpart.

What's in a (Range) Name?

Besides being able to refer to cells by using descriptive names rather than their addresses, you gain other advantages when using range names. A few follow:

- You can quickly move to a distant area of your worksheet by choosing the Formula ⇨ Goto command and specifying the name of your worksheet range.

- You can name a value or formula for use in other formulas. Excel automatically updates any formulas that use the named value or formula if you change them. The named value or formula doesn't have to be located in a cell but can exist as part of your worksheet, independent of any particular cell.

- Creating formulas is easier. You can paste the name of a cell into a formula by using the Formula ⇨ Paste Name command.

- Names make your worksheets more understandable and easier to use. =INCOME-TAXES is more intuitive than =D20-D40.

- Macros are easier to create and modify when you use named ranges rather than cell addresses.

You can create, change, list, and delete range names. To get started using range names, you need to learn how to create one first.

Naming a range

Excel provides you with two commands to create a range name. Formula ⇨ Define Name enables you to use any name you can think of for your range, and Formula ⇨ Create Names enables you to create names by using labels in your worksheet.

The world is your oyster when it comes to choosing a range name. You can use any name you like that best suits your particular situation. You need to be aware of a few rules, however:

■ Begin your name with a letter.

■ You can have names up to a maximum of 255 characters.

■ You can have names that use letters and numbers.

■ You can use an underscore (_) in place of spaces in your name.

■ You can't use a number or cell reference as a name.

■ You can't use a space in your name or other characters, such as a colon or hyphen.

Avoid creating range names that can be misinterpreted as a cell reference. For example, naming a range B12 isn't a good idea.

Now that you understand the range name rules, you're ready to name ranges. If you want to use a name that exists on your worksheet, use Formula ➪ Create Names. If the name is new, use Formula ➪ Define Name.

Creating new names

Naming a range with Formula ➪ Define Name is easy. You have your choice of whether or not you want to select the range first (generally, doing so is easier). In either case, choose the Formula ➪ Define Name command, and the dialog box in Figure 9-3 appears. Type the range name in the Name text box or use the one Excel proposes. Now, if you've already selected a cell or range, that address appears in the Refers to text box. If not, select a cell or range using your keyboard or mouse, or type a cell address. Remember to begin the cell address with an equal sign (=) if you type it.

Figure 9-3: The Define Name dialog box is your gateway to creating range names.

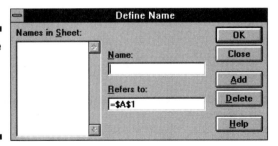

Figure 9-4: The Create Names dialog box enables you to use labels in your worksheet as range names.

If it obscures the cell range you want to name, move the Define Name dialog box by clicking on and dragging its title bar.

Choose OK to add the name to your worksheet and close the dialog box or choose Add to continue adding names to your worksheet.

Use File ⇨ Save or File ⇨ Save As to use new range names in future Excel sessions. Otherwise, names you've created in your current session are lost.

An even easier way to create names is to use the ones already in your worksheet.

Creating names using existing text

You may have an Excel application with labels you want to use as names in a worksheet. One advantage to using labels as names is that you can use them to move around your worksheet quickly. Another advantage is that you can create multiple range names rapidly in one step. And, as you become an Excel power user, this procedure makes naming your macro subroutines easy.

To use your worksheet labels as names, select the worksheet label and the range you want to name (the range must be adjacent to your labels). Then choose the Formula ⇨ Create Names command. When you do, the dialog box in Figure 9-4 appears. Check the box that corresponds to the location of your labels. For instance, if you're using the worksheet shown in Figure 9-5, you check the Top Row box. You can then quickly move to one of these database fields using the Formula ⇨ Goto command.

The position of your labels dictates which Formula ⇨ Create Names check box to use. In short, follow these guidelines:

Label location	Check box
Above the range	Top Row
Right of the range	Left Column
Below the range	Bottom Row
Left of the range	Right Column

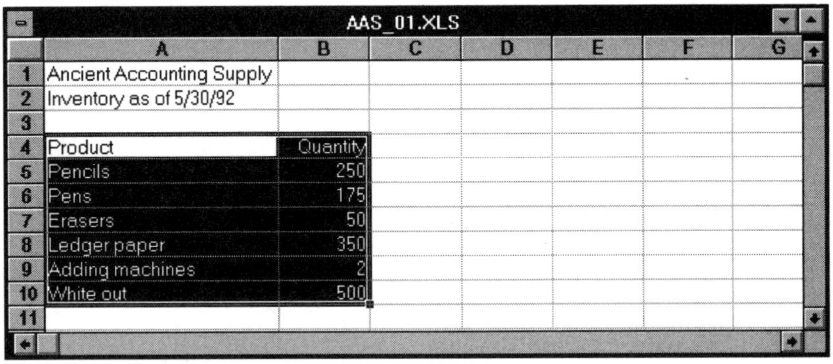

Figure 9-5:
You can use
your column
labels to
name the
fields in your
database
with Formula
⇨ Create
Names.

	A	B	C	D	E	F	G
	AAS_01.XLS						
1	Ancient Accounting Supply						
2	Inventory as of 5/30/92						
3							
4	Product	Quantity					
5	Pencils	250					
6	Pens	175					
7	Erasers	50					
8	Ledger paper	350					
9	Adding machines	2					
10	White out	500					
11							

Note, however, that you're not limited to checking only one box. If you choose more than one box, and the labels name the same range, the cells in the range have different names depending on their orientation, and the label at the intersection of your two options names the entire range. For example, if you check Top Row and Left Column for the worksheet shown in Figure 9-5, Product and Quantity are the names of the range B5:B10, and cells B5:B10 also have the names in column A.

Remember, your labels must follow the same rules as those for the Formula ⇨ Define Name command. The exception is that you can have spaces in your names — sort of. If you use a label for a name that contains spaces, say NET INC YTD, Excel creates the name NET_INC_YTD for you.

Choose unique names for your ranges. If you use a name that already exists, Excel displays a dialog box in which you can update the name using the new range (choose Yes), choose not to update the name with the new range (choose No), or choose not to update the name and stop creating range names (choose Cancel).

Naming formulas

Naming values and formulas you use often is a great way to make your worksheets easier to use and understand. Instead of entering values as arguments in an Excel worksheet function, for example, you can use range names of cells that contain those values. Then, to see the effect of changing a value (an increase in an interest rate, for example), all you need to do is change the value in the cell rather than edit the function's arguments.

Name values and formulas using the Formula ⇨ Define Name command, just as when naming worksheet ranges. But you don't necessarily need to select a cell or range before choosing Formula ⇨ Define Name; simply enter what you want the value or formula to be in the Define Name dialog box.

To name a value or formula in a cell, select the cell. After you've selected the cell, or if the value or formula isn't located in a cell, choose the Formula ⇨ Define Name command. In the Define Name dialog box, shown in Figure 9-3, type the name of the formula in the Name text box and your value or formula in the Refers to text box. After you choose OK or press Enter, the value or formula is named.

Naming rather than copying frequently used formulas saves worksheet memory and increases the recalculation speed of Excel applications. For example, you may have a monthly budget worksheet with totals at the bottom of each column. Move the cell pointer to the cell for your January total then choose Formula ⇨ Define Name and type MO_TOTAL (or something similar) in the Name text box. Next, use the SUM function with the appropriate range of values to total in the Refers to text box. You can use Edit ⇨ Copy to copy the formula name to your remaining cells and, in this manner, define only 1 formula that does the work of 12.

Listing names

You can identify the range names and their corresponding cell addresses in two ways. This information is important if you're in the process of modifying a worksheet you haven't seen for a while, you've acquired a worksheet from someone else, or you want to understand the worksheet's logic.

You can see an alphabetical list of the names in your worksheet in the Define Name dialog box. When you highlight a name, its cell address appears in the Refers to text box. Another way to determine your range name situation is to move your cell pointer to a blank area of your worksheet and then choose the Formula ⇨ Paste Name command. Choose Paste List, and Excel creates a two-column table of range name information. The first column at the bottom of Figure 9-6 illustrates the range names in alphabetical order (Product and Quality), and the adjacent column lists the name's cell address as an absolute reference.

Excel lists your range names in alphabetical order in your worksheet when you use the Formula ⇨ Define Name command with the Paste List option.

	A	B	C	D	E	F
	AAS_01.XLS					
1	Ancient Accounting Supply					
2	Inventory as of 5/30/92					
3						
4	Product	Quantity				
5	Pencils	250				
6	Pens	175				
7	Erasers	50				
8	Ledger paper	350				
9	Adding machines	2				
10	White out	500				
11						
12	Product	=$A$5:$A$10				
13	Quantity	=$B$5:$B$10				
14						

Figure 9-6:
Useful
range name
information
from the
Fo<u>r</u>mula ⇨
<u>P</u>aste Name
command.

Changing and deleting names

Every computer program requires maintenance, and your Excel worksheets are
no exception. You may find after modifying and improving your applications
that you want to do a little housekeeping in the way of changing or deleting
range names you no longer need.

An easier way to clean house

Your Excel Library subdirectory contains an add-
in macro that makes changing and deleting range
names a breeze. Use <u>F</u>ile ⇨ <u>O</u>pen and select
Changer.xla from the Library subdirectory and
then choose OK. Change Na<u>m</u>e appears on the
Fo<u>r</u>mula menu. Simply select the range name in
the From list box and choose Delete, or type the
new name of the range in the To text box, as
shown in the accompanying figure. As an added
bonus, if you change the name of a range,
Changer rummages through your worksheet and
replaces all instances of your old range name
with the new one (as with Fo<u>r</u>mula ⇨ <u>R</u>eplace
and <u>A</u>pply Names). Choosing Close returns you
to Ready mode.

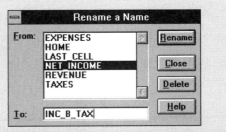

The Rename a Name dialog box enables you to
exchange or delete range names quickly and
easily.

Changing and deleting range names is an easy process and you can accomplish both tasks from the Define Name dialog box. In this dialog box, select the range name you want to change. Then type in a new name in the Name text box and/or edit the cell address in the Refers to text box. Finally, choose OK or press Enter.

Deleting a range name is similar to changing one. From the Define Name dialog box, select the range name you want to remove and then choose Delete. You can continue deleting (or adding or changing) range names until you choose Close or OK.

Changing the name of a range does not automatically delete the old name; the range has two names, which may confuse macros that operate on the range. Changing the name of a range is actually a two-step process: In the Name text box, first change the name of the range and then remove the old name by choosing Delete. Choose OK or press Enter to complete the process.

Applying range names

You may be in the middle of building a worksheet when you create a range name that you can use in other formulas that you've already entered. If this situation occurs, existing formulas will continue to use the corresponding cell

---

But wait! All I wanted to do was . . .

The Apply Names dialog box contains two options: Ignore Relative/Absolute and Use Row and Column Names. In addition, choosing Options expands the dialog box to provide you with three additional selections: Omit Column Name if Same Column, Omit Row Name if Same Row, and Name Order.

Essentially, these options give Excel wide latitude in replacing cell references with range names. For example, Ignore Relative/Absolute replaces references with names regardless of reference type (absolute, relative, or mixed). Turning off this check box keeps reference types from changing (absolute remains absolute, and so on). The other options enable Excel to use the labels in a table or another matrix (row and col-

umn labels, such as in a monthly budget) in your worksheet to name your cells.

In almost all instances, you'll merely want to exchange a cell reference for its range name counterpart (a range name you've created). To do so, select the names you want to apply; then deselect the Ignore Relative/Absolute and Use Row and Column Names check boxes. In this manner, Excel replaces a cell reference with a range name only when an *exact* match exists between the two.

Remember, you can always use Edit ⇨ Undo if the result of a Formula ⇨ Apply Names operation isn't what you expected.

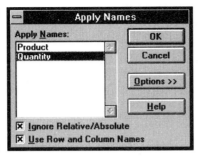

Figure 9-7: The Apply Names dialog box enables you to choose which range names get substituted for cell references.

reference rather than the range name. To exchange a cell reference with its corresponding name, you can use the Formula ➪ Apply Names command.

The Apply Names dialog box, shown in Figure 9-7, enables you to select the range names you want to substitute for cell references. Select the name you want; holding down one of the Shift keys enables you to make multiple selections. (Keyboard users should press Ctrl and use the up and down arrow keys to move the selection cursor and then press the spacebar to add or remove selected range names.) Choosing OK or pressing Enter sends Excel on its way.

Basic Range Operations

You can use several fundamental worksheet operations with ranges to make your Excel sessions more productive. You save time by working with groups of cells rather than on a cell-by-cell basis. You'll want to know how to move your cell pointer to a range and erase, move, and copy ranges of cells.

As you know, before you can carry out a worksheet operation you must select a cell or range. After you do so, you can perform multiple operations on it — move it, copy it, format it, and so on. Erasing, moving, and copying ranges are up to bat next.

Moving to a cell or range — quickly

After you name a range, you can quickly move to that cell address from anywhere on your worksheet. Simply choose the Formula ➪ Goto command (or press F5), and when the dialog box shown in Figure 9-8 appears, select the name of the range you want to move the cell selector to or type a cell address in the Reference text box. When you choose OK, Excel moves your cell selector to the range name or cell address you selected.

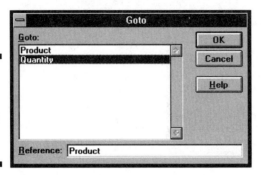

Figure 9-8:
The Goto
dialog box
helps you go
places
quickly.

You can also move rapidly to named ranges on other open worksheets. In the Reference text box of the Goto dialog box, type the name of the worksheet, an exclamation point, and the range name or cell address, such as PLAN92!TOTAL. When you select OK, Excel moves your cell pointer to the range named TOTAL on the PLAN92 worksheet.

If your named range is a multiple cell range, Excel selects the entire range and moves your cell pointer accordingly:

Range shape	New cell pointer position
A row of cells	Far left cell in row
A column of cells	Top cell in column
A rectangle of cells	Cell in upper-left corner

Erasing cell contents

You can erase the contents of cells almost as easily as you can move your cell pointer to them. Select the cell or range whose contents you want to erase; then choose the Edit ➪ Clear command or press Del. When you do either, the dialog box in Figure 9-9 appears, which gives you the following removal options:

Option	Action
All	Clears cell contents, notes, and format; format returns to General
Formats	Clears format only and returns it to General
Formulas	Clears formulas only
Notes	Clears notes only

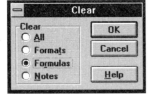

Figure 9-9: The Clear dialog box gives you pinpoint disposal choices.

If you've erased something unintentionally, remember Edit ⇨ Undo is only a mouse-click away, or you can close the file and try again, using the version of your worksheet last saved to disk.

If you use a mouse, you can quickly erase a cell or range by selecting the range and then moving the range's Drag-and-Drop indicator (the little square at the lower-right corner of a cell or range) inward (in a northwest direction). Just make sure that you've selected Drag and Drop from the Options Workspace dialog box.

Moving cell contents

Moving the contents of cells from one worksheet location to another involves "cutting" them out of one range and "pasting" them into another — or "picking them up" from one location on your worksheet and "putting them down" in another. (Recall that you were introduced to cutting and pasting in Chapter 7.) In any event, moving cell contents is a simple four-step procedure. To move cell contents, perform the following steps.

Make sure that you use the correct eraser

If you want to remove the contents of cells only, use Edit ⇨ Clear or press Del. If you want to re-move the cell(s) completely from your worksheet, use Edit ⇨ Delete. These two commands have vastly different results. As you learned in Chapter 8, Excel removes cells and moves the rest of your cell contents to take the place of the vacant space with Edit ⇨ Delete. Edit ⇨ Clear, on the other hand, leaves the cells undisturbed but re-moves contents you specify. Consequently, if you're looking for an eraser for your electronic worksheet, reach for Edit ⇨ Clear.

Steps: Moving cell contents

Step 1. Select the cell or range with the contents you want to move.

Step 2. Choose Edit ⇨ Cut.

Step 3. Select the upper-left cell of the range where you want to move the cell contents to.

Step 4. Choose Edit ⇨ Paste or press Enter.

The cells that originally held your cell contents are now blank and formatted as General. You should choose the destination for your cell contents carefully. Although you only need to specify the cell in the upper-left corner of the range you want to move your cell contents to (which may be blank), Edit ⇨ Paste overwrites any existing cell contents (which may not be blank) without warning. As always, you can use Edit ⇨ Undo to reverse an undesirable outcome.

 If you're a mouse user and have Drag and Drop selected, select the range of cells you want to move and then position your mouse on a border of the selection. Simply drag the selection to its new location.

You have another alternative if you need to move cell contents into an area with existing cell contents without overwriting them. When you select a range and choose Edit ⇨ Cut or Copy, the Edit ⇨ Insert Paste command is available. Edit ⇨ Insert Paste enables you to move a cell or range to another location without overwriting existing cell contents (Excel moves the cell entries for you).

The procedure to use Edit ⇨ Insert Paste is virtually identical to Edit ⇨ Paste when moving cells. To move a cut cell or range and place it among existing cell entries, perform the following steps:

Steps: Moving and placing a cut cell or range

Step 1. Select the cell or range with the contents you want to move.

Step 2. Choose Edit ⇨ Cut.

Step 3. Select the cell of the range where you want to insert the cell contents.

Step 4. Choose Edit ⇨ Insert Paste.

Step 5. Choose Shift Cells Right or Shift Cells Down from the Insert Paste dialog box.

Step 6. Choose OK or press Enter.

In addition to inserting the range, Excel closes up the cut area and shifts the existing cells down or to the right, depending on what you chose in Step 5.

If you need to move a range that has a name, be sure you move the entire named range. If you don't, worksheet formulas or macros that depend on the range become confused and cause errors. To ensure that you select the entire range, select Formula ⇨ Goto and choose the name of your range. Excel selects the entire named range for you; then you can cut and paste with confidence.

If you use a mouse, you can move a cell or range by pointing to a border of the selection (the mouse pointer turns into an arrow), clicking, and then dragging to the desired location. This method doesn't work with a multiple selection.

Copying cell contents

Making copies of cell contents can be one of your biggest time-savers. Instead of repeatedly entering the same data into a cell, you can have Excel do that task for you. That's what makes Excel so efficient; it performs repetitive tasks quickly so you have time for more important things.

Excel comes with many copying tools for your worksheet toolbox. To perform basic copying, however, perform the following steps:

Steps: Copying cell contents

Step 1. Select the cell or range with the contents you want to copy.

Step 2. Choose Edit ⇨ Copy.

Step 3. Select the upper-left cell of the range where you want to move the cell contents to.

Step 4. Choose Edit ⇨ Paste.

Because Excel continues to surround your selected range with a marquee, you can paste this range as many times as you want; just select the upper-left cell of the next range to paste to and choose Edit ⇨ Paste. If you want to copy only once, however, press Enter after Step 3.

If you choose Edit ⇨ Paste after choosing Edit ⇨ Copy and are finished copying cell contents, you can turn off the marquee by pressing Esc or selecting a new range to copy.

You can copy the selected range to another open worksheet by making the worksheet active, selecting the paste range, and choosing Edit ⇨ Paste or pressing Enter.

Remember, Edit ⇨ Insert Paste is also available if you want to insert the contents of the selected range into a range of existing cell contents. You use Edit ⇨ Insert Paste the same way to copy ranges as you do to move them. With Edit ⇨ Insert Paste, however, you can only copy once rather than multiple times, as with Edit ⇨ Paste.

Mouse users can copy a cell or range by pointing to a border of the selection (the mouse pointer turns into an arrow). Then hold down Ctrl and drag the selection to make a copy of it. While you do the procedure, a small plus sign appears near the mouse pointer as a reminder that you're copying.

Copying with Edit ⇨ Fill

Another way to copy is to use the Edit ⇨ Fill commands. Edit ⇨ Fill enables you to copy adjacent cell contents across a row (Right, as shown in Figure 9-10) or down a column (Down). Using Edit ⇨ Fill to duplicate cell contents is slightly different from using Edit ⇨ Copy:

- You select the cells you want to copy and the cells you want to copy to (they must be adjacent).

- The cells you want to copy to the right must be on the left edge of the selected range, and the cells you want to copy down must be on the top of the selected range.

- You don't use Edit ⇨ Paste.

Steps: Copying with Edit ⇨ Fill

Step 1. Select the cell or range whose contents you want to copy and include the range you want to copy to.

Step 2. Choose Edit ⇨ Copy.

Step 3. Choose Edit ⇨ Fill Right or Down.

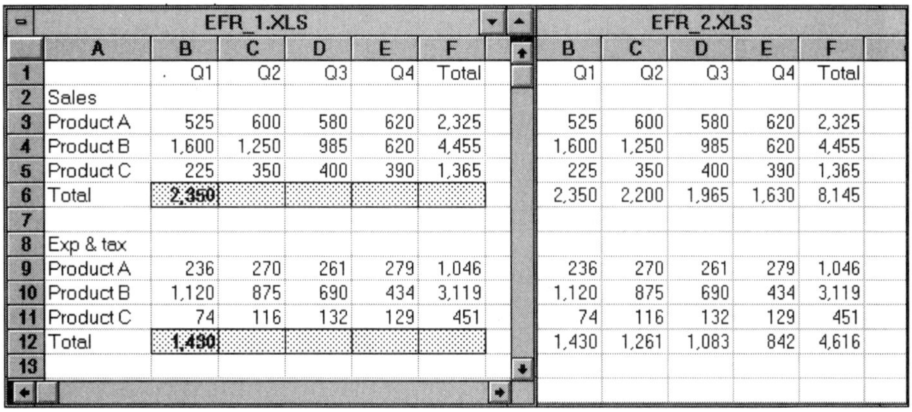

	A	B	C	D	E	F		B	C	D	E	F
		Q1	Q2	Q3	Q4	Total		Q1	Q2	Q3	Q4	Total
2	Sales											
3	Product A	525	600	580	620	2,325		525	600	580	620	2,325
4	Product B	1,600	1,250	985	620	4,455		1,600	1,250	985	620	4,455
5	Product C	225	350	400	390	1,365		225	350	400	390	1,365
6	Total	2,350						2,350	2,200	1,965	1,630	8,145
7												
8	Exp & tax											
9	Product A	236	270	261	279	1,046		236	270	261	279	1,046
10	Product B	1,120	875	690	434	3,119		1,120	875	690	434	3,119
11	Product C	74	116	132	129	451		74	116	132	129	451
12	Total	1,430						1,430	1,261	1,083	842	4,616
13												

EFR_1.XLS / EFR_2.XLS

Figure 9-10:
Edit ➪ Fill Right before and after. Keep the Edit ➪ Fill commands in mind for fast worksheet setup.

You're rarely likely to need them, but if you hold down one of the Shift keys while you choose Edit, you can use Fill Left (h) and Fill Up (w). If you do use one of these options, make sure that the range you want to copy is in the far right column and bottom row, respectively, of the selected range.

You can quickly copy the contents of a cell or range with Edit ➪ Fill by selecting the cell or range, clicking on and dragging the Drag-and-Drop indicator, and selecting an adjacent range. And you can have Excel copy the contents of a cell immediately after you enter it by selecting the range(s), entering the label, value, or formula in the active cell, and then pressing Ctrl+Enter.

Having it your way — Paste Special

The Edit ➪ Paste Special command is an advanced version of Edit ➪ Paste. Paste Special goes well beyond simple copying by enabling you to choose what you want copied from the selected range and how you want Excel to treat the selected range and the paste range. Paste Special offers these options:

Paste option	Action
All	Pastes cell contents, notes, and format
Formulas	Pastes formulas only
Values	Pastes values only
Formats	Pastes formats only
Notes	Pastes notes only

Operation option	Action
None	Places selected range in paste area only
Add	Adds selected cells to those in paste area
Subtract	Subtracts selected cells to those in paste area
Multiply	Multiplies selected cells to those in paste area
Divide	Divides selected cells by those in paste area

Skip Blanks prevents Excel from overwriting cell contents in your paste area with blank cells from your selected range, and Transpose changes the orientation of your selected area when it is pasted. That is, selected columns are pasted as rows (as shown in Figure 9-11), and selected rows are pasted as columns.

Examining commands used with named ranges

Three sets of commands perform operations on ranges. The first, found on the Edit menu, enables you to cut, copy, and paste ranges onto worksheets. You were introduced to these commands in Chapter 7 and learned how to put them to work in the preceding section.

The third set, on the Format menu, enables you to format your ranges. You learned about formatting, such as formatting numbers and specifying row height and column widths, in Chapter 8. Applying whiz-bang formats (fonts, shading, and outlining) is discussed in Chapter 12. The following discussion summarizes the second set of range commands, located on the Formula menu.

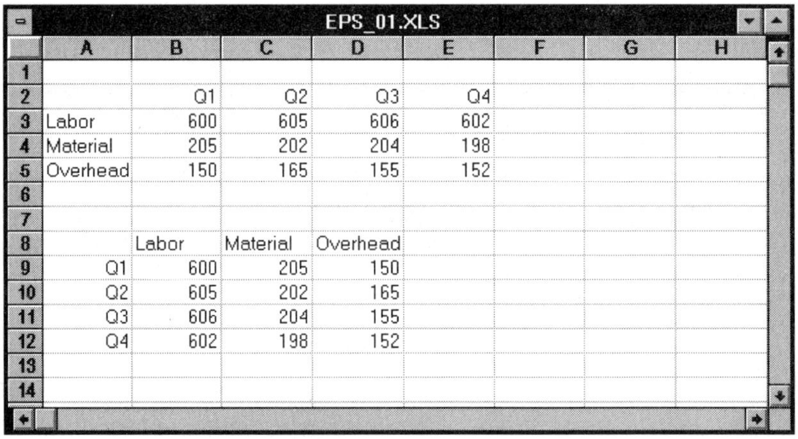

Figure 9-11:
Edit ⇨ Paste
Special can
do some quick
furniture
rearranging
with your
selected
range.

	A	B	C	D	E	F	G	H
1								
2		Q1	Q2	Q3	Q4			
3	Labor	600	605	606	602			
4	Material	205	202	204	198			
5	Overhead	150	165	155	152			
6								
7								
8		Labor	Material	Overhead				
9	Q1	600	205	150				
10	Q2	605	202	165				
11	Q3	606	204	155				
12	Q4	602	198	152				
13								
14								

EPS_01.XLS

As you work with these commands, remember that you can use Edit ⇨ Undo if you run into trouble. Also, don't forget that you need to open the Changer add-in macro file located in your Excel Library subdirectory to use the Formula ⇨ Name Change command. (See the sidebar "An easier way to clean house" earlier in this chapter for information about Changer.)

Formula ⇨ Paste Name

The Formula ⇨ Paste Name command enables you to paste a range name in the Formula bar. You can also create a table of range names and their cell references in your worksheet by choosing the Paste List option. This action gives you the advantage of being able to print and/or sort your range names, thus providing you with a handy reference — not to mention another entry into your worksheet documentation handbook.

Formula ⇨ Define Name

The Formula ⇨ Define Name command gives you the ability to give a descriptive name to a single- or multicell range in your worksheet. You can also name formulas and values, which don't necessarily have to reside in a cell. You can also use the Delete option to remove unneeded range names.

Formula ⇨ Create Names

The Formula ⇨ Create Names command enables you to use the labels in your worksheet as names. Those labels, however, must follow the rules for range names you create with Formula ⇨ Define Name. You can use labels that are adjacent to the cells to the left, right, top, or bottom of the cells you want to name.

Help! I have too many choices!

If you're new to Excel or spreadsheets, you may be overwhelmed by the number of ways you can copy cell contents. Edit ⇨ Copy, Paste, Paste Special, and clicking and dragging are available; the variety may make you feel like pulling your hair out.

Like anything else, the copying method you use depends on the task you want to perform and your personal preferences — copying technique and keyboard or mouse method. If you're just starting out with Excel, or you just want to copy one nonadjacent range to another, use Edit ⇨ Copy and Paste. Later, when you're more comfortable with Excel, you may want to experiment with the Edit ⇨ Fill commands — one of a worksheet builder's best friends. Finally, as your needs become more specialized and users start coming to *you* for answers, Edit ⇨ Copy and Paste Special have enough horsepower to handle just about any duplicating job. Keep in mind, though, that you can use your mouse to accomplish many copying tasks without relying on commands.

Formula ⇨ Apply Names

The Formula ⇨ Apply Names command enables you to substitute range names for cell references in formulas that you've already created. You can substitute range names exactly as their cell reference counterpart, have Excel ignore the reference type (absolute, relative, or mixed) during the substitution, or use row and column labels to name the cells adjacent to them.

Formula ⇨ Change Names

The Formula ⇨ Change Names command gives you a way to quickly change the names of ranges in your worksheet. Change Names works similar to a search-and-replace function in that it scans your worksheet and replaces every occurrence of your old range with the new one. In addition, you can use Change Names to delete unwanted range names. Note that Change Names ⇨ Delete removes range names only and leaves labels in your worksheet undisturbed.

Formula ⇨ Goto

The Formula ⇨ Goto command enables you to move your cell pointer quickly to any point in your worksheet with a minimum of keystrokes (or mouse clicks). You can specify the name of a range or a cell address to move to. If you use Formula ⇨ Goto with a range name, Excel moves your cell pointer to the upper-left corner of the range and selects the entire named range. You can then cut or copy the range without fear of missing anything.

Summary

▶ A range is a rectangular group of cells on your worksheet and can be as small as a single cell or as large as your entire worksheet. Ranges can be in contiguous or noncontiguous cells.

▶ Use Edit ➪ Clear to erase contents of ranges. Use Edit ➪ Cut and Edit ➪ Paste to move ranges from one area to another on your worksheet. Use Edit ➪ Copy and Edit ➪ Paste to copy ranges.

▶ With Edit ➪ Fill, you can quickly copy cell contents to adjacent ranges.

▶ Use Edit ➪ Paste Special to do specialized copying operations, such as specifying what to copy, perform arithmetic operations on the cells in the paste area, and transpose rows and columns.

▶ If you use a mouse, you can do the following:

   ▪ Erase a selected range by dragging the Drag-and-Drop indicator toward the top-left cell in the range.

   ▪ Move a selected range by dragging one of the range's borders.

   ▪ Copy a selected range by pressing Ctrl and dragging one of the range's borders.

   ▪ Copy a range similar to Edit ➪ Fill by selecting a cell or range and then dragging the range's Drag-and-Drop indicator.

▶ Formula ➪ Paste Name enables you to paste a range name into the Formula bar.

▶ Formula ➪ Define Name enables you to create and delete range names. Formula ➪ Create Names enables you to create range names from the labels in your worksheet. Formula ➪ Change Name enables you to rename and delete range names.

▶ Formula ➪ Goto enables you to move your cell pointer quickly to a cell address or range name.

Chapter 10
Creating Formulas

In this chapter . . .

▶ How to create formulas — including complete details on the operators used in formulas.

▶ Many examples of formulas, using both numeric and text data.

▶ The difference between relative, absolute, and mixed cell references.

▶ How to spot circular references and what to do about them.

▶ How to control how your worksheets are calculated.

Chemists use them. Baby food companies sell them. Soft drinks have "secret" formulas. Spreadsheets have formulas too. In every instance, formulas are a key to a successful product, and the worksheet you develop is no different. This chapter introduces you to the essence of spreadsheets — formulas. If you've used spreadsheets prior to Excel, you should at least scan this chapter to learn about any subtle differences between Excel formulas and those used by your former spreadsheet program. If you're a newcomer, reading this chapter teaches you about formulas and helps you understand why they're essential.

What Are Formulas?

Without formulas, a spreadsheet would be nothing more than a word processor that has a lot of fancy row and column manipulation commands. In fact, a worksheet without formulas just sits there and stares back at you. Formulas are the engines of a worksheet; they enable you to calculate results from the data in the worksheet.

A worksheet formula is entered into a cell like any other item of data. You can erase, edit, move, and copy it if you want. Unlike values and labels, however, you combine arithmetic operators with values, labels, worksheet functions, and other formulas to calculate a value in the cell. Values and labels can be located in other cells, which makes changing data easy. That's what gives worksheets their dynamic nature; you can quickly recalculate a result if an assumption (represented by data) changes. In short, you can see multiple scenarios quickly by changing the data in a worksheet and letting formulas do the work.

As we touched on in Chapter 7, Excel has three types of formulas:

- Numeric
- Text
- Logical

The following sections contain detailed information about the individual types of formulas you can use in worksheets. But first, examine some nuts-and-bolts information about formulas in general.

Examining Formula Building Blocks

Excel needs two key types of information from you before it can calculate a formula. One is something to operate on, known as an *operand*; the other is an instruction to tell Excel what you want to do, called an *operator*.

Operands are the inputs or quantities in a formula. They can be part of the formula itself or stored in other cells in your worksheet. The most common operand is a value or number.

Operators are commands you give to formulas that specify how you want a formula to treat operands. One operator you're likely to use often is the plus sign (+).

Each category of formulas (numeric, text, and logical) has its own set of operators. Excel's worksheet functions, explained in the next chapter, can be looked on as another type of operator.

Numeric formulas

Numeric formulas, as the name implies, operate on numbers, or values, such as 1, 2, 2.5, 100, and so on. You use the arithmetic operators with numbers to calculate numeric formulas. They are as follows:

Operator	Name
+	Addition
–	Subtraction
*	Multiplication
/	Division
^	Exponentiation

N_FORM.XLS	
A	**B**
1 2	=A1
2	
3 2	=A1+A3
4	
5	=A3+4
6	
7	=4+4
8	
9	=B1+B3+B5+B7
10	
11	=SUM(B1:B7)
12	

VALUES.XLS			
A	**B**	**C**	**D**
1 2	2		
2			
3 2	4		
4			
5	6		
6			
7	8		
8			
9	20		
10			
11	20		

Figure 10-1: A sampling of numeric formulas, with formulas displayed in the left worksheet and corresponding values in the right worksheet.

A simple example of a numeric formula is:

```
1 + 1
```

where the plus sign is the symbol for the addition operator.

 You begin a formula in Excel with the equal sign (=), which tells Excel to expect a formula.

In Excel, you enter the preceding formula as =1+1 in a cell, which displays 2.

In addition to values, you can create a formula that references cells in your worksheet and thus use the values in those cells for calculations. For example, the formula =A1+A2 results in the addition of the contents in cells A1 and A2 in the cell containing the formula.

Figure 10-1 illustrates several examples of numeric formulas. The worksheet on the left displays the formula using the Options ➩ Display command (with Formulas checked), and the one on the right displays the result of the same formula. Excel's default setting (the one you should use most of the time) shows the results of formulas — not the formulas themselves.

Text formulas

As you've probably guessed, text formulas operate on labels. The text in your formula, however, differs from a text entry in your worksheet in one important aspect: You must enclose text in formulas in quotation marks. Some examples follow:

T_FORM.XLS		T_RESULT.XLS			
	A	**B**		**A**	**B**	**C**	**D**

	T_FORM.XLS A	T_FORM.XLS B	T_RESULT.XLS A	T_RESULT.XLS B	T_RESULT.XLS C	T_RESULT.XLS D
1	net	sales	net	sales		
2						
3	="net"&"sales"		netsales			
4	="net"&" "&"sales"		net sales			
5	=A1&" "&B1		net sales			
6	=LEN(A1)		3			
7	=UPPER(A5)		NET SALES			
8	=PROPER(A5)		Net Sales			
9	=REPT(A1,3)		netnetnet			
10						
11						
12						

Figure 10-2: A sampling of text formulas, with formulas displayed in the left worksheet and corresponding values in the right worksheet.

```
"m"
"Net"
"Fiscal Year"
"Income and Expense"
```

Only one text operator, the ampersand symbol (&), exists. Note, however, that you can use a number of worksheet functions with text formulas. The ampersand enables you to concatenate text operands, which is the text equivalent of saying to add them together (or combine them). For example, the formula

```
="For the week ending"&" "&"February 29, 1992"
```

creates the label and displays

```
For the week ending February 29, 1992
```

in the cell containing the formula.

Figure 10-2 shows several examples of text formulas. Similar to the numeric formulas, text formulas are displayed in the left worksheet, and their corresponding results are shown in the right worksheet.

Logical formulas

Logical formulas are somewhat different from their numeric and text counterparts. Logical formulas perform a test, or comparison, between operands. The result of the test is either True (Yes) or False (No). The logical operators are as follows:

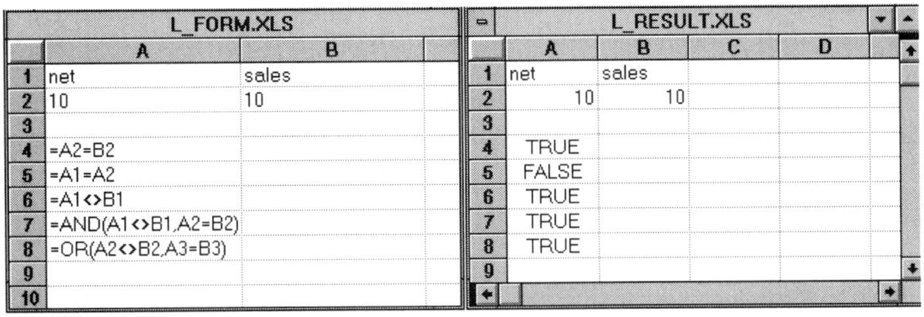

Figure 10-3: A sampling of logical formulas, with formulas displayed in the left worksheet and corresponding values in the right worksheet.

Symbol	Test
=	Equal to
>	Greater than
>	Less than
>=	Greater than or equal to
<=	Less than or equal to
<>	Not equal to

Thus a simple logical formula is:

    =1=1

Because 1 is in fact equal to 1, this formula results in True being displayed in the cell containing the formula. The following logical formula yields False because 1 isn't equal to 2:

    =1=2

Although logical formulas use logical operators, values and text are used as the operands. Figure 10-3 illustrates several examples of logical formulas in action. Again, note that the formulas are displayed on the left and the results on the right. But just as important, notice that the real power of logical tests is when you compare operands located in cells rather than in the formula itself.

Table 10-1: Reference operators in Excel			
Operator	**Name**	**Example**	**Description**
:	Range	=SUM(A1:F20)	Refers to cells in the rectangle between the upper-left (A1) and lower-right (F20) corners.
space	Intersection	=SUM(A1:A5 A1:E1)	Refers to the cell(s) at the intersection of the two references. #NULL is displayed if no cells are in common.
,	Union	=SUM(A1:A5,A9:E9)	Refers to the cell(s) in both references as one.

Still more operators

Excel has a set of operators that enable you to specify what you want your formulas to calculate. These operators are called the *reference* operators because they let your formulas reference a contiguous range of cells (:), the cells in the intersection of several different ranges (*space*), or several ranges as one (,). The reference operators are defined in Table 10-1.

You're likely to use the range operator (:) most of the time in your formulas. The intersection and union references, however, are helpful when you need to refer to several cells or ranges in one formula. Without them, in some instances you would have to create several formulas to achieve the same result as one formula with an intersection or union reference.

The order of operation

As you ascend the Excel learning curve, you'll probably be creating formulas that perform several calculations in one cell. You may, for example, have a formula that sums a range of values, adds a value from another cell, and then divides the result by 2 to arrive at a final result. In arithmetic, some operations occur before others, and the same is true with Excel. Your formulas perform and some operations before others, depending on the operator. This order of operation, called *precedence*, follows basic arithmetic rules, as shown in Table 10-2.

If you have operators with the same level of precedence, Excel evaluates the operations from left to right — again, the same as in basic arithmetic. If you need to control which expression is calculated first, however, your tools are only a few keystrokes away.

Table 10-2: Operator precedence in Excel formulas		
Symbol	**Operator**	**Precedence**
:	Range	1
space	Intersection	1
,	Union	1
–	Negation	2
%	Percentage	3
^	Exponentiation	4
*	Multiplication	5
/	Division	5
+	Addition	6
–	Subtraction	6
&	Concatenation	7
=	Equal to	8
<	Less than	8
>	Greater than	8
<=	Less than or equal to	8
>=	Greater than or equal to	8
<>	Not equal to	8

Parentheses to the rescue

You can override the order of precedence by enclosing operations in parentheses. In effect, parentheses give you the ability to control calculation in your formulas. Enclose the operations you want calculated with a left parenthesis in the beginning of the expression and a right parenthesis at the end. Notice how parentheses affect the result of the following formula:

Formula	Result
=5*12-6	54
=5*(12-6)	30

If you have more than one set of expressions enclosed within parentheses, Excel first calculates the results of each enclosed expression and then uses the normal order of precedence to finish calculating the rest of your formula.

Creating Formulas

Now that you know the formula ground rules, here's how you create and then enter a formula into an Excel worksheet cell (remember, only one formula per cell).

Entering a basic formula

Entering a basic formula into a worksheet cell is an easy process: You type an equal sign, enter your operand, an operator, your next operand, your next operator, and so on, until you have built a formula. Then press Enter. Excel enters the formula in the selected cell and immediately calculates the result. The step-by-step procedure follows:

Steps: Entering a formula

Step 1. Select the cell by clicking it or by using the arrow keys.

Step 2. Type an equal sign. Excel's status indicator displays `Enter`.

Step 3. Type the first operand or cell address (or range name). You can also select rather than type the cell by clicking it or by selecting it with the arrow keys.

Step 4. Type the first operator.

Step 5. Repeat Steps 3 and 4 until you enter all your operands and operators.

Step 6. Click the Enter box in the Formula bar or press Enter.

The result of the formula appears in the cell, and the Formula bar continues to display the formula itself, as shown in Figure 10-4. The formula in cells C2 and C8 displays repeating number signs because the result is longer than the width of the cell.

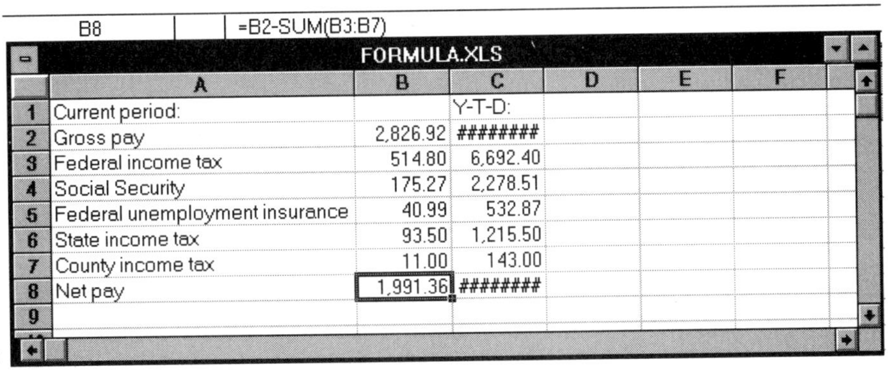

B8		=B2-SUM(B3:B7)					

FORMULA.XLS

	A	B	C	D	E	F
1	Current period:		Y-T-D:			
2	Gross pay	2,826.92	#######			
3	Federal income tax	514.80	6,692.40			
4	Social Security	175.27	2,278.51			
5	Federal unemployment insurance	40.99	532.87			
6	State income tax	93.50	1,215.50			
7	County income tax	11.00	143.00			
8	Net pay	1,991.36	#######			
9						

Figure 10-4: You can see a cell's formula in the Formula bar by making the cell the active cell.

If typing operators becomes tedious or the keyboard isn't your forte, you can create a toolbar that contains many of the arithmetic operators as tools.

Remember, if the result of a formula is too long to display in a cell, widen the column or use another format that permits you to see the formula's value.

Creating advanced formulas

Excel has two commands that can help you create more capable formulas, and you don't need to be a spreadsheet wizard to use them (don't let the "advanced" heading intimidate you). The Formula ⇨ Paste Name and Formula ⇨ Paste Function commands enable you to quickly combine range names and/or functions in your formulas. By using these commands, you can save time and avoid having to correct typos, and you can take advantage of the range names in your worksheet and the functions available in Excel.

To reference a named cell or range in a formula, select the cell that will hold the formula and type an equal sign, just as you do to create any other formula. Then choose the Formula ⇨ Paste Name command and select the range name you want in the formula, as shown in Figure 10-5. When you choose OK or press Enter, Excel pastes a copy of the range name in the Formula bar. You can continue pasting names or pressing Enter to complete the formula.

If you haven't defined any named cells or ranges, the Paste Name command is grayed so you can't select it.

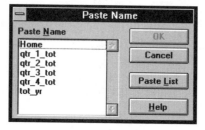

Figure 10-5: Select a range name from the Paste Name dialog box to include it in your formulas.

You can find formulas that depend on a range name by using the Formula ⇨ Find command.

Entering a function in a formula using the Formula ⇨ Paste Function command works similarly to the Paste Name command. Choose the Formula ⇨ Paste Function command, which displays the dialog box shown in Figure 10-6. Select the worksheet function you want from the list box and choose OK or press Enter. Excel pastes a copy of the worksheet function name in the Formula bar (don't forget to supply the function's arguments). Continue pasting names or functions, or entering operands and operators, and press Enter when you're finished.

When you begin a formula by pasting a worksheet function, you don't need to type an equal sign; Excel enters it for you.

Of course, a range name or worksheet function doesn't have to be the first operand in your formula. You can use as many names and functions as you need in your formula and at any point. Just position the insertion point with your mouse or arrow keys in the Formula bar where you want the range name or function.

Figure 10-6: The Formula ⇨ Paste Function command enables you to quickly enter functions directly into your worksheet or into formulas.

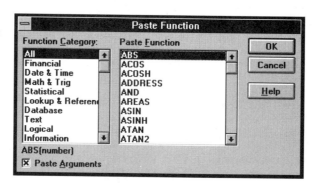

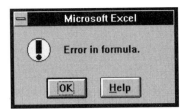

Figure 10-7: This warning message appears if your formula contains an error. Choose OK to close the box and correct the formula; choose Help to display the Help window with correction suggestions.

Correcting Formulas

Now and then, every Excel user makes a mistake trying to create a formula. If you construct a formula incorrectly, Excel doesn't let you enter it into the worksheet. Rather, Excel beeps and displays a message box, shown in Figure 10-7, warning you of an error. Most errors are due to typographical mistakes, a combination of values and text operators, incorrect or missing operators, and mismatched or extra parentheses. Other errors are a result of misspelled names or missing or incorrect arguments in worksheet functions. A few examples of common mistakes follow:

Formula	Reason for error
A1+B1	Missing equal sign
=A1+B1&C1	Combining numeric and text operators
=((A1+B1)*(C1+D1)	Extra parenthesis

To correct the error, first choose OK to close the message box. Notice that Excel highlights the portion of the formula that may be causing the error in the Formula bar. To correct a wayward formula, edit it in the Formula bar.

If you add a missing parenthesis, Excel displays in boldface for a few seconds the expression's matching left and right parentheses in the Formula bar. By moving the Formula bar cursor, you can check all the corresponding left and right parentheses in the formula and see whether they match up properly.

Press Enter when you're satisfied that the formula is correct. If you receive another error message, repeat the process or use the following tip. Pressing Esc or clicking the Cancel box removes the formula from the Formula bar and enables you to start over.

If you are still having trouble tracking down the error in your formula, delete the formula's equal sign while in Edit mode and Excel accepts your formula as a text entry. In this manner, you don't have to reenter the formula, and you can correct it later after you've had a chance to mull it over.

Using Values Only

Some of your worksheets, depending on their purpose or life cycle, can use the results of formulas rather than the formulas themselves. For example, if you perform bookkeeping or accounting tasks, you probably can use your formulas' values after the books are closed for your reporting. When you "lock in" a value from its corresponding formula, you take another step in ensuring the accuracy of your worksheet. In addition, your worksheet calculates more quickly and uses less memory because formulas are a little more demanding than values.

You have two ways to substitute a formula for its value. If you want to substitute a formula here and there, select the cell containing the formula and activate the Formula bar. Then press F9 (the shortcut key for recalculating) and press Enter. Excel substitutes the formula with its result in the cell you selected.

If you have a range of cells, such as a row or column of totals, select the range and then choose Edit ⇨ Copy. Next (without moving your cell pointer) choose Edit ⇨ Paste Special ⇨ Values and choose OK. Excel overwrites your formulas with their resulting values.

After you copy over formulas with their values, your formulas are history. If your values-for-formulas swap isn't exactly what you had in mind, choose Edit ⇨ Undo pronto.

Addressing Your Cells with Respect

In Chapter 9, you learned how to cut, copy, and paste cell contents. As with any other cell entry, you can save time by cutting, copying, and pasting formulas.

What happens when you cut or copy and paste formulas that contain range addresses? Although the cell address of your formula may change, the range of cells it references will not. Consequently, you can move a formula around your worksheet and still obtain the same result.

Similarly, you can copy a formula in one cell to the rest of the selected cells, in the process duplicating the formula in each cell. Excel automatically adjusts the range argument and cell references (if any) in the function or formula. This feature is known as *relative cell addressing,* because Excel modifies cell references *relative* to the location of the formula, and is Excel's default. For example, if you want to total values in columns A through F in a worksheet, you need only to enter the SUM function at the bottom of column A. As you copy the SUM

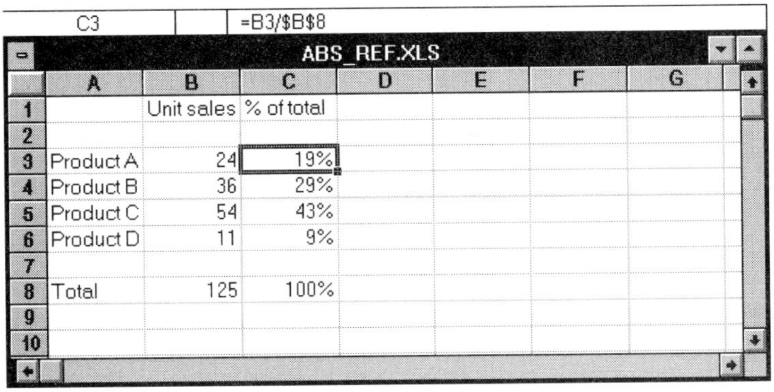

Figure 10-8:
Absolute
references
enable you to
hold cell
addresses still
as you copy
formulas that
reference
them.

	C3		=B3/$B$8					
			ABS_REF.XLS					
	A	B	C	D	E	F	G	
1		Unit sales	% of total					
2								
3	Product A	24	19%					
4	Product B	36	29%					
5	Product C	54	43%					
6	Product D	11	9%					
7								
8	Total	125	100%					
9								
10								

function across columns B through F, Excel uses each column's values to arrive
at a total for that column. You don't need to manually adjust the range reference for each SUM function or enter a separate SUM function in each column.

At times, however, you may need an *absolute* cell reference in your formula — a
reference that you *absolutely* do not want to change as you copy a formula. You
may encounter a situation similar to that as displayed in Figure 10-8. Note the
formula in cell C3. The dollar signs in the reference to cell B8 make cell B8 absolute; cell B8 will be in each formula in column C. If cell B8 weren't absolute, the
divisor in the formulas in range B4:B6 would be B9, B10, B11, and so on.

You may also come across a circumstance that requires you to use a mixed cell
reference — one where either the column letter or the row number of the cell
stays fixed as you copy. In this case, a dollar sign precedes the column letter or
row number, respectively. You can change between absolute and relative cell
addresses in several ways. As you enter your formula, do the following:

■ Type the dollar sign(s) in front of the column letter or row number you
want absolute.

■ After you select a cell (with the arrow keys or mouse) but before you type
an operator, choose Formula ➪ Reference or press F4.

To edit a cell's reference in a formula, do the following:

■ Select the cell containing the formula and activate the Formula bar on any
part of the cell whose address you want to make absolute (or relative).
Keyboard users should press F2 and then move the insertion point to the
cell address.

■ Choose Formula ➪ Reference or press F4.

Repeat the Formula ⇨ Reference command or keep pressing F4 to cycle through the four available reference types until you get the type of address you need, as follows:

Cell Reference

Cycle	Current	New	Type
First	B9	$B$9	Absolute
Second	$B$9	B$9	Mixed
Third	B$9	$B9	Mixed
Fourth	$B9	B9	Relative

Be careful if you copy formulas that use relative cell addresses. Because the cell addresses that comprise each copied formula change, your formulas may reference the incorrect cells. You can make sure that your copied formulas are referencing the correct cells by making the cell containing the formula the active cell and tracing through the logic of the formula, or by using some of the techniques described in Chapter 30.

Working with Circular References

Occasionally you may create a formula that refers to its own cell address. For example, in cell A3, you may have the formula =A1+A2+A3. If you try to enter this formula, Excel displays the message box shown in Figure 10-9 and displays Circular:A3 on the Status bar after you choose OK.

Excel is telling you that the worksheet contains a *direct* circular reference, a formula that will try to calculate a result indefinitely because its own cell address is included in the formula. In short, it's caught in an endless calculation loop. You can untangle your formula in two ways.

Figure 10-9: This warning message appears if your formula contains a circular reference. Choose OK to close the box and correct the formula (if the circular reference is unintentional) or choose Help to display the Help window with circular reference helpful hints.

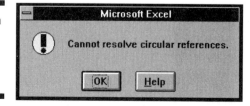

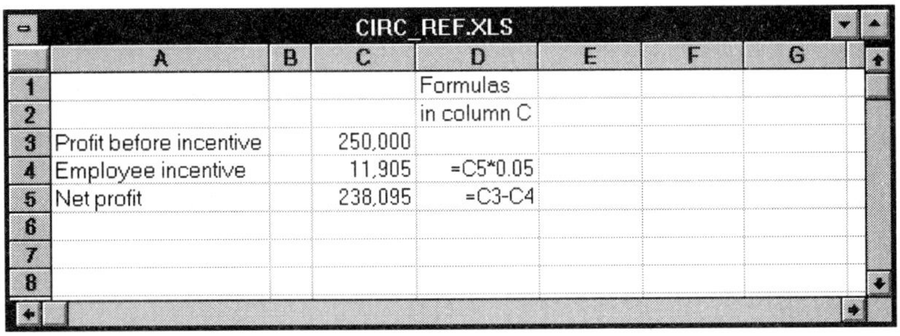

Figure 10-10: A circular reference in some situations (in cell C5) is necessary to solve a problem (net profit).

	A	B	C	D	E	F	G
			CIRC_REF.XLS				
1				Formulas			
2				in column C			
3	Profit before incentive		250,000				
4	Employee incentive		11,905	=C5*0.05			
5	Net profit		238,095	=C3-C4			
6							
7							
8							

The first is to select the cell and activate the Formula bar to correct it. Delete or change the address of the offending cell; then click the Enter box or press Enter. The second solution involves *iteration*. With iteration, you specify how many times you want Excel to calculate the formula — the intention being that you want to converge on a result. In this case, you probably have a circular reference that is deliberate or intentional, such as the one in Figure 10-10. In Figure 10-10, the amount of employee incentive is based on 5 percent of net profit. But net profit equals profit less employee incentive. And there's the rub: Net profit indirectly depends on itself through the employee incentive, creating a circular reference in cell C5.

If you want Excel to attempt to find an answer to a formula with a circular reference, you need to use the Options ➪ Calculation command and specify the number of iterations (the default setting is 100, which usually is plenty) in the Maximum Iterations box. Next, you can also select the amount of change in the cells involved in the circular reference with each calculation pass (the default is 0.001) in the Maximum Change box. When you select OK, Excel calculates your formula the number of times you specified in Maximum Iterations, using the previous cycle's result, or until the affected cells change less than the number in Maximum Change, whichever comes first.

As your proficiency with Excel increases, you may create worksheets that depend on so many cells containing formulas that identifying the location of the circular reference may be difficult. In this case, you may have an *indirect* circular reference. You can track down indirect cell references by using the Info window, discussed in Chapter 30.

You may encounter a formula with a circular reference that, after using the iteration options, is *diverging*, or calculating results farther and farther away from a solution. In this case, your formula is probably unsolvable, and you need to go back and take another look at its logic. It may require simple editing or recreating from scratch.

Selecting When To Calculate

As you saw earlier, you can choose which operands and expressions in your formulas Excel calculates first with the use of parentheses. You can also choose when Excel calculates *all* the formulas in your worksheet.

Examining calculation basics

Normally, Excel automatically calculates your worksheet when a change occurs — for example, when you enter or edit data or formulas. In addition, Excel only recalculates formulas that depend on new or edited data. Excel also temporarily suspends calculation if you need to perform other worksheet tasks, such as issuing commands, and resumes when you're finished. Finally, Excel keeps tabs on your worksheet for calculation and determines the order by which formulas are calculated. The more a formula depends on other formulas for its result, the later its turn comes up for recalculation.

Sometimes, however, you may want Excel to calculate only when you want it to. For example, suppose that you've created a worksheet the size of a football field. You can increase your data entry speed by going to manual calculation, so Excel doesn't recalculate each time you enter a new number. You may also want to use manual calculation if you have complex open charts and change the data they depend on.

Changing calculation

You change from automatic to manual calculation by choosing Manual from the Calculation Options dialog box, as shown in Figure 10-11. After you choose OK, Excel only calculates open worksheets and charts on command. Excel displays Calculate along the Status bar after you make a change to your worksheet that affects a formula, as a reminder that your worksheet needs to be updated. To calculate your worksheet, you can use the Options ➪ Calculation ➪ Calc Now command or press F9. When you do so, Calculate isn't displayed on the Status bar until you make another change to your worksheet. If you want to only calculate your active worksheet, charts on the worksheet, and any charts linked to your worksheet, use Options ➪ Calculation ➪ Calc Document or press Shift+F9.

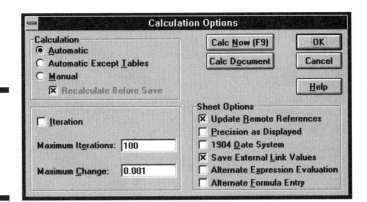

Figure 10-11: The Calculation Options dialog box enables you to choose when and how you want your worksheet calculated.

If you have a large worksheet application that requires calculation, you can change to another Windows program while Excel calculates and perform other tasks.

Make sure that you calculate your worksheet after you're through making changes and before you print it. Otherwise, the results on paper (and on-screen) don't reflect the most current data.

Learning other fast calculation techniques

When you choose Manual calculation, Excel automatically chooses the Recalculate Before Save box for you. This option protects you from not saving your latest worksheet changes to disk. You may prefer, however, to calculate immediately after making a change and so won't need this option, which can somewhat slow down file saving. Simply turn off Recalculate Before Save if you don't want Excel to calculate before saving.

If your worksheet contains a data table (explained in Chapter 27), calculation can in some instances take a while. You can have Excel calculate only the formulas in your worksheet if you choose the Automatic Except Tables option. In this manner, you have the best of both worlds: You can keep your worksheet updated with responsive data entry and quick calculation time and calculate the data table portion when you're ready. With Automatic Except Tables, you update your data table(s) with Options ⇨ Calculation ⇨ Calc Now or by pressing F9.

Torpedo your calculator

If you're digging your calculator out of a desk drawer to calculate a number for use in a worksheet, or you need a quick calculation, a better way is available. Simply type an equal sign, the values, and operators and press F9. Excel performs the calculation in the Formula bar, which you can enter into your worksheet or clear. For example, enter =SQRT(184) into the Formula bar and press F9. Excel displays the value 13.5646599662505. Press Enter to insert the value rather than the formula into your worksheet.

You can also calculate a portion of a formula. To do so, select the cell, select the part of the formula you want calculated, and then press F9. The selected part of the formula is replaced with its calculated value — a method you can use to debug long, complex formulas.

Summary

▶ Formulas are entered into cells and calculate a result.

▶ Three types of formulas are available: numeric, text, and logical. Worksheet functions, a fourth type, are built-in formulas that come with Excel.

▶ Formulas consist of operands and operators. Operands consist of your data (values and text), a reference to a cell containing data, or a worksheet function. Operators are arithmetic symbols.

▶ Excel calculates the operands from left to right in a cell, unless the cell has several types of operators. Excel follows an order of precedence when calculating a formula similar to arithmetic rules, but you can change the order of calculation by using parentheses in formulas.

▶ You can easily build powerful formulas by using range names in worksheets and Excel worksheet functions.

▶ You can correct a formula in the Formula bar rather than clearing it and starting over from scratch.

▶ Cell addresses in formulas can be relative, absolute, or mixed. Be aware of how a cell's address type will affect the duplicates of a formula if you copy the original to other ranges.

▶ Circular references occur when a formula refers to itself directly or indirectly. Most of the time, you'll want to edit your formula so it will produce the correct result.

▶ You can choose when and how Excel calculates your worksheet. If you have a large worksheet or one that contains a data table, you may want to change from automatic recalculation to enhance your worksheet's responsiveness.

Chapter 11
Using Functions in Worksheets

In this chapter . . .

▶ Spreadsheet functions and why you need to be on speaking terms with them.

▶ The rules for using functions plus many examples to get you started.

▶ General tips on using functions in worksheets.

▶ An overview of the functions available in Excel, arranged by category.

Chapter 10 covered worksheet formulas. Excel's arsenal of built-in functions greatly increases the power of the formulas you create and use in your worksheets. All spreadsheet products have functions, but Excel has more of them than any other product on the market. Becoming familiar with them is well worth your time; you never know when you may need to calculate the payment on a loan, convert a list of words to uppercase, or determine the ASCII code for a character. Although some of the functions may appear esoteric, familiarity with them will make you a more proficient spreadsheet user.

What Are Functions?

Functions are procedures that are built into Excel. They enable you to perform calculations and operations on your data that would otherwise be difficult or impossible. For example, Excel has a function to calculate the average of a range. You could, of course, develop a formula to calculate an average on your own, using the + operator to add the values and the / operator to divide by the number of values. But what if you added a new value to your range? You would then have to adjust the formula by adding in the new entry and change the number of values that you divide by. As you'll see, the AVERAGE function can make this process much simpler and less prone to errors.

Excel actually has two classes of functions: worksheet functions and macro functions. Worksheet functions can be used on macro sheets, but macro functions cannot be used in worksheets. This chapter covers only the worksheet functions. Macro functions are covered in Chapter 26.

Worksheet functions work with one or more arguments, perform their specified calculation, and return a result. The result is calculated immediately when you enter the function. Excel's worksheet functions are classified into 11 categories:

- Database
- Date and time
- Financial
- Information
- Logical
- Lookup
- Mathematical
- Matrix
- Statistical
- Text
- Trigonometric

Getting overwhelmed by the sheer number of available functions is easy. You'll probably find, however, that you use only a dozen or so functions frequently and will soon be comfortable with them. You'll periodically need to use other, less frequently used functions, and looking up their syntax is a simple matter. Excel makes the task easy by providing superb on-line help and a special command to help you select functions and their arguments. We discuss how to use the Formula ⇨ Paste Function command later in this chapter.

The Excel worksheet functions are described in the Quick Reference booklet that comes with this book. The remainder of this chapter consists of general information about worksheet functions and examples of how some of the more commonly used functions can be used in your worksheets.

Using Function Arguments

Most functions use *arguments* that tell them what data to act on. For example, you may enter the following formula into cell C21:

```
=AVERAGE(C1:C20)
```

In this case, the formula computes the average of the 20 values in the range C1:C20, and the result is displayed in cell C21. The argument for this function is the range C1:C21. If you change the argument, the function returns a different result — as with any other function in Excel. Arguments for worksheet functions can be of the following types:

- Actual values
- Cell or range references (including named ranges)
- Formulas
- Logical values
- Error values

Some functions do not require arguments, and others use optional arguments. Arguments are always placed to the right of the function name and are enclosed in parentheses. Functions that do not require an argument must include a set of *empty* parentheses. For example, the RAND function (which returns a random number from 0 to 1) does not use any arguments. You enter this function into a cell as follows:

```
=RAND()
```

Actual values as arguments

In some cases, you may want to supply a function with actual values — numbers or text that you enter directly. An example of a function written to use actual values for arguments follows:

```
=AVERAGE(12,15,18,18,22,17,23)
```

In this case, the AVERAGE function returns the average of the seven value arguments supplied (17.8571).

Cell or range references as arguments

Not too surprisingly, Excel can use named ranges as arguments as well as cell coordinates. The following example calculates the average of the values in the named range scores. The range scores may be defined as cells C1:C20.

```
=AVERAGE(scores)
```

You can use noncontiguous cell references or range names as arguments. For example, =AVERAGE(A1:A10,C1:C10,E1:E10) averages the 30 values in these three ranges.

Formulas as arguments

Functions can use the result of a formula for an argument. Importantly, the formula can include other functions. These are referred to as *nested functions*. An example of a function that uses a formula for its argument follows:

```
=SQRT((A4^2)*(A5^2))
```

This function first computes the formula for the argument, which is the value in cell A4 squared times the value in cell A5 squared. It then takes the square root of the result. An example of a simple nested function follows:

```
=SQRT(SUM(D1:D16))
```

This function first evaluates its argument, which is the sum of the values in the range D1:D16. It then computes the square root of this result. You can nest functions as deeply as you want (as long as you don't exceed the 255-character maximum number for a cell).

Logical values as arguments

Function arguments can also be logical values. Logical values are either True or False but can also be statements that evaluate either of these values. For example, the formula =A5>20 evaluates to True only if the value in cell A5 is greater than 20. An example of a function that uses a logical argument and equals True follows:

```
=ISLOGICAL(TRUE)
```

The ISLOGICAL function returns True if its argument evaluates to a logical value; otherwise, it returns False.

Error values as arguments

The final type of argument is error values. The error values in Excel indicate a specific type of error:

Error	Reason
#DIV/0	Division by zero
#N/A	Referring to a cell with no value
#NAME?	A name Excel doesn't recognize
#NULL!	Two worksheet ranges that do not intersect
#NUM!	A problem with a number
#REF!	Referring to a cell that is not valid
#VALUE!	Incorrect argument or operand

An example of a function that uses an error value for an argument follows:

```
=ISERROR(B10)
```

This function returns True when cell B10 contains one of the previously listed errors.

Entering a Function

Now that you've examined the rules of using Excel's functions, you're ready to use them in your formulas. When building a formula that uses a function, you have three ways to enter the function:

- Type the function manually.
- Paste the function with the Formula ➪ Paste Function command.
- Use a combination of the preceding two techniques.

Entering a function is no different from entering any other data in your worksheet. First, select the cell that will hold your function. You enter the function in the Formula bar, and it can be as simple as a single function:

```
=SUM(A1:A10)
```

Or it can be as complex as several functions that create a formula:

```
=IF(SUM(A1:A10)=SUM(B1:B10),"Equal","Not Equal")
```

Each method of entering functions is discussed next.

You can save time by entering the same function in a multicell range by selecting the range (a row or column, for example), entering the function in the Formula bar, and then pressing Ctrl+Enter.

Typing a function

The most basic way to enter a function into your worksheet is to type it, as when entering a value or label into a cell. After selecting the cell, type an equal sign, then the function name, and finally its argument(s). Press Enter to complete the process.

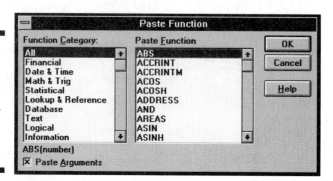

Figure 11-1: The Paste Function dialog box is your no-muss, no-fuss way to copy a function's name and arguments into the Formula bar.

If you're good at typing, or if you won't be using many functions, entering a function in this manner may be your best option. But, if you're prone to typos or use some of Excel's more exotic functions with hard-to-remember arguments, you may want to have Excel help you by pasting them into your worksheet.

Pasting a function

Another way you can enter functions into your worksheet is to paste them. In Chapter 10, you received the cook's tour of how you can paste range names and functions to help you create powerful formulas quickly. Letting Excel help you enter functions by pasting them ensures that they are spelled correctly and reminds you of their argument requirements and the order in which they are expected.

Typing a function and pasting it both begin the same way: You first select the cell where you want the function to calculate a result. To paste a function, however, you choose the Formula ⇨ Paste Function command, and the dialog box in Figure 11-1 appears. Next, you scroll the Paste Function list box until the function you want is selected. When you choose OK or press Enter, Excel places a copy of the function with argument names in the Formula bar, as follows:

A1	☒☑	=PV(rate,nper,pmt,fv,type)

As you become more proficient with functions, you may want to turn off the Paste Arguments check box in the Paste Function dialog box. If you know the function's argument requirements, you can enter them directly into the Formula bar after using Formula ⇨ Paste Function and avoid having to replace the argument names Excel provides you.

You can display the Paste Function dialog box by pressing Shift+F3.

At this point, you need to supply the arguments the function needs to calculate properly. Select the argument name you want to replace with your actual argument by double-clicking the name of the argument or by pressing Ctrl+Shift+right arrow to select the name.

Type a value, cell address, or range name, or select the cell or range containing the argument with your mouse. The reference replaces the highlighted text. Select the next name with the mouse or keyboard and substitute the name for the actual reference. Continue this process until all the argument names have been replaced. If you make a mistake, reselect the argument by clicking it or by pressing Ctrl+Shift+left arrow.

When you're finished and satisfied with your specified arguments, press Enter. If everything is OK, Excel enters the function into the cell and calculates the result.

 If you press Enter before you replace the function's argument names, Excel displays the #NAME? error in your selected cell because the formula is using a nonexistent reference. Go back and edit the formula so it includes a valid reference.

Copying for quick results

If you need to enter one function many times into your worksheet, don't forget that Excel has a boatload of copying tools for entering functions in a hurry. For example, if you have a 12-month budget worksheet, you only need to total the

---

Finding functions fast

Even if you're not a touch typist, you can quickly find the function you need from the Paste Function list box by typing the first letter of the function's name. Excel scrolls the function list to select the first function that begins with the letter. From there, you can select the function or pinpoint the one you need fairly rapidly.

 You can also use the Function Category list box as a filter to narrow your function choices displayed in the Paste Function list box. For example, if you know that the function

you need is a logical function, choosing Logical from the Function Category list box displays the six logical functions in the Paste Function list box. In this manner, you don't have to wade through a lot of unneeded functions to find the one you want.

Keyboard users can use the PgUp and PgDn keys to scroll the Paste Function list up and down one screen at a time. In addition, you can use the Home and End keys to select the first function (ABS) and last function (ZTEST).

first column with SUM or with Excel's Autosum tool (discussed next). Then use Edit ⇨ Copy to copy the function and Edit ⇨ Paste to paste it to the remaining months and annual total column. Better still, if you select the range where you need totals that includes the entered SUM function, Edit ⇨ Fill Right or Down copies the SUM (or any other) functions in rapid-fire fashion.

If you're a mouse user, the world is your oyster (if you have Options ⇨ Workspace ⇨ Cell Drag and Drop selected). Simply select the cell containing the function and drag on the cell's Drag-and-Drop indicator.

Getting fast totals with Autosum

No function is used more frequently than SUM. As with accounting ledger paper, Excel is most commonly used to total columns and rows of numbers. For this reason, you should keep Autosum in mind if you need to enter the SUM function quickly into your worksheet. Autosum is located on Excel's default toolbar and resembles the Greek letter Sigma (Σ).

You may find that invoking the Autosum tool by pressing Alt+= is even faster.

To total a range of cells using Autosum, first select the cell where you want Excel to enter the SUM function, such as at the bottom of a column or in the cell immediately to the right of a row of numbers. Then select the Autosum icon on the toolbar (or press Alt+=). Excel surrounds the range to be totaled with a marquee, as shown in Figure 11-2. You can change the selected range at this time or choose the Autosum icon a second time to enter the function. Autosum is your one-stop totaling tool.

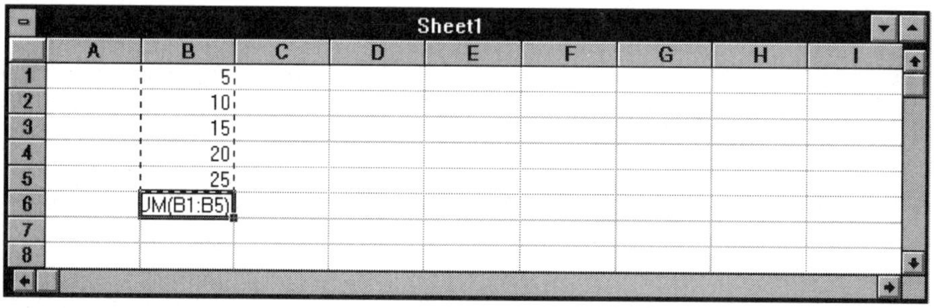

Sheet1								
	A	B	C	D	E	F	G	H	I
1		5							
2		10							
3		15							
4		20							
5		25							
6		UM(B1:B5)							
7									
8									

Figure 11-2: Autosum about to total a range of values. The marquee helps you see what's included in the range to be totaled.

Correcting a Function _____

Sometimes you'll want to edit a function in order to change a reference for an argument or because of an error message (hopefully you won't have too many of the latter). In either case, making a change to a function is easy.

When you enter a formula, Excel automatically capitalizes all functions and cell references if they are syntactically correct. Consequently, entering formulas and functions in lowercase is a good idea. That way, if you make a mistake, you can quickly spot the problem; it will be the part of the formula that wasn't converted to uppercase.

To change an aspect of your function, make the cell containing the function the active cell. Then click the Formula bar as close as possible to the point in the function you want to change (or press F2 then use Excel's cursor-movement keys — Home, End, and the arrow keys — to do the same thing if you're a keyboard user). You can use any combination of cell selections — entering, deleting, or pasting additional functions into the Formula bar to correct or enhance the function (or formula). Press Enter when you're finished.

If you need to edit your function due to an error message, choose OK in the Error dialog box. Excel then moves the insertion point to the place in your function where a problem exists. Follow the previous procedures to repair your function and enter it into your worksheet.

If you choose Help in response to a function error, Excel displays a help screen relative to that context. That is, you see a help screen that directly relates to your function error, such as *Parentheses do not match,* which can help you solve the problem.

Getting Help with Functions _____

You shouldn't feel badly if you need a little function help from your spreadsheet program now and then. Let's face it, the number of functions and their argument requirements can be overwhelming to the beginner and guru alike.

Fortunately, as the saying goes, help is only a keystroke away. Excel's on-line Help function is outstanding; each function has its own screen of information, which includes a description of the function, how to use it, and examples

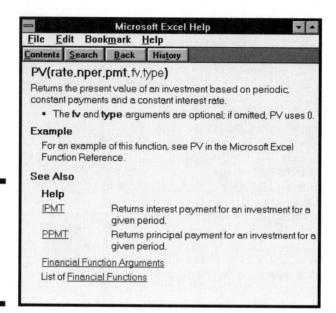

Figure 11-3:
Everything you always wanted to know about the PV (present value) function, courtesy of Excel's help system.

(Figure 11-3 shows a sample). The following steps explain an easy way to get help on the function you have a question about:

Steps: Getting help in Excel

Step 1. Press F1 or choose Help ⇨ Contents.

Step 2. From the Help Contents screen, choose Worksheet Functions (near the bottom of the screen).

Step 3. From the Worksheet Functions screen, choose the category of the function you need help on. If you're unsure of the category, choose All.

Step 4. From the selected category or the All screen, choose the name of the worksheet function.

If you need help on more than one function, don't close the Help window and start over. After you're through getting help on your current function, click the Back button and you are returned to the Worksheet Function category help

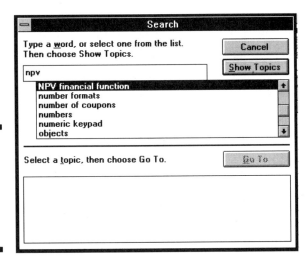

Figure 11-4: You also can get worksheet help by using <u>H</u>elp ⇨ <u>S</u>earch and typing the letters of the function. Choosing Show Topics and then Go To opens the Help window with the corresponding information.

screen (either All or the one you selected). You can then select the next function you need help with.

You can also get help quickly if you know the function's name. Choose <u>H</u>elp ⇨ <u>S</u>earch and then type the letters of the function name in the Search text box (for example, NPV), as shown in Figure 11-4. Choose Show Topics and then Go To. Excel displays the Help window for that function.

Nesting Functions

You've already seen how you can use various operators and operands to create customized formulas that calculate what you want when you want it. By using functions and parentheses, you elevate your formulas to a higher level of capability. Combining functions with multiple sets of parentheses is known as *nesting* functions, because your formulas rely on many levels of intermediate calculations (performed by functions) to arrive at a final result. For example, the formula

```
=SQRT(AVERAGE(SUM(A1:A10),SUM(B1:B10)))
```

has three levels of nesting. The first level uses the SUM function to total the values in A1:A10 and B1:B10, respectively. The second level computes the average of these two results. The third level takes the square root of the AVERAGE function using the SQRT function.

You're most likely to encounter nested functions using the IF function, either through formulas you create or worksheets you inherit from others. Formulas that use nested IF functions commonly have many levels of nested IF statements, making them complex, but they provide your worksheet with a great deal of decision-making, timesaving capabilities. For example, the formula

```
=IF(A2=1,IF(A3=2,SUM(A12:I12),0),0)
```

only totals the range A12:I12 if the cell A2 contains the value 1 *and* A3 contains the value 2. Otherwise, if A2 or A3 contain a value other than 1 and 2, respectively, the cell containing the IF formula returns 0.

The best way to understand formulas comprised of nested functions is to work through their logic in the order Excel calculates them. You mentally walk through each level of nesting, from the lowest to the highest, whether the nesting is due to parentheses controlling the calculation or to the function's argument requirements. In the case of multiple expressions enclosed in parentheses, begin with the expression enclosed by the greatest number of parentheses and work your way out to the next set of parentheses. In multiple IF functions, step through your formula remembering the IF function syntax: IF(*test_cond,do_this,else_this*), while keeping in mind that each of these arguments can be another IF function.

 If nested parentheses are driving you up a wall, you may want to print the formula and use a pencil to connect sets of matching parentheses. This is the most efficient way we know of to determine parentheses-related problems.

Using Worksheet Functions

Excel has more than 100 worksheet functions, and although you may not have a need for them all, this section shows you how you can put the most frequently used functions to work. Note that the following sections don't correspond exactly to the function categories listed in your Excel documentation or in the function help screens but are presented in groups showing how you can view and use functions together.

Calculating basic statistics

Figure 11-5 shows several functions you can use to compute some basic but practical statistics from a range of values. These functions are listed in the following table.

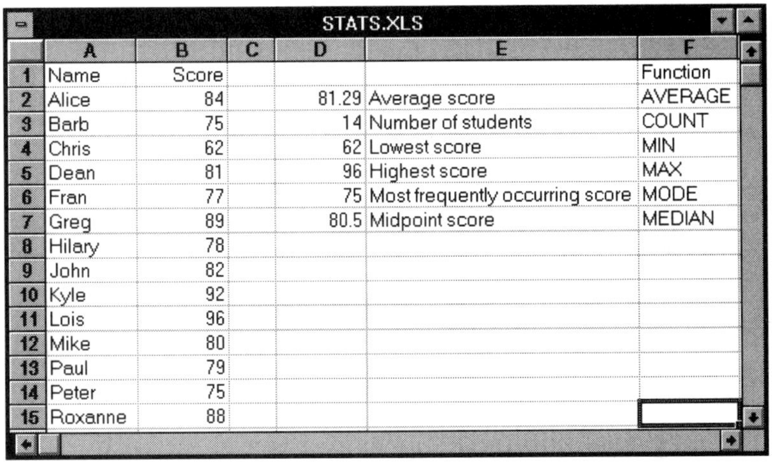

	A	B	C	D	E	F
1	Name	Score				Function
2	Alice	84		81.29	Average score	AVERAGE
3	Barb	75		14	Number of students	COUNT
4	Chris	62		62	Lowest score	MIN
5	Dean	81		96	Highest score	MAX
6	Fran	77		75	Most frequently occurring score	MODE
7	Greg	89		80.5	Midpoint score	MEDIAN
8	Hilary	78				
9	John	82				
10	Kyle	92				
11	Lois	96				
12	Mike	80				
13	Paul	79				
14	Peter	75				
15	Roxanne	88				

STATS.XLS

Figure 11-5: Basic but revealing statistics every spreadsheet user should know how to use.

Function	Action
AVERAGE	Calculate an average
COUNT	Count the number of values in a range
MAX	Find the largest value in a range
MEDIAN	Find the midpoint value in a range
MIN	Find the smallest value in a range
MODE	Find the most frequently occurring value in a range
SUM *(not shown)*	Calculate a total

Analyzing investments

Excel provides three tools to perform capital budgeting: IRR (internal rate of return), MIRR (modified internal rate of return), and NPV (net present value), shown in use in Figure 11-6.

Internal rate of return is the rate at which an investment is predicted to earn. Modified internal rate of return performs the same analysis but uses an interest rate for the cost of the investment and another for reinvestment of the positive cash flows generated from the investment. Net present value is the value of all future cash flows in today's dollars, discounted (or reduced) by the interest

	A	B	C	D	E	F
				CAP_BUD.XLS		
	Year	Cash flow		IRR guess	10%	
1	0	($1,000,000)		MIRR finance rate	9%	
2	1	$150,000		MIRR reinvest rate	7%	
3	2	$150,000		NPV rate	7%	
4	3	$150,000				
5	4	($250,000)		IRR =	20.21%	
6	5	$175,000		MIRR =	16.35%	
7	6	$175,000		NPV =	$2,529,549.80	
8	7	$175,000				
9	8	$175,000				
10	9	$175,000				
11	10	$3,500,000				

Figure 11-6: These capital budgeting tools (IRR, MIRR, and NPV) are at your disposal.

rate that's available for investment for each of the cash flows (except the initial outflow). These functions use the following syntax:

Function	Syntax
IRR	Values,*guess*
MIRR	Values,finance_rate,reinvest_rate
NPV	Rate,value(s)

Excel uses a guess of 0.10 if you don't furnish one for the IRR function. If Excel returns #NUM!, change your guess and allow Excel to try again.

Excel assumes that cash flows occur at the end of the period for the NPV function.

If you are analyzing an investment with more than one negative cash flow (a project with multiple internal rates of return), use the MIRR function. In general, MIRR is more accurate than IRR and calculates more realistic results, as you can see from Figure 11-6. IRR assumes you can reinvest positive cash flows at your guess rate, which may not be possible.

Performing loan and annuity calculations

Excel offers numerous functions to help you perform calculations involving loans and annuities. Here's what's available, with their syntax (items in italic are optional variables):

Name	Function	Syntax
Future value	FV	Rate,nper,pmt,*pv,type*
Present value	PV	Rate,value(s)
Payment	PMT	Rate,nper,pv,*fv,type*
Principal payment	PPMT	Rate,per,nper,pv,*fv,type*
Interest payment	IPMT	Rate,per,nper,pv,*fv,type*
Rate	RATE	Nper,pmt,pv,*fv,type*
Number of periods	NPER	Rate,pmt,pv,*fv,type*

You should keep a few things in mind as you use these functions. First, *type* (1 or 0) refers to when the payment is made. Specifying 1 or 0 tells Excel that the payment occurs at the beginning and end, respectively, of the period. If you don't specify a type, Excel uses 0 (end of period).

Second, Excel considers cash outflows as negative and cash inflows as positive. As a result, make sure that you specify values with the correct sign for function arguments. Excel displays #NUM! in a cell, for example, if a cash outflow isn't a negative number.

Third, these functions lend themselves particularly well to using cell addresses or range names as arguments. The functions are eaiser to create, and you merely change a cell's value instead of editing the cell containing the function to calculate a new result.

With that in mind, the following descriptions give you a flavor for Excel's loan and annuity worksheet functions.

Future value

FV calculates the future value of a series of cash-flow-of-equal-payment (PMT) amounts made at regular intervals (NPER) at a constant interest rate (RATE). If you make an investment, the cash outflow can be represented as *pv*. For example, if, for your child's education, you deposit $100 at the beginning of each month for 15 years at the rate of 6.5 percent interest, its future value is

```
=FV(.065/12,15*12,-100,1) = $30,351.83
```

which isn't too shabby and a good habit to begin as soon as possible.

Present value

PV calculates the present value of a series of cash-flow-of-equal-payment (PMT) amounts made at regular intervals (NPER) at a constant interest rate (RATE). (Note the similarity with future value.) For example, you're finally ready to purchase your dream home and you've determined (through an Excel worksheet) that the family budget can withstand a monthly mortgage payment of $990. You can get a 30-year fixed-rate loan at 9 percent interest. When you go hat in hand to your friendly banker, your maximum mortgage amount is:

```
=PV(0.09/12,30*12,990) = $123,039.05
```

Payment

PMT calculates the payment needed on a principal amount (PV) for a specified interest rate (RATE) and number of time periods (NPER). For example, if you want to know the monthly payment (principal and interest) on a mortgage of $120,000 at 9.25 percent interest over 30 years, you use

```
=PMT(0.0925/12,30*12,120000) = -987.21
```

or $987.21 monthly.

Principal portion of a payment

PPMT enables you to know what portion of a payment is for the principal only, for a specified period number. From the preceding example, as a new homeowner you're curious about just how much of your first payment will go toward knocking down that $120,000 mortgage. To find out, you use:

```
=PPMT(0.0925/12,1,12*30,120000) = $62.21
```

Compare apples to apples

It's vitally important that your interest rate and payment period cover the same time frame. If they don't, the results will be wild, unpredictable, and incorrect. If you specify a monthly interest rate, for example, make sure that the time increments are also in months. To illustrate, 180 could have been used just as easily as 15*12 in the example in the "Future value" section.

One way to help ensure that you avoid this pitfall is to enter labels into your worksheet that describe the time period, such as *Monthly interest rate* and *Number of monthly payments*. In the corresponding cell immediately to the right, enter the formula to calculate the appropriate amounts. Then all you need to do is reference these cells as arguments in your functions and thus bypass a potentially embarrassing situation.

Interest portion of a payment

IPMT, as you'd expect, enables you to know what portion of a payment is for interest only, for a specified period number. From the previous example, you'd be astounded that only about $62.21 of your first payment goes toward reducing your mortgage balance; surely Excel made a mistake. To double-check by determining the interest portion of your first payment, use:

```
=IPMT(0.0925/12,1,12*30,120000) = $925.00
```

Rate

RATE calculates the interest rate of an annuity. For example, suppose that you want to live a life of leisure in your golden years. A well-regarded life insurance company has approached you with an offer to cough up $15,000 in 5 years if you hand over $200 at the beginning of each month. You want to determine the interest on this investment in comparison with other alternatives. To do so, you use

```
=RATE(60,-200,15000,1) = 0.007 monthly or 8.51% annually
```

which is pretty good. You may want to shop around a little more, however.

Number of periods

NPER calculates the number of periods required to reach a specified annuity at a given interest rate. For example, suppose that you want to know how many months are needed for you to accumulate $5,000 if you put $50 at the beginning of each month in your savings account, which pays 5 percent interest. You use

```
=NPER(0.05/12,-50,5000,0,1) = 128.92
```

or 129 months (about 10 ¾ years).

Calculating depreciation

In the dizzying world of high finance, firms are allowed to write down, or *depreciate*, the cost of certain types of assets over time. You should, as closely as possible, match the increased revenue or decreased cost the asset contributes to your firm to the cost of the asset for that period. Figure 11-7 is an

	A	B	C	D	E	F	G	H
	DEPREC.XLS							
1	Asset cost	1000						
2	Salvage	100						
3	Life	3						
4	Period			1	2	3	4	Total
5								
6	Straight-line		SLN	$300.00	$300.00	$300.00		$900.00
7	Declining balance		DB	$536.00	$248.70	$115.30		$900.00
8	Double-declining balance		DDB	$666.67	$222.22	$11.11		$900.00
9	Sum-of-the-year's digits		SYD	$450.00	$300.00	$150.00		$900.00
10	Variable declining balance		VDB	$250.00	$375.00	$187.50	$87.50	$900.00
11								
12	Start period for VDB			0.00	0.50	1.50	2.50	
13	End period for VDB			0.50	1.50	2.50	3.00	
14								

Figure 11-7: Excel has a variety of depreciation functions (SLN, SYD, DB, DDB, and VDB) for every asset amortization need. Note the differing amounts depending on method and year.

example of the depreciation method and corresponding function available in Excel, which follow. Items in italic text are optional variables:

Depreciation method	Function	Syntax
Straight-line	SLN	Cost,salvage,life
Sum-of-the-year's digits	SYD	Cost,salvage,life,period
Declining balance	DB	Cost,salvage,life,period,*month*
Double-declining balance	DDB	Cost,salvage,life,period,month,*factor*
Variable-declining balance	VDB	Cost,salvage,life,start_period,end_period, *factor,no_switch*

Excel uses 200 percent double-declining balance if you do not specify otherwise in the VDB function. In Figure 11-7, 150 percent was used.

Because every business has its own unique circumstances, and tax laws are a moving target, be sure to consult your accountant or tax advisor to select the method that's right for you. You can see from Figure 11-8 that each method produces different results.

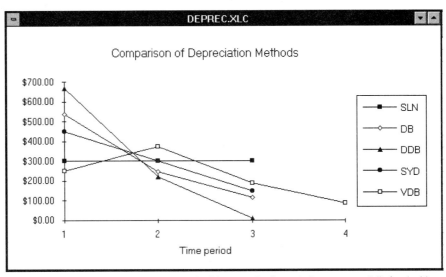

Figure 11-8: Choose the depreciation method for your firm's capital assets carefully (and with the help of your tax professional) because the depreciation expense varies depending on the year and method selected.

The ins and outs of VDB start and end periods

The VDB function requires you to furnish the point your asset to be depreciated is put into service. In Figure 11-7, it was the beginning of the third quarter, so 0.50 was used because half the year is gone. But what if the asset is placed into service in the middle of the first quarter or at the end of the second?

You can quickly calculate start and end periods by first remembering that the start and end periods of the asset correspond to its beginning and end periods for that particular year. Consequently, the start period for the first year in most cases is zero.

Calculating the end period for the first year is the most difficult, but after you do, all subsequent

periods and years are easy. One approach is to divide the current week of the year by 52 and then subtract this number from 1.00. This value is your end period for the asset's first year. Use your company's reporting calendar for accuracy.

You can see from Figure 11-7 that the next year's starting period is the same as the prior year's end period, and the next year's end period is incremented by the same amount as the first year's end period. You can set up a table to perform these calculations for you (so you can reference them in the VDB functions) using either formulas or the Data ⇨ Series command.

	A	B	C	D	E	F	G	H
1	Serial number	33638.58	1992	YEAR				
2	Formatted number	2/4/92	2	MONTH				
3			3	WEEKDAY				
4			4	DAY				
5			13	HOUR				
6			50	MINUTE				
7			52	SECOND				
8								

Figure 11-9: The date and time functions enable you to perform arithmetic by extracting the appropriate date or time increment from a serial number.

Finding dates and times

You can extract any date or time portion of a serial number by using the worksheet functions shown in Figure 11-9. These functions are useful for performing date and time calculations in worksheets, such as in accounts payable and accounts receivable. You can specify a date or time by using the DATE or TIME function or by typing it directly into a cell using a format Excel recognizes as a date or time, such as 11/15/92.

Two other functions, NOW and TODAY, enable you to quickly enter today's date into your worksheet as a serial number. Then you only need to format the number as a date. In addition, you can format NOW to display the time you entered it into your worksheet. Don't forget to include a set of empty parentheses for these functions.

 Use Edit ⇨ Copy and Edit ⇨ Paste Special (with the Values option) to freeze the date or time as a result of the NOW and TODAY functions. NOW and TODAY update each time you open or manually calculate your worksheet.

Finding data

Excel has a number of functions that enable you to select an item from a table of data. For example the CHOOSE(*index_num,value1,valuex*) function selects a value from a table based on *index_num*. For example, if *index_num* is three, CHOOSE selects *value3*:

```
=CHOOSE(3,5,10,15,20) = 15
```

CHOOSE returns the name of the day with this formula, if cell A1 contains a date:

```
=CHOOSE(MOD(A1,7),"Sat","Sun","Mon","Tues","Wed","Thu","Fri")
```

If you need an exact match

If you need your worksheet to look up a number and match it exactly with its counterpart number, HLOOKUP and VLOOKUP may not yield the right answer. The reason is that these two functions scan for an exact match with *lookup_value*, and if they can't find one, they look for the first value that is greater than *lookup_value* and then "back up" one cell. This cell may not point your worksheet to the right data item.

For example, suppose that you prepare a monthly report of actual vs. planned sales. You have an Excel worksheet set up with your plan amounts by product but have to wait until month-end to enter actual sales. Furthermore, your company is a bit behind the technology curve; you don't have the ability to directly download this data from your company's mainframe computer into Excel.

Fortunately, however, you're on good terms with your MIS department, and once a month they give you a disk with the information you need. But now what? Do you use a printout to visually match and then manually enter the actual data next to its corresponding plan amount? If you're

dealing with several hundred products, and some products with sales without a plan (such as a discontinued product), manually entering this data is a long and tedious process and not the best use of your time. And VLOOKUP in this case doesn't always return the correct answer.

You need a turbocharged version of VLOOKUP, as illustrated in the accompanying figure. The IF formula in the figure first checks whether the plan part number equals the actual part number by using the first VLOOKUP function. If so, then the actual data is selected for that part, using the second VLOOKUP function. If not, NA is entered into the cell, letting you know an actual value doesn't exist for that part. You can bring the sales data into your worksheet with Edit ➪ Copy and Edit ➪ Paste or, better yet, keep it in its own separate worksheet file.

Excel heavies will recognize that you can accomplish the same task by using the INDEX function with a MATCH argument. Either formula works fine, but you can share the IF formula with your spreadsheet friends who have Excel envy.

EX_MATCH.XLS						
	A	B	C	D	E	F	G
1							
2	Part ID	Plan	Actual		Part ID	Actual	
3	1001	50	55		1001	55	
4	1002	60	59		1002	59	
5	1003	70	40		1003	40	
6	1004	80	#N/A				
7							
8	Formula in cell C3:	=IF(A3=VLOOKUP(E3,range,1),VLOOKUP(E3,range,2),NA())					
9							
10	range	=$E$3:$F$5					

A turbocharged version of VLOOKUP.

HLOOKUP and VLOOKUP return data from a table based on a lookup value. They function similarly, but HLOOKUP scans tables horizontally and VLOOKUP vertically. Their syntax is:

```
HLOOKUP(lookup_value,table_array,row_index_num)

VLOOKUP(lookup_value,table_array,col_index_num)
```

The HLOOKUP function scans the top row of *table_array* until it finds *lookup_value*; then it looks down the same column to the row defined in *row_index_num*. The top row must be in numeric or alphabetic ascending order.

VLOOKUP, on the other hand, scans the far-left column of *table_array* until it finds *lookup_value*; then it looks across the same row to the column defined in *col_index_num*. The far-left column must be in numeric or alphabetic ascending order.

In both cases, Excel scans the top row and far-left column for each respective function and searches for the largest value that is less than or equal to *lookup_value*. Also, Excel refers to the rows in an HLOOKUP and columns in a VLOOKUP beginning with the number 1. Figure 11-10 shows an example of the VLOOKUP function in cell B4, which returned the value 0.075 from the range named `table`, A7:D12. The `Commission` amount, $900, in cell B5 is based on the $12,000 sale from the `Product` category 2, multiplied by 0.075 (75 percent).

Using general math functions

These functions are general-purpose in nature but are of a type that you won't appreciate fully until you need them:

Task	Function	Example	Result
Find the absolute value of a number	ABS	=ABS(−30)	30
Round to the integer portion of a number	INT	=INT(3.99)	3
Find the remainder in division	MOD	=MOD(5,3)	2
Round a number	ROUND	=ROUND(3.99,1)	4.0
Find the square root of a number	SQRT	=SQRT(144)	12
Find the integer portion of a number	TRUNC	=TRUNC(3.99)	3

	A	B	C	D	E	F	G	H
1			Formulas in column B					
2	Sale	$12,000.00						
3	Product	2						
4	Rate		0.075	=VLOOKUP(B2,table,B3)				
5	Commission	$900.00	=B2*B4					
6								
7	Sales category	1	2	3				
8	$2,500	0.030	0.040	0.050				
9	$5,000	0.040	0.050	0.060				
10	$7,500	0.050	0.060	0.075				
11	$10,000	0.075	0.070	0.080				
12	$12,500	0.080	0.080	0.085				
13								
14	table	=$A$7:$D$12						
15								
16								

VLOOKUP.XLS

Figure 11-10: VLOOKUP can automatically locate the correct value from a table based on the arguments you specify.

INT and TRUNC function similarly. INT rounds down to the nearest integer, and TRUNC removes the decimal portion of the number entirely. INT and TRUNC are different, however, in their treatment of negative numbers: INT(–6.4) equals –7, and TRUNC(–6.4) equals –6.

If you need the root of a number other than the square root, use the following formula:

```
=number^(1/root)
```

where *number* is the value you want the root of and *root* is the nth root. For example, =540^(1/6) is the sixth root of 540, or 2.8536. Remember, you can use cell references in the formula in place of actual numbers.

Examining a useful text function

Of the several text functions, you may find TEXT one of the most useful. TEXT enables you to change a value to text with a specific format. For example,

```
=TEXT(-1200,"$#,##00;(#,##00)")
```

displays ($1,200.00) as a text entry. TEXT is helpful when you want to create custom dialog boxes and need numbers as text.

Create a worksheet with frequently used format codes. In this manner, you can copy them to your active worksheet and reference them as an argument and not have to type them manually each time you enter a TEXT function.

Considerations when using functions

The key to successful function use is planning ahead on what you want to do. Are you summing a range or calculating subtotals? In this instance, the SUM function and a formula are the ways to go. Do you need a formula when its respective value will do? You can reduce calculation time and memory usage by substituting your formulas with values using Edit ⇨ Copy and Edit ⇨ Paste Special (with the Values option). In summary, creating worksheets is like doing home improvements; you want to use the right function for the right job.

Summary

▶ Functions are built-in Excel formulas that calculate results that would be difficult or impossible with a formula.

▶ Excel contains 11 classes of more than 100 functions.

▶ Functions in most cases require arguments, or information, to calculate a result. Arguments can be values, cell or range references, named ranges, formulas, other functions, and logical or error values.

▶ You enter a function by typing it or using the Formula ⇨ Paste Function command. You can also enter functions by copying them with Edit ⇨ Copy and Edit ⇨ Paste, using the Edit ⇨ Fill commands, or dragging on the cell's Drag-and-Drop indicator.

▶ The Autosum tool on the toolbar enables you to total values quickly.

▶ Press Shift+F3 to display the Paste Function dialog box and quickly select the function you need.

▶ Excel's on-line help system offers help for each individual worksheet function. Press F1 and then choose Worksheet Functions to see a list of function categories. From there, you can select the function name you need help on.

Chapter 12
Formatting
Spreadsheet Output

In this chapter . . .

▶ The advantages of on-screen formatting.

▶ Detailed information on using different fonts and typefaces.

▶ How to add lines, borders, shading, and other features to your worksheets.

▶ Miscellaneous tips, techniques, and things to watch out for.

Excel goes well beyond providing you with quick and accurate calculations; you can apply all sorts of drop shadows, colors, shading, lines, and fonts to your worksheets that not only make them easier to understand, but also draw attention to your worksheets and the story you want to tell.

In Chapter 7 you learned how to change the appearance of your worksheet data by specifying alignment and number formatting options. This chapter is the sequel that deals with customizing the appearance of your worksheet — how you can apply stylistic formatting to your spreadsheets for dramatic or attention-getting results. If you're new to Excel or haven't used a publishing add-in with your previous spreadsheet, this chapter is about as close to required reading as you'll get. Excel, Windows, and other GUI-program pros will be traveling familiar territory here, but you never know when you'll unearth a useful nugget — so don't go away.

The WYSIWYG Advantage

Back in the old days (which wasn't that long ago), a spreadsheet displayed one color (green or white) on a dark background. You could draw attention to selected ranges, however, by increasing the *intensity* of that one color. Needless to say, after a long day of spreadsheeting, this setup was a little rough on the eyes.

Printing had its own set of challenges. Because your printer is in a sense a computer (remember, it has its own memory but receives data through a cable as opposed to a keyboard or disk), getting exactly on paper what was on-screen was a tedious process because the computer and printer were often singing from different song books. Each used its own technology, which forced you to format a worksheet on-screen, print it on paper, look at the printout, change the formatting on-screen (page length, margins, headers, footers, and so on), hope that it's right, print it again, and on and on.

The advent of the Apple Macintosh, OS/2 Presentation Manager, and Microsoft Windows has changed all that. Besides offering you a more attractive screen display, these computer operating systems provide a WYSIWYG (pronounced WIZ-zy-wig) capability, or "what you see is what you get." This term simply means that your screen display is a very close approximation of what will come out on paper. So the boxes and shading you apply to your worksheet as displayed on-screen will be reproduced on paper by your printer. In short, it's no-nonsense printing.

You don't have to do anything to take advantage of WYSIWYG; you can create, use, and print your worksheets as you always have, but now you won't need to repetitively print them to determine whether they're what you had in mind. Instead, you have a whole arsenal of style tools that can add pizzazz to worksheets, which includes fonts, lines, shading, and colors. These formatting tools are explained next.

What Is a Font?

If you're coming over from the character-based computing world, you may be asking yourself just that. A *font*, simply, is the shape, size, and weight of the letters and values you want to display. You can choose from many shapes of fonts. For example, telephone books commonly use a font similar to one known as Lotica, and newspapers use Times Roman. These font names have their origin in the typefaces printers would use to print a newspaper or book. So referring to fonts as typefaces isn't uncommon

You can change the default font by editing your `excel 4.ini` file, located in your Windows directory. Use a text editor such as Notepad and locate the section labeled `[Microsoft Excel]`. Insert a line with the font name and size you want to use as the default. For example, if you want to use a fixed-space font that's smaller than normal, enter a line such as `Font=Courier New, 8`. Make sure that you actually have this font available. When you start Excel, this font is the new default.

A font also has more than one size, and the larger the point size, the larger the font.

Figure 12-1:
Members of
the Helvetica
family, in 10-
and 12-point
sizes.

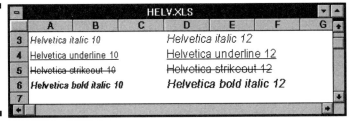

Other characteristics can affect the display of your selected font. You can also use an italic or a boldface font, and a font that is *serif* (pronounced SAIR-if). A serif font has short lines at the upper and lower ends of the strokes of a character, usually at an angle. In this book, the text you're reading now is a serif font. Most Excel users, however, prefer to use the corresponding font that is *sans* (without) *serif*. The headings and subheadings in this book use a sans serif font. You can also mix and match font characteristics. Figure 12-1 shows one font, Helvetica, in 10 and 12 points, with several different attributes, also referred to as a *font family*. The fonts available to you depend on your printer, your version of Windows, and any additional software installed in your computer.

Available fonts may change, depending on the paper orientation (Landscape or Portrait) selected through File ⇨ Page Setup.

Using fonts in your worksheet couldn't be easier, as you'll find out next.

Applying Fonts

You can use up to a maximum of 256 fonts per worksheet, but unless you're going for some sort of "ugly worksheet" record, you're better off sticking with only a few at a time. You have several ways to add additional fonts or change their attributes in your worksheets:

- Commands, accessed through the menu bar or by clicking the left mouse button

- The toolbar

- Shortcut keys

- Styles (discussed later in the chapter)

Before you begin mixing and matching fonts, note that applying fonts is no different from any other worksheet procedure; first select the cell or range for which you want to make a font change. The various methods are explained in the sections that follow.

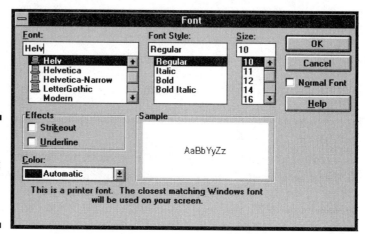

Figure 12-2: You can use the Font dialog box to select the fonts and attributes you want to use.

Remember, you can apply fonts and other formatting to noncontiguous ranges, such as in a report that contains subtotals. Mouse users can do this procedure by pressing and dragging on the first range and then holding down the Ctrl key and pressing and dragging on subsequent ranges.

Selecting fonts with command menus

Applying fonts via Excel's menu system is done from the Format menu. To apply fonts in this manner, perform the following steps:

Steps: Apply fonts from the Format menu

Step 1. Select the cell or range to which you want to apply the font.

Step 2. Choose Format or click the right mouse button.

Step 3. Choose Font and the dialog box in Figure 12-2 appears.

Step 4. Select the font you want from the Font list box or the attribute you want to change from the Size and Color list boxes. Check (or uncheck) the attribute(s) you want from the Effects box.

Step 5. Choose OK or press Enter.

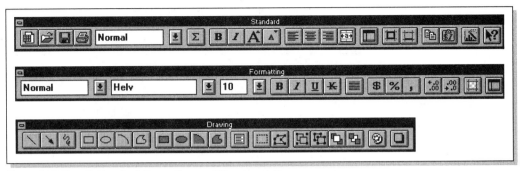

Figure 12-3: Excel's Standard, Formatting, and Drawing toolbars.

To apply fonts from the shortcut menu, position the mouse pointer anywhere over the selected range and then click the right mouse button. Choosing Font from the menu displays the Font dialog box.

If you want to start over after changing fonts for your selected range, check the Normal Font check box to return to the default font style.

As you select fonts and attributes, keep your eyes on the Sample box. Excel displays how the text will look with the options you selected. If you don't like what you see, you can change it before applying it to the selected range.

If the selection includes more than one font, the Sample box is empty because Excel doesn't know which font to show you.

Selecting fonts with the toolbar

The toolbar is a quick-access method for mouse users to apply fonts and attributes to worksheets. Select the cell or range containing the data you want to change the appearance of and then click any combination of icons for Bold, Italic, and Increase or Decrease font size (these icons appear directly below Options on the command menu bar.). If you increase or decrease the size of your fonts using the toolbar icons, Excel changes their size one point per click. If you display the Formatting toolbar, shown in Figure 12-3 along with the Standard and Drawing toolbars, you can also specify underlining, strikeout, font type, and size which are pull-down menus similar to the Style pull-down menu.

Selecting fonts with shortcut keys

If you prefer to keep your hands on the keyboard, you can use the following shortcut keys to quickly format a selected range:

Format	Shortcut keys
Normal font	Ctrl+1
Bold	Ctrl+B
Italic	Ctrl+I
Underline	Ctrl+U
Strikeout	Ctrl+5

Note that, except for the Normal attribute, these shortcut keys act as a toggle. For example, you can turn boldface on and off by repeatedly pressing Ctrl+B. You can also access the following pull-down menus with these key combinations:

Toolbar	Pull-down menu	Shortcut keys
Standard	Style list	Ctrl+S
Formatting	Font name	Ctrl+P
Formatting	Font size	Ctrl+F

Excel displays the Standard toolbar (the rectangle of icons below the command menu bar and above the Formula bar) by default. Choose Options ➪ Toolbars, select Formatting, and then select Show to display the Formatting toolbar.

After you activate the pull-down menu (the first choice is highlighted when you do so), use Alt+down arrow to display the pull-down menu so you can choose the style or type and size of font you need.

Some formatting may cause cell contents not to be displayed. If this is the case, widen the column (by dragging on the line separating your worksheet's column letters or using Format ➪ Column Width) or choose another format option.

Shading Ranges and Drawing Lines _____

From elementary school we all remember drawing a line between the last number in a column of numbers and its total. If you've used a spreadsheet other than Excel, you may have placed a dashed line in a cell directly above cells that contained a subtotal or total. With Excel, you have an elegant way of drawing lines below or on any side of a cell or range. When used with effective shading, lines added to your worksheet can make important areas of your application stand out. These tools are discussed in the sections that follow.

Figure 12-4: The Border dialog box enables you to choose which sides of your range you want bordered.

Drawing lines

Drawing single and double underlines draws attention to subtotals and totals and helps anyone reading your worksheets use them properly. You can add a line along any side of a cell or range which is known as *bordering*. You can also draw a line along the outside edges of a cell or range, which is known as *outlining*.

Lines are easier to see and more effective if you turn off the display of gridlines with the Options ⇨ Display command.

To add lines to a cell or range, select the cell(s), then choose the Format ⇨ Border command. When you do, the dialog box in Figure 12-4 appears. Choose the sides of the cell or range you want bordered from the Border box and then choose the type of border from the Style box. The style of the line is displayed next to the corresponding border in the dialog box. Figure 12-5 illustrates the available border styles.

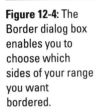

Figure 12-5: Choose from these border styles to draw lines around your ranges.

At this time you can also choose a color for your border from the Color drop-down list box in the Border dialog box. Click the the Color down arrow or press Alt+C and then Alt+down arrow to select the color for your border.

Don't close that dialog box yet. The Shade check box gives you the option of shading your selected range, which is explained next.

Applying shading

Shading, in combination with bordering, enables you to draw attention to important areas in your worksheet. You may want to shade column labels, totals, or other cells that display results of interest. Two ways are available to apply shading to your worksheet.

Option 1: Format ⇨ Patterns

The Format ⇨ Patterns command enables you to apply a black-and-white pat-terned shading to a range, or a pattern with a foreground and background in color. After you select the range to shade, choose the Format ⇨ Patterns command. The dialog box shown in Figure 12-6 appears. For black-and-white or color patterns, choose a pattern from the Pattern pull-down list. Then, for colored patterns, choose a color from the Foreground and Background pull-down lists. As with choosing a font, watching the Sample box as you select patterns and colors helps you find the combination that's right for your spreadsheet.

You can display up to 16 colors in your worksheet at one time. If you prefer a color that's not available on the Foreground and Background pull-down color lists, use the Options ⇨ Color Palette command to modify your worksheet's color choices.

Outline or border: Which one for you?

Adding a line around a cell or range can be confusing; do you use a border or an outline? An easy way to determine what you need is to decide whether you want a line around *every* side of your cells, or just the outside sides, for the selected range. Then just follow the guidelines in this table:

Range	Border	Option(s)
Single cell	A line around all edges	Outline
Multiple cells	A line around all edges	Left, Right, Top, Bottom
Multiple cells	A line around outside edge only	Outline

Figure 12-6:
Customize your shading by using the options in the Patterns dialog box.

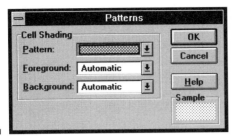

If you assign a color to a shade pattern and use a black-and-white printer, your printed output may contain unexpected results. The best way to see how your printer handles color is to do some tests. For example, you may want to set up a spreadsheet with a matrix showing all colors in columns and all shades in rows to test the possible combinations when you print.

Option 2: The Shade box

Recall that after you choose the Format ⇨ Borders command, the dialog box that appears has a Shade option. If you check this box, Excel shades the selected range with a light shade pattern (black and white). After you select OK or press Enter, Excel shades the range.

Which method you use depends on your needs. If you want to apply several shading patterns or shading with color to your worksheet, use Format ⇨ Patterns. If you only need a light shade, specifying borders and a light shade is a simple one-step process with Format ⇨ Border. Later in this chapter you learn how to name a set of styles so you can apply them to ranges quickly.

Your cell entries may become somewhat obscured if you apply shading to them. If you haven't already done so, select the cells in the shaded region and then boldface them.

Dropping a shadow

The advent of desktop publishing brought us many important new capabilities, one of which is drop shadows. Drop shadows enable you to highlight your worksheet titles (or other ranges) in a dramatic way, as shown in Figure 12-7. As you can see, a drop shadow combines lines and shading to produce a three-dimensional effect. Remember, of course, that in Excel drop shadows apply to boxes, not to fonts.

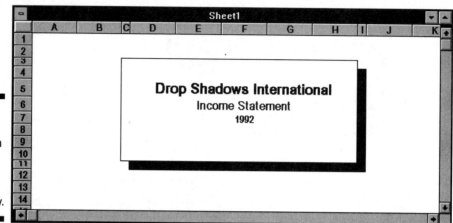

Figure 12-7:
A drop
shadow can
wow your
audience
when used
appropriately.

You can use two methods to create a drop shadow. The first method is to display the Drawing toolbar using the Options ⇨ Toolbars command. Next, select the range of cells you want drop-shadowed and then click the Drop shadow icon (the last icon on the Drawing toolbar). Excel creates a drop shadow around the cells you've selected. You can enter or edit the data contained within the drop shadow like any other data in your worksheet.

Drop shadows created this way actually consist of a graphic object placed over the cells of your worksheet, not as entries in cells. Think of graphic objects being placed on a piece of plexiglass that's over your worksheet. As such, you can move the object anywhere on your worksheet, delete it, or format it, much like numbers or text. See Chapter 16 for information about moving and sizing graphic objects.

With the second method, you use Format ⇨ Borders ⇨ Outline to draw a single line around the range containing your data and then adjust the width of the far-left column inside the range and the column to the immediate right of the range with the Format ⇨ Column Width command, reducing their widths to 1. Next, reduce the height of the row immediately below the range and the first row of the drop shadow, with Format ⇨ Row Height to 9. Use Format ⇨ Patterns and apply a solid shade to the column to the right and to the row below the range so it appears similar to the one in Figure 12-7. You can control the amount of shadow by adjusting the row height and column width.

You can call attention to a cell or range in your worksheet by adding lines, arrows, or even freehand drawings. Refer to Chapter 16 for detailed information about adding graphics objects to your worksheet.

Using Styles

If you find yourself applying the same combination of fonts, lines, and shading repetitively in your worksheets, creating and using named styles is to your advantage. Named styles save time and reduce formatting errors by applying formats you specify in a single procedure. If your firm uses company-wide formats and logos, you can create and name them so your worksheets have a standard appearance matching other company documents.

The *real* advantage of styles, however, is that you can change a component of a style, and all the cells with that style change to reflect it. Say, for example, that you applied a particular style to a dozen or so cells scattered throughout your worksheet. Later, you realize that these cells should really be 14 points rather than 12 points. Rather than change each one, just edit the style. All cells with that particular style change automatically.

You can have up to a maximum of six style attributes associated with a named style:

- Number format
- Font (type and size)
- Alignment
- Border
- Pattern
- Protection

Naming styles has similar advantages as naming ranges and provides you with another productivity tool. You learn how to put styles to work for you next.

Applying worksheet styles

Applying styles is another easy process, and several ways are available to do it. First, as always, select the cell or range you want to apply the style to. Then choose one of the methods that follow.

Applying styles from the toolbar

Click the Style list down arrow on the default toolbar and then click the name of the desired style (few are available until you define them). Keyboard users can select a style by pressing Ctrl+S or Alt+' and by pressing the down arrow key to highlight the style name. When you press Enter, the style is applied to your cell or range. Alternatively, after you press Ctrl+S or Alt+', pressing Alt+down arrow pulls down the style name list so you can view all available named styles for quick selection.

Figure 12-8: The
dialog box that
appears when you
choose Format ⇨
Style — your
gateway to creating
named styles.

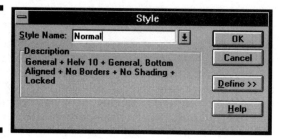

Applying styles from the menu bar

After selecting a cell or range to format, choose the Format ⇨ Style command.
When the dialog box in Figure 12-8 appears, select or type in the name of the
style you want to use in the Style Name text box. Choosing OK or pressing Enter
applies your selected style to the range.

Applying a style overwrites any formatting already assigned to the range, unless
the style does not include that attribute. For example, if you have a shaded
range and apply the Percent style, the shading remains unscathed.

Creating styles

Every business situation is unique, and you're likely to have a need for a named
style that doesn't come with Excel out of the box. Creating custom-named
styles, like applying them, is a straightforward process, and a number of ways
are available to get the job done.

Setting a good example

If you've formatted a cell with all the attributes you want and would like to
apply it to other cells in your worksheet, you can use the formatted cell as an
example. After you have the cell or range formatted the way you want, be sure
it's selected and then click the Style box on the Standard toolbar (keyboard
users should press Ctrl+S or Alt+') Type the name of the new style and press
Enter, or press Esc if you make a mistake or change your mind and want to start
over.

If you prefer working with commands, you can use the Format Style dialog box
to define a new style name. From the dialog box, type the new name in the Style
Name text box. When you choose OK or press Enter, Excel will include the new
style name in its repertoire of styles.

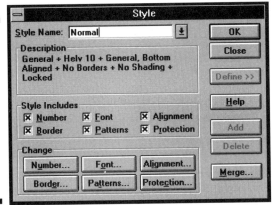

Figure 12-9:
Choosing
Define from
the Style
dialog box
expands the
box so you
can
customize
your named
styles.

Choosing between defining a new style name through example and the toolbar or through the Format ⇨ Style command is personal preference. Either method works fine. The Format ⇨ Style command, however, enables you to see the attributes assigned to the name in the description box — something you may like if you're just beginning your spreadsheet journey with Excel.

Revisiting the Style dialog box

You can use the Style dialog box to create a new style from scratch (that is, not from an example cell or range). Creating a style in this fashion enables you to select the attributes you want. If you're a new Excel user, this method may be the easiest way for you.

To create a style in this manner, select Format ⇨ Style. When the dialog box appears, type the name for your style in the Style Name text box and then choose Define. The dialog box then expands, as shown in Figure 12-9, so you can choose the attributes you want from the Style Includes box. All attributes are selected by default; uncheck the box of the attribute you don't want included in your style.

Choosing a button from the Change box enables you to specify the option you want for that particular attribute. For example, if you select Font, the Font dialog box appears so you can choose the type and size of font you need. When you're finished selecting font attributes and have closed the Font dialog box, you are returned to the Style dialog box.

Excel does *not* warn you if you attempt to define a name that already exists. A good idea is to scan through all the named styles from the Style Name pull-down list by clicking on the Style Name arrow or by pressing Alt+S and then Alt+down arrow.

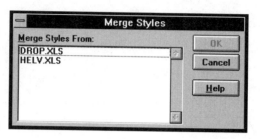

Figure 12-10: From the Merge Styles dialog box you can select a source worksheet that contains the styles you want to copy to your open worksheet.

After you've selected formatting options, you can continue creating more styles by selecting Add, or you can choose Close to add the style to your formatting arsenal.

You aren't required to select a range before using Format ➪ Style to create a style, but if you do, and choose OK or press Enter after you've defined your style, Excel applies your new style to the selected range.

Merging styles

If you feel confident with your Excel skills, you can create a new style by merging existing styles. When you merge styles, you take named styles from a "source" worksheet and merge them into another "target" worksheet. Depending on the style you want to transfer to the other worksheet, and if a style of the same name doesn't exist in the second worksheet, you can freely copy the style from the first worksheet. If the name of the style exists in both worksheets, however, merging the style from the first to the second overwrites the style in the second, so be sure that this is really what you want to do. Other than this caution, merging styles is a relatively simple process. First, open the source and target worksheets — the worksheet that contains the named styles and the one to receive the style. Make the worksheet to receive the style the active worksheet.

Next, choose Format ➪ Style; from the Style dialog box that appears, choose Define and then Merge. Select the name of your source worksheet from the Merge Styles From list box in the Merge Styles dialog box, as shown in Figure 12-10, and choose OK. If you are merg-ing a named style that doesn't exist in the target worksheet, Excel completes the operation by copying all named styles to the target worksheet, and you're returned to the Style dialog box.

If you want to merge a named style that exists in both worksheets, Excel displays the warning message shown in Figure 12-11. Here are your choices:

Figure 12-11: Red alert! Excel asks you to confirm whether you really want to copy a named style from the source worksheet that already exists in your target worksheet.

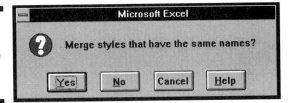

Option	Result
Yes	The named style from the source worksheet replaces the same named style in the target worksheet.
No	Only dissimilar named styles are merged from the source worksheet to the target worksheet.
Cancel	No styles are transferred, and the Style dialog box is redisplayed.

Changing a style

At times you may need to update your named styles for changes. For example, suppose that you work for a firm that produces component parts for ion-drive engines for spacecraft. Your firm is acquired by another, larger firm, but later it sells your firm to a competitor, who has the wherewithal and vision for this untested but promising propulsion method. You want your worksheets to conform to company standards, and to keep up with the rapid ownership changes, so you modify your named styles and avoid the rigmarole of recreating them.

When you redefine your styles, you not only avoid reinventing the wheel, but Excel rummages through your worksheet and applies the style modifications to those cells with that style. So you save time both ways. As with creating a style, you have two options for changing an existing style: by example or by menu commands.

Changing styles by example

Little difference exists between redefining a style and creating one through an example cell or range. To redefine an existing style, select a cell formatted with the style you want to change. Then apply the formats you want to use as the new style. Next, activate the Style box on the Standard toolbar. Select the name

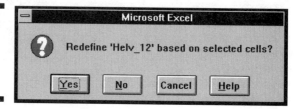

Figure 12-12: Another heads-up: Excel is checking whether you're sure that you want to redefine a named style from an example cell.

of the style you want to change and then select one of the following alternatives from the dialog box (as shown in Figure 12-12):

Option	Result
Yes	Redefines existing style as specified.
No	Retains style as defined and reapplies it to the example cell.
Cancel	Halts named style modification process with no changes made.

If you don't want to use the toolbar to modify a named style, select an example cell; then choose Format ⇨ Style and select the name of the named style from the Style Name text box.

Changing styles by command

Redefining a style, like creating one using commands, enables you to see the attributes assigned to the format. In this manner, if you're new to Excel or have a style with extensive formats associated with it, you can set your desired formats with confidence and precision.

Start by issuing the Format ⇨ Style command and then choosing Define. Choose the name of the style from the Style Name text box. Uncheck the Style Includes boxes that correspond to the attributes you don't want your style to contain and select the Change buttons to customize the formats you do want your style to contain. Finally, after you've selected the formatting options you want for your revised style, you can continue creating or redefining other styles by selecting Add, or you can choose Close to wrap it up (to add the style to your list of available formats but not apply it).

You can, if you want, redefine Excel's default style, Normal. If you do, all cells in your worksheet *without* formatting are formatted with your new Normal style. This method is a quick way to make global font or size changes.

Deleting style names

If you no longer have a need for a named style, you may want to consider putting it out to pasture, to reduce the possibility of a formatting error. To delete a style name, choose Format ➪ Style and then the name you want to delete from the Style Name text box. Next, choose Define and then Delete.

At this point, you have the opportunity to format any selected cells by choosing another named style and then choosing OK, or applying the Normal format by choosing OK.

You cannot delete Excel's Normal style, but you can change it.

Automated Range Formatting _____

If you're in a rush (and who isn't these days) and need to create an attractive report quickly, consider having Excel format your selected ranges for you. Excel's automatic range formatting is a feature new to version 4 and is similar in function to named styles — except you can't create your own customized automatic formats. Automatic formats contain these attributes:

- Number format

- Font (type and size)

- Alignment

- Border

- Pattern

- Row height/column width

- Colors

Suppose, for example, that you have a worksheet similar to the simple one shown in Figure 12-13. By selecting a range and then using the Format ➪ AutoFormat command, you can transform your worksheet to the one shown in Figure 12-14. If you don't care for that particular style, you can choose from ten others or select the attributes you don't want to apply. Putting Format ➪ AutoFormat in action is explained next.

Automatic formatting looks best if you turn off the display of worksheet gridlines with Options ➪ Display ➪ Gridlines.

	A	B	C	D	E	F	G	H
				NON_AF.XLS				
1								
2			Expenses	Income after				
3	Month	Gross sale	and taxes	tax				
4	Jan-92	654032	606813	47219				
5	Feb-92	668321	619810	48511				
6	Mar-92	676954	625543	51411				
7	Apr-92	678684	623170	55514				
8	May-92	697576	637658	59918				
9	Jun-92	699891	639501	60390				
10	Jul-92	708426	645721	62705				
11	Aug-92	712081	647699	64382				
12	Sep-92	715034	647152	67882				
13	Oct-92	718441	647803	70638				
14	Nov-92	734638	659129	75509				
15	Dec-92	740057	660572	79485				
16	Total	8404135	7660571	743564				
17								
18								

Figure 12-13: A typical monthly income report before it is dressed up.

	A	B	C	D	E	F	G	H
				AF.XLS				
1								
2			Expenses	Income after				
3	Month	Gross sales	and taxes	tax				
4	Jan-92	$654,032.00	$606,813.00	$47,219.00				
5	Feb-92	668,321.00	619,810.00	48,511.00				
6	Mar-92	676,954.00	625,543.00	51,411.00				
7	Apr-92	678,684.00	623,170.00	55,514.00				
8	May-92	697,576.00	637,658.00	59,918.00				
9	Jun-92	699,891.00	639,501.00	60,390.00				
10	Jul-92	708,426.00	645,721.00	62,705.00				
11	Aug-92	712,081.00	647,699.00	64,382.00				
12	Sep-92	715,034.00	647,152.00	67,882.00				
13	Oct-92	718,441.00	647,803.00	70,638.00				
14	Nov-92	734,638.00	659,129.00	75,509.00				
15	Dec-92	740,057.00	660,572.00	79,485.00				
16	Total	$8,404,135.00	$7,660,571.00	$743,564.00				
17								
18								

Figure 12-14: The monthly income report after the make-over, courtesy of Format ⇨ AutoFormat (Financial 1).

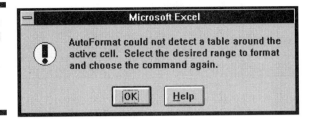

Figure 12-15: This dialog box appears if you don't specify a range and Excel can't detect a table to automatically format. Take another crack at it by choosing OK, selecting a range, and choosing Format ⇨ AutoFormat.

Applying automatic formats

Applying an automatic format starts out like any other formatting process; you select the range you want to format, but you must select a multicell range (if you do not select a range, Excel displays the warning message in Figure 12-15 and asks you to try again). Choose OK, select a range, and then choose Format ⇨ AutoFormat. Excel displays the dialog box in Figure 12-16.

Think of the Format ⇨ AutoFormat command as a "smart" formatting command. That is, if you do not select a range but have your cell pointer located anywhere within a range bordered by empty rows and columns, Format ⇨ AutoFormat selects the range for you, determines detail and summary ranges, and applies predefined formatting options appropriately.

Choose a format from the Table Format list box. As you scroll through the list, watch the Sample box to see how the various formats will display your data. When you find the one you want, choose OK. Excel applies the format to the selected range.

You can apply the last AutoFormat table format by selecting the icon from the Standard or Formatting toolbar. (The icon is the one below and a little to the left of Help in the menu bar.)

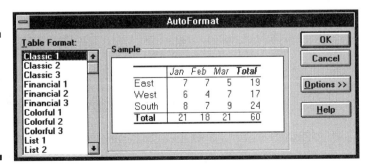

Figure 12-16: Numerous automatic format combinations are available through the AutoFormat dialog box.

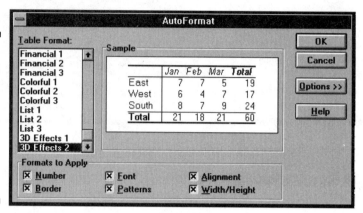

Figure 12-17: The AutoFormat dialog box expands when you choose Options so you can tailor your autoformatting to your (or your supervisor's) liking.

If you get cold feet, you can reverse the effects of the Format ⇨ AutoFormat command by choosing Edit ⇨ Undo immediately after the command.

Selecting automatic format attributes

You may have ranges in your worksheet already partially formatted and want to use automatic formatting to finish the job. For example, you like the Classic 1 format but want to retain the column widths you've set. You can have the best of both worlds — formatting you've applied and formatting applied by AutoFormat — all applied to the same range.

Select the range and choose Format ⇨ AutoFormat, just like you do in a normal AutoFormat operation. Next, however, click the Options button. The AutoFormat dialog box expands to show you the attributes you can turn off, as shown in Figure 12-17. Uncheck the box corresponding to the format you do not want applied (in the previous example, you'd uncheck Width/Height). Choosing OK overlays the automatic formats over the formats already in place on your selected range.

You can't modify automatic formats like you can named styles (we'll probably have to wait for Excel 5 for that). If you want a particular format, apply it to your range first and then let AutoFormat loose on it.

You can also combine Table Formats to create the one you want. For example, suppose that you like Classic 1 and Colorful 2 automatic formats. Select the range you want to format, choose Format ⇨ AutoFormat, select Classic 1, and then choose OK. Now, select Format ⇨ AutoFormat ⇨ Options and uncheck the Border and Font options. Excel applies the Classic 1 formats with the colors of Colorful 2 format.

In most cases, you'll want to set your own column widths rather than have AutoFormat do this task for you (they tend to get too narrow). If, however, you want AutoFormat to change column widths or row heights, leave the Width/Height box checked.

Because you can't change the colors of the AutoFormat ➪ Table Format options, apply the colors you want to the aspects of your range with Format ➪ Border, Font, and Patterns. Be sure to uncheck the appropriate box if you use a Table Format that includes colors.

If you have a worksheet that has been set up as an outline (see Chapter 23), Excel may on occasion become confused when applying an automatic format. If this is the case, choose Edit ➪ Undo, tweak your outline structure, and try again. If Excel still has problems, consider opening a new worksheet and copying a version of your original worksheet to the new one that is easier on AutoFormat.

Guidelines for Formatting Spreadsheets _____

The final section of this chapter is an opportunity for us to share some of our spreadsheet formatting experience in the form of miscellaneous tips and guidelines. Although these points are general in nature, you may find them useful in your quest for stylish spreadsheets:

■ Don't go overboard with the number of style attributes you apply to your worksheet. A worksheet loaded up with too many fonts, colors, and shading looks garish and unprofessional, and your supervisor will wonder what you've been doing all afternoon. In general, limit the number of font types to two, but you can be a little more liberal with font sizes. The bottom line is that you want to create worksheets with substance that have a clear, crisp look, much like the Classic 1 automatic format.

■ For the best shading effect, surround shaded ranges with a border.

■ For better visibility, boldface cell entries that have a light shading applied to them.

■ If you add borders or underlines, you'll probably want to turn off the display of gridlines with the Options ➪ Display command. And, of course, you'll want to remove gridlines from your printed output. Use the File ➪ Page Setup command.

■ Emphasize important ranges, such as column labels and totals, with a light shade and a border.

■ Use the same font but in progressively smaller sizes for your worksheet titles and subtitles.

- Don't hesitate to borrow attractive numeric table formats from other sources, such as annual reports, magazines, or technical reports. You can get some good ideas from these sources.

- Use the File ➪ Print Preview command to view your worksheet on-screen before you send it off to the printer.

- Keep your printer's capabilities in mind as you add style attributes to worksheets. If you use colors, for example, a black-and-white printer may not be capable of producing exactly what you want.

- Don't use screen fonts (or sizes) that you don't have for your printer — unless, of course, you won't be printing the worksheet.

- For best appearance, center or right-align column labels over values.

- Use the Format ➪ Column Width and Format ➪ Row Height commands to fine-tune the height and width of rows and columns.

Summary

▶ WYSIWYG is a prominent feature of today's computer operating system software. WYSIWYG helps you be more productive by creating more attractive and accurate screen displays and reports, thus reducing the time required to print worksheets the way you want them.

▶ Fonts are different typefaces and come in different point sizes. You can apply different attributes to fonts, such as underlining, boldface, and italic.

▶ You apply assorted fonts to your worksheet through the Standard toolbar or the Format ➪ Font command.

▶ You can add lines to your worksheet with Format ➪ Border; you can shade ranges with Format ➪ Patterns or by checking the Shade box on the Border dialog box.

▶ The Font, Border, and Patterns dialog boxes provide options that enable you to set colors.

▶ Use the Drop Shadow icon on the Drawing toolbar to quickly add a drop shadow to your worksheet.

▶ You can use named styles to quickly apply a set of formatting options to a cell or range. Create styles through an example cell or by using Format ➪ Style.

▶ You can modify existing styles, and all cells with that particular style change automatically to reflect your changes.

▶ Format ➪ AutoFormat enables you to automatically format a range with a set of style attributes.

▶ Use discretion when you apply style attributes to worksheets.

Chapter 13
Printing Worksheets

In this chapter . . .

▶ All about printers — the various types available and some of the pros and cons of each.

▶ How to set up your printed page so it comes out like you want it.

▶ How to deal with page breaks and arrange horizontal and vertical titles.

▶ How to use the page preview feature to see what your printed output will look like.

▶ Everything you need to know to get your spreadsheet data from the screen to paper.

▶ How two Excel add-ins (Views and Reports) can help you manage complex printing chores.

▶ Miscellaneous tips to reduce the frustration level that often accompanies printing.

The goal of most spreadsheet tasks is to get something on paper, in the form of a report or handout, or simply for your own reference. To obtain this goal, of course, you need a printer. We focus on printing Excel worksheets in this chapter. Chapter 17 discusses printing Excel charts.

The simplest way to print a worksheet is to simply select File ➪ Print from the menu. Excel prints the entire worksheet, using its default settings. In some cases this setup is all you need. But more often, you'll want to change some settings and make sure that everything's the way you want it. That's what this chapter is all about.

A Few Words About Printers

Printers vary widely in their capacity to use fonts, graphics, spacing, alignment, and character formats. The appearance of your printed spreadsheets depends on the printer you use and the formatting you assign. Printers have evolved considerably over the years. They've become faster and more versatile, produce better quality output, and have even come down in price. What more could you want?

Examining printer types

The current crop of printers used with PCs follow:

Dot-matrix printers: These printers come in a variety of styles, and the output ranges from barely acceptable to great. The image is made by pressing pins against a ribbon to form dots in a matrix. The matrix size varies, so the more pins in the matrix, the higher the resolution. An advantage of dot-matrix printers is that they are impact printers and therefore can work with multipart forms. They're also relatively inexpensive.

Ink-jet printers: This class of printers produces output on a par with dot-matrix printers. Ink-jets, however, are much quieter because small dots of ink are sprayed on the page and no physical impact occurs. The printing method means that you can't use multipart forms in an ink-jet printer. Ink-jet printers are usually inexpensive. A disadvantage to some of these printers is that the ink is water-soluble and smears if it gets damp or wet.

Daisy-wheel printers: These printers were quite popular about 5 to 10 years ago because they could produce "letter quality" output at a time when laser printers were either unheard of or outrageously expensive. The image is formed

About printer drivers

Excel (and all other Windows applications) uses printer drivers as the link between your applications and your printer. Windows includes an assortment of printer drivers, and the files have a DRV extension.

A printer driver contains all the information that Windows needs to know about a specific printer — details about the hardware itself and the interface, a description of fonts, character width definitions, and the control sequences the printer uses to achieve various effects such as boldface, italic, and font changes.

If Windows includes a printer driver for your printer, you probably installed it when you ran the Windows Setup program. If you want to add an additional printer driver after you've installed Windows, you can use the Control Panel to install it (select the Printers icon). The install procedure will probably ask you to insert one or more of the Windows disks so it can transfer the printer driver to your hard drive. After you install a printer, you must configure it before you can print. See your Windows documentation or the on-line help for more information.

If Windows does not have a printer driver for your specific printer, you may still be able to print documents with Excel because most printers emulate another more popular printer such as the Epson FX or Hewlett-Packard Series II. Read your printer manual carefully to find out whether it emulates any other printer. If so, simply install that printer driver and printing should work OK. You may find a few glitches here and there, however, because most emulations aren't 100 percent accurate. You may also want to contact your printer manufacturer or Microsoft to find out whether a printer driver has been made available for your printer.

by striking a key against a ribbon, much like a typewriter. The disadvantages include slow output, noisy operation, and incapacity to print graphics. Most daisy-wheel printers have been retired from service, and Windows does not even support such printers.

Laser printers: Now the standard office printer, laser printers are available at prices starting around $600. Laser printers are fast and quiet, handle both graphics and text, and come in a variety of models. Two laser "standards" have emerged: Hewlett-Packard PCL language LaserJet printers and PostScript printers. You can't go wrong choosing either of these printers. PostScript printers are a bit more expensive than PCL printers but are more capable of handling sophisticated graphics. Laser printers can't handle multipart forms, so many offices use dot-matrix printers in addition to lasers.

Telling Windows about your printer

Printing from Excel is actually performed by Windows. Excel — like all other Windows applications — merely sends its output to a printer driver (that is, software), and Windows takes care of the details. Consequently, if you purchase a new printer, you need only configure it once, and all your Windows programs work properly with the new hardware.

Configuring your printer correctly within Windows is important. Otherwise, the output may not be what you expect, or you may not be fully utilizing the printing capability that you have.

 If your system is connected to a LAN, you should not make any changes to your printer setting unless you notify your system administrator (or someone who understands how the network is set up).

You can set up Windows for multiple printers, but only one printer at a time can be the "active" printer. You can select and configure your printer from the Windows Control Panel (a program accessible from Program Manager). You get a dialog box like the one shown in Figure 13-1. If the printer you want to use is listed in this box, make sure that it's highlighted. If it's not listed, you may be using a printer that emulates a specific printer. For example, most laser printers can emulate a Hewlett-Packard LaserJet printer. You can change the printer setting for all your Windows applications by selecting the Setup button. This action brings up another dialog box that's specific to the printer you selected.

You can also select a printer from Excel by using the File ➪ Page Setup command (select the Printer Setup button). As you'll see, Excel gives you almost complete control of your printer via its dialog boxes.

```
┌─────────────────────────────────────────────────────┐
│ ─                        Printers                     │
│ ┌─Default Printer──────────────────────┐  ┌─────────┐ │
│ │ NEC Silentwriter2 90 on LPT1:        │  │ Cancel  │ │
│ ├─Installed Printers:──────────────────┤  ├─────────┤ │
│ │ NEC Silentwriter2 90 on LPT1:     ▲  │  │ Connect...│ │
│ │                                      │  ├─────────┤ │
│ │                                      │  │ Setup...│ │
│ │                                   ▼  │  ├─────────┤ │
│ │      Set As Default Printer          │  │ Remove  │ │
│ └──────────────────────────────────────┘  ├─────────┤ │
│ ☒ Use Print Manager                        │ Add >>  │ │
│                                            ├─────────┤ │
│                                            │ Help    │ │
│                                            └─────────┘ │
└─────────────────────────────────────────────────────┘
```

Figure 13-1: Use this dialog box to select a printer. In most cases, only one printer is installed.

Working with fonts

The actual typefaces and fonts you can use in your spreadsheets depend on your printer. Printers have a selection of built-in fonts and may take plug-in cartridges or ROM cards that provide additional fonts. Still another way to get fonts is via software. You may have a program such as Adobe Type Manager (ATM) installed on your system. If so, you'll have some additional fonts available for on-screen display, as well as for printing.

If you're using Windows 3.1, you have access to additional fonts called TrueType. These fonts are scalable fonts that work with any printer. The advantage of using scalable fonts is that you can print text in any size (and also display it properly on-screen). Windows 3.1 includes five TrueType fonts: Arial (like Helvetica), Times New Roman (like Times Roman), Courier New (like Courier), Symbol, and Wingdings. These last two fonts contain special-purpose symbols and pictures.

Before You Print

Before you issue the command to send your worksheet to the printer, you'll normally want to perform a few preliminary steps.

We refer to printing worksheets throughout this chapter. The same procedures also apply to printing macro sheets. In addition, if you are displaying an Info Window (specified in the Workspace dialog box), you can print that window by making it active before issuing the File ➪ Print command.

Selecting what gets printed

Unless you tell it otherwise, Excel prints the entire active worksheet when you issue the File ➪ Print command. Included are all drawings, charts, and other objects that have been placed on the worksheet.

Because charts and drawings tend to take longer to print, in some situations you may not want to print one or more such objects. The solution is simple: Select the object you don't want to print and click the right mouse button to bring up the shortcut menu. Select Object Properties and then clear the check box that is labeled Print Object.

You can make a multiple selection of all objects that you don't want to print and then issue the command only once. To make a multiple selection, hold down Ctrl while you click the objects.

Selecting a print area

If you don't want to print the entire active worksheet area, you must set a print area. To set a print area, select the range or ranges that you want to print using the normal range selection techniques. When you're satisfied with your selection, select Options ➪ Set Print Area.

You can set a print area that consists of noncontiguous ranges by holding down the Ctrl key while you select ranges. You can also hide rows and/or columns prior to printing. Such hidden elements are not printed.

To remove a print area, select the entire worksheet by clicking the button at the intersection of the row and column borders. Then select Options ➪ Remove Print Area.

Selecting Options ➪ Set Print Area actually defines a named range called Print_Area. As with any other named range, you can modify it with the Formula ➪ Define Name command (see Figure 13-2). For example, you can increase or decrease the size of Print_Area by changing the range designation. This method is usually much easier than redefining the print area from scratch. Similarly, you can eliminate the print area simply by clicking the Delete button in the Define Name dialog box.

Setting up your page

Before you print, checking your page setup is a good idea to make sure that the margins, headers, footers, and other details are to your liking. In Excel, you do

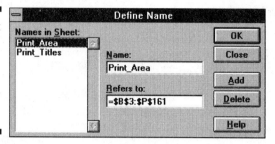

Figure 13-2: When you set a print range or specify row or column print titles, Excel stores this information in a named range, which you can easily modify.

this task with the File ⇨ Page Setup command, which brings up the dialog box shown in Figure 13-3.

Users of previous versions of Excel will note that the Page Setup dialog box is a much more efficient way of getting ready to print. Everything you may need to change is directly accessible in this dialog box.

This dialog box contains a wealth of settings that are valid for the current worksheet only and are saved along with the worksheet. The options follow:

Orientation   Select either portrait (for tall pages) or landscape (for wide pages printed sideways).

Paper   This pull-down box enables you to choose the paper size. Make sure that this setting corresponds to the paper that you're actually using.

Margins   Here you specify how wide you want each margin. The measurement unit (English or Metric) corresponds to your global Windows setting (which you can change with the Windows Control Panel program — select the International icon).

Center Horizontally   Checking this box centers your print range horizontally on the page.

Center Vertically   Checking this box centers your print range vertically on the page.

Page Order   You can choose how Excel orders your pages within the print area. This option is appropriate only for large print ranges. Normally, Excel prints from the top page of the print area down. If you prefer, you can print from the left page of the print area to the right.

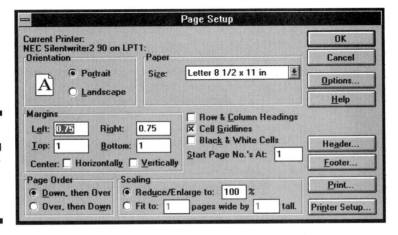

Figure 13-3: The Page Setup dialog box provides one-stop shopping for all your printing setup needs.

Scaling	If you want your printout to be larger or smaller than normal, specify a scaling factor. The valid range is 10 percent up to 400 percent (100 percent is normal size). Another option here enables you to specify how many pages to use; Excel automatically scales your output to fit.
Row & Column Headings	Check this box if you want the row numbers (1, 2, 3, and so on) and column letters (A, B, C, and so on) to appear on your printed output.
Cell Gridlines	Check this box if you want the dotted gridlines that delineate the cells to be printed. This setting has no effect on borders that you add to your worksheet and does not affect the display of gridlines on-screen.
Black & White Cells	Check this box if you want Excel to ignore any background colors or text colors that you've added. This option eliminates a common problem in which the colorful screen looks great on-screen but the printed output comes out muddy or unreadable due to poor contrast.
Start Page No.'s At	This option enables you to start your page numbering with a number other than 1.

Notice that the Page Setup dialog box has a number of buttons along the right side. These buttons take you into other dialog boxes related to printing. The Options button enables you to select your particular printer, and the Printer

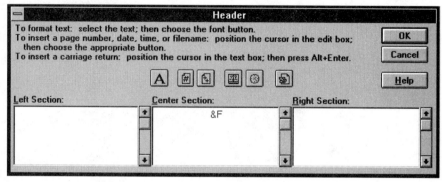

Figure 13-4:
Specifying
headers and
footers for
your printed
output has
never been
easier.

Setup button enables you to change some printer settings that will apply to all your Windows printing.

The buttons labeled Header and Footer enable you to specify information that will appear on the top (header) or bottom (footer) of each of your printed pages. Clicking these buttons brings up the dialog box shown in Figure 13-4. The same dialog box appears for both the Header and Footer buttons.

Notice that Excel provides three scrollable text boxes. The reason is that a header or footer can consist of three parts: flush-left text, centered text, and flush-right text. You simply enter the text in each box (you can leave any or all of them blank). A header or footer can consist of as many lines as you like — as evidenced by the scroll bars.

In addition to printing text that you enter here, Excel can interpret various codes in its headers and footers. For example, &P inserts the page number, &D inserts the date, and so on. Conveniently, Excel provides some icons that insert some of these codes for you. The icon with the big A on it brings up the Font dialog box, which enables you to change the appearance of selected text. This dialog box explains what the icons do. When the header and footer are to your liking, choose OK and you return to the Page Setup dialog box.

The Options button enables you to control how graphics are printed. If you find that graphics objects aren't printing well, experiment with different settings.

The Print button in the Page Setup dialog box enables you to jump to the Print dialog box (discussed shortly) without exiting the Page Setup dialog box. When you're satisfied with your page settings, choose OK to close the dialog box.

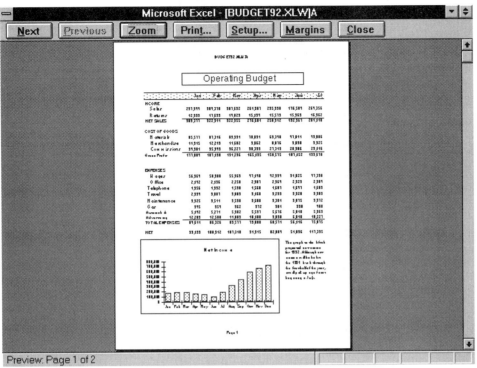

Figure 13-5: The Print Preview window also enables you to adjust margins and column widths without returning to the worksheet.

Previewing your work

Before you print, previewing your document on-screen is a good idea. You do so with the File ⇨ Print Preview command. Selecting this command opens a new window that shows a miniature version of how your printout will look. An example is shown in Figure 13-5.

The Print Preview window is a handy feature of Excel. Notice the buttons displayed at the top of the window. Here's what they do:

Next   Displays the next page. If no additional pages are available, this button is grayed. Pressing Enter or the down arrow key accomplishes the same thing. Pressing End displays the last page of your output.

Previous Displays the preceding page. If no previous pages are available, this button is grayed. Pressing the up arrow key accomplishes the same thing. Pressing Home displays the first page.

Zoom Enables you to zoom in to see more detail. You can accomplish the same thing by clicking the mouse button when the mouse pointer resembles a magnifying glass, which is any time the cursor is over the previewed page. When the preview is zoomed, you can use the scroll bars or the arrow keys to scroll through the display. Click Zoom again and it returns you to the full-page view.

Print Sends you to the Print dialog box so you can start printing your worksheet (you don't have to exit from the preview window and select the File ⇨ Print command).

Setup Brings up the Page Setup dialog box — handy if you discover that you forgot to remove the gridlines or need to make some other change.

Margins Changes the display to show margins and column borders on the preview. This is a great feature because you can drag the margin or column rules and see the effect in the preview window. For example, if you discover that one column of your worksheet will print on a page by itself, you can adjust the column widths and/or margins until enough room is available on the page to hold the column. Unfortunately, you cannot adjust row heights in the preview window.

Close Closes the preview window and returns you to your worksheet.

Controlling page breaks

You may have noticed that Excel takes care of page breaks automatically if your worksheet does not fit on one page. The File ⇨ Preview command shows you where the page breaks will occur when you print your worksheet.

After selecting this command, you'll find that your worksheet now contains some new dotted lines. These lines represent the vertical and horizontal page breaks. Understanding that these page break displays are dynamic is important; they adjust automatically when you insert or delete rows or columns, or change column widths or row heights. This convenient feature helps you spot the all-too-common occurrence of a single row or column being printed on a page by itself.

 Excel doesn't display the automatic page breaks in your worksheet until you choose the File ⇨ Print or File ⇨ Print Preview command.

You can also manually insert page breaks and override the automatic page breaks made by Excel. You can insert three types of page breaks:

- **Both a horizontal and a vertical page break.** Select the cell below and to the right of the gridline where you want to insert the breaks. Select the Options ⇨ Set Page Break command.

- **A horizontal page break only.** Select the cell in column A that is just below the gridline where you want the page to end. Select the Options ⇨ Set Page Break command.

- **A vertical page break only.** Select a cell in row 1 that is to the right of the gridline where you want the page to end. Select the Options ⇨ Set Page Break command.

Manual page breaks are depicted on-screen slightly darker than the automatic page breaks. To remove a manual page break, select any cell directly below or to the right of the manual page break and then issue the Options ⇨ Remove Page Break command. If the Remove Page Break command is not available from the Options menu, the page break you're trying to remove is an automatic break.

To remove all manual page breaks at once, select the entire worksheet by clicking the button at the intersection of the row and column borders. Then select Options ⇨ Remove Page Break from the menu.

Fixing titles

When you're printing a lengthy report, you often want to print row headings and/or column headings on each page. Excel enables you to specify row titles, column titles, or both.

These print titles have nothing to do with headers. Headers appear at the top of each page. Print titles are usually used to describe the data being printed — field names in a database, for example.

To specify rows and/or columns that will serve as print titles, select Options ⇨ Set Print Titles. This action brings up the dialog box shown in Figure 13-6.

To specify rows that will print at the top of each page, click in the upper text box and then select the rows in your worksheet (they must be adjacent). Excel interprets your selection in terms of rows only. To specify columns that will print at the left of each page, click in the lower text box and then select the columns in your worksheet (they must be adjacent). Excel interprets your

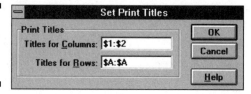

Figure 13-6: The Set Print Titles dialog box enables you to specify rows and/or columns that will be printed on each page.

selection in terms of columns only. You can specify either rows, columns, or both. When you've made your selection, choose OK to close the dialog box.

If you set print titles, you must manually set a print area (see the previous section). Make sure that the print area doesn't overlap with the print titles, or the titles will print twice on the first page. To clear print titles, use the Options ⇨ Set Print Titles command and simply delete the selection or selections from the text box.

Another way to remove print titles is to select the entire worksheet by clicking the button at the intersection of the row and column borders. Then select Options ⇨ Remove Print Titles from the menu. Or select Formula ⇨ Define Name and delete the range named `Print_Titles`.

Printing Your Work

With all the preliminary details out of the way, you're ready for the final step of actually printing. Select File ⇨ Print from the menu. Excel displays a dialog box like the one shown in Figure 13-7. This dialog box offers you more options:

Print Range   All and Pages are radio buttons that enable you to print just a portion of your worksheet. If you select Pages, you need to enter the beginning and ending page numbers. You can figure out what's on which page by using the File ⇨ Print Preview command.

Print Quality   This pull-down box enables you to select the quality of the printing. The actual effects of these selections vary by printer, and in some cases (PostScript laser printers) they are equivalent. Lower resolution means faster printing.

Print   This box contains three more radio buttons. You can print only the worksheet (the default), only cell notes, or both. Cell notes can be attached to cells with the Formula ⇨ Note command.

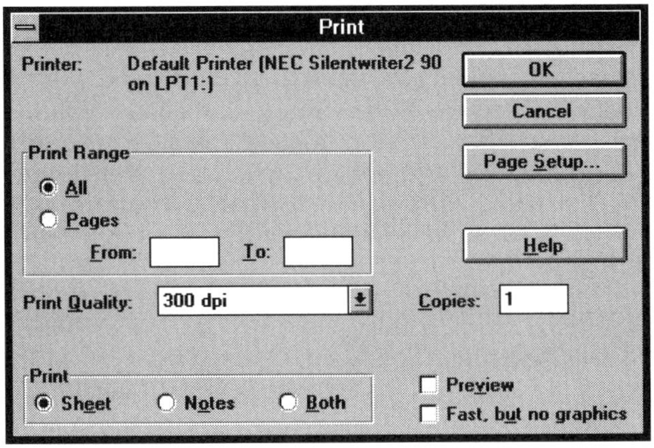

Figure 13-7: The Print dialog box enables you to set some more options before sending your work to the printer.

Copies	This is a text box in which you can enter the number of copies you want to print.
Preview	Check this box if you want to go into the preview window prior to printing.
Fast, but no graphics	Check this box to print the worksheet only, without any charts or graphics objects.

Printing to a file

At times you may want to send your output to a file on disk rather than to a printer. To do this task, you need to change the port assigned to the printer by using the Printers icon in the Control Panel. Select the printer and then click the Connect button. Scroll through the list of ports until you find one called FILE:. Click OK. Now, when you want to print, Excel displays a dialog box that asks for a filename.

The result of this operation is an "encoded" file that includes all the printer control commands appropriate to the active printer. Then, at a later time, you can simply copy this file to the appropriate printer, using the DOS copy command, and the results will be exactly as if you printed the worksheet directly.

When would you want to print to a file? Say you use a PostScript printer at your office, but you only have a dot-matrix printer at home. You can install the PostScript printer driver on your home system and make it active. You can then format your worksheet to use the fonts and capabilities of a PostScript printer and print to a file. When you return to the office, you can send this file to the PostScript printer with a DOS command such as the following:

```
c:\:>copy results.enc prn
```

This command assumes that the filename is results.enc and that the PostScript printer is accessible as device PRN.

Note that you can also jump to the Page Setup dialog box by clicking the Setup button. When you are satisfied with your selections, choose OK and the printing begins (unless Preview is checked, in which case you go to the preview window first). Excel sends your output to the Print Manager, which prepares it for your printer. Print Manager is also a spooler, so it works in the background. As a result, you may be able to continue working while your worksheet is printing. You'll notice, however, that things slow down quite a bit — not unexpected because you're actually sharing your computer's time with Print Manager.

To cancel a job before it finishes printing, press Esc. If the job has already been sent to Print Manager, you need to cancel it from Print Manager. Press Ctrl+Esc to bring up the Windows Task List, select Print Manager from the list of open applications, and then click the Switch to button. This action takes you to the Print Manager window, where you can cancel the print job. You may need to eject the last page in your printer to avoid overprinting it with your next print request.

After you set your print range and select other print options, you can quickly print your worksheet by clicking the Print icon on the Standard toolbar. The Print icon is the fourth icon from the left on the Standard toolbar and resembles a printer.

You can use the Print icon at any time, of course, but because the icon prints your worksheet directly without displaying any print-related dialog boxes, you may want to make some print settings before using the icon.

Complex Print Jobs

If you find yourself constantly rearranging your worksheet before printing, you should take advantage of two new add-ins that are included with Excel 4: Views and Reports.

The Views add-in

The Views add-in enables you to set up different views of your workspace and assign names to them. For example, you may define a view that hides a few columns of numbers, another view with a print range defined as just a summary range, another view with the page setup set to landscape, and so on. A view, as defined for the Views add-in, includes the following:

- Print settings as specified in the Page Setup dialog box (optional)
- Hidden rows and columns (optional)

Figure 13-8: The View dialog box (available only if you've loaded the `views.xla` add-in) enables you to switch to a predefined view, which can include a print area and printer settings.

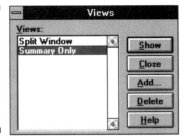

■ Display settings as specified in the Options Display dialog box

■ Selected cells and ranges

■ The active cell

■ Window sizes and positions

■ Frozen panes

To activate the Views add-in, select File ➪ Open from Excel's menu, locate the file named `views.xla` (it should be located in your `\excel\library` directory), and choose OK. The add-in is attached to Excel, and you have a new menu option: Window ➪ View. This command brings up the dialog box shown in Figure 13-8.

Before you issue the Window ➪ View command, make sure that your worksheet view is set up like you want it — including print area, print titles, and settings available in the Page Setup dialog box. Then choose the Add button. This displays another dialog box (see Figure 13-9) in which you provide a name. The two check boxes enable you to determine whether to include print settings and hidden rows and columns in the view definition.

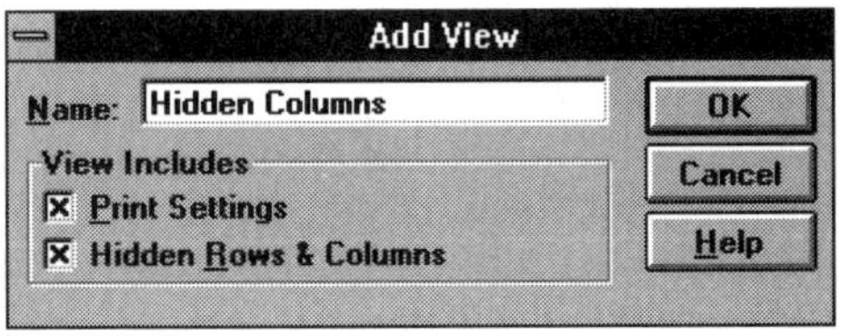

Figure 13-9: When you add a view, you can specify whether it will include print settings and hidden rows and columns in the definition.

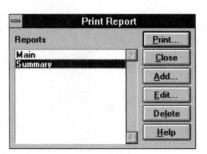

Figure 13-10: With the Print Report dialog box (available only if you've loaded the `reports.xla` add-in) you can easily print a report that has already been set up.

The trick here is to set up and provide names to views that have different print areas (and perhaps different print settings). Then, when it's time to print a specific job, select the appropriate view by using the Window ⇨ View command and then select File ⇨ Print.

The Reports add-in

You can use the Reports add-in with the Views add-in to provide even more functionality to your printing. This add-in enables you to set up a sequence of views and print them as a single report. You can also specify different scenarios within each view, if you've defined them with the Scenario add-in (covered in Chapter 27). In other words, it can automate what would otherwise be a tedious manual task.

To activate the Reports add-in, select File ⇨ Open from Excel's menu, locate the file named `reports.xla` (it should be located in your `\excel\library` directory), and choose OK. The add-in is attached to Excel, and you have a new menu option: File ⇨ Print Report.

After loading the Reports add-in, you can select File ⇨ Print Report to access the dialog box shown in Figure 13-10. This dialog box enables you to name your report, as well as select different views to be included in the report. In addition, you can specify one or more scenarios for a particular view if you've defined multiple scenarios for a view.

When you click the Add button, another dialog box appears (see Figure 13-11). This dialog box enables you to select specific views to be added to the report. The net effect is that you can develop different reports, each of which uses one or more views. And then you can select a report with a few mouse clicks.

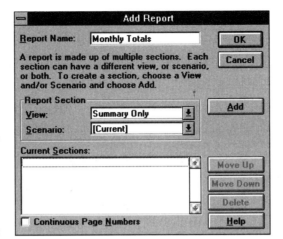

Figure 13-11: You can build a custom-named report by adding predefined views.

General Printing Tips

Following are some things to keep in mind when you're printing from Excel:

■ If your system has enough memory, you may want to set up a RAM disk to hold the temporary files Print Manager generates. This setup greatly increases the speed with which your file is sent to the printer. Windows includes RAM disk software, called ramdisk.sys. Make sure you include a command in your autoexec.bat file that says set temp=d:\ (assuming that your RAM disk is designated drive D:).

■ When you specify a print area in Excel, make sure that it covers the entire area to be printed, including long labels that may spill over to adjacent columns.

■ If you find that some parts of your worksheet are printing twice, the print area is probably overlapping with print titles. To correct the problem, redefine your print area so that it doesn't include the title areas.

■ A print range doesn't have to consist of a rectangular range of cells. You can make a multiple selection (hold down the Ctrl key while you highlight ranges) and then issue the Options ➪ Set Print Area command. Each part of the selection is printed on a separate page, in the order that you made your selections.

■ Become familiar with the options for your printer. For example, most HP LaserJet printers can print in three different resolutions: 75, 150, and 300 dots per inch (dpi). Printing at 75 dpi is the fastest, but nonresident characters will be poorly formed and graphics will not look all that great. You may want to print your drafts at 75 or 150 dpi and your final printout at 300 dpi. You can control this setting with the Print Quality setting in the Page Setup dialog box.

■ The Windows black-and-white printer drivers convert colors to dot patterns. Develop a test sheet so you'll know in advance how various colors will translate on your printer. Or instruct Excel to ignore colors by selecting the Black & White Cells setting in the Page Setup dialog box.

■ You can cancel a job that's being printed by accessing the Print Manager program. Press Ctrl+Esc to bring up the Windows Task Manager and double-click on Print Manager. In the Print Manager window, select the job being printed and then choose Delete. Note that you can also change the priority of print jobs. If you find that your system slows down too much while you're printing, try selecting Options ⇨ Low Priority from the Print Manager menu. This action makes your print job take longer, but your system is more responsive so you can keep working.

■ You may occasionally receive a message stating that Windows cannot write to the printer. Make sure that the printer is turned on and it's connected properly. Clear any paper jams and make sure that paper is loaded. Then activate Print Manager and select Resume to try printing again.

■ With the Control Panel, you can install a printer that you don't actually have. For example, if you normally use a PostScript printer at the office, you may want to install the PostScript printer driver on your home system. That way, when you bring work home from the office, you can avoid some complications due to different fonts on different systems. This setup is also useful for situations in which you send your output to a file rather than a printer.

■ You can get a printout of all the formulas in a worksheet by first selecting Options ⇨ Display and then choosing Formulas. Print this worksheet as usual. This setup may be useful for debugging purposes.

■ If you like the idea of naming views and using the Reports add-in, you can load these two add-in files automatically whenever you run Excel. Use the Add-in Manager to create this setup, which eliminates the need to manually open the add-in files when you need them.

Summary

▶ Windows (and therefore Excel) supports most printers, including dot-matrix, ink-jet, and laser printers.

▶ When you configure and set up your printer in Windows, the printer settings are functional in all Windows applications. Excel, however, enables you to override these settings for each document by the settings in the Page Setup dialog box.

▶ You can only print in fonts that are available to your printer. Software-based types of programs such as Adobe Type Manager and TrueType (included with Windows 3.1) display high-quality fonts on-screen and also work with most printers.

▶ By default, Excel prints the entire worksheet when you issue the File ➪ Print command, but you can override this setting and specify your own print area.

▶ Excel provides many options for controlling how your printed page will look. These settings are available in the Page Setup dialog box.

▶ Excel's File ➪ Print Preview command enables you to see exactly how your printed output will look before it hits the paper. In addition, you can adjust margins and column widths directly in the preview window.

▶ Excel automatically determines page breaks, but you can easily override them and insert manual page breaks.

▶ For multipage printouts, you may elect to print row and/or column headings on each page.

▶ The File ➪ Print command enables you to specify the number of copies and also specify a range of pages to print.

▶ If you tend to print many different reports from a single worksheet, consider using the Views add-in to create named views and then the Reports add-in to save named reports.

Chapter 14
Controlling Your Spreadsheet Display

In this chapter . . .

▶ How to change the colors used in your display.

▶ How to modify other properties of your spreadsheet, such as row and column borders, gridlines, and scroll bars.

▶ How to freeze worksheet titles so you can see what you're dealing with, regardless of where you are.

▶ How to split a window into panes so you can see more at one time.

▶ How to arrange and hide windows.

▶ All about the View Manager, and why you should understand it.

Back in the days of monochrome computer monitors, you had a choice of two colors for viewing your spreadsheet on-screen: black or green. CGA arrived and provided some new color choices, but the resolution left a lot to be desired. EGA and VGA monitors opened up the possibility for a rainbow of colors at better resolutions, but it wasn't until the advent of Windows that spreadsheet users could get the most from their color monitors.

Today, you can not only choose the colors you want to display, but also customize those colors; you can even adjust the brightness and intensity of the color. And with Excel, you can choose what parts of the program or worksheet you do or do not want displayed. In short, you can tailor your spreadsheet display to your particular liking.

The number of display options Excel offers can be a bit overwhelming to beginning or experienced users alike. So no matter what your spreadsheet experience, be sure to read on for information on choosing the display attributes that are right for you.

Choosing Colors

You might like Excel's default display colors well enough, but why walk when you can fly? It's easy to take full advantage of your VGA monitor and Excel's color capability and make certain ranges or tables stand out. You have the option of changing the color of the following items that comprise your worksheets:

- Contents of cells

- Ranges

- Borders

- Patterns of shades

- Gridlines, row numbers, and column letters

Instructions on how to select colors for each of these worksheet elements are presented next. If you have a color printer, such as an HP PaintJet, the screen colors will translate well to the printed page.

 If your printing options are limited to monochrome, you can still use the screen colors you like without affecting the printed output. Normally your printer driver translates colors into various dot patterns. You can override this and essentially tell Excel to ignore all the colors when you print and stick with pure black and white. You do this via the File ⇨ Page Setup command. When the Page Setup dialog box displays, simply select the Black & White Cells option.

Choosing colors for cells

You have two ways to customize the colors of the content of cells: by using a predefined or custom numeric format or by changing the color of the font.

By using a numeric format

Creating a custom format that includes two colors helps you draw attention to results that are above or below expectations (hopefully you won't have too many of the latter). You can use a numeric format that includes color with dates as well as values. Recall from Chapter 7 that you can use or modify a number format that includes a color. For example, if you want to display negative values in red with a dollar sign and two decimal places, you'd use this built-in format:

```
$#,##0.00_);[RED]($#,##0.00)
```

You can use a color in addition to red for negative values by selecting from one of the 16 available colors,. The first 8 are listed here:

Color	Number
[BLACK]	1
[WHITE]	2
[RED]	3
[GREEN]	4
[BLUE]	5
[YELLOW]	6
[MAGENTA]	7
[CYAN]	8
[COLOR #]	

where # is the color number 1 through 16, beginning with black as color 1 and dark gray as color 16, as displayed in the dialog box you get when you select the Options ⇨ Color Palette command.

You can also change the format by adding a color symbol at the point in the format that represents what you want to color. Suppose you have a holiday version of your worksheet and want to display positive values as green. The new format for the previous example is:

```
[GREEN]$#,##0.00_);[RED]($#,##0.00)
```

If you prefer another color set to work with, you can customize one or more of the colors on the color palette. This process is explained later in the chapter.

 If you want to change the color of just your data, without affecting everything else, use a numeric format that includes one or more colors or change the color of the font.

By choosing colors for fonts

Changing the color of a font is done through the Format ⇨ Font command. You may remember that this command lets you change many aspects of the fonts in your worksheet. To select another color, you simply select a range and then choose Format ⇨ Font. The Color pull-down list is your ticket to changing colors. Select a color from the list and notice how the selected font type and size appears in the Sample box. If you're satisfied with your choice, choose OK, and the data in the range you've selected now sports the new color.

Choosing colors for borders

Choosing a color for your borders is similar to choosing colors for fonts. The Format ⇨ Border command's dialog box also has a Color pull-down list that you can pick a color from. You can color your borders as you're applying them to your spreadsheet cells or after you have the lines the way you want them. In

What is the Automatic color?

The Automatic color found on all Color pull-down lists is based on the colors selected from the Windows Control Panel. You can easily select another Automatic color without leaving Excel. Click the Excel Control box menu (or press Alt+spacebar) and choose Run. When you do, the Run dialog box appears.

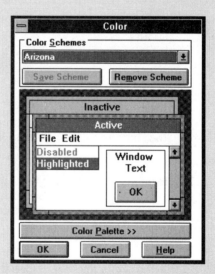

Choose Control Panel and then Colors to display the Color dialog box. Select another color arrangement from the Color Schemes pull-down list. As with other dialog box Sample boxes, watch how the colors for various windows elements will appear. In addition, you can customize the colors for each element within a color scheme by selecting Color Palette.

When you're finished changing or customizing colors, choose OK or press Enter. You'll return to the Control Panel group, and Windows will dis-

play the new colors you selected. Choose Close from the Control box menu to return to Excel.

The color scheme you display is entirely up to you. But if you spend as much time in front of your computer as we do, do your eyes a favor and pass on the Fluorescent color scheme!

Keep in mind that choosing or changing colors through the Control Panel mainly affects colors of windows. To change the 16 colors available to your worksheet window elements, see the section "Modifying Colors."

either case, select the range of cells that contain borders, choose Format ⇨ Border ⇨ Color and choose the color for your lines. When you select OK, Excel displays the borders around your selected cells with the chosen color.

Choosing colors for ranges

Recall from Chapter 12 that you can select a color for the shade pattern you apply to ranges. As always, after you select a range, use Format ⇨ Patterns and select a black-and-white pattern from the Pattern drop-down list. Next, select Foreground and Background colors from the corresponding drop-down color list. Make sure you select colors that won't make your data illegible. Watch the Sample box to see beforehand how your colors will look before you choose OK. If you pull down the Patterns list again, you can see how the various patterns will appear with the color combination you've chosen.

Choosing the gridline and heading colors

Two final areas you can control the color of in your worksheet are the gridlines and the headings. Headings are the row numbers and column letters along the left side and top of the worksheet, respectively. To change this color, choose Options ⇨ Display, then pull down the Gridline & Heading Color list. Select the one you want and then choose OK. That's all there is to it. Excel displays each worksheet's gridlines and headings with this color. These colors apply to the current document only.

To quickly change the font or background colors in your entire worksheet, select the entire worksheet by clicking the button at the intersection of the row headings and column headings. Then, use the Format ⇨ Font or Format ⇨ Patterns command to make your color choice.

Modifying Colors

Excel comes with 16 standard colors that you can use out-of-the-box or customize to your liking. If you use a different set of 16 colors, you can keep this modified set in a template worksheet for use in other Excel models. Creating your own custom set of colors is a relatively painless process, as you'll see.

Colors contained in your custom color palette are also available for your charts.

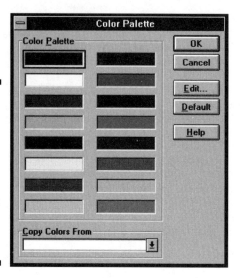

Figure 14-1: The Color Palette dialog box is the first step toward customizing the colors you want your worksheets to display. Select the color you want to change here.

Colors previously assigned to fonts, borders, ranges, gridlines and headings, and objects will change if you change the color palette they were assigned from. Depending on how you look at it, you can consider this to be a feature since it's a quick way to change all the colors to a different color scheme.

First, make the worksheet active that contains the color palette you want to modify. Next, choose Options ⇨ Color Palette, and the dialog box shown in Figure 14-1 appears.

Monochrome display users (including most laptop users) will see the name of each color on the palette in the Color Palette dialog box and will not be able to modify colors.

Now, choose the color you want to change by selecting it with the mouse or using the arrow keys. When you've selected the one you want, choose Edit. The dialog box in Figure 14-2 appears. First, click on an area inside the large square on the left of the dialog box to select a color. Second, click then drag up and down on the pointer to the right of the narrow rectangle to change the luminance, or brightness, of the color.

You change degrees of red, blue, and green because these are the basic display colors of your monitor — much like a color television set.

Second, you may want to change the hue of your color. Enter a number from 0 to 239 in the Hue box, where 0 is the least and 239 the largest amount of hue at the left and right edges of the large square in the dialog box.

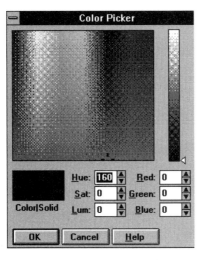

Figure 14-2:
The Color Picker dialog box is the second step when customizing colors.

Third, you may also want to change the saturation, or purity, of your color. Enter a number from 0 to 239 in the Sat box, where 0 is the least and 239 the largest amount of saturation at the bottom and top edges of the large square in the dialog box.

Fourth, and finally, you may want to change the luminance, or brightness, of your color. Enter a number from 0 to 240 in the Lum box, where 0 is the least and 240 the largest amount of luminance at the bottom and top edges of the narrow rectangle in the dialog box.

Watch the Color/Solid box to see how your selections affect the color — just as you do when you select a color for a font, border, or pattern. When you're satisfied you have the right combination of color and brightness, choose OK. Excel replaces the old color with the new color on the palette of the active document. Repeat this process if you want to modify another color.

If you return to your worksheet and chart and have second thoughts about how a modified color appears on your display, you can revert to Excel's default color palette by selecting Options ➪ Color Palette and choosing Default.

Finally, you can copy color palettes between worksheets or charts. Copying color palettes from one worksheet to another (or from one chart to another) is similar to copying named styles among worksheets. Open the source and target worksheet (or charts) and make the target worksheet the active worksheet. Next, choose Options ➪ Color Palette (Chart ➪ Color Palette for charts) and then the name of your source worksheet from the Copy Colors From list box.

When you choose OK, the target (active) worksheet (or chart) receives the source worksheet's color palette. Fonts, borders, ranges, gridlines and headings, and objects in the target worksheet will display colors based on the new palette.

Choosing What to Display

With Excel, you have wide latitude for which areas of your worksheet, and even Excel itself, that you want to display on-screen. The next two sections illustrate how you can select what you want displayed on-screen.

The options that follow affect how Excel displays itself and your worksheet on-screen only, and not how the worksheet is printed.

Displaying Excel's elements

Changing Excel's appearance on-screen means changing the window Excel resides in. In general, this is the area that surrounds your open worksheets and includes these screen regions:

- The toolbar
- The Formula bar
- The vertical and horizontal scroll bars
- The Status bar

You use two commands to select the elements of Excel you want (or don't want) displayed. These are the Options ▷ Toolbars and the Options ▷ Workspace commands. Note that Excel displays all these screen elements by default.

Hiding toolbars

To hide any toolbar, choose the Options ▷ Toolbars command. When the dialog box shown in Figure 14-3 appears, select the toolbar you don't want to display and choose Hide. Repeat this process for any other toolbars you want to hide. Alternatively, you can display toolbars by selecting the name of the toolbar and choosing Show.

The Show and Hide buttons toggle appropriately between these two options as you scroll through the toolbar list, based on the display status of the individual toolbar.

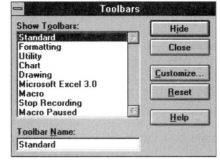

Figure 14-3:
Select the toolbar(s) you need or don't need with the Toolbars dialog box.

When you're finished hiding and displaying toolbars, choose OK, and Excel modifies your screen display.

A faster way to hide and display toolbars is to right-click on any displayed toolbar. The resulting shortcut menu lets you select and deselect specific toolbars.

Hiding other workspace elements

Use the Options ⇨ Workspace command to hide or show the Formula bar, the scroll bars, and the Status bar. Remember, by default, these elements display when you fire up Excel. When you choose this command, the dialog box shown in Figure 14-4 opens. Simply uncheck the appropriate box of the element you don't want displayed, and Excel removes that element from your display.

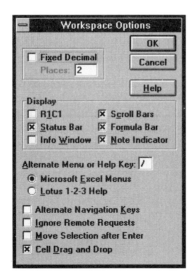

Figure 14-4:
Choose which elements you want displayed from the Workspace Options dialog box.

If you're a former Microsoft MultiPlan user (there must be a few of you out there), or prefer column numbers over letters, check the R1C1 box. Column A will display as 1, column B as 2, and so on. Most people find this option to be confusing beyond belief, but at least Excel lets you be in control.

If you primarily use the keyboard, consider turning off the display of the scroll bars. Without a mouse, there's really no purpose for displaying them, and you'll be able to see a bit more of your active worksheet.

In general, hiding the Formula bar is not a good idea, especially if you have cells that contain long formulas. Hiding the Formula bar forces you to edit cell contents directly in the cell, which can be tedious since you can't see a formula in its entirety.

Displaying worksheet elements

The various elements of the worksheet itself can also be hidden or shown. They are as folllows:

- The display of a formula's results or the formula itself
- Worksheet gridlines
- Row numbers and column letters
- Zeros
- Outline symbols
- Page-break symbols

By default, Excel displays each of these elements, except page-break symbols and, as you know, formula results. The exception is with macro sheets, which display formulas rather than results.

Displaying formulas can help you understand the logic of a worksheet you're unfamiliar with. Note, however, that displayed formulas do not spill over into the cell to the right (even if it's empty). Consequently, you'll probably want to increase your column width to see the entire formula.

Changing any of these options is much like using the Options ⇨ Workspace command. When you choose Options ⇨ Display, the dialog box in Figure 14-5 appears, and you need only to check or uncheck the option of the corresponding element you want displayed or hidden. Choosing OK or pressing Enter completes the operation and Excel makes the changes you request.

Figure 14-5: Choose the options you'd like to see displayed on your worksheet from the Display Options dialog box.

If the Options ➪ Display and Options ➪ Workspace commands seem a bit confusing, here's a way to keep them separate. The settings you make in the Display Options dialog box affect only the current worksheet. The settings you make in the Workspace Options dialog box are saved and are in effect for all of your worksheets.

Recall from Chapter 12 that worksheets you've added borders to appear much more attractive with worksheet gridlines turned off. And a worksheet with many formulas that calculate to zero may be more attractive and understandable if you suppress the formulas' display.

Taking Advantage of Multiple Views _____

Thus far you've displayed your worksheet in a single window. In the sections that follow, you'll learn how to benefit from viewing different areas of your worksheet simultaneously. You can do this by creating "panes" of a worksheet, additional windows of a single worksheet window, or a combination of both. First up, however, is separating a worksheet display into segments.

Creating window panes

You may have a large Excel application that doesn't lend itself well to multiple worksheets. If this is the case, you can view different areas of a worksheet's window at the same time. For example, in Figure 14-6, you can see range A1:H10 and A18:H24 at the same time. Creating different views of your worksheet is

	A	B	C	D	E	F	G	H	I
				AMORT.XLS					
1									
2			First payment date				3/31/92		
3			Amount of loan				$12,000		
4			Number of months				60		
5			Annual interest rate				8.75%		
6			Payment amount				$247.65		
7									
8									
9		Payment	Payment	Interest		Interest	Principal	Remaining	
10		number	date	rate	Payment	amount	amount	balance	
18		8	31-Oct-92	8.75%	$247.65	$79.14	$168.50	$10,685.65	
19		9	30-Nov-92	8.75%	$247.65	$77.92	$169.73	$10,515.92	
20		10	31-Dec-92	8.75%	$247.65	$76.68	$170.97	$10,344.95	
21		11	31-Jan-93	8.75%	$247.65	$75.43	$172.21	$10,172.73	
22		12	28-Feb-93	8.75%	$247.65	$74.18	$173.47	$9,999.26	
23		13	31-Mar-93	8.75%	$247.65	$72.91	$174.74	$9,824.53	
24		14	30-Apr-93	8.75%	$247.65	$71.64	$176.01	$9,648.52	
25		15	31-May-93	8.75%	$247.65	$70.35	$177.29	$9,471.23	

Figure 14-6:
Window panes enable you to view separate areas of your worksheet simultaneously.

known as creating *panes*, because you're separating your worksheet's window into sections. Unlike many Excel commands, you don't have to select a range before completing this procedure. It's helpful, however, to display the portion of your worksheet that you want to view most of the time through one of the panes before going ahead and creating the panes. You'll also want to decide ahead of time if you want two vertical panes, two horizontal panes (such as in the example), or four panes. In any event, here's how you do it:

Making panes with a mouse

Notice the small black rectangles at the top of the vertical scroll bar and the far left of the horizontal scroll bar. If you move your mouse pointer to one of these areas, the pointer changes to the corresponding black two-headed arrow.

To create two horizontal panes, move your pointer to the rectangle above the vertical scroll bar — the horizontal split box — then press and drag. As you do, a gray horizontal line appears on your worksheet and follows the direction (up and down) of your mouse movements. Stop and release the mouse button when the gray line is at the point in your worksheet where you'd like the two panes to be separated. You now have two horizontal panes on your worksheet window.

To create two vertical panes, you use the same procedure as for horizontal panes, only you press and drag on the rectangle to the far left on the horizontal scroll bar — the vertical split box.

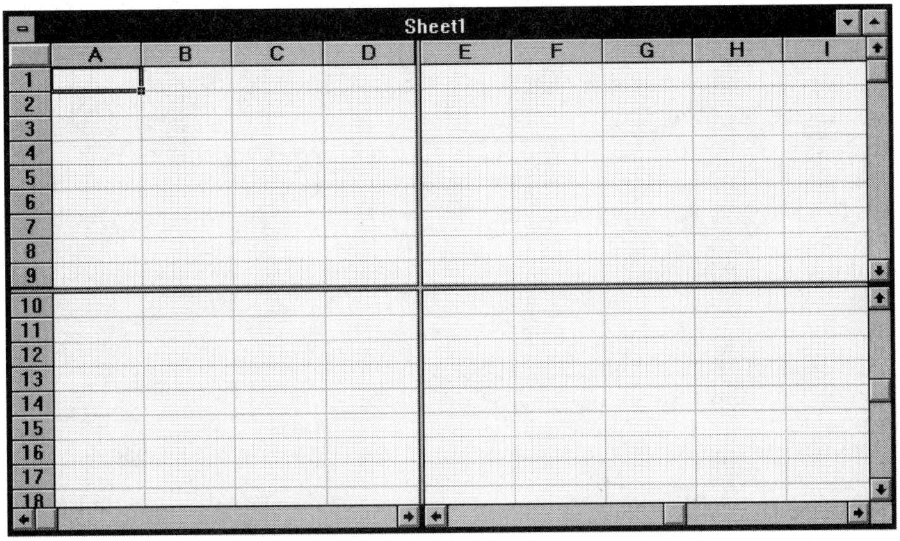

Figure 14-7: These movable lines help you specify the position of four window panes.

If you already have two panes on your window, you can quickly add two of the opposite orientation by clicking and dragging on the appropriate split box. For example, if you decide you need four panes on your worksheet, and already have two horizontal panes, press and drag on the vertical split box to add two vertical panes.

Making panes with the keyboard

To make window panes with the keyboard, use your worksheet window's Control menu. Start by pressing Alt+–, and then choose Split by pressing P or by using the down-arrow key to highlight the command and pressing Enter. When you do, the four gray lines appear, as shown in Figure 14-7. Use the up and down arrow keys to specify which rows will appear in the horizontal panes, and your left and right arrow keys to specify which columns will appear in the vertical panes.

If you only want two horizontal panes, press the left arrow key until the vertical gray line disappears. Similarly, if you only want two vertical panes, press the up arrow key until the horizontal gray line disappears. When you're satisfied you have the panes the way you want them, press Enter and you're all set.

Making panes with both mouse and keyboard

Whether you're a keyboard or mouse user, you can use the Window ➪ Split command to create two or four window panes The number and size of panes depends on the location of the cell pointer when you invoke Window ➪ Split.

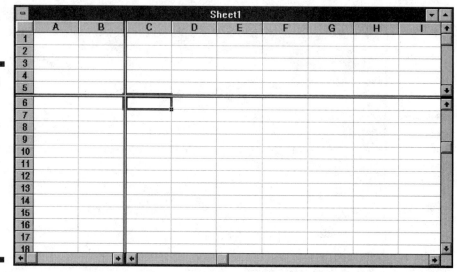

Figure 14-8:
Selecting
cell C6 and
then choos-
ing the
Window
⇨ Split
command
produces
these four
window
panes.

The rule to remember is that Window ⇨ Split will create a *horizontal* pane *above* the location of the cell pointer and a *vertical* pane to the *left* of the cell pointer. For example, if you position the cell pointer at cell C6 and choose the Window ⇨ Split command, Excel displays four panes, as shown in Figure 14-8.

To create two horizontal panes, move the cell pointer to column A and to the row that will be the first row of the lower pane, then choose Window ⇨ Split. To create two vertical panes, you'll need to use a mouse or the worksheet window's Control menu Split command and the procedures described previously.

Moving between panes

Moving the cell pointer between window panes is easy. If you use a mouse, just click on any cell in the pane you want to move to. To use your keyboard, press the F6 key. Each press of F6 moves the cell pointer to the next pane, in clockwise order. Shift+F6 moves the cell pointer counterclockwise between panes.

Removing panes

As with displaying worksheet window panes, you have several alternatives for removing them. When you display your worksheet window with panes, the Window ⇨ Split command becomes the Window ⇨ Remove Split command. If you no longer have a need for panes, choose Window ⇨ Remove Split. Procedures specific to the mouse and keyboard follow.

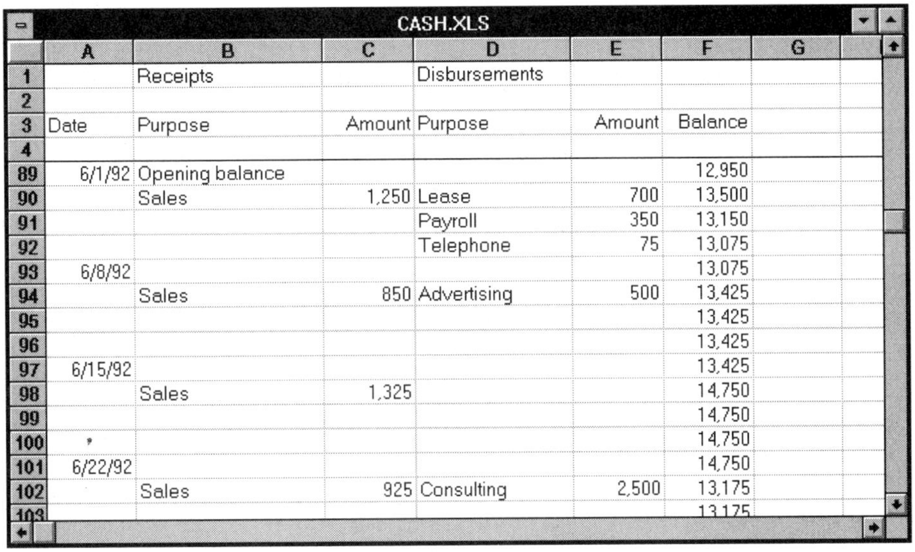

	A	B	C	D	E	F	G
1		Receipts		Disbursements			
2							
3	Date	Purpose	Amount	Purpose	Amount	Balance	
4							
89	6/1/92	Opening balance				12,950	
90		Sales	1,250	Lease	700	13,500	
91				Payroll	350	13,150	
92				Telephone	75	13,075	
93	6/8/92					13,075	
94		Sales	850	Advertising	500	13,425	
95						13,425	
96						13,425	
97	6/15/92					13,425	
98		Sales	1,325			14,750	
99						14,750	
100						14,750	
101	6/22/92					14,750	
102		Sales	925	Consulting	2,500	13,175	
103						13,175	

CASH.XLS

Figure 14-9:
By freezing the top pane in this worksheet, we can have column headings available as we scroll through the worksheet.

Removing panes with a mouse

Press and drag the vertical split box all the way to the left of the horizontal scroll bar, then release the mouse to remove vertical panes. Press and drag the horizontal split box all the way to the top of the vertical scroll bar, then release the mouse to remove horizontal panes.

Removing panes with a keyboard

Press Alt+– to display the worksheet window's Control box menu, then choose Split. Use the left arrow key to move the vertical gray line all the way to the left of the worksheet, then use the up arrow key to move the horizontal gray line all the way to the top of the worksheet, and then press Enter.

Holding a pane in place

When you display window panes and scroll your worksheet, both panes scroll in the same direction together — they're synchronized. For example, if you display two vertical panes on your worksheet and press the PgDn key, both window panes scroll down by one screen.

At times, however, you may want to hold one pane in place while the other scrolls. For example, you might have a worksheet with many line items. As you move down your worksheet, it's easy to lose your place. (Figure 14-9 is an example of how to prevent this.) You can create a horizontal pane that displays column titles (most likely, the months of the year) and freeze the upper pane in place, so it doesn't scroll with the lower pane. This is also known as freezing titles, because you're freezing them in place so you can view them at all times. You can freeze column titles, row titles, or both, as follows:

To freeze	Create this pane	Then issue this command
Row titles	A vertical pane that encloses row labels	Window ⇨ Freeze Panes
Column titles	A horizontal pane that encloses column labels	Window ⇨ Freeze Panes
Both	A vertical pane that encloses row labels, and a horizontal pane that encloses column labels	Window ⇨ Freeze Panes

 When you freeze panes, note that you have only one set of horizontal and vertical scroll bars.

Unfreezing panes

The Window ⇨ Freeze Panes command works similar to the Window ⇨ Split command. When you have a worksheet that displays a frozen window pane, Window ⇨ Freeze Panes becomes Window ⇨ Unfreeze Panes. Use this command to unfreeze any window panes in the active worksheet.

Creating windows

Another tool available for viewing distant portions of your worksheet is, appropriately enough, windows. Creating another window of your worksheet is easy. Just choose Window ⇨ New Window, and Excel creates and numbers the window for you. Though a new worksheet is displayed in one window, you can create multiple windows to display other areas of the same worksheet. The number of windows you can create is limited only by your computer's memory and (perhaps) your imagination. And since your new windows are bona fide, you can move and size them like any other window.

 Keep in mind that when you create new windows you're not creating new worksheets (as you do with File ⇨ New). Rather, you're looking at different parts of the same worksheet, and changes to a cell are reflected in every window, if that cell is displayed. You can, however, change the display options of the window. For example, you can see the results of formulas and the formulas themselves, as shown in Figure 14-10. Notice that each window is numbered in the title bar: The original window is 1, the new window is 2, and so on.

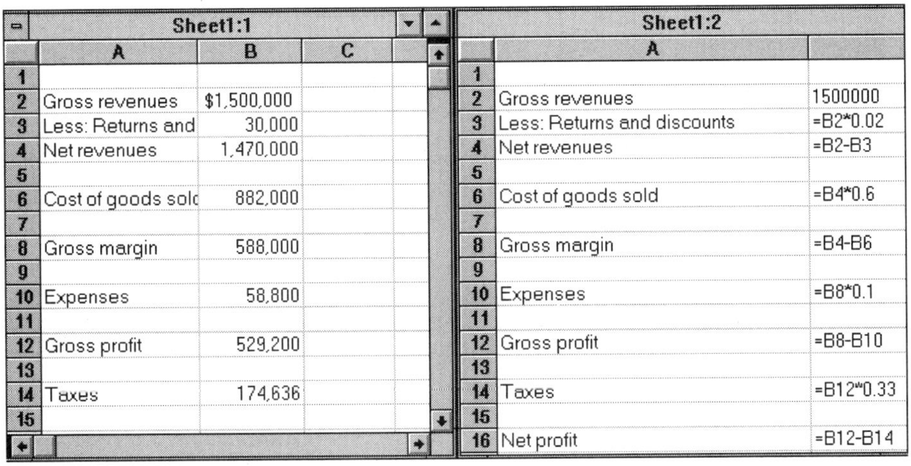

Sheet1:1				Sheet1:2	
	A	B	C		A	
1				1		
2	Gross revenues	$1,500,000		2	Gross revenues	1500000
3	Less: Returns and	30,000		3	Less: Returns and discounts	=B2*0.02
4	Net revenues	1,470,000		4	Net revenues	=B2-B3
5				5		
6	Cost of goods sold	882,000		6	Cost of goods sold	=B4*0.6
7				7		
8	Gross margin	588,000		8	Gross margin	=B4-B6
9				9		
10	Expenses	58,800		10	Expenses	=B8*0.1
11				11		
12	Gross profit	529,200		12	Gross profit	=B8-B10
13				13		
14	Taxes	174,636		14	Taxes	=B12*0.33
15				15		
				16	Net profit	=B12-B14

Figure 14-10: Same worksheet, two windows: Results of formulas and the formulas themselves in separate windows.

Arranging windows

You can move and size your worksheet's windows by choosing Move and Size from the window's Control menu or by pressing and dragging with your mouse. If you need to quickly display all Excel windows simultaneously on-screen, the Window ⇨ Arrange command is your ticket. Your Window ⇨ Arrange options are shown in the table on the next page.

Panes or windows: Which are better?

Using window panes or additional windows to view different areas of your worksheet depends on your personal preference and what you need to do. Remember, panes let you lock your row and column titles, while additional windows may make it a little easier to see separate areas of a worksheet, especially if those areas are diagonal to each other. Your best bet may be to experiment and see which method works best for you.

Nevertheless, you shouldn't look at window panes and multiple windows as an either-or proposition. You can team them up so you can gain the benefits of both. For example, if you have a large budget worksheet, you might want to create horizontal and vertical frozen panes to view row and column labels, a second window to view row totals, and even a third window to view column totals.

Option	Window display
Tiled	Windows displayed as same-sized rectangles. The more windows you have, the smaller the rectangles.
Horizontal	Windows displayed evenly from top to bottom as wide rectangles.
Vertical	Windows displayed evenly from left to right as tall rectangles.

 If you want to arrange only the windows of your active worksheet, make sure you check the Windows of Active Document box. If you don't do this, Excel arranges all unhidden windows of a worksheet and all other open worksheet windows.

 You can create a cascade effect by moving and sizing your windows in the direction you want them to cascade (from bottom left to top right, or bottom right to top left). Use Window ⇨ Arrange ⇨ Horizontal to give you a head start in moving and sizing.

Specifying synchronization

Unlike window panes, windows of the same worksheet will not scroll together by default. However, if you check the Windows of Active Document box in the Arrange Windows dialog box, Sync Horizontal and Sync Vertical become available. Check the appropriate box for the direction you want to scroll windows.

 Choose None from the Arrange box if you only want your windows to scroll together and do not want Excel to arrange them for you.

Hiding and showing windows

You may have one or more windows you want to hide from casual or deliberate snooping, such as a salary planning worksheet. You can keep confidential windows from displaying, whether those windows are from the same or other open worksheets.

To hide a window, first make the window you want to hide the active window. Next, choose Window ⇨ Hide, and the window and its contents disappear from view. If you want to redisplay a hidden window, use Window ⇨ Unhide and then select the name of the window you want to display from the list box shown in Figure 14-11. Select OK and Excel displays the hidden window you selected.

Figure 14-11: Select the windows you want to decloak from the Unhide dialog box, available from the Window menu.

Saving windows

Saving the number, size, and position of open windows and panes happens automatically when you save your worksheet to disk. The next time you open your worksheet, the windows will display just as you left them, with all other modifications intact (including data, formulas, and range names).

Closing windows

If you no longer need a window, you can remove it from your worksheet. First, make the window you want to remove the active window. Then, choose Close from the window's Control box menu. The window is permanently removed from your worksheet.

You can also use Close from the File menu to close a single window containing a worksheet. With either method, Excel prompts you with a warning message if you attempt to close a worksheet window that has been changed but not saved.

Zooming in and out

A handy feature — new to version 4 — lets you expand or contract the display of your worksheet by a percentage using the Window ⇨ Zoom command. Zooming a worksheet is helpful when you want to position a chart or object precisely or you want to get a bird's-eye view if you inherit a worksheet the size of an aircraft carrier and want to see how it's laid out.

When you choose Window ⇨ Zoom, the dialog box in Figure 14-12 appears. Select one of the magnifications from the dialog box, or enter a percentage from 10 to 400 percent in the Custom text box. When you choose OK, Excel expands or contracts your worksheet's display by the percentage you specified. Figure 14-13 shows a condensed view (50 percent) of a worksheet.

Figure 14-12: The Zoom dialog box (available from the Window menu) lets you select the display percentage of your worksheet.

Window ➪ Zoom affects only the display of your worksheet on-screen and not how it appears on paper. You can control zooming in your printed output in the Page Setup dialog box.

To redisplay your worksheet at normal size, choose Window ➪ Zoom, then 100% from the Zoom dialog box, and choose OK. Your worksheet appears as it did prior to zooming.

BUDGET-R.XLS

Operating Budget

	Jan	Feb	Mar	Apr	May	Jun	Jul	Aug	Sep	Oct	Nov	Dec	TOTAL
INCOME													
Sales	297,344	304,778	307,632	261,487	235,338	176,504	264,756	397,134	516,274	671,156	738,272	812,099	4,982,773
Returns	12,433	17,633	14,823	15,194	15,573	15,963	16,362	16,771	17,190	17,620	18,060	18,512	196,134
NET SALES	309,777	322,411	322,455	276,681	250,912	192,467	281,118	413,905	533,464	688,776	756,332	830,611	5,178,906
COST OF GOODS													
Materials	85,577	87,716	83,331	70,831	63,748	47,811	49,006	50,231	51,487	52,774	54,094	55,446	752,053
Merchandise	11,915	12,213	11,602	9,862	8,876	9,098	9,325	9,558	9,797	10,042	10,293	10,550	123,131
Commissions	34,481	35,343	36,227	30,793	27,713	28,406	29,116	29,844	30,590	31,355	32,139	32,942	378,950
Gross Profit	177,804	187,138	191,296	165,195	150,575	107,152	193,670	324,271	441,589	594,604	659,806	731,672	3,924,772
EXPENSES													
Wages	56,964	58,388	55,469	47,148	42,434	31,825	47,738	71,607	93,089	121,015	133,117	146,428	905,221
Office	2,142	2,196	2,250	2,307	2,364	2,423	2,484	2,546	2,610	2,675	2,742	2,810	29,550
Telephone	1,456	1,492	1,530	1,568	1,607	1,647	1,689	1,731	1,774	1,818	1,864	1,910	20,086
Travel	2,934	3,007	3,083	3,160	3,239	3,320	3,403	3,488	3,575	3,664	3,756	3,850	40,476
Maintenance	3,425	3,511	3,598	3,688	3,781	3,875	3,972	4,071	4,173	4,277	4,384	4,494	47,250
Gas	345	354	362	372	381	390	400	410	420	431	442	453	4,759
Automobile	5,142	5,271	5,402	5,537	5,676	5,818	5,963	6,112	6,265	6,422	6,582	6,747	70,937
Advertising	12,203	12,508	11,883	10,100	9,090	6,818	5,113	3,835	2,876	2,157	1,618	1,213	79,415
TOTAL EXPENSES	84,611	86,726	83,577	73,880	68,571	56,116	70,761	93,800	114,782	142,460	154,504	167,906	1,197,694
NET	93,193	100,412	107,718	91,315	82,004	51,036	122,909	230,471	326,807	452,145	505,302	563,766	2,727,078

Figure 14-13: Viewing this worksheet at 50 percent of its real size enables you to see the entire worksheet.

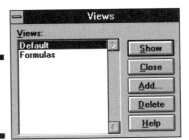

Figure 14-14: The Views dialog box (available from the Window menu) lets you add or delete named views to and from worksheets.

Retaining Display Attributes

If you want to view selective parts of your worksheet, such as values, formulas, a collapsed outline, or hidden columns, you can use a command that's new to version 4 of Excel. The Window ⇨ View command lets you save window settings so you don't need to create additional worksheets of your original to see your worksheet from other perspectives.

With Window ⇨ View, you can save the following settings:

- Size and position of windows

- Frozen window panes

- The active cell

- Selected cell range

- All Options ⇨ Display choices

In addition, you can specify print settings and hidden rows and columns from the Window View dialog box. Before you invoke Window ⇨ View, customize the display of your worksheet the way you want to see it in future Excel sessions. Use Options ⇨ Display and the Window commands to create panes or windows and arrange them appropriately. Next, choose Window ⇨ View, and the dialog box shown in Figure 14-14 appears. Choose Add and type the name of your view in the Name text box of the Add View dialog box, shown in Figure 14-15. If you *don't* want to save print settings or hidden rows and columns, uncheck the

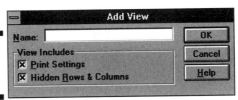

Figure 14-15: Name views and specify print settings and/or hidden rows and columns with the Add View dialog box.

appropriate box. Choosing OK saves the view. You can have as many views as your computer's memory can handle. Use File ⇨ Save or File ⇨ Save As to save your view to disk along with your worksheet.

If you plan on having many views of a worksheet, you may want to create a default view. In this manner, you can return to an uncustomized display of Excel, without having to choose commands or close and reopen your worksheet.

To display other views, select the view from the Views list box in the Views dialog box and choose Show. Excel displays your worksheet with the attributes defined in the selected view.

Summary

▶ You can change the color of numeric data through predefined or custom formats. Changing the color of fonts is another way to control the color of your data.

▶ You can change the color of borders and apply color to ranges.

▶ Select the color for your gridlines and worksheet headings with the Options ⇨ Display command.

▶ You can customize the 16 colors available to your worksheets using Options ⇨ Color Palette.

▶ You can choose whether you want to display Excel's toolbar, Formula bar, the scroll bars, or the Status bar. You can also specify which toolbars you want to display, if any.

▶ You can choose whether you want to display formulas or the results of formulas, as well as worksheet gridlines and worksheet headings.

▶ You can view your worksheet through two or four window panes, which also can be frozen to prevent scrolling.

▶ Worksheets can also be viewed through more than the one default window. Multiple worksheet windows can be moved, sized, closed, and saved with your worksheet.

▶ The display of your worksheet can be decreased or increased with Window ⇨ Zoom.

▶ Window ⇨ View lets you save views of your worksheet with customized display characteristics.

Chapter 15
Creating Charts

In this chapter . . .

▶ Why charts are important for most spreadsheet users.

▶ What types of charts Excel can generate.

▶ How Excel handles charts.

▶ How to create charts — with and without the help of the ChartWizard.

▶ How to make basic modifications to your charts.

As you know by now, a nicely formatted table of numbers is easy enough to generate in Excel. And it's just as easy to transform the numbers into a chart or graph. All spreadsheets provide the ability to produce charts, and Excel's prowess in this area leaves little to be desired. In fact, there's so much capability here that we've split charting into three chapters. This chapter tells you everything you need to know to produce handsome charts from Excel. Chapter 16 continues the adventure with details on customizing charts, and we wrap it up in Chapter 17 with instructions on how to get your charts on paper with minimal frustration.

Why Use Charts?

You know the old saying that claims a picture is worth a thousand words. When dealing with data, it may be more appropriate to say that a chart can tell you much more than a table of numbers. Presenting numbers graphically in the form of a well-conceived chart can make your point quickly — and maybe even save you a thousand words in the process. And since charts are linked to worksheet data, if your numbers change the charts will reflect these changes instantly.

Charts are particularly useful for getting a visual picture of a lengthy series of numbers and their relationships. Making a quick chart often shows you trends and patterns that are nearly impossible to spot in a range of numbers.

Fortunately, Excel makes it easy to convert numbers into a chart. Even better, you can easily experiment with different chart types to determine the best way to make your case. And if that weren't enough, you can make all sorts of adjustments to the standard charts and even add annotations, clip art, and other bells and whistles.

Suffice it to say that mastering the charting features of Excel is necessary if you plan to get the most out of the program. We know of very few Excel users who don't use this feature — either for their own use or for major presentations.

Chart Types

Excel can generate many types of charts — from familiar column and line charts, to esoteric "radar" and surface charts. Table 15-1 shows a complete list of Excel's basic chart types and the number of variations of each that you can select from.

Do the arithmetic and you'll discover that this adds up to 90 basic chart types. Each of these is highly customizable and you can overlay one chart on top of another, so there's almost no limit to the number of different chart types you can create. Figures 15-1a through 15-1f show a small sample of the charts that you'll be able to generate with Excel.

Table 15-1: The basic chart types available in Excel, and the number of variations you can choose from	
Chart type	**Number of variations**
Area	5
Bar	10
Column	10
Line	9
Pie	7
Radar	5
XY (Scatter)	5
Combination	6
3-D Area	7
3-D Bar	4
3-D Column	7
3-D Line	4
3-D Pie	7
3-D Surface	4

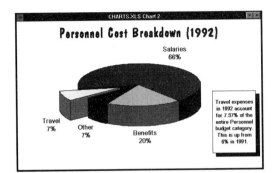

Figure 15-1a: A 3-D pie chart with added text in a shadowed box.

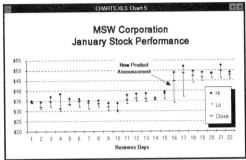

Figure 15-1b: This line chart type is useful for plotting stock market data. Free-floating text has been added to this chart, along with an arrow.

Figure 15-1c: This combination chart consists of columns and a line, each with its own vertical axis.

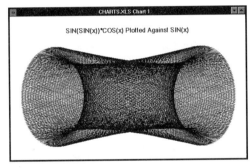

Figure 15-1d: An example of what you can do when you play around with trigonometric functions. This chart has the axes removed.

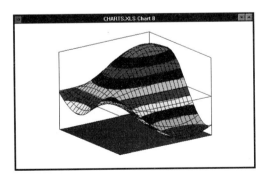

Figure 15-1e: An example of a surface chart.

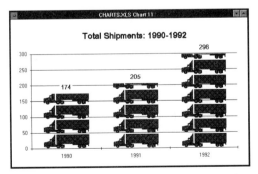

Figure 15-1f: Excel lets you paste graphic images into bars and columns — similar to the types of charts you might see in USA Today.

We don't have space in this book to discuss all of the possible chart types and what they are most suitable for. In fact, there are no hard and fast rules for choosing the appropriate graph type for your data. The best advice is to use the type of chart that gets your message across in the simplest way possible. Don't be afraid to experiment; it only takes a few seconds to convert a graph to a different type.

A Quick Example

Believe it or not, you can generate a chart from existing data with one mouse click and one keystroke. The worksheet in Figure 15-2 shows some monthly sales data for two regions. To generate a quick chart, select the data in the range A3:D9, and press F11 (the shortcut key for File ⇨ New with the Chart option).

Excel creates a default chart in a new window — shown in Figure 15-3. The default (or "preferred") chart type is a standard column chart with no gridlines and no legend. You can change the chart type with a few mouse clicks, and the entire chart can easily be customized with a title, a legend, gridlines, and practically anything else you would want. For example, the selected data might be displayed better as a 3-D chart with legends — an easy change to make with Excel. And, of course, you can insert the chart into a worksheet file to augment your reports. These topics make up the remainder of this chapter.

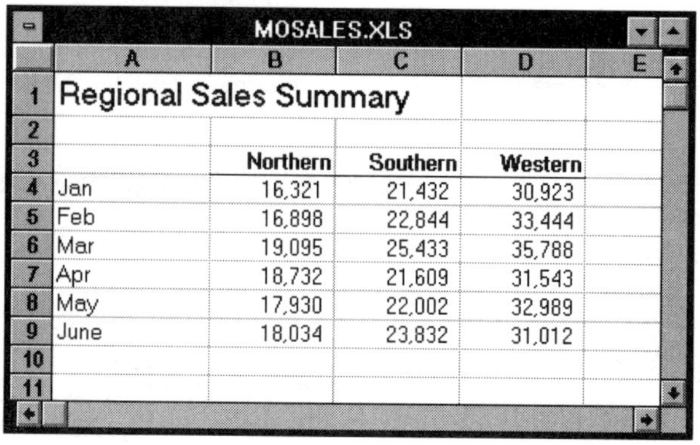

Figure 15-2:
Worksheet
data that can
be converted
into a chart
with one
mouse click
and one
keystroke.

	A	B	C	D	E
			MOSALES.XLS		
1	Regional Sales Summary				
2					
3		Northern	Southern	Western	
4	Jan	16,321	21,432	30,923	
5	Feb	16,898	22,844	33,444	
6	Mar	19,095	25,433	35,788	
7	Apr	18,732	21,609	31,543	
8	May	17,930	22,002	32,989	
9	June	18,034	23,832	31,012	
10					
11					

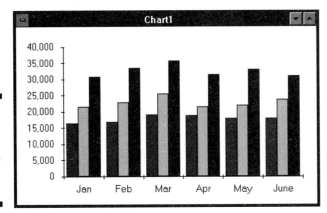

Figure 15-3:
Excel's
default
chart type is
a column
chart.

How Excel Handles Charts

When you create a chart in Excel, you have two options:

■ Insert the chart directly into a worksheet as an object (that is, as an "embedded" chart). Such a chart is stored within the worksheet file.

■ Create the chart as a new document in its own window (a chart window, as opposed to a worksheet window). When you're working in a chart window, you have full access to the chart menu, including a command to print the chart independent of any worksheet range.

After you insert a chart into a worksheet, you can move it, resize it, change the proportions, and do other tricks. You can access all of the Chart menu options simply by double-clicking anywhere within the chart frame. This opens up a chart window for editing the chart. When you finish with your changes and close the chart window, the chart object in your worksheet reflects the changes you made.

When you're working in a chart window, you can save a chart as a separate xlc file. When you do this, Excel automatically creates a link to the original data. In practice, however, it's more efficient to store charts in worksheet files.

Inserting a chart directly into a worksheet is the preferred method of creating a chart, since the chart is then saved with the worksheet and you don't have to keep track of separate chart files that are associated with a worksheet file. Storing a chart in a separate file may be useful, however, if you need to pass an electronic copy to a coworker, and you do not want to give that person the entire worksheet file.

Creating Charts

 A new feature in Excel 4 is the ChartWizard tool which you activate from the toolbar. (We'll explain how to do this in a moment.) The ChartWizard displays a series of dialog boxes that walk you through all of the steps necessary to create a chart. You can invoke the ChartWizard when creating a new chart or when modifying an existing one.

 The ChartWizard is optional but it's handy for changing the row and column orientation of a chart. In previous versions of Excel, this was often a problem that had to be approached by making multiple selections.

Preparing data to be charted

Excel plots information using one or more sets of data called a *series*. For example, a line chart with three lines has three data series. A pie chart, on the other hand, can have only one series. Your data series can be arranged in a worksheet either horizontally (by rows) or vertically (by columns). Figure 15-4 shows a worksheet with some data that's well-suited for charting. In this case, it contains two data series, each with ten values. To create a chart from this data, select the range A4:C14 and then click the ChartWizard tool:

Making a chart is easiest if the data you'll be plotting is all together in a worksheet. This isn't a requirement, however, since a chart can contain data from ranges scattered throughout a worksheet or even spread across different worksheets.

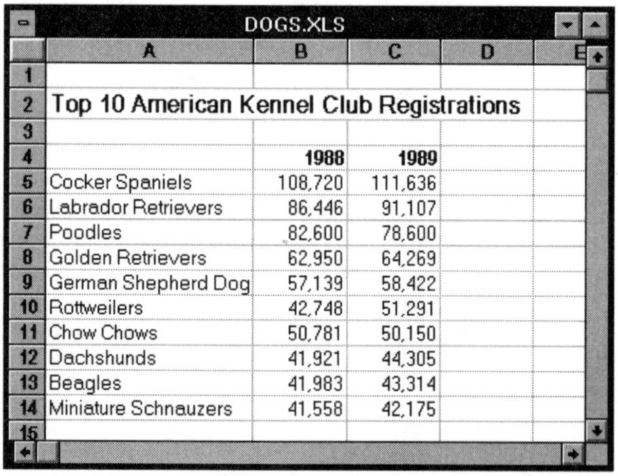

Figure 15-4: This range can easily be plotted. It has two data series, each with ten values. You can select the entire range.

	A	B	C	D	E
1					
2	Top 10 American Kennel Club Registrations				
3					
4		1988	1989		
5	Cocker Spaniels	108,720	111,636		
6	Labrador Retrievers	86,446	91,107		
7	Poodles	82,600	78,600		
8	Golden Retrievers	62,950	64,269		
9	German Shepherd Dog	57,139	58,422		
10	Rottweilers	42,748	51,291		
11	Chow Chows	50,781	50,150		
12	Dachshunds	41,921	44,305		
13	Beagles	41,983	43,314		
14	Miniature Schnauzers	41,558	42,175		
15					

DOGS.XLS

DRUGS.XLS

	A	B	C	D	E	F	G	H
1	High School Graduating Classes							
2	Percent who have never used a particular drug							
3								
4				Illegal Drugs				
5		1984	1985	1986	1987	1988	1989	
6	PCP	5.0	4.9	4.8	3.0	2.9	3.9	
7	LSD	8.0	7.5	7.2	8.4	7.7	8.3	
8	Cocaine	16.1	17.3	17.0	15.2	12.1	10.3	
9	Marijuana/Hash	54.9	54.2	50.9	50.2	47.2	43.7	
10								
11								
12				Legal Drugs				
13	Cigarettes	69.7	68.8	67.6	67.2	66.4	65.7	
14	Alcohol	92.6	92.2	91.3	92.2	92.0	90.7	
15								
16								

Figure 15-5: If the data to be plotted isn't adjacent, you can use Excel's multiple-selection techniques.

If the data you're plotting isn't contiguous you can make a multiple selection by holding down the Ctrl key while you select the data ranges. Alternatively, you can set up another contiguous range with formula references to the noncontiguous data. This option lets you create a chart with a single selection.

Figure 15-5 shows data that's not arranged together, but has been selected using the multiple-selection technique.

How Excel determines chart series

When you select a range of data to be charted, how does Excel determine if the series are arranged vertically or horizontally? Good question. Excel examines the shape of the range and assumes that you want fewer data series than categories. As a result, if the data selection has more rows than columns, it uses columns for the series. If there are more columns than rows, it uses each row as a separate series.

Excel also checks the data selection for content. If the upper-left cell is blank, or if the first row and column contain text or dates, Excel uses the first row and column for the series names and category names.

Before Excel 4, overriding Excel's guess about the data series was a real pain that required making multiple selections and pasting data. The issue is greatly simplified if you use ChartWizard — you change row vs. column settings with the click of a button, and you can see the results immediately.

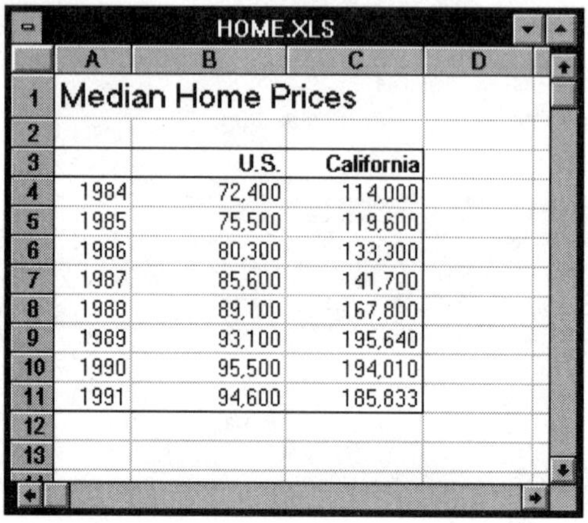

	A	B	C	D
1	Median Home Prices			
2				
3		U.S.	California	
4	1984	72,400	114,000	
5	1985	75,500	119,600	
6	1986	80,300	133,300	
7	1987	85,600	141,700	
8	1988	89,100	167,800	
9	1989	93,100	195,640	
10	1990	95,500	194,010	
11	1991	94,600	185,833	
12				
13				

HOME.XLS

Figure 15-6:
Data used to
demonstrate
ChartWizard's
features.

Using the ChartWizard

The easiest way to transform a range of numbers into a chart is to use Excel's ChartWizard to guide you through the five steps. To demonstrate how to use the ChartWizard, we'll walk through these steps and create a chart from the worksheet data shown in Figure 15-6. If you're new to charting, you might want to set up the data in a worksheet and follow along on your own computer.

First, select the data for the chart — including the category labels (specifically, the years) and legend text. In this case select the range A3:C11.

When selecting data to be charted, make sure the selection doesn't include any empty rows or columns.

With the data selected, click the ChartWizard icon. You'll notice that the mouse pointer changes shape, and a message appears at the bottom of the screen that reads "Click and drag in document to create a chart." Use the mouse to point out an area in the worksheet where you want the chart inserted. You can always move and resize the chart later, so don't be too concerned about its location at this point. When you release the mouse button, the first Chart-Wizard dialog box appears as shown in Figure 15-7.

The first dialog box asks you to indicate the data range that you're plotting. Since we preselected the data, the range already appears in the text box. If you discover that you selected the wrong data (or if you did not select data before invoking the ChartWizard), you can simply click in the text box and then select the range in the worksheet. When you're satisfied that the proper data range is selected, choose the Next button to move on to the next step.

Figure 15-7: The first of five ChartWizard dialog boxes lets you enter a range to be plotted or displays the range you've selected.

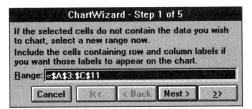

The ChartWizard dialog box controls were designed to resemble those found on a VCR. For example, the ⇨ button represents fast forward — which is a shortcut way of skipping the subsequent steps in the ChartWizard and displaying your completed chart. You can get detailed help at any time by clicking the Help button. If you change your mind about creating a chart, click the Cancel button.

The second ChartWizard dialog box is shown in Figure 15-8. This is where you select the general chart type from the 14 categories. For this example, we'll select the Column chart type. You can double-click this icon to move on to the next step, or click once on the chart icon to select it and then choose the Next button.

The next ChartWizard dialog box will vary, depending upon your previous selection. If you select the Column chart type, the dialog box shown in Figure 15-9 appears. Excel offers ten varieties of column charts. For this example, we'll select format number 1. Double-click the first chart icon to move on to the next step.

Figure 15-8: The second ChartWizard dialog box lets you select a chart from the general chart types.

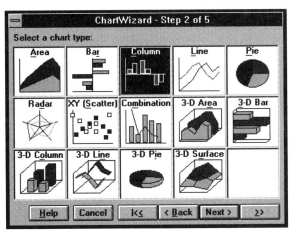

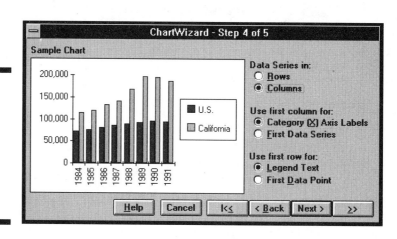

Figure 15-9: The third ChartWizard dialog box lets you select a specific chart type.

The fourth dialog box in the series (Figure 15-10) displays the actual chart. Excel makes its best guess as to how your data series are organized (either by rows or by columns). If it guessed wrong, you can change it by selecting the appropriate radio button. In this example, Excel figured out that we wanted to use the first column for Category Labels and the first row for Legend Text to distinguish the series. If you want to correct either of these assumptions, do it here. Otherwise, select Next to move on.

You can experiment with these options to see their effects by clicking the buttons. The ChartWizard will show the changes to the graph in this dialog box but they will not become permanent until you choose Next.

The fifth dialog box (Figure 15-11) lets you delete the legend it added if you like, and also gives you an opportunity to add a Chart Title and provide titles for the Category and Value axes. Before you enter text, select the appropriate text box.

Figure 15-10: The fourth ChartWizard dialog box previews your chart. You can easily change some options at this point.

Figure 15-11:
The final
ChartWizard
dialog box lets
you add a title
and labels.

You're not limited to the box size shown — your entry will scroll to the left as
each box fills with text. For this example, remove the legend by clicking the No
button and enter the following title: *Median Resale Home Prices*. We won't need
any Axis Titles since they are self-explanatory. Since this is the last ChartWizard
dialog box, there is no Next button. Select OK or press Enter. When the dialog
box disappears, the chart will be inserted in the worksheet in the area you
originally specified. Your screen should resemble Figure 15-12.

You can select the new chart in the worksheet by clicking on it. This lets you
move it or change the size. If you double-click on it, the chart will be displayed
in a chart window where you can edit it.

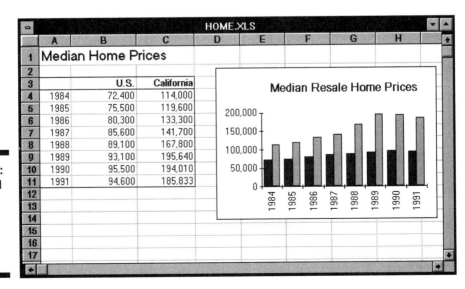

Figure 15-12:
ChartWizard
inserts the
chart in the
area you
originally
indicated.

You can insert a chart directly into a worksheet without using the ChartWizard if you use the Options ⇨ Toolbars command and display the Chart toolbar. Simply select the data to be charted and choose the chart tool that corresponds to the chart type you want. You'll get a message at the bottom of the screen instructing you to press and drag in the worksheet. The chart appears where you indicate.

Creating a chart in a separate window

If you won't be inserting a chart into a worksheet, you can create it in its own window. If you decide later that you want to put it in a worksheet, you can easily copy and paste it wherever you like.

Why would you want to create a chart in a window, rather than in a worksheet? There are several reasons:

- You might want to print the chart separately using the chart window's File ⇨ Print command.

- You might be creating the chart for use in another application. For example, you can create a chart in Excel and then copy it to a word processing document.

- You might have many charts to create, and you don't want them cluttering up your worksheet. Creating a chart directly in a window can be faster than going through the ChartWizard.

To create a chart in a separate chart window, select the data and then choose File ⇨ New from the worksheet menu. This pops up a dialog box that lets you pick the type of file you want (see Figure 15-13). Double-click Chart to create a chart from the selected data.

You can also press F11 — a shortcut key for creating a new chart.

Excel will open a new window and display the chart in the current preferred format (this is explained later). You can then use the chart window menu to make any changes or modifications. If you want to save the chart, you can do one of two things:

- Select File ⇨ Save from the chart window menu to save the chart as an xlc file. It will retain its links to the worksheet.

- Select the entire chart (using the Chart ⇨ Select Chart command), copy it to the clipboard (with Edit ⇨ Copy), and then paste it into a worksheet by activating the worksheet and selecting Edit ⇨ Paste from the worksheet menu. The chart can then be saved in the worksheet file.

Figure 15-13: The New dialog box lets you select the type of document you want to open. To create a chart, select Chart.

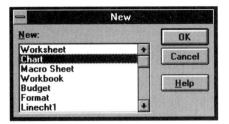

Setting a preferred chart format

You may have noticed that when you create a chart (using either the Chart-Wizard or the Chart toolbar) Excel always generates a standard column chart with no gridlines — this is the default "preferred" chart format. If you'll be creating several charts of the same general style, you can save yourself a lot of work by telling Excel to change its default chart format to one that you select. After you create a chart and customize it, you can specify that chart as your new preferred chart format. Change the default chart format by selecting the Gallery ⇨ Set Preferred command on the chart window menu.

The preferred chart type that you set remains in effect only for the current session (or until you specify a different preferred chart). When you use the File ⇨ Save Workbook command, however, the preferred chart format is saved in the workbook. Consequently, when you reopen the workbook and create more charts, your preferred chart format will be used.

You can also create a template file which includes the preferred chart type that you set. For example, you might create a worksheet template file called lines that has a preferred chart type of line charts. All charts that you create from worksheets using that template will start out as line charts. You'll see these templates listed in the File ⇨ New dialog box (Figure 15-13) when you select File ⇨ New.

Basic Chart Modifications_____

Unless you're generating a quick and dirty chart for your own purpose, the initial chart that Excel generates is rarely good enough. You'll usually want to make at least a few modifications to it. This section discusses some of the basic edits you can perform on a chart. The topic is explored more fully in the next chapter.

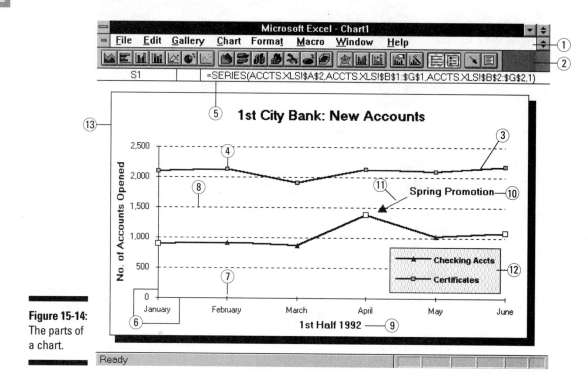

Figure 15-14:
The parts of
a chart.

Chart parts

Figure 15-14 shows a typical Excel chart displayed in a chart window, with the various components numbered. The following discussion tells you everything you need to know about these parts.

① **Chart menu bar:** This provides access to the commands you use to modify the chart (it's different from the menu displayed in a worksheet window). Many of these commands are also accessible from the Chart toolbar.

② **Chart toolbar:** This has 23 charting tools (including ChartWizard) and displays automatically when you activate a chart window or when you select an embedded chart in a worksheet window. As with all toolbars, you can move it to a more convenient screen location.

③ **Data series:** This corresponds to a group of related values in a worksheet. A data series can be represented as bars, columns, a line, a pie, and so forth. This example plots two data series, each as a line.

④ **Data marker:** A bar, symbol, or some other image that represents an individual data point or value.

⑤ **Series formula:** When you select a data series in a chart, Excel displays a series formula in the Formula bar. This is actually a rather complicated function that you can edit, but in most cases, you'll have no need to mess with series formulas.

⑥ **Axis:** A line that displays the reference values for the chart data. A two-dimensional chart has two axes, with an optional second vertical axis on the right. Three-dimensional charts have three axes.

⑦ **Tick mark:** A small line that intersects an axis and may or may not have an axis label attached to it. Tick marks are used to demarcate units along an axis.

⑧ **Gridlines:** Extensions of all or some of the tick marks through the plot area to help the viewer determine values.

⑨ **Attached text:** Text you provide that is associated with a particular component of the chart. Attached text can be a title, an axis label, or a data label. Attached text cannot be moved independently.

⑩ **Unattached text:** Free-floating text you can add anywhere in a chart.

⑪ **Arrow:** A free-floating arrow you can add anywhere in a chart to point out something. You can remove the arrowhead to transform an arrow into a line.

⑫ **Legend:** A chart key that identifies what each of the series corresponds to.

⑬ **Chart border:** An optional border that surrounds the entire chart.

Editing an embedded chart

A chart inserted into a worksheet is called an *embedded* chart. When you double-click an embedded chart, Excel opens a chart window where you can edit the chart. When you exit the chart window, the changes will be reflected in the embedded chart.

 Clicking an embedded chart one time selects it. Clicking it twice displays it in a chart window for editing.

You can also perform a few modifications to an embedded chart using the Chart toolbar, which is activated whenever you select an embedded chart (see Figure 15-15). As with all toolbars, you can move it anywhere you like. The

Figure 15-15:
The Chart
toolbar.

toolbar shown in the figure is free-floating. Here's what you can do to an embedded chart using the Chart toolbar:

- Change the chart type

- Add or take away gridlines

- Add or take away the legend

- Add an arrow

- Add a free-floating text box

Two charting tools accessed when an embedded chart is selected do not work as you might expect. The arrow icon and the text box icon do not affect the chart itself. Rather, these tools add new objects on *top of* the chart. You can see this for yourself by adding an arrow to an embedded chart and then moving the chart. The arrow will stay put. This is useful for drawing a line from a worksheet to the chart representing the data, for example. Note, however, that you can select all of the objects (the chart, arrows, text boxes, and so on) and then issue the Format ⇨ Group command to bind them into a single object. This new object can then be moved and sized (but it's no longer a chart object). To convert it back to a chart object so you can edit it in a chart window, select it and issue the Format ⇨ Ungroup command.

You can make other modifications to an embedded chart by double-clicking it. This action opens up a chart window. If the worksheet is maximized, the chart window will also be maximized. If the worksheet is not maximized, the chart window will be the same size as the embedded chart.

If you plan to present charts embedded in worksheets, it's a good idea to work on charts at their actual size. If you work on a maximized chart and then reduce it to its original size in the worksheet, some of the elements may not be positioned or displayed properly.

In the chart window, you have access to all of Excel's chart commands. Any chart component that you can select has a shortcut menu associated with it — accessible by clicking the right mouse button. When you are finished editing the chart in the chart window, click anywhere in the worksheet to close the chart window and update the chart. If the chart window is maximized, select the File ⇨ Close command from the chart menu.

Inserting a chart in a worksheet

If you created a chart directly in a chart window, you can embed it in a worksheet. First, select the entire chart with the Chart ➪ Select Chart command from the chart window menu. Next, copy the chart to the Windows Clipboard by using the Edit ➪ Copy command or the Ctrl+C key combination.

Activate the worksheet in which you want to insert the chart and select Edit ➪ Paste (or use the Ctrl+V key combination). The chart object will be copied from the Clipboard to the worksheet. You can then move and resize this object to your liking (see next section).

After you embed the chart in a worksheet, you can close the chart window without saving any changes, since you can always get the chart object back into a chart window by double-clicking it from the worksheet.

Moving and resizing an embedded chart

A chart object in a worksheet is just like any other worksheet object. You can move it around, change its size and proportions, adjust the border, and so on.

Changing the size or proportions of an embedded chart can drastically alter the way it looks and prints. For example, legends are typically oversized on smaller charts. After you resize an embedded chart, make sure it's still legible.

Before you can do anything with an embedded chart, you must select it by clicking once (double-clicking will open up a chart window so you can edit it). As you move the mouse over the selected chart and its borders, you'll notice that the mouse pointer changes shape.

Moving a chart object: When the mouse pointer is a large arrow, you can click and move the object anywhere you want by dragging it.

If you want to move an embedded chart a long distance in a worksheet, or move it to another worksheet, use the Windows cut-and-paste procedure.

Resizing a chart object: When you drag the mouse over the small square "handles" of the chart, the mouse pointer turns into a double-headed arrow. This means that you can press and drag the border to change its size. If the chart has no handles, it's not selected.

When you resize an object using the "handles" of the chart, you can hold down the Shift key to keep the same relative proportions.

Opening a chart window for more adjustments

To change colors, add text, and modify gridlines in an embedded chart, you need to open a chart window. You do this by double-clicking the embedded chart. Excel displays the chart in its own window at the same size and location as the embedded chart. If the worksheet is maximized, the chart window will also be maximized.

When you're working with a chart in a chart window, you can modify most aspects of the chart: colors of the bars, line widths, types of markers, axis scaling, font sizes, and so on. There are three basic ways to edit and modify elements in a chart:

1. Select an element by clicking it and then use the chart window menus to make your modifications. Only the appropriate menu commands will be available (the others will be grayed out).

2. Double-click an element to bring up a dialog box, which may or may not be appropriate for what you want to do. In the vast majority of cases, however, the dialog box will have a button that leads you to the dialog box you had in mind.

3. Click a chart element with the right mouse button to display a context-sensitive shortcut menu. Use this menu to bring up the appropriate dialog box.

Chapter 16 goes into quite a bit of detail on modifying charts. You might find, however, that it's all fairly straightforward. If you're the type who likes to tinker around, Excel's charts provide you with plenty of territory to explore. Dig in and check it out. If you prefer to go about your learning a bit more systematically, the next chapter explains how to make your charts sing (well . . . at least look better).

 Contrary to what you might think, you cannot use the normal Windows copy-and-paste procedures with elements of a chart. You can select the entire chart and copy it to the clipboard, but the Edit ⇨ Copy command is not available for individual components such as arrows, the title, and so on.

After you've made your changes you can exit the chart window using any of the following techniques:

■ Click anywhere in the worksheet (this works only if you haven't maximized the chart window).

■ Select File ⇨ Close from the chart window menu.

■ Double-click the chart window's Control box (the small horizontal bar in the upper-left corner of the chart window).

The embedded chart will then include the changes you made.

Some General Charting Tips

- The numerical format of the values on the chart axes are always the same as the worksheet data for the series. If you're working with large numbers, you might want to create a custom numeric format that hides some of the digits. You can then add an annotation that reads something like *(dollars in thousands)* or *($,000,000)*. Here are two examples of useful custom formats to hide digits:

Value	Appearance	Custom Format
123,456,789	123,457	#,##0,
123,456,789	123	#,##0,,

- Use caution when you manipulate the values that are used for a chart. For example, if you move any of the cells in a charted range, the chart no longer refers to the right cells. If you move an entire range, however, the chart will adjust its cell references.

- If you find yourself using a particular chart type most often, consider setting up a template with that chart as the preferred chart type.

- Don't forget that you can copy charts to the Clipboard and then paste them into other applications.

Summary

▶ Using a chart can make a table of numbers more easy to understand, and can also expose trends that are not apparent from numbers alone.

▶ Excel offers an excellent selection of chart types (90 basic types), and each chart can be modified and annotated extensively.

▶ The ChartWizard feature (new to Excel 4) simplifies chart making for both beginners and advanced users.

▶ You can create a chart directly in a worksheet (embedded) or in its own chart window. Most of the time, you'll probably embed your charts in a worksheet.

▶ Excel has a default "preferred" chart type. You can override the default type and set your own preferred chart type. This is valid only for the current session unless you save your work in a workbook.

▶ You can easily move and resize an embedded chart.

▶ When you double-click an embedded chart, Excel opens a chart window the same size as the embedded chart (or maximized if the worksheet is maximized) and gives you access to all of the chart editing menus. After you've made your modifications, simply click anywhere in the worksheet to close the chart window and update the embedded chart (or select the File ⇨ Close command if the chart window is maximized).

Chapter 16
Modifying and Annotating Charts

As you learned in Chapter 15, creating a chart in Excel is simple and straight-forward. ChartWizard provides a foolproof way to generate a basic chart with only a few mouse clicks. But that's just the first step — the tip of the proverbial iceberg with regard to Excel's charting capabilities. This chapter builds on the basic concepts covered in the preceding chapter and shows you how to create some truly stunning charts and presentations.

Why Modify a Chart?

In some cases, the basic chart that Excel creates is all you need. If you're using charts to get a better idea of what your data looks like, a simple chart does just fine. But if you're preparing an important presentation, you'll want to take advantage of the additional charting tools available in Excel. Besides the most obvious modification — changing the chart type — adjustments to your charts typically involve one or more of the following:

- Changing the data range that the chart uses.

- Adding titles for the chart or any of the axes.

- Changing the fonts and sizes used for text items.

- Changing the colors or hatch patterns of bars, columns, or areas — or of the entire chart.

- Changing line attributes (width or type of line) and selecting different line markers.

- Adding one or more additional data ranges to the chart after the fact.

- Changing the type of overlay used.

- Adding free-floating text and/or arrows (which can be moved anywhere you like).

- Changing the scaling on the axes. For example, you may want to tell Excel what the minimum and maximum values are on the value axis.

- Converting bars or columns to bitmap images.

- Moving the legend (or adding one if it's not present).

- Adding or modifying gridlines.

- Modifying the tick marks displayed on the axes.

- Changing the color palette used by the chart.

- Rotating or changing the viewing perspective of 3-D graphs.

- Changing the scale to logarithmic.

Obviously, when you create a chart, what you see initially is only a starting point.

Examining Chart Items

A chart is made up of many different items — the series you plot, axes, the title, any text you add, and so on. Most of the chart items can be selected and modified in one way or another. For example, you can change the font and size of the title, move the legend, and change the scaling on the axes; you can change almost everything.

 Most of this chapter assumes that you're working in a chart window. If your chart is embedded in a worksheet, double-click it to open it in a chart window.

You can first select a chart item and then use the chart menus to make your modifications. Or you can double-click an item to bring up a dialog box. The best method, however, is to point to an item and then click the right mouse button to display a shortcut menu. Figure 16-1 shows the shortcut menu that appears when you right-click the chart's title. The menu that appears depends on the type of item.

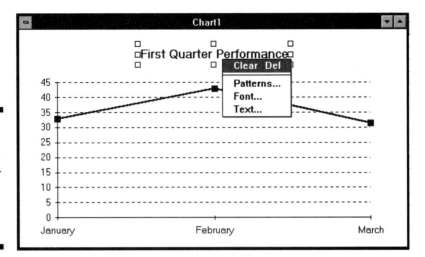

Figure 16-1:
Excel's shortcut menus (which pop up when you right-click something) provide an easy way to modify chart elements.

Being able to select the correct chart item takes some practice. Sometimes you may have to make two or three click attempts before the intended item gets selected. Notice that the formula bar displays the name of the currently selected item. You can also use the arrow keys to cycle through all the chart items. Use the up and down arrows to cycle through classes of objects and the left and right arrows to cycle through items within a class.

Here's a summary of the different types of chart items that you can select and modify. These names are displayed in the Formula bar when the particular item is selected:

Plot   The area within the chart window that is not occupied by any other item (including the gridlines).

Chart   The entire chart. Select this setting by clicking outside of the plot area where no other items exist or use the Chart ⇨ Select Chart command on the menu.

Sn   The data series, where *n* is a number beginning with 1. Select a data series by clicking the marker (such as the line, column, or bar). When a data series is selected, a series formula is displayed in the edit bar. You can modify this formula if you know what you're doing.

SnPm   Individual data points within a series. For example, the first data point in the first series is called S1P1. The only way to select individual data points is to hold down the Ctrl key while you click (or you can use the arrow keys to cycle through all items until you get to the one you want).

Title	The chart's title.
Legend	The chart's legend.
Axis _n_	One of the axes in the chart. A chart can have up to four axes (two for the main chart and two for the overlay chart). A 3-D chart has three axes.
Text Axis _n_	The label assigned to the axis.
Text _n_	Free-floating text that you add to the chart. The first text added is called Text 1, the next is Text 2, and so on.
Arrow _n_	An arrow you add to the chart. The first arrow added is called Arrow 1, the next is Arrow 2, and so on.
Gridlines _n_	Any gridlines that you added to the chart. You can have up to four gridlines in 2-D charts: category axis (major and minor) and value axis (major and minor). 3-D charts provide two more gridline options.
Walls	On 3-D charts only (except 3-D pie charts).
Floor	On 3-D charts only (except 3-D pie charts).
Corners	Only 3-D charts (except 3-D pie charts) have corners. You select the corners if you want to rotate a 3-D chart using a mouse.

Working with a Data Series

Understanding that Excel creates a link between worksheet data and the chart is important. If you change the data, the chart adjusts automatically. Consequently, you need to know how to work with the individual data series that make up a chart.

Adding a new data series

You'll often want to add a new data series to an existing chart. You can, of course, just start over by clearing the current chart and creating a new one. By the way, if you issue the Gallery ⇨ Set Preferred command before you clear the chart, you can retain most of the customizations you already did, and the next

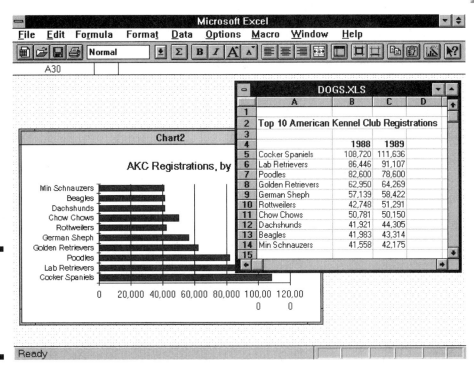

Figure 16-2: This chart needs to have another series added to it.

chart takes on these formats. But no reason really exists to start over just because you want to add more data to a chart. With Excel you can easily add a new data series to an existing chart using familiar copy and paste procedures.

Figure 16-2 shows a chart that uses the data in range A4:B14. After the chart was customized, we decided that the data in range C4:C14 should also be plotted. Here's how to add a new series to the chart:

Steps: Adding a new series to a chart

Step 1. Activate the worksheet that holds the data you'll be adding. This data can be in the same worksheet or in a different worksheet.

Step 2. Select the worksheet data, including the series title, if any.

Step 3. Issue the Edit ⇨ Copy command to copy the data to the Clipboard.

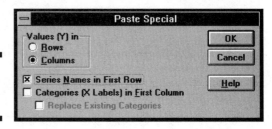

Figure 16-3: The Paste Special dialog box enables you to tell Excel how your data is set up before it gets copied into a chart.

Step 4. Activate the chart window.

Step 5. Issue the Edit ⇨ Paste Special command. You'll see the dialog box shown in Figure 16-3. This dialog box enables you to inform Excel about what the copied data contains.

Step 6. In this case, the series name (specifically, 1989) is in the first row, so click this option. Excel then pastes the data as a new chart series.

If there's no ambiguity about series names, you can simply use the Edit ⇨ Paste command to let Excel guess about your data. Usually, however, using Edit ⇨ Paste Special to paste new data into a chart is best.

After performing these steps, the chart should look like the one shown in Figure 16-4.

You can also use the chart window's Chart ⇨ Edit Series command to add a new data series to a chart. Select New Series and then choose the Define button.

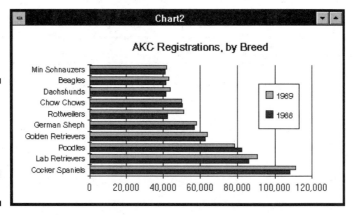

Figure 16-4: The chart from Figure 16-2, after pasting in another data series.

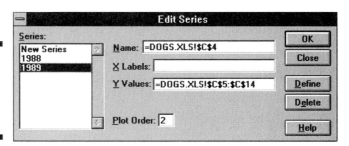

Figure 16-5: The Edit Series dialog box enables you to add a new series, change or delete a series, or change the order in which the series are plotted.

Deleting a data series

Getting rid of a data series in a graph is easy. Actually, you have several ways to do this task. Here's the easiest method:

Steps: Deleting a data series

Step 1. Select the series by clicking one of its elements — a bar, a column, or a point on a line, for example. Excel then displays its series formula on the Formula bar.

Step 2. Select the Edit ⇨ Clear command (or press the Del key). A small dialog box appears.

Step 3. Select the Series option and then choose OK to delete the series.

You can also use the Edit ⇨ Clear command to simply remove any formatting you have added to a series.

Changing the number of data points plotted

The preceding discussion focused on adding or deleting entire data series. But what if you just want to extend a data series to include more data? Or plot less data? Again, you don't need to start over. In the chart window menu, select Chart ⇨ Edit Series which takes you to the dialog box shown in Figure 16-5. If you're working on a 3-D chart, this dialog box has additional options.

The list box on the left displays all the chart series names, plus an extra name called New Series (used for adding a series to a chart). When you select one of the series names, the text boxes to the right display the series' name (which is used in the legend), the range that holds the x-axis labels, and the range itself. To change any of these items, click in the appropriate box and edit the range manually — for example, shorten or lengthen the range it refers to (don't forget to adjust the x-labels accordingly). Or you can highlight the *entire contents* of a text box, activate the worksheet, and point out a new range with the mouse or keyboard. The range that you select replaces the contents of the text box.

If you don't select the entire contents of the text box before pointing out a new range, only the highlighted part is replaced with the selected range. Alternatively, you can erase the contents of the text box with the Del key before pointing to a new range.

Continue in this dialog box until you've completed your changes. Make sure that you choose the Define button before moving on to the next range. When you're done, choose OK. The graph reflects your new range designations.

If you're going to modify any of the data series, you may want to have the worksheet displayed on-screen before you issue the Chart ⇨ Edit Series command. This practice makes pointing out ranges with the mouse or keyboard easier. Note, however, that you can always access the Window command and activate a different Excel window while you're pointing out a range.

Notice that this dialog box also enables you to change the order in which the series are plotted and delete series altogether via the Delete button.

Using chart overlays

As you explore the chart window menus, you'll eventually see references to something called *overlays*. An overlay is essentially one chart plotted on top of another — that is, a combination chart. An overlay chart doesn't necessarily have to have the same number of data elements as the main chart, and it can have its own category axis. An overlay chart type is useful in two situations:

- When you want one or more of the data series to be of a different chart type than the others — for example, plotting a line chart on top of a column chart.

- When you want one or more of the data series to use a different axis scale than the others. For example, if you want to plot two data series that have drastically different scales, Excel can display a second value axis on the right.

In most cases, you can simply choose Combination as the chart type and then make any necessary adjustments after the chart is created. Excel offers six variations on combination charts:

- Columns and lines, with one value axis

- Columns and lines, with two value axes

- Lines and lines, with two value axes

- Area and columns, with one value axis

- Columns and hi-low-close. This is actually a stock market chart that also shows trading volume and is referred to as a volume-hi-low-close chart.

- Columns and open-hi-low-close. This too is a stock market chart that shows trading volume and opening price. It's also referred to as a volume-open-hi-low-close chart.

These last two chart types are for special purposes, and unless you're plotting stock market data you probably won't have much use for them.

 If you've been working on a chart and realize that you need to plot another data series as an overlay, you don't need to start over. The chart window menu has a command that enables you to add an overlay to an existing chart. Select the Chart ⇨ Add Overlay command. This command essentially changes the chart type to Combination. You can then copy data from the spreadsheet and paste it into the chart.

In combination charts, Excel normally assigns half of the data series to the main chart and the other half to the overlay chart. For example, if six data series exist, the first three are for the main chart and the remaining three are for the overlay. However, you have a fair amount of control over the assignment of the data series. Change the assignments with the Format ⇨ Overlay command. Additionally, you can change the plot order of the series by using the Chart ⇨ Edit Series command.

Changing a data series' look

Excel has a set of default colors that it uses for your charts. You don't have to be content with these colors because you can easily change the color, pattern, line width, line style, and markers used for data series.

To do so, select a series by clicking one of its elements. For example, click a column, a bar, or a line. Then select Format ⇨ Patterns (or right-click the object to get to the shortcut menu). In either case, you bring up the dialog box shown

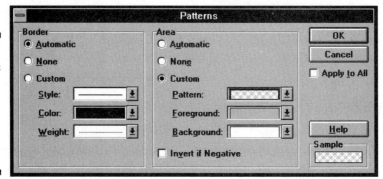

Figure 16-6:
The Patterns
dialog box
enables you
to manip-
ulate colors
and border
attributes.

in Figure 16-6. This figure shows the Patterns dialog box for a bar or column chart.

You can modify the lines that make up the border or change the colors and patterns used. The check box labeled Apply to All applies these patterns to all the series in the chart.

You can hide a data series by selecting None in both the Border and Area sections of the dialog box.

Figure 16-7 shows the dialog box that appears if you first select a line chart before you issue the Format ⇨ Patterns command. Here you can change the line width, style, and color and also select a different marker and change the colors used.

Figure 16-7: If a
line series is
selected, the
Patterns dialog
box enables you
to change the line
attributes and
markers.

Adding Text to a Chart

Most charts require some sort of explanatory text — at the very minimum, a title. Excel enables you to add two types of text items to a chart: attached text and free-floating text.

Attached text

Attached text is just that — text that is attached to a specific chart item. To attach text, select the Chart ⇨ Attach Text command from the Chart menu. This action brings up the dialog box shown in Figure 16-8. You can attach text to the following chart items:

Chart Title	The title of the chart. It is always positioned above the plot area and centered. The only way to get a title "uncentered" is to insert free-floating text in place of the title and move it where you want.
Value (Y) Axis	The title that appears next to the value axis. You cannot reposition this title.
Category (X) Axis	The title that appears next to the category axis. You cannot reposition this title.
Series and Data Point	The data values that appear next to a chart series marker. To add a data point, you must specify the series number and the point number. If you want to add data values to all your points, choose a chart type that shows numbers in its icon.
Overlay Value (Y) Axis	The title that appears next to the overlay values axis (if one exists). You cannot reposition this title.

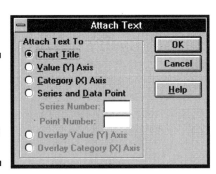

Figure 16-8: The Attach Text dialog box enables you to insert text that is attached to a specific chart element.

Overlay Category (X) Axis   The title that appears next to the overlay category axis (if one exists). You cannot reposition this title.

After you've entered text, you can adjust its properties to your liking — change the font, change the patterns, add a box, and so on. The easiest way to do this procedure is to right-click the object and use the shortcut menu.

Free-floating text

The second type of text you can add to a chart is *unattached*; you can add it anywhere and move it around as you like. The easiest way to add such text is to simply start typing and press Enter when you're finished. Excel positions the text near the middle of the chart, and you can move it to its position by dragging it with the mouse. And, of course, you can change its properties by right-clicking the text. To edit such text, select it and use the Formula bar in the usual way.

Free-floating text may not appear where you want it after you resize the chart or add additional values to a data series. Consequently, you may have to make some manual adjustments to such text.

While you're entering text, you can force a line break by pressing Ctrl+Enter. But on the other hand, you can always resize the text box. Long text strings automatically wrap around as you size the box.

Lines and arrows

A common addition to a chart is an arrow, which is often used in conjunction with free-floating text to emphasize a specific data point. To add an arrow, select the Chart ⇨ Add Arrow command. Excel places the arrow on-screen. Simply drag it to its proper place and orientation. Click the end of an arrow and drag to change its length. As with all other chart items, if you right-click an arrow you get a shortcut menu that enables you to change its attributes. An arrow without an arrowhead is a line.

Adding Chart Legends

A legend in a chart identifies what the various series represent. A chart doesn't have to have a legend. For example, you don't need to specify a legend if you're only plotting one data series. Alternatively, you can use free-floating text and arrows to identify data series, as shown in Figure 16-9.

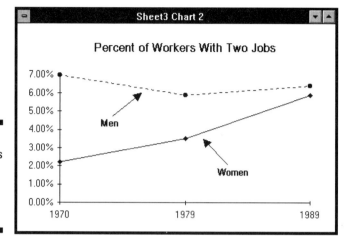

Percent of Workers With Two Jobs chart

Figure 16-9: This chart demonstrates the use of free-floating text and arrows in lieu of a legend.

If a chart doesn't have a legend, you can add one by selecting the Chart ➪ Add Legend command. Conversely, you can remove a legend from a chart with the Chart ➪ Delete Legend command. One of the icons in the Chart toolbar serves as a toggle; it adds a legend if no legend exists and takes it away if one does exist.

If you didn't include legend text when you originally selected the cells to create the chart, Excel displays Series 1, Series 2, and so on, in the legend. To add more descriptive names, select Chart ➪ Edit Series and enter series names in the Name box.

You can click a legend displayed in a chart and move it around wherever you like. Right-clicking the legend displays its shortcut menu, which enables you to adjust its patterns, fonts, and placement.

Adding Chart Gridlines

If you want a reader to be better able to determine what the chart elements represent numerically, you can add gridlines to your chart. Gridlines simply extend the tick marks on the axis. You can specify which gridlines you want to display with the Chart ➪ Gridlines command in the chart window menu. This command leads you to the dialog box shown in Figure 16-10.

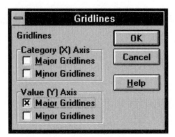

Figure 16-10: Excel provides a great deal of flexibility in the area of gridlines. This dialog box enables you to turn specific gridlines on or off.

This dialog box enables you to specify the gridlines to display. Major units are the units that have a label displayed. Minor units are those in between. You can override the default units used, if you want. First, select the appropriate axis and then issue the Format ⇨ Scale command (see the following section for more information).

When gridlines are displayed in a chart, you can right-click one of them to bring up a shortcut menu. Select Patterns and then select the line style and line width in the resulting dialog box. For example, you may want to make your gridlines dashed.

Changing a Chart's Scale

When you create a chart, Excel determines the chart's scale automatically. By scale, we mean the upper and lower numerical limits on the axes. You can easily change the scales on your charts. You may want to do so to emphasize differences between values or to deemphasize them if they're not significant.

Figure 16-11 shows two charts generated from the same data. The chart on the left uses the default scale determined by Excel, and the one on the right was

Figure 16-11: Two charts that use identical data. The only difference is the y-axis scale.

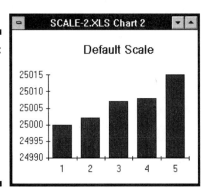

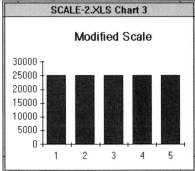

Figure 16-12:
These two charts don't use the same scale. They should, to make comparing one with the other easier.

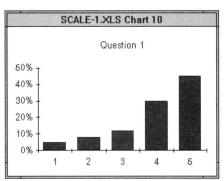
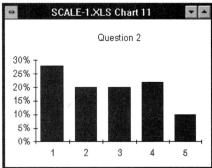

changed to better reflect the data. The differences among the data points are not very significant (they differ by about 0.05 percent), but the chart on the left makes it seem like the numbers vary dramatically. In fact, the fifth data point looks to be about twice as much as the first. In the second chart, we instructed Excel to use zero for the minimum scale value.

The actual scales you use depend on the situation. You will find no hard and fast rules, but you should avoid misrepresenting data by manipulating the chart to prove a point that doesn't exist.

If you're preparing several charts that use similarly scaled data, keeping the scales the same for all of them is a good idea so they can be compared more easily. Figure 16-12 shows an example of what we mean. These charts show the distribution of responses for a survey. Because the scales used are not the same, comparing the responses across survey items is difficult.

You adjust the scales used by charts by first selecting the axis and choosing the Format ⇨ Scale command. A faster method is to right-click the axis and then select Scale from the shortcut menu. The resulting dialog box varies, depending on which scale you selected. Figure 16-13 shows the dialog box that pops up for the value axis (y-axis). These are your options:

Auto   The series of check boxes under Auto indicate that you want Excel to calculate various components of the scale for you. Alternatively, you can enter your own values in the text boxes. When you do so, the corresponding Auto box is automatically unchecked for you.

Logarithmic Scale   Check this box if you want Excel to use a logarithmic scale for the axis. This option is useful mainly for scientific applications in which the values to be plotted have an extremely large range.

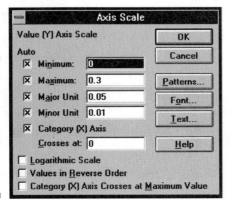

Figure 16-13: The Axis Scale dialog box enables you to adjust many aspects of the axis.

Values in Reverse Order	Check this box to reverse the order of the values on the scale. In the default column chart, this option moves the category axis to the top of the chart.
Category (X) Axis Crosses at Maximum Value	Checking this box makes the category axis cross the value axis at its maximum value (not its minimum, which is the normal way).

Each of the axes has the appropriate variations on the dialog box shown in the figure. The best way to learn how this all works is to create a simple chart and then make changes to the scale, one component at a time. Seeing the effects is easier than describing them.

Creating Chart Templates

If you have several chart formats that you use frequently, creating chart templates for them is worthwhile. This practice saves you the trouble of modifying Excel's default every time you create a chart. A template can include a customized setting for the colors in a column chart, heavier lines for the axes, a preformatted title (such as 16-point Helvetica bold), and practically any other element that you can adjust in a chart window. Templates are discussed in Chapter 6.

If your template files (with an xlt extension) are stored in your excel\xlstart directory, you can select the template when you create a new chart with the File ⇨ New command.

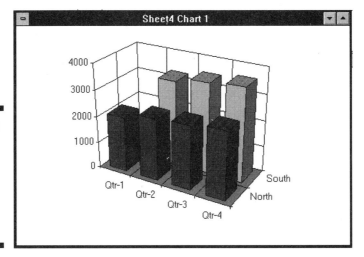

Figure 16-14:
One of the columns in this 3-D bar chart is obscured by the columns in front.

Rotating 3-D Charts

3-D charts are useful in certain situations, because you can depict changes over two different dimensions. Figure 16-14 shows a 3-D bar chart that displays sales data by quarter and by region. Note, however, that not all of the bars are visible. Rather than move on to another chart type, you can salvage this one simply by rotating the chart to a more favorable position, in one of two ways:

■ Select the Format ⇨ 3-D View command from the Chart menu. The dialog box shown in Figure 16-15 appears. You can make your rotations and perspective changes by selecting the appropriate buttons. The changes you see in the sample chart in the dialog box are *not* your actual chart; it looks the same regardless of the chart you're editing. Make the adjustments and choose OK to make them permanent.

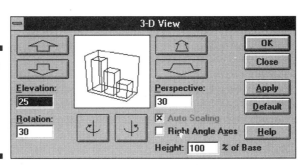

Figure 16-15: The 3-D View dialog box enables you to rotate and change the perspective of a 3-D chart. You can also drag it with the mouse.

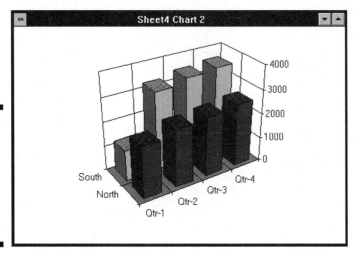

Figure 16-16:
The chart
from Figure
16-14, after
rotating it.
Now all the
columns are
visible.

■ Rotate the chart in real time by dragging corners. Right-click one of the corners of the chart. Black handles appear. You can simply click one of these black handles and rotate the chart's 3-D box to your satisfaction. This method definitely takes some practice. If your chart gets totally screwed up, select Format ⇨ 3-D View and then select the Default button to return to the original view.

If you hold down the Ctrl key while you drag, you can see an outline of the entire chart, not just the axes.

The rotated chart is shown in Figure 16-16. Now all the bars are visible, and you can clearly see the Southern region's poor first-quarter performance.

Changing a Worksheet Value by Dragging ____

Excel provides an interesting feature that can also be somewhat dangerous. You can change the value in a worksheet by dragging the data markers on 2-D line charts, bar charts, column charts, and x-y charts. Hold down the Ctrl key and click the data point on the chart. Then drag the black square in the direction you want to adjust the value. A small line appears on the y-axis to show the value as you drag (and you can move the pointer only within the scale on the value axis). If the chart is an x-y chart, you see the lines on both axes.

If the value of a data point you move is the result of a formula, Excel switches to the worksheet (which must be open) and displays the Goal Seek dialog box (goal seeking is covered in Chapter 28). Use this dialog box to specify the cell that you want Excel to adjust in order to make the formula produce the result you pointed out on the chart. Obviously, this feature can be abused because you may inadvertently change some values that you shouldn't, so be careful.

Creating Picture Charts

One of the slickest features in Excel charts is the capacity to replace bars, columns, or line chart markers with pictures. Figure 16-17 and Figure 16-18 show two examples. In the first chart, we replaced the columns with a picture of a cow — the topic of the chart. In the second, we replaced the line markers with gender symbols. This feature not only makes the chart more interesting, but it also eliminates the need for a legend.

Unfortunately, you're rather limited in what you can do with this technique. In fact, Excel only enables you to paste pictures into three chart items (2-D charts only):

■ Columns

■ Bars

■ Line markers

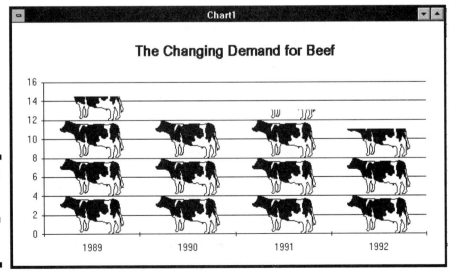

Figure 16-17: An example of a picture pasted into a column chart.

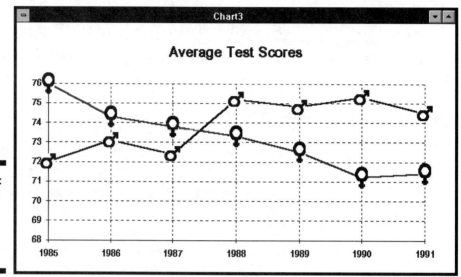

Figure 16-18:
An example
of pictures
pasted into
line chart
markers.

Whatever the limitations, the process is really quite simple and uses the standard Windows copy and paste techniques, as follows:

Steps: Creating a picture chart

Step 1. Locate the image that you want to use in the chart. This image can come from a variety of sources and is not limited to those available from Excel. Actually, most anything that you can select and copy to the Windows Clipboard can be inserted in a chart, but sometimes the results may be surprising.

Step 2. Select the image and copy it to the Windows Clipboard by using the application's Edit ⇨ Copy command.

Step 3. Activate the chart and make sure that it's a column, bar, or line chart.

Step 4. Select one of the charts' series, such as a bar, a column, or a line.

Step 5. Select Edit ⇨ Paste from Excel's Chart menu (or press Ctrl+V). The chart item is replaced with the contents of the Clipboard.

Step 6. In the case of bar or column charts, you can adjust how the image appears by right-clicking the item and selecting the Patterns option. This action displays the dialog box shown in Figure 16-19. You can specify that the image be stretched or repeated.

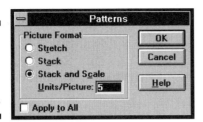

Figure 16-19: When you paste a picture into a bar or column, you can specify how you want it to appear.

The key thing to remember is that only graphics images can be pasted in this manner. Graphics images fall into two categories: bitmaps and pictures. A bitmap is made up of discrete dots, and a picture is made up of lines and shading (or color). Generally, pictures work better because bitmaps tend to get distorted when resized. As always, experiment until you understand what's going on.

You can preview the image you'll be pasting by running the Windows Clipboard application. Select the Display command from the Clipboard's menu to see whether the copied image can be displayed as a bitmap or picture. If the copied item cannot be displayed in either of these formats, the Excel chart Edit menu does not display the Paste option.

You don't have to paste the image into the entire series. You can select a single item — one column in a column chart, for example — by pressing the Ctrl key while you select the item. As a result, the Edit ⇨ Paste command works only with the single selected item. This is a good way to make one particular part stand out in a chart.

Be creative in your quest for graphics images. You can use the clip art that's provided with most word processors, drawing packages, presentation graphics programs, or desktop publishing programs. If your software resources are limited, don't forget that you can use Excel's drawing tools (discussed in a following section) to create your own design, and this image can be pasted to a chart. Don't underestimate what you can do with these simple tools. You can group the elements together (with the Format ⇨ Group command) to create some attractive images for pasting into charts.

Pasting Graphics on a Chart

Except for picture charts (discussd earlier), you may have noticed that Excel doesn't enable you to paste graphics information into a chart window. For example, you may want to add your company's logo to a chart. Even if you have a logo available as a bitmap copied to the Clipboard, you cannot paste it into a

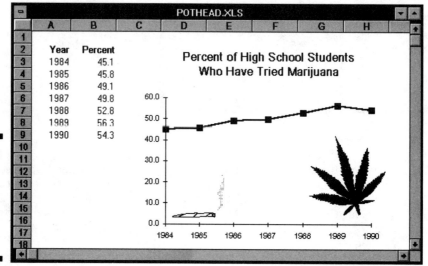

	A	B
1		
2	Year	Percent
3	1984	45.1
4	1985	45.8
5	1986	49.1
6	1987	49.8
7	1988	52.8
8	1989	56.3
9	1990	54.3

Percent of High School Students Who Have Tried Marijuana

Figure 16-20: An example of an embedded chart embellished with clip art.

chart. You can get around this limitation by embedding the chart into a worksheet (if it's not already embedded) and then using the Edit ➪ Paste command to copy other images on top of it. Figure 16-20 shows an example.

Augmenting Your Worksheets

A worksheet doesn't have to consist of just numbers and text. Besides embedding charts, you can also create drawings and paste clip art images directly into a worksheet. And don't forget about the new Object Linking and Embedding (OLE) feature that enables you to embed linked objects from other programs. With these capabilities you can add some interest to an otherwise boring report.

Using Excel's drawing tools

Excel comes with a fairly decent set of drawing tools that enable you to create diagrams and images directly in a worksheet. The only way to access these drawing tools is from the Drawing toolbar.

If the Drawing toolbar is not displayed, select the Options ➪ Toolbars command and select the Drawing toolbar to display it. Or right-click the toolbar that

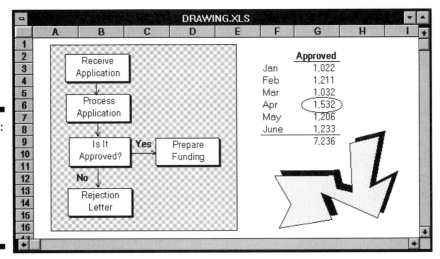

Figure 16-21:
A modest
example of
what you
can do with
Excel's
drawing
tools.

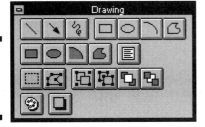

Figure 16-22:
The default
Drawing
toolbar.

is displayed to bring up a shortcut menu that enables you to select the toolbar(s) you want displayed.

When would you want to use Excel's drawing tools? Figure 16-21 shows a few examples that were created with these drawing tools. As you can see, with these tools you can liven up an otherwise dull report. Using these tools is easy. Just click the tool icon and start drawing. Figure 16-22 shows the default Drawing toolbar. Here's what these tools do:

 Insert a line. You can change the length and orientation with the mouse.

 Insert an arrow. You can change the length and orientation with the mouse.

 Insert a freehand drawing. Use the mouse to draw free-form lines.

 Insert a text box. Press and drag to insert a box into which you can enter whatever text you like.

 Add drop shadow. This tool lets you add drop shadows to rectangles or objects.

Select one or more graphics objects. This tool is useful if you have several objects and you want to select a group of them. Just drag the outline so it covers the objects.

 Reshape an object. This tool enables you to modify an existing object by dragging its handles. It's particularly useful for changing polygons.

 Draw a rectangle (or square). Press and drag to draw a rectangle. Hold down the Shift key while you drag with the mouse to produce a perfect square.

 Draw an oval (or circle). Press and drag to draw an oval. Hold down the Shift key while you drag with the mouse to produce a perfect circle.

 Draw an arc. Press and drag.

 Draw a polygon. Click and move the mouse to create connected lines. If you hold down the mouse button while you drag, it gives the same effect as the freehand drawing tool.

 Draw a filled rectangle (or square). This tool is the same as the rectangle tool, but it's filled with a pattern.

 Draw a filled oval (or circle). This tool is the same as the oval tool, but it's filled with a pattern.

 Draw a filled arc. This tool is the same as the arc tool, but it's filled with a pattern.

 Draw a filled polygon. This tool is the same as the polygon tool, but it's filled with a pattern.

 Group objects together. Select multiple objects and then use this tool to combine them into a single item. This tool is useful if you want to resize or move a group of separate items.

Ungroup objects. First select an object that has been grouped. This tool ungroups them.

 Move the object to the front. Select an object that is partially obscured by another. This tool brings it to the front of the stack.

 Move the object to the back. Select an object that is on top of one or more items. This tool drops it to the bottom of the stack.

 Change the object or cell color. Selecting this tool cycles through the colors. It works on both drawn objects and selected cells.

When objects are inserted into a worksheet, you can modify them as you like. The easiest way is to use the shortcut menu. You can change the line width or style and modify patterns with the Patterns option. If you have objects stacked on top of each other, you can move the selected item to the front or back of the stack (tool icons are also available for doing this procedure). Choosing Format ⇨ Object Properties displays the dialog box shown in Figure 16-23. With this dialog box, you can control how the object interacts with the worksheet cells on which it is placed. You have these options:

Move and Size with Cells	The object changes, depending on what happens to the cells.
Move but Don't Size with Cells	The object is moved with the cells but not resized.
Don't Move or Size with Cells	The object always remains in the same position, regardless of what happens to the cells.
Print Object	When this option is checked, the object is printed with the worksheet.

The best way to understand how these drawing tools work is to experiment. Start with a blank worksheet and go for it. You may want to turn off the gridline

Figure 16-23: With the Object Properties dialog box, you can control how an object interacts with the cells on which it is located.

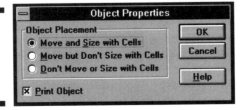

display with the Options ⇨ Display command. Create several objects, move them around, and change their sizes. Make a group selection and combine several objects into one. Change the line colors and patterns. You'll soon learn how easy — and fun — this Excel feature can be.

Using clip art

Besides creating your own drawings with Excel's drawing tools, you can insert existing drawings or pictures into an Excel worksheet. Although you can't paste an image into a chart window, you can paste it on top of a chart that is embedded in a worksheet. A good source of such images is electronic clip art.

What is clip art? Graphic artists have always had access to books and books of "clip art." *Clip art* is simply a collection of images that can be used freely without any copyright restrictions. Electronic clip art is the computer equivalent of these books. In fact, most word processors, drawing packages, and desktop publishing programs provide a collection of clip art files.

Clip art comes in two main categories: bitmapped and vector (picture). Bitmapped images are made up of discrete dots. They normally look pretty good at their original size but lose clarity if you increase or decrease their size. Vector-based images, on the other hand, retain their crispness regardless of their size.

Examples of common bitmapped file formats include: `bmp`, `pcx`, `dib`, and `gif`. Examples of common vector file formats include `cgm`, `wmf`, `eps`, and `drw`.

Excel doesn't have a command to import such files directly, but the Windows Clipboard works well for this task. You need to bring up the image in another Windows program (such as a word processor), copy it to the Clipboard, and then paste it into your Excel worksheet. After it's pasted, you can move and resize it as needed.

Inserting linked embedded objects

OLE is a useful Windows feature that enables you to insert an object from another program and use the other program's editing tools to manipulate it whenever you need to. This is a relatively new concept, but a growing number of Windows applications support OLE.

If you own Word for Windows 2.0, you may have discovered the additional "applets" that you can install with WinWord. These applets include a graphics package, a drawing package, an equation package, and a "word art" package. After you install these packages, they are also available in other applications that support OLE — including Excel.

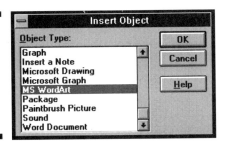

Figure 16-24: This dialog box enables you to embed an object into Excel. The choices vary depending on which OLE-compatible applications are installed on your system.

If you don't have WinWord 2.0 installed on your system, the following discussion won't make much sense, but it'll probably make you want to trade in your current word processor for a copy of Word for Windows.

The Edit ➪ Insert Object command in the Worksheet menu enables you to insert an OLE object into your worksheet. For this example, use the WordArt applet that comes with Word for Windows. When you select Edit ➪ Insert Object, the choices you see vary, depending on which OLE-supporting applications are installed (this information is stored in your win.ini file). Figure 16-24 shows the choices on a system that has several such applications installed.

If your system includes a sound card and you're running Windows 3.1 (or Windows 3.0 with Multimedia Extensions), you can also embed and link a sound object, which can be a waveform wav audio file that you recorded yourself or got from somewhere else.

Selecting the WordArt option calls up the appropriate application in which you can create a graphics object (see Figure 16-25). When you exit this application,

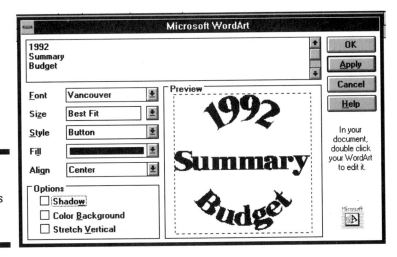

Figure 16-25: This is an example of an embedded WordArt object. WordArt is an applet included with Word for Windows.

the object is inserted onto the Excel worksheet. It can be moved and resized like any other object. But here's the good part: If you double-click an embedded object, Windows launches the application that it came from and loads the object for further editing. When you exit the application, the changes appear in Excel.

You may have a sense of *deja vu* here. Double-clicking an embedded chart brings up a chart window for editing. Actually, Excel's chart editing features use OLE.

Using Excel for Slide Show Presentations

If you need to make a presentation before a group of people, consider using Excel rather than the customary overheads or slides. If the group is small, you can even use a normal computer monitor. For larger groups, however, you need an overhead projection system that feeds the output from your video card or monitor to a projector (many such devices are available).

Excel provides a template (which uses an add-in) that makes setting up impressive slide shows easy. If your computer is equipped for multimedia, you can even add sound to your presentations. This is a fun feature, with lots of useful applications.

To create a slide show, select File ➪ New and choose Slides. This action opens up a special blank worksheet, as shown in Figure 16-26. This worksheet has buttons at the top that you use to create and edit slides. Information for each slide is stored in a separate row and occupies five columns. Images for the slides are copied from the Clipboard and can consist of almost anything that can be

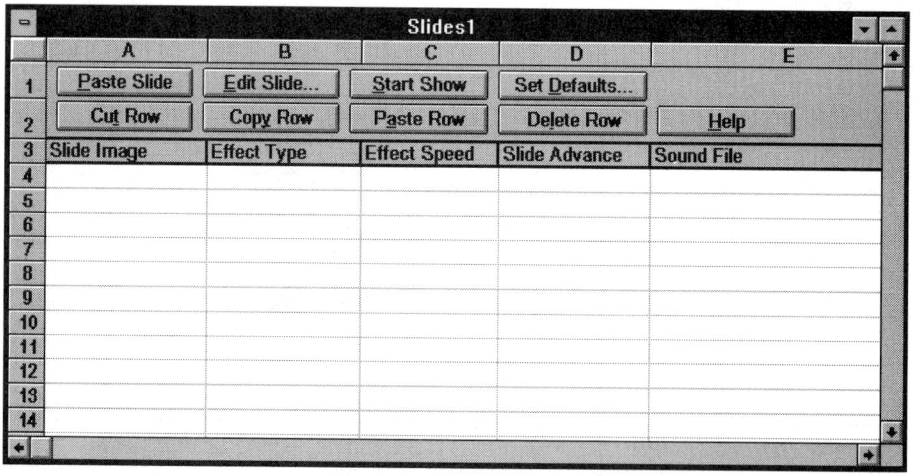

Figure 16-26: The first step in creating a slide show is to create a new slide document.

	A	B	C	D	E
1	Paste Slide	Edit Slide...	Start Show	Set Defaults...	
2	Cut Row	Copy Row	Paste Row	Delete Row	Help
3	Slide Image	Effect Type	Effect Speed	Slide Advance	Sound File
4					
5					
6					
7					
8					
9					
10					
11					
12					
13					
14					

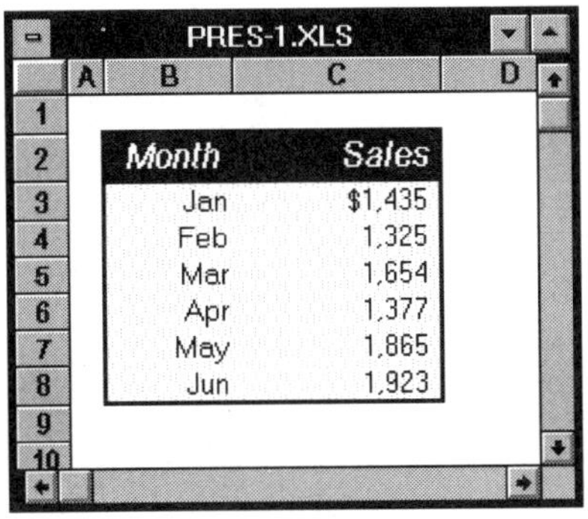

Figure 16-27: This worksheet holds some of the information for use in an Excel slide show.

displayed on the Clipboard — including ranges of cells in Excel. Let's jump right in with an example. Figure 16-27 shows part of a worksheet that you'll copy information from for use as slides. Range B2:C8 contains a formatted table that will be transformed into a slide. Here are the steps involved:

Steps: Creating a slide show

Step 1. Select the range B2:C8 and copy it to the Clipboard with Edit ⇨ Copy.

Step 2. Open a blank slide sheet by selecting File ⇨ New and then choose Slides. You get a new, specially formatted worksheet to hold your slide information.

Step 3. Select the Paste Slide button. Excel copies the Clipboard contents into the first slide row, which is row 4.

Step 4. Excel then displays the dialog box shown in Figure 16-28. This dialog box enables you to set the transition effect, specify how the slide is advanced (manually or automatically), and attach a sound file if your system is properly equipped. You can test both the transition effect and the sound by choosing the Test button.

Step 5. When you're satisfied with your selection, choose OK. The information is transferred to the slide sheet in the following format:

Column 1 Holds a miniature version of the slide image.

Column 2 Holds a label that indicates the type of transition effect.

Column 3 Holds a value that determines how fast the transition effect will take using an arbitrary 10-point scale.

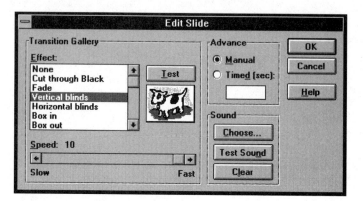

Figure 16-28: Each slide can have a different transition effect and sound file associated with it. You can also specify manual or automatic advancement.

Column 4   Specifies how the slide is advanced. It contains either the label Manual or a number that indicates the number of seconds it will be displayed.

Column 5   Holds the path and filename of the sound file that will begin playing when the slide is displayed.

Figure 16-29 shows how this setup looks. Repeat this procedure until you have your slide information entered. You can use the buttons on this sheet to change the defaults, to copy, cut, and paste slide information to different locations, and to start the actual slide show. When you select Start Show, Excel displays a dialog box that enables you to specify which slide to start with and whether you want to repeat the slide show until you press Esc.

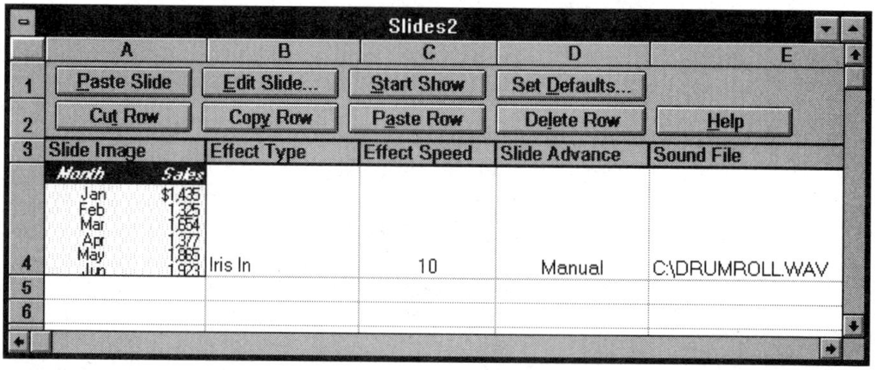

Figure 16-29: A miniature version of the copied picture appears in the slide worksheet, along with the other information you specified in the dialog box.

Your slides can consist of a range of cells (which are copied as a "picture"), a chart, or any other object such as a drawing or imported clip art.

If you're using a drawing on a worksheet, select the underlying cells before you copy it to the Clipboard (don't copy the drawing object itself; it won't work, and Excel will tell you so).

The information that you paste into a slide sheet can come from any number of different worksheets. This slide information is stored in a normal Excel x1s file. This feature is really easy to use, and you should be able to figure it out in no time.

Tips on Modifying Your Charts

- Don't go overboard. You may be tempted to dress up every chart with all sorts of clip art, text objects, multiple colors, and more whistles and bells. Remember that the ultimate goal is to present your ideas clearly. Too much window-dressing may detract from your message.

- You can also "steal" graphics images from non-Windows applications, but you must be running Windows in 386 enhanced mode. Start your DOS application from Windows and display the graphic that you're interested in. Then press Print Screen. This action transfers the complete graphics screen to the Windows Clipboard. If you don't want the full screen, copy the Clipboard contents to a program such as Windows Paintbrush and select the part you want to copy. Copy the selected part to the Clipboard and then paste it into Excel.

- You can make global changes to the 16-color palette available for each chart window. Select Chart ⇨ Color Palette to display the current color palette. To change a color, double-click it and then move the mouse through the 2-D color display until you find the color you want. Select OK, and the chart is updated with the new color(s).

- When you're creating a chart, explore the other chart-type options Excel offers. Often, the choice of a chart type can make a major difference in the impact of your chart.

- You can copy worksheet data and paste it into a chart to add a new series. You can also copy a series from a chart and paste it into another chart.

- And finally — experiment. This chapter provided some background information about charts. But you'll learn more by doing than by reading.

Summary

▶ You can modify virtually every component in an Excel chart. In most cases you right-click a chart item to bring up its shortcut menu. Choose the appropriate command and make your modifications.

▶ When you select an item in a chart, the item name appears on the Formula bar. You can also use the arrow keys to cycle among all the chart items.

▶ The Chart ⇨ Edit Series command provides an easy way to add a new series, delete an existing series, or change the ranges that you're plotting.

▶ Overlay charts are combination charts. This feature essentially enables you to plot two charts as one.

▶ Text that you add to a chart can be either attached to an item or free-floating.

▶ Chart legends are optional, and sometimes they are not needed.

▶ You have a great deal of control over the display and type of gridlines.

▶ You can change the scale used on any chart axis.

▶ Often, you need to rotate a 3-D chart so columns or lines are not obscured. Excel provides two ways to do this task.

▶ Excel provides a good assortment of drawing tools (which are functional only in a worksheet window).

▶ OLE enables you to insert all kinds of objects into a worksheet. Double-clicking such an object enables you to edit it using its original source application.

▶ With Excel, you can produce attractive on-screen presentations, consisting of text, charts, drawings, and even sound.

Chapter 17
Printing Charts

Getting a great-looking chart on-screen is one thing. Getting it to look good on paper is another. If you're fortunate enough to have access to a color printer or plotter, congratulations. Most of us are still living in a black-and-white world when it comes to computer output. Either way, this chapter tells you how to get great-looking charts on paper. It's a pretty short chapter because the background information on printing was provided in Chapter 13.

Printing Charts

Excel provides two ways to print charts:

■ If your chart is embedded in a worksheet, you can use the normal worksheet printing techniques. Just make sure that your print_area range includes the embedded chart or charts. The chart prints exactly as it appears on-screen.

■ If your chart is in a separate chart window, use the File ⇨ Print command from the chart menu. This method provides you with a few additional options and is most useful if you want optimum quality output and charts printed on separate pages.

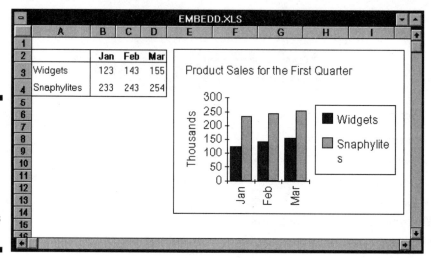

Figure 17-1:
When you reduce the size of an embedded chart, the size of the text remains the same.

Printing from a Worksheet Window

As you know, you can embed charts directly in a worksheet. These chart objects are just like any other embedded objects, and they get printed when you print the worksheet. The advantages of printing charts from a worksheet include the following:

- You can print multiple charts with a single command.
- You can size and proportion the charts any way you like.
- You can position the chart next to the data that it uses.

The disadvantages of printing charts from a worksheet are the following:

- You will probably have to adjust the size and proportions so it looks right.
- Excel does not automatically scale the text when you change the size. Consequently, smaller charts may look terrible.

When a chart is displayed in a worksheet window, you can easily change its size and proportions simply by selecting it and dragging the handles. As you make these changes, you'll notice that the chart changes appearance; it adjusts some of its elements to correspond to the new scale. Note, however, that Excel does not scale the text in the chart; it always remains its original size. Consequently, making an embedded chart small often distorts it, as shown in Figure 17-1. In particular, legends tend to look bad in small embedded charts because the text is too large. You have two ways to get around this problem:

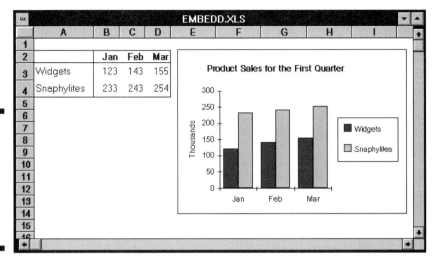

Figure 17-2:
Reducing
the size of
the text
makes the
embedded
chart look
better.

■ Adjust the chart's size and proportions so it looks good on-screen; usually, you have to make it larger.

■ Reduce the size of all or some of the text in the chart.

To change the size of all the text in an embedded chart with one command, double-click the chart to open a chart window. Choose the Chart ⇨ Select Chart command to select all the chart elements. Then select Format ⇨ Font and specify a smaller font size in the dialog box. All the text in the chart is adjusted. At this point, you may want to select the title and make it a bit larger than the other text.

Figure 17-2 shows the embedded chart after the text was made smaller.

When you're printing embedded charts, remember that WYSIWYG is the name of the game. If the chart looks good on-screen, what you see is what you get, and it'll look good when it's printed.

To prevent an embedded chart from being printed with the worksheet, select the chart (click once, not twice) and then choose the Format ⇨ Object Properties command. From the dialog box, deselect the option labeled Print Object. This setup may be useful if you're printing a quick draft and don't want to wait the additional time necessary to print the chart.

Before you print

The preliminary steps involved in printing charts are exactly the same as for printing worksheets. Rather than repeat ourselves, we refer you to Chapter 13. If you prefer not to thumb back through the book, here's a quick summary of what you need to do before you attempt to put a chart on paper:

- Unless you specify otherwise, Excel prints the entire active worksheet when you issue the File ⇨ Print command — including all drawings, charts, and other embedded objects.

- To select only a portion of the worksheet to print, you must specify a print area. Select the range or ranges that you want to print by using the normal range selection techniques. When you're satisfied with your selection, select Options ⇨ Set Print Area.

- Before you print, check your page setup to make sure that the margins, headers, footers, and other details are to your liking. In Excel, you do this task with the File ⇨ Page Setup command.

- You may want to preview your printed output on-screen. You do so with the File ⇨ Print Preview command.

Printing

When you are satisfied with the page setup and preview, select File ⇨ Print. Make any necessary adjustments to the dialog box settings and choose OK.

When you're printing a worksheet with embedded charts, the results look better if you don't print with cell gridlines. Use the File ⇨ Page Setup command to remove cell gridlines from your printed output.

Printing from a Chart Window _____

The second way to print a chart is directly from a chart window. As you know, a chart can be either embedded into a worksheet or created in its own chart window. In either case, you're not stuck with your original decision. You can double-click an embedded chart to open it in a chart window, and you can copy an entire chart to a worksheet. Printing a chart directly from its chart window offers the following advantages:

- You can easily print the chart alone, without any worksheet information.

■ Excel offers several different options as to how the chart comes out on the page.

■ The scaling of chart elements is taken care of automatically; you don't have to adjust the proportions so everything looks right.

The disadvantages of printing from a chart window follow:

■ You can only print one chart at a time.

■ You can only print one chart per page.

■ The chart cannot appear along with the data that produced it.

As you may expect, at times printing charts from your worksheet is the best solution, and at other times you'll want to print a chart from the chart window.

Before you print

For you to print a chart from a chart window, the chart window must be active. If the chart is embedded in a worksheet, simply double-click it to open a chart window. If the worksheet is not maximized, the chart window is the same size as the embedded chart. If the worksheet is maximized when you double-click the embedded chart, the resulting chart window is maximized. When a chart window is active, a different set of menus is available.

The first step is to select the File ➪ Page Setup command. This action brings up a similar dialog box as when you select this command in a worksheet window (see Figure 17-3). In this case, however, some of the page setup options that apply to worksheets are grayed (so you can't change them). The options that you can change follow:

Orientation	Select either Portrait (for tall pages) or Landscape (for wide pages printed sideways).
Paper	This pull-down box enables you to choose the paper size. Make sure that this setting corresponds to the paper that you're actually using.
Margins	Here you specify how wide you want each margin. The measurement unit corresponds to your global Windows setting (which you can change with the Windows Control Panel program; select the International icon).
Header	Select this button to change the header used on the printed page.

Figure 17-3: When you select File ⇨ Page Setup from a chart window, a few additional options are available.

Page Setup

Current Printer:
PostScript Printer on LPT1:

Orientation
● Portrait
○ Landscape

Paper
Size: Letter 8 1/2 x 11 in

OK
Cancel
Options...
Help

Margins
Left: 0.75   Right: 0.75
Top: 1   Bottom: 1
Center: ☐ Horizontally ☐ Vertically

☐ Row & Column Headings
☐ Cell Gridlines
☐ Black & White Cells
Start Page No.'s At: 1

Page Order
○ Down, then Over
○ Over, then Down

Scaling
● Reduce/Enlarge to: 300
○ Fit to: ___ pages wide by ___ tall.

Chart Size
○ Size On Screen   ● Scale to Fit Page   ○ Use Full Page

Header...
Footer...
Print...
Printer Setup...

Footer   Choose this button to change the footer used on the printed page.

Chart Size   This group box consists of three radio buttons (only one can be active). Your selection here drastically affects the way your chart is printed. The options follow:

Size On Screen: This option prints the chart the same size as shown on-screen. The results depend on the current size of the chart window. If the chart window is maximized, the chart may actually run off the page (as shown in Figure 17-4).

Scale to Fit Page: This option prints the chart as large as possible, but it doesn't change the chart's proportions. In other words, the ratio of the height to width always remains intact.

Use Full Page: This option adjusts the chart's height-to-width ratio to fill the page completely. This option usually works best when you print in landscape mode because that's the normal orientation of charts. This option uses the size of the page specified by the Margins option in the Page Setup dialog box.

When you select Size On Screen, you can also adjust the Scaling factor — anywhere from 10 percent to 400 percent of its size. When the other two Chart Size options are selected, this option is grayed in the dialog box.

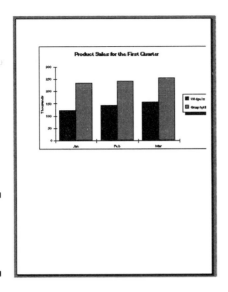

Figure 17-4: A chart previewed with the Size On Screen option set.

Figures 17-4, 17-5, and 17-6 show page previews of how these options affect your output (the chart window was maximized when we issued the File ➪ Page Preview command). Fortunately, Excel's File ➪ Print Preview window has a button that sends you to the Page Setup dialog box. This feature enables you to try out the three options to see which is most appropriate.

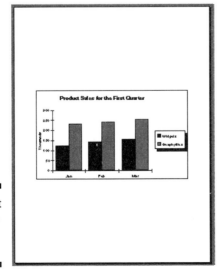

Figure 17-5: A chart previewed with the Scale to Fit Page option set.

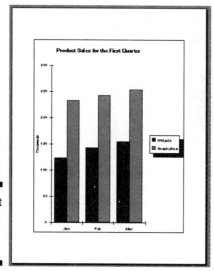

Figure 17-6: A chart previewed with the Use Full Page option set.

 None of these chart printing options scales the text in the chart. Text always prints in the size you specify. In many cases, you need to adjust your fonts to fit the size of the printed chart.

Printing

When you're satisfied with the appearance of the chart (as seen via the File ⇨ Print Preview command), you can simply issue the File ⇨ Print command to send it on its way. A button in the preview window also provides an express route to the Print dialog box. Here you can specify the print quality and the number of copies you want.

Printing a Chart in Another Application

Yet another option is available for printing a chart — printing it in another application. You can accomplish this task by copying the chart to the Windows Clipboard and then pasting it into an application such as a word processor or desktop publishing program.

Begin from a chart window and select the entire chart with the Chart ➪ Select Chart command. Issue the Edit ➪ Copy command to copy the chart to the Windows Clipboard. Next, activate the application that you're pasting it to and select the program's Edit ➪ Paste command to insert the chart in the application's document. You can then use the other application's printing commands to get the chart on paper.

Depending on the application you're using, the chart is copied as either a "picture" or a "bitmap." Remember, a bitmap is a collection of dots that makes up the picture. If you change the size or proportion, it will probably not look very good. If the application supports pictures, you can generally resize it with no loss in clarity.

When you paste the chart into drawing applications such as CorelDRAW, you can further manipulate the chart elements by using that application's drawing tools. For example, you can use the product's fountain fill option to add pizzazz to columns or to the chart background. Or you can change the fonts (Corel DRAW, for example, provides more than 100 different fonts).

Troubleshooting Tips _____

- If nothing comes out of your printer, first check that the power is on, the connections are made properly, it has paper, and it's switched on-line (selected). Next, make sure that the printer is configured properly in Windows.

- If an embedded chart isn't printing, check to make sure that its "object properties" are set properly. Right-click the chart and select Object Properties from the shortcut menu. If the check box labeled Print Object is not checked, select it.

- If you're sending your output to a pen plotter rather than a printer, be warned that you may not always get what you expect when chart elements are placed behind other objects (such as with a 3-D column chart). As far as we can tell, no solution exists except to use another chart type.

- Predicting how colors will appear on a black-and-white printer is difficult. Our only advice is to experiment with different colors and patterns.

- If your embedded charts look distorted, you probably need to change the size of the chart or of the fonts used in the chart.

Summary

▶ Excel provides two options for printing your charts. You can print embedded charts directly from the worksheet window by using the normal printing commands, or you can print directly from a chart window.

▶ The results you get when you print from a chart window can vary dramatically, depending on the setting you choose for Chart Size (in the Page Setup dialog box).

▶ Yet another option is to copy your chart to the Windows Clipboard and paste it into another application for printing.

Chapter 18

What Every Excel User Should Know

In this chapter . . .

▶ Things you should know to get the most out of Excel.

▶ Essential shortcuts that are guaranteed to make you more efficient.

▶ A summary of the best ways to perform common operations.

One of us authors once had a coworker who was considered a fairly proficient Excel user. One day, this fellow remarked that it would be nice if Excel could automatically update his formulas. Upon further questioning, it became obvious that this user didn't know anything about built-in functions. He laboriously entered formulas such as =A1+A2+A3+A4+A5, which had to be updated manually if he entered a new row. Hopefully, this chapter will prevent such a thing from happening to you.

If you're following this book chapter by chapter, you'll notice that this is the final chapter of "The Basic Concepts" section. Before you graduate and move on to "The Advanced Features," it's important that you haven't overlooked one or more essential components. You'll notice that much of this information has already been covered in other chapters so you might think of this chapter as an optional review session.

Considering All the Options _____

Excel is a flexible program and usually offers several ways to do any one thing. For example, you can select a range of cells using different mouse and keyboard techniques. When a range is selected, you can operate on it using any of the following methods:

■ Select a menu command with the mouse.

■ Issue a menu command from the keyboard.

- Select an icon on a toolbar to perform an action.
- Click the right mouse button for a shortcut menu.
- Drag the selection to a different location.
- Make a copy of the selection by holding Ctrl while you drag.
- Copy the selection across or down by dragging the "drag and drop" handle.
- Press a shortcut key combination (sometimes).
- Invoke a custom macro to perform the operation or operations.

Although newcomers might find all of these options a bit confusing, more experienced users will welcome the choices since they add flexibility and improve efficiency. Every user eventually settles on his or her own combination of techniques. The key is to be at least aware of all of the available options so you won't overlook something that may be more efficient. Efficiency, after all, is one of the reasons we use a spreadsheet program in the first place.

Examining Essential Shortcuts

The following sections summarize some of the essential shortcuts that you should at least know about and experiment with.

Using the keyboard for menu selections

Many Excel users seem to think that the mouse is the only way to access the command menus and make selections. Actually, you might find the keyboard faster in many cases.

If you're entering data from the keyboard, it stands to reason that it takes less time to issue a command from the keyboard rather than by way of the mouse. Pressing the Alt key or F10 activates the menu bar, and you can use the arrow keys or spacebar to scroll through the menu items. Actually, it's more efficient to simply press one of the underlined letters to pull down a menu. You'll soon memorize some of the more common commands. For example, pressing the three keys Alt+F+S is much faster than pulling down the File menu with the mouse and then locating the Save option, especially if your hands are already on the keyboard.

It would be nice if the underlined hotkey was always the first letter of the command (this is how the Lotus 1-2-3 menus are arranged). Nevertheless, you'll soon associate the proper letter with the commonly used commands.

You don't have to wait for the menu to drop down if you know which key you're going to press. You can issue a command in rapid succession — something that the original version of 1-2-3 was famous for.

Working with dialog boxes

Command options on a pull-down menu with ellipsis (three periods) after them produce a dialog box if you select that command. Since dialog boxes are prevalent in Excel, it's worth your while to understand how to work with them efficiently. This knowledge applies to other Windows applications as all Windows dialog boxes essentially work the same way.

Some dialog boxes simply require that you check or uncheck a few options which can be done most efficiently with a mouse. Other dialog boxes, however, require some type of keyboard input. If you're already entering information from the keyboard, you'll usually save some time by using the keyboard for the entire dialog box rather than reaching for the mouse. Here are a few dialog box pointers:

- When a dialog box appears that you don't want, you can cancel it by selecting the Cancel button or pressing Esc.

- The Tab and Shift+Tab keys allow you to move among the components of a dialog box. This is often more efficient than clicking with the mouse.

- You can hold down the Alt key and press an underlined letter to move or make selections in a dialog box.

- Many dialog boxes have text boxes. When the text in a text box is highlighted (it will be white type on black background), you can simply start typing to replace what's already there — there's no need to press Del first.

- In some check boxes, you can use the spacebar to turn an option on or off.

- When you're satisfied with what you've entered in a dialog box, you can simply press Enter — which is usually faster than selecting the OK button.

Using shortcut menus

If you're moving up from Excel 3, it may be hard to remember that the right mouse button is no longer dormant. When something is selected in Excel — a cell, range, chart element, graphic object, or whatever — you can press the right mouse button and pop up a shortcut menu. This is a great time-saver, since it prevents trips to the menu bar.

The exact shortcut menu the right mouse button produces depends on what is selected. The menus are context-sensitive, so only the appropriate choices will appear.

Selecting a range

One of the most frequent operations performed in Excel is selecting a range of cells to operate on. You could, of course, press and drag the mouse over the range. While this is fine for small ranges that fit on one screen, there are better ways to select larger ranges.

Shift

We've found that many users, for one reason or another, don't realize that the Shift key plays an important role in selecting ranges. When you hold down Shift and move the cell pointer with the arrow keys, all of the cells in its path are selected. And if you go too far, you can back up. When you release the Shift key, the range remains selected.

Shift+Ctrl

The Ctrl key, when used in conjunction with the arrow keys, quickly moves the cell pointer to the end of a block of numbers or to the first nonblank cell (whichever comes first). Assume that the cell pointer is in cell A1, all of the cells in row 1 between column A and column W are blank, and there's an entry in column X. Ctrl+right arrow will instantly move the cell pointer to cell X1.

This technique, when used in conjunction with the Shift key, is a fast way to select a range of cells. Assume you have a large rectangular range of data. Move the cell pointer to the upper-left cell. Hold down Ctrl and Shift and press the down arrow key to select the first column of data. Keep Ctrl and Shift pressed and then press the right arrow key to extend the selection across all columns of the data.

 A handy icon that you should consider adding to your toolbar is the select current region tool:

Clicking this icon selects the current block of cells (defined as the area bounded by any combination of blank rows or blank columns). The icon is in the Utility category and does not appear on any of the default toobars. Ctrl+* accomplishes the same thing.

Shift+Click

The best way to select a very large range is the Shift+Click method. Move the cell pointer to one corner of the range. Next locate the opposite corner of the range using the scroll bars. Hold down the Shift key and click the opposite corner of the range to select all cells between the original cell pointer location and the new cell pointer location.

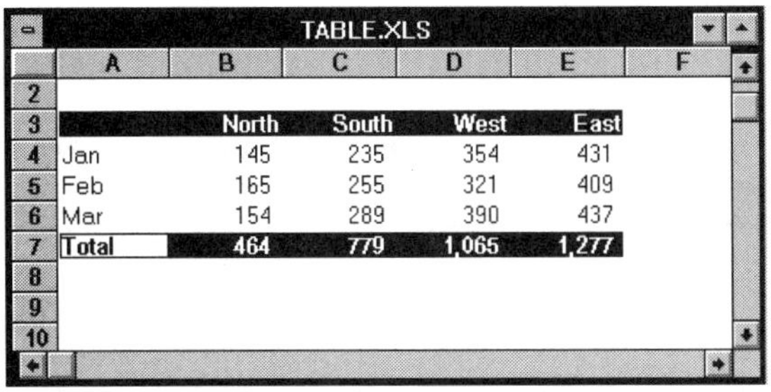

	A	B	C	D	E	F	
				TABLE.XLS			
2							
3		North	South	West	East		
4	Jan	145	235	354	431		
5	Feb	165	255	321	409		
6	Mar	154	289	390	437		
7	Total	464	779	1,065	1,277		
8							
9							
10							

Figure 18-1:
An example
of using a
multiple
selection.

Formula ⇨ Goto

Another method of selecting a range is to use the Formula ⇨ Goto command (or F5). If the range you want to select has a name, just double-click it in the Goto dialog box. Otherwise, simply enter a valid range designation in the Reference box of the Goto dialog box.

Multiple selections

Unlike most spreadsheets, Excel lets you make multiple selections. This means that you can select cells or ranges that aren't adjacent to each other. You can even assign a range name to nonadjacent cells, but that's another issue.

Figure 18-1 shows a worksheet with a table. We want to add top and bottom borders to the first row and last row of the table — a perfect use for a multiple selection. With a mouse, select the first row using any of the techniques we've discussed. Next, hold down the Ctrl key and select the last row.

To use the keyboard, select the top row and then press Shift+F8 (you'll see the word ADD in the status bar at the bottom of the screen). Move to the last row and select it. If you wanted to add another range to the selection, press Shift+F8 again since Add mode is turned off automatically.

Copying and Moving _____

Copying and moving cells and ranges are common operations. As with most other basic operations, there are several ways to accomplish this.

Edit ⇨ Copy and Edit ⇨ Paste

The most obvious method of copying cells or ranges is through the menu. Select the range and issue the Edit ⇨ Copy command to copy the information to the Clipboard. Then, move the pointer where you want to copy the information to and select the Edit ➪ Paste command.

Keep in mind that when you're pasting a range, you do *not* have to select a complete range. You can designate the paste location with only a single cell. Excel will use this as the upper-left corner of the pasted range.

When you copy a range, Excel displays a message: "Select destination and press Enter or choose Paste." If you move to the destination location and press Enter, the information is copied to the location but is cleared from the Clipboard (so you can't paste it somewhere else). If you use Edit ➪ Paste, the Clipboard contents remain intact and you can copy that information over and over.

Don't forget about the shortcut menu. When a cell or range is selected, you can right-click to get quick access to the Copy command. Move to the destination and right-click again for access to the Paste command.

All Windows applications use a standard keyboard shortcut for copy (Ctrl+Ins) and paste (Shift+Ins). This lets you quickly copy and paste cells or ranges using only the keyboard. The advantage to pasting (whether you use the menu or the shortcut) is that you can continue to paste multiple copies of what's on the Clipboard.

Note: Many products, including Excel, also use Ctrl+C for copy, Ctrl+V for paste, and Ctrl+X for cut.

Edit ➪ Fill commands

Another handy way to copy a cell over to adjacent cells is with the Fill commands. Select the cell or range you want to copy and drag the selection to include the area you want to copy to. Select the Edit ➪ Fill Down or Edit ➪ Fill Right command to perform the copy. If you hold down Shift, the Edit menu displays two alternative options: Fill Up (w) and Fill Left (h). Notice that the hotkeys are the same as for Fill Down and Fill Right

Autofill

If you're copying to an adjacent range that's not too large, the Autofill method is a good alternative. Select a cell or cells (in a single row or column) and then grab the drag and drop handle at the lower-right corner of the selection. Drag this handle down or across to copy.

When you're editing a formula, the Edit ⇨ Copy command is still accessible. This lets you copy all or part of a formula to paste into another formula and can be very handy.

Edit ⇨ Cut and Edit ⇨ Paste

If you want to move a cell or range, the most obvious approach is probably to use the menu commands: Edit ⇨ Cut to move the selection to the Clipboard, and Edit ⇨ Paste to paste it in another location.

Remember when you're pasting a range, you do *not* have to select a complete range — you can designate the paste location with only a single cell. Excel will use this as the upper-left corner of the pasted range.

 All Windows applications are standardizing a common keyboard shortcut for cut (Ctrl+X) and paste (Ctrl+V). This lets you quickly copy and paste cells or ranges using only the keyboard.

Drag and drop

Excel 4 is the first version of this product that lets you move and copy cells or ranges simply by dragging them. First, select the cell or range (the range must consist of adjacent cells). Now move the mouse over the borders of the selection. When the mouse pointer changes to an arrow, you can press the left mouse button and drag the selection anywhere you want. If you drag the selection against the edge of the window, it will scroll automatically. To make a copy of the selected range, hold down Ctrl while you drag it.

Edit ⇨ Paste Special

Edit ⇨ Paste Special is a useful command that every user should learn thoroughly. This command is only available when information is on the Clipboard from a copy or cut procedure. Selecting this command when there's a cell or range on the Clipboard brings up the dialog box shown in Figure 18-2. If there's a graphic object on the Clipboard, you'll get a different dialog box.

This command lets you paste just certain aspects of the selection: everything, the contents with no formatting, just the values, the formatting alone, or just the cell notes. This is handy if you have part of your worksheet formatted and you want to reproduce the formats elsewhere — it can save a lot of steps. It's also useful for converting formulas to their values. In such a case, you select the

Figure 18-2: The Paste Special dialog box provides many useful options.

Values option from the dialog box and paste the information right over the copied cells.

The Operation group box is useful if you want to perform a simple numeric operation on a range of cells without using formulas. For example, you can copy a range of cells and add the values to another range in the paste destination by checking the Add box. The Transpose box lets you convert a horizontal range to a vertical range and vice versa.

It's a good idea to experiment with this command until you understand exactly what it can do.

Entering and Editing Data

You probably spend much of your spreadsheeting time entering data into a worksheet. The most obvious way to do this is to make an entry into a cell, move to the next cell with the arrow keys, make another entry, and so on. But this is not the only way — alternatives are available.

Preselecting the range

If you preselect the range that you'll be entering data into, you can press the Enter key to enter the data and Excel will automatically move the cell pointer to the next cell. If the selection consists of multiple rows, Excel moves down the column and then up to the top of the next column when it reaches the end. This can save you quite a few keystrokes if you have a lot of data entry.

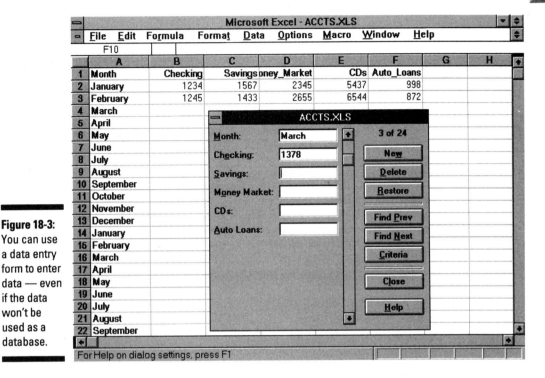

Figure 18-3:
You can use a data entry form to enter data — even if the data won't be used as a database.

Defining a database

If you're entering data that's arranged in rows, you might find it easier to define a database and then use the built-in database form to enter. You can do this even if you won't be using the data as a database. Figure 18-3 shows an example.

The task involves entering numbers for several accounts for each of 12 months. First, we set up a row with the account names, and then used the Autofill feature to fill in the months in the first column. Then we select A1:F13 and choose the Data ⇨ Set Database command. Next, we select Data ⇨ Form to display the data entry form. Excel displays the existing data (specifically, the month) and lets you quickly enter the appropriate data for the remaining fields. Use the Tab key to move to the next field and the Enter key to move to the next record. You also have the scroll bar to quickly move to the appropriate row.

Using Ctrl+Enter for repeated information

If you need to enter the same information into multiple cells, your first inclination would probably be to make one entry and then copy it to the remaining cells. Here's a better way: Select all of the cells that will contain the information, enter the value, text, or formula in the Formula bar, and then press Ctrl+Enter. The entry will be inserted into every cell in the selection. In the case of a formula, the cell references are adjusted properly.

Using the pointer when building formulas

When you're entering a formula, you *could* simply enter the cell references or range names manually. A better way is to point to the cells and ranges you want to refer to. As you enter a formula into the formula bar, you can move the cell pointer with the arrow keys or with the mouse to insert specific cell references. This is usually faster than typing them in and is much less prone to errors, since you won't have to figure out which column letter and row number you need to refer to in making up cell references.

Letting Excel enter the decimal points

If you're entering financial data with two decimal places, you can eliminate the need to enter the decimal points. Select the Options ⇨ Workspace command and then select the Fixed Decimal box (make sure the text box reads 2). Now, when you enter a number such as 12345, it will be entered as 123.45.

To get back to normal, select Options ⇨ Workspace and deselect the Fixed Decimal box.

Using the Formula ⇨ Paste Function

When you need to insert a built-in function into a formula, consider using the Formula ⇨ Paste Function command. This displays the dialog box shown in Figure 18-4.

All of the functions are displayed in the right group box, and the categories of functions are shown in the left group box. When you select a category, only the relevant functions are shown on the right. Simply double-click on a function name and it will be inserted into the Formula bar.

Figure 18-4: The
Paste Function
dialog box can
save you the
effort of typing a
function and can
also insert dummy
arguments for
you.

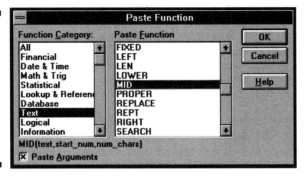

Notice the check box labeled Paste Arguments. If this is checked, Excel will also
paste dummy names for the arguments. This is useful if you can't remember
which arguments a function takes or forget what order they go in.

When the function is pasted to the Formula bar, you can double-click a dummy
argument and then point out the cell or range that you want to insert, using the
mouse or keyboard for this. When all of the arguments have been completed,
press Enter to insert the formula.

When you're editing a formula, the Edit ⇨ Copy command is still accessible and
lets you copy all or part of a formula to paste into another formula.

Converting a formula to a string

In some situations you might want to copy a formula, but don't want the
references to change relatively. To do this, first convert the formula to a text
string by adding a space character at the beginning. Then copy the formula and
paste it wherever you like. Finally, remove the space character from the original
and the copy. You'll have an exact duplicate of the original formula, and the cell
references will be identical.

Using Other Excel Features _____

The following miscellaneous hints don't really fall into any specific categories,
but are important timesaving commands to be aware of nonetheless.

Repeating a command

You may spend a lot of time repeating commands over and over for different ranges. There's no need to do this manually, thanks to the Edit ⇨ Repeat command. For example, you might select a range and format it as Helvetica 16 bold and red. If you want to apply the same formatting to another cell or range, simply select the range and choose the Edit ⇨ Repeat command. When you pull down the Edit menu, the command changes to tell you what it will repeat. The shortcut key for this operation is Alt+Enter. In this particular example, using a style may be an even better option.

Using Edit ⇨ Undo

Another time-saver that's easy to forget about is the Edit ⇨ Undo command (Alt+Backspace on the keyboard). Like the Edit ⇨ Repeat command, this command changes in the menu to tell you what will be undone when the command is selected. This is handy for recovering from mistakes — such as clearing a range of data when you only meant to clear the formatting.

Function keys

Excel provides many command shortcuts that use the function keys on your keyboard. Although you'll probably never be able to remember them all, you should take a quick look and figure out which ones you might want to memorize.

Table 18-1 lists all of Excel's function keys and function key combinations.

Table 18-1: Shortcut function key and function key combinations for most commands and operations	
Function key	**Action**
F1	Help
Shift+F1	Context-sensitive help
F2	Activates the formula bar for editing
Shift+F2	Formula ⇨ Note
Ctrl+F2	Displays an Info window
F3	Formula ⇨ Paste Name

Function key	Action
Shift+F3	Formula ⇨ Paste Function
Ctrl+F3	Formula ⇨ Define Name
Ctrl+Shift+F3	Formula ⇨ Create Names
F4	Changes type of reference while editing
Ctrl+F4	Exit Excel
Alt+F4	File ⇨ Exit
F5	Formula ⇨ Goto
Shift+F5	Formula ⇨ Find
Ctrl+F5	Restore window
F6	Next pane
Shift+F6	Previous pane
Ctrl+F6	Next window
Ctrl+Shift+F6	Previous document window
F7	Formula ⇨ Find (finds next occurrence)
Shift+F7	Formula ⇨ Find (finds previous occurrence)
Ctrl+F7	Move window
F8	Turns Extend mode on or off
Shift+F8	Turns Add mode on or off
Ctrl+F8	Size window
F9	Recalculate
Shift+F9	Recalculate Document
Ctrl+F9	Minimize the window
F10	Activate the menu bar
Shift+F10	Activate the shortcut menu
Ctrl+F10	Maximize the window
F11	New chart window
Shift+F11	New worksheet window
Ctrl+F11	New macro sheet window
F12	File ⇨ Save As
Shift+F12	File ⇨ Save
Ctrl+F12	File ⇨ Open
Ctrl+Shift+F12	File ⇨ Print

Using Named Ranges

One of the best pieces of advice we can give to any Excel user is to get in the habit of using named ranges. This makes it easier to create formulas, makes your worksheet more readable, and ensures that things don't get messed up when you move cells and ranges around. You owe it to yourself to learn about and understand this concept thoroughly.

Fortunately, Excel makes it easy to name ranges. You can do it manually with the Formula ⇨ Define Name command or automatically using worksheet text with the Formula ⇨ Create Names command.

Dealing with Errors

No matter how careful you are, you'll eventually find yourself in a predicament. Here are some examples:

- You accidentally erased an important range of data.

- You used File ⇨ Save As and wrote over a good file.

- Your system crashed, and you hadn't saved your file in the last several hours.

- You pasted a range of data over another range.

In some cases, you can recover from your screw-ups by immediately accessing the Edit ⇨ Undo command.

If you find your worksheet totally messed up, you might be better off by abandoning it and reverting to the last saved version. Do this by selecting File ⇨ Open and then specifying the same filename that you're working on. Excel will respond with a dialog box similar to that in Figure 18-5. Select OK to abandon the worksheet in memory and start over with the latest version on disk.

Obviously, you should not save your file before you issue the File ⇨ Open command. You *can* use File ⇨ Save As, however, and save it under a different name.

You might also want to create a backup file. Choose File ⇨ Save As, select Options, and then choose Create Backup File. Now, whenever Excel saves the file, it renames the existing file with a bak extension. The best precaution is to make regular backups — preferably to a floppy disk or some other removable media.

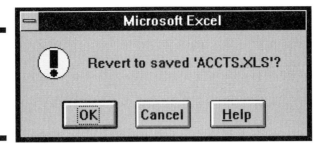

Figure 18-5: Excel displays this dialog box if you want to revert to the most recently saved version of your file.

Maximizing Excel

If your goal is to maximize the benefits of Excel, first you need to know what it can do. This book provides you with that knowledge, but the next step is really up to you: You need to learn how to do it. This requires practice and experimentation.

Start with a blank worksheet and explore the menus and dialog boxes. Enter some data and see what happens when you select various commands. And don't forget about the on-line help. This can usually provide some relevant information if you get stuck. Go for it!

Summary

▶ Excel is a flexible program and usually provides several different ways to accomplish any given task.

▶ Often, using the keyboard rather than the mouse is the most efficient approach. This applies to selecting ranges as well as selecting commands.

▶ It's important that you understand how to work with dialog boxes. In most cases, it's more efficient to use the keyboard.

▶ Excel's shortcut menus can save you a lot of time. Make a selection and then click the right mouse button to display a context-sensitive menu.

▶ The Edit ⇨ Repeat command can be a real time-saver. Don't forget to use it.

▶ Many of Excel's menu commands can be carried out by pressing a function key or a function key in combination with Alt, Shift, or Ctrl. You should learn the commands that you use most often.

▶ Using named ranges is an excellent habit to get into.

▶ If you find your worksheet completely messed up, you might want to revert to the last saved version of your file.

▶ If you want to be an Excel guru, the best approach is to experiment — try out new things and see what happens.

The Advanced Features

Chapter 19
Customizing Toolbars

In this chapter . . .

▶ How Excel's toolbars can improve your efficiency.

▶ What tools are available in the default toolbar.

▶ How to use the tools and learn what they do (and how to get double duty out of some of them).

▶ How to customize the toolbars to suit your working habits.

Imagine a computer program where all you need to do is push a button and the work is done for you. Push a button, and a file opens. Push another button, and ranges format themselves with custom styles. Push yet another button, and your worksheet starts printing. It sounds too good to be true.

Well, you can stop imagining — the future is here, right now. You can do these things and much more with Excel's toolbars. Tools, represented as icons, perform many common worksheet tasks. There's no need to pull down menus, navigate dialog boxes, or press shortcut keys — clicking a tool replaces all that. You can also create your own tools and toolbars to suit your work habits.

To take advantage of Excel's toolbars, you'll need a mouse. If you don't have a mouse and don't plan on getting one, you're really missing out on a capability that can not only make you more productive, but is equally as fun.

This chapter is for Excel users of all stripes who want to get the most from their toolbars. Since Excel's toolbar capability has been substantially enhanced with version 4, experienced users should also check into this chapter. If you thought the *single* toolbar in Excel 3 was pretty cool, wait until you find out the *multiple* toolbars available in version 4.

What Is a Toolbar?

A toolbar is a collection of frequently used commands represented by icons grouped together. Excel comes with seven predefined toolbars, as listed here:

- Standard
- Drawing
- Formatting
- Microsoft Excel 3
- Utility
- Macro
- Chart

Each toolbar contains tools of a similar nature. For example, the Chart toolbar helps you quickly select the type of chart you want to create and makes it simple to change chart types. The Drawing toolbar contains the tools that let you create simple drawings on your worksheet. When you're finished with a toolbar that you use for a particular task such as drawing, you can hide it so it doesn't take up valuable screen real estate.

When you select a tool, Excel performs the task assigned to the tool. Excel comes with more than 130 tools with commands or tasks preassigned to them, but not all these tools are located on the predefined toolbars. You can reassign what a tool does by creating a macro for it. You can also create your own custom tools with blank tool icons provided by Excel or use tools you create with a Windows graphics program.

By default, Excel displays the Standard toolbar, positioned between the command menu bar and the Formula bar. The Standard toolbar is comprised of general-purpose tools that you're likely to use most often. These tools are listed in Table 19-1 (as they appear from left to right on the toolbar).

Excel provides enormous flexibility with its toolbars. You can hide or show as many toolbars as you want, choose where you want a toolbar displayed, and create your own toolbars (by selecting the tools you want on a toolbar and/or by creating new tools). As a first step, we'll provide some background information as an introduction.

Using Tools

At first, you might be overwhelmed by all of these tiny images. There's no way you can ever remember what they do, right? Fortunately, Excel makes it easy to learn the function of a tool. Normally, to use a tool you select or click it. But if you click a tool and don't release the mouse button, Excel displays the tool's function in the Status bar at the bottom of the screen. For example, if you click on the Summation tool, Excel displays the following text at the bottom of the

Table 19-1: Shortcut tool icons for performing common spreadsheet tasks	
Tool	**Command equivalent**
New worksheet	File ⇨ New (with Worksheet option)
Open file	File ⇨ Open
Save file	File ⇨ Save
Print	File ⇨ Print (using current or default settings)
Style box	Format ⇨ Style
AutoSum	none
Bold	Format ⇨ Font (Bold)
Italic	Format ⇨ Font (Italic)
Increase font size	Format ⇨ Font (Size)
Decrease font size	Format ⇨ Font (Size)
Left align	Format ⇨ Alignment (Left)
Center align	Format ⇨ Alignment (Center)
Right align	Format ⇨ Alignment (Right)
Center across columns	Format ⇨ Alignment (Center across selection)
AutoFormat	Format ⇨ AutoFormat
Outline Border	Format ⇨ Border (Outline)
Bottom border	Format ⇨ Border (Bottom)
Copy	Edit ⇨ Copy
Paste cell formats	Edit ⇨ Paste Special (Formats)
ChartWizard	none
Help	Help

screen: "Inserts SUM function and proposes sum range." Or, you can click the Help tool and point at the icon, which displays a description in the Status bar.

In some cases, the tools act as a toggle. Select the Bold tool, and the data you've highlighted becomes bold. Selecting the Bold tool again removes the bold attribute.

You'll also find that some tools serve double duty. If you hold down the Shift key when you select a tool, it may perform the *opposite* function. For example, if you hold Shift while you click the tool for increasing the font size of selected data, it actually *decreases* the font size. This means that you can often get by with fewer tools on a toolbar — there's really no reason to have separate tools for both increasing and decreasing font size.

The best way to become familiar with how the tools work is to try them. Usually, the one-line description provides a pretty good idea of the tool's function, but sometimes you'll need to do some testing before you're comfortable using a tool. And, of course, if you select the wrong tool by accident, you can use the Edit ➩ Undo command to reverse its effects.

Displaying and Hiding Toolbars _____

In Chapter 12 you learned how to display certain aspects of Excel and its worksheet windows. To display and hide toolbars, use the Options ➩ Toolbar command. When you choose this command, the dialog box in Figure 19-1 appears. Select the toolbar you want to display or hide from the Show Toolbars box. If the selected toolbar is not already displayed, the Show button is available in the dialog box. If the selected toolbar *is* already displayed, the Show button becomes the Hide button. Depending on the display status of the toolbar you select, the Show and Hide buttons toggle to the appropriate option. Choosing Show or Hide displays or hides the toolbar you selected, then closes the dialog box and returns you to your active worksheet.

You can hide or display the Standard toolbar by pressing Ctrl+7.

If you position your mouse pointer over a toolbar (but not on an icon) and click the *right* mouse button, the toolbar shortcut menu appears, just like other right-button shortcut menus. The toolbar shortcut menu, shown in Figure 19-2, displays the names of the toolbars and the commands that lead to the Toolbars and Customize dialog boxes.

Figure 19-1: The Toolbars dialog box enables you to select the toolbars you'd like to display or hide.

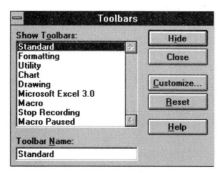

Figure 19-2: The toolbar shortcut menu is available any time you click on a blank area of a toolbar with the right mouse button.

Notice that the upper portion of the menu is similar to the bottom portion of the Window menu — a check mark appears to the left of the name of the toolbar that is on-screen. To display or hide a toolbar, simply click on its name.

If you've caught toolbar mania and have created more toolbars than the toolbar shortcut menu can display, choose More Toolbars (which appears under such a condition) to display the Toolbars dialog box. You can then select the name of the toolbar from the Show Toolbars list box and display or hide the toolbar as desired.

Moving and Sizing Toolbars

As you know, everything in Windows (program groups, Excel, worksheets, charts, and so on) appears in windows, and toolbars are no exception. Toolbar windows can be moved and sized just like all windows. Because toolbars are totally mouse-oriented, there are no keyboard Control menu command equivalents for controlling a toolbar as a window. Consequently, to move a toolbar, position your pointer in a blank area in the toolbar, then press and drag. As you drag the mouse, a gray outline of the toolbar appears. What happens next depends on where you're moving your toolbar from and to. Some terminology is in order.

Make sure you position your mouse pointer carefully to move a toolbar. If you don't, and click on an icon, you may experience unwanted results. If this should occur, choose Edit ⇨ Undo pronto.

Positioning toolbars

You can move your toolbars anywhere in the Excel application window or worksheet window. If you place a toolbar above the Formula bar or along an edge of the Excel application window, Excel will park your toolbar in a *toolbar*

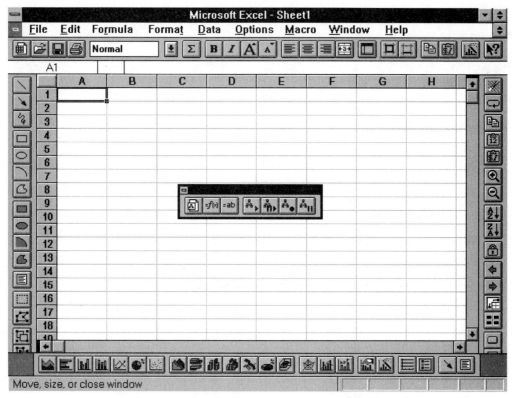

Figure 19-3: Toolbars on parade: four docked toolbars, one per dock, and a floating toolbar.

dock. The four toolbar docks are: to the left of the row numbers, to the right of the vertical scroll bar, below the horizontal scroll bar, and between the command menu and Formula bars. Figure 19-3 displays four docked toolbars and a *floating toolbar.* Floating toolbars have a title bar and appear in their own window on your worksheet. You can display floating toolbars across columns or down rows.

Once you've displayed a toolbar, you can move it into a toolbar dock or float it over your worksheet. The placement of toolbars has a direct bearing on their size.

Moving toolbars

To move a toolbar, position your mouse pointer in a blank area of the toolbar, then press and drag it to a toolbar dock or onto your worksheet. How to do each is described in the following sections.

Docking toolbars

To place a toolbar in the left or right toolbar dock, drag the toolbar to the respective edge of your worksheet, below the Formula bar. As you do, the toolbar outline changes its shape from a horizontal to a vertical rectangle. When your pointer is directly below the top line of the Formula bar (the Reference area on the left, to be precise) and along one of the edges of the worksheet, release the mouse. Excel then places the toolbar in the appropriate dock. If you already have another toolbar in the dock, Excel displays the new toolbar to the left or right of the original toolbar, depending on the position of the toolbar outline when you released the mouse.

To place a toolbar in the top or bottom toolbar dock, press and drag on the toolbar and position the toolbar outline above the Formula bar. If you already have a toolbar there, move the outline above or below the existing toolbar and release the mouse. Excel then places the toolbar in the top or bottom toolbar dock.

Toolbars are easier to dock if your worksheet window is maximized. And the Standard, Formatting, and Microsoft Excel 3 toolbars cannot be placed in the left or right toolbar docks because of their pull-down list boxes. This also applies to any custom toolbars that contain pull-down list boxes.

You can also position toolbars within the dock by clicking and dragging on a blank area of the toolbar. As you drag, a white outline of the toolbar appears, helping you place the toolbar where you want it in the dock. Release the mouse when your toolbar is positioned correctly. Figure 19-4 shows the Macro toolbar centered in the left toolbar dock.

If the white toolbar outline suddenly increases in height, this indicates that you've sailed out of the toolbar dock, and the extra height accommodates a title bar for the now floating toolbar.

If you've previously docked a floating toolbar, double-clicking on a blank area of the toolbar will return it to its former toolbar dock. Double-clicking a floating toolbar that's never been docked places it in the top toolbar dock, immediately above the Formula bar.

Making toolbars float

Making a toolbar float is easy. If your toolbar is in a dock, point to a blank area of the toolbar, then press and drag it to the desired location on the worksheet. When you release the mouse button, the gray outline disappears and the toolbar reappears with a title bar. You can move the toolbar again, or a new toolbar you've displayed with Options ⇨ Toolbars Show, by pressing and dragging on its title bar.

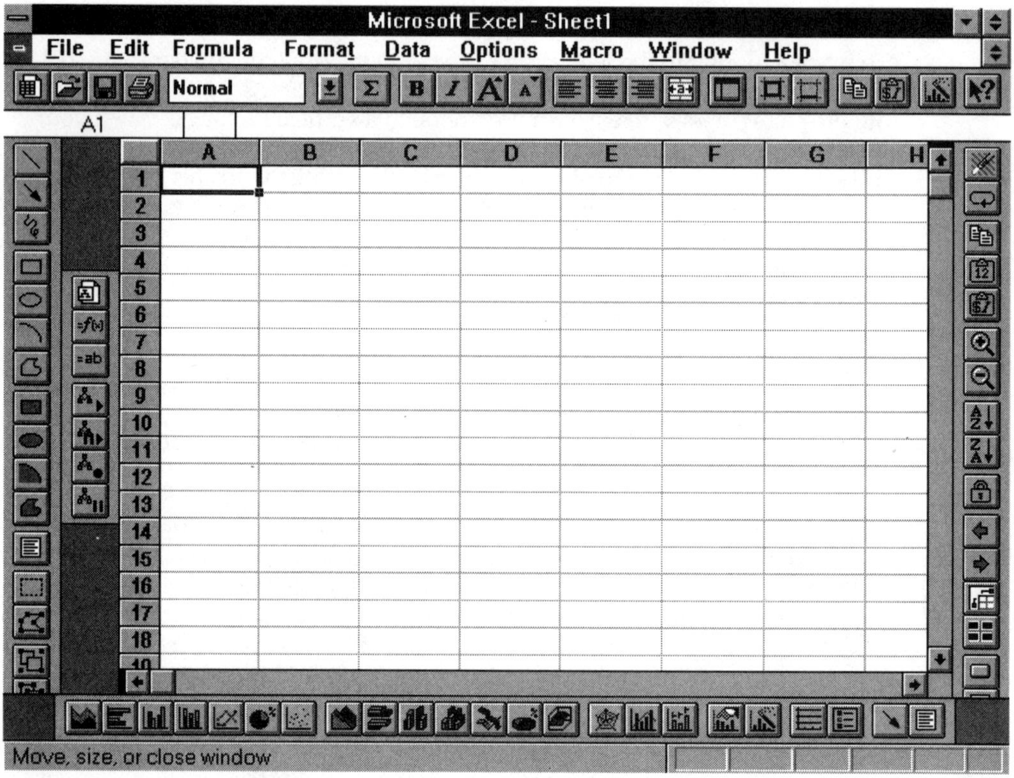

Figure 19-4: The Macro toolbar centered vertically in the left toolbar.

You can also resize floating toolbars. Position the mouse pointer at either side or the bottom border of the toolbar window. When the pointer appears as a white two-headed arrow, press and drag on the border. Dragging on the right or left border increases the window's width, while dragging on the bottom border increases its length. A toolbar window can appear as a wide rectangle, a square, or a long rectangle. Figure 19-5 illustrates some of the various shapes floating toolbars can have.

Figure 19-5: Various toolbar shapes you can create by pressing and dragging on either side or the bottom of the toolbar.

Customizing Toolbars and Tools _____

As we've mentioned, Excel's toolbars are especially flexible. You can customize the toolbars that come with Excel by adding, deleting, moving, and copying the tools on the toolbar.

In addition, you can customize the individual tools themselves. You can change a tool's appearance by copying one tool's face to another or by creating your own. Or you can change the action of a preexisting tool or a tool you create by assigning a macro to it. The next two sections explain how to customize and create toolbars so you can get the most from Excel.

Customizing existing toolbars

You can change the composition of Excel's toolbars so they better fit the way you use Excel. You do this by adding and deleting tools and by changing the order in which the tools appear on one or more of the toolbars. Keep two things in mind as you read these sections:

■ You must display the toolbar you want to customize before you make any changes to it, much like selecting a range before you choose an Excel command.

■ We'll be using the toolbar shortcut menu, which you access by positioning your mouse pointer on a blank area of the toolbar and clicking the right mouse button. You can access Toolbars from the Options menu, but the shortcut menu is faster.

To customize an existing toolbar, first display the toolbar by selecting it from the toolbar shortcut menu and then choose Customize. The Customize dialog box appears, as shown in Figure 19-6. Refer to Table 19-2 for the various customizations you can make to toolbars.

Figure 19-6:
The Customize dialog box contains over 130 tools for adding to existing toolbars or toolbars you create on your own.

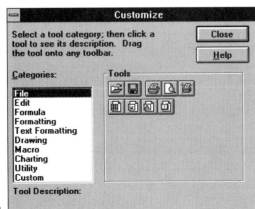

Table 19-2: Toolbar customizations		
Goal	**Action**	**Excel's response**
Add a tool	Select a tool category, then drag a tool from the Tools box to a location on the toolbar.	Adds the tool and resizes the toolbar.
Delete a tool	Drag the tool off the toolbar to anywhere other than a toolbar or the dialog box.	Deletes the tool and resizes the toolbar.
Move a tool	Drag the tool to its new location on an existing toolbar or another displayed toolbar.	Changes the order the tools are displayed on the toolbar and closes up extra space.
Copy a tool	Press Ctrl and drag the tool to its new location on the same toolbar or another visible toolbar.	Inserts a copy of the tool and resizes the toolbar to accommodate the duplicate.

Creating new toolbars

You can create a toolbar from scratch and include any of the tools that come with Excel. This section discusses how to create toolbars with tools provided by Excel; the next section shows how to create your own tools that you can add to Excel's toolbars or to those you create yourself. Either way, creating your own toolbars is easy. Choose Toolbars from the toolbar shortcut menu and type a name in the Toolbar name box. Next, choose Add or Customize, and a blank toolbar appears, as well as the Customize dialog box.

Change your mind? No need to panic . . .

The bad news is that if you delete a tool that comes with Excel you can't use Edit ⇨ Undo to retrieve the tool and put it back on the toolbar. The good news is that Excel tools can't be permanently deleted. Although you can remove them from a toolbar, they're still available in the Customize dialog box. Simply drag the tool from the Tools box back onto your toolbar.

If you've added, moved, or deleted so many tools you've lost track of what you were trying to accomplish, you can restore a toolbar that came with Excel by displaying the toolbar and choosing Reset from the Toolbars dialog box.

Select a tool category from the Categories box, then drag a desired tool from the Tools box to add it to your new toolbar. If you change your mind, drag the tool off the toolbar to anywhere over your worksheet, and the tool won't be added to the toolbar. When you're finished selecting categories and tools, choose Close to complete the toolbar, which is now ready for action.

You can add tools from another displayed toolbar by holding down the Ctrl key and dragging the tool to your new toolbar. This copies the tool and leaves the original in place.

Spacing tool icons

You can add or delete spaces between the tools on your toolbars and thus group tools with similar functions together. For example, the four formatting tools (Bold, Italic, Increase font size, Decrease font size) are grouped together, as well as the four alignment tools (Left, Center, and Right justify, and Center across columns).

To add space between tools, display the toolbar you want to change, then choose Customize from the toolbar shortcut menu. Press on the tool you want to insert a space in front of (or above, for a vertical toolbar), then take one of the following actions.

Creating toolbars on the fly

You can create new toolbars at warp speed using either of these methods:

- Drag a tool from the Tools box and place it anywhere over your worksheet, as long as it isn't on another toolbar.

- Press Ctrl and drag a tool from a displayed toolbar anywhere over your worksheet. In either case, Excel creates a toolbar for the tool, with its own title bar and Close box, and names it Toolbar1, Toolbar2, and so on.

You can continue to add tools from the Tools box or another toolbar, or forge ahead and put your toolbar to work.

To rename your new toolbar with a more-descriptive name, choose Toolbars and select the name of the toolbar in the Show Toolbars list box. Type a new name in the Toolbar Name text box and choose Add. Repeat the process but select the original toolbar name and Delete from the Toolbars dialog box to remove the old name.

Tool position	Action
Not followed by a space	Drag the tool to the right until it is halfway over the next tool (down for vertical toolbars).
Followed by a space you want to retain	Drag the tool to the right so it is just touching the next tool (down for vertical toolbars).
Followed by a space you don't want to retain	Drag the tool to the right so it is past its original position but not past the next tool (down for vertical toolbars).

To remove space between tools, press and drag the tool toward the extra space you want to delete, but don't drag the tool past the next tool immediately adjacent to it. Be careful that you don't drag to far — if you drag more than half way past the next tool, Excel inserts a space on the opposite side of the tool you're dragging.

Customizing tools

In addition to customizing existing toolbars and creating new ones, you can customize and create tools for your toolbars. You can change the appearance (*face*) or function of tools that come with Excel, or create new tools for specific needs you may have.

You follow the same procedure to change the appearance or function of a tool, whether its a built-in tool or a tool you create. To change the appearance of a tool, you can copy the face from another tool or copy a picture you create from a Windows graphics program. To change the function of a tool, assign a macro to it.

In the previous section, you used the toolbar shortcut menu to customize your toolbars. In this section, you'll use both the toolbar shortcut menu and a *tool* shortcut menu. You access the tool shortcut menu by opening the Options Toolbars Customize dialog box (available through the toolbar shortcut menu), then pointing at the tool you want to customize and clicking the right mouse button. The dialog box in Figure 19-7 appears. It enables you to change the face of a tool or assign a macro to it.

Figure 19-7: The tools shortcut menu is your express lane to creating new tools.

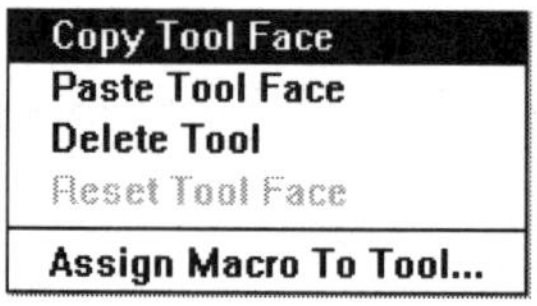

Copy Tool Face
Paste Tool Face
Delete Tool
Reset Tool Face
Assign Macro To Tool...

Changing the face

You can change the appearance of tools in two ways: by copying the face of one tool to another or by importing a picture from a graphics program such as Windows Paintbrush. These methods are discussed next.

 You can change the appearance of tools displayed on toolbars only. Changing the face of tools in any of the Tools boxes is off limits.

Copying another face

Changing the face of a tool by copying another is the easier of the two ways to modify a tool's appearance. For example, you might prefer (from the Custom tools category) the tool face that resembles a 3 ½-inch disk with an arrow pointing toward it rather than the disk on the Standard toolbar that represents and performs a File ⇨ Save operation.

To copy a tool face from one tool to another, display the toolbar you want to copy the tool face to or from and then choose Customize from the toolbar shortcut menu. Next, click the tool you want to copy *from* the toolbar or the Customize dialog box Tools box. Now, choose Edit ⇨ Copy Tool Face, or if you're copying a tool from a toolbar, choose Copy Tool Face from the tool shortcut menu. Click on the tool you want to copy *to*, then choose Edit ⇨ Paste Tool Face.

 If you want to start over and return a tool to its original appearance, click on the tool and then choose Reset Tool Face from the tool shortcut menu. The selected tool will be returned to its original appearance.

Creating your own face

You can use the Paintbrush program that comes with Windows (or some other Windows bitmap graphics program) to create tool faces. Note, however, that using Paintbrush to do this is a rather tedious process (calling all shareware and third-party software developers) and requires a lot of time and patience. If you have the wherewithal, however, you can create some handy customized tools that will increase your productivity and give you a toolbar with sizzle.

As with most Excel operations, there's more than one way to use Paintbrush to create tool faces. You can build one from scratch, but the easier method is to take one of the Custom blank tools and modify its appearance, as we explain next. Whichever way you choose, your tool face should ideally be the same size as the tools that come with Excel (16 pixels wide by 15 pixels high) and have a light gray background (unless you want it to *really* stand out). You should be familiar with Windows Paintbrush, specifically the Paintbrush tools and color palette. Check out the *Microsoft Windows User's Guide* for more information.

Steps: Using Paintbrush to create a tool face

Step 1. Display the toolbar that contains a tool you want to change the appearance of. You can add a blank tool to the toolbar if you don't want to change an existing tool face.

Step 2. Choose Customize from the toolbar shortcut menu, select Custom from the Categories box, click on a blank tool, and choose Copy Tool Face from Excel's Edit menu. This copies the image to the Clipboard.

Step 3. Start Paintbrush.

Step 4. Select Options ⇨ Image Attributes, specify 250 in the Width and Height text boxes, and select the pels radio button from the Units box (pels = pixels).

Step 5. Select File ⇨ New, then View ⇨ Cursor Position. The first command creates a new file with the dimensions specified in Step 4; the second command exhibits the position of the mouse pointer on-screen. Note that the coordinates of the upper-left corner of the window are 0,0 while the lower-right coordinates are 249,249.

Step 6. Select Edit ⇨ Paste to copy the blank tool face from the Clipboard.

Step 7. Press and drag the tool face to the center of the drawing area.

Step 8. Select View ⇨ Zoom In and position the square mouse pointer so it surrounds the blank tool, then click. The zoom window appears, as shown in Figure 19-8.

Step 9. Modify the tool face pixel by pixel with the Brush and fill tools (to use other tools, exit ZOOM mode). Use light gray for the background and black for the foreground. You can press and drag on the pixels to change their color quickly. Don't go beyond the gray area, as this part won't be saved. An example of what you can do is shown in Figure 19-9.

Step 10. When you're finished modifying the image, select View ⇨ Zoom Out.

Step 11. Select the 15 × 16 pixel area with the Pick tool (the Scissors tool in the upper-right corner in the Paintbrush toolbox). Refer to the Cursor Position window to zero in on the correct coordinates.

Step 12. Select Edit ⇨ Copy to copy the image to the Clipboard.

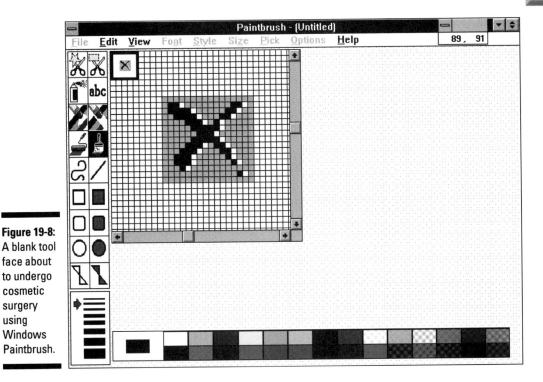

Figure 19-8:
A blank tool face about to undergo cosmetic surgery using Windows Paintbrush.

Step 13. Return to Excel and select Customize from the toolbar shortcut menu.

Step 14. Right-click the tool on the toolbar you want to change and select Paste Tool Face from the tool shortcut menu. The new icon appears, as shown here:

These steps detail the method for making "perfect" icons. Actually, you can paste a bitmap of any size (not just 15 × 16 pixels) and Excel will scale it to fit on the tool face. Large images lose a lot in the scaling, so experiment with this until you're satisfied.

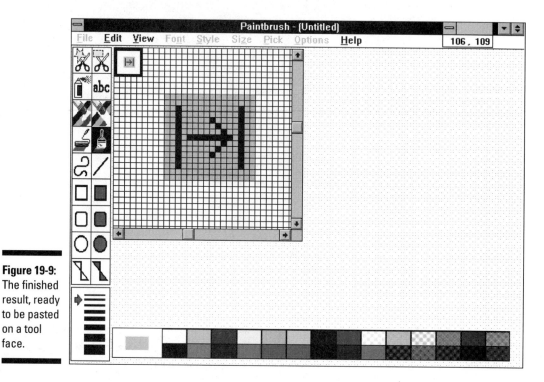

Figure 19-9:
The finished
result, ready
to be pasted
on a tool
face.

Assigning macros

A custom tool without a macro is like a parked car in neutral: the tool will just sit there and do nothing. If you create a tool, you must assign it a macro so the tool performs an action when clicked. You can also reassign the function of tools that come with Excel. For example, you may prefer the File ⇨ Save tool to perform as File ⇨ Save As instead (although you could create a separate tool to do this). In either case, the procedure for assigning macros to built-in or custom tools is pretty much identical.

If you've created a custom tool, press and drag it from the Custom category in the Tools box (located in the Customize dialog box) to the toolbar where you want to add it. Excel then displays the Assign To Tool dialog box, as shown in Figure 19-10.

Figure 19-10:
The Assign To
Tool dialog box
lets you assign a
macro to a
predefined or
custom tool.

If you want a tool (preexisting *or* custom) to perform a different action, click on
the tool on the displayed toolbar and choose Assign To Tool from the tool
shortcut menu. At this point, you can assign an existing macro, or one that you
create right now.

Assigning an existing macro

Before you assign a macro to a tool, open the sheet that contains the macro you
want to assign. To assign a macro, you need only select the name of the macro
from the Assign Macro list box and choose OK (you can assign macros on
unopened macro sheets by typing the complete filename and address in the
Reference text box, but this is taking the long way around).

Assigning a macro on the move

You can create a macro from the Assign Macro To dialog box if you don't have
an existing macro to assign to your selected tool. Choose Record and then OK.
Excel displays the Stop Recording Macro tool and the message "Recording" on
the Status bar. Perform the worksheet operations (choosing commands, making
dialog box choices, and so on) *exactly* the way you want your tool to do it.
When you're finished, select the Stop Recording Macro tool. Your tool now has
a new macro assigned to it.

If you create and assign a macro in this manner, make sure you carry out the
steps you want your macro to take precisely. If you perform any extraneous
keystrokes, they will be recorded by your macro and played back when you
select the tool, sometimes with disastrous results (especially if you've recorded
keystrokes that erase or overwrite cell contents). For more information about
creating, testing, and debugging macros, see Chapter 26.

Changing your mind, part 2

Unlike unsaved changes to your worksheets, Excel "remembers" what toolbars you displayed and any changes to them from your last session, without any intervention from you. If you want to save your toolbar layout that came with Excel, do one of the following:

■ Display only the Standard toolbar and reverse any changes to all toolbars by displaying the toolbar and choosing Reset from the Toolbar dialog box.

■ Choose File ▷ Open and select excel.xlb.

If you wish to save the original and new toolbar layouts, switch to File Manager and rename the file excel.xlb. to excel.old (or another file extension that has meaning to you). At this point you can share your toolbars with your fellow Excel users by giving them a copy of your latest version of excel.xlb (and your corresponding macro sheets) on disk.

Also, note that if you move a custom tool off a toolbar, it's gone for good. One way you can save custom tools without displaying them on a toolbar is to create a toolbar just for custom tools — a warehouse to store the tools you create. In this manner, you can hide and display the toolbar, though you still won't be able to select custom tools from the Customize dialog box's Tools box. But you'll still have them in one convenient place so you can quickly add them to other toolbars.

Summary

▶ Toolbars are one of the latest advances in spreadsheet technology and let you perform common tasks quickly by pointing and clicking on an icon.

▶ Toolbars hold tool icons and can be positioned in four docks located along the edges of the Excel workspace. You can also have floating toolbars that hover over your worksheet.

▶ Floating toolbars can be moved or sized just like any other window. They also have a Close box and a title bar.

▶ The Standard toolbar appears in the top toolbar dock, between the menu bar and Formula bars.

▶ The Standard toolbar tools include commonly used commands, such as File ▷ New, Open, Save, and Print, plus a variety of Format options.

▶ You can hide or show any of the toolbars that come with Excel using Options ▷ Toolbars ▷ Hide and Show, respectively.

▶ Access the *toolbar* shortcut menu by pointing to a blank area of a toolbar and clicking the right mouse button. Access the *tool* shortcut menu by pointing to a blank area of a toolbar, clicking the right mouse button, choosing Customize, selecting a tool, then clicking the right mouse button a second time.

▶ You can customize existing toolbars by adding and/or deleting tools that come with Excel or those you create yourself.

▶ You can customize tools by changing their appearance, by copying from one tool face to another, or by creating a tool face using a graphics program such as Windows Paintbrush.

▶ You can also customize tools by changing their function. You can assign a macro to a tool that comes with Excel or change a macro assigned to a custom tool. A custom tool, however, must have a macro assigned to it in order to be functional.

Chapter 20
The Excel Add-Ins

In this chapter . . .

▶ How to use Excel add-ins and the features they provide.

▶ How to make a custom group of add-ins available automatically every time you start Excel.

▶ How to load (and unload) add-ins.

When you first install Excel, you might be overwhelmed by all the features available to you. Actually, the product has even more features that can be added on as needed. These features are called *add-ins* — supplementary or third-party features "added in" to the program. Although many of the add-ins included with Excel address rather esoteric topics, several of them are quite useful for all users. Add-ins are also available from third-party vendors, and advanced users can create their own with macros.

What Is an Add-In?

An add-in is a file you load into memory that adds additional functionality to Excel. Add-ins can provide:

- New commands to the menu system
- New functions to use in your formulas

Once an add-in is loaded, it works seamlessly with Excel. For example, the commands appear right on the menu along with the standard commands, and any new add-in functions are listed in the Paste Function dialog box.

Examining Excel's Add-Ins _____

Many types of add-ins ship with Excel. This section describes them so you can determine which, if any, can be of use to you. Some of these provide significant new capabilities (like the Analysis ToolPak), and others are handy utilities (such as the View Manager add-in). A few are only of marginal value (such as the What-if add-in).

Automatically installed add-ins

During the Excel installation process, one option is to set up the program so certain add-ins are automatically placed on the menu when you start Excel (the actual add-ins aren't loaded until you invoke the menu command). If you installed Excel with this option, the following add-ins should be available to you with no additional steps:

Add-in	New command or functions
Add-In Manager	Options ⇨ Add-ins
Analysis ToolPak	Options ⇨ Analysis Tools
Crosstab	Data ⇨ Crosstab
Report Manager	File ⇨ Print Report
Solver	Formula ⇨ Solver
View Manager	Window ⇨ View

If you did not choose this option when installing Excel, you can run the Setup program again and specify that you want these add-ins available. If you find that you do not need one or more of these add-ins, you can remove them. Instructions for removing add-ins are provided later in this chapter.

Add-in library

Excel includes an extensive list of add-ins, located in the \library directory off the main \excel directory. The \library directory has additional directories which hold more add-ins. Add-in files have an \xla file extension.

The add-ins are described in the following sections.

Add-in Functions

Purpose: Provides five new worksheet functions for use in your formulas.

Filename: `library\addinfns.xla`

Commands added: None

Functions added: BASE, DEGREES, FASTMATCH, RADIANS, and RANDBETWEEN

Add-In Manager

Purpose: Lets you work with other add-ins. Use it to add or remove add-ins from your *working set* — a selection of add-ins that are made available automatically whenever you start Excel.

Filename: `library\addinmgr.xla` (Automatically loaded when you start Excel, as specified at installation time.)

Commands or functions added: Options ➪ Add-ins

Alternate Startup

Purpose: Lets you designate or change the alternate startup directory. Normally, Excel automatically loads all the files in the `\xlstart` directory. This add-in lets you specify another directory to serve this purpose. This is most useful for users on a network.

Filename: `library\altstart.xls`

Commands or functions added: None

Analysis ToolPak

Purpose: Provides extensive analytical tools, primarily in the areas of engineering, statistics, and finance. Loads other add-ins as needed.

The Analysis ToolPak is the topic of Chapter 25.

Filename: `library\analysis\analysis.xla` (Provided as an option when you install Excel.)

Commands or functions added: Options ⇨ Analysis Tools. The following new functions are provided:

ACCRINT	DEC2OCT	IMLN	ODDLPRICE
ACCRINTM	DEGREES	IMLOG10	ODDLYIELD
BESSELI	DELTA	IMLOG2	PMT
BESSELJ	DISC	IMPOWER	PPMT
BESSELK	DOLLARDE	IMPRODUCT	PRICE
BESSELY	DOLLARFR	IMREAL	PRICEDISC
BIN2DEC	DURATION	IMSIN	PRICEMAT
BIN2HEX	EFFECT	IMSQRT	PV
BIN2OCT	ERF	IMSUB	RADIANS
COMPLEX	ERFC	IMSUM	RATE
CONVERT	FV	INTRATE	RECEIVED
COUPDAYBS	FVSCHEDULE	IPMT	SLN
COUPDAYS	GESTEP	IRR	SYD
COUPDAYSNC	HEX2BIN	MDURATION	TBILLEQ
COUPNCD	HEX2DEC	MIRR	TBILLPRICE
COUPNUM	HEX2OCT	NOMINAL	TBILLYIELD
COUPPCD	IMABS	NPER	VDB
CUMIPMT	IMAGINARY	NPV	XIRR
CUMPRINC	IMARGUMENT	OCT2BIN	XNPV
DB	IMCONJUGATE	OCT2DEC	YIELD
DDB	IMCOS	OCT2HEX	YIELDDISC
DEC2BIN	IMDIV	ODDFPRICE	YIELDMAT
DEC2HEX	IMEXP	ODDFYIELD	

AutoSave

Purpose: Lets you save your documents automatically as you work. Choose the time interval and decide whether or not to be prompted before saving. Figure 20-1 shows the dialog box where you set your options.

Filename: library\autosave.xla

Commands or functions added: Options ⇨ AutoSave

Checkup

Purpose: Displays a window of technical information about Excel and your system environment. This might be useful if you have a problem with Excel and

Figure 20-1: The AutoSave add-in automatically saves your files at an interval you specify.

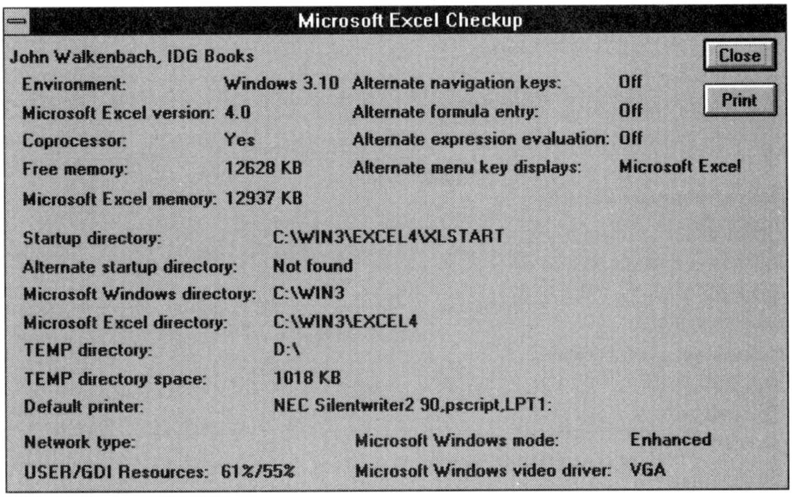

Figure 20-2: The Checkup add-in displays useful information about your system environment.

you're on the phone with someone from Microsoft's technical support department. Figure 20-2 shows a sample output window.

Filename: `library\checkup\checkup.xlm`

Commands or functions added: None

Crosstab

Purpose: Starts the Crosstab Wizard, which guides you step-by-step in creating crosstabulation tables for databases.

Filename: `library\crosstab\crosstab.xla` (Automatically loaded when you start Excel.)

Commands or functions added: Data ⇨ Crosstab

Custom Color Palettes

Purpose: Lets you change the color palette for a chart or embedded chart. Uses a group of worksheet files stored in the `library\colors` directory. Figure 20-3 shows the dialog box in which you select the color choices.

Filename: `library\color\palettes.xla`

Commands or functions added: Options ⇨ Custom Palettes

Figure 20-3: The Custom Palettes add-in lets you quickly change the color scheme of a chart.

Document Summary

Purpose: Lets you store explanatory information with a file: author, subject, creation date, and comments. An example of the dialog box you complete is shown in Figure 20-4.

Filename: library\summary.xla

Commands or functions added: Edit ⇨ Summary Info

File Functions

Purpose: Provides you with four new macro functions that work with directories.

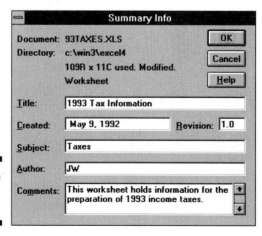

Figure 20-4: You can keep track of file details with the Summary add-in.

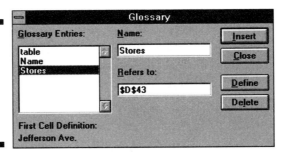

Figure 20-5: The Glossary add-in gives you access to a word processor-like glossary in which you can store frequently used data or formulas.

Filename: `library\filefns.xla`

Commands or functions added: CREATE.DIRECTORY, DELETE.DIRECTORY, FILE.EXISTS, and DIRECTORIES

Flat File

Purpose: Lets you parse imported labels and export selected data to a space-delimited text file.

Filename: `library\flatfile.xla`

Commands or functions added: Data ⇨ Smart Parse and Data ⇨ Export

Glossary

Purpose: Lets you store frequently used formulas or data in a glossary (similar to the glossary feature found in most word processors). Once defined, you can quickly paste a glossary entry into a worksheet or macro sheet. An example of the dialog box for this command is shown in Figure 20-5.

Filename: `library\glossary.xla`

Commands or functions added: Edit ⇨ Glossary

Macro Debugger

Purpose: Helps you locate and correct logical errors in macros that you write. This is discussed further in Chapter 26.

Filename: `library\debug.xla`

Commands or functions added: Macro ⇨ Debug

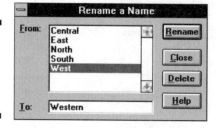

Figure 20-6:
Changing range names is a snap with the Name Changer add-in.

Name Changer

Purpose: Makes it easy to change or delete range names. The dialog box that results from this command is shown in Figure 20-6.

Filename: library\changer.xla

Commands or functions added: Formula ⇨ Change Name

Q+E

Purpose: Lets you access remote data using the Q+E application that's included with Excel.

Filename: library\qe\qe.xla (Provided as an option when you install Excel).

Commands or functions added: Data ⇨ Paste Fieldnames, Data ⇨ SQL Query, Data ⇨ Activate Q+E

Report Manager

Purpose: Works in conjunction with the View Manager and the Scenario Manager. Lets you define and print reports that consist of multiple views and scenarios. Automatically loads the View Manager and the Scenario Manager if they are not already loaded.

Filename: library\reports.xla (Automatically loaded when you start Excel.)

Commands or functions added: File ⇨ Print Report

Scenario Manager

Purpose: Lets you set up and manage various what-if scenarios by storing alternative values for a set of input cells. An example dialog box is shown in Figure 20-7.

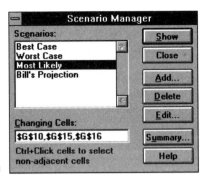

Figure 20-7: The Scenario Manager add-in makes it easy to manage multiple scenarios.

Filename: library\scenario.xla (Automatically loaded when you start Excel.)

Commands or functions added: Formula ⇨ Scenario Manager

Slide Show

Purpose: Works in conjunction with the Slide template (provided with Excel) and lets you create and display on-screen slide shows.

Filename: library\slides\slides.xla

Commands or functions added: None. Activated only when you access a document created with the Slide template.

Solver

Purpose: Provides access to Excel's Solver — an advanced analytical tool that can solve optimization problems involving constraints.

Filename: library\solver\solver.xla (Provided as an option when you install Excel.)

Commands or functions added: Formula ⇨ Solver

Switch

Purpose: Provides tools (which you can add to a toolbar) that let you quickly switch to any of three other Microsoft applications: Word for Windows, PowerPoint, or Project.

Filename: library\switchto.xla

Commands or functions added: New tools on the toolbar of your choice.

Figure 20-8: The View Manager is one of the most useful add-ins provided with Excel.

View Manager

Purpose: Lets you save specific views by name (see Figure 20-8). A view consists of window placement, gridline display, row and column borders, hidden columns and rows, and print settings. This add-in is very useful, and every Excel user should become acquainted with it.

Filename: library\views.xla (Automatically loaded when you start Excel.)

Commands or functions added: Window ⇨ View

What-if

Purpose: Lets you set up alternative values for specific input cells and then cycle through them while observing the effects on your worksheet.

Filename: library\whatif.xla

Commands or functions added: Formula ⇨ What-If

Worksheet Auditor

Purpose: Generates several reports that help you identify errors or potential errors in a worksheet. Also provides an interactive trace facility to identify cell dependencies. The dialog box in which you select your options is shown in Figure 20-9.

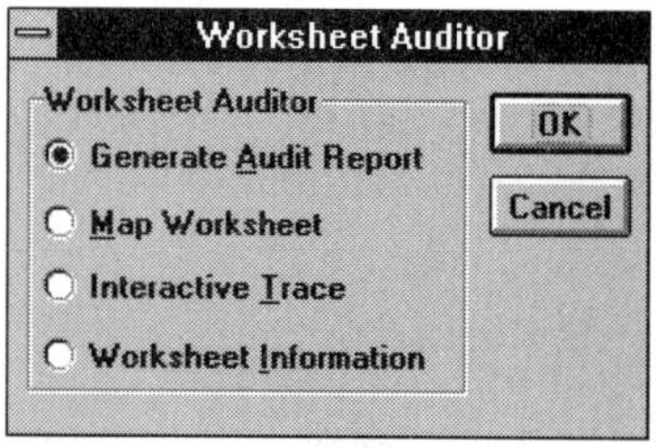

Figure 20-9: The Worksheet Auditor add-in can help you track down errors and potential errors.

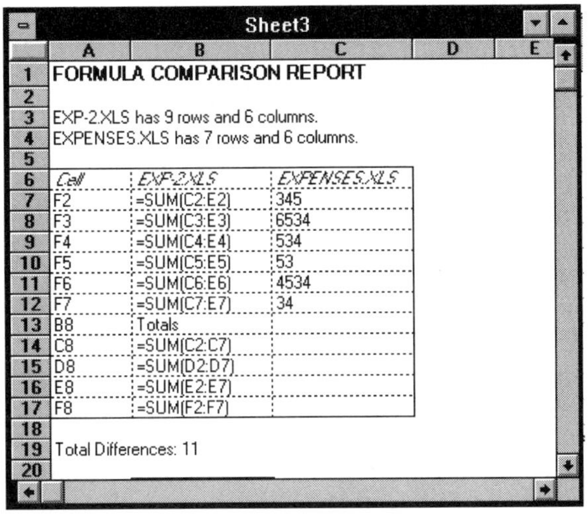

Figure 20-10: The Worksheet Comparison add-in generates a report that shows the differences between two worksheets.

Filename: `library\audit.xla`

Commands or functions added: Formula ➪ <u>W</u>orksheet Auditor

Worksheet Comparison

Purpose: Generates reports that identify which cells are different in two worksheets. Useful for documenting changes that you make to a worksheet. Figure 20-10 shows a sample report that summarizes the differences between two worksheets.

Filename: `library\compare.xla`

Commands or functions added: Formula ➪ Co<u>m</u>pare

Managing Add-Ins

The Add-In Manager lets you manage other add-ins. It's accessed through the <u>O</u>ptions ➪ Add-<u>i</u>ns command. When you select this command, you'll get the dialog box shown in Figure 20-11. This dialog box lists all the add-ins that are automatically available when you start Excel — referred to as your "working set." If you find that you use an add-in regularly, add it to your working set. On the other hand, you may want to remove add-ins that you never use.

Figure 20-11: The
Add-In Manager
add-in lets you
determine which
add-ins are available
when you start Excel.

These add-ins are not actually loaded until you invoke the command to use them.

The Add-In Manager is straightforward. To remove an add-in from your working set, select the add-in and then choose Remove. To add a new add-in to your working set, choose Add and then select the add-in file using the File Open dialog box. To change the path to the add-in file, select the add-in and then choose Edit. This lets you modify the path. When you've made all your changes, close the dialog box by choosing Close.

The Add-In Manager accesses the `excel4.ini` file, which is stored in your main Windows directory. This file keeps track of which add-ins are loaded at start-up.

Browsing through add-ins

Add-in files are actually macro files. Many add-ins provided with Excel contain calls to Dynamic Link Libraries (DLLs) — compiled code written in a programming language. These DLLs are loaded as necessary.

When an add-in is loaded into memory, it is not visible. In fact it's not even hidden, so you can't use the Window ➪ Unhide command to view it. This is done to prevent the file from being tampered with and to keep it out of your way. A normal end-user has no need to examine an add-in file.

If you're curious, however, you can open an add-in file and browse through it. The secret is to hold down the Shift key when you click OK in the

File Open dialog box. This technique opens the add-in file so it's visible in its own window. In some cases, the window may be hidden, but you can unhide it with the Window ➪ Unhide command. You'll find that these files are complex, but you might be able to pick up some hints on how Excel macros are structured and organized. At the very least, it's interesting to see some actual code written by Microsoft programmers.

 If you browse though any add-in files provided with Excel, make sure you don't save the files. One minor change could make it inoperable —in which case you would have to reinstall it from the original Excel disks.

Loading an Add-In

If you want to load an add-in for use during the current session (and don't want it to be available every time you start Excel), you can use the normal File ⇨ Open command. To display only add-in files, use the pull-down list box labeled List files of type and select MS Excel Macros. This will display only files with an xlm or xla extension. Locate the add-in file you want to load and then choose OK.

Unloading an Add-In

Using normal methods, you cannot unload an add-in once it has been loaded. This is unfortunate, since you may need to free up some memory by getting rid of an unwanted add-in. Nevertheless, there is a trick you can use if you *really* want to unload an add-in file.

Unloading an add-in file involves loading another copy of the add-in file — but hold down the Shift key when you click OK in the File Open dialog box. Excel will ask if you want to revert to the saved copy (that is, the copy on disk). Reply in the affirmative. The add-in will be replaced with the same add-in, but since you opened it with the Shift key held down, you can access it in its own window. You may have to unhide the window with the Window ⇨ Unhide command. Next, activate the add-in window and then close it with the File ⇨ Close command.

Add-In Functions

Some add-ins simply provide new functions you can use. As you might expect, the appropriate add-in must be loaded whenever you use a worksheet that uses an add-in function. If the add-in function is not available, the formula will return #REF, which means the reference could not be located. To solve this, simply load the add-in file that contains the add-in function or functions required by the formula.

You can create your own add-ins using Excel's macro language. This includes new commands as well as new functions. Complete coverage of this topic is beyond the scope of this book, but Chapter 26 provides enough information to get you started.

Summary

▶ Excel provides many add-in files that extend the functionality of the product.

▶ When you install Excel, you have the option of setting it up so several add-ins are automatically loaded when you start Excel.

▶ The Add-In Manager is an add-in that lets you modify your working set — a group of add-ins that are loaded automatically whenever you start Excel.

▶ You can load an add-in file using the standard File ⇨ Open command.

Chapter 21
Workbooks, File Linking, and Consolidation

In this chapter . . .

▶ How to make the most of Excel's new workbook feature.

▶ How to use linking formulas to access data from other worksheets.

▶ Three ways to consolidate data from multiple worksheets.

▶ Working with a group of worksheets to simulate a 3-D worksheet.

If you tend to use more than one Excel document for your projects, this chapter is for you. On the other hand, if you *don't* use multiple documents for projects, maybe you should. In either case, this chapter will show you the ropes involved in dealing with multiple Excel documents. Besides discussing the ins and outs of workbooks, we'll get into file linking and consolidating information from multiple worksheets.

Using More Than One Worksheet

Probably most of the projects that you use Excel for are relatively small. For example, you might store monthly sales figures and calculate percentage changes. Or, you might keep a list of products and prices and update the file periodically. Other worksheets might be used simply to print nice-looking tabular data (since Excel is better at this than most word processors).

But as you gain experience with Excel, you'll see its potential for handling more complex projects — for example, a complete sales tracking and incentive system that generates custom letters and prints mailing labels. You might find yourself allocating different parts of a worksheet for different types of related information. For instance, one section might list the sales people by region, another the components of the incentive plan, another the results, another the mailing address information, and so on. If you find yourself in this position, it's time to consider working with groups of related documents.

Using Excel's Workbooks

One of the most exciting new features in Excel 4 is workbooks. A workbook is a collection of related Excel documents — worksheets, chart sheets, and macro sheets. You can (optionally) store multiple documents in a single file, making it much easier to open them all and close them all. You can identify workbook files by their xlw extension.

 Excel 3 users should note that a workbook is an extension of the concept of a workspace (both use the same file extension). A workspace simply saves information about a group of files. A workbook, on the other hand, can actually store the multiple documents in one file. When you open an Excel 3 workspace file, it is automatically converted to a workbook (with all documents unbound — see further). Unfortunately, you will not be able to save your work as an Excel 3 workspace.

Why use workbooks?

Following is a list of benefits you can realize by using a workbook:

- **Easier file management.** You can open a group of related documents with a single command. You can also close a group of documents with one command when you are finished working with them.

- **Easier navigation among documents.** A workbook gives you three additional icons that make it easy to quickly jump to the document you want to activate.

- **Simplifies file distribution.** If you need to give a coworker several related Excel documents, it's much easier to store them in a workbook and provide a single file rather than several files.

- **More descriptive names.** Bound documents in a workbook need not conform to DOS's eight-character filenames. Rather than have a file named wregsals.xls, you can refer to your document as *Western Regional Sales*.

- **Ensures macros will be accessible.** If you have a worksheet that uses macros, you can store the worksheet and the macro sheet together in a workbook — thereby ensuring that the macros will always be available when the worksheet is loaded.

A workbook is actually another type of Excel document. The workbook contents window consists of a list of documents in that workbook. Figure 21-1

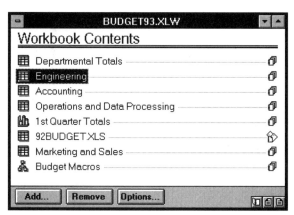

Figure 21-1: The workbook contents window displays the documents contained in the workbook, along with icons that describe what type of document each is and whether it is bound or unbound.

shows an example of a workbook contents window. This particular workbook consists of eight Excel documents: six worksheets, one chart, and one macro sheet (notice the extended names used for some of the worksheets).

The workbook window serves as sort of a table of contents for groups of documents. The icon to the left of each document name tells you what type of document it is (if there is no icon to the left, it means the document is part of the workbook, but is hidden). Documents in a workbook can be bound or unbound. You can tell if a document is bound or unbound by looking at the icon to the right of the name in the workbook contents window.

 Bound   A bound document is actually stored in the workbook file. Bound documents can be used in only one workbook at a time.

 Unbound An unbound document is part of a workbook, but is stored as a separate file. This means that such a document can be part of more than one workbook.

Also notice the "paging" icons at the bottom of the workbook window. Actually, each document in a workbook displays these icons in the lower-right corner of its window. These icons are used for navigation through the workbook, as follows:

 Displays the workbook contents window.

 Activates the previous document in the workbook.

 Activates the next document in the workbook.

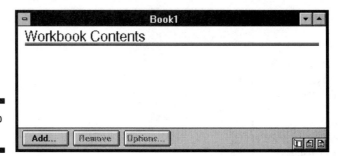

Figure 21-2: The first step in creating a workbook.

Figure 21-2: The first step in creating a workbook.

These paging icons will not appear if scroll bars have been turned off with the Options ⇨ Workspace command.

You can also right-click on any of the paging icons to display a shortcut menu that lists all of the documents in the workbook, the File ⇨ New command, and the Options ⇨ Group Edit command.

Creating a workbook

To create a new workbook, use the File ⇨ New command and choose the Workbook option. Excel displays a blank workbook contents window, as shown in Figure 21-2. The next step is to add documents to the workbook. You can add existing documents or create new documents. You do this by selecting Add, which pops up the dialog box in Figure 21-3. The dialog box lists all of your open documents.

Add an open document to a workbook: Select the document name from the list and choose Add.

Add a document that's not open: Select Open. Excel displays the familiar File Open dialog box, from which you can select a document to add to the workbook.

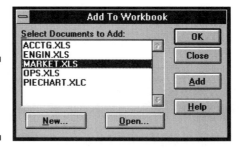

Figure 21-3: The Add To Workbook dialog box lets you add open files or files on disk to a workbook.

Figure 21-4: The Document Options dialog box lets you substitute a more descriptive name for your file (up to 31 characters).

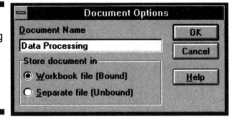

Add a new document: Select New. Excel displays its File New dialog box, and you can select the type of document you want to create.

Continue this process until your new workbook contains all the documents that you'll be using. You can always add new documents to a workbook at any point — or remove those that you no longer need.

Using the workbook contents window

The workbook contents window is the control center for the workbook. It lists all of the documents, and the icon to the right of each document name tells you if each document is bound or unbound.

Change a bound document to an unbound document (and vice versa): Click the icon to the right of the document name.

Change the order in which the documents are listed: Select the document name and drag it up or down. When you release the mouse button, the document name appears in the new location. (Keyboard users can use the Edit ⇨ Cut and Edit ⇨ Paste commands for this.)

Eliminate a document from the workbook: Select the document and then choose Remove. The document remains open, but is no longer part of the workbook. You can also simply select the document name and drag it out of the window.

Add a more descriptive name to a document: Select Options. Excel displays the dialog box shown in Figure 21-4. Simply enter a new name, using up to 31 characters (including spaces). You can also use the dialog box to change the bound/unbound status of the document.

Activate a document: Double-click the document name (or select it and press Enter). The selected document is activated in a window the same size as the workbook contents window. Or, you can use the paging icons to scroll through each document in order. When a workbook document is active, you can quickly get back to the contents window by clicking the first paging icon.

Workbook considerations

■ You can work with more than one workbook at a time. For example, you might have one project that uses eight documents and another that uses five. Arranging these projects in two workbooks is much simpler than dealing with 13 separate documents.

■ Unbound documents can be part of more than one workbook. For example, you might have a macro sheet that you use in three different workbooks. In this case, it's best to leave the macro sheet unbound, yet keep it as part of each workbook that needs it.

■ The workbook stores all of Excel's settings, so you can easily pick up where you left off. For example, it stores the preferred chart type, the workspace options, the display options, global calculation settings, and the position and size of the workbook's document windows.

■ If you open a multisheet 1-2-3 file (that is, a file from 1-2-3 Release 3 or 1-2-3 for Windows), Excel converts it to a workbook. Each sheet becomes a bound document, and 3-D references are converted to workbook references.

■ When you use a reference to a worksheet that's part of a workbook, you need to precede the filename with the workbook name. If you've assigned a nonstandard name to the document, you need to include the full name and include it in single quotes. This can get rather unwieldy. For example, a simple reference to a cell in a workbook might appear as:

```
='[budget93.xlw]Operations and Data Processing'!$B$4.
```

If you're going to use a lot of external references, you might consider keeping document names on the short side.

■ You can apply password protection to a workbook that applies to all bound documents in the workbook. Since unbound documents are stored separately, you need to protect those documents separately.

When you work with a group of related files, you'll often need these files to interact with each other. This is accomplished by setting up links between the files — the topic of the next section.

Linking Worksheets

By now, you should be thoroughly familiar with the concept of copying and pasting. For example, you can copy a range of data from one worksheet and paste it in another. This is one way to share data between worksheets. But as you know, if the original data is changed, the changes do not appear in the worksheet that it was copied to — you need to repeat the copy and paste procedure.

Setting up links between worksheets is a way around this problem. Through linking, a worksheet that depends on values in another worksheet remains up-to-date. First, a few definitions are in order:

External reference A reference to another Excel worksheet cell, range, or range name. External references are used in formulas, just like other references.

Dependent worksheet A worksheet that contains an external reference. In other words, the worksheet *depends* on another worksheet.

Source worksheet The worksheet that is the source of the data being supplied to a dependent worksheet.

 The types of links we're talking about here are links between Excel documents. Excel provides other methods to link to data in other applications. These topics — Dynamic Data Exchange (DDE) and Object Linking and Embedding (OLE) — are discussed in Chapter 29.

Linking Techniques

There are three ways to create worksheet links:

- Pointing to cells or ranges while creating a formula.
- Entering the external references manually.
- Using the Edit ➪ Paste Link command.

Entering references by pointing

Figure 21-5 shows two worksheets. The *source* worksheet, on the left, contains data that is used by the *dependent* worksheet, on the right. Column C in the dependent worksheet lists the formulas that are used in column B. These formulas were created by pointing — just like any other formula. The only difference is that we activated the source worksheet after entering the initial equal sign to start the formula. Excel provided the file reference automatically.

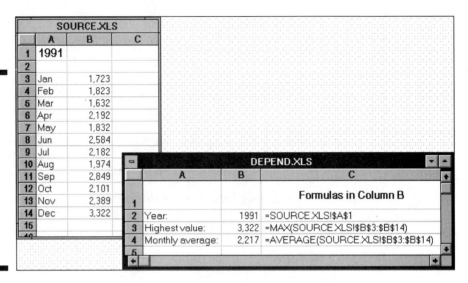

Figure 21-5:
The source
worksheet
contains data
used by the
dependent
worksheet.
They are
connected via
link formulas
(external
references).

The file reference is always separated from the cell reference by an exclamation point.

NOTE

When you create link formulas, Excel always makes the references absolute (that is, it uses two dollar signs in the cell references). If you want to copy a formula that uses an external reference, change the references so they are relative (remove the dollar signs).

The formula in cell B2 is a simple reference to a cell in the source worksheet (it simply returns the value in the cell, without using a formula). The other two formulas refer to an entire range. As you might expect, you can change any of the values in the source worksheet and the dependent worksheet recalculates to reflect the changes.

If the source worksheet is a bound sheet in a workbook, the file reference is preceded with the workbook's name in brackets. In the previous example, if `source.xls` was a bound document in a workbook named `summary.xlw`, the formula in cell B2 would be: `=[summary.xlw]source.xls!$A$1`.

Entering external references manually

Although pointing is much easier, you *could* have created the link references manually. It involves a lot more typing and is more prone to errors. Just remember the following rules:

- Precede the cell reference with the full filename, followed by an exclamation point. If the file is not stored in the default directory, precede the filename with the drive and path.

- If the source worksheet is bound in a worksheet, precede the filename with the workbook name, enclosed in brackets. If the bound document uses a nonstandard name, enclose the workbook name and document name in single quotes.

- The cell reference can be either absolute, relative, or mixed.

Using the Edit ⇨ Paste Link command

The final method of creating external links is available through the command menu. This technique is somewhat limited, since it creates only simple cell links — not links that are used in formulas. In the example presented earlier, we could have used this technique to create the formula in cell B2 (but not the other formulas).

Activate the source worksheet and select the cell or range that you want to link. Choose Edit ⇨ Copy from the menu to copy this information to the Clipboard. Next, activate the dependent worksheet and move the cell pointer to the location where you want the link formula(s) to be. Select Edit ⇨ Paste Link, and Excel inserts the link formula.

If you copy more than one cell using this method, Excel creates a single array formula. See Chapter 22 for more information.

Working with File Links _____

As you might expect, you'll need to make sure that the source worksheets are available when the dependent worksheet needs them. If all of these files are stored together in a workbook, you'll have no problem since the files will always open together.

Linked files, however, are not required to be in a workbook. When you retrieve a file that uses data in a source worksheet, Excel asks if you want to update the links by displaying the dialog box shown in Figure 21-6.

When you save a worksheet that depends on cells in another worksheet, Excel stores the most recently calculated source sheet values in the dependent worksheet. If you know that the source worksheet has not changed since you last used it, there's no need to update the links. If you've modified the source

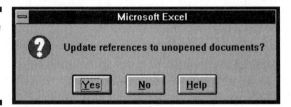

Figure 21-6: When you retrieve a file that has external reference formulas, Excel asks you if you want to update the links.

worksheet in the interim, however, you'll probably want Excel to update the links when you open a dependent worksheet. If Excel can't find the source file because you moved it or renamed it, it will display the standard File Open dialog box for you to specify the file.

If you move or rename a source worksheet, the link cannot be updated unless you change the formulas. The only exception to this is when both the source and dependent worksheets are active, and you use Excel's File ⇨ Save As command to change the source file's name. In this case, Excel makes the changes for you.

If you move a source file to another directory, there's an easy way to respecify the links — use the File ⇨ Links command. Selecting this command displays the dialog box shown in Figure 21-7. This command is used for other types of links as well. Consequently, make sure that the pull-down list labeled Link Type has Excel files selected. This dialog box lets you change the source file to something else (with the Change button) and also lets you refresh the links (with the Update button).

You can open a source document that's not already open by double-clicking on a cell that contains an external reference. Excel opens the source file for you and selects the cell or range referred to in the dependent worksheet.

One of the most common uses for linking worksheets is to consolidate data. For example, you might receive monthly sales reports from several regions and need to roll them up into a single consolidated report. You can do this fairly easily with link formulas, but there's another method you should consider. If consolidating worksheets is important to you, keep reading.

Consolidating Multiple Worksheets

Data can be consolidated across multiple worksheets in three different ways:

■ Using link formulas

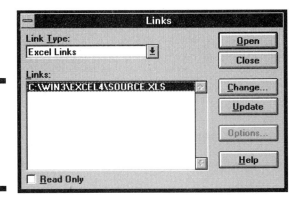

Figure 21-7: The Links dialog box lets you specify a different source document for your external references.

■ Using the Edit ➪ Paste Special command

■ Using the Data ➪ Consolidate command

We discuss all three of these methods in the sections that follow.

Consolidating with link formulas

Figure 21-8 shows a simple budget for four departments, plus a consolidated budget called total.xls. The departmental budget sheets are laid out identically, and we used linking formulas in total.xls to sum the corresponding values in the four worksheets. For example, the formula in cell B4 is:

```
=ops.xls!B4+market.xls!B4+acctg.xls!B4+engin.xls!B4
```

This formula was copied to the other cells and gives us the total consolidated budget amounts. total.xls is the dependent worksheet, since it depends on the values in four other source worksheets.

When you create a link formula by pointing, Excel uses absolute references. Before you copy such a formula, you need to change the absolute references to relative references. For example, we changed all instances of $B$4 to B4 in the previous formula.

This consolidation technique is straightforward and fairly easy to do — especially if all of the source worksheets have an identical layout — since we can then create one formula and copy it. On the other hand, if the source files were different, creating the link formulas in total.xls would be more difficult. For example, if the budget items were not in the same order across all four departmental sheets, we couldn't simply create one =SUM formula and copy it.

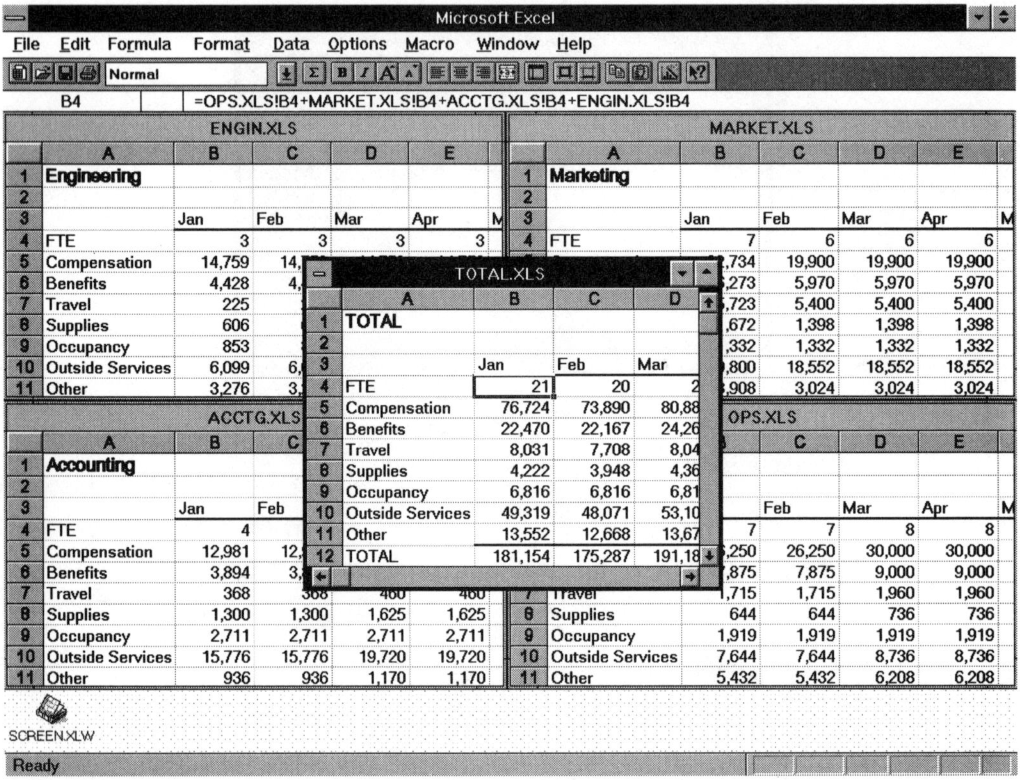

Figure 21-8: One way to consolidate multiple files is to use link formulas, like the one in the Formula bar in this figure.

Consolidating with the Edit ⇨ Paste Special command

The second method of consolidating multiple files uses the Edit ⇨ Copy and Edit ⇨ Paste Special commands. As you can see in the Paste Special dialog box shown in Figure 21-9, this command has a group box labeled Operation, with five options. These options perform the specified operation on the data in the destination worksheet *and* the data on the Windows Clipboard. For example, if you select the Add option, it adds the existing data in the destination worksheet to the data on the Clipboard. The other mathematical options work similarly, but subtract, multiply, or divide the data.

In the four-worksheet consolidation example, we can use the Edit ⇨ Copy and Edit ⇨ Paste Special command sequence four times — one for each source

Figure 21-9: The Paste Special dialog box provides several options for combining worksheet data with data on the Clipboard.

worksheet. We then select the Add option to create a consolidation of the four worksheets.

The disadvantage to this method is that it's a one-time operation. So if the data changes in any of the source files, the consolidation total won't change. And, the data must be laid out identically in all of the worksheets.

Consolidating with the Data ⇨ Consolidate command

The final consolidation method is the most robust of all. The Data ⇨ Consolidate command quickly consolidates data by matching row and column labels, so it works even if the categories aren't laid out identically in the source files. In addition, it can create link formulas and a worksheet outline if you like. This command lets you consolidate in two ways:

■ **By position:** This is similar to how Edit ⇨ Paste Special works and can be used only if the worksheets are laid out identically.

■ **By category:** In this case, Excel uses row and column labels to match data in the source worksheets.

We'll start out with the four departmental budget files we used in the example from Figure 21-8. Open a new blank worksheet to hold the consolidated data. The first step is to select the destination range — the range that will hold the consolidated results. It's easiest to select a single cell — Excel will use as much space as it needs. If you select a range, Excel stops consolidating when the range is full.

If you want to rearrange the category labels differently from the source documents, enter the labels (in any order) in the destination sheet and include these labels in the destination range.

Select <u>D</u>ata ⇨ Co<u>n</u>solidate, and Excel displays the dialog box shown in Figure 21-10. This dialog box has several parts:

Function   This pull-down list contains 11 consolidation functions you can choose from. Most of the time you'll want to use the =SUM function (which is the default choice), but you can also select options such as =AVERAGE, =MIN, and =MAX.

Reference   This text box holds a range from a source file that will be consolidated. You can enter the range manually or use any of the standard pointing techniques. Once the range is selected, use the Add button to add it to the All References list. If you're consolidating by position, do not include labels in the range. If you're consolidating by category, *do* include the labels in the range.

All References   This box contains the list of references that you've added with the Add button.

Use Labels In   This option tells Excel to examine the labels in the top row, the left column, or both to perform the consolidation. This is useful if the source worksheets are not laid out the same, or if some are missing information.

Create Links to Source Data   If you select this option, Excel creates external reference formulas in the destination worksheet and a structural outline. All of the data from the source files is duplicated in the destination file. A collapsed outline shows only the consolidation totals.

	D	E	F	G	H	I	J	K
			TOTAL.XLS					
1								
2								
3			Jan	Feb	Mar	Apr	May	Jun
4		Acctg	4	4	5	5	5	
5		Engin	3	3	3	3	4	
6		Market	7	6	6	6	6	
7		Ops	7	7	8	8	9	
8	FTE		21	20	22	22	24	
9		Acctg	12,981	12,981	16,226	16,226	16,226	16
10		Engin	14,759	14,759	14,759	14,759	19,678	19
11		Market	22,734	19,900	19,900	19,900	19,900	19
12		Ops	26,250	26,250	30,000	30,000	31,875	31
13	Compensation		76,724	73,890	80,885	80,885	87,679	87
18	Benefits		22,470	22,167	24,265	24,265	26,304	26
23	Travel		8,031	7,708	8,045	8,045	8,243	8
28	Supplies		4,222	3,948	4,365	4,365	4,613	4
33	Occupancy		6,816	6,816	6,816	6,816	6,816	6
38	Outside Services		49,319	48,071	53,107	53,107	55,686	55

Figure 21-11: This worksheet shows data that was consolidated with the Data ⇨ Consolidate command. In this case, Excel also created an outline.

Browse button	This button displays a dialog box that lets you select a file from disk. It inserts the filename in the Reference box, but you need to fill in the range reference yourself.
Delete button	This deletes the selected reference from the All References list.

Figure 21-11 shows the consolidated data from our example. Note that Excel inserted link formulas to pick up the data from the source worksheets and created an outline, which can be expanded to show all of the source data or collapsed to show only the totals. We discuss outlines extensively in Chapter 23.

Here are a few things to keep in mind when using the Data ⇨ Consolidate command:

- You can consolidate up to 255 worksheets with this method.

- The source worksheets do not need to be open. If they aren't open, however, you need to specify the reference manually (no pointing).

- Excel remembers the references, so you can perform a new consolidation without opening the source worksheets.

- Make sure all of the labels match exactly, since Excel consolidates only exact matches (it won't match "January" with "Jan"). Excel doesn't distinguish between uppercase and lowercase, however, so "Jan" *will* be matched to "JAN." Excel won't inform you if the labels don't match, since it only uses the labels you insert in the dependent worksheet.

Using Group Edit Mode

You may have several worksheets that all need to look the same and share common information, such as performance reports for each district or sales office. Except for the numbers, the headings and formatting in these worksheets can be identical.

Excel's Group Edit mode makes it easy to set up such files and edit them as a group. You enter Group Edit mode by selecting the Options ➪ Group Edit command, which displays the dialog box shown in Figure 21-12. This box shows all of the open worksheet files. You select the files that you want to work with as a group by highlighting the worksheet names. Hold down the Ctrl key while you click the worksheet names. When you've selected the desired worksheets, choose OK. Excel displays the word [Group] in the title bar of all grouped documents as a reminder. If a workbook is active, you can select individual documents in the workbook, plus any other open documents.

You can include worksheets and macro sheets in a group, but not chart sheets.

At this point, nearly everything you do in one document is repeated in the others. This includes making cell entries and all the formatting commands (but not drawing commands). For example, if you change the column width in one sheet, it changes in all of the grouped sheets. If you format a range as bold, it is bold in all the grouped worksheets.

A good way to become familiar with Group Edit mode is to display several worksheets at once (using the Window ➪ Arrange command), enter Group Edit mode, and then watch what happens when you go about your business in one worksheet.

You exit from Group Edit mode when you activate a different document (even if it's part of the group). As a result, it's fairly easy to get out of Group Edit mode by accident — so keep your eye on the title bar. To get back into Group Edit mode, select Options ➪ Group Edit again.

A new command is available when you're in Group Edit mode: Edit ➪ Fill Group (see Figure 21-13). This command lets you copy a cell or range (or just the

Figure 21-12: The Group Edit dialog box lets you select open worksheets that you can work with as a group.

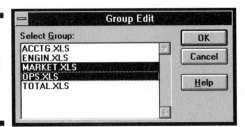

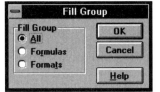

Figure 21-13: The Fill Group dialog box will copy a cell or range from one worksheet to all the others in the group.

formatting) from one sheet in the group to all the others. For example, you can start with a formatted worksheet, open three more blank worksheets, and then enter Group Edit mode. Select a range in the original worksheet and select Edit ⇨ Fill Group. That range is then copied to the other documents in the group. If you want to copy only the formats, select the Formats option in the dialog box. This command gives you many of the advantages of a 3-D worksheet (found in 1-2-3 Release 3, 1-2-3 for Windows, and Quattro Pro for Windows).

Summary

▶ If your projects use multiple Excel documents, you may want to consider using the workbook feature.

▶ You can store multiple Excel files in a single workbook file — making it easier to open the files, save the files, and distribute them to others. In addition, files can be unbound (saved separately).

▶ The workbook contents window displays all of the documents in the workbook and lets you quickly activate the desired document. You also have access to three paging icons to let you jump to the contents window or scroll through all the documents in the workbook.

▶ Workbooks are saved with an xlw extension.

▶ You create a workbook with the File ⇨ New command (select the Workbook option). You can then add documents to the workbook. You can add or remove documents at any time and change their status from bound to unbound (or vice versa).

▶ You can create linking formulas that work with or without a workbook. Do this by preceding the cell or range reference with a file reference.

▶ Excel provides three ways to consolidate data across multiple worksheets: with link formulas, with the Edit ⇨ Paste Special command, and with the Data ⇨ Consolidate command.

▶ The Data ⇨ Consolidate command provides the most flexibility and can even set up an outline of the consolidated data.

▶ Group Edit mode lets you work with a group of worksheets at once. It can give you many of the advantages of a 3-D worksheet.

Chapter 22
Array Formulas

In this chapter . . .

▶ What are array formulas, and why would you want to use them?

▶ Examples of useful (and undocumented) techniques that use arrays and array formulas.

▶ Some of the limitations and potential problems involved in using array formulas.

This chapter covers arrays and array formulas. Once you understand how Excel works with arrays, you'll discover a whole new world of analytical capability. Working with arrays, rather than individual cells, requires a different type of mind set. Some people can never quite get the hang of arrays, while others take to this concept quickly. If you fall into the former group, don't despair. Using arrays can be considered an "optional" skill.

Using Arrays — A Unique Concept

Excel is the only spreadsheet product available that uses arrays. An array is simply a collection of cells or values that is operated on as a group. You can write an array formula by entering a single formula that performs an operation on multiple inputs and produces multiple results — with each result displayed in a separate cell. Here's a working definition of what we mean by an *array formula*.

Array formula   Any formula that uses one or more arrays either as operands or as arguments for a function. An array formula can occupy one or more cells. You enter an array formula in Excel by holding down the Ctrl and Shift keys while you press Enter.

Here's an example. If you multiply a 1×5 array by another 1×5 array, the result will be a 1×5 array consisting of each element in the first array multiplied by each corresponding element in the second array. Because Excel can only fit one value in a cell, the results of an operation such as this will occupy five cells — and the same array formula will be in each of the five cells.

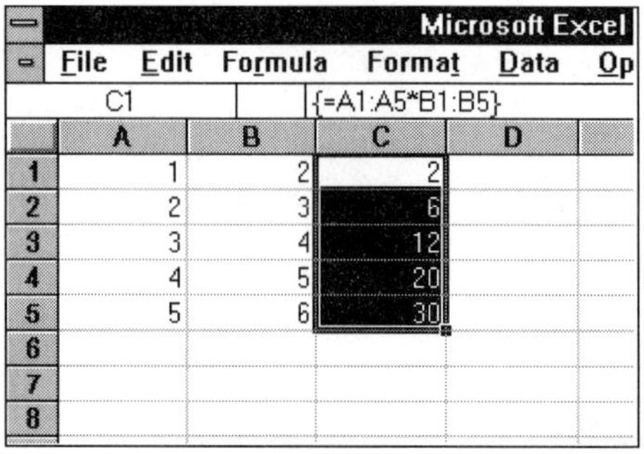

Figure 22-1:
A simple
example of
an array
formula that
produces
results in
five cells.

This is illustrated in the worksheet in Figure 22-1. Each cell in the range C1:C5 holds the same formula: {=A1:A5*B1:B5}. The result occupies five cells and contains each element of the first array multiplied by each corresponding element in the second array. The brackets around the formula designate it as an array formula.

As we'll see, arrays have their pros and cons. At the very least, this feature provides an alternative way of doing some operations — and is the only way to perform some others.

Advantages

Some of the advantages of using array formulas (as opposed to single-cell formulas) are:

- They use less memory.
- They can be much more efficient to work with.
- They can eliminate the need for intermediary formulas.
- They can let you do things that would be difficult or impossible otherwise.

Disadvantages

A few disadvantages of using array formulas are:

- Some large arrays can slow your spreadsheet recalculation time to a crawl.
- They can make your worksheet more difficult for others to understand.
- You must remember to enter an array formula with a special key sequence (Ctrl+Shift+Enter). Otherwise, the result will not be what you expect.

Some of Excel's functions require array constants or references to cell ranges as arguments and return array constants. We'll discuss these later in the chapter.

Understanding Arrays

This section introduces arrays by presenting several examples. As always, you'll get more out of this chapter if you follow along on your own computer.

Operating on one array

Let's jump right into this with an example. Figure 22-2 shows two worksheets: the top one uses normal single-result formulas, and the lower sheet uses a single-array formula to produce the same result. Both examples use the SQRT function to calculate the square roots of the values in column A. In the first example, we entered =SQRT(A3) into cell B3 and copied it down to the three cells below. This example uses four different formulas to calculate the results in column B.

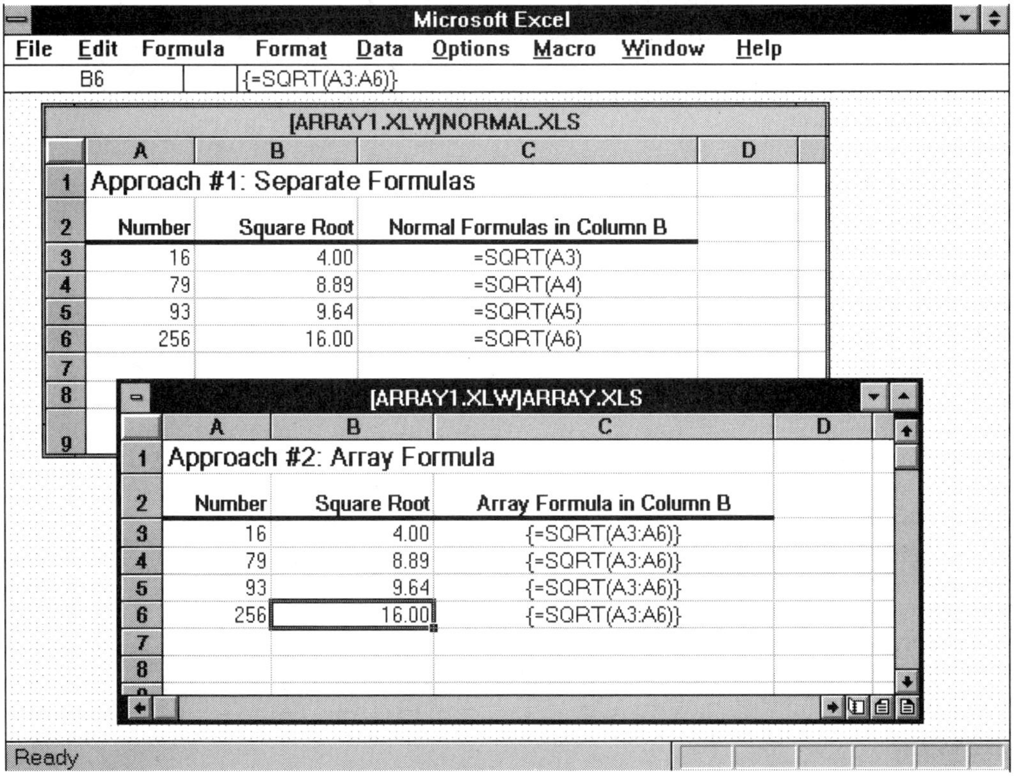

	Microsoft Excel						
File	Edit	Formula	Format	Data	Options	Macro	Window	Help

B6   {=SQRT(A3:A6)}

[ARRAY1.XLW]NORMAL.XLS

	A	B	C	D
1	Approach #1: Separate Formulas			
2	Number	Square Root	Normal Formulas in Column B	
3	16	4.00	=SQRT(A3)	
4	79	8.89	=SQRT(A4)	
5	93	9.64	=SQRT(A5)	
6	256	16.00	=SQRT(A6)	
7				
8				

[ARRAY1.XLW]ARRAY.XLS

	A	B	C	D
1	Approach #2: Array Formula			
2	Number	Square Root	Array Formula in Column B	
3	16	4.00	{=SQRT(A3:A6)}	
4	79	8.89	{=SQRT(A3:A6)}	
5	93	9.64	{=SQRT(A3:A6)}	
6	256	16.00	{=SQRT(A3:A6)}	
7				
8				

Ready

Figure 22-2: Producing the same result with normal formulas (top worksheet) and an array formula.

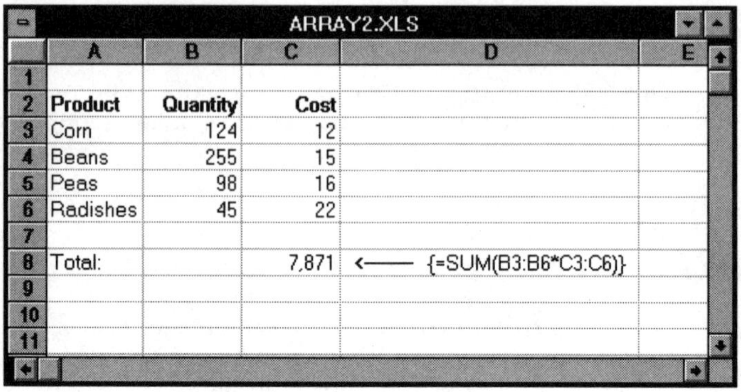

	A	B	C	D	E
				ARRAY2.XLS	
1					
2	Product	Quantity	Cost		
3	Corn	124	12		
4	Beans	255	15		
5	Peas	98	16		
6	Radishes	45	22		
7					
8	Total:		7,871	←——— {=SUM(B3:B6*C3:C6)}	
9					
10					
11					

Figure 22-3: An array formula that operates on two arrays and produces one result.

The lower example uses one array formula to produce the same result. Note that only one formula is used, and it is inserted into all four cells. We entered the formula by first selecting the range B3:B6, entering SQRT(A3:A6) into the edit line, and ending with Ctrl+Shift+Enter to designate it as an array formula. Excel provided the brackets around the formula to indicate that it's an array formula. We emphasize again that this second example uses only one formula, but the results appear in four different cells because it's operating on a four-cell array.

Operating on two arrays

Figure 22-3 shows another example of an array formula. This one, however, resides in only one cell because the result is a single value. The formula in cell C8 is:

```
{=SUM(B3:B6*C3:C6)}
```

This array formula operates on two arrays. It multiplies each corresponding element of the two arrays together and then adds them up with the SUM function. Since the SUM function returns only a single value, the result of this formula occupies a single cell. Normally, one would approach this problem by creating intermediary formulas that multiply the cells together and then use the SUM function to add the intermediary results together. Using an array formula eliminates the need to create the intermediary formulas.

You can, by the way, use the SUMPRODUCT function to accomplish this same result, instead of using an array formula.

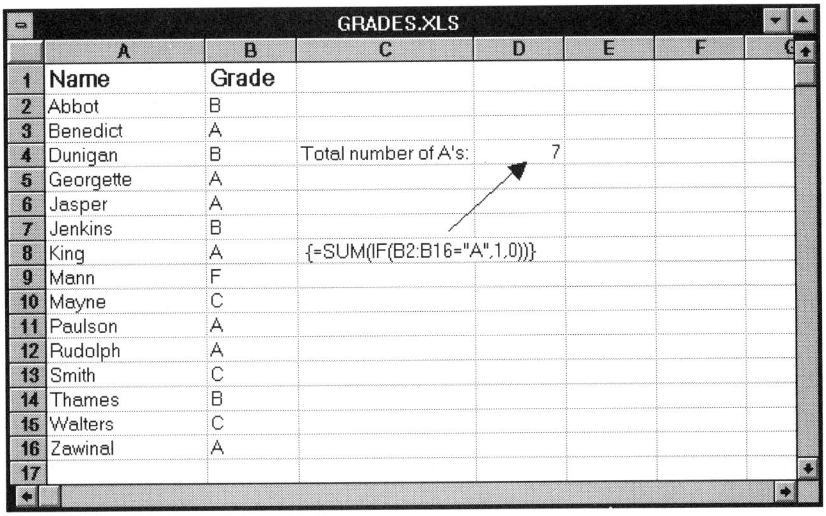

Figure 22-4:
Counting
the number
of occur-
rences of a
specific
item with an
array
formula.

"Looping" with arrays

Excel's array concept lets you perform individual operations on each cell in a range — in much the same way as a program language's looping feature allows you work with elements of an array.

For example, an instructor's spreadsheet might contain a range of data consisting of names and test grades. How can you get a count of the number of students earning each letter grade? You *could* perform some database operations — or you could use array formulas. In the latter case, an array formula would provide you with the power to count the number of A's, for example, using a single formula. Better yet, the formula is *dynamic,* which means that if your input data changes, the formula recalculates automatically. If you use database commands to accomplish this, you have to reissue the commands if you change any of the data. This is illustrated in the example in Figure 22-4. Letter grades for each student are entered in B2:B16. The formula in cell D4 is:

```
{=SUM(IF(B2:B16="A",1,0))}
```

The IF function in this formula checks each element in the input range to see if it's equal to "A." If so, the IF function returns a value of 1, otherwise it returns 0. At the same time, the SUM function is adding together the results of this IF function as it evaluates each element in the range B2:B16. The array formula returns 7, which is the number of A grades in the range.

We'll cover more useful examples using arrays later in this chapter. First, it's time to provide some rules on how to work with arrays and array formulas.

Working with Arrays

This section deals with the mechanics of entering, editing, and selecting arrays. As you'll see, these procedures are a bit different from working with ordinary cells and ranges.

Entering an array formula into a cell

When you enter an array formula into an Excel worksheet, you must follow a special procedure so Excel knows you want an array formula. You enter a normal formula into a cell by pressing Enter. You enter an array formula into one or more cells by pressing Ctrl+Shift+Enter.

You can identify array formulas because they are enclosed in brackets in the edit line. For example, {=SQRT(A1:A12)} is an array formula. Do not enter the brackets when you create an array formula. Excel inserts them for you.

Entering an array formula into a range

If the result of an array formula consists of more than one value, you must enter the array formula into all of the cells at once. If you fail to do this, only the first result will show. The following describes how to enter a formula into multiple cells.

Steps: Entering a formula into multiple cells

Step 1. Select the range (the selection should have the same dimensions as the resulting array).

Step 2. Enter the formula using normal methods (that is, you can point to ranges, insert functions, and so on).

Step 3. When the formula is correct, enter it into the selected cells by pressing Ctrl+Shift+Enter.

Editing an array formula

If an array formula occupies multiple cells, you must edit the entire range as if it were a single cell. The key thing to remember here is that you can't change just one element of an array formula. In fact, the following are some rules regarding multicell array formulas. If you try to do any of these things, Excel lets you know about it.

Rules: Multicell array formulas

Rule 1. You cannot change the contents of any cell that makes up an array formula.

Rule 2. You cannot move cells that make up part of an array formula. You can, however, move an entire array formula.

Rule 3. You cannot delete cells that form part of an array formula. But you can delete an entire array.

Rule 4. You cannot insert new cells into an array range; this includes inserting rows or columns that would add new cells to an array range.

To edit an array formula, select any cell in the array range and activate the Formula bar as usual (click on it or press F2). You'll notice that Excel removes the brackets from the formula while you're editing it. Edit the formula and then use Ctrl+Shift+Enter to enter the changes. You'll notice that all of the cells in the array now reflect the editing changes you made.

Formatting arrays

Although you can't change any part of an array formula without changing them all, you are free to apply formatting to the entire array, or just parts of it, as you like. This includes numeric formatting as well as stylistic formatting.

Selecting an array range

You can select an array range manually using the normal selection procedures or by using one of the following shortcuts:

■ Move to any cell in the array range and press Ctrl+/ to select the range.

■ Move to any cell in the array range. Issue the Formula ⇨ Select Special command and then select the Current Array option. Choose OK to close the dialog box.

Using Array Constants

So far, this discussion has used cell ranges for arrays. You can also use constant values as an array. These can be used in array formulas in place of a reference to a range of cells. To use an array constant in an array formula, type the set of values directly into the formula and enclose them in braces ({ }).

Specifiying array dimensions

Array constants can be either one-dimensional or two-dimensional. One-dimensional arrays can be either vertical or horizontal. The elements in a one-dimensional horizontal array are separated by commas. The following is an example of how we represent some one-dimensional horizontal arrays. The first example is a 1×4 array, and the second example is a 1×7 array:

```
{1,2,3,4,5}

{"Sun","Mon","Tue","Wed","Thu","Fri","Sat"}
```

The elements in a one-dimensional vertical array are separated by semicolons. Following are some examples. The first example is a 6×1 array, and the second is a 4×1 array.

```
{10;20;30;40;50;60}

{"1st-Q";"2nd-Q";"3rd-Q";"4th-Q"}
```

Two-dimensional arrays also separate the elements in a single row with commas and separate the rows with semicolons. The next example is a 3×4 array (three rows, each of which occupies four columns):

```
{1,2,3,4;5,6,7,8;9,10,11,12}
```

 You cannot list cell references, names, or formulas in an array formula as you would list constants. For example, {2*3,3*3,4*3} is not valid because it lists formulas. Also, {A1,B1,C1} is not valid because it lists cell references. Rather, you should use a range reference such as {A1:C1}.

It's important that you keep an array's dimensions in mind when you're performing operations on it. Consider the following array formula:

```
={2,3,4}*{10,11}
```

This formula is multiplying a 1×3 array by a 1×2 array. Excel returns an array with three values: 20, 33, and #N/A. Because the second array wasn't large enough, Excel generated #N/A as the third element of the result.

Using Arrays — Some Real-Life Examples ____

Perhaps the best way to learn about array formulas is by following some examples and adapting them to your own needs. It just so happens that we've pulled together some examples that should give you a good idea of how you can use this feature; we also provide some useful techniques.

Calculating data distributions

It's often desirable to summarize the number of occurrences of particular values in a range. Consider the range of data shown in the worksheet in Figure 22-5. How many 4's are there in this range? Excel's array formula makes this an easy task. For simplicity, we've named the data range Data. To determine the number of 4's in the range, enter this formula in any cell:

```
{=SUM(IF(Data=4,1))}
```

To indicate that this is an array formula, hold down the Ctrl and Shift keys when you press Enter. Excel places brackets around the formula to remind you that it's an array formula. The formula will return the value of 21, indicating that there are 21 occurrences of the value 4 in the Data range.

Now let's make this more general. Enter the numbers 1 through 6 in cells K3:K8. In cell L3, enter the following array formula (remember to hold down the Ctrl and Shift keys when you press Enter):

```
{=SUM(IF(Data=K3,1))}
```

	A	B	C	D	E	F	G	H	I	J	K
1											
2		1	3	4	4	5	4	2	2		
3		2	3	1	6	3	2	6	5		
4		3	5	6	6	5	4	6	2		
5		5	4	2	2	2	5	4	5		
6		3	2	6	5	5	6	3	2		
7		5	4	6	2	2	6	6	4		
8		2	5	4	5	6	6	5	4		
9		5	6	3	2	4	5	6	6		
10		4	3	5	6	4	2	2	2		
11		2	4	1	3	3	4	4	5		
12		1	5	2	2	2	6	6	4		
13		3	6	4	1	4	2	1	5		
14		4	3	4	2	1	5	2	2		
15											

Figure 22-5: An array formula can quickly count the number of occurrences of any value in this range.

	A	B	C	D	E	F	G	H	I	J	K	L	
								DIST.XLS					
1													
2		1	3	4	4	5	4	2	2		Value	Count	
3		2	3	1	6	3	2	6	5		1	7	
4		3	5	6	6	5	4	6	2		2	25	
5		5	4	2	2	2	5	4	5		3	12	
6		3	2	6	5	5	6	3	2		4	21	
7		5	4	6	2	2	6	6	4		5	20	
8		2	5	4	5	6	6	5	4		6	19	
9		5	6	3	2	4	5	6	6				
10		4	3	5	6	4	2	2	2				
11		2	4	1	3	3	4	4	5				
12		1	5	2	2	2	6	6	4				
13		3	6	4	1	4	2	1	5				
14		4	3	4	2	1	5	2	2				
15													

Figure 22-6: Using array formulas to calculate a dynamic data distribution.

Next, copy this formula down to the five cells below. Your spreadsheet should look like Figure 22-6. Change some of the numbers in the Data range and watch the frequencies change.

So what's going on here? Each of the array formulas is essentially going through a loop for each of the 104 elements in the Data range according to the following "pseudocode":

```
Sum=0
For i = 1 to 104 do
   if Data[i] = Cell_to_the_left, then Sum = Sum + 1
Next i
Display Sum
```

Note that the SUM function adds a 1 each time the element in Data is equal to the value being tested. The value being tested is in the cell directly to the left of the array formula.

It's important to understand that this example uses six different array formulas — not one array formula that occupies six different cells.

But what if your data range consisted of nonintegers, as in Figure 22-7? The previous formula would not work, since it tests for exact values. The solution is to modify the basic formula we used before as follows:

```
{=SUM(IF(Data>=K3,1))-SUM(IF(Data>=K4,1))}
```

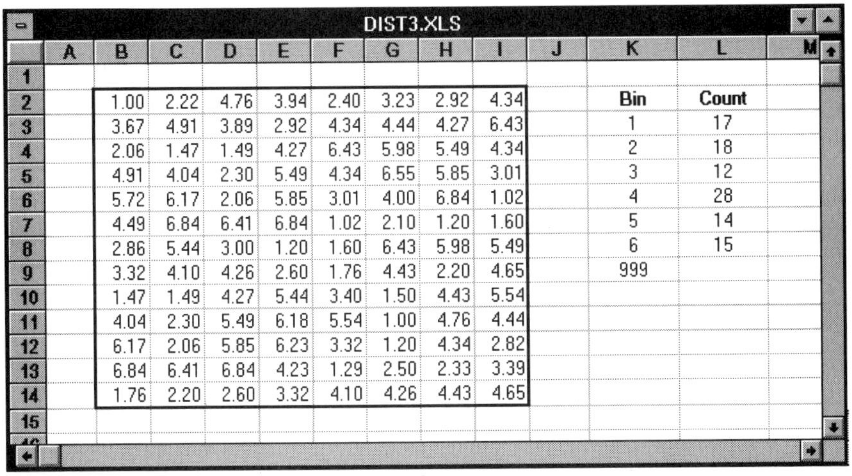

	A	B	C	D	E	F	G	H	I	J	K	L	M
1													
2		1.00	2.22	4.76	3.94	2.40	3.23	2.92	4.34		Bin	Count	
3		3.67	4.91	3.89	2.92	4.34	4.44	4.27	6.43		1	17	
4		2.06	1.47	1.49	4.27	6.43	5.98	5.49	4.34		2	18	
5		4.91	4.04	2.30	5.49	4.34	6.55	5.85	3.01		3	12	
6		5.72	6.17	2.06	5.85	3.01	4.00	6.84	1.02		4	28	
7		4.49	6.84	6.41	6.84	1.02	2.10	1.20	1.60		5	14	
8		2.86	5.44	3.00	1.20	1.60	6.43	5.98	5.49		6	15	
9		3.32	4.10	4.26	2.60	1.76	4.43	2.20	4.65		999		
10		1.47	1.49	4.27	5.44	3.40	1.50	4.43	5.54				
11		4.04	2.30	5.49	6.18	5.54	1.00	4.76	4.44				
12		6.17	2.06	5.85	6.23	3.32	1.20	4.34	2.82				
13		6.84	6.41	6.84	4.23	1.29	2.50	2.33	3.39				
14		1.76	2.20	2.60	3.32	4.10	4.26	4.43	4.65				
15													

DIST3.XLS

Figure 22-7:
Extending the
data distribution
array formula to
work with
nonintegers.

This formula was entered into cell L3 as an array formula and copied down. This modification counts the number of values in data that are greater than or equal to the value in the cell to the left and then subtracts the number that are greater than or equal to next highest number (the cell directly below). You need to make sure you add an additional value in column K so the last array formula won't refer to an empty cell (we added a value of 999). It should be clear that you can set up the "bins" any way you like — as long as they are in increasing order.

 You can also use the Analysis ToolPak to compute distributions. An advantage of this technique is that it's dynamic and displays the correct values even if you change the input data.

Crosstabulating data

Now we're ready to tackle a slightly more sophisticated version of this formula that lets you create dynamic crosstabulation tables. Take a look at the sample spreadsheet in Figure 22-8. This shows a simple expense account listing. Each item consists of the date, the expense category, and the amount spent. Each column of data is a named range, indicated in the first row.

Excel's array formulas can be used to summarize this information into a handy table that shows the total expenses, by category, for each day. The summary

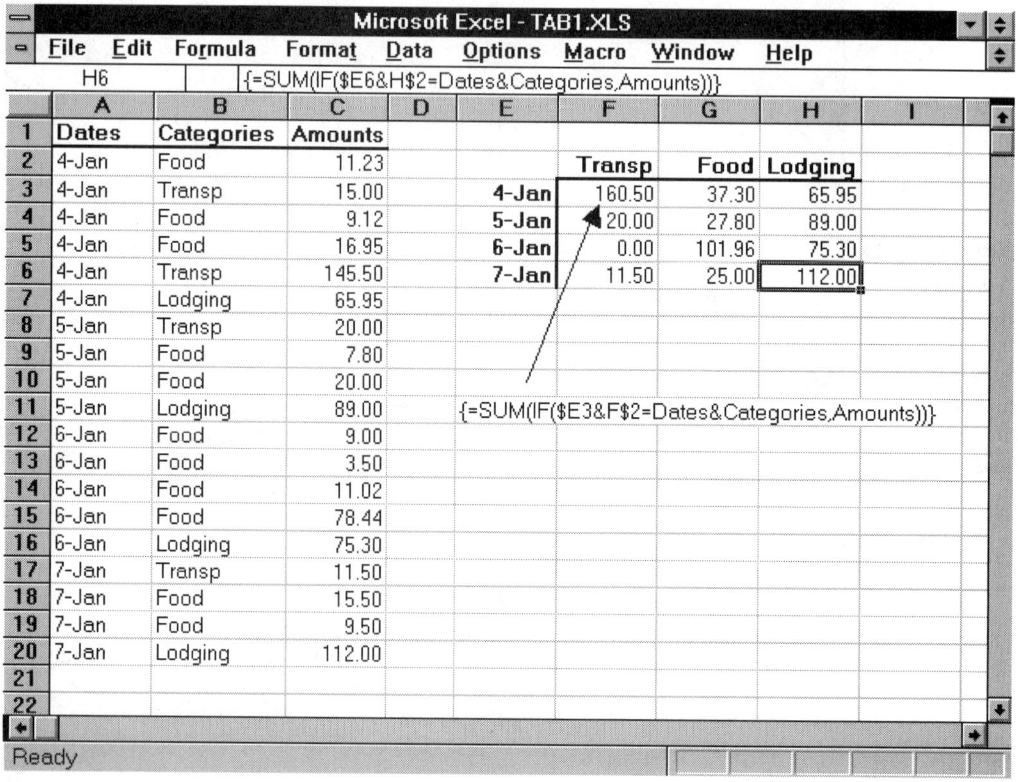

	A	B	C	D	E	F	G	H
1	Dates	Categories	Amounts					
2	4-Jan	Food	11.23			Transp	Food	Lodging
3	4-Jan	Transp	15.00		4-Jan	160.50	37.30	65.95
4	4-Jan	Food	9.12		5-Jan	20.00	27.80	89.00
5	4-Jan	Food	16.95		6-Jan	0.00	101.96	75.30
6	4-Jan	Transp	145.50		7-Jan	11.50	25.00	112.00
7	4-Jan	Lodging	65.95					
8	5-Jan	Transp	20.00					
9	5-Jan	Food	7.80					
10	5-Jan	Food	20.00					
11	5-Jan	Lodging	89.00					
12	6-Jan	Food	9.00					
13	6-Jan	Food	3.50					
14	6-Jan	Food	11.02					
15	6-Jan	Food	78.44					
16	6-Jan	Lodging	75.30					
17	7-Jan	Transp	11.50					
18	7-Jan	Food	15.50					
19	7-Jan	Food	9.50					
20	7-Jan	Lodging	112.00					
21								
22								

Figure 22-8: You can use array formulas to summarize data like this in a dynamic crosstab table.

table occupies the range E2:H6. Enter the category names in the first row (cells F2:H2) and the dates in the first column of the table (cells E3:E6). Next, enter the following array formula in cell F3 (remember to hold down Ctrl and Shift while you type Enter):

```
{=SUM(IF($E3&F$2=Dates&Categories,Amounts))}
```

Copy this formula to the remaining 11 cells of the table, and you'll see the totals for each day, by category. Again, note that there are 12 different array formulas at work here, not one formula in 12 cells.

This formula operates similarly to the more simple formula developed previously, but with a few new twists. Rather than counting the number of entries, the formula adds the appropriate value in the `Amounts` range. But it does this only if the row and column names in the summary table matche the corresponding entries in the `Dates` and `Categories` ranges. It does the comparison by concatenating (using the & operator) the row and column names and

	A	B	C	D	
				RANKS.XLS	
1	Salesperson	Sales	Rank	Formula in Col C	
2	Adams	123,844	8	{=SUM(IF(B2<=Sales,1))}	
3	Bigelow	143,578	7	{=SUM(IF(B3<=Sales,1))}	
4	Fredericks	98,723	11	{=SUM(IF(B4<=Sales,1))}	
5	Georgio	231,233	3	{=SUM(IF(B5<=Sales,1))}	
6	Jensen	224,090	4	{=SUM(IF(B6<=Sales,1))}	
7	Juarez	101,840	9	{=SUM(IF(B7<=Sales,1))}	
8	Klein	324,576	1	{=SUM(IF(B8<=Sales,1))}	
9	Lynch	145,898	6	{=SUM(IF(B9<=Sales,1))}	
10	Mayne	96,722	12	{=SUM(IF(B10<=Sales,1))}	
11	Roberton	100,000	10	{=SUM(IF(B11<=Sales,1))}	
12	Slokum	275,000	2	{=SUM(IF(B12<=Sales,1))}	
13	Wu	150,020	5	{=SUM(IF(B13<=Sales,1))}	
14					

Figure 22-9: You can use array formulas to compute dynamic rankings of a range of values.

comparing this to the concatenation of the corresponding Dates and Categories values. If the two match exactly, the =SUM function kicks in and adds the corresponding value in the Amounts range. Rather clever, eh?

This technique, of course, can be customized to hold any number of different categories and any number of dates. In fact, you can eliminate the dates and substitute people's names, departments, regions, and so forth.

You can also crosstabulate data using the Crosstab Wizard. The advantage of the technique just described is that it's dynamic; if you change any of the numbers, the table is updated automatically. The Crosstab Wizard, on the other hand, is much more flexible and easier to use.

Ranking data

It's often desirable to compute rank orders for a range of data. For example, if you have a worksheet with the annual sales figures for 20 salespeople, you might want to know how each person ranks from highest to lowest.

One way to do this is to sort the data, use the Data ⇨ Series command to insert ranks based on the sorted data, and then re-sort back to the original order. A better alternative is to use array formulas to compute dynamic ranks. The worksheet in Figure 22-9 shows an example of this. The array formula in cell C2 is:

```
{=SUM(IF(B2<=Sales,1))}
```

This formula was entered as an array formula (that is, it was entered with Ctrl+Shift+Enter) and then copied to the 11 cells below it. The formula essentially counts the number of elements in the Sales range (B2:B13) that are less than or equal to the number being ranked. The highest ranked value is less than or equal to only one value (itself). The second ranked value is less than or equal to two values (itself and the first ranked value), and so on.

Note that if you change any of the sales figures, the ranks recalculate — something that wouldn't happen if you used the sorting method described earlier to insert ranks.

A problem is that this simple formula doesn't handle ties properly (the tied values are all given the highest rank). Normally, if two or more values are tied, they would all be assigned a middle rank. For example, if four numbers are tied for third, each should receive a rank of 4.5 — the midpoint of 3, 4, 5, and 6. The formula as written returns a rank of 6 for each of these.

The following formula correctly handles tied ranks, but is too complex to explain adequately here.

```
{=IF(((SUM(IF(Sales=B2,1)))=1,(SUM(IF(Sales>=B2,1,0)))),
    (SUM(IF(Sales>=B2,1)))-((SUM(IF(Sales=B2,1)))-1)*0.5)}
```

 You can also use the RANK function to determine dynamic ranks. On the other hand, the preceding formula is preferable since it handles ties better. Also, if you'll be sharing your worksheet with someone who uses a prior version of Excel, you can't use the RANK function since it's new to version 4.

Determining if a range contains a specific value

Array formulas are also useful for determining if a range contains a specific value or label. Examine the worksheet in Figure 22-10. This worksheet contains a list of names in a range named Names (A4:C13). You can use the logical OR function to compare each element of the range with a test value. In this case, the formula in cell E4 is:

```
{=OR(B1=Names)}
```

The formula returns the logical value true if the label entered in cell B1 is found in the range named Names, otherwise it returns False. Note that if you don't enter the formula as an array, Excel checks only the first element in Names.

	A	B	C	D	E	F
1	Test value:	Jack				
2						
3		Names				
4	John	David	Bud		TRUE	
5	Bill	Carl	Jeremy			
6	Frank	Herman	Annette			
7	Louis	Jack	Warren			
8	Lori	Homer	Phil			
9	Jill	Bart	Toby		{=OR(B1=names)}	
10	Joice	Marge	Shirley			
11	Ken	Gail	Anthony			
12	Jeff	Sally	Tanya			
13	Stephanie	Al	Gomer			
14						

NAMES.XLS

Figure 22-10: An array formula can quickly tell you if a specific value or label is in a range of cells.

Calculating a dynamic correlation matrix

Excel 4 includes a new function called CORREL, which calculates the correlation coefficient for two ranges of data. If you'll be creating worksheets for use by people with previous versions of Excel, you can't use this function. But we've developed a complex formula that uses arrays to compute a correlation matrix for any number of ranges.

Figure 22-11 shows some sample data for correlation, nine variables for each of 13 people. We assigned range names to each column of data, and the names appear in row 1 (this is an important step).

CORMATRX.XLS

	A	B	C	D	E	F	G	H	I	J
1	NAME	HEIGHT	WEIGHT	SEX	IQ	TEST1	TEST2	TEST3	TEST4	TEST5
2	Bill	74.2	176	1	110	90	86	134	65	9
3	Mike	68.5	132	1	123	90	87	122	31	67
4	Carol	65.0	157	0	95	82	75	145	2	6
5	Scott	73.2	199	1	120	90	79	109	7	92
6	Jill	65.8	154	0	131	100	92	132	79	73
7	Francis	52.4	101	0	100	78	89	176	18	50
8	Helen	69.2	157	0	143	90	84	103	64	87
9	Marci	69.0	148	0	94	65	54	123	100	32
10	Benedict	77.0	225	1	145	92	85	132	74	22
11	Hank	71.0	179	1	85	70	60	144	36	78
12	John	73.5	190	1	86	69	58	156	12	1
13	Susan	66.9	155	0	111	80	86	157	68	22
14	Gloria	67.1	190	0	113	89	77	98	23	25
15										

Figure 22-11: You can use a complex array formula to compute a dynamic correlation matrix of these variables.

	A	B	C	D	E	F	G	H	I	J
				CORMATRX.XLS						
15										
16										
17		HEIGHT	WEIGHT	SEX	IQ	TEST1	TEST2	TEST3	TEST4	TEST5
18	HEIGHT	—	0.84	0.67	0.22	0.10	-0.28	-0.44	0.23	-0.10
19	WEIGHT	0.84	—	0.52	0.21	0.16	-0.22	-0.38	0.00	-0.18
20	SEX	0.67	0.52	—	-0.02	0.00	-0.15	-0.01	-0.21	0.05
21	IQ	0.22	0.21	-0.02	—	0.83	0.70	-0.52	0.37	0.37
22	TEST1	0.10	0.16	0.00	0.83	—	0.84	-0.45	0.08	0.29
23	TEST2	-0.28	-0.22	-0.15	0.70	0.84	—	-0.02	0.07	0.21
24	TEST3	-0.44	-0.38	-0.01	-0.52	-0.45	-0.02	—	-0.15	-0.37
25	TEST4	0.23	0.00	-0.21	0.37	0.08	0.07	-0.15	—	0.01
26	TEST5	-0.10	-0.18	0.05	0.37	0.29	0.21	-0.37	0.01	—
27										

Figure 22-12: This correlation matrix was generated with array formulas (and could be done much simpler using the CORREL function).

We want to create a matrix that shows the correlation coefficient for each variable vs. every other variable (a 13×13 matrix of correlation coefficients) — without using the CORREL function.

The actual formula we developed is too complex to explain here. It uses indirect referencing based on the range names. The results are shown in Figure 22-12. The huge formula below was entered into cell B18 as an array formula (using Ctrl+Shift+Enter) and then copied to the range B18:J26.

```
{=IF(INDIRECT(B$17)<>INDIRECT($A18),((COUNT(INDIRECT(B$17))*SUM(INDIRECT(B$17)*INDIRECT($A18)))-
(SUM(INDIRECT(B$17))*SUM(INDIRECT($A18))))/
(SQRT((COUNT(INDIRECT(B$17))*SUM(INDIRECT(B$17)*INDIRECT(B$17)))-
SUM(INDIRECT(B$17))^2)*SQRT((COUNT(INDIRECT(B$17))*SUM(INDIRECT($A18)*INDIRECT($A18)))-
(SUM(INDIRECT($A18))^2))),"—   ")}
```

The net result is a dynamic correlation matrix. To speed things up, you could erase the formulas in one of the diagonals of the matrix (since one is a mirror image of the other). This technique is provided to demonstrate just how complex formulas can get.

Examining Functions that Use Arrays _____

Several of Excel's worksheet functions require the use of arrays for arguments — and others can use either arrays or ranges. A list of these functions follows. If you are interested in using arrays with functions, we urge you to check out the complete coverage of these in Excel's on-line help.

COLUMN	MDETERM
COLUMNS	MINVERSE
GROWTH	MMULT
HLOOKUP	ROW
INDEX (ARRAY FORM)	ROWS
LINEST	SUMPRODUCT
LOGEST	TRANSPOSE
LOOKUP (ARRAY FORM)	TREND
MATCH	VLOOKUP

Avoiding Potential Limitations and Pitfalls _____

If you've followed along in this chapter, you probably understand the advantages of using array formulas. As you gain more experience with arrays, you'll undoubtedly discover some disadvantages.

The primary problem with array formulas is that they slow down your worksheet's recalculations, especially if you use large arrays. If speed is of the essence, you'll probably want to avoid using large arrays. But on the other hand, if you're flirting with out-of-memory errors, you might find that converting copied formulas to array formulas provides some additional memory.

Array formulas are probably one of the least understood features of Excel. Consequently, if you plan to share a worksheet with someone else who may need to make modifications, you should probably avoid using array formulas.

You may discover that it's easy to forget to enter an array formula with Ctrl+Shift+Enter. If you edit an existing array, you still must use these keys. Except for logical errors, this is probably the most common problem users have with array formulas.

There is a limit on the number of elements in an array — about 6,500 elements. There shouldn't be too many occasions where you need arrays of this size. If so, you can break the array into smaller divisions and use separate array formulas.

Summary

▶ Array formulas are considered one of the advanced features in Excel — and Excel is the only spreadsheet that offers this feature.

▶ An array is a collection of cells or values that is operated on as a group.

▶ You can write an array formula by entering a single formula that performs an operation on multiple inputs and produces multiple results — with each result displayed in a separate cell.

▶ This chapter provided several useful techniques involving array formulas. Some of the techniques can be performed in other ways, but some require array formulas to do their thing.

Chapter 23
Working with Outlines

In this chapter . . .

▶ An overview of Excel's outlining feature, and when you would use it.

▶ How to create an outline from scratch.

▶ How to convert existing data into an outline.

Remember how some of your elementary school teachers stressed the importance of creating an outline before you wrote a report? And if you followed through, how much easier your writing would be?

Many of today's software companies also realize the importance of outlining. Most word processing programs now have an outlining feature that helps you write by revealing your organization in a compact form. This capability makes creating a document easier, since you can zero in and concentrate on what's important at the moment — and easily reorganize a document by moving complete outline sections around.

Now you can do the same thing with Excel. While not a required function of spreadsheeting, outlining a spreadsheet can make you more productive and is a good spreadsheet habit to get into. This chapter is for Excel users who want to get the most from their software investment (not to mention Excel sessions).

Understanding the Concept of Spreedsheet Outlining

Spreadsheet outlining for the PC is another unique, but powerful, feature of Excel. Well, sort of unique — there's an outlining add-in available for Release 2 of 1-2-3, but it's not nearly as rich in features.

Before you get too far into this, it's important to understand that not all worksheets are candidates for outlining. Outlining is appropriate for applications that have multiple "levels" of information. A classic example is a budget that could be collapsed across categories, departments, time units, and so on.

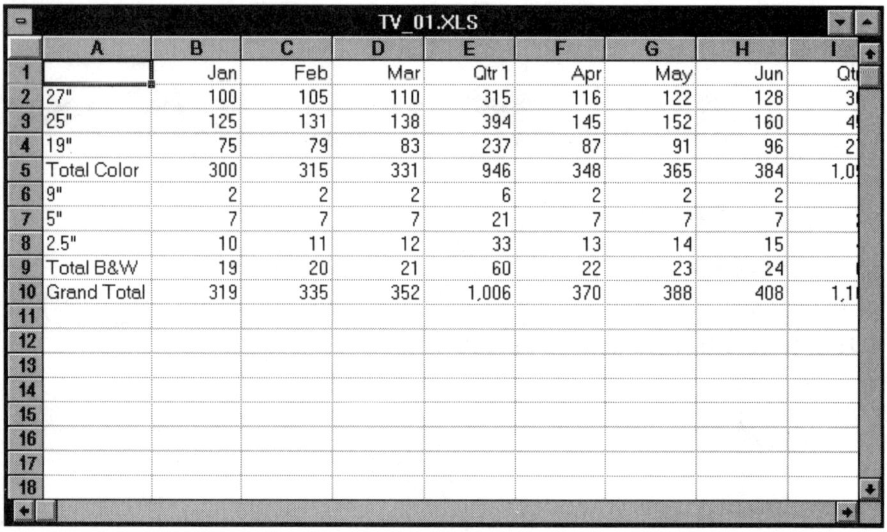

	A	B	C	D	E	F	G	H	I
		Jan	Feb	Mar	Qtr 1	Apr	May	Jun	Qt
2	27"	100	105	110	315	116	122	128	3
3	25"	125	131	138	394	145	152	160	4
4	19"	75	79	83	237	87	91	96	2
5	Total Color	300	315	331	946	348	365	384	1,0
6	9"	2	2	2	6	2	2	2	
7	5"	7	7	7	21	7	7	7	
8	2.5"	10	11	12	33	13	14	15	
9	Total B&W	19	20	21	60	22	23	24	
10	Grand Total	319	335	352	1,006	370	388	408	1,1

Figure 23-1: A monthly unit sales plan spreadsheet before outlining.

Outlining enables you to view either summary levels (such as subtotals and grand totals) or both detail and summary levels. This information can be arranged vertically, horizontally, or in both directions. Some of the advantages of outlining follow:

- An outlined spreadsheet has better design and logic than a nonoutlined version and is therefore easier to maintain and enhance.

- Detail and subordinate summary levels can be hidden to protect confidential data or to allow you to simply look at the "big picture."

- You can quickly display or print only necessary information, such as summary levels.

- You can quickly create charts from worksheet ranges that normally would be noncontiguous.

Outlining is particularly advantageous for planning and budgeting, especially if you deal with hundreds of line items that have subgroupings. When you need to see all the details, you can display an entire spreadsheet, as in Figure 23-1; when all you need is a bottom-line summary or only subtotals and a grand total, you can use the outlining feature, as illustrated in Figure 23-2. The outline elements displayed in Figure 23-2 are as follows:

- **Collapse symbol:** Indicates that a row or column has visible detail subordinate summary levels which can be collapsed. Click to hide the corresponding rows or columns that fall under the row or column level bar connected to the collapse symbol.

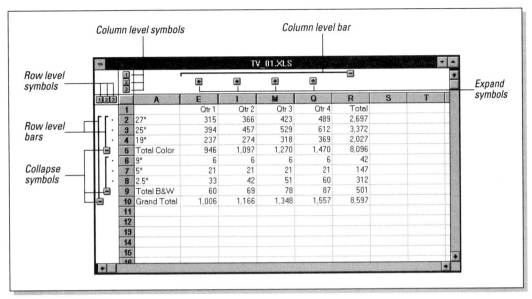

Figure 23-2: An outline of Figure 23-1.

■ **Expand symbol:** Indicates that a row or column has invisible detail subordinate summary levels, which can be expanded by clicking the expand
symbol.

■ **Row and column level bars:** Indicates what rows or columns are included
in a specified level. Click to collapse detail or subordinate rows or columns.

■ **Row and column level symbols:** Indicates levels of the outline. Click to
display or hide rows or columns of the corresponding level for the entire
outline.

The next section will help you quickly get up and running with outlining in
Excel.

Examining Outline Basics

Creating an outline from spreadsheet data may be foreign to you, especially if
you're new to Excel. But relax — this section explains what you need to know
and do to make outlining part of your spreadsheet regimen.

You cannot "hurt" an existing spreadsheet by adding an outline to it. No data, function, or formulas are overwritten by outlining. You can always remove the outline if you don't like its results or appearance.

The jargon

To use outlining effectively, you need to know the language of outlining. Spreadsheet outlining uses the following key terms:

Level

Level refers to the hierarchy of the data in your spreadsheet. You can have up to eight outline levels in each row or column of a spreadsheet. There are two types of levels: *summary* (highest) and *detail* (lowest). Summary levels are comprised of detail rows or columns or of lower summary levels, which are known as *subordinate summary levels*.

Summary

A *summary* level of information summarizes data, usually below (if it is in rows) or to the right (if it is in columns). A level is designated as a summary level by Excel if the row or column contains a total of the data in detail rows or columns. In Figure 23-2, rows 5 and 9 are summary levels, because they comprise rows 2–4 and 6–8, respectively.

Row 10 in Figure 23-2 is also a summary level, because it summarizes the summary rows 5 and 9. Rows 5 and 9 are subordinate summary levels to row 10, making row 10 the highest summary level.

Detail

Detail is the lowest point on the outlining hierarchy. Detail levels are typically rows or columns of data, such as rows 2–4 and 6–8 in Figure 23-2.

Collapse

When you *collapse* a level, you temporarily hide detail or subordinate summary levels. Note that rows or columns are not deleted from your spreadsheet, but are hidden, as when using the Hide option in the Format ➪ Column Width and Row Height commands. Rows or columns that are summary levels are identified by the collapse symbol (–), indicating there are detail or subordinate summary levels that can be displayed. You can also tell if an outline is collapsed by looking at the row and column borders. If the row numbers or column letters are not contiguous, it means that data is collapsed.

Expand

When you *expand* a level, you display formerly hidden detail levels or subordinate summary levels. This is similar to using the Unhide option in the Format ⇨ Column Width and Row Height commands. Rows or columns that are summary levels display the expand symbol (+), indicating the detail or subordinate summary levels.

Promote

When a level is *promoted*, it is assigned to a higher outline level. Higher levels usually denote a summary level. The highest level is 1. You promote a level with the Promote tool or by pressing Alt+Shift+left arrow.

Demote

When a level is *demoted*, it is assigned to a lower outline level. Lower levels are usually detail or subordinate summary levels. The lowest level is 8. You demote a level with the Demote tool or by pressing Alt+Shift+right arrow.

The display

When you create and use spreadsheet outlining, Excel automatically displays some symbols unique to outlining that you might not have encountered before, as illustrated in Figure 23-2. The symbols appear to the left of the row numbers and/or above the column letters of your spreadsheet. These symbols enable you to expand or collapse detail or subordinate summary levels (the plus and minus signs), display or hide entire levels of data (the number buttons), and hide detail or subordinate rows or columns (level bars):

Tool	Purpose
+ (Expand symbol)	Displays collapsed detail or subordinate levels for a summary row or column.
− (Collapse symbol)	Collapses and hides detail or subordinate levels of rows or columns.
Number symbols	Displays or hides a specified level of data throughout your outline.
Level bars	Indicates the detail or subordinate rows or columns of a level; can hide the detail range.

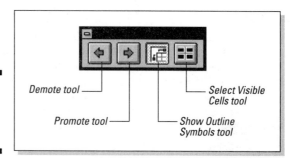

Figure 23-3: A custom Outline toolbar with the Promote, Demote, Show Outline Symbols, and Select Visible Cells tools.

Demote tool

Promote tool

Select Visible Cells tool

Show Outline Symbols tool

The toolbar

Four toolbar tools can make your outlining sessions more productive. If you're moving from Excel 3, note that these tools have moved from the Standard toolbar to the Utility toolbar. You can display the Utility toolbar for outlining, or you can create a custom Outline toolbar with the four outline tools (see Chapter 19 for more information about tools and creating toolbars). The tools on the Utility toolbar, shown in Figure 23-3, are as follows:

Tool	Purpose
Promote	Assigns selected rows or columns to a higher level.
Demote	Assigns selected rows or columns to a lower level.
Show Outline Symbols	Toggles between displaying or hiding outline symbols.
Select Visible Cells	Selects visible cells only.

The keys

Excel has a few shortcut keys for outlining. If you're a keyboard user, you'll want to know about these outlining shortcuts:

Key combination	Result
Alt+Shift+left arrow	Promotes a row or column.
Alt+Shift+right arrow	Demotes a row or column.
Ctrl+8	Toggles between displaying and hiding outline symbols.

Make sure your cell pointer is in the correct row or column before using the first or second key combination.

Now that you have some outlining background under your belt, you're ready to get down to outline business.

Creating an Outline

You have two methods to choose from to add outlining to your spreadsheet:

- **Automatic:** Excel creates the outline for you.
- **Manual:** You do the outlining yourself.

Regardless of the method you choose, you can have only one outline per worksheet. You can, however, open new worksheets, copy your data from the original to the new spreadsheets, and create a different outline on each document.

Letting Excel have a go at it

If your spreadsheet is straightforward and you've invested some forethought in it by creating an appropriate structure, it's usually faster to let Excel set up the outline for you. But before you push the On button, remember these two key points:

- Excel scans your spreadsheet for formulas to determine detail and summary levels.
- Formula references must always occur in the same direction. Usually this means summary rows refer *up* to detail rows and summary columns refer *left* to detail columns.

Having said all that, make the worksheet you want to outline the active document. Next, select the range that you want to add an outline to (that is, if you don't want to outline your entire spreadsheet, which is the default). Then you need to decide if you want to use menu commands or the outlining tools to create your outline. The next two sections can help you tip the scales one way or the other.

 If you want some control over how Excel creates your outline, use menu commands. If you have a spreadsheet that lends itself well to outlining, you may save some time by using the outline tools.

Using commands

To add an outline using menu commands, choose Formula ➪ Outline. When the dialog box shown in Figure 23-4 appears, make the following selections that are appropriate for your spreadsheet:

Automatic Styles   Check this box if you want Excel to apply predefined format styles to your various outline levels. The default is *no*. If you don't check this box, you can apply styles later by choosing Formula ➪ Outline again and choosing Apply Styles.

Summary rows below detail   Keep this Direction box checked if your summary rows (the rows that contain functions or formulas) are *below* your detail (data) rows. Figure 23-2 has Summary rows below detail, because the SUM function, in row 5, for example, is located *below* rows of data (2, 3, and 4).

Summary columns to right of detail   Keep this Direction box checked if your summary columns (the columns that contain functions or formulas) are to the *right* of your detail (data) columns. Figure 23-2 has Summary columns to the right of detail, because the SUM function, in column E for example, is located to the right of columns that contain data (B, C, and D).

If you have a spreadsheet similar to Figure 23-2 (containing row and column totals), be sure to select both Direction boxes, as shown in Figure 23-4. After you make your selections and choose Create, Excel builds an outline from your data and displays the outline symbols.

Using tools

Whether you're using the Utility toolbar or a custom outline toolbar, you can add an outline to your spreadsheet in rapid-fire fashion. This method works only if your spreadsheet does not already have an outline. Note also that your

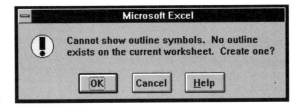

Figure 23-5: This dialog box appears after you click the Show Outline Symbols tool (if your spreadsheet is not yet outlined).

spreadsheet should have the same structure as the defaults in the Outline dialog box: Summary rows below detail and Summary columns to right of detail, as this is what Excel assumes as it outlines.

To outline using toolbar tools, remember that you need to select a range if you don't want to outline the entire worksheet. Then select the Show Outline Symbols tool. If your spreadsheet doesn't contain an outline, Excel displays the message box in Figure 23-5 and asks if you want an outline. If you select OK, Excel creates an outline and displays the outline symbols.

Do-it-yourself outlining

You may have an existing worksheet that you want to add an outline to, but it doesn't always follow the rules for automated outlining. For example, you may have a row of totals that rely on data in one direction (down), and another row of totals that depend on data in another direction (up). In such a case, you'll need to create the outline manually. You can also make changes to an existing outline using the method explained in this section.

 If you're creating a new outline manually, and the structure of your spreadsheet does not adhere to these options, uncheck the Summary rows below detail and Summary columns to right of detail boxes in the Outline dialog box.

Manual outlining isn't difficult, but the rows and columns you assign (or reassign) as summary levels should make sense. That is, don't specify a range of data as either a subordinate summary level or the highest summary level (such as a grand total) that includes subordinate summary levels *and* detail levels.

To create an outline manually, then, or to make changes to an existing one, display the Utility toolbar (or a custom Outline toolbar, if you have one). Then select the rows or columns you want to assign a new level to. Select the Promote or Demote tools, or press Alt+Shift+left arrow and Alt+Shift+right arrow, respectively, to make the corresponding level assignment change. Do this for each set of rows or columns you want to change. Excel redisplays your worksheet data with the levels you specified and their associated outline symbols.

When creating an outline manually, Excel displays outline symbols that are appropriate for the rows or columns you've promoted or demoted. Remember, you can hide or display these symbols by selecting the Show Outline Symbols tool or by pressing Ctrl+8.

Modifying your outline

You may need to make a few changes in a spreadsheet to which you've added an outline. For example, you want to add 21-inch color televisions to the example in Figure 23-2 but don't want to disturb the structure of your outline.

Not to worry. You add or remove items just as you would if your spreadsheet wasn't outlined. To add 21-inch color televisions, use Edit ⇨ Insert (or select Insert from the shortcut menu), insert a new row below row 3, and enter the corresponding information. Excel takes care of all the outline work for you automatically by including the new row as a detail level in the outline. Edit ⇨ Insert Paste (available when you cut or copy something) can also be used to include new rows or columns.

The same goes for inserting columns and deleting rows and columns. Excel adjusts your outline accordingly based on the changes you make to your underlying spreadsheet. You may, however, want to choose the Entire Row and Entire Column options from the Insert and Delete dialog boxes to ensure your change affects the entire worksheet and outline. And displaying the level that contains the row or column is essential if you want to make accurate modifications.

Tapping the Power of Outlines

Now that you know how to add an outline to your worksheet, you can put your knowledge to work. The ability to collapse or expand levels creates another dimension of flexibility and ease of use in your worksheets. In outline mode, for example, you can quickly select a single print or chart range; this might ordinarily be a multistep process, depending on the size of the range. The following sections explain how you can use outlining to make your Excel sessions more efficient (and fun).

Viewing your outline

Before outlining capability, you may have needed to prepare two worksheets — a detailed sheet for your own use and a summary sheet for your manager. Outlining lets you create charts quickly, print only specified information (such as totals), hide sensitive information, and see the big picture without getting bogged down by details. Conversely, you can expand and display detail or summary rows or columns when you need to dig a little deeper and determine what your function and formula results are based on.

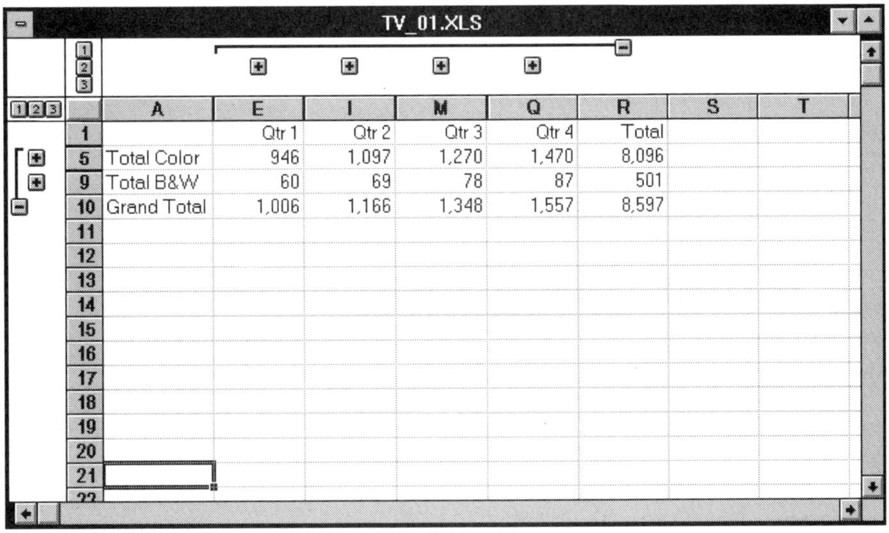

TV_01.XLS							
	A	E	I	M	Q	R	S	T
1		Qtr 1	Qtr 2	Qtr 3	Qtr 4	Total		
5	Total Color	946	1,097	1,270	1,470	8,096		
9	Total B&W	60	69	78	87	501		
10	Grand Total	1,006	1,166	1,348	1,557	8,597		

Figure 23-6: Figure 23-2's outline collapsed to level 2, displaying only summary information.

To work with your outline, make sure both the Utility toolbar (or your custom Outline toolbar) and the outline symbols are displayed. Then expand or contract rows, columns, or levels as follows:

Goal	Action
Expand a specified row or column	Select the expand (+) symbol
Expand a level	Select a level number button (1, 2, 3, and so on)
Collapse a specified row or column	Select the collapse (–) symbol
Collapse a level	Select a level number button (1, 2, 3, and so on) or bar

Figure 23-6 shows the rows and columns in Figure 23-2 collapsed to level 2.

To display all levels of your outline, select the highest level number. Conversely, to hide all levels of your outline, select the lowest level number. Choosing a level number displays or hides the detail for that level, plus any lower levels.

You can also expand and collapse selected rows and columns by choosing Format ➪ Row Height and Format ➪ Column Width, respectively, and then choosing Hide and Unhide.

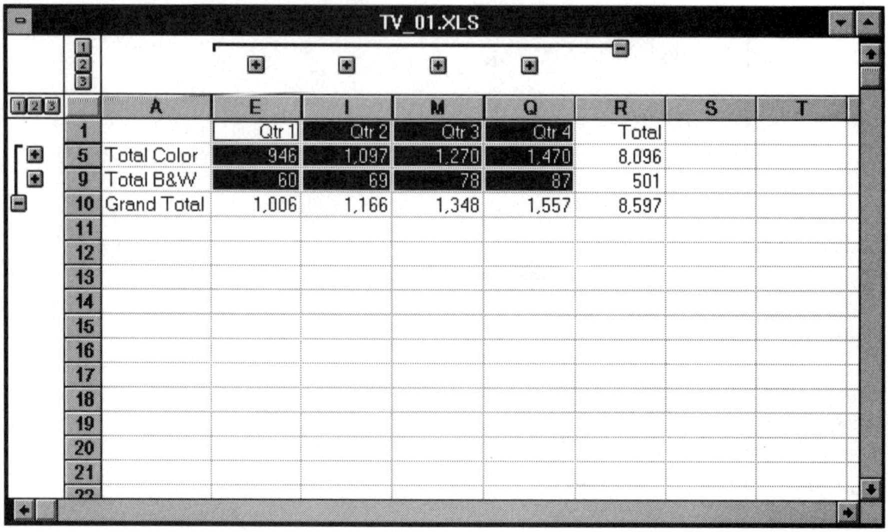

		A	E	I	M	Q	R	S	T
	1		Qtr 1	Qtr 2	Qtr 3	Qtr 4	Total		
	5	Total Color	946	1,097	1,270	1,470	8,096		
	9	Total B&W	60	69	78	87	501		
	10	Grand Total	1,006	1,166	1,348	1,557	8,597		
	11								
	12								
	13								
	14								
	15								
	16								
	17								
	18								
	19								
	20								
	21								
	22								

TV_01.XLS

Figure 23-7:
An outline range selected with Select Visible Cells, ready for charting, copying, printing, or what have you.

Selecting data

When all levels of your outlined spreadsheet are expanded, you select ranges as you normally would. If you've collapsed one or more levels, however, you should be aware of a few twists to cell selection that affect some worksheet operations.

First, if you want to select only summary level ranges for copying and charting and exclude collapsed (hidden) data, you need to use the visible cells option. If you don't, hidden data will also be selected, even though it's not displayed.

The visible cells option is an important concept. Be sure you understand it, or you won't get the results you expect.

To select only displayed ranges, select the range as usual. Then click the Select Visible Cells tool or choose Formula ⇨ Select Special and specify the Visible Cells Only option. When you do, Excel highlights the range of cells you selected, as shown in Figure 23-7. You can now copy or print the cells or create a chart. Excel ignores all data that is not displayed. Figure 23-8 shows a chart created from the selected data in Figure 23-7.

Second, if you want to copy or move rows or columns in an outline, you can quickly select the row or column and all its subordinate rows or columns. Hold down the Shift key, then choose the collapse (–), expand (+), or level bar to select the data.

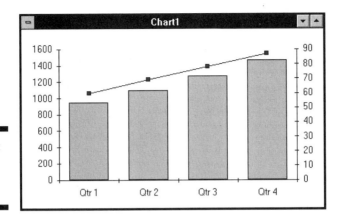

Figure 23-8: A chart created from the selected range in Figure 23-7.

Formatting an outline

When you create an outline with the Formula ▷ Outline command, you can select the Automatic Styles option from the Outline dialog box and Excel formats the outline for you. Or you can format it later by selecting the range of data that is outlined and then choosing the Apply Styles option from the Outline dialog box. You can format an outline with named styles, attributes you choose from the Format menu (Font, Border, Pattern), or Format ▷ AutoFormat.

Figure 23-9 shows the worksheet from Figure 23-2 formatted using Apply Styles, while Figure 23-10 shows the same information formatted with Format ▷ AutoFormat (using the Classic 1 format, with Width/Height unselected and

What is an automatic outline style?

The Formula ▷ Outline command brings up the Outline dialog box, from which you can choose either the Automatic Styles or Apply Styles options. Excel formats your outline just enough to show you the differences in summary levels. While there isn't a defined style exclusively for outlines, Excel uses individual styles for summary levels. For example, in Figure 23-9, row and column level 1 is Helvetica 10-point bold, while row and column level 2 is Helvetica 10-point italic.

You can determine the name of the style by placing your cell pointer on any cell in the row or column that is a summary level, and the name of the level will appear in the Style box. For example, row 10 has the style name RowLevel.1. Choose Format ▷ Style, and the Description box displays the attributes assigned to that level, which you can modify by choosing Define. When you choose OK, Excel applies the modified style to all cells in the level.

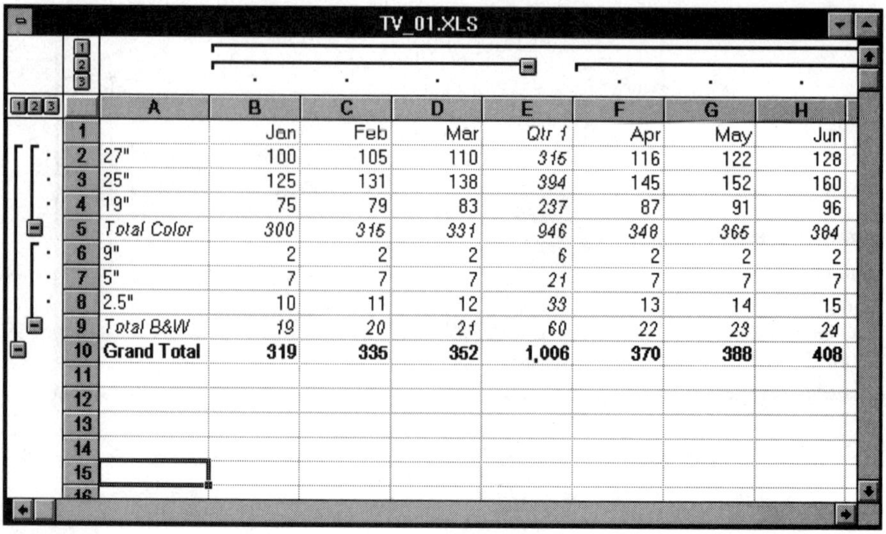

TV_01.XLS

	A	B	C	D	E	F	G	H
1		Jan	Feb	Mar	*Qtr 1*	Apr	May	Jun
2	27"	100	105	110	*315*	116	122	128
3	25"	125	131	138	*394*	145	152	160
4	19"	75	79	83	*237*	87	91	96
5	*Total Color*	*300*	*315*	*331*	*946*	*348*	*365*	*384*
6	9"	2	2	2	*6*	2	2	2
7	5"	7	7	7	*21*	7	7	7
8	2.5"	10	11	12	*33*	13	14	15
9	*Total B&W*	*19*	*20*	*21*	*60*	*22*	*23*	*24*
10	**Grand Total**	**319**	**335**	**352**	**1,006**	**370**	**388**	**408**

Figure 23-9: Figure 23-2's new and improved appearance using the Apply Styles option from the Outline dialog box.

guidelines hidden). Notice that when you choose Apply Styles, the formatting that results is fairly basic; the italic attribute has been applied to the subordinate summary levels, and boldfacing has been applied to the highest summary level (row 10).

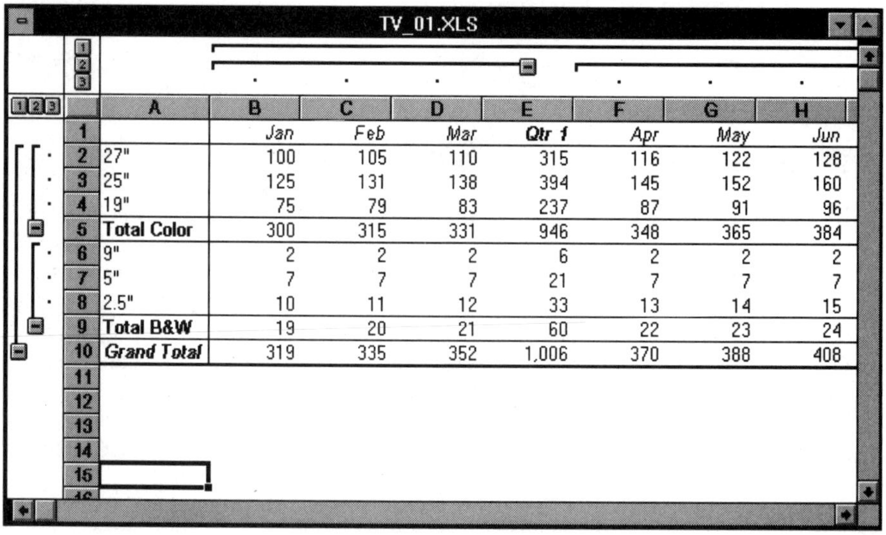

TV_01.XLS

	A	B	C	D	E	F	G	H
1		*Jan*	*Feb*	*Mar*	***Qtr 1***	*Apr*	*May*	*Jun*
2	27"	100	105	110	315	116	122	128
3	25"	125	131	138	394	145	152	160
4	19"	75	79	83	237	87	91	96
5	**Total Color**	300	315	331	946	348	365	384
6	9"	2	2	2	6	2	2	2
7	5"	7	7	7	21	7	7	7
8	2.5"	10	11	12	33	13	14	15
9	**Total B&W**	19	20	21	60	22	23	24
10	***Grand Total***	319	335	352	1,006	370	388	408

Figure 23-10: The Classic 1 look: Figure 23-2 formatted with Format ⇨ AutoFormat (without gridlines).

Removing Outlines

If you have a change of heart and prefer a nonoutlined spreadsheet, you can remove all or part of the outline. You do this by repeatedly promoting rows or columns (in effect, by displaying hidden rows and columns). If you remove an outline, you delete the outline only, and the cell contents remain intact. If you plan on using the Promote tool, the outline symbols must be displayed, either by selecting the Show Outline Symbols tool or by pressing Ctrl+8.

You may not want to completely abandon an outline. Use File ⇨ New and copy your spreadsheet to another file, then remove the outline from one of your spreadsheets. In this manner, you'll have both outlined and nonoutlined versions of your work.

Removing an entire outline

Begin by selecting the entire spreadsheet, either by clicking on the box at the intersection of the worksheet window's row and column headings, or by pressing Shift+Ctrl+spacebar. Then select the Promote tool or press Alt+Shift+left arrow. When you do, a dialog box appears, as shown in Figure 23-11. Choose Rows or Columns and then choose OK or press Enter. Excel displays the rows or columns of the level you selected. Continue this process until all rows and columns are displayed.

Removing part of an outline

Removing sections of an outline is similar to removing an outline entirely. In this case, select the row or column you no longer want outlined by clicking on the row's number or the column's letter. (You can select an entire row or column with your keyboard by pressing Shift+spacebar and Ctrl+spacebar, respectively.) Then select the Promote tool or press Alt+Shift+left arrow. Repeat this process for other rows or columns you don't want outlined.

Figure 23-11: Here's your opportunity to remove outlining if you've selected an entire spreadsheet for outlining demolition. Keep promoting all rows and columns until they're all back up to the highest level.

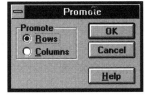

Summary

▶ Outlining, a feature that originated in word processing programs, is now available in Excel.

▶ Outlining lets you choose the ranges you want to display on-screen, and thus makes it easier for you to view important calculations, select ranges for printing and charting, and hide sensitive data.

▶ A detail level contains data, while a summary level contains calculations based on detail levels or other subordinate summary levels.

▶ Expanding and collapsing levels displays and hides them, respectively. You do this by clicking on the expand (+) and collapse (–) symbols, or by using the Format ➪ Column Width and Row Height Hide and Unhide options.

▶ Promoting and demoting increases and decreases a row or column's level, respectively. You do this with the Promote and Demote toolbar tools, or by pressing Alt+Shift+left arrow and Alt+Shift+right arrow.

▶ You can have Excel create an outline for you by choosing Format ➪ Outline or by selecting the Show Outline Symbols tool (if your spreadsheet isn't already outlined).

▶ You can add an outline to an existing spreadsheet or make outline changes by promoting or demoting selected rows or columns.

▶ Outlines can be formatted as you create them by choosing Format ➪ Outline and then Automatic Styles, or later by choosing Format ➪ Outline and then Apply Styles. You can also use other cell formats you prefer.

▶ Remove all or part of an outline from your spreadsheet by selecting a range or the entire spreadsheet and promoting rows or columns in succession.

Chapter 24
Working with Databases

In this chapter . . .

▶ What is a database, and what does it have to do with Excel?

▶ How to set up a database within a worksheet and modify it as needed.

▶ What you can do with a database.

▶ An introduction to the Q+E external database program.

Excel, of course, is known primarily for its spreadsheet and graphing powers. But it's also a pretty decent database manager. It certainly doesn't have all the bells and whistles of products such as Paradox or dBASE, but many people find that Excel's database capability is all they ever need. If you find yourself using Excel for things like mailing lists, inventory, price lists, and other structured data, this chapter can make you more efficient.

What Is a Database?

A database is a collection of similar data stored in a structured manner, as shown in Figure 24-1. Some databases you're already familiar with — including a telephone book, a Rolodex, and your checkbook. Database data is organized so that you can easily perform analyses with it, such as listing, sorting, and searching its contents for entries that meet certain criteria.

In a database, information is stored as records. Each record contains separate items of information, or *fields*. In a telephone book, for example, each entry is a record, consisting of fields with similar information for every record (name, street address, and telephone number). There are plenty of uses for databases in your day-to-day work. For example, you can:

- Calculate sales statistics.

- Analyze stock market trends.

- Maintain a name, address, and phone book.

- Monitor accounts receivable.

- Target direct mail promotions.

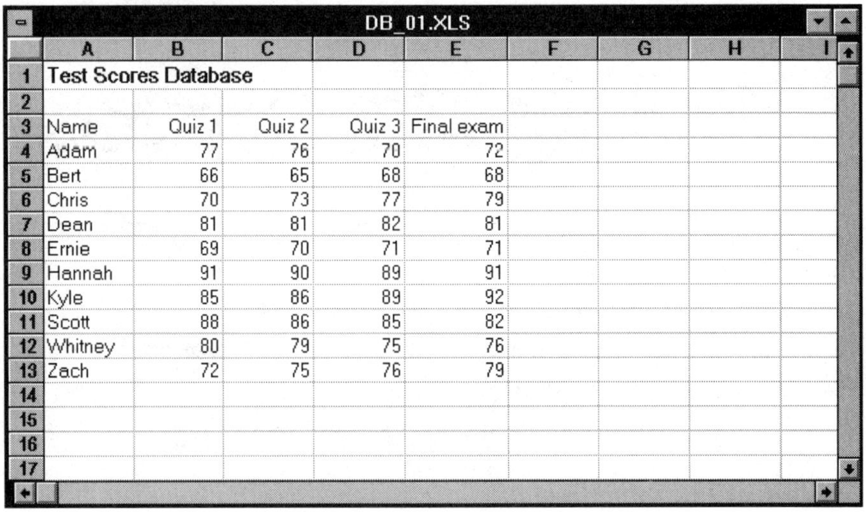

	A	B	C	D	E	F	G	H	I
1	Test Scores Database								
2									
3	Name	Quiz 1	Quiz 2	Quiz 3	Final exam				
4	Adam	77	76	70	72				
5	Bert	66	65	68	68				
6	Chris	70	73	77	79				
7	Dean	81	81	82	81				
8	Ernie	69	70	71	71				
9	Hannah	91	90	89	91				
10	Kyle	85	86	89	92				
11	Scott	88	86	85	82				
12	Whitney	80	79	75	76				
13	Zach	72	75	76	79				
14									
15									
16									
17									

Figure 24-1: The labels we'll use for our example database's field names.

A variety of computer programs perform database operations. Some run on humongous mainframe computers that keep customers' bank accounts, keep track of phone bills, and manage health insurance claims. Others are personal computer programs dedicated to database management; you may have heard of dBASE, Paradox, and Q&A, to name a few. Finally, there's your spreadsheet program. Excel as a database manager? You bet.

Using a Worksheet for a Database

You *can* use Excel for database management operations, and what it does, it does well. But like anything else, you'll discover pros and cons to doing so.

The good news

You already have Excel and so don't need to spend the time or money researching, comparing, shopping, and buying another computer program (though magazines such as *PC World* and *InfoWorld* review such programs periodically) to find out if you like or need database capability. Try it out with Excel first before you go out and plunk down more money.

Excel's row and column spreadsheet structure makes it a perfect candidate for databasing, since each row in the database can represent a record of information, and each column in the record can be considered a field.

If you've gotten this far in the book, you probably have a fairly good comfort level with Excel and know how to take advantage of Excel features and put them to work with your database. Printing and charting are two good examples, not to mention the database worksheet functions and commands that are specific to using Excel as a database.

Finally, you probably haven't realized it, but it's likely you already use Excel as a database. To perform calculations, you've entered data into your spreadsheet, and some of that data is probably already in a structured arrangement in a range — a database.

The not-so-good news

As you know, Excel loads a copy of your spreadsheet from disk when you use the File ⇨ Open command. Since your entire spreadsheet is in memory, your computer's memory may limit the size of the database you can have (unless you're using Q+E, as we'll describe later). Most dedicated database management programs read and write records as needed to and from the hard disk and therefore don't face this limitation. But if your database needs are relatively simple, what you lose in capacity is more than made up in speed and flexibility. You don't have to wait around while your database is performing intensive disk operations. Because your entire database resides in the computer's memory, you'll enjoy fast calculation and short task-completion times.

Examining a Database Example

The best way to learn is by doing, and this section shows you how to design and create a database, how to enter, edit, and delete records, and how to query. We'll use a database application most accountants and small business owners will be familiar with: an accounts receivable database.

Designing the database

The first step in creating a database is to resist the urge to charge in and begin making entries in a blank Excel worksheet. Rather, like any other spreadsheet application, you should invest some time in thinking about what you want your database to do and the best way to accomplish it. Consider the type and quantity of data you're dealing with, what information you want to gather from your database, the ways you'll want to upgrade and enhance it, and so forth. You should concentrate on the database fields: their selection, placement, and names.

To get a head start on database fields, examine the data you'll be working with, if available. Select the fields that appear most often in your data; consider whether you need to separate these fields into smaller units and whether you need to add additional fields for calculations or other database operations.

Selecting fields

The fields you choose for your database are of paramount importance, as they determine the information in each database record, and ultimately, the effectiveness of the database itself. You should decide, for example, if an accounts receivable database at a minimum should include the company name, date of the invoice, amount, and date due.

We could, however, provide the database with more firepower by breaking the fields down into more detail. For example, we could change "amount" to "total" and have separate "amount" and "tax" fields. It all depends on what your current and future database uses are. In general, however, more fields mean greater flexibility. The tradeoff is added set-up time and, in some cases, a slight decrease in performance.

Placing fields

Field names comprise the top row of your database, so you need to place them across contiguous columns in a single row. It is best to place field names in a logical order, grouping similar information together. For instance, your database will be more understandable and useful if descriptive information such as invoice number, date, and company name are all adjacent to each other.

Designating key fields

Each record in your database should be unique. A record is unique if one or more fields contain exclusive information, such as a date or an amount. Such a field is called a *key* field, because the field identifies a unique feature by which the record can be accessed.

If you have records that aren't unique, you can include an extra field to make them so. This field would include a serial number, a record number, or another such entry. For example, if your employee database has to support two different employees with identical names, you can add a "tie-breaker" field — a number that is used in combination with the name field.

Naming fields

Field names are a critical component in databases. Excel does all its sort and search operations on field names, so you should choose these names carefully (although you can always change them). Similar to range names and filenames, database field names have their own set of rules.

Rules: Naming database fields

Rule 1. You can use text or text formulas, including those that look like numbers (for example, = "1992").

Rule 2. You cannot use numbers, formulas, logical values, error values, or blanks.

Rule 3. Field names can have from 1 to 255 characters per name.

Rule 4. Field names should be different from one another.

In general, shorter field names are easier to understand and permit you to display more fields on your screen at a time. You should also know Excel is interested only in the row of field names directly above your first database record. You can have two or more rows of names to help you understand a field, but it's the single row above your database records that counts with Excel.

 Steer clear of field names that resemble cell addresses, such as AB1, as Excel and your macros may become confused and calculate database results improperly.

Creating a Database

Once you have your database design firmly in hand, you can place it in a spreadsheet. You can use a new, empty spreadsheet or one that already contains data. Begin by choosing a blank area of a spreadsheet with plenty of empty rows for database records. You can now enter data and specify your database.

Entering database data

Place your field names across a row in your spreadsheet. Make sure they're in the same row in adjacent cells and follow the rules for names. Figure 24-1 shows the field names we've chosen for the example. Notice we've applied some formatting to the field names and the yet-to-be database records (row 1 is shaded and boldface, range A1:H9 has a border, and guidelines are turned off). Formatting makes it easier to understand the database and its contents and won't affect how Excel goes about its database business. There are several options for entering database records:

- Use the standard data entry method.

- Use a form.

- Use a macro-driven custom dialog box.

- Import data from another source.

- Copy the data from another worksheet.

For now, we'll stick with the familiar and go with the first option. Later in the chapter you'll learn how to create a fill-in-the-blanks form that you can use for data entry and other database tasks. And if you're so inclined, you can use the Dialog Editor and Excel's macro commands to create a custom dialog box for data entry that looks and operates like an Excel dialog box. Chapter 26 touches on this technique.

In any event, to enter your first database record, place your cell pointer in the row directly under your field names, in the cell that is the first field of the first record. Type data for the field and then press the right arrow key. If you don't have data for a cell, press the right arrow key to continue. Database data can be text, values, or formulas, as with any other worksheet cell entry.

Repeat this process for each field in the record. For the last field, press the down arrow key and then the left arrow key repeatedly (or use your mouse) to make the first field of the second record the active cell. Continue this process for each record you want in your database. If you prefer, you can enter the same field for each record first (entering data by column) rather than rows, but it's a little easier to lose your place if you're entering data from a piece of paper. Figure 24-2 shows some sample data in our database.

To facilitate data entry, select the entire database data area before starting to enter data. Make an entry and press Tab to move the cell pointer to the right. When you get to the end of the row, Excel moves the cell pointer down to the first column in the next row. To move the cell pointer by rows, press Enter instead of Tab.

Consider splitting your database into two horizontal panes and freezing the pane containing your database field names. That way, if you have many records to enter, you won't lose your place as you scroll your worksheet.

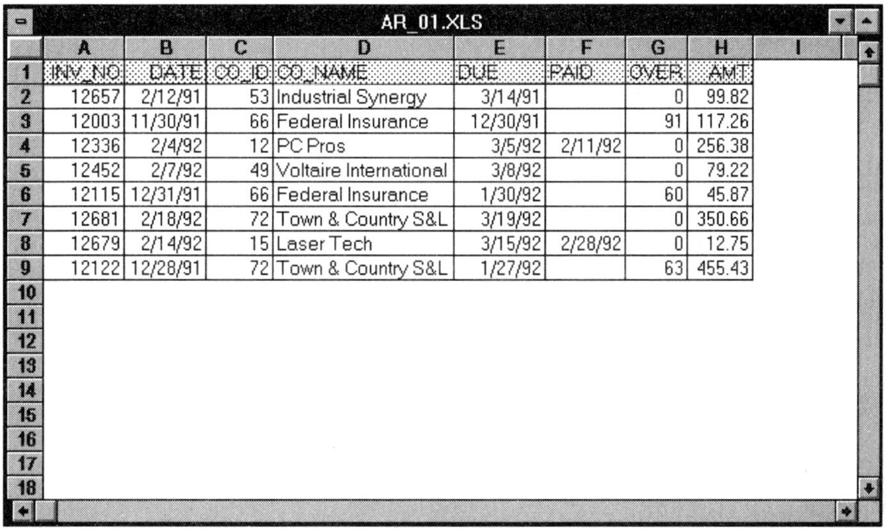

	A	B	C	D	E	F	G	H	I
1	INV_NO	DATE	CO_ID	CO_NAME	DUE	PAID	OVER	AMT	
2	12657	2/12/91	53	Industrial Synergy	3/14/91		0	99.82	
3	12003	11/30/91	66	Federal Insurance	12/30/91		91	117.26	
4	12336	2/4/92	12	PC Pros	3/5/92	2/11/92	0	256.38	
5	12452	2/7/92	49	Voltaire International	3/8/92		0	79.22	
6	12115	12/31/91	66	Federal Insurance	1/30/92		60	45.87	
7	12681	2/18/92	72	Town & Country S&L	3/19/92		0	350.66	
8	12679	2/14/92	15	Laser Tech	3/15/92	2/28/92	0	12.75	
9	12122	12/28/91	72	Town & Country S&L	1/27/92		63	455.43	

AR_01.XLS

Figure 24-2:
Our database, complete with field names and records.

Specifying a database

After you finish entering data, you can tell Excel that your spreadsheet contains a database. Select the database field names (exclude any cell entries above the field names) and all the records in the database. Then choose Data ➪ Set Database to define your database. When you do, Excel creates the range name Database and recognizes the range as such.

You can have more than one database on your spreadsheet at a time, but only one defined as a database. To specify another range as the database, select the range and choose the Data ➪ Set Database command. Excel now recognizes the new range as the database. You may, however, be better off placing multiple databases on separate worksheets and creating a workbook file of them.

Once you save your worksheet to disk, that's all there is to it. Before you put a database to work, however, you may want to modify it, which we cover next.

Modifying a Database

Most databases are constantly growing and changing. You add new records to the database or update the fields in certain records. You may even decide to add a new field to all of your records — such as an area code and telephone number on your direct mail database. Because a database is stored on a worksheet, modifications are made with familiar worksheet commands. Modifying your database isn't difficult, but you need to be careful what the left hand and the right hand consider as your new and improved database.

Changing fields

At some point, you may want to add a new field or eliminate a field whose data becomes extraneous. Changing database fields isn't a difficult process, though depending on the operation, it may change the database's fundamental structure.

If you want to change the name of a field, all you need to do is move the cell pointer to the cell containing the field name, click on the Formula bar or press F2, and edit the name (or create a new name). Then continue using your database as before.

Adding or deleting fields is a bit trickier, depending on the location of the field. Adding or deleting a field simply entails adding a new column or removing an existing column from your database. To do so, use the Edit ⇨ Insert and Edit ⇨ Delete commands, respectively. In both cases, use the Entire Column option to ensure the complete column (field) is inserted or deleted from your database.

Unless you have data immediately to the right of existing data, you don't need to "add" a field to your database as just described. You can enter the data of the new field directly into your spreadsheet.

If you use Edit ⇨ Insert or Edit ⇨ Delete with a Shift Cells option, and you haven't selected all the records in your database, adjacent fields in the database records will not align properly and so ruin the integrity of your data. If this happens, use the Edit ⇨ Undo command immediately to restore your database structure.

Now comes the tricky part. If you're adding a field or deleting a field, you're home free — Excel adjusts the range address of Database for you. But if you add a field adjacent to your database's extreme left or right columns, you'll need to select the entire range of the database and redefine it using the Data ⇨ Set Database command. If you don't, Excel won't realize you've enlarged your database, and you may be in for a surprise later.

Changing records

Making a change to your records is the converse of making a change to your fields. Changing records has its own set of avoidable pitfalls, however. As with changing the name of a field, you change a record by making the field in the record you want to change the active cell, pressing F2, and then editing the cell contents. You can also enter a completely different label, value, or formula. But remember, you're making a change to your data, so in any case make sure it's accurate.

To add or delete a record, use the Edit ➪ Insert and Edit ➪ Delete commands, respectively, with the Entire Row option. As with adding or deleting fields, you'll want to ensure you add or remove an entire row (record) from your database. You can also select records (make sure you select every field) and choose Edit ➪ Clear All to remove records.

Sound familiar? If you use Edit ➪ Insert or Edit ➪ Delete with a Shift Cells option and you haven't selected all the fields in your database, corresponding fields of your database records will not align properly, which, once again, leaves your data in ruins. Using the Edit ➪ Undo command immediately reverses such mishaps.

Now for the interesting part. If you add a row (record) between the field names and the last record or delete a record, Excel automatically makes the appropriate adjustment to the range name Database. If you add a record immediately following the last record at the bottom of the database, however, you won't need to insert a row to do so, but you'll need to remember to select the entire range of your expanded database and use the Data ➪ Set Database command.

An easier way to do this is to use the Formula ➪ Define Name command and simply edit the range specification for the Database range name. For example, if you add a row to the database that was originally defined as the range $A$1:$D$50, simply edit the range designation to be $A$1:$D$51. This method becomes especially appropriate as your databases get larger and larger.

You can avoid redefining your database every time you add a new record to the bottom of your database if you take the following steps.

Steps: Expanding range names automatically

Step 1. Define your database with an extra blank row at the bottom of the database.

Step 2. Insert a new row at the location of the blank row.

Step 3. Enter your new record where you've inserted the new row. Excel automatically expands the range name Database for you when you insert the new row.

So far, you've seen how to create and fine-tune a database. Now it's time to discover how the power of an Excel database can be put to good use.

Sorting a Database

If you've entered new records in the middle of your database, you've probably realized your records are out of order (assuming, of course, that the order is important). Or perhaps you'd like to perform an analysis of your accounts receivable database that shows largest to smallest amount owed, or longest to shortest in age.

Welcome to *sorting,* the first stop along the way to database productivity. Sorting a database rearranges the order of the records. You can sort by rows (the most common sort) or by columns (less frequently used, but still useful). The way a sort is performed is based on sort keys you specify. If you want to sort by rows, select a cell in a column to specify the column to sort on. If you want to sort the columns of your database, select a cell in a row to specify the row to sort on. You can specify up to three sort keys.

You don't have to define a database in order to use Excel's <u>D</u>ata ⇨ <u>S</u>ort command.

Many times you'll need more than one sort key to break "ties." A tie occurs when records with duplicate key fields remain unsorted. For example, suppose your wedding invitation list includes names, addresses, and telephone numbers, and you'd like to have it in alphabetical order for easy envelope addressing. But first you need to specify the last name as your first sort key and the first name as the second sort key, to sort your list in ascending order. That way, the Jones's (Indiana, John Paul, and Tom) will be alphabetized within the last name category. Excel sorts records based on the entries in key field(s) as follows:

Ascending order	Descending order
Numbers (. . . -1, 0, 1 . . .)	Error values
Text (a, b, c . . .)	Logical values
Logical values	Text (z, y, x . . .)
Error values	Numbers (. . . 1, 0, -1 . . .)
Blanks	Blanks

Excel always sorts blank rows or columns last, regardless of sort order (ascending or descending).

Sorting a database, like most operations in Excel, is easy once you know which button to push. Sorting is, however, an opportunity to make the greatest number of changes to the worksheet in one step, so be sure to save your spreadsheet to disk before beginning any sort operation, so you can revert to it later, if need be.

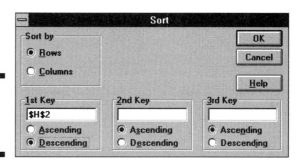

Figure 24-3: The Data Sort dialog box gives you all the options you need to rearrange database records in ascending or descending order.

Begin sorting by selecting the database records. Make sure you select every field of every record you want sorted. Next, choose Data ⇨ Sort, and when the Sort dialog box appears, as shown in Figure 24-3, choose Rows if you want to sort the order of your rows or Columns if you want to sort the order of your columns. Next, enter a cell reference in the 1st Key text box. You can enter the cell reference by selecting a cell or by typing its address. The cell reference can be any cell in the column or row to sort rows and columns, respectively. Now, choose Ascending or Descending depending on the direction of your sort. Repeat this process if you plan on using 2nd and 3rd sort keys (that is, if you have more ties to break). When you're finished specifying sort key information, choose OK and Excel sorts your records; our sample database is shown sorted in Figure 24-4.

When you select a range to sort, make sure you do *not* include the field names. If you do, this row may end up last instead of first.

Figure 24-4: Our database's records sorted from largest to smallest amount owed (descending order).

	A	B	C	D	E	F	G	H	I
1	INV_NO	DATE	CO_ID	CO_NAME	DUE	PAID	OVER	AMT	
2	12122	12/28/91	72	Town & Country S&L	1/27/92		63	455.43	
3	12681	2/18/92	72	Town & Country S&L	3/19/92		0	350.66	
4	12336	2/4/92	12	PC Pros	3/5/92	2/11/92	0	256.38	
5	12003	11/30/91	66	Federal Insurance	12/30/91		91	117.26	
6	12657	2/12/91	53	Industrial Synergy	3/14/91		0	99.82	
7	12452	2/7/92	49	Voltaire International	3/8/92		0	79.22	
8	12115	12/31/91	66	Federal Insurance	1/30/92		60	45.87	
9	12679	2/14/92	15	Laser Tech	3/15/92	2/28/92	0	12.75	

You can use range names in place of cell addresses in the key text boxes. In multicell ranges with names, Excel uses the cell in the upper-left corner as the key. Consequently, if you name a column or row, Excel uses the *top* and *left* cell in the range as the key when you sort rows and columns, respectively.

If you don't like the results of a sort operation or have inadvertently selected the database's field names with the range to be sorted, choose Edit ➪ Undo immediately after the sort.

Querying a Database

In addition to sorting the records of a database, you can ask a database questions about its records. This is known as *querying*. Our example database contains few records, but what if the database you use (or will use) contains several hundred rows of information? It'll probably be more difficult to find records to update (edit) or delete, or that match a certain set of conditions. Excel can do these things for you quickly and easily, but you'll need to give Excel a little head start first, in the form of a *criteria range*.

A criteria range contains conditions you specify that exist in some or all of the database records. You can place a criteria range on the same spreadsheet as the database or on another open spreadsheet. Specifically, a criteria range is a multirow range. The first row contains a copy of your database's field names, and one or more of the following rows contain criteria characters or formulas (explained later on). Figure 24-5 shows our example database with a criteria range (rows 11 and 12) ready to receive criteria.

What if three isn't enough?

What do you do if you need more than three keys for sorting operations? For example, recall your wedding invitation list. You have relatives, friends, and business associates that live in close proximity. You've sorted your list by last name, first name, and city, but it still wasn't enough to sort all your records in ascending order. Now what?

You can sort on more than three keys with Excel by performing multisort operations. To do this successfully, however, you start by sorting the *least* important key fields *first*, because your final sort takes precedence over all other sorts. In our example, then, you could choose to sort on telephone number as your first sort. In effect, this would be your "fourth key." Then do a second sort with 1st, 2nd, and 3rd sort keys, sorting as before. That should be enough so everyone in your close-knit group will be alphabetized and get their invitation on time.

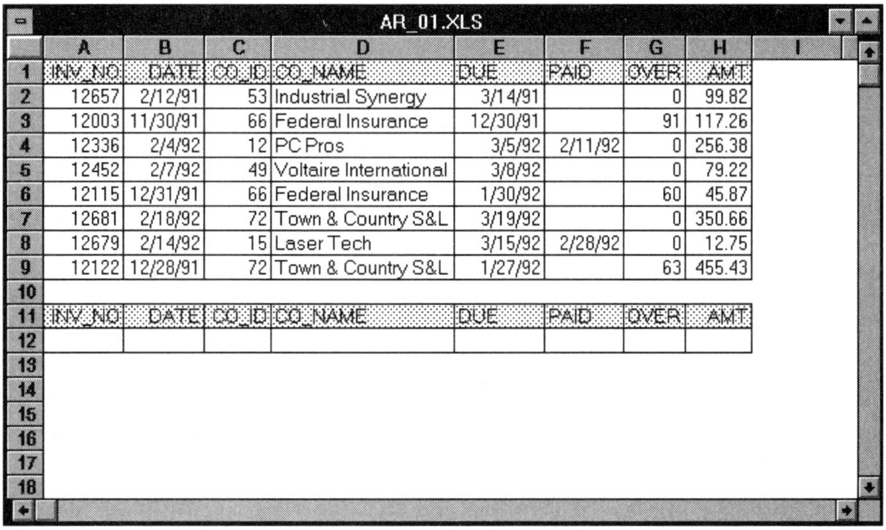

	A	B	C	D	E	F	G	H	I
1	INV_NO	DATE	CO_ID	CO_NAME	DUE	PAID	OVER	AMT	
2	12657	2/12/91	53	Industrial Synergy	3/14/91		0	99.82	
3	12003	11/30/91	66	Federal Insurance	12/30/91		91	117.26	
4	12336	2/4/92	12	PC Pros	3/5/92	2/11/92	0	256.38	
5	12452	2/7/92	49	Voltaire International	3/8/92		0	79.22	
6	12115	12/31/91	66	Federal Insurance	1/30/92		60	45.87	
7	12681	2/18/92	72	Town & Country S&L	3/19/92		0	350.66	
8	12679	2/14/92	15	Laser Tech	3/15/92	2/28/92	0	12.75	
9	12122	12/28/91	72	Town & Country S&L	1/27/92		63	455.43	
10									
11	INV_NO	DATE	CO_ID	CO_NAME	DUE	PAID	OVER	AMT	

AR_01.XLS

Figure 24-5:
Our database with a criteria range added.

Another way to restore order

All dedicated database programs number their records sequentially. You can do the same; the benefit is that if your operation doesn't go as planned, you can sort your records on the field that contains the numbers, in ascending order, and restore your database records to their original order.

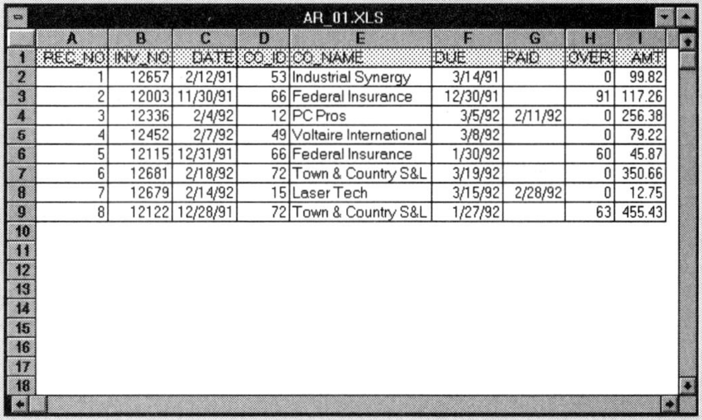

To number the records in the database as shown in the accompanying figure, insert a column in column A, then move your cell pointer to cell A2 and enter the number 1. Select the range A2:A9, choose Data ➪ Series, and then OK. Excel will enter the numbers 2 through 9. Remember to include this new column in the range name Database (use the Data ➪ Set Database command).

	A	B	C	D	E	F	G	H	I
1	REC_NO	INV_NO	DATE	CO_ID	CO_NAME	DUE	PAID	OVER	AMT
2	1	12657	2/12/91	53	Industrial Synergy	3/14/91		0	99.82
3	2	12003	11/30/91	66	Federal Insurance	12/30/91		91	117.26
4	3	12336	2/4/92	12	PC Pros	3/5/92	2/11/92	0	256.38
5	4	12452	2/7/92	49	Voltaire International	3/8/92		0	79.22
6	5	12115	12/31/91	66	Federal Insurance	1/30/92		60	45.87
7	6	12681	2/18/92	72	Town & Country S&L	3/19/92		0	350.66
8	7	12679	2/14/92	15	Laser Tech	3/15/92	2/28/92	0	12.75
9	8	12122	12/28/91	72	Town & Country S&L	1/27/92		63	455.43

AR_01.XLS

To return your database records to numerical order, select all the database records (including the new field) and choose Data ➪ Sort. Specify any cell in column A as the 1st Key, choose Ascending and then OK. Excel will return your database back to square one.

Table 24-1: Comparison operators for criteria ranges			
Operator	**Definition**	**Example criteria**	**Result**
=	Equal to	=500	Records with a field equal to 500
>	Greater than	>500	Records with a field greater than 500
<	Less than	<500	Records with a field less than 500
>=	Greater than or equal to	>=500	Records with a field greater than or equal to 500
<=	Less than or equal to	<=500	Records with a field less than or equal to 500
<>	Not equal to	<>500	Records with a field not equal to 500
?	Matches single	="j?nes"	Records with a field with character matching text and any single character at that position
*	Matches multiple	="j*nes"	Records with a field with characters matching text and any multiple characters at that position

Database and criteria field names must match exactly for any query operation to work properly. To ensure that they do, use Edit ⇨ Copy to copy database field names and then Edit ⇨ Paste to paste them to your criteria range.

There are two types of criteria, comparison and computed, with several flavors among them.

Comparison criteria

You use comparison criteria when you want to find records that exactly match your criteria or fall within a specified range. Comparison criteria consists of text, a value, or a date you want to search for, preceded by one of the comparison operators detailed in Table 24-1.

If you want to use these criteria comparison operators with text, enclose your text in double quotation marks. For example, `="Jones"` finds all records with a field containing the text `Jones`. Because Excel considers them serial numbers, dates operate similarly to values. For example, `=10/31/92` finds records with a field that contains the date October 31, 1992. You can use dates in any standard spreadsheet date format.

Entering criteria in a single cell in the row below criteria fields is known as *single comparison criteria*. In some instances, however, you need to use *multiple comparison criteria* — criteria that meet more than one set of conditions. You can have multiple criteria that meet two or more conditions, or multiple criteria that meet one or another criteria.

Entering criteria in more than one field in the same row instructs Excel to search for records that meet more than one condition. For example, entering `>500` under Amount and `>60` in Overdue in the second row of your criteria range would tell Excel to search for records that were over $500 *and* over 60 days.

Entering criteria in more than one row instructs Excel to search for records that meet one or another condition. For example, entering `>500` under Amount in the second row and `>60` under Overdue in the third row of your criteria range would tell Excel to search for records that were over $500 *or* overdue 60 days.

 You can use the AND and OR worksheet functions in formulas to create "and" and "or" criteria.

To create multiple criteria based on the same field, add an appropriate dupli-cate field name to the criteria range. Using the example in Figure 24-5, in order to find records with amounts greater than 500 and less than 600 you would enter the label `amt` in cell I11, `7500` in cell H12, and `<600` in cell I12.

Calculated criteria

Calculated criteria is similar to comparison criteria, but differ in two ways: The criteria is a formula, and you need to use a name for your criteria that doesn't exist as a database field name. Your formula should be the relative reference of your first database record (so all records will be searched) and evaluate to `True` or `False`. Figure 24-6 shows the result of the criteria formula `=TAX>28%*income`, which causes Excel to search the database for individuals paying greater than 28 percent of their income in taxes.

Once you've set up your criteria range, select it and then choose the Data ⇨ Set Criteria command. Like the Data ⇨ Set Database command, this tells Excel the location of the criteria range. Now you can search your database records and extract and delete records.

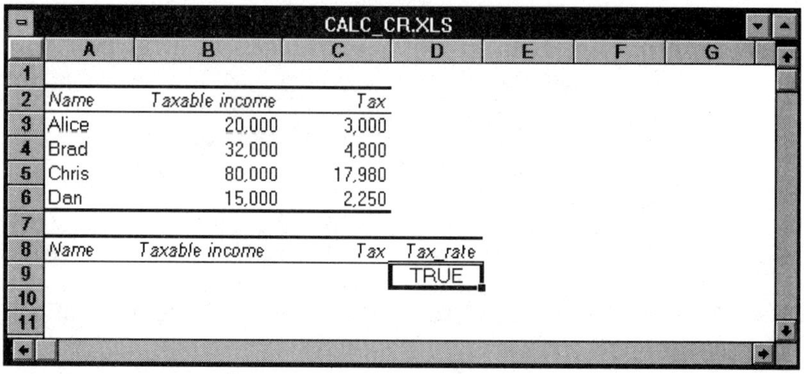

Figure 24-6: Calculated criteria in action: The search for individuals coughing up more than 28 percent of their income for taxes.

	A	B	C	D	E	F	G
			CALC_CR.XLS				
1							
2	Name	Taxable income	Tax				
3	Alice	20,000	3,000				
4	Brad	32,000	4,800				
5	Chris	80,000	17,980				
6	Dan	15,000	2,250				
7							
8	Name	Taxable income	Tax	Tax_rate			
9				TRUE			
10							
11							

Finding Records

Records in large databases can be found quickly using criteria you specify and the Data ⇨ Find command. Excel selects the first record that meets your criteria, as shown in Figure 24-7. If no records meet your criteria, you'll be greeted by a message box telling you so. To move to the next record that meets your criteria, take one of the following actions:

You can only scroll within the boundaries of your database in Find mode.

■ To move to the next or previous matching record, click the down or up scroll arrow or press the down or up arrow keys.

■ To move to the next or previous record one screen away, click in the vertical scroll bar or press PgDn or PgUp.

■ To scroll right or left, click in the horizontal scroll bar or press right or left arrow keys.

■ To make the right or left cell active, click on the cell or press Tab or Shift+Tab.

Hold down Shift while you select Data ⇨ Find to search your database backward.

While you have a record selected, you can edit it by selecting the cell and then pressing F2. After you make changes, press Enter. Select Data ⇨ Find to restart finding records. To exit Find mode, choose Data ⇨ Exit Find, press Esc, or select a cell outside the database range.

	A	B	C	D	E	F	G	H	I
				AR_01.XLS					
1	INV_NO	DATE	CO_ID	CO_NAME	DUE	PAID	OVER	AMT	
2	12657	2/12/91	53	Industrial Synergy	3/14/91		0	99.82	
3	12003	11/30/91	66	Federal Insurance	12/30/91		91	117.26	
4	12336	2/4/92	12	PC Pros	3/5/92	2/11/92	0	256.38	
5	12452	2/7/92	49	Voltaire International	3/8/92		0	79.22	
6	12115	12/31/91	66	Federal Insurance	1/30/92		60	45.87	
7	12681	2/18/92	72	Town & Country S&L	3/19/92		0	350.66	
8	12679	2/14/92	15	Laser Tech	3/15/92	2/28/92	0	12.75	
9	12122	12/28/91	72	Town & Country S&L	1/27/92		63	455.43	
10									
11	INV_NO	DATE	CO_ID	CO_NAME	DUE	PAID	OVER	AMT	
12						>0			
13									
14									
15									
16									
17									
18									

Figure 24-7:
A found
record, as a
result of the
criteria in
range
A11:H12.

Extracting Records

You can extract records from your database to another range in your spread-sheet or another open spreadsheet. When you extract records, you copy the records in your database to another area that meets your criteria. In effect, extracting records is a "smart" copy and paste operation.

Before you get rolling, however, you need to add another range to your spread-sheet. You guessed it — an *extract range*. Extract ranges must include at least one field name from your database field names and should include all fields if you want to extract exact copies of your records, as shown in Figure 24-8.

Creating an extract range is similar to creating a criteria range. Select the data-base field names, choose Edit ⇨ Copy, and then paste the field names (with Edit ⇨ Paste) to an extract area of your choice. You need to tell Excel what range you're extracting the records to, just as when you specify a criteria range. More on that in a moment.

You can quickly create a new database from an existing database by choosing only the field names you need and using Data ⇨ Extract.

After you've entered (or copied) the extract field names, select the names and the rows beneath your names to hold the copied records. If you select only the field names, the extract range will include the names and all rows beneath the names to the bottom of your spreadsheet (row 16,384).

	A	B	C	D	E	F	G	H	I
1	INV_NO	DATE	CO_ID	CO_NAME	DUE	PAID	OVER	AMT	
2	12657	2/12/91	53	Industrial Synergy	3/14/91		0	99.82	
3	12003	11/30/91	66	Federal Insurance	12/30/91		91	117.26	
4	12336	2/4/92	12	PC Pros	3/5/92	2/11/92	0	256.38	
5	12452	2/7/92	49	Voltaire International	3/8/92		0	79.22	
6	12115	12/31/91	66	Federal Insurance	1/30/92		60	45.87	
7	12681	2/18/92	72	Town & Country S&L	3/19/92		0	350.66	
8	12679	2/14/92	15	Laser Tech	3/15/92	2/28/92	0	12.75	
9	12122	12/28/91	72	Town & Country S&L	1/27/92		63	455.43	
10									
11	INV_NO	DATE	CO_ID	CO_NAME	DUE	PAID	OVER	AMT	
12						>0			
13									
14	INV_NO	DATE	CO_ID	CO_NAME	DUE	PAID	OVER	AMT	
15									
16									
17									
18									

AR_01.XLS

Figure 24-8: Our example with database and criteria and extract ranges.

Any existing cell entries below an unlimited extract range will be overrun by extracted records without warning from Excel.

If you know how many records will be extracted, you can specify that number of rows in your extract range. If there are more records than rows in your extract range, however, Excel displays the message box shown in Figure 24-9. Choose OK, enlarge the extract range, and choose Data ⇨ Extract to try again.

Once you've created an extract range, choose Data ⇨ Set Extract to let Excel know the whereabouts of your extract range. Now when you choose Data ⇨ Extract and press Enter, Excel copies the records from your database that meet the criteria in your criteria range, as shown in Figure 24-10.

Figure 24-9: Oops! Excel's way of letting you know you need to enlarge your extract range.

Microsoft Excel

Extract range is full.

OK   Help

	A	B	C	D	E	F	G	H	I
1	INV_NO	DATE	CO_ID	CO_NAME	DUE	PAID	OVER	AMT	
2	12657	2/12/91	53	Industrial Synergy	3/14/91		0	99.82	
3	12003	11/30/91	66	Federal Insurance	12/30/91		91	117.26	
4	12336	2/4/92	12	PC Pros	3/5/92	2/11/92	0	256.38	
5	12452	2/7/92	49	Voltaire International	3/8/92		0	79.22	
6	12115	12/31/91	66	Federal Insurance	1/30/92		60	45.87	
7	12681	2/18/92	72	Town & Country S&L	3/19/92		0	350.66	
8	12679	2/14/92	15	Laser Tech	3/15/92	2/28/92	0	12.75	
9	12122	12/28/91	72	Town & Country S&L	1/27/92		63	455.43	
10									
11	INV_NO	DATE	CO_ID	CO_NAME	DUE	PAID	OVER	AMT	
12						>0			
13									
14	INV_NO	DATE	CO_ID	CO_NAME	DUE	PAID	OVER	AMT	
15	12336	2/4/92	12	PC Pros	3/5/92	2/11/92	0	256.38	
16	12679	2/14/92	15	Laser Tech	3/15/92	2/28/92	0	12.75	
17									
18									

AR_01.XLS

Figure 24-10:
Records
copied from
your database
to the extract
range that
matched the
criteria.

In Figure 24-10, the criteria >0 was used in the cell under PAID in the criteria range as a way for Excel to distinguish between a blank and nonblank cell, since a date is a serial number and blank cells are evaluated as zero.

Choose Unique Records Only from the Data Extract dialog box to copy nonduplicate records to your extract range.

Deleting Records

If you work with databases frequently, especially those such as accounts receivable, you know that your database requires maintenance to stay current. In our example, for instance, you may need to remove a record when a company pays its bill in full. Earlier in the chapter you learned how to delete records using the Edit ➪ Delete command. You can also use the Data ➪ Delete command to remove records that are no longer current.

You should use Data ➪ Delete with caution, however, as it's a potentially destructive command. If you delete records inadvertently, you cannot use Edit ➪ Undo to reclaim them. Instead, use File ➪ Save or File ➪ Save As before you delete records regardless of which method you use. That way, you have a backup copy of your database on disk if your Data ➪ Delete (or Edit ➪ Delete) operation goes awry.

Figure 24-11: Your last chance to halt a <u>D</u>ata ⇨ <u>D</u>elete operation rests with this alert box.

To delete records from your database, you need only your named database and a criteria range. Enter a criteria that represents an attribute that describes the records you want deleted. For example, if you want to delete all records greater than $500, you'd enter >500 in the cell under the AMT field of your criteria range. After you enter the criteria and choose <u>D</u>ata ⇨ <u>D</u>elete, the message box shown in Figure 24-11 appears. Choose OK to proceed, and your records are removed, as in the example in Figure 24-12.

You can determine which records will be removed using <u>D</u>ata ⇨ <u>F</u>ind. <u>D</u>ata ⇨ <u>F</u>ind selects all records that qualify for removal based on your criteria if you choose <u>D</u>ata ⇨ <u>D</u>elete.

AR_01.XLS

	A	B	C	D	E	F	G	H	I
1	INV_NO	DATE	CO_ID	CO_NAME	DUE	PAID	OVER	AMT	
2	12657	2/12/91	53	Industrial Synergy	3/14/91		0	99.82	
3	12003	11/30/91	66	Federal Insurance	12/30/91		91	117.26	
4	12452	2/7/92	49	Voltaire International	3/8/92		0	79.22	
5	12115	12/31/91	66	Federal Insurance	1/30/92		60	45.87	
6	12681	2/18/92	72	Town & Country S&L	3/19/92		0	350.66	
7	12122	12/28/91	72	Town & Country S&L	1/27/92		63	455.43	
8									
9									
10									
11	INV_NO	DATE	CO_ID	CO_NAME	DUE	PAID	OVER	AMT	
12						>0			
13									
14	INV_NO	DATE	CO_ID	CO_NAME	DUE	PAID	OVER	AMT	
15	12336	2/4/92	12	PC Pros	3/5/92	2/11/92	0	256.38	
16	12679	2/14/92	15	Laser Tech	3/15/92	2/28/92	0	12.75	
17									
18									

Figure 24-12: Our updated database with old records deleted.

Using Database Forms

Excel, like most dedicated database programs, has a database form feature that enables you to view, edit, add, or delete records one at a time. Excel is no exception. Excel's data form is a dialog box and is created by Excel using your database field names. Once you define a database with Data ⇨ Set Database, you can invoke the Data ⇨ Form command, and Excel displays a handy form for the current database. The database form for our example database is shown in Figure 24-13. The following sections explain how to maintain your database with a form.

Finding records

To search your database records, choose the Criteria button, then use criteria appropriate for your search in the corresponding text box. (The record number indicator in the upper-right corner of the form changes to Criteria.) To remove criteria from previous searches, choose Clear, and to bail out of searching altogether, choose Form.

Choose Find Prev and Find Next to move to the previous and next records, respectively, that meet your criteria. Excel displays the matching record's fields in the form's text boxes. When Excel has found the last record, your computer will beep. Choose Close to exit your data form.

Criteria you set in the data form works independently of any criteria defined with Data ⇨ Set Criteria on your spreadsheet.

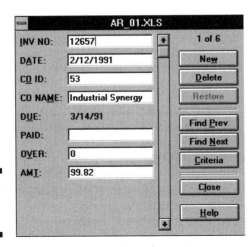

Figure 24-13: Our database's easy-to-use, fill-in-the-blanks form.

Since the data form is in its own window, you can move and close it like any other window. If you're a keyboard user, you can also use all the usual keys (arrow keys, for instance) to view records in the data form. If you're a mouser, click or drag as follows:

- To move to the next or previous matching record, click the down or up scroll arrow.

- To move to the next or previous matching record 10 records away, click below or above the scroll box in the vertical scroll bar.

- To move to the last or first matching record, drag the scroll box to the bottom or top of the vertical scroll bar.

- To scroll right or left, click in the horizontal scroll bar.

Editing records

Once you've found the record you're searching for, you can change it. Move to the text box by clicking on it or by pressing Tab. Edit the contents of the record in the form as you would any spreadsheet cell entry (pressing F2 or clicking the Formula bar isn't necessary, however). If you change your mind, make sure you choose Restore before pushing on to the next record, though you can always recover by editing the record again after you exit your form.

Fields you can change appear with a text box. Fields that are off-limits (such as a calculated field) have no text box.

Adding records

Adding new records with a form helps you enter data properly — you don't need to worry about data going into the wrong field. In fact, using a database form is ideal for creating your database in the first place. In addition, forms make it easy for data entry users who may not be well-versed in spreadsheet applications.

To add a record to your database, choose New. The record number indicator will display New Record, indicating you can now enter data. Type the data for the first field and then press Tab or select the next field. Repeat this for every field and press Enter when you're through. Another blank record will appear for you to fill out. If you're finished with data entry, choose Close. Excel extends the range name Database to include your new records and redisplays your database form.

Deleting records

Deleting records from your database with a form is similar to deleting them using the Data ⇨ Delete command. In both cases, you should use caution with this procedure, since a backup copy of your spreadsheet on disk is the only way to recover from unwanted deletions.

To delete a single record using a form, find the record using your form and then choose Delete. Excel displays a message box. When you choose OK, the record is removed and the resulting space in your database is closed up.

To delete multiple records in one step, enter appropriate criteria in the corresponding field's text box, then proceed with the delete operation as before.

Analyzing a Database

Excel has several worksheet functions you can use with databases. These functions enable you to quickly calculate results that would otherwise be tedious. The functions available to you are detailed in Table 24-2. All the database functions have the format:

```
=DFUNCTION(Database,field,criteria)
```

where *Database* is a range of cells, and *field* and *criteria* are as their name implies (you can use the range names Database and Criteria if you've applied the Data ⇨ Set Database and Data ⇨ Set Criteria command to the respective range).

As an example of the utility of database functions, it'd be a fairly easy process to determine the amount of money owed by Federal Insurance in our example database. You could visually scan all the instances of amount owed and use

Data forms: Are they for you?

Database data forms are great if your database needs are relatively simple, and data forms are especially helpful if your database is primarily for data entry. If you need to extract records or use calculated criteria, however, you'll need to go the nonform route, unless you create a macro-driven custom application. You may also find searching for more than one record easier with the Data ⇨ Find command.

Table 24-2: Worksheet functions for use with databases	
Function	**Result**
DAVERAGE	Averages values
DCOUNT	Counts values
DCOUNTA	Counts nonblank cells
DGET	Extracts a single value
DMAX	Finds a maximum value
DMIN	Finds a minimum value
DPRODUCT	Multiplies numbers
DSTDEV	Calculates standard deviation — sample population
DSTDDEVP	Calculates standard deviation — entire population
DSUM	Totals values
DVAR	Calculates variance — sample population
DVARP	Calculates variance — entire population

(gasp!) your calculator, or enter the values in another area of your spreadsheet and total the numbers. A faster and less error-prone solution would be to use the DSUM function (especially if you're dealing with a database containing hundreds of records).

Figure 24-14 shows the result of using DSUM to quickly find the total. (Note that the extract range has been removed, as it isn't a requirement for use with database worksheet functions.) The DSUM function uses the name Database for the range database, Amt for the field, and the range D11:D12 as the criteria.

You can specify a field name (as long as it's enclosed in quotation marks) from your database. You can also use the column number of the database as the field argument in a database function (database column numbers begin with 1). In the example, INV_NO would be column number 1, so the function would then be =DSUM(Database,8,D11:D12).

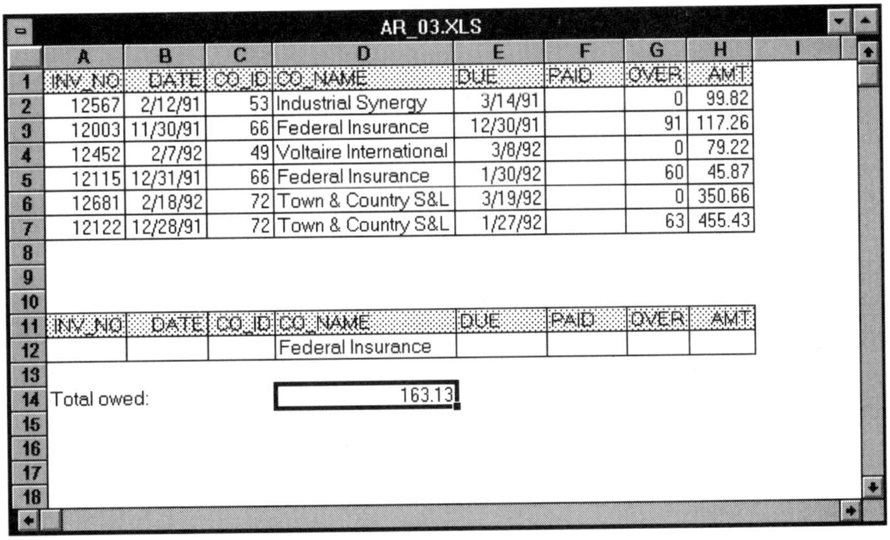

	A	B	C	D	E	F	G	H	I
1	INV_NO	DATE	CO_ID	CO_NAME	DUE	PAID	OVER	AMT	
2	12567	2/12/91	53	Industrial Synergy	3/14/91		0	99.82	
3	12003	11/30/91	66	Federal Insurance	12/30/91		91	117.26	
4	12452	2/7/92	49	Voltaire International	3/8/92		0	79.22	
5	12115	12/31/91	66	Federal Insurance	1/30/92		60	45.87	
6	12681	2/18/92	72	Town & Country S&L	3/19/92		0	350.66	
7	12122	12/28/91	72	Town & Country S&L	1/27/92		63	455.43	
8									
9									
10									
11	INV_NO	DATE	CO_ID	CO_NAME	DUE	PAID	OVER	AMT	
12				Federal Insurance					
13									
14	Total owed:			163.13					
15									
16									
17									
18									

Window title: AR_03.XLS

Figure 24-14:
DSUM quickly calculates a total from databases with a common field.

If you need to repeat this exercise for each account, product, or company in your database, you can team up DSUM with the <u>D</u>ata ➪ <u>T</u>able command to quickly calculate a total for each item. Chapter 27 shows how to be an Excel data table expert in no time — and also demonstrates Excel's new Crosstab Wizard.

Using External Databases

Thus far, you've learned how to use a database on your Excel worksheet. You can also access databases that aren't on your worksheet, called *external* databases. External databases can reside on other personal computers (accessed via a LAN) or on mainframe computers. To access external databases, you use a separate Windows program that comes with Excel, Q+E. You install Q+E when you install Excel (you can always install Q+E later with the Excel Setup program if you chose not to install it initially). When installed, Q+E is a member of your Excel for Windows program group. Q+E enables you to access files created by these database programs:

- dBASE III Plus or dBASE IV database files on other personal computers

- SQL Server, Oracle, and OS/2 Extended Edition LAN databases

- Text (ASCII) files

Q+E, as a database query and edit program, can be used as a stand-alone program or with Excel. As a stand-alone program, it can sort, edit, and query data like any other database program. If you have Excel running, you can use Edit ⇨ Copy and Edit ⇨ Paste, or link data via DDE between Q+E and your Excel spreadsheet. (For a primer on DDE, see Chapter 28.)

 You must use Q+E to modify existing records or to add records to external databases.

To run Q+E, return to the Windows Program Manager and open the Excel program group. Double-click the Q+E icon to start the Q+E program.

You can also use Q+E from within Excel. When you do, commands on Excel's Data menu are modified for use with external databases. The following commands are also added to the Data menu:

Command	Purpose
Paste Fieldnames	Adds database field names from the external database to your worksheet to use as criteria and extract field names.
SQL Query	Provides a dialog box to enter an SQL query.
Activate Q+E	Starts Q+E or makes Q+E the active window.

To use Q+E from within Excel, select File ⇨ Open and choose the QE subdirectory. Next, choose the qe.xla macro and then select OK. The macro starts Q+E, modifys existing Data commands, and adds new Data commands so you can work with external databases.

Summary

▶ A database is a collection of similar data organized in a structured manner. Database data consists of *records*, which are rows of data. Each cell, or *field*, in the record, contains a unique data item.

▶ Excel can be used for database management, thereby taking advantage of Excel's analytical, charting, and printing capabilities and its familiar environment, and thereby avoiding the expense and learning time of using a dedicated database program.

▶ Database design is the first and crucial step to creating a useful database.

▶ You can enter database records using your normal data entry manner, use a form, or create a macro-driven dialog box.

▶ You can modify the structure of a database by adding, deleting, or moving fields (columns). You can modify the contents of a database by editing, adding, or deleting records. You can rearrange the order of your database records by sorting them.

▶ You can find, extract, and delete database records that match specified criteria.

▶ A fill-in-the-blanks form is available to use with your database for simple database find, add, and delete operations.

▶ Excel's worksheet functions include a set of database functions that enable you to analyze your database.

▶ Q+E is a powerful Windows program included with Excel that provides access to external databases (databases not on your worksheet).

Chapter 25
The Analysis ToolPak

Most spreadsheet products are designed with business users in mind. Yet these products are used in a variety of other disciplines, including education, research, statistics, and engineering. Microsoft, for the first time, specifically addresses these nonbusiness users with its Analysis ToolPak collection of add-ins for Excel. This provides new analytical capability that's not found in any other spreadsheet product — including a slew of new functions for technical users. But don't think you have to wear a white lab coat or a plastic shirt pocket protector to use these add-ins. Many of the features and functions in the Analysis ToolPak are well-suited for business applications as well.

What Is the Analysis ToolPak?

The Analysis ToolPak is a collection of several add-ins that provide new analytical capability to Excel. These features are easily accessible via a menu where you can select from 19 new procedures. In addition, the ToolPak provides 89 new built-in functions — which appear conveniently in the Paste Function dialog box.

This analytical grab bag offers some exciting features that will surely be welcomed by advanced users and those in the scientific, engineering, and educational communities, not to mention business users who need tools that extend beyond the normal spreadsheet fare.

Making the Analysis ToolPak Available

Depending on how Excel was originally installed on your system, you may or may not have access to the Analysis ToolPak. To see if this add-in is available, select the Options menu. If the Options pull-down menu displays Analysis Tools as an option, you're all set.

If the Options ⇨ Analysis Tools command is not available on your system, you'll need to run Excel's Setup program to add the appropriate files. After running Setup, choose the Custom Installation option and select the Analysis ToolPak option (you can leave all of the other options unchecked). Unlike the original installation, this only takes a few minutes. When you restart Excel, the Options ⇨ Analysis Tools command should be at your disposal.

An Overview of Analysis Tools

Before we get into the meat of this chapter, here's a quick overview of the types of analyses you can conduct with the Analysis ToolPak add-in, broken down by the category of user that is most appropriate for each type of analysis.

Business, or general interest

Many of these procedures are actually classified as statistical tools, but they have widespread application in business and many other disciplines.

- Descriptive statistics
- Correlation
- Histogram
- Moving average
- Covariance
- Sampling
- Rank and percentile
- Exponential smoothing
- Random number generation
- Regression

Statistical

These procedures perform statistical significance tests on worksheet data. They inform you if differences among groups are large enough to be considered statistically significant.

- Analysis of variance (single-factor)
- Analysis of variance (two-factor with replication)
- Analysis of variance (two-factor without replication)

- *F*-Test (two-sample for variance)
- *t*-Test (paired two-sample for means)
- *t*-Test (two-sample assuming equal variances)
- *t*-Test (two-sample assuming unequal variances)
- *z*-Test (two-sample for means)

Engineering

This last procedure is primarily for engineering applications.

- Fourier analysis

As you can see, this add-in offers quite a bit of new functionality to Excel. These procedures have limitations, however, and in some cases you might prefer to create your own formulas to do some of the calculations.

New functions

Besides the procedures just listed, the Analysis ToolPak provides a load of new worksheet functions. These functions cover mathematics, engineering, unit conversions, financial analysis, and dates. The functions are listed as follows.

Engineering and mathematical functions

BESSELI	Modified Bessel function In(x)
BESSELJ	Bessel function Jn(x)
BESSELK	Modified Bessel function Kn(x)
BESSELY	Bessel function Yn(x)
DELTA	Tests whether two numbers are equal
ERF	Error function
ERFC	Complementary error function
FACTDOUBLE	Returns the double factorial of a number
GCD	Returns the greatest common divisor of two or more integers
GESTEP	Tests whether a number is greater than a threshold value
IMABS	Absolute value (modulus) of a complex number
IMAGINARY	Imaginary coefficient of a complex number
IMARGUMENT	The angle theta, expressed in radians
IMCONJUGATE	Complex conjugate of a complex number
IMCOS	Cosine of a complex number
IMDIV	Quotient of two complex numbers
IMEXP	Exponential of a complex number
IMLN	Natural logarithm of a complex number
IMLOG2	Base-2 logarithm of a complex number

IMLOG10	Common logarithm (base 10) of a complex number
IMPOWER	Complex number raised to an integer power
IMPRODUCT	Product of two complex numbers
IMREAL	Real coefficient of a complex number
IMSIN	Sine of a complex number
IMSQRT	Square root of a complex number
IMSUB	Difference of two complex numbers
IMSUM	Sum of complex numbers
ISEVEN	Returns 1 if the argument is even, otherwise 0
ISODD	Returns 1 if the argument is odd, otherwise 0
LCM	Returns the least-common multiple of integers
MROUND	Returns a number rounded to a specified multiple
MULTINOMIAL	Ratio of the factorial of a sum to the product
QUOTIENT	Returns the integer portion of a divisor
SERIESSUM	Sum of a power series
SQRTPI	Square root of the argument times pi

Conversion functions

BIN2DEC	Converts a binary number to decimal
BIN2HEX	Converts a binary number to hexadecimal
BIN2OCT	Converts a binary number to octal
COMPLEX	Converts real and imaginary coefficients into a complex number
CONVERT	Converts a number from one measurement system to another
DEC2BIN	Converts a decimal integer to binary
DEC2HEX	Converts a decimal number to hexadecimal
DEC2OCT	Converts a decimal integer to octal
DEGREES	Converts radians to degrees
HEX2BIN	Converts a hexadecimal number to binary
HEX2DEC	Converts a hexadecimal number to decimal
HEX2OCT	Converts a hexadecimal number to octal
OCT2BIN	Converts an octal number to binary
OCT2DEC	Converts an octal number to decimal
OCT2HEX	Converts an octal number to hexadecimal
RADIANS	Converts degrees to radians

Financial functions

ACCRINT	Accrued interest for a security paying periodic interest
ACCRINTM	Accrued interest for maturity security paying periodic interest
COUPDAYBS	Days between beginning of coupon period to settlement date
COUPDAYS	Days in the coupon period that contains settlement date
COUPDAYSNC	Days from settlement date to next coupon date
COUPNCD	Next coupon date after the settlement date

COUPNUM	Number of coupons payable between settlement and maturity dates
COUPPCD	Previous coupon date before settlement date
CUMIPMT	Cumulative interest paid on a loan between start and end periods
CUMPRINC	Cumulative principal paid on a loan between start and end periods
DISC	Discount rate for a security
DOLLARDE	Converts fractional dollar price to decimal
DOLLARFR	Converts decimal dollar price to fraction
DURATION	Annual duration for security with periodic interest payments
EFFECT	Effective annual interest rate, given nominal rate and period
FVSCHEDULE	Future value of initial principal after compounding rates applied
INTRATE	Interest rate for a fully invested security
MDURATION	Annual modified duration for a security
NOMINAL	Nominal annual interest rate given effective rate and compounding
ODDFPRICE	Price per $100 face value of security with odd first period
ODDFYIELD	Yield of security with odd first period
ODDLPRICE	Price per $100 face value of security with odd last coupon period
ODDLYIELD	Yield of security with odd last period
PRICE	Price per $100 face value of security paying periodic interest
PRICEDISC	Price per $100 face value of discounted security
PRICEMAT	Price per $100 face value of security paying interest at maturity
RECEIVED	Amount received at maturity for fully invested security
TBILLEQ	Bond-equivalent yield for treasury bill
TBILLPRICE	Price per $100 face value for treasury bill
TBILLYIELD	Yield for a treasury bill
XIRR	IRR for cash flows that may not be periodic
XNPV	NPV for cash flows that may not be periodic
YIELD	Yield on security that pays periodic interest
YIELDDISC	Annual yield for discounted security
YIELDMAT	Annual yield of security that pays interest at maturity

Date functions

EDATE	Date that is a specified number of months before or after a date
EOMONTH	Last day of month that is a specified number of months after a date
NETWORKDAYS	Number of working days between two dates
WORKDAY	Date that is specified number of working days from a date
YEARFRAC	Year fraction representing days between two dates

Using the Analysis ToolPak

We've broken this section down into two parts: the tools and the functions.

The tools

The procedures in the Analysis ToolPak add-in are straightforward. Typically, you select the Options ⇨ Analysis Tools command, which displays the dialog box shown in Figure 25-1. Then you scroll through the list until you find the analysis tool you want to use. Select OK, and you'll get a new dialog box that's specific to the procedure you selected.

Normally, you need to specify one or more input ranges, plus an output range (one cell will do). The procedures vary in the amount of additional information required.

An option that you'll see in many of the dialog boxes is whether or not your data range includes labels. If so, you can specify the entire range, including the labels, and indicate to Excel that the first column (or row) contains labels. Excel then uses these labels in the tables it produces.

In some cases, the procedures produce their results using formulas. Because of this, you can change your data and the results update automatically. In other procedures, the results are in the form of values, so if you change your data the results do not reflect your changes. Make sure you understand what Excel is doing.

Space limitations prevent us from discussing each and every option available in these procedures. We assume that if you need to use some of these advanced analysis tools, you know what you're doing.

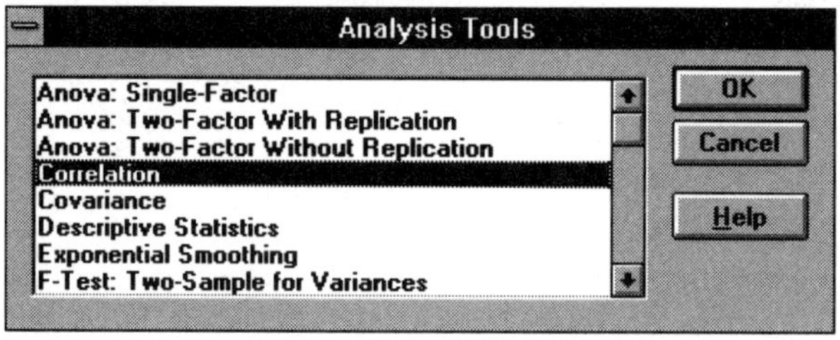

Figure 25-1: The Analysis Tools dialog box, where you select the tool you're interested in.

Analysis Tools	
Anova: Single-Factor	OK
Anova: Two-Factor With Replication	
Anova: Two-Factor Without Replication	Cancel
Correlation	
Covariance	
Descriptive Statistics	Help
Exponential Smoothing	
F-Test: Two-Sample for Variances	

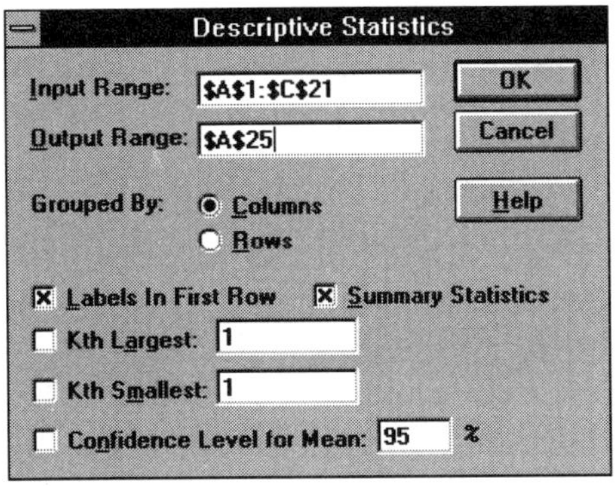

Descriptive Statistics

Input Range:	$A$1:$C$21
Output Range:	$A$25

OK

Cancel

Help

Grouped By: ● Columns
○ Rows

☒ Labels In First Row   ☒ Summary Statistics

☐ Kth Largest: 1

☐ Kth Smallest: 1

☐ Confidence Level for Mean: 95 %

Figure 25-2:
The
Descriptive
Statistics
dialog box.

The functions

Once the Analysis ToolPak is installed, you'll have access to all of the additional functions (which are described fully in the on-line help system). You can access these functions just like any other function, and they appear in the Paste Function dialog box.

If you will be sharing worksheets that use these functions, make sure the user has access to the add-in functions.

Now, on to a description of each of the 19 analysis tools.

Business or general-interest procedures

This first category of tools is useful for a wide variety of users and includes several standard statistical procedures often used in business applications.

Descriptive statistics

This tool produces a handy table that describes your data with some standard statistics. It uses the dialog box shown in Figure 25-2. The Kth Largest and Kth Smallest option display the data value that corresponds to a rank you specify. For example, if you check Kth Largest and specify a value of 2, the output shows the second largest value in the input range (the standard output already includes the minimum and maximum values).

Sample output for the Descriptive Statistics tool is shown in Figure 25-3. Note that the output uses the labels to describe the groups. Unfortunately, the output for this procedure consists of values, not formulas. Consequently, you should use this procedure only when you're certain that your data will not change — otherwise you'll need to reexecute this procedure.

	A	B	C	D	E
24					
25	Control		Method1		
26					
27	Mean	39.25	Mean	46.00	
28	Standard Error	1.85	Standard Error	2.11	
29	Median	37.50	Median	45.50	
30	Mode	37.00	Mode	52.00	
31	Standard Deviation	8.26	Standard Deviation	9.43	
32	Variance	68.30	Variance	88.84	
33	Kurtosis	1.47	Kurtosis	-0.48	
34	Skewness	1.18	Skewness	0.14	
35	Range	32.00	Range	34.00	
36	Minimum	28.00	Minimum	28.00	
37	Maximum	60.00	Maximum	62.00	
38	Sum	785.00	Sum	920.00	
39	Count	20.00	Count	20.00	
40					

DESCRIP.XLS

Figure 25-3: Output from the Descriptive Statistics tool.

If your data is subject to change, you may want to set up formulas that produce identical results. Figure 25-4 shows formulas that produce the same results as the Descriptive Statistics tool. These formulas use indirect references and assume that the data is in a named range and that the range name is inserted at the top of the column. In this case, the name of the range is inserted in cell G1.

	F	G	
1		Control	
2			
3	Mean	=AVERAGE(INDIRECT(G1))	
4	Standard Error	=G7/SQRT(G15)	
5	Median	=MEDIAN(INDIRECT(G1))	
6	Mode	=MODE(INDIRECT(G1))	
7	Standard Deviation	=STDEV(INDIRECT(G1))	
8	Variance	=VAR(INDIRECT(G1))	
9	Kurtosis	=KURT(INDIRECT(G1))	
10	Skewness	=SKEW(INDIRECT(G1))	
11	Range	=ABS(MIN(INDIRECT(G1)-MAX(INDIRECT(G1))))	
12	Minimum	=MIN(INDIRECT(G1))	
13	Maximum	=MAX(INDIRECT(G1))	
14	Sum	=SUM(INDIRECT(G1))	
15	Count	=COUNT(INDIRECT(G1))	
16	Confidence Level (95%)	=CONFIDENCE(1-G17,G7,G15)	
17	Confidence Level	0.95	
18			

DESCRIP.XLS

Figure 25-4: These formulas produce the same results as the Descriptive Statistics tool (and are updated if your data changes).

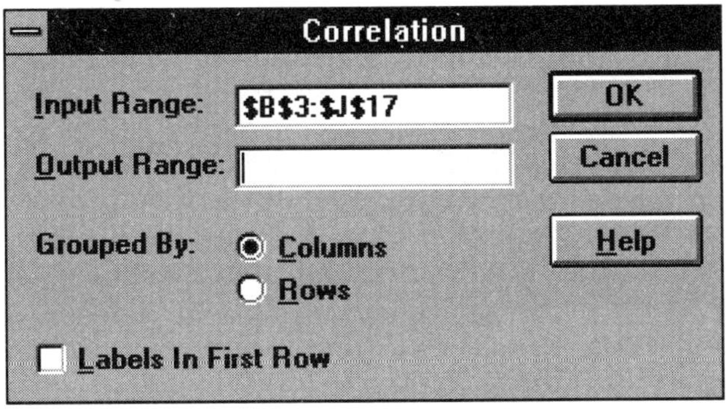

Figure 25-5: The Correlation dialog box.

Correlation

Correlation is a widely used statistic that measures the degree to which two sets of variables vary together. The result is a correlation coefficient that ranges from −1.0 (a perfect negative correlation) to +1.0 (a perfect positive correlation). A correlation coefficient of 0 means that the two variables are not correlated.

The Correlation dialog box is shown in Figure 25-5. Specify the input range, which can include any number of variables arranged in rows or columns. The output consists of a correlation matrix that shows the correlation coefficient for each variable paired with every other variable.

In this case, Excel *does* use formulas to calculate the results. The correlation matrix is updated whenever you change any values in the input range. Figure 25-6 shows an example of a correlation matrix generated by this tool. Note that a variable correlated with itself produces a correlation coefficient of 1.0.

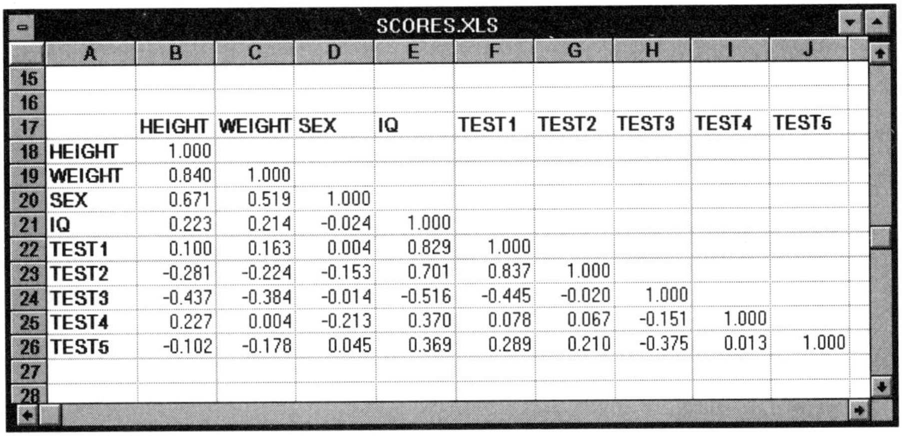

Figure 25-6: A correlation matrix generated by the Correlation tool.

	A	B	C	D	E	F	G	H	I	J
15										
16										
17		HEIGHT	WEIGHT	SEX	IQ	TEST1	TEST2	TEST3	TEST4	TEST5
18	HEIGHT	1.000								
19	WEIGHT	0.840	1.000							
20	SEX	0.671	0.519	1.000						
21	IQ	0.223	0.214	-0.024	1.000					
22	TEST1	0.100	0.163	0.004	0.829	1.000				
23	TEST2	-0.281	-0.224	-0.153	0.701	0.837	1.000			
24	TEST3	-0.437	-0.384	-0.014	-0.516	-0.445	-0.020	1.000		
25	TEST4	0.227	0.004	-0.213	0.370	0.078	0.067	-0.151	1.000	
26	TEST5	-0.102	-0.178	0.045	0.369	0.289	0.210	-0.375	0.013	1.000
27										
28										

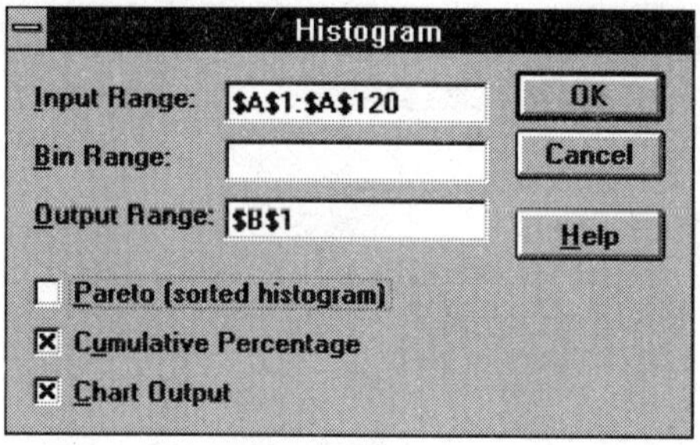

Figure 25-7:
The Histogram tool
lets you generate
distributions and
graphical output.

```
┌─────────────────────────────────────────────┐
│  ─              Histogram                     │
├─────────────────────────────────────────────┤
│  Input Range:   $A$1:$A$120    ┌────────┐    │
│                                │   OK   │    │
│  Bin Range:                    └────────┘    │
│                                ┌────────┐    │
│  Output Range:  $B$1           │ Cancel │    │
│                                └────────┘    │
│  ☐ Pareto (sorted histogram)   ┌────────┐    │
│  ☒ Cumulative Percentage       │  Help  │    │
│  ☒ Chart Output                └────────┘    │
└─────────────────────────────────────────────┘
```

Covariance

The Covariance tool produces a matrix similar to that generated by the Correlation tool. Again, the matrix is made up of formulas, so when you change your data the table updates automatically. The formulas along the diagonal of the matrix are population variance (=VARP) functions; the other formulas are covariance (=COVAR) functions.

Histogram

This procedure is useful for producing data distributions and histogram charts. It accepts an input range and a "bin" range. A bin range is a range of values that specify the limits for each column of the histogram. If you omit the bin range, Excel creates ten equal-interval bins for you. The size of each bin is determined by a formula of the following form:

```
=(MAX(input_range)-MIN(input_range))/10
```

The Histogram dialog box is shown in Figure 25-7. As an option, you can specify that the resulting histogram be sorted by frequency of occurrence in each bin.

If you specify the sorted histogram option, the bin range must consist of values and cannot contain formulas. If there are formulas in the bin range, the sorting done by Excel will not work properly and your worksheet will display error values.

Figure 25-8 shows some sample output from this procedure. If you specify a chart output, the chart is created in a separate window. This is not a dynamic procedure, so if you change any of the input data you need to repeat the Histogram procedure to update the results.

Refer to Chapter 22 for a method to calculate these types of distributions dynamically using array formulas.

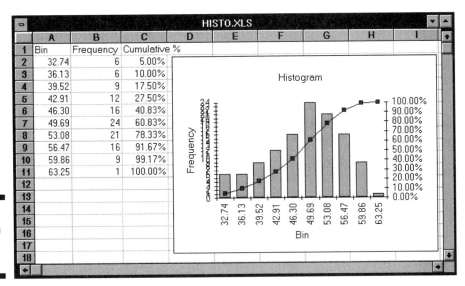

Figure 25-8:
Output from
the Histo-
gram tool.

Moving average

The Moving Average tool is useful to smooth out a data series that has a lot of variability. This is best done in conjunction with a chart. Excel does the smoothing by computing a moving average of a specified number of values. In many cases, a moving average lets you spot trends that would otherwise be obscured by the "noise" in the data.

Figure 25-9 shows the Moving Average dialog box. You can, of course, specify the number of values to be used for each average. When you exit this dialog box, Excel creates =AVERAGE formulas that reference the input range you specify. You'll notice in Figure 25-10 that the first few cells in the output are #NA. This is because there are not enough data points to calculate the average for these initial values.

Figure 25-9: The
Moving Average
dialog box.

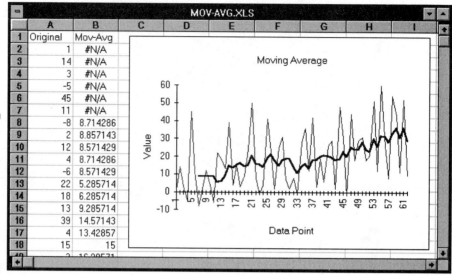

Figure 25-10: Output from the Moving Average tool (including a chart that was gene-rated auto-matically).

An option in this procedure calculates standard errors and places formulas for these calculations next to the moving average formulas. The standard error values indicate the degree of variability between the actual values and the calculated moving averages.

Exponential smoothing

Exponential smoothing is another technique for smoothing out random varia-tions in a data series. This technique is useful when the average appears to change over time but is obscured by variations. You can specify the *damping factor* (also known as a *smoothing constant*), and it can range from 0 to 1. As with the Moving Average tool, you can also request standard errors and a chart.

Random number generation

Although Excel already has a built-in function to calculate random numbers, this tool is a lot more flexible because you can specify what type of distribution you want the numbers to have. The Random Number Generation dialog box appears in Figure 25-11.

The Parameters box varies, depending on the type of distribution selected.

The Number of Variables refers to the number of columns you want, and the Number of Random Numbers refers to the number of rows you want. For example, if you want 200 random numbers arranged in 10 columns of 20 rows, you would specify 10 and 20, respectively, in these text boxes.

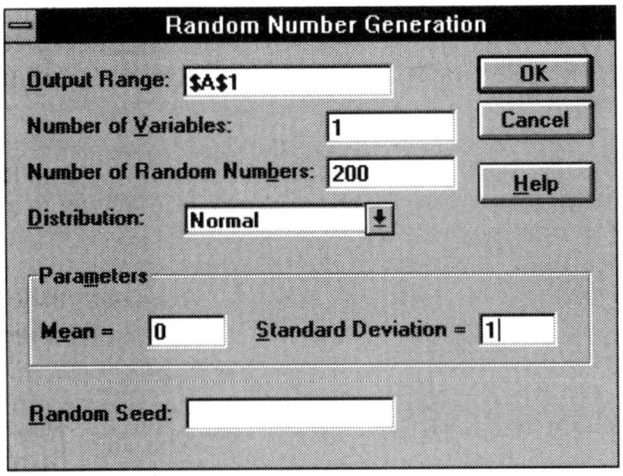

Figure 25-11:
This dialog box lets you generate a wide variety of random numbers.

The Random Seed box lets you specify a starting value that Excel uses in its random number generating algorithm. Normally, you would leave this blank. If you want to generate the same random number sequence, however, you can specify a seed between 1 and 32,767 (integer values only). The distribution options available are:

Uniform   Every random number has an equal chance of being selected. You specify the upper and lower limits.

Normal   The random numbers correspond to a normal distribution. You specify the mean and standard deviation.

Bernoulli   The random numbers will be either 0 or 1, determined by the "probability of success" you specify.

Binomial   This returns random numbers based on a Bernoulli distribution over a specific number of "trials," given a probability of success that you specify.

Poisson   This option generates values in a Poisson distribution. This is characterized by discrete events that occur in an interval, where the probability of a single occurrence is proportional to the size of the interval. The lambda parameter is the expected number of occurrences in an interval. In a Poisson distribution, lambda is equal to the mean, which is also equal to the variance.

Patterned   We're a bit confused over this option, since it doesn't actually generate random numbers. Rather, it repeats a series of non-random numbers in steps that you specify. If you can figure out a use for this option, let us know.

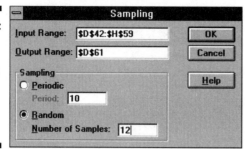

Figure 25-12:
The
Sampling
dialog box is
useful for
selecting
random
samples.

> **Discrete**   This option lets you specify the probability that specific values
> are chosen. It requires a two-column input range: the first
> column holds the values, and the second column holds the
> probability of that value being chosen. The sum of the prob-
> abilities in the second column must equal 100 percent.

To get a visual depiction of the random numbers generated, use the Histogram
tool to plot them.

Sampling

The Sampling tool generates a random sample from a range of input values.
This is useful for working with a subset of a large database, for example to
select winners in a raffle. The Sampling dialog box is shown in Figure 25-12. This
procedure has two options: periodic and random.

A periodic sample selects every *n*th value from the input range, where *n* equals
the period you specify. With a random sample, you simply specify the size of
the sample to be selected, and every value has an equal probability of being
chosen.

Rank and Percentile

The Rank and Percentile tool creates a table that shows the ordinal and percentile ranking for each value in a range. Personally, we don't find this tool all that
useful and prefer to use functions for this. For example, the =RANK function
returns the relative ranking (and we presented a better method using arrays in
Chapter 21). If you need percentiles, the =PERCENTRANK function returns the
percentage rank among the values in an array or range.

Regression

The Regression tool calculates a regression analysis from worksheet data.
Regression is used to analyze trends, forecast the future, build predictive
models, and often make sense out of a series of seemingly unrelated numbers.

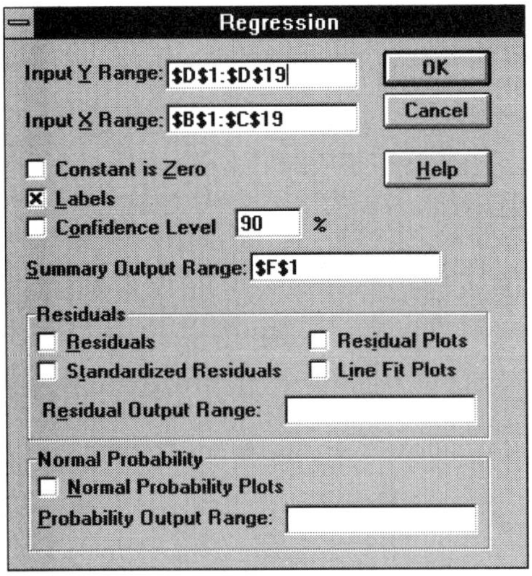

Figure 25-13:
The
Regression
dialog box.

Regression analysis lets you determine the extent to which one range of data (the dependent variable) varies as a function of the values of one or more other ranges of data (the independent variables). This relationship is expressed mathematically, using values that are calculated by Excel. You can use these calculations to create a mathematical model of the data and predict the dependent variable, using different values of one or more independent variables. This tool can perform simple and multiple linear regressions and automatically calculate and standardize residuals. Figure 25-13 shows the Regression dialog box. As you can see, it offers quite a few options.

Input Y Range   This is the dependent variable.

Input X Range   This is one or more ranges of independent variables.

Constant is Zero   If checked, this forces the regression to have a constant of 0 (which means the regression line passes through the origin — when the X values are 0, the predicted Y value will be 0).

Confidence Level   The confidence level for the regression.

Residuals   These options specify whether to include residuals in the output. Residuals are the differences between observed and predicted values.

Normal Probability   This generates a chart for normal probability plots.

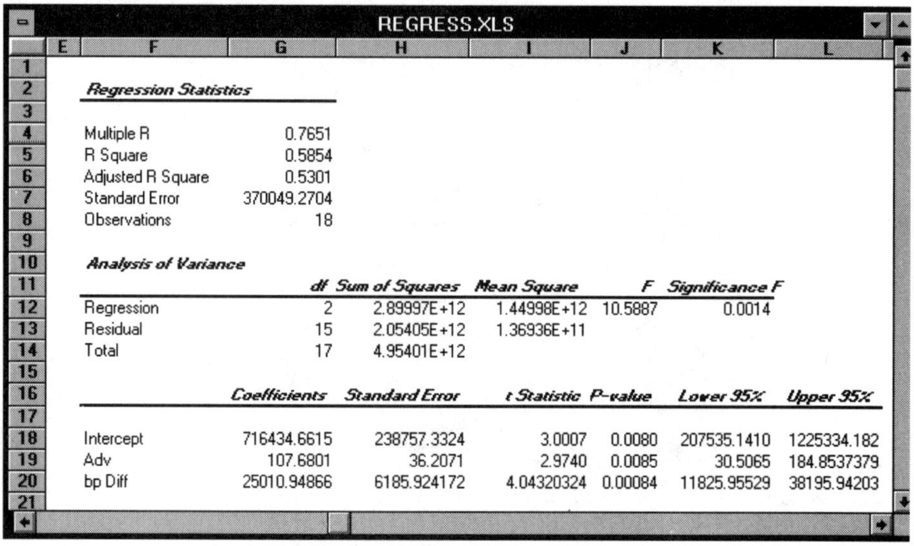

Figure 25-14:
Sample output
from the
Regression
tool.

The following is the spreadsheet content (REGRESS.XLS):

Regression Statistics

Multiple R	0.7651
R Square	0.5854
Adjusted R Square	0.5301
Standard Error	370049.2704
Observations	18

Analysis of Variance

	df	Sum of Squares	Mean Square	F	Significance F
Regression	2	2.89997E+12	1.44998E+12	10.5887	0.0014
Residual	15	2.05405E+12	1.36936E+11		
Total	17	4.95401E+12			

	Coefficients	Standard Error	t Statistic	P-value	Lower 95%	Upper 95%
Intercept	716434.6615	238757.3324	3.0007	0.0080	207535.1410	1225334.182
Adv	107.6801	36.2071	2.9740	0.0085	30.5065	184.8537379
bp Diff	25010.94866	6185.924172	4.04320324	0.00084	11825.95529	38195.94203

The results of a regression analysis are shown in Figure 25-14. If you understand regression analysis, the output from this procedure will be familiar to you.

Statistical tools

These tools are designed to perform statistical significance tests on your worksheet data. The appropriate test depends on the data. These tests fall into four categories:

t-Test — This tests the hypothesis that means from two samples are equal.

z-Test — This tests the hypothesis that means of two populations are equal.

Analysis of variance — This tests the hypothesis that means from several samples are equal.

F-Test — This compares the variances of two populations.

t-Test (paired two-sample for means)

The *t*-Test is used to determine if there is a statistically significant difference between two small samples. This form is for paired samples, in which you have

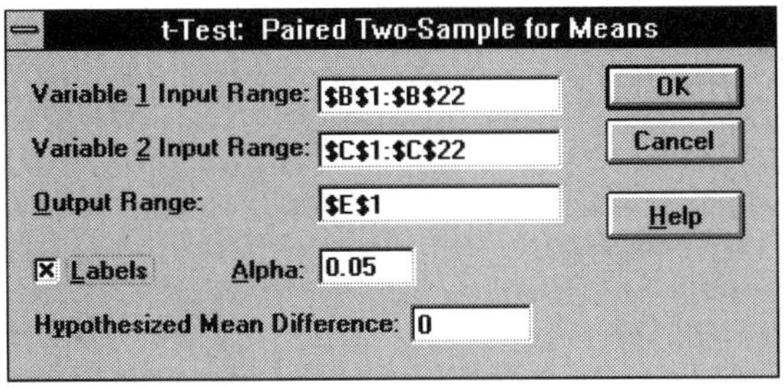

t-Test: Paired Two-Sample for Means

Variable 1 Input Range:	$B$1:$B$22
Variable 2 Input Range:	$C$1:$C$22
Output Range:	$E$1

OK

Cancel

Help

[X] Labels   Alpha: 0.05

Hypothesized Mean Difference: 0

Figure 25-15: The Paired t-Test dialog box.

two observations on each subject (such as a pretest and a posttest). Figure 25-15 shows the dialog box for this test.

A paired test requires the same sample size for both variables.

You specify the significance level (alpha) and the hypothesized difference between the two means (that is, the null hypotheses). Sample output from this test is shown in Figure 25-16. As you can see, Excel calculates *t* for both a one-tailed and two-tailed test.

t-Test (two-sample assuming equal variances)

This option is similar to the previous tool, except that it is for independent, rather than paired, samples. It assumes equal variances for the two samples.

t-Test (two-sample assuming unequal variances)

This option is similar to the previous tool, but assumes unequal variances for the two samples.

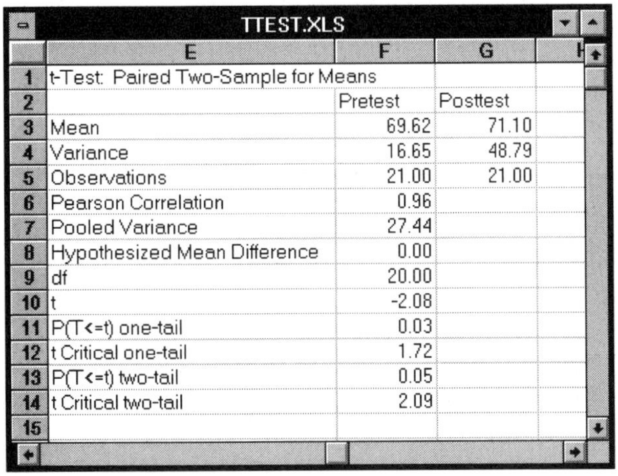

TTEST.XLS

	E	F	G
1	t-Test: Paired Two-Sample for Means		
2		Pretest	Posttest
3	Mean	69.62	71.10
4	Variance	16.65	48.79
5	Observations	21.00	21.00
6	Pearson Correlation	0.96	
7	Pooled Variance	27.44	
8	Hypothesized Mean Difference	0.00	
9	df	20.00	
10	t	-2.08	
11	P(T<=t) one-tail	0.03	
12	t Critical one-tail	1.72	
13	P(T<=t) two-tail	0.05	
14	t Critical two-tail	2.09	
15			

Figure 25-16: Sample t-Test output.

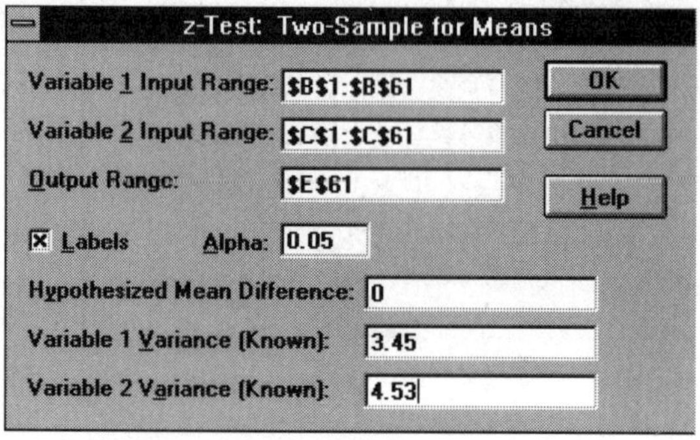

Figure 25-17: The *z*-Test dialog box.

z-Test (two-sample for means)

While *t*-Tests are used for small samples, the *z*-Test is used for larger samples or populations. You need to know the variances for both input ranges, as seen in the dialog box in Figure 25-17.

Analysis of variance (single-factor)

This is the simplest form of analysis of variance (also known as one-way analysis of variance) and helps you determine whether two or more samples were drawn from the same populations. The dialog box for this tool is shown in Figure 25-18 The input range must contain at least two blocks of data. This test calculates the *F* statistic, as seen in the sample output in Figure 25-19.

Analysis of variance (two-factor without replication)

This performs a two-way analysis of variance, with only one sample for each group of data.

Analysis of variance (two-factor with replication)

This tool extends upon the previous one and allows more than one sample (or replication) for each group of data.

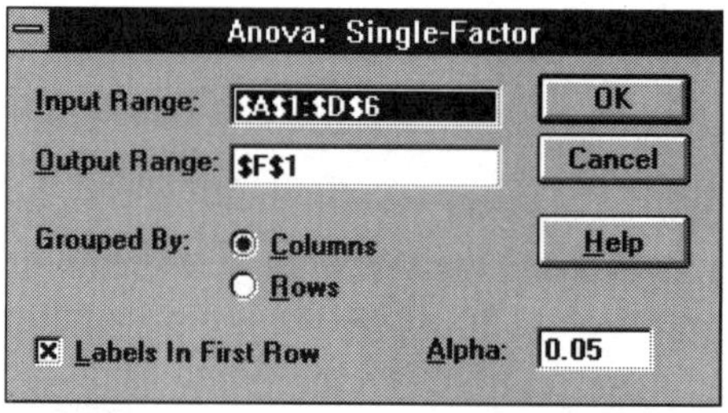

Figure 25-18: Excel provides three types of analysis of variance. This is the dialog box for one of them.

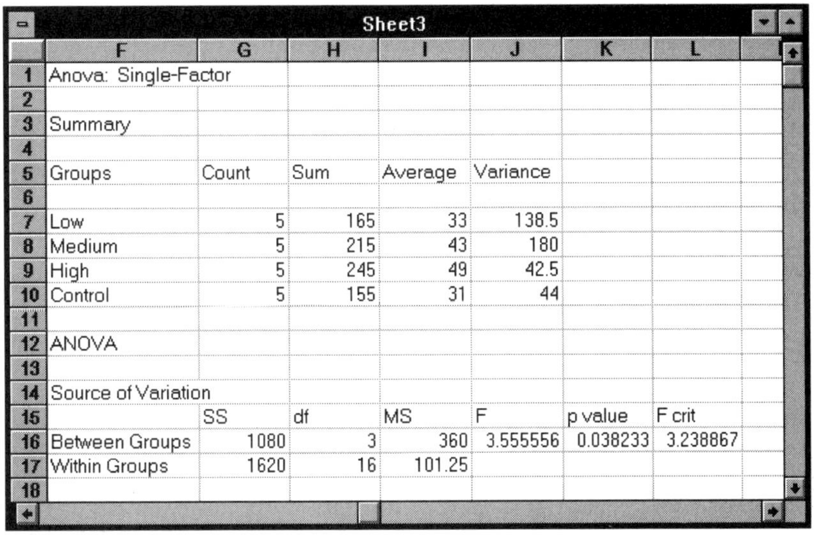

Figure 25-19:
Analysis of
variance
output.

	F	G	H	I	J	K	L
1	Anova: Single-Factor						
2							
3	Summary						
4							
5	Groups	Count	Sum	Average	Variance		
6							
7	Low	5	165	33	138.5		
8	Medium	5	215	43	180		
9	High	5	245	49	42.5		
10	Control	5	155	31	44		
11							
12	ANOVA						
13							
14	Source of Variation						
15		SS	df	MS	F	p value	F crit
16	Between Groups	1080	3	360	3.555556	0.038233	3.238867
17	Within Groups	1620	16	101.25			
18							

F-Test (two-sample for variance)

The *F*-Test is a commonly used statistical test that lets you compare two population variances. The dialog box for this tool is shown in Figure 25-20. The output for this test consists of the means and variances for each of the two samples, the value of F, the critical value of F, and the significance of F.

The engineering tool

The last category of Analysis ToolPak tools has only one entry: Fourier analysis (a tool that deals with the analysis of waveforms).

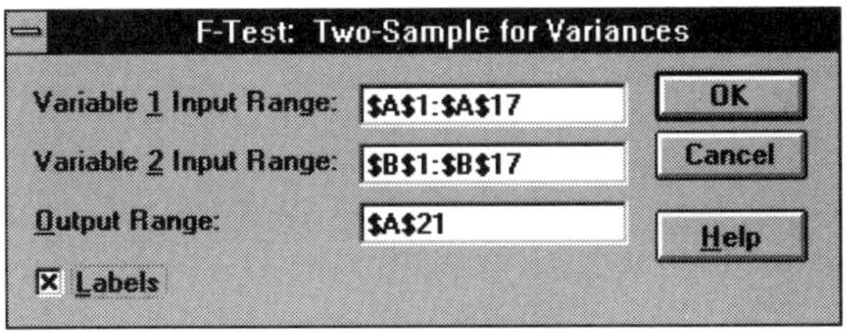

Figure 25-20:
The *F*-Test
dialog box.

F-Test: Two-Sample for Variances

Variable 1 Input Range:	$A$1:$A$17
Variable 2 Input Range:	$B$1:$B$17
Output Range:	$A$21
X Labels	

OK
Cancel
Help

Fourier analysis

This performs a "fast Fourier" transformation on a range of data. The range is limited to the following sizes: 1, 2, 4, 8, 16, 32, 64, 128, 256, 512, or 1024 data points.

This procedure accepts and generates complex numbers, which are represented as labels.

Summary

▶ The Analysis ToolPak is a series of add-ins that greatly extend the analytical powers of Excel. It includes 19 analytic procedures and nearly 100 new functions.

▶ If you didn't choose full installation when you installed Excel, the Analytical ToolPak may not be available. If this is the case, run the Excel Setup program again and select the Custom Installation option.

▶ You access the tools with the Options ⇨ Analysis Tools command.

▶ You can use the additional functions just like you would any other function. They are described completely in the on-line help system.

▶ Many of the tools are useful for general business applications, and others are for more specialized uses, such as statistical tests and Fourier analysis.

Chapter 26
Creating Macros

In this chapter . . .

▶ An introduction to macros: what they are, how they are used, and why you may or may not want to use them.

▶ The differences between the two types of macros (command macros and function macros).

▶ How macro sheets differ from normal worksheets.

▶ Step-by-step instructions for creating a command macro using the macro recorder feature, and how to enter macros directly.

▶ The different ways to execute macros.

▶ An introduction to the Excel macro language, and an overview of various macro programming concepts.

▶ Tips and techniques for debugging macros, and how to use the Macro toolbar.

▶ How to create your own custom functions for use in your worksheets.

▶ Why — and how — to document your macros.

Macros are usually considered one of the "advanced" features of Excel, since you need to have a pretty thorough understanding of Excel in order to put them to good use. Truth is, the majority of Excel users have never created a macro and probably never will. But if you want to get the most out of Excel, the macro feature has a lot to offer. To reduce the frustration level, we suggest that you become very familiar with Excel before you start pursuing macros. This chapter starts with the basics and covers all of the essential topics related to macros. Because of the depth of Excel's macro capability, we can't treat some of the more advanced topics as thoroughly as we'd like. But this chapter will provide the foundation for you to continue as far as you like.

What Is a Macro?

In its broadest sense, a macro is a "program" that automates some aspect of Excel so you can work more efficiently and with fewer errors. For example, you might create a macro to format and print your month-end sales report. Once the macro is developed and debugged, you can invoke the macro with a single command to perform many time-consuming procedures automatically.

All spreadsheets have macro capability, but Excel's macro features are among the most extensive in any spreadsheet. If you have experience with macros in other spreadsheets, you should know that Excel deals with macros much differently than most products (see the sidebar "Moving up from 1-2-3?" for more information).

In Excel, a macro consists of a series of functions that are executed upon command. These functions can either be normal worksheet functions or special macro functions. While a worksheet function typically performs a calculation, a macro function usually specifies an *action* to be performed.

Moving up from 1-2-3?

If you're moving up from 1-2-3, you'll find that Excel implements macros in a completely different way. You'll eventually discover that Excel does it right.

1-2-3's macros consist of keystrokes and commands that are played back. This is fine, but it's ultimately limiting because the macros only work under the exact user interface under which they were developed. For example, the 1-2-3 macro command /FR stands for /File Retrieve. This means that Lotus is stuck with this exact command name — if they changed it to /File Open, for example, any macros that use /FR won't work.

Excel, on the other hand, translates keystrokes and mouse movements into their command equivalents. Excel's =OPEN macro command will always work, regardless of how the user interface may change in the future. By the way, Quattro Pro offers the user a choice: You can either record macros using keystrokes or command equivalents.

If you're used to 1-2-3 macros, you'll probably find Excel's macros somewhat confusing until you get used to them. The macro commands are actually functions that evaluate to values or logical values. We authors cut our teeth on 1-2-3 macros, but now find Excel's system to be far superior and easier to work with — not to mention more powerful. Excel's macros can do wonders that 1-2-3 macros could never do. In the meantime, Excel can execute most 1-2-3 macros directly. Simply load a 1-2-3 worksheet and execute macros by pressing Ctrl plus a macro's name.

One last thing to keep in mind: Excel macros can include blank cells (which are simply ignored). So if you've relied on blanks to end your 1-2-3 macros, you'll need to change your habits.

Typical uses for macros

Here are a few examples of how you might use macros:

- **To insert a text string or formula.** If you need to enter your company name into worksheets frequently, it makes sense to create a macro to do the typing for you. (Excel's Glossary add-in can also do this.)

- **To automate a procedure that you perform frequently.** For example, you may need to prepare a month-end summary. If this task is straightforward, you can develop a macro to do it for you.

- **To avoid having to perform repetitive operations.** If you've got 50 columns of data that you need to perform some action on individually, you can record a macro while you perform the task once — and then let the macro do it the other 49 times. (But don't forget about the Edit ➪ Repeat command — which is easier if you're only using one command.)

- **To create a "custom command."** You could, for example, combine several of Excel's menu commands so they are executed with a single keystroke.

- **To create a custom tool.** You can customize Excel's toolbars with your own unique tools, which are actually macros.

- **To create a simplified "front end" for users who don't know much about Excel.** For example, you could set up a foolproof data entry template.

- **To develop a new function.** Although Excel includes a wide assortment of built-in functions, you can create your own customized functions with a macro.

- **To create complete turnkey macro-driven applications.** As you'll see, Excel macros can display custom dialog boxes and even add new commands to the menu bar.

- **To create custom add-ins for Excel.** All of the add-ins that are shipped with Excel were created with Excel macros (although most of them use external library files to help out).

Macros can be used at many levels. If you're not interested in becoming a macro guru, don't fret. Creating simple macros is actually quite easy, and they can save you a lot of time. Virtually every Excel user can benefit by learning how to create and use simple macros.

Two types of macros

Excel provides two classes of macros: command macros and function macros.

Command macros

These can be thought of as new commands that can be executed by the user or by another macro. A command macro can combine several Excel commands into one, or perform a series of operations automatically. You can execute a command macro via the <u>M</u>acro ⇨ <u>R</u>un command or by typing its Ctrl key shortcut.

Function macros

The second type of macro is a custom function that jumps into action only when necessary. Unlike command macros, function macros can be used in formulas, just like normal Excel functions. Let's say you use a lot of cube roots in your work. Excel, of course, has a built-in function for square roots, but not cube roots. Without too much effort, you can develop a macro function that returns the cube root of the value in a cell.

We'll be discussing both types of macros in this chapter.

How Excel handles macros

The following points summarize some of the key things you need to know about how Excel uses macros:

- A macro (whether it is a command macro or a function macro) consists of a series of commands, arranged in a single column.

- Each command in a macro places a single value in the cell in which it resides. Each macro command is a special macro function that returns a result.

- Macros are stored in macro sheets, not worksheets.

- The macro sheet must be open in order to run a macro. It can be hidden or minimized, however.

- Excel maintains a global macro sheet that's always available. This is a good place to store general-purpose macros that you might use with several different worksheets.

- The normal display mode of a macro sheet is to display the formulas, not the results of the formulas. This is the equivalent of selecting the Options ⇨ Display command and then selecting the Formulas option.

- Each macro must be assigned a name, and the name must be designated as a macro. This works like normal cell and range naming and is done via the Formula ⇨ Define Name command accessed from a macro sheet.

- You can execute a macro by selecting Macro ⇨ Run from the menu and then selecting the appropriate macro from the list. Or, you can assign a shortcut key to a macro so you can execute it directly from the keyboard (with the Ctrl key).

- A macro can be executed from any window, including worksheet windows and chart windows.

The remainder of this chapter provides details regarding these points. But for now, let's jump in with an example.

An Example of a Command Macro

Figure 26-1 shows a macro sheet with a short macro displayed in A1:A5. This macro, when executed, inserts a text string into the current cell, formats it as 12-point Helvetica bold, and then moves the cell pointer down one row.

 You'll benefit most from this example if you take a few minutes to enter the macro into a macro sheet. Select File ⇨ New and then choose Macro Sheet to open a blank macro sheet. Enter the formulas exactly as they appear in Figure 26-1.

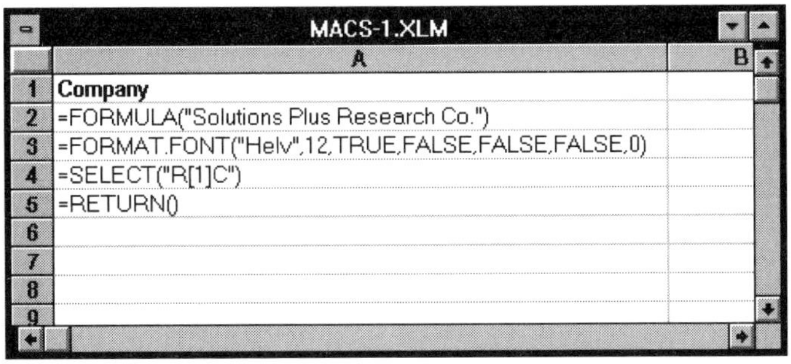

Figure 26-1: This simple macro inserts a text string, formats the cell, and moves the cell pointer down one row.

	MACS-1.XLM	
	A	B
1	Company	
2	=FORMULA("Solutions Plus Research Co.")	
3	=FORMAT.FONT("Helv",12,TRUE,FALSE,FALSE,FALSE,0)	
4	=SELECT("R[1]C")	
5	=RETURN()	
6		
7		
8		
9		

This macro consists of five cells. Note that the macro sheet is showing the formulas, not the results of the formulas (this is the default for macro sheets). Here's a rundown of what each command does:

```
Company
```

This is the first cell of the macro and holds a label for identification purposes. It's also the name of the macro.

```
=FORMULA("Solutions Plus Research Co.")
```

This macro function inserts a formula into the currently selected cell. In this case, the formula is just a simple text string.

```
=FORMAT.FONT("Helv",12,TRUE,FALSE,FALSE,FALSE,0)
```

This macro function formats the current selection according to the seven arguments enclosed in parentheses. The =FORMAT.FONT macro function is a command-equivalent

About Excel macro sheets

Excel macros must reside on an official macro sheet — they won't work if you create them on a normal worksheet. A macro sheet is stored with an xlm extension (as opposed to the xls extension for worksheets). What's the difference? A macro sheet is similar to a worksheet, with a few major differences:

■ The default view is to show formulas, rather than the values they produce. When you enter a formula, the result is not normally visible. Rather, you see the formula itself in the cell. You can display the values by selecting the Options ⇨ Display command and then choosing the Formula option.

■ The default column width is wider — which makes it handy for viewing formulas. As with a worksheet, you can widen the columns if you like. This is actually a good idea, since displayed formulas don't run over to adjacent cells.

■ When a macro sheet is the active document, the Formula ⇨ Paste Function command lists macro functions as well as worksheet functions.

■ Cells on a macro sheet are calculated only when they are run in a macro. In other words, Excel handles recalculation of macro sheets differently than worksheets.

You can do pretty much the same procedures on macro sheets as you can on worksheets. The menus are nearly identical, and you can move and resize a macro sheet window, minimize it, and hide it. You can store a macro sheet in a workbook so it's always available in the workbook for the worksheets that use it.

function. In other words, it performs the same action as the Format ⇨ Font command. The arguments correspond to various items in the Font dialog box.

```
=SELECT("R[1]C")
```

This macro function moves the cell pointer down one row.

```
=RETURN()
```

This macro function signals the end of the macro and returns control back to whatever executed the macro. This is either the user or another macro (macros can execute other macros, as we'll see).

Defining a macro name

Before you can use this macro, you need to define it as such and provide a name. The following steps show you how to do this:

Steps: Defining a macro name

Step 1. Activate the macro sheet and select the first cell of the macro (in this case, cell A1), and then issue the Formula ⇨ Define Name command. As seen in Figure 26-2, you'll get a variation on the familiar worksheet version of the Define Name dialog box.

Step 2. Give the first cell of the macro a name. You can give it any valid range name you like, but it's a good practice to place the macro name in the first cell of your macros. In this case, the macro is named *Company*.

Step 3. To define this range name as a command macro (as opposed to a function macro), select the Command option in the Macro group box.

Step 4. If you like, you can also assign a shortcut key by entering a letter in the text box next to the Key option. In this case, we assigned it to Ctrl+c. That way, when you press Ctrl+c, the macro executes (and inserts the formatted text into the current cell).

Excel distinguishes between uppercase and lowercase for macro key names. Ctrl+c is different from Ctrl+C. In the latter case, you must actually press Ctrl+Shift+c to execute the macro. If you have two macros with the same shortcut key, Excel invokes the macro on the sheet that comes first in alphabetical order.

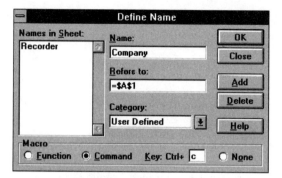

Figure 26-2: The Define Name dialog box that appears when a macro sheet is active is different from the worksheet version.

Executing a macro

Now that the macro has a name, you can activate a worksheet and invoke the macro from the worksheet. The easiest way is to type Ctrl+c. Or, you can select the Macro ➪ Run command, which pops up the dialog box shown in Figure 26-3. This displays a list of the names of the macros available in all of the open macro sheets. Note that it also shows the shortcut key to the left of the name. Select the macro named *Company* and choose OK. If everything was done properly, your worksheet should display the formatted text in the currently selected cell, and the cell pointer should be located directly below the cell (see Figure 26-4).

Macro function arguments

Even if you followed this example exactly, you may still be somewhat confused about macro functions. They certainly look daunting, with all the arguments and strange notation. Let's take a look at the arguments in a typical macro function — we'll examine the =FORMAT.FONT function. The official syntax of this function is as follows:

=FORMAT.FONT(*name_text,size_num,bold,italic,underline,strike,color,outline,shadow*)

Here's what the arguments represent:

name_text   This argument specifies the font name as a text string. For example, "Helv," or "Courier."

size_num   This argument specifies the size of the font, in points, as a value. For example, 12 for 12-point type.

bold   This is a logical argument. It's True if you want the text bold, otherwise it's False.

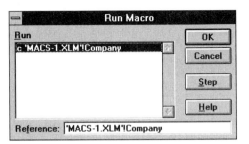

Figure 26-3: The Run Macro dialog box lets you select a macro to execute.

italic	This is a logical argument. It's True if you want the text italic, otherwise it's False.
underline	This is a logical argument. It's True if you want the text underlined, otherwise it's False.
strike	This is a logical argument. It's True if you want the text to be strike-through, otherwise it's False.
color	This argument specifies the color of the text as a number in the current palette.
outline	This argument is not necessary and has no effect if it's included. It's part of the syntax only for compatibility with the Macintosh version of Excel (which supports outlined text).
shadow	This argument is not necessary and has no effect if it's included. It's part of the syntax only for compatibility with the Macintosh version of Excel (which supports shadow text).

As we pointed out earlier, the =FORMAT.FONT macro function is an example of a command-equivalent function. It is the same as selecting the Format ⇨ Font command from the menu and then selecting certain options from the dialog box. Excel has macro commands for all of the menu commands.

Figure 26-4: The results of the macro from Figure 26-1.

	PROPOSAL.XLS					
	A	**B**	**C**	**D**	**E**	**F**
1	Solutions Plus Research Co.					
2						
3						
4						
5						
6						

Editing the macro

Now that you understand how these arguments work, you can change some of them — edit the macro. Editing a macro is exactly the same as editing cells in a worksheet, and all the same editing commands work as you would expect.

For example, change "Helv" to "Tms Rmn" or change the 12 to some other point size. You can also change the fourth argument to `True` to produce italic type. Experiment until you understand how this works.

What's all this RC business?

In the normal course of spreadsheeting, you reference cells by their column letter and row number — for example, cell D16 for the cell at the intersection of the fourth column and sixteenth row. You may not know it, but Excel gives you a choice in this matter. You can select the <u>W</u>orkspace ⇨ <u>O</u>ptions command and then choose the R1C1 option. Your column borders in your worksheets and macro will display as numbers rather than letters. Furthermore, all cell references in your formulas will use this different notation.

When you're working with macros, you'll need to understand RC (or row-column) notation because Excel uses this notation to refer to cells and ranges when you record macros. When you enter macros manually, you can use either RC notation or the normal letter-number notation.

Below are some examples showing how normal formulas (assumed to be in cell A11) would translate to RC notation:

Formulas using column letters and row numbers	Formulas using RC notation
=SUM(A1:A10)	=SUM(R[-10]C:R[-1]C)
=SUM(A1:B10)	=SUM(R[-10]C[-1]:R[-1]C)
=A1+A3+A5+A7+A9	=R[-10]C+R[-8]C+R[-6]C+R[-4]C+R[-2]C
=$A$1+$A$3+$A$5+$A$7+$A$9	=R1C1+R3C1+R5C1+R7C1+R9C1
=SUM($A$1:$A$10)	=SUM(R1C1:R10C1)

If you find RC notation confusing, you're not alone. Actually, RC notation isn't too bad when you're dealing with absolute references. But when relative references are involved, the brackets can drive you nuts.

The numbers in the brackets refer to the relative position of the reference. For example R[-5]C[-3] specifies the cell that's five rows above and three columns to the left. On the other hand, R[5]C[3] references the cell that's five rows *below* and three columns to the *right*. If the brackets are omitted, it specifies the same row or column: R[5]C means the cell five rows below in the same column.

Unfortunately, you'll have to understand this notation if you'll be working with macros. You'll get used to it soon.

Take this a step further and modify the argument in =SELECT("R[1]C"). For example, to move the cell pointer down two rows rather than one, change the argument to read "R[2]C".

Recording Macros

If you went through the trouble of entering the macro in the previous section, you've already created a macro. But simply copying a macro from a book is different than creating one from scratch. You're probably thinking that there's no way you could ever remember all these arguments — especially since Excel has nearly 400 macro functions, each of which may have several variables. Fortunately, Excel lets you *record* macros simply by making the appropriate keystrokes or mouse movements. It translates these actions into corresponding macro commands and inserts them into a macro sheet. In fact, that's how we created the previous sample macro — the whole thing took about ten seconds.

Basic steps

The easiest way to create simple macros is to record them and let Excel handle the specifics of inserting the functions and filling in the arguments.

Steps: Macro recording basics

Step 1. Normally, you should start out in the window you'll be running the macro from — typically a worksheet window. Move the cell pointer to the place where you want it to be and then start the macro recorder with the <u>M</u>acro ⇨ Re<u>c</u>ord command.

Step 2. Specify the macro sheet that will store the macro being recorded. Excel prompts you for this information with a dialog box.

Step 3. Perform the task, using keystrokes or the mouse. Don't be afraid of making mistakes. For example, if you select the wrong menu command you can choose Cancel from the dialog box. Excel won't record your mistake.

Step 4. Stop the macro recorder with the <u>M</u>acro ⇨ Stop Re<u>c</u>order command.

Step 5. Save your worksheet. This is not necessary, but it's a good idea since macros can sometimes act in ways you don't expect.

Step 6. Test the macro to see how it works.

An example

Let's now get more specific and try it out for real. The goal here is to create a macro that will serve as a new formatting "command." This command will format the left-most cell in a horizontal selection as Helvetica 14-point bold, provide a yellow background, center the contents across the entire selection and vertically in the row, insert a thick border around the selection, and make the row 28 points high. This macro might be useful for quickly formatting titles for a series of tables.

Steps: Creating a formatting macro

Step 1. Start with a new worksheet or move to an empty area of an existing worksheet.

Step 2. Enter some text (any text) into a cell (any cell).

Step 3. Select the cell that you entered the text in, along with a few cells to the right. (Remember, we want to center the cell contents over a selected horizontal range, so we're setting it up before we start recording.)

Step 4. Select the Macro ⇨ Record command to start the macro recorder.

Step 5. Excel displays the dialog box shown in Figure 26-5. It proposes a name for the macro (Record1) and a Ctrl+key shortcut (Ctrl+a). It also proposes recording the macro on a macro sheet rather than on the global macro sheet. Accept these defaults. Excel then opens a new macro sheet automatically.

Step 6. Now, simply execute all of the worksheet commands that accomplish the formatting you want. You can use the normal menus, toolbar icons, or the right mouse button shortcut menus.

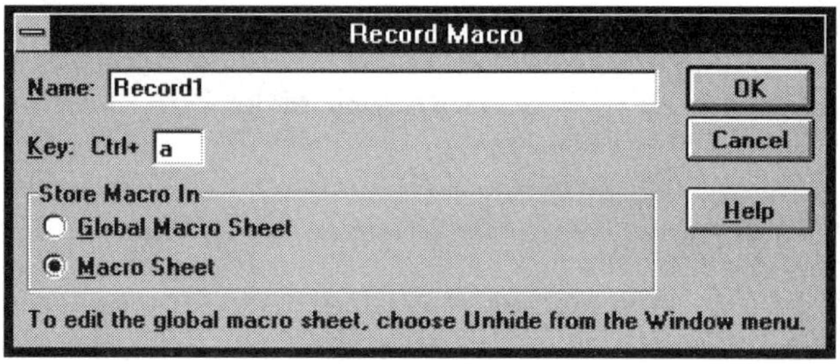

Figure 26-5: The Record Macro dialog box lets you specify a name and shortcut key before you record a macro.

```
┌─────────────────────────── Record Macro ───────────────────────────┐
│                                                                      │
│  Name: [Record1                                    ]      [  OK  ]   │
│                                                                      │
│  Key: Ctrl+ [a  ]                                        [ Cancel ]  │
│  ┌─ Store Macro In ─────────────────────────────────┐               │
│  │  ○ Global Macro Sheet                             │   [  Help  ]  │
│  │  ● Macro Sheet                                    │               │
│  └───────────────────────────────────────────────────┘              │
│  To edit the global macro sheet, choose Unhide from the Window menu. │
└──────────────────────────────────────────────────────────────────────┘
```

Step 7. When you're finished with all of the formatting, select the Macro ➪ End Recording command to turn off the recorder.

Step 8. Activate the macro worksheet to examine your work. Select the Window command and then click the `Macro1` sheet name. Your macro should look something like the one shown in Figure 26-6. The functions may be in a different order, depending on the order in which you issued your formatting commands. Notice that the first cell holds the macro name, plus the shortcut key in parentheses.

Step 9. Activate the worksheet again and test it. First enter some text in a cell and then extend the selection to include a few more columns to the right. Press Ctrl+a, and the text should take on the formats you defined.

Congratulations, you just recorded your first macro.

The Macro Record dialog box

When you select the Macro ➪ Record command, Excel displays a dialog box that gives you some options:

- **The name of the macro.** Excel always provides a default name, in the form `Record1`, `Record2`, and so on. This name is inserted in the first cell of the macro. You can enter a different name if you like — and you can always change the name later with the Formula ➪ Define Name command.

- **The shortcut key.** This is optional, but Excel always proposes a default key, starting with *a*, continuing through *z*, and then starting with uppercase *A*, and so on. You can change it to any letter you like or leave it blank. If you select an uppercase shortcut key, you must use the Shift key along with the Ctrl key to invoke the macro.

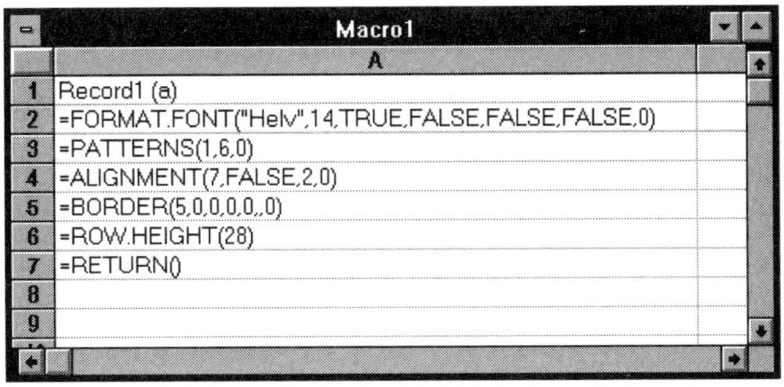

Figure 26-6: Excel records your actions and translates them into these functions.

	A
1	Record1 (a)
2	=FORMAT.FONT("Helv",14,TRUE,FALSE,FALSE,FALSE,0)
3	=PATTERNS(1,6,0)
4	=ALIGNMENT(7,FALSE,2,0)
5	=BORDER(5,0,0,0,0,0)
6	=ROW.HEIGHT(28)
7	=RETURN()
8	
9	

■ **Where to store the macro.** You have two choices here: the global macro sheet (see the next section) or a normal macro sheet. If a macro sheet is open, Excel displays its name in the dialog box and you can select it to record the macro there. If no macro sheet is open, Excel opens a blank one.

When you close the dialog box, the recording begins.

The global macro sheet

Whether you use it or not, Excel always loads a global macro sheet. Macros stored on this sheet are always available for use, with no extra effort on your part. The global macro sheet is ideal for general-purpose macros that you might want to use with all types of worksheets.

The global macro sheet is in a hidden window. If you record a macro to this sheet, you'll need to unhide the window before you can edit or view the macro. Use the <u>W</u>indow ➪ <u>U</u>nhide command for this.

The main advantage to storing macros on the global macro sheet is that you don't have to remember to load a macro sheet when you load a worksheet that uses macros. By the same token, you don't have to remember to save it — Excel handles all these details for you. Excel stores this file as global.xlm, and places it in your \xlstart directory.

If you unhide the global macro sheet, make sure you hide it before you exit Excel. Otherwise, the global macro sheet will not be hidden the next time you start Excel. Before you exit the program, Excel prompts you and asks if you want to save changes to the global macro sheet. Unless you're just experimenting and don't want to save you work, answer in the affirmative.

Specifying the cells where a macro is recorded

When you record several macros in succession, Excel normally starts each in a separate column. Every macro sheet has a range named Recorder, which is the location that will hold the next recorded command. Normally, you don't have to worry about this, but you can change this so you can start recording at a desired location in the macro sheet. This might be useful if you want to add to an existing macro by recording more commands. In such a case you could specify the exact cell in which you want the recording to start. You can change the Recorder definition in either of two ways:

■ Activate the macro sheet, select the cell where you want recording to begin, and then select the <u>M</u>acro ➪ Se<u>t</u> Recorder command.

■ Activate the macro sheet and select the For<u>m</u>ula ➪ <u>D</u>efine Name command to change the cell location for the name Recorder.

You can arrange your macros any way you like on a macro sheet — one per column, stacked in a single column, or whatever. You should at least try to be consistent, so your macros will be easier to read and modify.

Pausing macro recording

Just like a tape recording, you can pause while recording a macro. This might be useful if you discover you want to do something that shouldn't appear in the macro — such as open a file to check on something. To pause a macro, select Macro ⇨ Stop Recorder. You can then do whatever you like. To resume recording where you left off, select Macro ⇨ Start Recorder.

Even though they sound similar, Macro ⇨ Start Recorder is different than Macro ⇨ Record. Use Macro ⇨ Record when you want to start a new macro. To continue recording where you left off before, use Macro ⇨ Start Recorder.

Relative vs. absolute recording

If you're going to work with macros, it's important that you understand the concept of relative vs. absolute recording. Normally, when you record a macro, Excel stores references to the actual cells you select (that is, it performs absolute recording). For example, if you select the range A1:A10 while you're recording a macro, Excel records this as =select("R1C1:R10C1"). This means *select the cells in row 1 column 1 through row 10 column 1.* When you invoke this macro, the same cells are always selected, regardless of where the active cell is.

You may have noticed the Macro pull-down menu command has an option labeled Relative Record. When you select Macro ⇨ Relative Record, Excel changes its recording method from absolute to relative. Selecting a range of ten cells would be translated as =select("RC:R[9]C"). This means *select the current cell and nine more cells down in the same column.* In other words, a macro recorded in Relative mode starts out using the active cell as its "base" and then stores relative references to this cell. As a result, you'll get different results depending on the location of the active cell.

When Excel is recording in Relative mode, the pull-down menu changes from Macro ⇨ Relative Record to Macro ⇨ Absolute Record. Select the command to change back to Relative mode recording.

The recording mode — either absolute or relative — can make a major difference in how your macro performs. Figure 26-7 shows two macros, both designed to switch two columns by cutting and pasting columns. The macro named Relative was recorded in Relative mode, and the one named Absolute

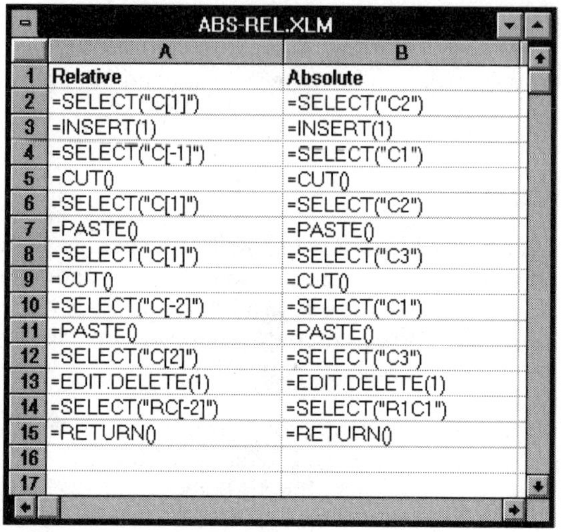

Figure 26-7: The macro in column A was recorded in Relative mode. The macro in column B was recorded in Absolute mode. They produce drastically different results.

	A	B
1	Relative	Absolute
2	=SELECT("C[1]")	=SELECT("C2")
3	=INSERT(1)	=INSERT(1)
4	=SELECT("C[-1]")	=SELECT("C1")
5	=CUT()	=CUT()
6	=SELECT("C[1]")	=SELECT("C2")
7	=PASTE()	=PASTE()
8	=SELECT("C[1]")	=SELECT("C3")
9	=CUT()	=CUT()
10	=SELECT("C[-2]")	=SELECT("C1")
11	=PASTE()	=PASTE()
12	=SELECT("C[2]")	=SELECT("C3")
13	=EDIT.DELETE(1)	=EDIT.DELETE(1)
14	=SELECT("RC[-2]")	=SELECT("R1C1")
15	=RETURN()	=RETURN()
16		
17		

ABS-REL.XLM

was recorded in Absolute mode (big surprise, eh?). The Relative macro is a lot more useful, since it switches the column that holds the cell pointer with the column to the right of it. The Absolute macro, on the other hand, always switches column A with column B, regardless of where the cell pointer is.

When recording macros, be careful when you use commands like Shift+Ctrl+right arrow or Shift+Ctrl+down arrow (that is, commands that extend the selection to the end of a block of cells). Excel doesn't record this type of command as you might expect. Rather, it records the actual cells you made in the selection (either in an absolute or relative manner, depending on the mode). When you play the macro back with a different size range, the selection may not be correct (and you may not even realize it).

Entering Macros Directly

Recording macros is appropriate for simple macros, but for more complex macros, you'll usually need to enter the macro functions manually — or at least some of them. Often, you'll be able to record part of the macro and then tweak it by adding some other functions.

Why can't you record all macros? If you think about it, the only macro functions that you can record are the command-equivalent functions and the functions that make selections. Many of the macro functions don't fall into this domain. Examples of these include functions that create loops or dialog boxes and functions that modify or create menus.

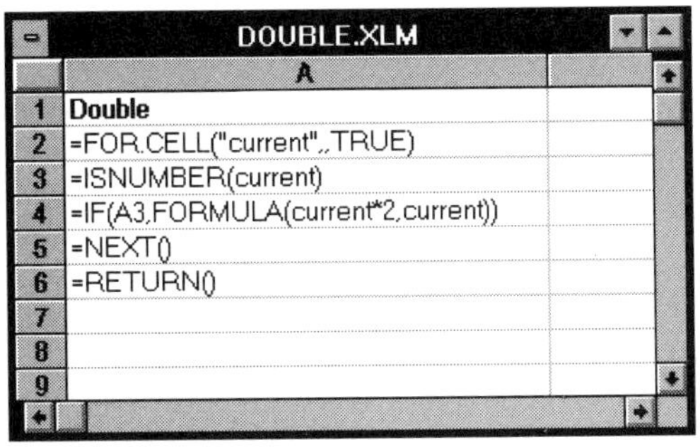

Figure 26-8: This macro contains functions that cannot be recorded via the macro recorder.

An example

Figure 26-8 shows a macro that cannot be recorded because it uses functions that are not command equivalents. This macro works with the current worksheet selection and loops through each cell, multiplying the contents by 2. But it also checks the current cell to make sure it's a number. Here's a play-by-play description:

```
Double
```

> The name of the macro.

```
=FOR.CELL("current",,TRUE)
```

> This function starts a loop. All of the functions between the =FOR.CELL function and the =NEXT function are executed once for each cell in the current selection. The name for the cell being worked on is current.

```
=ISNUMBER(current)
```

> This is a normal worksheet function. It returns True if current is a number, otherwise it returns False.

```
=IF(A3,FORMULA(current*2,current))
```

> This =IF function checks the value in the previous cell. If it's true (that is, the current cell is a number), it evaluates the =FORMULA function, which multiplies the current value by 2. If the current cell is not a formula, macro execution continues to the next cell. (By the way, this formula uses a cell reference — A3 — rather than a name. This is not really a good practice, but we did it for simplicity.)

```
=NEXT()
```

This signals the end of the loop, so macro execution jumps back up to the statement following the =FOR.CELL command — but only if there are more cells to process.

```
=RETURN()
```

The end of the macro.

To try out this macro, enter it into a macro sheet and give it a name with the Formula ⇨ Define Name command. You might want to assign it a shortcut key such as Ctrl+d. Then, select a range on your worksheet and invoke the macro. The macro goes through each cell in the selection. If the cell contains a number, it multiplies it by 2. Otherwise it skips the cell.

Be careful if you use this macro, since it will also replace formulas with their values doubled.

Pasting macro functions

Recording macros, as you've seen, is relatively painless because Excel takes care of all the details for you. Entering macro functions manually is a bit more tedious. Nevertheless, Excel comes to the rescue again with its Formula ⇨ Paste Function command.

Although we couldn't record the previous macro example, we did take advantage of the Formula ⇨ Paste Function command to help insert the =FOR.CELL function. It didn't save us a whole lot of typing, but it *did* help us out with the arguments (which we don't happen to have memorized). Furthermore, the Formula ⇨ Paste Function ensures that you spell the function name correctly.

When you issue the Formula ⇨ Paste Function command from a macro sheet, it displays the dialog box shown in Figure 26-9. (It's different if you invoke this command from a worksheet.) Notice that there are two list boxes. The box on the left shows categories of functions. When you select a category from this box, the box to the right displays the functions in that category. As you scroll through the function list, the function and its arguments are displayed in the lower-left corner. The Paste Arguments option box, if checked, pastes dummy arguments (placeholders) into the function. To insert a function into the active cell, double-click the function name (or choose OK).

Unfortunately, the Help button isn't all that helpful. Microsoft did not include help for the specific macro functions in the on-line Help program. For specific information and examples of functions, consult the *Microsoft Excel Function*

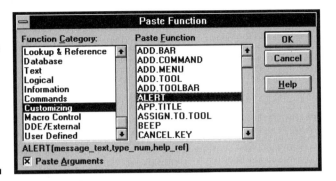

Figure 26-9: The Paste Function dialog box will insert a function plus place-holders for its arguments.

Reference guide included with your software package (or refer to Appendix B of this book for a brief description of each macro function).

Figure 26-10 shows the results of a pasted function in the Formula bar. Note that it inserts argument placeholders and automatically selects the first one for you. You must replace the placeholders with actual arguments. To do so, you can use all the normal cell-editing techniques. For example, you can double-click on an argument and then point to the location in the worksheet or macro sheet. Excel then replaces the dummy argument with the argument you pointed out. When you've specified all the arguments, press Enter to enter the function into the cell.

Combining recording with direct entry

Often, you'll be able to combine the two macro creation techniques — recording and direct entry. For example, it's usually much easier to record the command-equivalent functions since their number of arguments can be lengthy. Then, you can combine what you've recorded with other functions that you

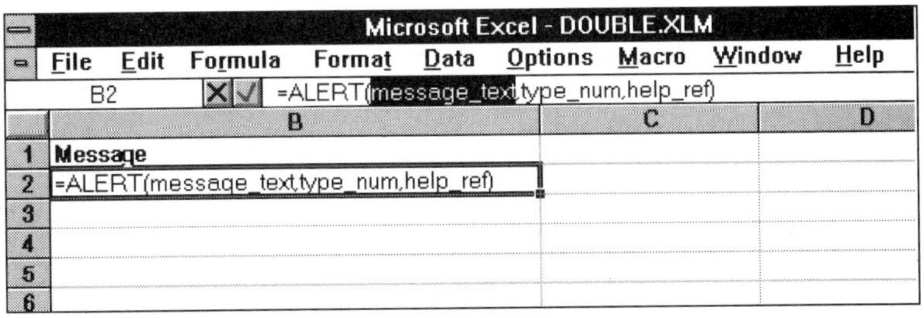

Figure 26-10: This function was pasted into a macro sheet and is waiting for the user to substitute actual arguments in place of the placeholders.

enter directly. For example, if your macro needs to do something simple like remove gridlines from the screen, rather than enter the =DISPLAY function and its nine arguments manually, take a few seconds and record it. By the way, this is a good use for the Macro ⇨ Set Recorder command because you can specify the exact location to record the command.

The best advice is to become familiar with both methods and use macro recording whenever you can. But remember that you can copy and paste recorded functions into other macros.

Excel's Macro Functions

All told, Excel provides you with nearly 400 macro functions. These can be classified into several different categories based on the type of action they perform and what they are used for. These categories are somewhat loose because some functions clearly fall into more than one category. Nevertheless, the following discussion will give you a feel for what type of macro functions are available.

The best way to learn macro functions

If you want to learn how Excel translates your actions into macro functions, here's a great way to go about it. Set up your screen so a worksheet and a macro sheet are both visible, as in the accompanying figure. Make sure the *recorder* range is visible in the macro sheet. Now, go about your normal business — and watch as your actions are recorded before your very eyes in the macro sheet. Spend some time doing this, selecting various commands and making selections, and see what happens. We guarantee you'll gain some new insights about macros.

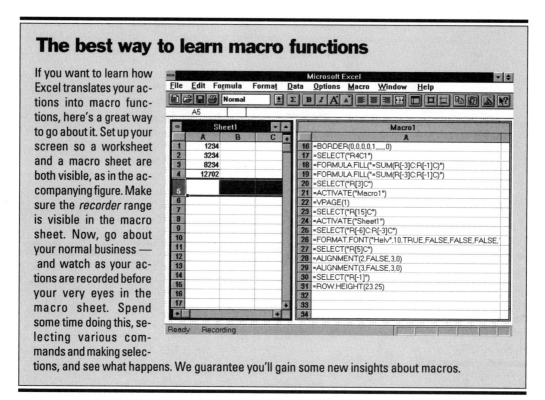

Appendix B contains a complete listing and description of all the macro functions.

Command-equivalent functions

These functions simulate selecting commands from the menu bar and comprise the bulk of the total macro functions. The arguments in these functions correspond to items in the dialog boxes that result from selecting the command from the menu.

 Command-equivalent macro functions usually have a "dialog box" version that pops up the appropriate dialog box for the user to complete. You specify this by adding a question mark after the command name, but before the arguments. For example, the following macro function:

```
=FORMAT.FONT?("Helv",12,TRUE,FALSE,FALSE,FALSE,0)
```

formats the text with the arguments supplied and then displays the Format Font dialog box for the user to make any modifications to these settings. Alternatively, you can omit the arguments to display the dialog box with no settings made — for example, =FORMAT.FONT?().

Information functions

These functions typically return information about a worksheet or the environment, and also include logical functions that return True or False. These functions are often used to determine conditions in order to direct subsequent macro execution.

Macro control functions

These functions are used to control how a macro behaves and the order in which the macro functions are calculated. For example, you can design a macro so it behaves differently depending on conditions in the worksheet (given the value of a specific cell, for instance). See the section "Macro Programming Concepts" for more details on this.

Customizing functions

This group of macro functions is for customizing the Excel environment and is often used by developers who want to produce complex applications using Excel macros. You can choose functions to display messages, solicit user input, add commands to a menu bar, create a new menu bar, create custom dialog boxes, and other things. This category also includes event-triggered functions that monitor your system for certain events such as an error, data entry, a specific key press, or a specific time of day. When the event occurs, you can specify a macro to be executed.

DDE/external functions

These functions let macros work with other applications via the Windows DDE feature. Make sure you understand DDE before you attempt to use these — and give yourself a lot of time for testing and experimenting, as this can get very complicated.

User-defined functions

This category of macro functions may or may not exist. These are the function macros that you have defined (if any). They appear in the Paste Function dialog box, just like other functions.

Macro Programming Concepts

When developing more complex macros, it helps to have some programming experience. Excel's macro language includes many basic programming constructs. Following are a few that you should be familiar with.

Branching

Normally, macros execute one cell at a time starting with the first cell and continuing down the column. You can create macros, however, that display some intelligence and execute functions based on a certain value. This normally involves one or more =IF and =GOTO functions. The =IF function can make a logical test and then send macro execution to another location with the =GOTO function. A more sophisticated type of branching involves the use of the =IF, =ELSE, and =END.IF functions. This can be conceptualized as follows:

```
=IF(condition)
[functions that execute if condition is true]
=ELSE()
[functions that execute if condition is false]
=END.IF()
```

This concept can be extended even further with Excel's =ELSE.IF function to include additional logical tests.

Subroutines

As you might expect, macros can execute other macros. This is done by treating the macro name as a function. For example, if your macro needs to execute another macro named Getinput, simply insert the following command in the appropriate spot in your macro: =GETINPUT( ). Normally, there are no arguments. You can write macros so they use arguments, however. In such a case, you would need to provide the appropriate arguments.

Looping

If you need a macro to repeat a task, you can create a loop within the macro. Excel's macro language provides for three types of loops:

- **FOR-NEXT loop:** This executes the functions between the =FOR function and the =NEXT function a specified number of times.

- **FOR.CELL-NEXT loop:** This performs a function or group of functions for every cell in a reference you specify.

- **WHILE-NEXT loop:** This lets your macro loop until a certain condition is true.

In each of these cases, a =NEXT function is paired with either a =FOR, =FOR.CELL, or =WHILE function.

Soliciting user input

Many times, a macro is designed to require input from the user. It may require a filename, a value, a text string, and so on. Excel provides several ways to accomplish this. The simplest is with the =INPUT function. This displays a simple dialog box with a message, and the user makes the entry and chooses OK. You can get fancier and develop custom dialog boxes (discussed in Chapter 31).

Other Ways to Execute Macros

So far, we've discussed two ways to invoke command macros: via the Macro ⇨ Run command or by using a shortcut key assigned to it. Besides these methods, you have several other ways to execute a macro.

Assign a macro to a tool

You can assign a command macro to a tool on the toolbar and create custom tools. Use the Options ⇨ Toolbars command and select Customize. The Custom category provides a selection of button icons to choose from. Drag one to a toolbar and Excel displays its Assign to Tool dialog box. This lets you specify an existing macro or gives you the opportunity to record one on the spot.

Assign a macro to a macro button

The Utility toolbar has a Button tool that lets you insert a button on a worksheet. This 3-D image looks like a common button, can have a label, and can be clicked with a mouse to execute a macro. When you click the Button tool, your cursor becomes a crosshair. You can then press and drag a button shape onto the worksheet. When you release the mouse button, Excel pops up its Assign To Object dialog box that lets you select an existing macro or record one (see Figure 26-11). After you specify the assignment, clicking the button in the worksheet executes the specified macro.

Assign a macro to any graphic object on the worksheet

The tools on the Drawing toolbar are used to add graphic objects directly to a worksheet. Any of these objects (including charts) can have a macro assigned to them. After adding an object (such as a circle), select it by clicking once and then select the Macro ⇨ Assign to Object command. You'll get the same dialog box used for assigning a macro to a button.

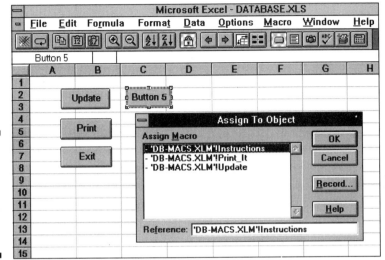

Figure 26-11: You can assign a macro to a graphic object (such as a button) placed on a worksheet.

When you assign a macro to a button or graphic object, Excel stores a link between the object and the assigned macro. This link includes the filename of the macro sheet, so if you rename the sheet outside of Excel, the link will be severed and the macro won't be located. To restore these links, use the File ⇨ Links command, with the Change option.

Assign a macro to an event

Another way to execute a macro is to assign it to an event, such as a specific keystroke, a time of day, or a worksheet recalculation. This is done using the macro "On" functions. For example, you can design a macro that uses the =ON.TIME function that monitors the system clock and runs another macro when a specific time occurs.

Execute a macro automatically

Another way to execute macros is whenever you open, close, switch to, or switch from a specific worksheet. The trick here is to assign one of four special range names in the Define Name dialog box (available from the Formula menu)

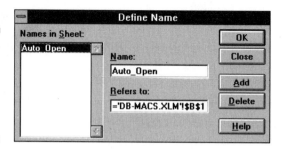

Figure 26-12: If a worksheet has a range named Auto_Open that refers to a macro sheet, that macro will execute whenever the worksheet is opened.

and provide a reference to the macro you want to execute (see Figure 26-12). Note that you define the range in the worksheet, not the macro sheet. The names are as follows:

Auto_Open	This macro executes whenever the document is opened.
Auto_Close	This macro executes whenever the document is closed.
Auto_Activate	This macro executes whenever the document window is activated (but not when the document is opened).
Auto_Deactivate	This macro executes whenever the document window is deactivated (but not when the document is closed).

You can avoid executing an Auto_Open or Auto_Close macro if you hold down Shift while you click the OK button in the File Open or File Close dialog box.

Run a macro from a macro

It should go without saying that macros can execute other macros. This is analogous to calling a subroutine from a programming language.

Place a macro on a custom menu bar

As discussed in Chapter 31, Excel lets you create new menu bars and modify existing menu bars. This makes it possible to create new commands that are actually macros.

Use a custom dialog box

Another feature of Excel is the capability to create custom dialog boxes (this is also discussed in Chapter 31). For example, you could create a dialog box that executes a specific macro, depending on how the user responds to the dialog box.

Macro Debugging

If your macros don't work properly the first time, don't despair — you've got lots of company. As you may have surmised by now, working with macros can be a tedious chore. Getting them to work properly often requires systematic testing and every other method you can think of to track down errors — a process commonly known as *debugging*.

In order to debug a macro, you have to be able to see what's going on. Consequently, if your macro uses any =ECHO(FALSE) functions (which turns off screen updating), you should remove them.

A macro that doesn't work properly is usually worse than no macro at all. As a result, you'll want to make sure your macro works as intended before you trust anything important to it. A completely bomb-proof macro is a rarity, but you can do several things to prevent errors. Macro errors fall into two categories:

- **Syntax errors:** Errors that arise because you didn't specify the arguments properly, misspelled the function name, or some similar problem.

- **Logical errors:** Errors that result from faulty thinking on your part. The macro simply isn't doing what you think it should.

If your macro isn't working properly, your first action should be to examine the offending statement carefully. Are the arguments correct? Is the function spelled properly? Refer to the *Microsoft Excel Function Reference* for examples and details on the function. Many problems are solved at this stage.

If everything looks OK, you might want to try Single-step mode (described further) in which you can execute the macro one line at a time. Often, slowing the macro down lets you see things you overlooked. If Single-step mode doesn't help, it's time to fire up Excel's Debug add-in. This add-in is discussed later in this chapter.

If you still can't figure out the problem, try simplifying the problem. Set up a test situation that uses the function that's giving you problems. Try various alternatives until you determine the cause of the problem.

Common macro problems

Besides logical errors on the part of the macro developer, we've found that most macro problems fall into these categories:

- **Nothing happens when you invoke a macro with a Ctrl+*key* shortcut.** This could mean several things: you didn't assign the macro to a key, you assigned it to a different key than you thought, or the macro sheet that holds the macro is not loaded. If the key is uppercase, invoke it with Ctrl+Shift+*key*.

- **The macro doesn't appear in the Macro Run dialog box.** This could mean either of two things: you didn't assign it a name, or the macro sheet that holds the macro is not loaded.

- **You spelled the function name wrong.** You can avoid this problem by using the Formula ➪ Pas$\underline{t}$e Function command. If you enter functions manually, it's a good idea to use lowercase. If no syntax errors are detected, Excel converts the command into uppercase. Therefore, if your macro command doesn't display in uppercase, you need to change it.

- **The wrong macro executes when you invoke a macro with a Ctrl+*key* shortcut.** You either have your shortcut keys confused, or you have two or more macros that use the same shortcut key. In the latter case, Excel executes the macro in the sheet that comes first alphabetically.

- **Values in the macro sheet are not updated properly.** You probably used a =FORMULA function rather than a =SET.VALUE function. Use =FORMULA for worksheets and =SET.VALUE for macro sheets.

- **Your function macro returns an error value.** This can be caused by several things: the wrong number of arguments, the wrong type of arguments, or an unloaded macro sheet.

- **The macro seems to be operating on the wrong cells.** This is a pretty good sign that you recorded the macro using the Absolute mode, rather than the Relative mode.

- **The macro doesn't perform properly sometimes.** This could mean a lot of things. More than likely, you haven't taken into account all possibilities and built-in error handling procedures.

- **The macro used to work fine, but not any more.** This is often caused by using cell references instead of range names in your macros, and then moving things around on your worksheet or macro sheet. Using range names ensures that the formulas always refer to the correct cells (even if they are moved).

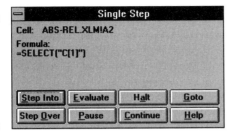

Figure 26-13:
Single-step mode lets you execute a macro in slow motion, one line at a time.

Single-step mode

If you're having problems with a macro and can't figure out the solution, Excel provides a Single-step mode that lets you step through your macro one line at a time. Normally, macros run so quickly that you can't really see what's going on. Single-step mode lets you control the execution, one line at a time.

 Single-step mode is only appropriate for command macros, not function macros.

Here's how single-stepping works:

Make sure the macro that you're working on is in a macro sheet that's loaded. Activate the document that you'll normally run the macro from and use the Macro ➪ Run command to display the Macro Run dialog box. Select the macro you want to work with and click the Step button. Excel displays the Single Step dialog box shown in Figure 26-13. This box always displays the contents of the cell that it is about to calculate or execute. As you can see, you have many options here:

Step Into   This executes the command shown in the dialog box and moves on to the next command step.

Step Over   Normally, Single-step mode goes through all commands one at a time, even those in subroutines. This button lets you skip over a subroutine that you know is working OK. The subroutine macro is executed, but not in Single-step mode.

Evaluate   This calculates the current formula one function or operation at a time and displays the result. You may have to select this button several times to completely evaluate a complex formula.

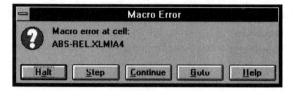

Figure 26-14: Excel lets you know when it discovers an error in your macro. This dialog box gives you the option of entering Single-step mode if you want.

Pause   This pauses the macro and removes the Single Step dialog box from the screen. In its place is a small toolbar with one tool — the Macro Resume tool. You can do anything you like while the macro is paused. When you click the Macro Resume tool, single stepping continues where you left off.

Halt   This button stops the macro.

Continue   This resumes running the macro at full speed.

Goto   This stops the macro and sends you to the displayed cell, where you can edit it as necessary. This automatically activates the macro sheet for you if it's not already activated. This is a handy way to jump directly to an incorrect function once you identify it.

Help   Displays a help window that describes your options.

If your macro has a syntax error, Excel displays a Macro Error dialog box (shown in Figure 26-14). One of your options is to click the Step button, which transfers you into Single-step mode and displays the Single Step dialog box.

Stepping through your problem macro one step at a time is often illuminating, but it can be tedious to pause and examine specific cells that you're interested in. If you still can't figure out the source of the problem, it may be time to load Excel's Debug add-in. This is useful for industrial-strength macro problems.

The Debug add-in

Microsoft provides an add-in that can help the macro developer track down problems. This add-in lets you set *tracepoints* and *breakpoints* (known collectively as *debug points*) in your macro. Here's what these terms mean:

Tracepoint   You can specify one or more locations in your macro where execution will automatically pause. These are known as tracepoints. This lets you run the "good" part of a macro

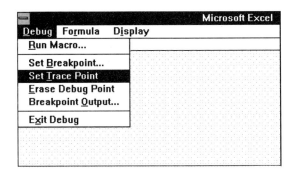

Figure 26-15: The Debug add-in displays a different menu bar, loaded with commands that are handy for working with macros.

quickly and stop when you get to your problem. At this point, you can enter Single-step mode, continue, or halt the macro.

Breakpoint   You can also set one or more breakpoints in your macro. Breakpoints are more informative than tracepoints. The macro will pause at each breakpoint and display the current values in the cells you specify in advance. You can then enter Single-step mode, continue, or halt.

As with all add-ins, the Debug add-in must be loaded before you can use it. The add-in file is located in your \library directory and is named debug.xla. Use the File ⇨ Open command to load the add-in.

The Debug add-in only works for command macros, not function macros.

After you load the Debug add-in, you'll have a new command on your menu: Macro ⇨ Debug. When you select this command, you are in Debug mode and Excel displays a new menu bar (see Figure 26-15). This menu has commands that are relevant only to working with macros. The menu option of most interest is the Debug command. When you pull this menu down, you have the following options:

Run Macro   This displays the familiar Macro Run dialog box that lets you start executing a macro.

Set Breakpoint   This option lets you set breakpoints in your macro. A small dialog box enables you to provide a message that will be displayed when the macro reaches the breakpoint.

Set Trace Point   This lets you set tracepoints in your macro.

Erase Debug Point This removes selected breakpoints or tracepoints that you set. Select the cell before you issue this command.

Breakpoint Output   This command brings up a dialog box that lets you specify one or more cells you would like to monitor. Enter the cell or range and choose Add to add it to the list. You can also remove variables from the list with the Delete button.

Exit Debug   This exits Debug mode and returns the normal menu system. You can reenter Debug mode by selecting Macro ➪ Debug again.

The best way to understand how this works is to use it. Start with a simple macro and set some tracepoints and breakpoints. Specify some cells to monitor and watch what happens. Once you understand how the Debug add-in works you can use it on more complex macros.

The Macro Toolbar _____

Excel provides a special toolbar that contains seven icons to help you work with macros (see Figure 26-16). Most of these icons are intended to be used while a macro sheet is active. The icons perform as follows:

 Creates a new macro sheet.

 Displays the Paste Function dialog box.

 Displays the Paste Name dialog box.

 Starts executing the macro at the active cell in the macro sheet.

 Steps through the selected macro, beginning at the active cell.

 Starts the macro recorder.

 Stops the macro recorder.

If you're working with macros, don't overlook the shortcuts available on this toolbar.

Figure 26-16: The Macro
toolbar contains shortcuts
for working with macros.

Function Macros

Up to this point, we've dealt exclusively with command macros — macros that
you can execute directly. Now it's time to cover the other class of Excel macros,
function macros.

Although most people find Excel's selection of worksheet functions more than
adequate, users with more specialized needs may be left wanting more. Microsoft recognizes this and gives Excel users the power to create custom
functions. Creating custom functions can make your worksheet easier to edit
and read. In many cases you can eliminate the need for a complex formula and
substitute a custom function in its place. In other cases, you can perform
operations with custom functions that could not be done using normal worksheet formulas.

This terminology can be confusing. A *function macro* is a macro that creates a
new function for use in worksheets. A *macro function* is a command that's used
in a macro.

About function macros

All function macros you create need two macro functions: =RESULT( ) and
=ARGUMENT( ).

=RESULT(*type_num*)

This function specifies the type of data a custom function returns. The options
for the *type_num* argument are:

1	Number
2	Text
4	Logical
8	Reference
16	Error
64	Array

These strange code numbers enable you to add them together for more than one possible result type. For example, if you specify 65 (1 + 64), the result can be either a number or an array.

=ARGUMENT(name_text,data_type_num)

This function describes the arguments you'll be using. The function macro must contain one ARGUMENT function for each argument it uses. The arguments for this function are:

name_text   This is the name of the argument or of the cells containing the argument.

data_type_num   This number determines what type of values the function will accept for the argument. It uses the same code number listed for the RESULT function.

How these functions are used will become clearer as we go through an example.

 As you might expect, using function macros slows things down a bit compared to using formulas. But unless you use many function macros, the slow-down is hardly noticeable.

Obviously, the macro sheet that holds the custom function macros you use must be open, or the formulas will return an error value. One way to make sure that custom functions are always available to you is to store them on your global macro sheet. Also, keep in mind that if you distribute a worksheet that uses custom functions to someone else, you must also provide the macro sheet that holds the functions.

Function macro examples

We'll demonstrate this with a few examples. You can get as complex as you like with this feature — but we'll start out simple. The first function macro we'll develop is called FIRSTNAME. This function extracts the first name from a label entered as last name, a comma and space, and then first name. For example, if a cell contained the label "Smith, Julia," the FIRSTNAME function should return "Julia." The function macro that can do the job is shown in Figure 26-17 and described as follows:

FIRSTNAME

The name of the function.

Figure 26-17: This macro provides you with a new function that extracts the first name from a specially formatted text string.

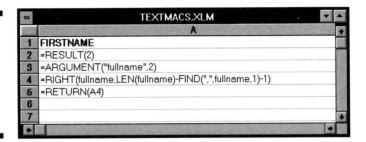

	A
	TEXTMACS.XLM
1	FIRSTNAME
2	=RESULT(2)
3	=ARGUMENT("fullname",2)
4	=RIGHT(fullname,LEN(fullname)-FIND(",",fullname,1)-1)
5	=RETURN(A4)
6	
7	

`=RESULT(2)`

This function specifies that the result is text (2 = text).

`=ARGUMENT("fullname",2)`

This function specifies that the argument is called `"fullname"` and it should be text.

`=RIGHT(fullname,LEN(fullname)-FIND(",",fullname,1)-1)`

This nested worksheet function does the work. It searches for the position of the comma and subtracts it from the length of the string. It then uses this as the argument for the RIGHT function. The formula returns the result.

`=RETURN(A4)`

This last function ends the macro and returns the result in cell A4.

After you enter this macro into a macro sheet, you must define it as a function macro. Click on the first cell, select the Formula ⇨ Define Name command, and complete the dialog box as usual. The only difference is that you must choose the Function option at the bottom of the dialog box. If you don't, Excel won't recognize this as a function macro.

You can also assign your custom function to a category (the default category is User Defined). This is useful since custom functions also appear in the Paste Function dialog box. If you create a group of new functions, you can even create your own category — just type the category name into the Category text box.

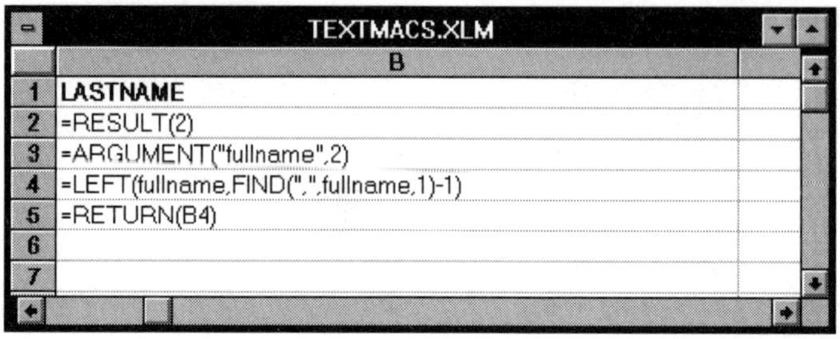

Figure 26-18:
This function
macro extracts
the last name
from a specially
formatted text
string.

```
TEXTMACS.XLM
                        B
1  LASTNAME
2  =RESULT(2)
3  =ARGUMENT("fullname",2)
4  =LEFT(fullname,FIND(",",fullname,1)-1)
5  =RETURN(B4)
6
7
```

To use a custom function in a worksheet, simply enter it as you would any
other worksheet function (including use of the Formula ⇨ Pas̲te Function
command). An important difference, however, is that you must precede the
function name with the macro sheet name, followed by an exclamation point.

If cell A1 contained the string "Roosevelt, Teddy" you could enter the following
into cell B1 to extract the first name: =textfunc.xlm!firstname(A1). This
assumes that the =FIRSTNAME function macro is stored on the textfunc.xlm
macro sheet.

The second example is similar to the first — it simply returns the last name
from a text string of the format described earlier. This macro function is shown
in Figure 26-18.

The third example is a bit more complex. This function, shown in Figure 26-19,
returns the number of words in a text string. Unlike the previous function
macro examples, this procedure could not be done using a worksheet formula.
This macro also demonstrates the use of macro variables. We use word_ct and
cleaned in the macro and store their values below the actual macro. These
variables are used by some of the functions in the macro. As with all function
macros, we use the =RESULT and =ARGUMENT functions to specify the type of
result and argument.

The macro works by counting the number of space characters in a string. The
False argument in the =VOLATILE function tells Excel not to recalculate the
macro formulas every time a calculation occurs on the worksheet. If this function were omitted, using this function would result in unnecessary calculations.

The first =IF function checks to see if the cell referred to in the argument is
empty. If so, the macro returns 0 and stops. The macro uses the =SET.VALUE
function to initialize the word_ct variable to 1. We start out with 1, rather than
0, to account for the fact that the last word will not have a space after it. Before
the string is processed by the macro, we use the =TRIM worksheet function to
strip away any leading spaces and trailing spaces and convert embedded
multiple spaces to one space. The "cleaned up" string is stored in cleaned, and
the macro actually operates on this variable rather than the original string. The

	C	D
1		**WORDS**
2		=RESULT(1)
3		=ARGUMENT("input_text",2)
4		=VOLATILE(FALSE)
5		=IF(input_text="",RETURN(0))
6		=SET.VALUE(word_ct,1)
7		=SET.VALUE(cleaned,TRIM(input_text))
8		=FOR("counter",1,LEN(cleaned))
9		=IF(MID(cleaned,counter,1)=" ",SET.VALUE(word_ct,word_ct+1))
10		=NEXT()
11		=RETURN(word_ct)
12	word_ct	3
13	cleaned	worksheet functions only.
14		

Figure 26-19: This function macro returns the number of words in a text string.

=FOR function sets up a loop so the next function is evaluated once for every character in the string. The function that begins with =IF simply increments `word_ct` whenever the current character is a blank. The =RETURN function returns the final value of `word_ct`.

 In general, you should use the =SET.VALUE function to assign values on a macro sheet and the =FORMULA function to assign values on a worksheet. Otherwise, the values in a macro sheet may not display up-to-date values due to the way Excel performs its calculations.

Creating your own add-in functions

If you can create your own function macros, you can also create your own add-in functions. The advantage to saving custom functions as add-ins is that you don't have to precede the function name with the filename and an exclamation point. Rather than enter something like =filefunc.xlm!firstname(C14), you can simply enter firstname(C14). Obviously, this makes your formulas easier to read and edit.

To save a macro sheet as an add-in, select the File ➪ Save As command and then access the

Save File as Type pull-down box and select Add-in. Excel saves the file with the name you specify, and adds an xla extension. Now, as long as the add-in is loaded, you can use your custom functions as if they were built-in functions.

To load an add-in, use the normal File ➪ Open command. Or, you can use the Options ➪ Add-ins command to set it up so your add-in is loaded automatically whenever you run Excel. If you ever want to edit an add-in file, use the File ➪ Open command and hold down Shift when you click OK.

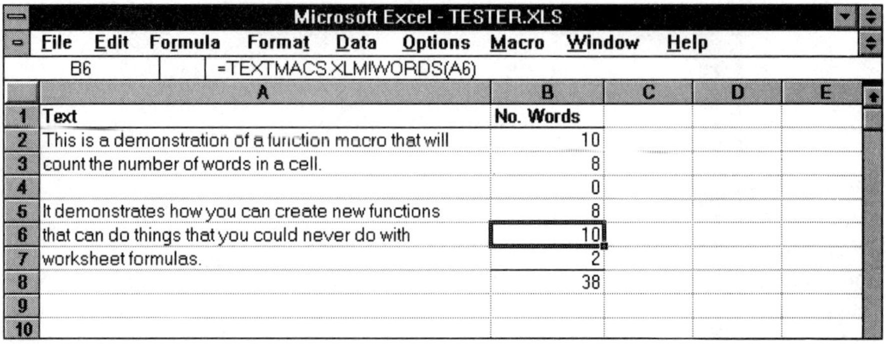

Figure 26-20:
The user-
defined
=WORDS
function in
action.

Figure 26-20 shows this function in use in a worksheet. Note that the function name is preceded by the filename. See the sidebar, "Creating your own add-in functions," for details on how you can get around this requirement.

Tips on defining custom functions

With a bit of practice, you'll find that creating simple macro functions is easy, and you'll be able to advance to more complicated functions. Here are a few things to keep in mind:

■ You can't use the macro record feature to develop function macros.

■ You can't use Excel's Debug add-in (described previously in this chapter) to debug function macros.

■ If the function isn't recognized in your worksheet, make sure that you specified it as a function macro in the Define Name dialog box.

■ Remember that the macro sheet that contains the function macro definition must be open in order for the custom functions to be used in worksheets.

■ Don't forget to include the filename and an exclamation point before the function name. If you use the Formula ⇨ Paste Function command, this is taken care of automatically.

■ If the custom function returns #NA, make sure you used the proper number of arguments.

■ If the custom function returns #VAL, one or more of the arguments is probably of the wrong type.

■ If your custom functions are of general use, you should keep them on your global macro sheet so they are always available.

■ If you don't like the idea of having to precede each custom function with a filename, consider defining your custom functions as add-in functions.

Documenting Macros

If you plan to use a macro beyond the current work session, it's a good idea to document your work. While you are developing a macro, your thought processes are undoubtedly crystal clear and every function is perfectly obvious to you. But come back in a week or two and it may seem like Greek. To avoid this pitfall, it's worth the time to document the macro to remind yourself (or whoever might need to modify the macro) what it's all about. You have two ways to do this:

■ Devote an adjacent macro sheet column to hold your explanatory comments.

■ Use cell notes to store your comments (use the Formula ➪ Note command). Cells with a note attached have a small red dot displayed in the upper-right corner. If you double-click a cell with a note, Excel displays a dialog box that lets you read or modify the note.

Now What?

This chapter has provided you with a fundamental overview of Excel's macro capability. At the very least, you should be able to appreciate the depth of this feature. If macro development appeals to you, the next steps are yours. We suggest starting simply, with short and simple macros. You can gradually build on your knowledge and before you know it things will start to click.

Experiment with small macros or macro fragments and combine them into larger, more complex macros when you're sure they work properly. Learning how to use the debugging tools will save you much time in the long run. If developing user-oriented applications sounds interesting, check out Chapter 31.

Summary

▶ A macro is a collection of functions that are designed to automate some aspect of working in Excel.

▶ Macros can be used at many different levels — from simple uses such as automatically typing a label, to complex macro-driven applications that may not even resemble a spreadsheet.

▶ Excel's macros fall into two categories: command macros and function macros.

▶ Macros are stored on macro sheets, not worksheets, and each macro must be named and designated as either a command macro or a function macro. Optionally, you can assign a shortcut key to execute the macro.

▶ The easiest way to create a simple macro is to use Excel's macro recorder. You can also enter macro functions directly (which is the only option in some cases). In the latter case, the Formula ⇨ Paste Function command can help out significantly.

▶ You execute macros with the Macro ⇨ Run command (or press its Ctrl key shortcut).

▶ Excel has a wide assortment of macro functions that perform actions and return values. You can use worksheet functions on a macro sheet, but you can't use macro functions on a worksheet.

▶ Macros can be written as programs, incorporating concepts such as branching, looping, and subroutine calls.

▶ Excel provides several tools to help you debug macros, including a special Debug add-in.

▶ The macro toolbar provides some shortcuts for working with macros.

▶ You can create your own worksheet functions using Excel macros.

▶ It's a good idea to document your macros in case you need to come back to them later. You can use an adjacent column or cell notes for this.

Chapter 27
Spreadsheet What-If Analysis

In this chapter . . .

▶ Why what-if analysis is a key spreadsheet concept.

▶ When you might want to perform what-if analyses.

▶ How to automate your what-if analysis using data tables.

▶ How to use Excel's What If add-in.

▶ How Excel's Scenario Manager can further simplify the process.

▶ How to decide which what-if technique is best for a particular situation.

One feature that every spreadsheet product has in common is the capability to develop dynamic formulas for performing calculations on cells. What's nice about spreadsheet formulas is that they can refer to cells and don't have to use actual values. As a result, if you change the value in a referenced cell, the formulas recalculate to display the correct results. When you change values in cells in a systematic manner and observe the effects on specific cells that contain formulas, you're performing what-if analysis — which just happens to be the topic of this chapter. Excel provides some great tools to help you in your what-if adventures.

What-If Analysis

In its most basic form, what-if analysis simply involves changing the value in one or more cells and observing the effects on other dependent cells. The dependent cells can be either in the same worksheet or in other worksheets. Consider the simple worksheet model in Figure 27-1. This model uses three input cells (named Loan_Amount, Interest_Rate, and Term) to calculate a fixed-rate mortgage loan payment amount. In addition, formulas calculate the total payments over the life of the loan and the amount of interest paid over the life of the loan. The formulas calculated in column B are displayed in column C.

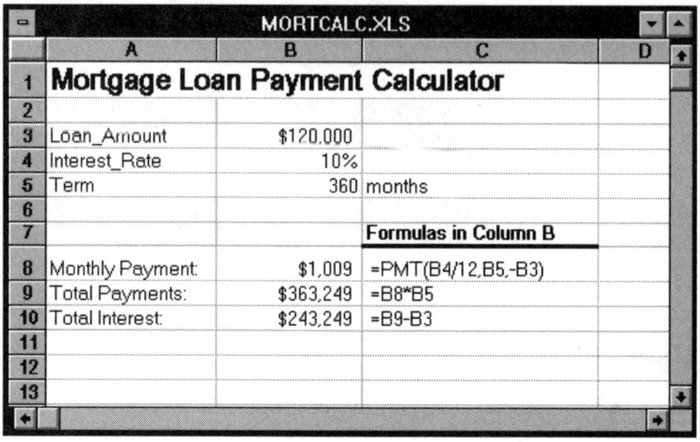

Figure 27-1: This worksheet model uses three input cells and provides a simple example of what-if analysis.

It should be obvious that when we change any of the three input cells the results change. In other words you can easily answer questions such as:

What if the interest rate were 10.5 percent?

What if the term were 15 years and the rate were 11 percent?

What if I bought a smaller house with a lower loan amount?

You can get answers to these questions quickly by plugging in different values in the cells in range B3:B5 and watching cells B8, B9, and B10 (the dependent

Keep it flexible

The mortgage calculation example, simple as it was, demonstrated an important point about spreadsheet design. You should always set up your worksheet so you have maximum flexibility to make changes. Perhaps the most fundamental rule of spreadsheet design is:

Never hard-code values in a formula. Rather, store the values in separate cells and use cell references in the formula.

The term "hard-code" refers to using actual values, or constants, in a formula. In the mort-

gage loan example, all of the arguments for the PMT function were references to cells, not values. For example, we *could* have used the value 360 for the third argument of the PMT function. Rather, we used a reference to a cell that contained this value. That way, we can easily change it without having to edit the formula. It may not seem like such a big deal when there's only one formula involved, but just think if this value were hard-coded into several hundred formulas scattered throughout a worksheet.

cells) change. When you do so, you're performing a what-if analysis. You can vary one cell at a time, two cells at a time, or all three input cells at a time.

As you might expect, Excel can handle much more sophisticated models involving thousands of dependent formulas. The remainder of this chapter gets into this topic in more depth. We'll demonstrate how you can do the following:

- Use the What If add-in macro (provided with Excel) to automatically display the results of different value substitutions.

- Automate the process of changing input cells by creating data tables.

- Use the Scenario Manager add-in to help you manage different sets of input cell values.

Excel's What If Add-In

As we've seen, one way to perform what-if analysis is to simply plug in values and observe the effect on dependent formulas. Microsoft includes an add-in file (`whatif.xla`) that can "semi-automate" this type of what-if analysis. The add-in file should be located in the `\library` directory off your `\excel` directory. Use the File ⇨ Open command to load this add-in.

If you use this add-in frequently, you might want it to be loaded automatically every time you start Excel. Use the Add-In Manager to specify this (see Chapter 20 for details).

The What If add-in consists of macros that use your worksheet, plus another worksheet that holds the different values of the variables you are investigating. Refer back to the mortgage loan worksheet presented at the beginning of this chapter (Figure 27-1). We'll use this to demonstrate the What If add-in. We'll use different values of the variables, as follows:

Loan_Amount	Interest_Rate	Term
120,000	10.0%	180
130,000	10.5%	360
150,000	11.0%	
160,000	11.5%	
175,000		

Simple arithmetic reveals 40 different combinations of these values. The What If add-in simply automates the process of plugging in these values. It cycles

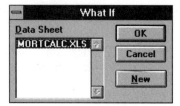

Figure 27-2: The first of a long series of dialog boxes generated by the Fo̲rmula ⇨ What I̲f command.

through all possible combinations and displays the worksheet's calculations. The add-in requires that these values be in a separate data sheet, laid out in a specific format.

OK, let's run through the example. Make sure you have the What If add-in loaded into memory. To begin, activate the worksheet and select Fo̲rmula ⇨ What I̲f. You'll see the What If dialog box, shown in Figure 27-2.

If your Fo̲rmula menu doesn't show the What I̲f command, the What If add-in is not loaded.

This dialog box wants to know which worksheet file holds the values of the variables. It displays a list of all open worksheets to choose from. It also presents a button labeled New, for creating a new worksheet. Choosing this button brings up the What If Variable dialog box, shown in Figure 27-3.

The What If Variable dialog box asks for the first variable reference. Enter B3, or Loan_Amount (the name for cell B3) and choose OK. Next it asks for the first value of the first variable. Enter 120000 and choose OK. Yet another box asks you for the second value of variable #1. Enter 130000 and choose OK. Continue until you've entered all five values of the Loan_Amount variable. Then choose Done.

Next, you'll have to repeat this process for the second variable: first enter the reference (cell B4, or Interest_Rate) and then provide the four values. Finally, do the same thing for cell B5 and provide the two values for Term.

Figure 27-3: This dialog box is used to enter the reference for a variable used in the what-if analysis.

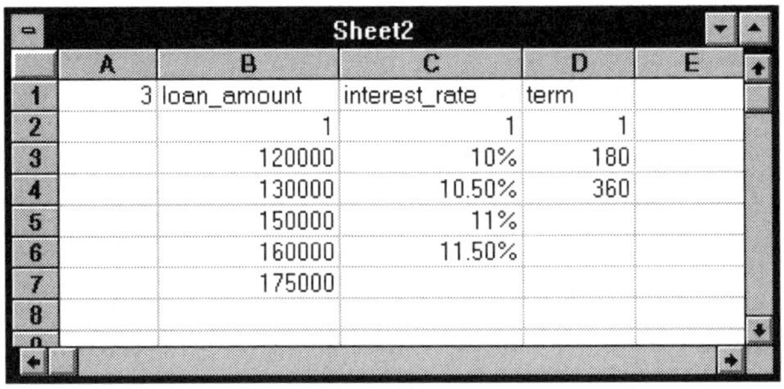

	A	B	C	D	E
1	3	loan_amount	interest_rate	term	
2		1	1	1	
3		120000	10%	180	
4		130000	10.50%	360	
5		150000	11%		
6		160000	11.50%		
7		175000			
8					

Figure 27-4: The series of dialog boxes results in this new worksheet.

When you've done this, choose Done. You should now have a new worksheet that looks like the one shown in Figure 27-4. Excel created this data sheet based on your entries in all of the dialog boxes.

The upper-left cell holds the number of variables — in this case, three. Each subsequent column holds the variable reference in the first row, an "index" number in the second row, and the values that you provided listed below. The index number is used by Excel to keep track of the current value.

To use the feature, move the cell pointer to cell B3. Press Ctrl+t to substitute the first value for Loan_Amount. Continue to press Ctrl+t to cycle through all of the values. Move to another input cell and press Ctrl+t to cycle through those values. To cycle through all of the possible combinations of values, press Ctrl+Shift+t. Note that this add-in doesn't create any tables for you — it just lets you observe the effects of changing the variables.

Although you can change the values used in the data sheet, you cannot add more variables. Furthermore, you cannot bypass the tedious series of dialog boxes and create your own data sheet. These faults seriously limit the usefulness of the add-in.

Automating What-If Analysis with Data Tables

Now we're ready for a slightly more complex example. Figure 27-5 shows a production model worksheet that calculates the total profit for a company that manufactures three products. Making each product requires a different number of production hours and resources, and each product is sold at a different price. Since the unit costs of production hours and resources are known, the formulas are set up to calculate the profit for each product and the total profit.

		PROD-MOD.XLS						
	A	B	C	D	E	F	G	H
1	Production Model							
2	Hourly_cost	30						
3	Resource_cost	57						
4								
5		Hrs per Unit	Res'ces per Unit	Cost to Produce	Sales Price	Unit Profit	Units Produced	Total Profit
6	Product A	12	6	702	925	223	12	2,676
7	Product B	14	9	933	1,200	267	12	3,204
8	Product C	20	12	1,284	1,600	316	12	3,792
9	TOTAL							9,672
10								
11								

Figure 27-5: A production model worksheet for use in the examples throughout this chapter.

 This spreadsheet model is used in the examples throughout this entire chapter. You'll benefit most if you take a few minutes to create the model on your system so you can follow along.

Here are the formulas used in the model:

=(B6*$B$2)+(C6*$B$3) in cell D6, copied to the two cells below.

=E6-D6 in cell F6, copied to the two cells below.

=G6*F6 in cell H6, copied to the two cells below.

=SUM(H6:H8) in cell H9.

All of the other cells contain values. If you change the Hourly_cost (cell B3) or Resource_cost (cell B4) cells, the worksheet recalculates so you can see the effects of these changes. The production manager, for example, might ask a question such as "What would be the impact on profit if our unit resource cost increases to $60?" In fact, this manager might be interested in looking at several different values of Resource_cost. He could, of course, plug in the values and write down the effect on the bottom-line profit. Or, he could take advantage of Excel's data table feature.

The Data ⇨ Table command lets you vary either one or two input cells and create a table of results. Actually, Excel provides two types of data tables:

1-Input Table This lets you vary one cell and create a table of the results on any number of other cells.

2-Input Table This lets you vary two different cells and create a two-dimensional table of how the changes affect another cell.

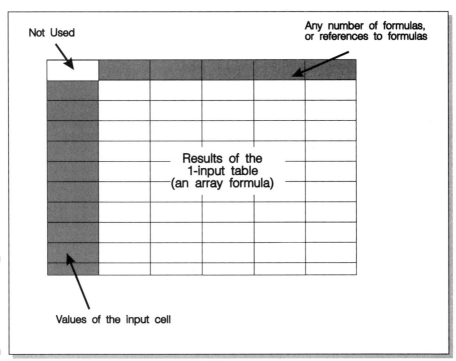

Not Used

Any number of formulas,
or references to formulas

Results of the
1-input table
(an array formula)

Values of the input cell

Figure 27-6:
A diagram
of how a
1-input table
is set up.

We'll demonstrate each of these data tables in the following sections, using the example production model worksheet.

If all of this seems too complicated for you, feel free to jump ahead to the section called "The Scenario Manager," which discusses a simpler approach to obtaining the same results.

1-input tables

For this example, we want to create a table that shows how different levels of Resource_cost will affect the profit. The table will show the profit for each of the three products, plus the total profit when the Resource_cost is $55, $56, $57, $58, $59, and $60.

Figure 27-6 is a diagram of how a 1-input table is set up. Such a table can reside anywhere in your worksheet. The first column of the table holds the values of the input variable. The first row holds references to the cells that you want to monitor. Excel calculates the values resulting from each level of the input cell and places them under each formula reference.

Figure 27-7:
The Table
dialog box.

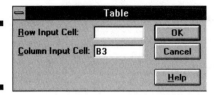

The first step is to enter the values of the input variable. We'll enter these
values in B12:B17. Next, we'll insert references to the cells that we want to look
at. In this case, we want to see how changing the Resource_cost cell affects
the profit for Product A, Product B, Product C, and the total profit. Insert the
following formulas into the worksheet.

    Cell C11:   =H6
    Cell D11:   =H7
    Cell E11:   =H8
    Cell F11:   =H9

Next, select the entire table area — the range B11:F17. We're now ready to issue
the Data ⇨ Table command, which brings up the Table dialog box, shown in
Figure 27-7. We need to specify the worksheet cell that we are using as the input
value. Since the input cell is located in a column rather than a row, we'll place
this cell reference in the text box called Column Input Cell. Enter B3 into this
box (or click in the box and then point to cell B3 in the worksheet). Choose OK,
and the table fills with the values.

A 1-input table can be arranged vertically (as we did here) or horizontally. If the
values of the input cell are placed in a row, you would enter the input cell
reference in the text box labeled Row Input Cell.

You'll note that the third row of this table is the same value that is currently in
cell B3 in the worksheet. As you would expect, the results in this row match
those that are displayed in the worksheet.

If you examine the cells that were entered as a result of this command, you'll
notice that Excel filled in formulas — more specifically, array formulas (see
Figure 27-8). As we discussed in Chapter 22, an array formula is a single formula
that produces multicell results. This means that the table you produced is not
static, it's dynamic. You can change the cell references in the first row, or plug
in different Resource_cost values in the first column, and the table updates
automatically. You can use any number of columns for this command —
including only one, if you want.

You might want to create a chart from the data in the data table to graphically
depict the result of changing a variable.

	A	B	C	D	E	F	G	H
	PROD-MOD.XLS							
1	Production Model							
2	Hourly_cost	30						
3	Resource_cost	57						
4								
5		Hrs per Unit	Res'ces per Unit	Cost to Produce	Sales Price	Unit Profit	Units Produced	Total Profit
6	Product A	12	6	702	925	223	12	2,676
7	Product B	14	9	933	1,200	267	12	3,204
8	Product C	20	12	1,284	1,600	316	12	3,792
9	TOTAL							9,672
10								
11			2,676	3,204	3,792	9,672		
12		55	2,820	3,420	4,080	10,320		
13		56	2,748	3,312	3,936	9,996		
14		57	2,676	3,204	3,792	9,672		
15		58	2,604	3,096	3,648	9,348		
16		59	2,532	2,988	3,504	9,024		
17		60	2,460	2,880	3,360	8,700		

Figure 27-8:
The results of the Data ⇨ Table command are stored in an array formula.

2-input tables

Now we'll take this one step further and vary *two* input cells. The setup up for this process is diagrammed in Figure 27-9. Although it looks similar to a 1-input table, there's one critical difference: a 2-input table can show the results on only one formula at a time. With a 1-input table, you can place any number of formulas or references to formulas across the top row of the table. In a 2-input table, this top row holds the values for the second input cell.

We'll continue with our product model example, but this time we'll look at different values for Resource_cost and Hourly_cost.

First, we'll enter the values of the first input variable (Resource_cost). We'll enter these values in B12:B17. Next, we'll enter some different values for the second input variable (Hourly_cost) in C11:G11. Since the table can only produce the result for one dependent cell, we'll choose the total profit cell, H9. The reference for this formula goes in the upper-left cell in the table range, which is cell B11. Next, select the entire table (range B11:G17) and select the Data ⇨ Table command. The row input cell is B2 and the column input cell is B3. You can enter these directly, or click in the appropriate text box and point to the cells in the worksheet. Choose OK to have Excel produce the table.

The result of this command is the table shown in Figure 27-10. Again, Excel creates an array formula that produces the desired results. As a check, examine

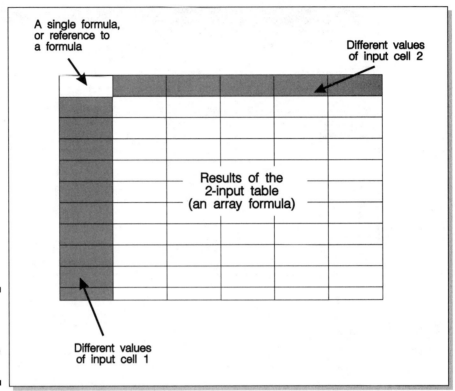

A single formula, or reference to a formula

Different values of input cell 2

Results of the 2-input table (an array formula)

Figure 27-9: A diagram of how a 2-input table is set up.

Different values of input cell 1

Figure 27-10: The results of the Data ⇨ Table command with two input variables.

	PROD-MOD.XLS						
	A	B	C	D	E	F	G	H

1 Production Model

	A	B	C	D	E	F	G	H
1	Production Model							
2	Hourly_cost	30						
3	Resource_cost	57						
4								
5		Hrs per Unit	Res'ces per Unit	Cost to Produce	Sales Price	Unit Profit	Units Produced	Total Profit
6	Product A	12	6	702	925	223	12	2,676
7	Product B	14	9	933	1,200	267	12	3,204
8	Product C	20	12	1,284	1,600	316	12	3,792
9	TOTAL							9,672
10								
11		9,672	30	31	32	33	34	
12		55	10320	9768	9216	8664	8112	
13		57	9672	9120	8568	8016	7464	
14		58	9348	8796	8244	7692	7140	
15		59	9024	8472	7920	7368	6816	
16		60	8700	8148	7596	7044	6492	
17		34	17124	16572	16020	15468	14916	

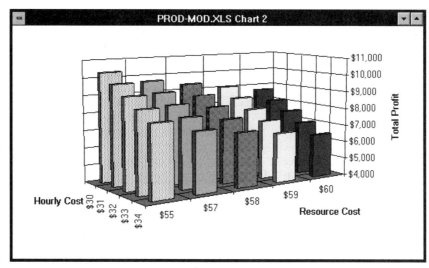

Figure 27-11:
A 2-input data
table is a
perfect
candidate for
a 3-D chart.

the value in the table for Resource_cost of 57 and Hourly_cost of 30 (these
are the values in the worksheet). The value in the table should be equal to the
value shown in cell H9.

Since Excel uses a formula to compute the values in the table, you can change
any of the values in the top row or first column to see what effect different
values would have on the total profit. By the same token, you could insert a
different formula reference into cell B11.

You might want to create a 3-D chart using the table data to graphically depict
the results of changing two variables. An example of such a chart for the 2-input
production model table is shown in Figure 27-11.

The Scenario Manager

It's easy to see the limitations of the What If add-in, and even data tables have a
few limitations:

- You can vary only one or two input cells at a time.

- It's not all that intuitive to set up a data table.

- A 2-input table shows the results on only one formula.

- More often than not, you're probably only interested in a few select combinations — not an entire table showing all possible combinations of two
input cells.

Apparently the designers of Excel also realized these limitations and included a new feature in version 4 — the Scenario Manager add-in. The Scenario Manager add-in makes it easy to automate your what-ifs. You can store different sets of input values for any number of variables and give a name to each set. You can then select a set of values by name, and Excel displays the worksheet using those values. You can also generate a summary report that shows the effect of various combinations of values on any number of result cells.

For example, your sales forecast for the year could depend on a number of factors. Consequently, you could define three scenarios: best case, worst case, and most-likely case. You can then switch to any of these scenarios simply by selecting from a list. Excel substitutes the appropriate input values in your worksheet.

We'll demonstrate the use of the Scenario Manager using the production model worksheet we've been using all along. Before that, however, we have to make sure you have access to the Scenario Manager add-in.

Loading the Scenario Manager add-in

When you select Formula from Excel's menu bar, you may or may not see a menu command labeled Scenario Manager. If you do, all is fine and you can skip on to the next section. If this command is not on your menu, you'll have to run Excel's Setup program to add it.

Using the Scenario Manager

When you select the Formula ⇨ Scenario Manager command for the first time after running Excel, it takes a few extra seconds for Excel to load the add-in file into memory. You'll soon see the Scenario Manager dialog box, shown in Figure 27-12.

The instructions in the dialog box tell you that there are no scenarios defined — not too surprising, since we're just starting out. It also tells you to select the changing cells. The changing cells are the input cells that take on different values in different scenarios. In our production model worksheet, the changing cells are cells B2 and B3.

We recommend that you give names to the changing cells and all of the cells that you want to examine. As you'll see, Excel uses these names in the dialog boxes and in the reports that it generates.

To specify the changing cells, simply select them in your worksheet (you can move the dialog box out of the way, if necessary). If the changing cells aren't

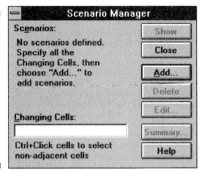

Figure 27-12: The Scenario Manager dialog box lets you assign names to different sets of assumptions.

contiguous, make a multiple selection by holding down the Ctrl key and selecting them with the mouse. Alternatively, you can simply type in the cell references or cell names, separated by commas (you're limited to nine changing cells). Once you've identified the changing cells, you can define your scenarios. For this example, we'll use three different scenarios:

Best case   Hourly_cost of 30 and Resource_cost of 54

Worst case   Hourly_cost of 35 and Resource_cost of 62

Most likely   Hourly_cost of 30 and Resource_cost of 57

The hourly costs are not going to go down, but there's a chance the resource cost could drop to $54. This represents the best case scenario. At worst, the hourly cost could increase to $35, and the resource cost could rise as high as $62. The manager's best estimate, however, is that the hourly cost will remain at $30 and the resource cost at $57.

To enter these scenarios into the Scenario Manager, choose the Add button. The Add Scenario dialog box that appears lets you enter a name for the scenario you're defining and also provide values for the changing cells that you identified (see Figure 27-13). This dialog box displays a row for each changing cell you specify. When you've entered this information, choose Add to define the next scenario. Fill in the blanks with the values for the worst case and

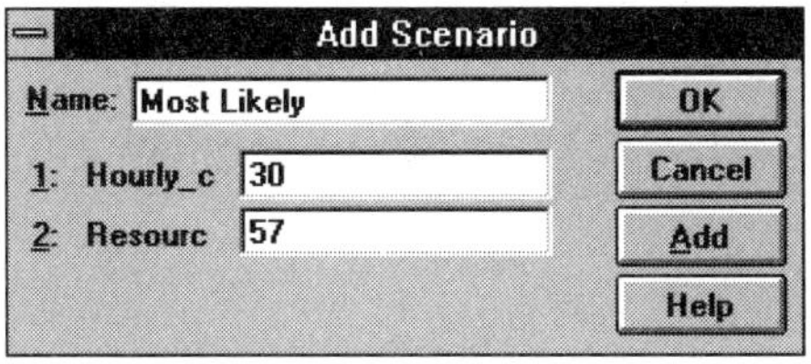

Figure 27-13: The Add Scenario dialog box is where you assign a name to the specific values for your changing cells.

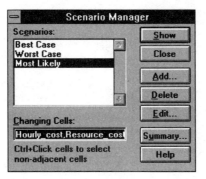

Figure 27-14: The Scenario Manager dialog box, with scenario names displayed. Double-clicking a name displays the worksheet under the selected scenario.

choose Add to enter the information for the most likely scenario. When you've entered all three scenarios, choose OK.

You'll return to the Scenario Manager dialog box, but now it displays the scenario names you entered, as shown in Figure 27-14. Select one of the scenarios and then choose Show. The worksheet will be updated using the Hourly_cost and Resource_cost values for the scenario you selected.

Double-clicking on a scenario name has the same effect as selecting the scenario and choosing Show.

At this point, the value of the Scenario Manager should be clear. The feature is even more useful when you have a larger number of input values (there is no limit to the number of changing cells you can define).

Now it's time to take the Scenario Manager through its final feat — generating a summary table. Choose Summary from the Scenario Manager dialog box. Excel displays the Scenario Summary dialog box, shown in Figure 27-15. This dialog box displays the changing cells (using cell names, if you named the cells) and provides a text box for you to enter the cells that are affected by changing the input cells. In this example, we want to see how the individual product profit

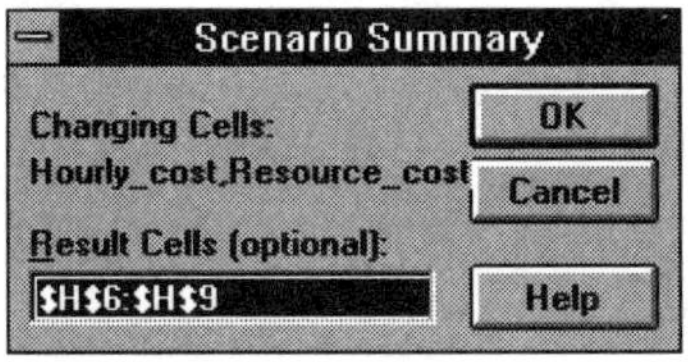

Figure 27-15: This dialog box lets you specify the dependent formulas that you want to appear in the summary table.

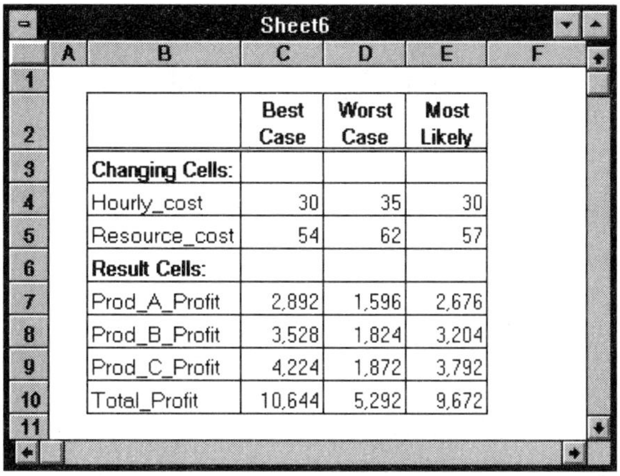

	Best Case	Worst Case	Most Likely
Changing Cells:			
Hourly_cost	30	35	30
Resource_cost	54	62	57
Result Cells:			
Prod_A_Profit	2,892	1,596	2,676
Prod_B_Profit	3,528	1,824	3,204
Prod_C_Profit	4,224	1,872	3,792
Total_Profit	10,644	5,292	9,672

Figure 27-16: The summary table produced by the Scenario Manager.

varies, plus the total profit. These cells are in the range H6:H9. As always, you can enter the cell references, type the cell names, or use the mouse to select the cells in the worksheet. When you've done so, choose OK.

Excel opens a blank worksheet to store the summary table, which is shown in Figure 27-16. Notice that it takes care of all the formatting — boldface text and borders. It displays your scenario names across the top row, lists the changing cells and the values for each scenario, and displays the result cells for each scenario.

You'll notice that this table is made up of values — not formulas. So if you make any changes in your worksheet, this table does not update automatically — you'll have to generate it again. You can, of course, copy or move this table to your original worksheet if you like. If you gave names to the changing cells and result cells, the table uses these names — otherwise, it simply lists the cell references.

The Edit button in the Scenario Manager dialog box does just what you'd think: it lets you edit a scenario. Select the scenario you want to change, choose Edit, and make your changes. Choose Add when you're finished.

There's no real limit to the number of changing cells and the number of result cells you can specify. Obviously, the time required to generate the table will be a function of the number of scenarios and the complexity of the worksheet, since it has to recalculate the worksheet for each scenario.

Which Technique?

If you've waded through this chapter, you should know that there are essentially four ways to perform what-if analyses:

- Simply plug in values for input variables and observe the effects.

- Use the What If add-in to do the plugging in for you.

- Create a data table to display the results of varying one or two input variables.

- Use the Scenario Manager add-in to name different scenarios and produce attractive summary tables.

The technique you use will, of course, depend on what you're trying to accomplish. For informal what-if analysis, plugging in values often tells you what you want to know. The What If add-in can automate this to some extent, but the up-front set-up time is probably not worth the effort.

Creating data tables is useful if you need to present several different alternatives. The Scenario Manager, however, makes data tables almost obsolete. Data tables still have a clear advantage, though: they use formulas, making it easy to change the input values once the table is generated. The Scenario Manager can generate nice tables, but it requires that you change the input values manually to create a new table.

Summary

▶ One of the key advantages of any spreadsheet is that it lets you perform what-if analysis by changing input values and observing the effects on dependent formulas.

▶ It's important that you set up your worksheet properly. In particular, you should avoid "hard coding" values in formulas. Rather, set up an assumptions area and refer to these values in your formulas.

▶ Excel's Data ⇨ Table command lets you create dynamic what-if tables.

▶ A 1-input data table shows the effects of varying a single input cell. The table displays the results for any number of dependent formulas.

▶ A 2-input data table lets you vary two input cells. The table displays the results of all combinations of these two variables on a single dependent formula.

▶ Excel provides an add-in called What If that lets you specify values for variables and then automatically cycles through them, displaying the results in your worksheet.

▶ Excel's Scenario Manager add-in provides an alternative to data tables and lets you assign names to sets of assumptions. It can also create a summary table of the results.

Chapter 28
Goal Seeking and Solver

In this chapter . . .

▶ What goal seeking is, and when you would use it.

▶ How Solver extends the concept of goal seeking.

▶ Some real-life examples of using Solver.

In the previous chapter, you saw how you can take advantage of the normal spreadsheet formula recalculation by changing input cells to observe the results on other dependent cells. This chapter looks at the process from the opposite perspective — finding the value of one or more input cells that will produce a desired result.

What Is Goal Seeking?

A typical what-if question posed daily in offices throughout the country is: "What will the total profit be if sales increase by 20 percent?" If your sales projection worksheet is set up properly, you can simply change the value in one cell to see what happens to the profit cell. Goal seeking takes the opposite approach. If you know what a formula result *should* be, Excel can tell you what values of one or more input cells are required to produce that result. In other words, you can ask a question such as, "What sales increase is needed to produce a profit of $1.2 million?" Excel provides two tools that are relevant here:

■ The Formula ⇨ Goal Seek command, which determines the value required in a single input cell to produce a desired result in a dependent cell.

■ The Formula ⇨ Solver command, which determines values required in multiple input cells that will produce a desired result. Moreover, you can specify certain constraints to the problem — giving you a significant problem-solving ability. (If the Solver command isn't available to you under the Formula menu, we'll fix that in a moment.)

Single-Cell Goal Seeking

Single-cell goal seeking is actually a rather simple concept. If you don't yet understand what this is all about, an example should clear things up.

 Single-cell goal seeking is sometimes referred to as *backsolving*.

Goal-seeking: An example

Figure 28-1 shows a worksheet that's designed to compute a monthly mortgage payment based on the loan amount, the interest rate, and the term. This might seem familiar to you, since it's a variation of the same example that kicked off the previous chapter on what-if analysis. This time, however, we're taking the opposite approach. Rather than supply different input cell values to look at the computed payment amount, we're going to supply the desired payment amount and let Excel determine the loan amount.

A house-hunter knows she can afford to pay only $1,200 per month in mortgage payments. She also knows that the bank will issue a fixed rate mortgage loan for 11.0 percent, based on an 80 percent loan-to-value (the loan amount will be 80 percent of the value of purchase price). The question is, "What's the maximum purchase price she can handle?" Here's how to do it:

Note that the worksheet is set up with formulas, shown in Column C. Select Formula ⇨ Goal Seek from the worksheet menu. Excel responds with the dialog box shown in Figure 28-2. Completing this dialog box is like forming a sentence. We want to set cell B8 to 1200 by changing cell B3. Enter this information into the dialog box either by typing the cell references or by clicking in the appropriate text box and pointing with the mouse. Choose OK to start the goal-seeking process.

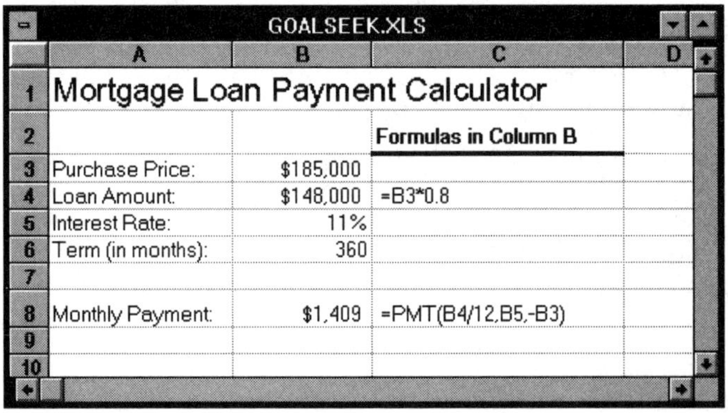

Figure 28-1: This simple worksheet computes a monthly mortgage payment and is a good demonstration of goal seeking.

	A	B	C	D
	GOALSEEK.XLS			
1	Mortgage Loan Payment Calculator			
2			Formulas in Column B	
3	Purchase Price:	$185,000		
4	Loan Amount:	$148,000	=B3*0.8	
5	Interest Rate:	11%		
6	Term (in months):	360		
7				
8	Monthly Payment:	$1,409	=PMT(B4/12,B5,-B3)	
9				
10				

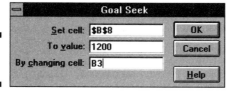

Figure 28-2: The Goal
Seek dialog box.

In about a second or so, Excel announces that it found the solution and displays
the Goal Seek Status box. This tells you what the target value was and what
Excel came up with. In this case, Excel found an exact value. The worksheet
now displays the found value in cell B3. As a result of this value, the monthly
payment amount is, in fact, $1,200. At this point, you have two options:

■ Choose OK. This replaces your original value with the found value.

■ Choose Cancel. This restores your worksheet to its form before you issued
the Formula ⇨ Goal Seek command.

If you accidentally choose OK and find that your original value was replaced by
the value Excel found, select Edit ⇨ Undo to reverse the effects of the goal
seeking.

It should be obvious that Excel can't always find a value that produces the
result you're looking for. As the song goes, you can't always get what you want.
In such a case, the Goal Seek Status box informs you of that fact.

Goal seeking through graphs

Excel provides another way to perform goal seeking — by manipulating a graph.
Look at the example in Figure 28-3. This is a sales projection for a start-up company. The CFO knows from experience that companies in this industry can
grow exponentially according to a formula like this:

$$y*(b^x)$$

where y is a constant equal to the first year's sales, b is a growth coefficient, and
x is a variable relating to time. The company knows that sales during the first
year will be $159,000, and they want to increase the company's sales to $10
million by the year 2002. The financial modelers need to know the growth
coefficient that will meet this goal. The worksheet has an embedded chart that
plots the annual sales and is set up as follows:

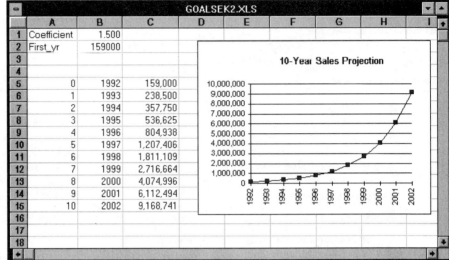

Figure 28-3:
This sales
projection
predicts
exponential
growth,
based on
the growth
coefficient
in cell B1.

Cell B1 is named `Coefficient` and cell B2 is named `First_yr`. Cell C6 contains the formula, `+first_yr*(coefficient^A6)`, and the formula is copied down through Cell C16. The initial guess for the coefficient is 1.50. As you can see, this is too low — it results in $9.168 million for the year 2002. Although we can use the Formula ⇨ Goal Seek command to arrive at the exact coefficient, we're going to demonstrate another way.

Maximize the embedded chart in its own window by double-clicking the chart and then clicking the maximize button, if necessary. In the chart window, hold down the Ctrl key and then click on the last data point — it turns into a black square. Now, drag the point upwards and observe the vertical axis on the left. You'll see a small indicator move up (you can also watch the value change in the Formula bar). When the indicator is exactly at the $10 million level, release the mouse button.

Excel responds with the usual Goal Seek dialog box, shown in Figure 28-4. You'll notice that it has filled in two of the boxes for you. It just needs to know which cell to use for the input cell. Specify cell B1 or enter `Coefficient` into the box. Excel will calculate the value of `Coefficient` needed to produce the result you pointed out on the chart. If you want to keep that number — which, by the way, is 1.51307441445218 — choose OK. Excel replaces the old coefficient with its new coefficient, and the chart updates automatically. You can probably appreciate the fact that it would take quite a while to arrive at this number by plugging in successive approximations.

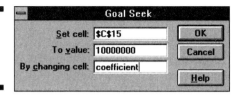

Figure 28-4: The Goal Seek dialog box appears when you directly manipulate a point on a chart that contains a formula.

You won't want to use this graphical method all the time, since the normal Formula ⇨ Goal Seek command is more efficient. But it does demonstrate another way to approach problems, for those who are more visually oriented.

As you might expect, goal seeking can get much more impressive when it's used with complex worksheets that have many dependent cells. In any event, it sure beats trial and error.

Goal-Seeking Tips

■ Excel's Formula ⇨ Goal Seek command can find the value for only one input cell. If you want to change more than one variable at a time, use Solver (which happens to be the next topic on the agenda).

■ If Excel reports that it could not find a solution (and you're pretty sure there is one), try changing the current value of the adjustable cell to a value closer to the solution and then reissue the command.

■ Another reason Excel may not be able to find a solution is if the formula does not depend on the specified adjustable cell.

■ Excel returns only one answer in the adjustable cell. There will be times, however, when multiple values of the adjustable cell produce the same desired result. For example =A1^2 returns 9 if cell A1 contains either –3 or +3.

■ Excel, like all computer programs, has limited precision. For example, for the purpose of goal seeking Excel considers 9.000022929 to be equal to 9.0. Unfortunately, there is no way to specify the level of precision you need.

Beyond Goal Seeking: Solver _____

Excel's goal-seeking feature is a useful tool, but it clearly has its limitations. For example, it can solve for only one adjustable cell, and it returns only a single solution. Excel's powerful Solver tool extends this concept in the following ways:

- It lets you specify multiple adjustable cells.

- It lets you specify constraints on the values that the adjustable cells can have.

- You can generate a solution that will maximize or minimize a particular worksheet cell.

- You can generate multiple solutions to a problem.

 If you've used Solver in Excel 3, you'll find that this feature is greatly improved in version 4. It's typically three to four times faster and can now handle integer programming problems. In addition, it's fully integrated with the Scenario Manager (see Chapter 27), so you can save a solution as a named scenario.

Using Solver for appropriate problems

Solver certainly isn't for everyone. In fact, most Excel users will have no use for this procedure. Problems that are appropriate for Solver fall into a relatively narrow range. They typically involve situations that meet the following criteria:

- There is a *target cell* that depends on other cells and formulas. Typically, you want to maximize or minimize this target cell or set it equal to some value.

- The target cell depends on a group of cells called *changing cells* that can be adjusted such that it affects the target cell.

- You must adhere to certain limitations or *constraints*.

Once your worksheet is set up appropriately, you can call on Solver to adjust the changing cells and produce the desired result in your target cell — and meet all the constraints you defined.

Accessing Solver

If you didn't choose the full installation option when you installed Excel, Solver may not be available to you. Here's how to check. Select Formula from the menu bar. If Solver appears on the pull-down command list, you're in good

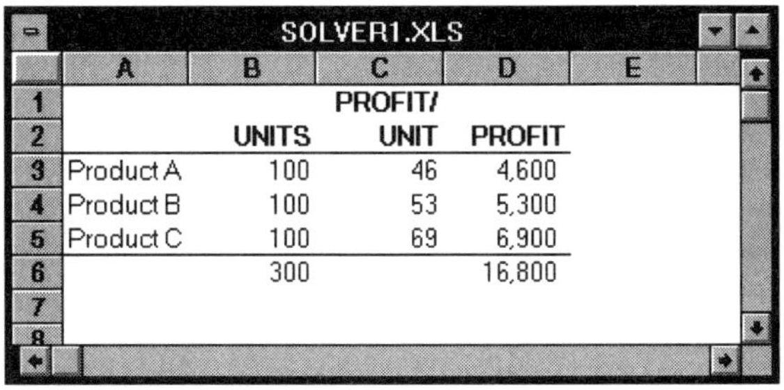

Figure 28-5: We use this worksheet to provide an introductory demonstration of Solver.

	UNITS	PROFIT/ UNIT	PROFIT
Product A	100	46	4,600
Product B	100	53	5,300
Product C	100	69	6,900
	300		16,800

shape. Otherwise, you'll need to run the Excel Setup program again. When you do so, select the Custom Installation option and select the Solver option (you can leave all the other options unchecked). Unlike the original installation, this only takes a few minutes. When you restart Excel, the Formula ⇨ Solver command should be at your disposal.

Starting with a simple example for Solver

Before we get into the details, we'll walk through a simple example to demonstrate some of Solver's features. Figure 28-5 shows a worksheet that's set up to calculate total profit to be made by producing different amounts of three products. Each product generates a different amount of profit for the company. The question we'll pose to Solver is, "What is the optimal mix of products that will maximize the profit?"

It doesn't take an MBA to realize that the greatest profit comes from Product C, so the logical solution is to produce only Product C. If things were this simple, we wouldn't need tools like Solver. As in most situations, this company has some constraints that it must adhere to:

- The company must produce at least 50 units of Product A to fill an existing order.

- The company also needs to produce at least 40 units of Product B to fill an anticipated order.

- The market for Product C is relatively limited, so they want to produce no more than 40 units of this product.

- The production capacity is 300 total units per day.

These four constraints make the problem a bit more realistic and slightly more challenging. This is a perfect problem for Solver.

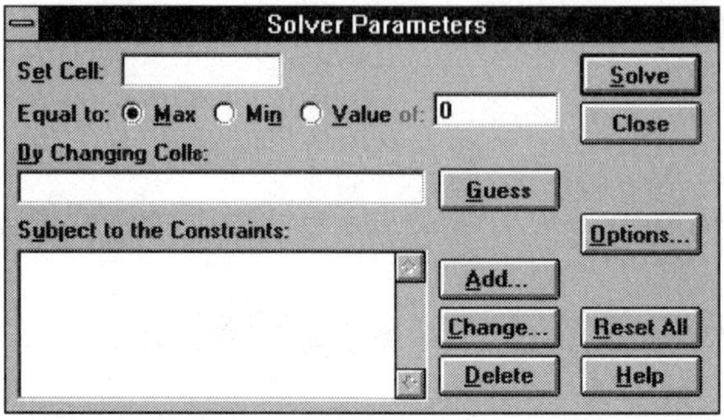

Solver Parameters

Se_t Cell: [   ]

Equal to: ⦿ _Max ○ Mi_n ○ _V_alue of: [0]

_B_y Changing Cells:

[   ] [_G_uess]

Su_b_ject to the Constraints:

[   ] [_A_dd...]

[_C_hange...] [_R_eset All]

[_D_elete] [_H_elp]

[_S_olve]

[Close]

[_O_ptions...]

Figure 28-6: The Solver Parameters dialog box.

We suggest that you set up this worksheet and follow along to get some hands-on experience with Solver. Cell D3 contains the formula =B3*C3, which is copied to the two cells below. Cell B6 contains =SUM(B3:B5), and cell D6 contains =SUM(D3:D5). The other cells contain values.

To start Solver, select Fo_r_mula ⇨ Sol_v_er. Excel displays the Solver Parameters dialog box, as shown in Figure 28-6. We want to maximize profit in cell D6, so we enter that cell reference into the Set Cell box and choose Max as the option. The model is set up so we can manipulate the quantities for each product — in the range B3:B5. These are known as the *changing cells*. Enter this range into the box labeled By Changing Cells.

The next step is to tell Solver about the constraints. The box labeled Subject to the Constraints is where we list the constraints. To add the first constraint, choose Add. This displays the Add Constraint dialog box, shown in Figure 28-7. The constraints we'll enter are:

    B3>=50

    B4>=40

    B5<=40

    B6=300

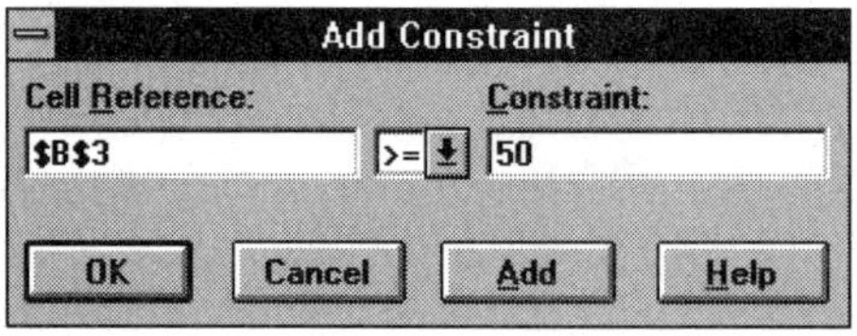

Figure 28-7: You add your problem's constraints one at a time in this dialog box.

Add Constraint

Cell _R_eference: Constraint:

[$B$3]   [>=] ⬍ [50]

[OK] [Cancel] [Add] [Help]

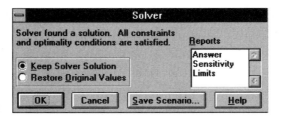

Figure 28-8: Solver displays this dialog box when it finds a solution.

To enter a constraint, specify the cell in the Cell Reference box, pull down the comparison list to specify a type of comparison, and then enter a value or cell reference in the Constraint box. To add the constraint to the list, choose Add. Enter the next constraint and choose Add again. Do this until you've specified all four constraints and then choose OK to return to the Solver Parameters dialog box, which now displays the constraints you specified. For every problem, Solver needs to know three pieces of information:

■ The cell that you want to maximize, minimize, or set equal to some value

■ The changing cells — cells that Solver can manipulate

■ The constraints

With the information in place, it's time to let Solver do its thing. Choose Solve and watch what happens. Solver runs through some options, which you can see flash by on-screen, and soon announces it has found a solution, displaying the Solver dialog box shown in Figure 28-8. At this point, you have some options:

■ Keep the values that Solver found.

■ Restore the original values.

■ Create any or all of three reports that describe what Solver did. Hold down the Shift key to select multiple reports from this list.

■ Choose Scenario to save the solution as a scenario so it can be used by the Scenario Manager add-in (see Chapter 27).

If you specify any report options, Excel creates each nicely formatted report on a new worksheet, with an appropriate name. Figure 28-9 shows an Answer report. Note that in the Constraints section of the report all of the constraints except one are "binding." This means the constraint was satisfied at its limit — with no more room to change.

This simple example illustrates what Solver can do, though you probably could have solved it just as quickly manually. That, of course, won't always be the case.

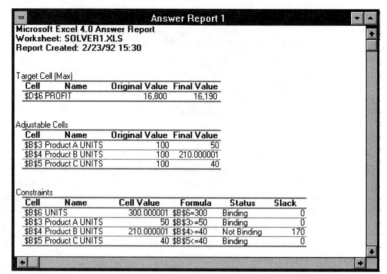

Figure 28-9: This is one of three reports that Solver can produce upon request.

Running Solver

Before we get into some more complex examples, let's discuss the Solver Parameter dialog box — one of the more feature-packed dialog boxes in Excel. Through this dialog box you control many aspects of the solution process, as well as load and save model specifications in a worksheet range.

When you choose Options from the Solver Parameters dialog box (see Figure 28-6) the Solver Options dialog box appears, as shown in Figure 28-10. Here's a description of its options:

Max Time	You can specify the maximum amount of time (in seconds) that you want Solver to spend on a problem.
Iterations	Enter the maximum number of trial solutions you want Solver to perform.
Precision	This specifies how close the Cell Reference and Constraint formulas must be to satisfy a constraint.
Tolerance	This is the maximum percentage of error allowed for integer solutions (only relevant if there is an integer constraint).
Assume Linear Model	This can speed up the solution process, but you can use it only if all the relationships in the model are linear.

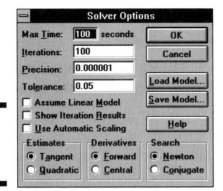

Figure 28-10: You can control many aspects of how Solver goes about solving a problem.

Show Iteration Results	If this option is set, Solver pauses and displays the results after each iteration.
Use Automatic Scaling	This turns on automatic scaling and is useful when the inputs (By changing cell) and outputs (Set cell and Constraints) have large differences in magnitude (see Figure 28-2) — for example, when you attempt to maximize a percentage by varying cells that are very large.

The Estimates, Derivatives, and Search group boxes let you control some of the technical aspects of the solution. In most cases, the default setting works fine.

Saving and loading models

Two buttons in the Solver Options dialog box let you save and load your model specification by using a range in your worksheet.

Save Model	Choosing this displays the Save Model dialog box, where you can specify a worksheet reference where the model parameters will be saved.
Load Model	Choosing this displays the Load Model dialog box, where you can specify a worksheet reference for the model you want to load.

Normally, you would want to save a model only when you are using more than one set of Solver parameters with your worksheet, since the first Solver model is automatically saved with your worksheet. This information is stored in the form of formulas that correspond to the specification you made (the last cell in the saved range is an array formula that holds the options settings).

More Solver Examples

This section presents a few more examples that use Solver for various types of problems.

Scheduling staff

Staff scheduling problems usually involve determining the minimum number of people that will satisfy staffing needs on certain days or times of day. The constraints typically involve such things as the number of consecutive days or hours a person can work.

Figure 28-11 shows a worksheet set up to analyze a simple staffing problem. The question is, "What is the minimum number of employees required to meet daily staffing needs?" At this company, each person works five consecutive days. As a result, employees start their five-day work week on different days of the week. The key to this problem — as with most Solver problems — is figuring out how to set up the worksheet.

 If you're trying to learn Solver, this is an excellent example to get hands-on experience.

Figure 28-11: This staffing model determines the minimum staff required to meet daily staffing needs.

	A	B	C	D	E	F	G
					No Who Start		
			Staff	**Staff**	**Work Week**	**Excess**	
		Day	**Needed**	**Scheduled**	**On this Day**	**Staff**	
4		Sun	60	125	25	65	
5		Mon	132	125	25	-7	
6		Tue	143	125	25	-18	
7		Wed	151	125	25	-26	
8		Thu	150	125	25	-25	
9		Fri	155	125	25	-30	
10		Sat	102	125	25	23	
11							
12					175	= Total staff needed	
13							
14							

STAFFING.XLS

The worksheet is laid out as follows:

Column B   Enter labels for the days of the week here.

Column C   These values represent the number of employees needed on each day of the week. As you can see, staffing needs vary quite a bit by the day of the week.

Column D   This holds formulas that use the values in column E. Each formula adds the number of people who start on that day to the number of people who started on the previous four days. Because the week "wraps around," we can't use a single formula and copy it. Consequently, each formula in column D is different:

        D4:   =E4+E10+E9+E8+E7

        D5:   =E5+E4+E10+E9+E8

        D6:   =E6+E5+E4+E10+E9

        D7:   =E7+E6+E5+E4+E10

        D8:   =E8+E7+E6+E5+E4

        D9:   =E9+E8+E7+E6+E5

        D10:   =E10+E9+E8+E7+E6

Column E   This holds the adjustable cells — the number to be filled in by Solver. We initialized these cells to 25 in order to give Solver something to start with. It's best to supply starting values that are at least in the ballpark of the anticipated answer.

Column F   This contains formulas that subtract the staff needed from the staff scheduled, to determine excess staff. Cell F4 contains =D4-C4, which is copied to the six cells below.

Cell E12   A formula that sums the number of people who start on each day — the total staff. The formula is: =sum(E4:E10).

We want Solver to minimize cell E12, the number of employees needed. We also need to make sure some constraints are satisfied — namely that the number of people scheduled each day is greater than or equal to the number of people required. Column F takes care of this. We just need to make sure that the formulas in column F all evaluate to 0 or greater.

	A	B	C	D	E	F	G
					No Who Start		
			Staff	Staff	Work Week	Excess	
		Day	Needed	Scheduled	On this Day	Staff	
4		Sun	60	60	-4.2	2.27E-13	
5		Mon	132	132	80.8	3.41E-13	
6		Tue	143	143	37.8	2.84E-14	
7		Wed	151	151	8.8	1.11E-12	
8		Thu	150	150	26.8	1.28E-12	
9		Fri	155	155	0.8	1.14E-13	
10		Sat	102	102	27.8	-1.42E-13	
11							
12					179	= Total staff needed	
13							
14							

STAFFING.XLS

Figure 28-12: This solution offered by Solver isn't quite right. We need to add some more constraints.

Once the worksheet is set up, select Formula ⇨ Solver and specify that you want to minimize cell E12 by changing cells E4:E10. Next, choose Add to start adding the constraints. The constraints are:

```
F4>=0
F5>=0
F6>=0
F7>=0
F8>=0
F9>=0
F10>=0
```

Choose Solve to start the process. You can watch as Solver goes through its motions. This problem takes longer than the first example. The solution Solver finds is shown in Figure 28-12 and indicates that a staff of 179 will meet the staffing needs, and there will be no excess staffing on any day.

The values in column F appear in scientific notation — a by-product of the fact that Solver doesn't have infinite precision. If you don't like this, simply format the cells with a numeric format other than "General."

But if you examine the results carefully, you'll notice a few things wrong here. First, Solver's solution involves fractional people. Second (and more critical) is the suggestion that a negative number of people should begin their work week on Sunday.

Figure 28-13: Many problems need to limit the solution to integers. You can easily do this by selecting the int option in the Constraint dialog box.

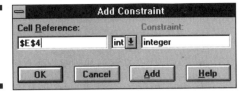

Both of these problems are easy to correct by adding more constraints. Fortunately, Solver lets you limit the solution to integers by using the int option in the Constraint dialog box. We need to add an additional constraint for each cell in E4:E10. Figure 28-13 shows how you can specify an integer constraint. To circumvent the negative people problem, we need to add seven more constraints of the form E7>=0.

If you find adding these constraints to be tedious, you can save the model to a worksheet range. Then, add new constraints to the range in the worksheet (making sure you don't overwrite the last cell in this range). Next, run Solver again and load the modified model from the range you edited.

After adding these 14 new constraints, run Solver again. This time, it arrives at the solution shown in Figure 28-14. You'll notice that this solution requires 180 people and results in excess staffing on several days of the week. This is the best solution possible that uses the fewest number of people — and almost certainly better than what you could arrive at manually.

This example illustrates two common problems people have with Solver: they need an integer solution, and they must have positive numbers. As we illustrated, both of these restrictions are easy to satisfy.

How does Solver do it?

Solver was developed by Frontline Systems, a company that specializes in computerized optimization products. Solver uses a variety of well-established numeric methods, including several techniques for solving linear and nonlinear optimization problems. Many of these methods involve iterative techniques in which calculations are made in a trial-and-error manner using successive approximations. If you watch the screen while Solver is working, you can see this for yourself.

Many problems appropriate for Solver have multiple solutions. Depending on the type of problem, Solver may or may not be able to find the "optimal" solution. In some cases, the solution depends on the initial values you supply. Consequently, you might want to try changing these starting values and see if Solver provides a different (perhaps better) solution.

Figure 28-14:
Rerunning Solver
after adding more
constraints produces
a better solution to
the staffing model
problem.

	Day	Staff Needed	Staff Scheduled	No Who Start Work Week On this Day	Excess Staff
4	Sun	60	64	0	4
5	Mon	132	132	78	0
6	Tue	143	145	38	2
7	Wed	151	151	10	0
8	Thu	150	151	25	1
9	Fri	155	155	4	0
10	Sat	102	102	25	0
12				180	= Total staff needed

Minimizing shipping costs

This next problem involves finding alternative options for shipping materials, while keeping total shipping costs at a minimum. In this example, a company has warehouses in Los Angeles, St. Louis, and Boston. Retail outlets throughout the United States place orders, which are then shipped from one of the warehouses. The object is to meet the product needs of all six retail outlets from available inventory in the warehouses and keep total shipping charges as low as possible.

This problem is set up in the worksheet in Figure 28-15. The Shipping Cost Matrix contains per-unit shipping costs from each warehouse to each retail outlet. For example, the cost to ship a unit from St. Louis to Atlanta is $30.

The range B12:B17 shows the product needs for each of the retail stores. Denver needs 150, Houston needs 225, and so on. The three columns to the right hold the adjustable cells that Solver will vary (we initialized them all to 25).

Row 18 contains =SUM formulas that add up the number of units to be shipped from each warehouse. Similarly, column G holds =SUM formulas that total the number of units to be shipped to each retail outlet. Both sets of =SUM formulas operate on the adjustable cells.

			Shipping Cost Matrix			
			L.A.	St. Louis	Boston	
		Denver	$58	$47	$108	
		Houston	$87	$46	$100	
		Atlanta	$121	$30	$57	
		Miami	$149	$66	$83	
		Seattle	$62	$115	$164	
		Detroit	$128	$28	$38	

	Number Needed	No. to ship from... L.A.	St. Louis	Boston	No. to be Shipped
Denver	150	25	25	25	75
Houston	225	25	25	25	75
Atlanta	60	25	25	25	75
Miami	175	25	25	25	75
Seattle	70	25	25	25	75
Detroit	150	25	25	25	75
Total	830	150	150	150	450

Starting Inventory:	390	400	525
No. Remaining:	240	250	375

Shipping Cost:	$15,125	$8,300	$13,750	$37,175 Total

Figure 28-15: This worksheet will determine the least expensive way to ship products from warehouses to retail outlets.

Row 20 contains the amount of inventory at each warehouse, and row 21 contains formulas that subtract the amount shipped (row 18) from the inventory. For example, cell D21 has this formula: =D20-D18.

Row 24 has the cost information. Cell D24 contains =SUMPRODUCT(D3:D8,D12:D17), which was copied to the two cells to the right. This formula calculates the total shipping cost from each warehouse. Cell G24 is the bottom line — the total shipping costs.

We'll ask Solver to fill in values in the range D12:F17 in such a way that each retail outlet gets the desired number of units *and* the total shipping cost is minimized. In other words, we want to minimize cell C24 by adjusting the cells in D12:F17 subject to the following constraints (a total of 27):

1. The number needed by each retail outlet equals the number shipped. This is represented by the following constraint specifications:

   C12=G12   C15=G15

   C13=G13   C16=G16

   C14=G14   C17=G17

2. The adjustable cells cannot be negative. This is represented by the following constraint specifications:

D12>=0	E12>=0	F12>=0
D13>=0	E13>=0	F13>=0
D14>=0	E14>=0	F14>=0
D15>=0	E15>=0	F15>=0
D16>=0	E16>=0	F16>=0
D17>=0	E17>=0	F17>=0

3. The number remaining in each warehouse's inventory must not be negative (that is, they can't ship more than what's available). This is represented by the following constraint specifications:

D21>=0	E21>=0	F21>=0

Before you solve this problem with Solver, you might want to try your hand at minimizing the shipping cost by changing the values in D12:F17 manually. Don't forget to make sure all of the constraints are met. Compare your best shot with what Solver comes up with.

When you've specified all of this information, select Solve to set Solver to work. This takes a while, but eventually Solver displays the solution shown in Figure 28-16. The total shipping cost is $43,460, and all of the constraints are met. Notice that shipments to Miami come from both St. Louis and Boston.

SHIPPING.XLS

Shipping Cost Matrix

	L.A.	St. Louis	Boston
Denver	$58	$47	$108
Houston	$87	$46	$100
Atlanta	$121	$30	$57
Miami	$149	$66	$83
Seattle	$62	$115	$164
Detroit	$128	$28	$38

	Number Needed	No. to ship from...			No. to be Shipped
		L.A.	St. Louis	Boston	
Denver	150	150	0	0	150
Houston	225	0	225	0	225
Atlanta	60	0	60	0	60
Miami	175	0	115	60	175
Seattle	70	70	0	0	70
Detroit	150	0	0	150	150
Total	830	220	400	210	830

Starting Inventory:	390	400	525
No. Remaining:	170	0	315

Shipping Cost:	$13,040	$19,740	$10,680	$43,460 Total

Figure 28-16: Solver comes to the rescue and potentially saves the company thousands of dollars.

	A	B	C	D	E	F
			CREDIT-U.XLS			
1	Portfolio	$5,000,000				
2						
3		Pct.	Amount		Pct of	
4	Investment	Yield	Invested	Yield	Portfolio	
5	New Car Loans	9.90%	1,000,000	99,000	20.00%	
6	Used Car Loans	13.50%	1,000,000	135,000	20.00%	
7	Real Estate Loans	10.90%	1,000,000	109,000	20.00%	
8	Unsecured Loans	17.00%	1,000,000	170,000	20.00%	
9	Bank CDs	8.60%	1,000,000	86,000	20.00%	
10	TOTAL		$5,000,000	$599,000	100.00%	
11						
12			Total Yield:	11.98%		
13						
14						
15				Auto Loans	40.00%	
16						

Figure 28-17: This worksheet is set up to maximize a credit union's investments — given some constraints, of course.

Optimizing an investment portfolio

Our last Solver example demonstrates how to use Solver to help maximize an investment portfolio. Portfolios consist of several investments, each of which has a different yield. In addition, you might have some constraints that involve reducing risk and diversification goals. Without such constraints, a portfolio problem becomes a no-brainer: Put all of your money in the investment with the highest yield.

This example involves a credit union — a financial institution that takes members' deposits and invests them in loans to other members, bank CDs, and other types of investments. Part of the yield on these investments is returned to the members in the form of dividends, or interest on their deposits. Our hypothetical credit union must adhere to some regulations regarding its investments, and the board of directors has imposed some other restrictions. These regulations and restrictions comprise the problem's constraints. The worksheet in Figure 28-17 shows the problem laid out and ready to solve. The formulas used are as follows:

D5:	=C5*B5, copied down through cell D9
E5:	=C5/$C$10, copied down through cell E10
C10:	=SUM(C5:C9)
D10:	=SUM(D5:D9)
D12:	=D10/C10
E15:	=E5+E6

	A	B	C	D	E	F
1	Portfolio	$5,000,000				
2						
3		Pct.	Amount		Pct of	
4	Investment	Yield	Invested	Yield	Portfolio	
5	New Car Loans	9.90%	2,400,000	237,600	48.00%	
6	Used Car Loans	13.50%	200,000	27,000	4.00%	
7	Real Estate Loans	10.90%	800,000	87,200	16.00%	
8	Unsecured Loans	17.00%	800,000	136,000	16.00%	
9	Bank CDs	8.60%	800,000	68,800	16.00%	
10	TOTAL		$5,000,000	$556,600	100.00%	
11						
12			Total Yield:	11.13%		
13						
14						
15				Auto Loans	52.00%	
16						

Figure 28-18: You can't always trust Solver's solution. Solver can do better if you adjust one of the parameters.

The constraints we must adhere to in allocating the $5 million portfolio are as follows:

- The amount in new car loans must be at least three times the amount in used car loans. This constraint is represented as C5>=C6*3.

- Car loans should make up at least 15 percent of the portfolio. This constraint is represented as E15>=.15.

- Unsecured loans should make up no more than 25 percent of the portfolio. This is represented as E8<=.25.

- At least 10 percent of the portfolio should be in bank CDs. This constraint is represented as E9>=.10.

- All investments should be positive or zero. In other words, we need to include five additional constraints to ensure that none of the changing cells go below 0.

The changing cells are C5:C9, and we want to maximize the total yield in cell D12. We supplied some starting values in the changing cells — $1,000,000 each. When we run Solver with these parameters, it produces the solution shown in Figure 28-18. The total portfolio yield of 11.13 percent looks pretty good, right? Actually, it's not the best. Since we're dealing with such a wide range of values (from percents up to millions), this is an example of when we need to use *automatic scaling*. Select the Options button in the Solver Parameters dialog box and choose Use Automatic Scaling. Start Solver again, and you'll get the results shown in Figure 28-19 — this time a total yield of 12.18 percent.

CREDIT-U.XLS						
	A	**B**	**C**	**D**	**E**	**F**
1	Portfolio	$5,000,000				
2						
3		Pct.	Amount		Pct of	
4	Investment	Yield	Invested	Yield	Portfolio	
5	New Car Loans	9.90%	562,500	55,687	11.25%	
6	Used Car Loans	13.50%	187,500	25,312	3.75%	
7	Real Estate Loans	10.90%	2,500,000	272,500	50.00%	
8	Unsecured Loans	17.00%	1,250,000	212,500	25.00%	
9	Bank CDs	8.60%	500,000	43,000	10.00%	
10	TOTAL		$5,000,000	$609,000	100.00%	
11						
12			Total Yield:	12.18%		
13						
14						
15				Auto Loans	15.00%	
16						

Figure 28-19: After selecting the Use Automatic Scaling option, Solver arrives at a more profitable solution.

This example demonstrates that you can't always trust Solver to arrive at the optimal solution with one try — even when its results dialog box tells you that "All constraints and optimality conditions are satisfied." If you play around with this example even more, you'll discover that Solver produces different results depending on the starting values you provide.

The best advice? Make sure you understand Solver well before you entrust it with helping you make any major decisions. Try different starting values and adjust some of the options to see if Solver can do better.

More About Solver

As you should have surmised by now, Solver is a complex analytical tool. Because of this, you'll need to spend some time working with it before you master all of its possibilities. Here are some things to keep in mind as you work with Solver:

■ The changing cells you specify in the Solver dialog box need not be contiguous. You can specify nonadjacent cells or ranges by separating them with commas.

■ Constraints must be of this form: single cell reference on the left, a relationship specification in the middle, and a number, formula, or cell reference on the right. Thus, $C$1>=0 is a valid constraint, but $C$1:$C$10>= is not.

■ You can interrupt Solver at any time by pressing Esc. A dialog box displays that lets you keep the current iteration solution or revert back to your original.

■ Don't forget that Solver works hand-in-hand with the Scenario Manager. You can save a solution as a named scenario with only a few mouse clicks.

■ If you request an integer solution by specifying integer constraints, Solver will probably take much longer to find the solution.

■ If you have a lot of constraints to enter, it may be more efficient to enter them in your worksheet (using the proper format) and then use the Load Model option. If you do this, make sure you use all absolute references.

■ If you find that a problem is taking too long to solve, you can often speed things up by entering starting values that are closer to the solution. If you have no idea what the solution is, try changing the precision to a lower value to get ballpark numbers and then reset it to a higher value for your final answers.

■ Solver has quite a few error messages that may occasionally pop up. Select the Help button to learn more about what may be causing the error.

■ When you installed Excel, it placed several sample Solver worksheets in your \examples\solver directory. You can use these to get a better understanding of how this feature works.

Summary

▶ Goal seeking is essentially what-if analysis in reverse. If you know what a formula's results should be, Excel's Formula ⇨ Goal Seek command can tell you the value in an input cell that will produce the desired result.

▶ Excel's Solver extends the concept of goal seeking by letting you specify multiple adjustable cells, constraints, and a cell to maximize or minimize.

▶ You need to run Excel's Setup program again and install Solver if the Formula ⇨ Solver command does not appear on your menu.

▶ Solver has many different parameters that can affect how it solves problems.

▶ Solver doesn't always produce optimal results, so you must check the calculations carefully for important problems.

Chapter 29

Communicating with Other Applications

In this chapter . . .

▶ Why it's necessary (or desirable) to share data with other applications.

▶ How to use the Clipboard to share data between Windows applications.

▶ An overview of Dynamic Data Exchange (DDE) — a technique that automatically updates changes to copied data.

▶ Using Object Linking and Embedding (OLE) to work with objects in other applications.

▶ How Excel can communicate with non-Windows applications: A discussion of the file types it can import and export.

▶ How to parse a text file so it's usable by Excel.

▶ Instructions for using an Excel add-in to create text files from Excel worksheet data.

Sooner or later — probably sooner — you may want to use data in Excel that already exists in a file created in another application. Or, you may want to use data from an Excel worksheet in another application. Both of these procedures are fairly easy to do. This chapter discusses all of the methods at your disposal for sharing data between Windows applications and non-Windows applications.

Why Share Data?

It's a rare computer user who works with only one application — or who doesn't interact with people using different applications. What if you are developing a spreadsheet model that uses data from last year's budget, which is stored in your company's mainframe? You could, of course, request a print-out of the data and manually enter it into Excel. If the amount of data isn't too large, this might be the most efficient route. But what if you had hundreds of entries to make? Chances are, your mainframe could produce a text file, which you could then import into an Excel worksheet. You could potentially save yourself several hours of work and virtually eliminate data entry errors.

This is just one example of sharing data. Here are some other reasons why you might need to transfer data from one application to another:

■ To bring an Excel chart into your word processor to include in a report.

■ To bring text from a word processing document into a worksheet. This might be done to add supporting text to a numeric model.

■ To bring a table of numbers from Excel into a desktop publishing package to include in a newsletter.

■ To bring more-sophisticated graphics or drawings into Excel. For example, you might develop a complex flow diagram in an illustration program and want to display it in a spreadsheet report.

■ To access clip art that's not supported by a specific application. For example, Excel can't directly read graphic files. If you have a Windows program with that capability, you can display the image and then copy it into Excel.

■ To share your data with someone who doesn't own Excel.

You have plenty of options at your disposal when it comes to data transfer. You need to know which technique is appropriate for each situation. We've broken the rest of this chapter into three parts:

■ Sharing data with other Windows applications.

■ Using data from non-Windows applications.

■ Exporting Excel files for use in other applications.

Sharing Data with Other Windows Applications

Excel provides three ways to transfer data to and from other Windows applications:

■ Copy and paste via the Clipboard

■ DDE

■ OLE

We'll discuss these three techniques and present an example for each.

Windows cut and paste

As you probably know, whenever Windows is running you have access to the Windows Clipboard — an area of your computer's memory that acts as a shared holding area for information that has been cut or copied from an application. The Clipboard runs behind the scenes, and you usually aren't even aware of it. Whenever you select the Edit ⇨ Copy or Edit ⇨ Cut commands, the selected data is placed on the Clipboard. Excel, as well as most other Windows applications, can then access the Clipboard data via the Edit ⇨ Paste command.

Data pasted from the Clipboard remains on the Clipboard after pasting, so you can use it multiple times. But the Clipboard can only hold one thing at a time, so when you copy something else, the old Clipboard contents are replaced.

 You can run the Windows Clipboard application to display the contents of the Clipboard. Your Windows Program Manager screen should have an icon set up for this program in one of your program groups. You can also run the Clipboard through Excel's control menu; select Run and then choose Clipboard from the option list (see Figure 29-1).

When you copy or cut data to the Clipboard, the source application places one or more formats along with it. Different applications support different Clipboard formats. When you paste Clipboard data into another application, the destination

---

Excel's Clipboard formats

The following table lists the Clipboard formats supported by Excel. When you run the Clipboard application, you can often display the contents in different formats by selecting the Display command.

Clipboard formats supported by Excel

Format	Description	Format	Description
Biff	Excel 2 file format	Object Link	A linked object format
Biff3	Excel 3 file format	OEM Text	Fixed-font text format
Biff4	Excel 4 file format	Owner Link	An embedded object format
Bitmap	Bitmapped graphics	Picture	Vector-based graphic
CSV	Comma-separated value	Rich Text	Text with formatting (RTF)
DIF	Data interchange format	SLK	MultiPlan format (symbolic link)
Display Text	Number of rows and columns in a range selection	Text	Text format (tab delimited)
		WK1	1-2-3 format
Link	A presentation format		
Native	An embedded object format		

Figure 29-1: You can run the Windows Clipboard application without leaving Excel.

application determines which format it can handle and typically selects the format that either provides the most information or is appropriate for where it is being pasted.

Copying from one Windows application to another is simple. The application you're copying from is considered the source application, and the application you're copying to is the destination application. Follow these steps:

Steps: Copying information from one application to another

Step 1. Activate the source document window that contains the information you want to copy.

Step 2. Select the information using the mouse or the keyboard. If Excel is the source application, this can be a cell, a range, a chart, or a drawn object.

Step 3. Select Edit ⇨ Copy. A copy of the information is sent to the Windows Clipboard.

Step 4. Activate the destination application. If it isn't open, you can run it without affecting the contents of the Clipboard.

Step 5. Move to the appropriate position in the destination application.

Step 6. Select Edit ⇨ Paste from the menu in the destination application. If the Clipboard contents are not appropriate for pasting, the Paste command will be grayed out (not available).

If you're copying a graphic image, you may have to resize it or crop it. If you're copying text, you may need to reformat it using tools available in the destination application. The information you copied from the source application remains intact, and a copy remains on the Clipboard until you copy something else.

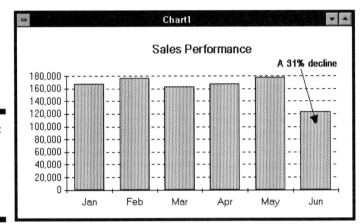

Figure 29-2:
An Excel
chart for
copying to
Word for
Windows.

In Step 3 of the previous exercise, you could also select Edit ⇨ Cut from the source application menu. This erases it from the source application after it is placed on the Clipboard.

Figure 29-2 shows an Excel chart. We can insert a copy of this chart into a word processing (Word for Windows) report easily. First, select the chart in Excel and copy it to the Clipboard with the Edit ⇨ Copy command (make sure you select the entire chart, not just a part of it). Next, activate the Word for Windows document, move to the place where you want the chart to go, and place the insertion point there. Select Edit ⇨ Paste from the Word for Windows menu and the chart is pasted from the Clipboard (see Figure 29-3).

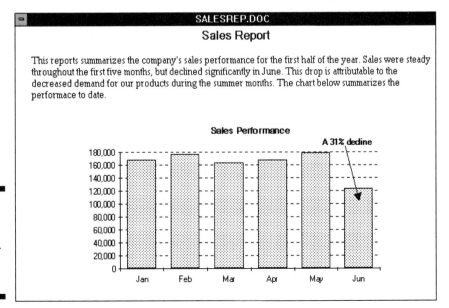

Figure 29-3:
The Excel
chart copied
to a Word for
Windows
document.

If the Excel selection is a range of data, Word for Windows creates a table when the data is pasted. Applications vary on exactly how they handle data pasted from Excel, so you'll need to experiment.

You'll notice that this copy and paste technique is static. In other words, there is no link between what gets copied from the source application and the destination application. If you're copying from Excel to a word processing document, subsequent changes in your Excel worksheet or charts are not reflected in the word processing document. Consequently, you would have to repeat the copy and paste procedure to update the source document with the changes. The next topic presents a way to get around this limitation.

Dynamic Data Exchange (DDE)

Windows DDE lets you set up a link between data copied from one Windows application to another. Not all Windows applications support DDE, so you need to make sure the application you'll be copying to is actually capable of handling a DDE link. If you're not sure, check your software documentation or on-line help. Before we get too far into this, you might want to consult the sidebar "DDE terminology" to become acquainted with some terms.

Setting up a DDE link from one Windows application to another isn't difficult. It assumes that the source application supports DDE as a server and the destination application supports DDE as a client. Here's how to set up a DDE link:

Steps: Setting up a DDE link

Step 1. Activate the window in the source application (the server) that contains the information you want to copy.

Step 2. Select the information using the mouse or the keyboard. If Excel is the server, you can select a cell, a range, or an entire chart.

Step 3. Select Edit ⇨ Copy from the server's menu. A copy of the information is sent to the Windows Clipboard.

Step 4. Activate the destination application. If it isn't open, you can start it without affecting the contents of the Clipboard.

Step 5. Move to the appropriate position in the destination application.

Step 6. Select the appropriate command in the destination application to paste a link. The actual command varies depending on the application. In Excel, the command is Edit ⇨ Paste Link. Some applications let you accomplish a DDE link through that application's Edit ⇨ Paste Special command.

Once the link is created, you can make changes to the server document and the changes will appear in the client application. The best way to test this is to display both applications on-screen.

Figure 29-4 shows an Excel worksheet with a table of data. We want to set up a DDE link to a Word for Windows document so it always reflects the current values in the worksheet. Select the range in Excel and copy it to the Clipboard. Activate the Word for Windows document, move to the appropriate position, and select Edit ➪ Paste Special from the menu. You'll be presented with the Paste Special dialog box, shown in Figure 29-5. Select Formatted Text (RTF) and the choose Paste Link. Word creates a table with the same numeric formats used in Excel. This table, however, is linked to the Excel worksheet. If you change any of the values in Excel, they are changed in the Word for Windows document.

DDE terminology

Dynamic Data Exchange is normally easy to use. But the terminology can sometimes be confusing. Here's a list of some DDE terms.

Server application: The application that provides the data. DDE links can go in either of two directions: from another application to Excel, or from Excel to another application. Most (but not all) applications that support DDE support it in both directions.

Client application: The application that receives the information from the server application.

Source document: The file that provides the information to the destination document.

Destination document: The file that receives the information from the source document. Also known as the *dependent document.*

Remote reference: A reference to a document in another application.

Conversation: Also known as a *channel.* This is the term for the link itself. A file can be both a source document and a destination document by sending and receiving information in different conversations, or channels.

Topic: An identifying factor in the server application — usually a filename.

Item: A further identifying factor in the server application. This is a named data item (such as a bookmark in Word for Windows), a cell reference, or a range name.

Format: The way the data appears. There are many Clipboard formats, and not all applications support them all.

Refresh: The process of updating the DDE links, bringing in new data if it has changed in the source document.

Update mode: How the links will be refreshed: either automatically, or upon request.

Link status: Whether the link is active or inactive.

Active link: A DDE link that is working.

Inactive link: A DDE link that has been turned off. The link still exists, but no fresh data is being transferred.

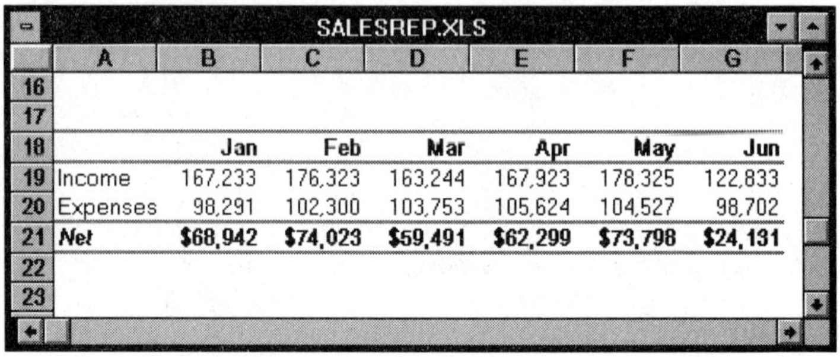

SALESREP.XLS
A B C D E F G
16
17
18 Jan Feb Mar Apr May Jun
19 Income 167,233 176,323 163,244 167,923 178,325 122,833
20 Expenses 98,291 102,300 103,753 105,624 104,527 98,702
21 Net $68,942 $74,023 $59,491 $62,299 $73,798 $24,131
22
23

Figure 29-4: An Excel range that will be dynamically linked to a Word for Windows document.

Here are a few things to keep in mind when using Windows DDE links:

- Not all Windows applications support DDE. Furthermore, some programs support DDE as a server, but not as a client (and vice versa). When in doubt, consult the documentation for the application you're dealing with. And good luck — documentation on DDE is usually scant or nonexistent.
- DDE is implemented differently by various applications. It's difficult to list hard and fast rules that apply in all situations.
- The server document must be open. If it's not, some applications will ask you if you want to open the document and then attempt to do so for you.
- DDE links can be severed rather easily. For example, if you move the source document to another directory or save it under a different name, the client document will be unable to update the link. You can usually reestablish the link manually, if you understand how the application manages the links.
- In Excel, a DDE link is stored in an array formula (a "remote reference formula") with the following syntax:

  {=*application_name* | *topic*!*item_name*}

  You can modify a link by editing the array formula.
- You can quickly jump to the source document by double-clicking a cell that contains a remote reference formula. If the application is not running, Excel will try to launch it and then load the appropriate document.

Paste Special
Source: Microsoft Excel Worksheet
SALESREP.XLS R18C1:R21C7
Data Type:
Microsoft Excel Worksheet Obje
Formatted Text (RTF)
Unformatted Text
Picture
Bitmap
Paste
Paste Link
Cancel

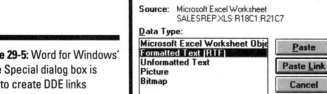

Figure 29-5: Word for Windows' Paste Special dialog box is used to create DDE links

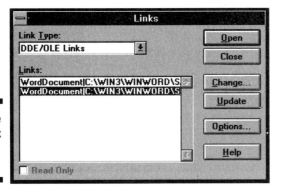

Figure 29-6: The Links dialog box lets you modify DDE links.

- Excel's <u>F</u>ile ➪ <u>L</u>inks command brings up the Links dialog box, shown in Figure 29-6. Here you can change DDE links from automatic to manual and also modify the array formulas that control the links.

- When Excel is running, it responds to DDE requests from other applications unless you've disabled remote requests. You do this by selecting the <u>O</u>ptions ➪ <u>W</u>orkspace command and then choosing Ignore Remote Requests.

- Having many DDE links takes its toll on system performance since Windows is doing quite a bit of work behind the scenes. If things get too slow, consider deactivating the links and updating them on request (rather than automatically).

Object Linking and Embedding (OLE)

The third method of sharing data between Windows applications is OLE. This relatively new Windows protocol is supported by only a few Windows applications. With the arrival of Windows 3.1, this situation will improve.

OLE extends the functionality of DDE and enables more powerful integration. The linked data is embedded in the document, but you can edit the data using the tools available in the application that it came from. There are two ways to set up an OLE link:

#1 Use the client application's <u>E</u>dit ➪ Paste <u>S</u>pecial command and select the "object" choice (the exact wording varies, depending on the application).

#2 Use the client application's <u>E</u>dit ➪ Insert <u>O</u>bject command (again, the actual command name may vary).

Some programs are designed to work only as server applications and can be run *only* from within a destination application that supports OLE. Some good examples are the applications included with Microsoft Word for Windows 2. This program includes server applications to create and edit equations, charts, drawings, and "word art." These applications can be run from any application that supports OLE, including Excel. Method #2 is the only way to access these programs.

Following are step-by-step instructions for each of these methods. The first method assumes that the client and server applications both support OLE.

Steps: Embedding an object in a Windows application using Edit ⇨ Paste Special

Step 1. Activate the window in the source application that contains the information you want to copy.

Step 2. Select the information using the mouse or the keyboard. In Excel, this can be a cell, a range, or a complete chart.

Step 3. Select Edit ⇨ Copy. A copy of the information is sent to the Windows Clipboard.

Step 4. Activate the destination (client) application. If it isn't open, you can run it without affecting the contents of the Clipboard.

Step 5. Move to the appropriate position in the destination application.

Step 6. Select Edit ⇨ Paste Special from the menu in the destination application. Then select the option that includes the word "object" (the exact wording varies from application to application).

The object — be it text or a graphic image — is now embedded in your document. But unlike DDE, a link is not created. Any changes you make in the source document are *not* reflected in the embedded object. Nevertheless, it is easy to access and modify an embedded object from its destination document.

To try out this procedure, copy a chart from Excel and then activate a document in Word for Windows. After copying the Excel chart to the Clipboard, select Edit ⇨ Paste Special from the Word for Windows menu and choose the Microsoft Excel Chart Object option from the dialog box. Note that when this option is selected the Paste Link button is grayed (not available). Choose Paste, and the chart is inserted into Word for Windows as an embedded objected. If you change the chart in Excel, these changes are not reflected in the embedded Word object.

The next method starts out with a blank document where you do your editing and then returns you to your original application. This assumes that both the source and destination applications support OLE.

Steps: Embedding an object in another Windows application using Edit ⇨ Insert Special

Step 1. Activate the application where you want to embed an object.

Step 2. Select the Edit ⇨ Insert Object command. The actual command name may vary, depending on the application. For example, it may be Insert ⇨ Object.

Step 3. The application displays a list of installed applications that support OLE. For Excel the options are Excel worksheet, Excel macro sheet, and Excel chart. Select one of the object types listed.

Step 4. The application then launches the server application (if it's not already running) and presents you with a blank document of the type you selected.

Step 5. Enter the information in the application or copy it from another file, if desired.

Step 6. To return to the original application, close the document (use the File ⇨ Close command) or close the application (use the File ⇨ Exit command).

The object is now embedded into your document.

We'll demonstrate this using one of the embedding applications included with Word for Windows. In Excel, select Edit ⇨ Insert Object. You'll see a dialog box similar to the one shown in Figure 29-7 (the actual choices varies depending on the OLE-supporting applications you have installed). For this example, we'll choose Microsoft Draw. The application is launched (see Figure 29-8) and we can use all the tools available. When you close Microsoft Draw, the picture will be embedded in the Excel worksheet.

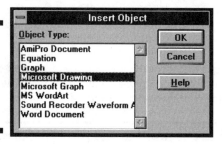

Figure 29-7: The Insert Object dialog box lets you select the type of object you want to embed in your Excel worksheet.

Modifying embedded objects

Regardless of which of the two options you use to embed an object, it's easy to modify the object — just double-click it. This sends you back to the server application where you can make your modifications. To update the original application, close the document or the application. You'll get a dialog box asking if you want to update the document. Normally, you'll respond Yes or OK to this query (unless you want to lose any changes you made and keep the object as it was).

If the embedded object is an Excel document, you'll have two new menu options: File ⇨ Update and File ⇨ Save Copy As. Choosing File ⇨ Update updates the changes in the application but keeps Excel active. Choosing File ⇨ Save Copy As saves the information in an Excel file. Embedded objects are normally stored along with the rest of the destination document, as opposed to being stored separately by the source application.

Figure 29-8: Microsoft Draw is an application that's included with Word for Windows 2.0. You can run it directly from Excel.

For example, if we wanted to modify the drawing we embedded in an Excel document from Microsoft Draw, we would simply double-click the object and we would be taken back into Microsoft Draw to make the changes.

OLE is most useful if you want to work on a type of object that is not supported by the application you're working in. For example, it's ideal for inserting a chart into a word processing document. OLE is still an evolving concept, and applications use OLE differently. The best advice is to experiment until you understand what's going on.

Your `win.ini` file keeps track of the applications on your system that support OLE. This information is stored under the `[Embedding]` heading.

You might notice that when you embed a Word for Windows document in an Excel worksheet all you get is an icon (not the text, as you may expect). This might lead you to suspect that you can't embed Word text into Excel (you're right). When you double-click on the icon, Word for Windows appears with the text displayed. This can be useful for some user-oriented applications; a user need only double-click on the icon and he or she can read the text — perfect for instructions or documentation.

Using Data from Non-Windows Applications ___

The preceding sections showed how to get data from other Windows applications into Excel. But what about non-Windows applications?

Importing non-Windows files

Excel provides direct support for several non-Windows file formats:

- Lotus 1-2-3 files (`wks`, `wk1`, and `wk3`)
- ASCII text files
- Comma-separated value files (`csv`)
- dBASE files (`dbf`)
- Data interchange format files (`dif`)
- MultiPlan symbolic link files (`slk`)

You can use the File ➪ Open command to bring these files directly into Excel. As shown in Figure 29-9, you can control which file types appear in the File Open dialog box by pulling down the list box labeled List Files of Type. Following are some pointers and things you need to keep in mind for each file type.

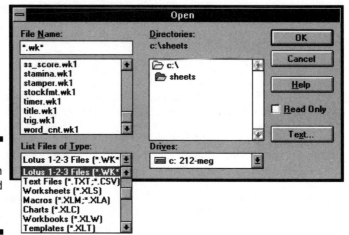

Figure 29-9: You can control which files are displayed in the File Open dialog box.

Lotus 1-2-3 files

Excel can read files produced by all versions of 1-2-3: Release 1 and 1A (wks), Release 2 (wk1), Release 3 (wk3) and 1-2-3 for Windows (wk3).

Excel generally does an excellent job of converting all the formulas and formats from all versions of 1-2-3. Check the conversion carefully, however, especially if it uses complex formulas.

If the 1-2-3 file has an associated format file (fmt or fm3), Excel applies the formats found in that file.

In the case of multisheet 1-2-3 files (from Release 3 or 1-2-3 for Windows), Excel creates a workbook, with a separate worksheet for each sheet of the source file. Formula references between sheets are converted to link formulas.

ASCII text files

ASCII files (often referred to as text files) contain only text, with no formatting information. Figure 29-10 shows an example of a text file typed at the DOS prompt.

ASCII files are often considered the "lowest common denominator," since most applications can read and write such files — providing a way to transfer raw data (without formatting information) between programs.

When you bring a text file into Excel, it normally reads each line as a label. If the text file contains numerical data, you can specify how the values are delimited

```
┌─────────────────────  Select COMMAND  ────────────────▼─▲─┐
│                                                           ↑│
│C:\>type month.txt                                         │
│                                                           │
│                                                           │
│Month        Region-1   Region-2   Region-3               │
│                                                           │
│January        89,323     11,233     10,878               │
│February       99,232     10,093      9,095               │
│March         113,220     13,656     14,092               │
│April         113,290     14,989     11,172               │
│May           121,778     12,098     13,768               │
│June          111,892     13,923     12,833               │
│                                                           │
│                                                           │
│                              Printed 5/7/92               │
│                                                           │
│                                                           │
│C:\>_                                                      │
│                                                          ↓│
└─◄─├──────────────────────────────────────────────►──────┘
```

Figure 29-10: An ASCII text file, displayed in a DOS window with the TYPE command.

by selecting Text in the File Open dialog box. The Text File Options dialog box appears, as shown in Figure 29-11. Select the character that's used as the delimiter and specify the source of the file (usually DOS).

If you specify the space character as the delimiter, Excel interprets multiple spaces between values as separate columns — usually not what you want. In this case, you can import the file as labels and then parse the labels into their component parts using the Data ⇨ Parse command (this is discussed later in this chapter).

Excel can actually read any file, with any extension. If the file type is not officially supported by Excel, the result is often garbage. For example Figure 29-12 shows a binary file loaded into Excel. If you end up with a screen

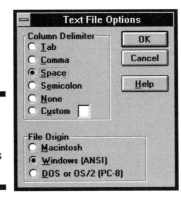

Figure 29-11: The Text File Options dialog box lets you specify the delimiter that separates columns of data.

	A	B	C	D	E	F	G	H
				HELVE.FON				
1	MZII ÿÿlle@@lèSThis program requires Microsoft Windows.							
2	$		ÍI¸ILÍINEIIÅ ñIOIÝIIII¹IIOIIIIIHELVE3FONTRES 100,96,96 ; Helv 8,10,12,14,1					
3	III ÿ˙çµII·IelvUIII(c) Copyright Microsoft Corp. 1987. All rights reserved.							
4	``							
5	IIIIIII ÿ˙IIzII·I ÿ˙sIÅ&HelvXIÿ1 Copyright (c) 1985 Xiphias, Los Angeles, Ca.I˙`IIIIIII ÿ˙II							
6	III ÿ˙É<IúII·PIIjIIwIIIIII¹IIIII«II¸IIÅIIOIIBIIùIIIIIII II-II¸IIGIITIIallnII{IIIIIIIIÊII¯II¼IIEIIOIIãI							
7	IIIII$II1II>I II		IôIIôIIôIIô I(		I5	IB	IO	I\
8	II							
9	II							

Figure 29-12: This binary file was imported into Excel as text.

that resembles this, you're trying to import a file that Excel does not support. Note, however, that Excel warns you if you ask to open a binary file that it does not recognize.

If you don't know if a file is a text file or not, read it into the Windows Notepad application. If the Notepad can read it, there's a pretty good chance it's an ASCII file. Or, you can use the DOS TYPE command. If you can read the displayed file and it doesn't have strange characters in it, it's probably a text file.

Comma-separated value files

Comma-separated value files are just that — each value is separated by a comma. In addition, text is usually enclosed in quotes. Figure 29-13 shows an example of a typical csv file.

Excel uses the commas to separate the variables into columns. Each row of the csv file occupies a separate row in the Excel worksheet. Excel reads these files properly only if they have a csv extension. You may therefore need to rename the file before you import it into Excel.

```
Select COMMAND

C:\>type employ.csv

FIRST_NAME,LAST_NAME,EMP_ID,HIRE_DATE,SALARY,DEPT,EXEMPT
Tyler,Bennett,E10297,06/01/77,32000.00,D101,Y
John,Rappl,E21437,07/15/87,47000.00,D050,Y
George,Woltman,E00127,08/07/82,53500.00,D101,Y
Adam,Smith,E63535,01/15/88,18000.00,D202,N
David,McClellan,E04242,07/27/82,41500.00,D101,Y
David,Motsinger,E27002,05/05/85,19250.00,D202,N,
Tim,Sampair,E03033,12/02/87,27000.00,D101,Y,
Kim,Arlich,E10001,07/30/85,57000.00,D190,Y,
Timothy,Grove,E16398,01/21/85,29900.00,D190,Y,

C:\>_
```

Figure 29-13: An example of a csv file. Each value is separated by a comma.

dBASE files

dBASE files are database files that contain information in record and field format. This translates nicely to Excel's row and column format.

Besides dBASE, many other programs can generate dBASE files (which are considered a somewhat "standard" file format).

Data interchange format files

The dif format used to be fairly common and was the format used by VisiCalc (the first DOS spreadsheet). dif files are not used very often these days.

MultiPlan (symbolic link) files

MultiPlan was Microsoft's first spreadsheet. It stands to reason that they would provide support for this file format (slk).

Excel generally does a good job of converting these files, including the formulas.

Parsing text files

In most cases, when you import a text file you can force Excel to split out the columns properly by specifying the appropriate delimiter in the Text File Options dialog box. Typical delimiters are the space character and commas.

At times, however, you may need more control over how the lines of text are split into columns. Excel provides two ways to do this.

The Data ⇨ Parse command

Excel's Data ⇨ Parse command lets you specify where the column breaks occur. Figure 29-14 shows a small file that we want to import into Excel. Note that the values are separated by several spaces.

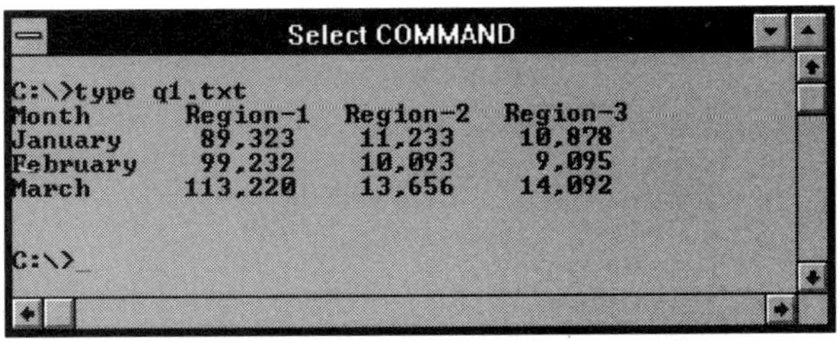

Figure 29-14: This text file will be imported into Excel and then parsed into its component parts.

```
C:\>type q1.txt
Month        Region-1   Region-2   Region-3
January       89,323     11,233     10,878
February      99,232     10,093      9,095
March        113,220     13,656     14,092

C:\>_
```

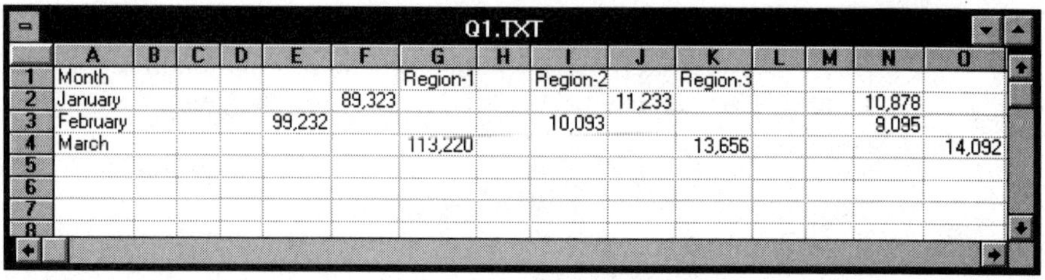

Q1.TXT														
A	B	C	D	E	F	G	H	I	J	K	L	M	N	O
Month						Region-1		Region-2		Region-3				
January				89,323					11,233				10,878	
February			99,232					10,093					9,095	
March						113,220				13,656				14,092

Figure 29-15: When Excel imports the file using the space character as a delimiter, each space adds a new column — not what we wanted.

If we import the file with the space character as the delimiter, we get the worksheet shown in Figure 29-15. You'll notice that each space resulted in a separate (blank) column. Cleaning this worksheet up would not be difficult — just delete the blank cells manually and move the data to the left. But just think of the task if the file were 200 lines instead of four. Data ⇨ Parse to the rescue.

First, we'll import the text file as labels. Select File ⇨ Open and enter the filename into the text box. Choose Text to open the Text File Options dialog box. Make sure the delimiter option is set to None. When the file is imported, Excel interprets each line as a label in column A. See Figure 29-16.

Notice that the columns do not appear to line up, as in the original file. This is only an illusion, due to the fact that Excel is using a proportionally spaced font (different characters take up a different amount of horizontal space). If you change the font to a fixed-space font such as Courier, the columns will align.

To parse the labels, select the range A1:A4 and then choose Data ⇨ Parse. Excel displays the Parse dialog box, shown in Figure 29-17. Excel makes its best guess as to how the labels should be parsed and displays brackets around what it proposes to be columns. Choose OK to parse the text. The labels in column A are now split into columns, as shown in Figure 29-18.

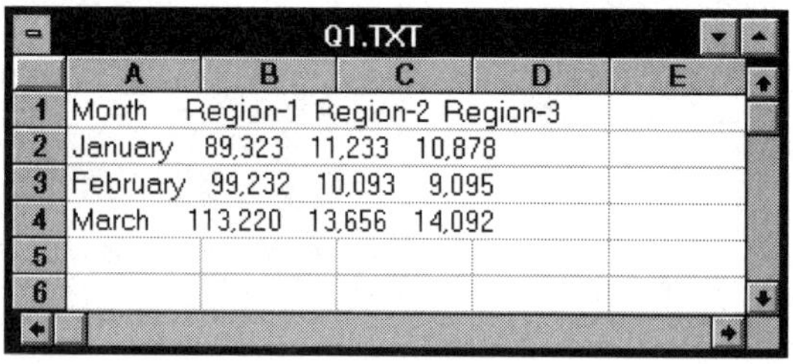

Figure 29-16: Importing the file with no delimiters results in a series of labels in column A.

Q1.TXT				
A	B	C	D	E
Month Region-1 Region-2 Region-3				
January 89,323 11,233 10,878				
February 99,232 10,093 9,095				
March 113,220 13,656 14,092				

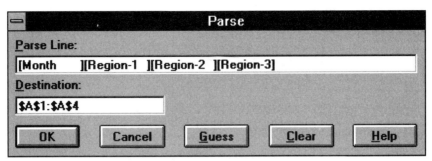

Figure 29-17: The Data Parse dialog box. Excel makes its best guess as to how the labels should be broken up — but you can edit this guess if it's wrong.

Smart Parse

Excel includes an add-in, Flat File, which has a command that makes such parsing even easier. First, you have to load the add-in. Select File ⇨ Open, and locate the flatfile.xla file. It should be located in the \library subdirectory in your excel directory. After loading this add-in, you'll have a new command available: Data ⇨ Smart Parse.

Select the labels that you want to parse and then select the Data ⇨ Smart Parse command. You'll see the dialog box shown in Figure 29-19. Specify the delimiter (usually spaces) and choose OK. The labels will divide into separate columns. This command is particularly useful if your labels have widely varying field lengths — something that would be difficult or impossible for the regular Data ⇨ Parse command.

	A	B	C	D	E
1	Month	Region-1	Region-2	Region-3	
2	January	89,323	11,233	10,878	
3	February	99,232	10,093	9,095	
4	March	113,220	13,656	14,092	
5					
6					

Figure 29-18: After parsing the labels, everything fits nicely in its own cell.

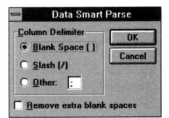

Figure 29-19: The Data Smart Parse dialog box is only available if you load the Flat File add-in.

Exporting Files

The final topic of this chapter covers how to save Excel data so it can be used by other applications. Earlier in this chapter we discussed the file types that Excel can import. It can export the same file types.

Applications supported

To save an Excel worksheet for use by another supported application, use the File ➪ Save As command. Click on the pull-down list box labeled Save File as Type and select the format that you want to save to. The options are as follows:

Choice	Format
Excel 3	Excel 3 file format
Excel 2.1	Excel 2.1 file format
Sylk	MultiPlan spreadsheet format (symbolic link)
Text	An ASCII text file
CSV	A comma-separated value file
WKS	A 1-2-3 Release 1 or 1A file
WK1	A 1-2-3 Release 2 file
WK3	A 1-2-3 Release 3, or 1-2-3 for Windows file
DIF	A data interchange format file
DBF 2	A dBASE II file
DBF 3	A dBASE III file
DBF 4	A dBASE IV file
Text (Macintosh)	A text file for the Macintosh
CSV (Macintosh)	A comma-separated value file for the Macintosh
Text (OS/2 or MS-DOS)	A text file for OS/2 or DOS
CSV (OS/2 or MS-DOS)	A comma-separated value file for OS/2 or DOS

Figure 29-20: The Data Export dialog box is only available if you load the Flat File add-in.

```
Data Export
To File Name: regions.txt          Export
[X] Retain cell formats             Cancel
```

Exporting a flat ASCII file

When you export an Excel worksheet with the Text option, each column of data is separated with a Tab character. In some cases, this is just what you want. At times, however, you may want the columns separated with spaces — lined up nicely in columns. If this is the case, you can use Excel's Flat File add-in.

This is the same add-in that provides the Data ⇨ Smart Parse command, which was discussed previously in this chapter.

First, you have to load the add-in. Select File ⇨ Open and locate the flatfile.xla file. It should be located in the \library subdirectory in your excel directory. After loading this add-in, you'll have a new command available: Data ⇨ Export.

To use this command, select the data that you want to export to an ASCII file. Then issue the Data ⇨ Export command. You'll see the dialog box shown in Figure 29-20. Enter a filename. If you want the file to contain the numeric formats shown on-screen, make sure the Retain cell formats option is checked. If this option is not checked, the file will contain the actual values. For example, a value displayed as 12.92 might actually be stored as 12.92017231234. Normally, you'll want to check the Retain cell formats box.

When you choose OK, the ASCII file is written. This file is now ready for use in any other application that supports ASCII text files.

Summary

▶ Most Excel users eventually need to access data that's not in Excel format, transfer data to another application, or share data with someone who doesn't own Excel.

▶ There are three ways to transfer data between Windows applications: copy and paste via the Clipboard, DDE, and OLE.

▶ Almost all Windows applications support copy and paste, but not all support DDE and OLE.

▶ Excel can directly read the files from quite a few sources, including all versions of 1-2-3, ASCII text files, comma-separated value files, and dBASE files. Use the File ⇨ Open command for this.

▶ When you import a text file, you can specify the character to be used to delimit columns.

▶ Excel's Data ⇨ Parse command lets you break text strings into component parts, which are stored in separate columns. Another command, Data ⇨ Smart Parse, is available via the Flat File add-in.

▶ Excel can export to several file formats, including previous versions of Excel, text files, comma-separated value files, all versions of 1-2-3, and all versions of dBASE.

▶ Excel's Flat File add-in provides additional flexibility be letting you select a range of cells to export to an ASCII file.

Chapter 30
Auditing Worksheets

In this chapter . . .

▶ Why it's so easy to make mistakes in a worksheet.

▶ How to use Excel tools to help you find and correct errors in a worksheet.

▶ Details on the auditing commands available in Excel.

Everyone makes mistakes now and then and, unfortunately, some may find their way into your worksheets. As with any other report, however, you need to ensure your worksheet is accurate.

Excel has several tools explicitly included for auditing, as well as other commands you can use to help you understand your worksheet. We'll show you what Excel has to offer in this department and share techniques you can use to troubleshoot and create accurate worksheets. As you should know by now, making a change in a single cell can affect dozens or hundreds of cells in the worksheet and other worksheets. In addition, it's easy to accidentally replace a formula with a value — possibly destroying the integrity of your work. For this reason, you should check your worksheet even if it *appears* OK. In this manner, you can avoid a major Maalox moment that could result in a career-limiting situation. Errors can occur at any stage of the worksheet process:

- By entering an incorrect formula and subsequently copying it.

- By entering incorrect data or entering data in the wrong location.

- In macros that process smoothly, but return erroneous results.

- When modifying your worksheet to reflect changes in your business.

Errors aren't the only reason you should make auditing part of your worksheet routine, however. If you have to use a worksheet created by a fellow Excel user who may not be readily available for help, you need to understand its logic quickly — before you distribute a report based on it.

You should definitely check the accuracy of your worksheet when you've finished creating it, when you make a change that impacts calculations, or when you inherit a worksheet from another user. In any case, auditing is a prerequisite to printing reports and basing decisions on your worksheet's results.

Auditing a Worksheet

You can use the same methodology to audit worksheets whether you're creating or inheriting them (or both). First, get a handle on what you're dealing with. In terms of rows and columns, how large is the worksheet? Which cells have formulas and which have values? Are there separate areas for data entry, calculations, and reports? Does it use any other worksheets?

Second, examine the worksheet for obvious signs of trouble, such as error values and circular references. Error values always begin with the pound (#) sign and can result from division by zero, use of a nonexistent range name, syntactical errors in functions, and more. Unintentional circular references always calculate incorrect results.

Third, carefully check the logic of your worksheet. Do formulas (dependent cells) refer correctly to data or other formulas (cells that have *precedence*)? Are your formulas themselves calculating the results you need?

Once your worksheet's been through the auditing gauntlet, you can use it with confidence. To determine a worksheet's accuracy, Excel has an entire suite of auditing tools at your disposal in the auditing toolbox.

Auditing Tools

Excel has a variety of features to help you navigate the sometimes turbulent worksheet currents. One set of auditing tools lets you see the big picture while another helps you understand the thinking that went into it. You can use any combination of the following commands and add-ins to assist you in comprehending your worksheet. Choose those that will help you the most, based on your particular needs and business situation.

Gaining a global perspective

If you've inherited a monster worksheet, or your pride and joy (worksheet-wise) is taking on a life of its own, you have several ways to keep abreast of things in terms of dealing with its size.

Zooming out

Recall from Chapter 14 the Window ⇨ Zoom command, which lets you expand or contract the display of your worksheet by a specified percentage. If you decrease the size of your worksheet display, you can see more of it on-screen at

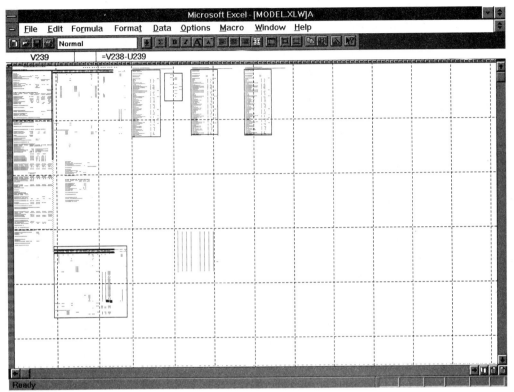

Figure 30-1: Seeing the big picture: On a high-resolution display, we selected <u>W</u>indow ⇨ <u>Z</u>oom and chose 10 percent magnification.

a time and therefore determine its dimensions. To shrink the display of the worksheet, select <u>W</u>indow ⇨ <u>Z</u>oom and choose a Magnification option, or choose Custom and type a value in the Custom text box. The magnification range is from 10 percent up to 400 percent. If you select small values, you probably won't be able to decipher the contents of the cells, but you can get a good idea of how the entire sheet is laid out.

If you're using a standard VGA display, consider going to a higher resolution mode to see more of your worksheet at once (assuming your hardware supports it). In 800 × 600 mode, you can see about 56 percent more information on-screen. In 1024 × 768 mode, you can view about 156 percent more information. Using zoom mode in these resolutions gives you a great bird's eye view. Figure 30-1 shows an example of a worksheet zoomed to 10 percent of its original size, using a 1024 × 768 display. You can see more than 300 rows and 100 columns.

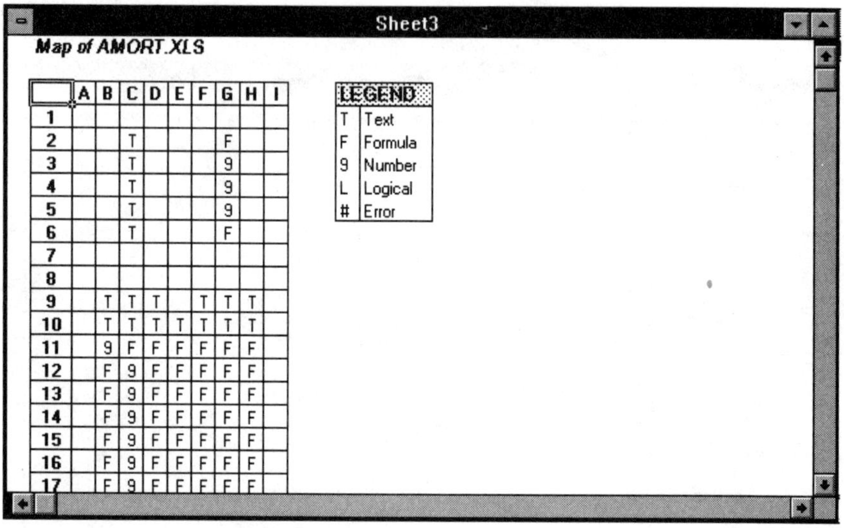

Figure 30-2: A treasure map to worksheet information, courtesy of the Worksheet Auditor's Map Worksheet option.

Mapping your worksheet

The second method of viewing a large worksheet uses the Worksheet Auditor add-in (the Worksheet Auditor is in the \library subdirectory under the excel directory). Choose File ⇨ Open and from the \library subdirectory select audit.xla. A new command appears: Formula ⇨ Worksheet Auditor.

Select this command and choose the Map Worksheet option from the dialog box. Excel opens a new worksheet and creates a grid that resembles a miniature version of your worksheet. Column letters and row numbers are across and down, respectively, and the intersection of each row number and column letter contains a code if a cell has an entry. These codes, representing the cells' contents, are described in the Legend box to the right of the worksheet grid, as shown in Figure 30-2.

You can also discover a great deal of general information about your worksheet if you choose Worksheet Information from the Worksheet Auditor dialog box. As before, Excel opens a new worksheet and places key details about the active worksheet in the new worksheet, as shown in Figure 30-3.

Viewing formulas and their results

Displaying formulas and their results is another way to understand a worksheet. You use the Options ⇨ Display command and select Formulas to display the formulas in your worksheet, rather than their results.

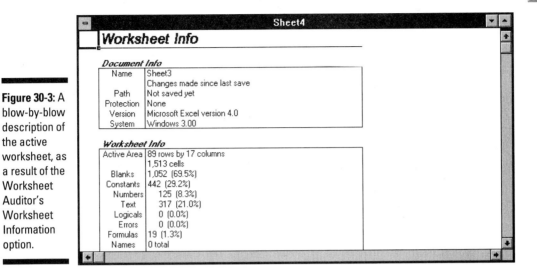

Figure 30-3: A blow-by-blow description of the active worksheet, as a result of the Worksheet Auditor's Worksheet Information option.

To display results and formulas simultaneously, make the worksheet you want to view the active document. Choose Window ⇨ New Window, then make the first window the active window. Now choose Window ⇨ Arrange and then Tiled and Windows of Active Document. Your screen arrangement should resemble the one shown in Figure 30-4. Saving the worksheet to disk saves this display arrangement for your next Excel session. Choose Window ⇨ View to create a view that you can use at your discretion. Either way, you can see the numbers and what's behind them at the same time.

Figure 30-4: Choose Options ⇨ Display and select Formulas to view the formulas behind the numbers.

	IS_01.XLS:1 A	B		IS_01.XLS:2 A	B
1	Gross sales	$125,000	1	Gross sales	125000
3	COGS	75,000	3	COGS	=B1*0.6
5	Gross Margin	50,000	5	Gross Margin	=B1-B3
7	G&A	4,500	7	G&A	=B5*0.09
8	Interest	1,000	8	Interest	=B5*0.02
10	Op Expense	5,500	10	Op Expense	=B7+B8
12	Gross Profit	44,500	12	Gross Profit	=B5-B10
14	Income taxes	14,685	14	Income taxes	=B12*0.33
16	Net income	$29,815	16	Net income	=B12-B14

Check Sync Horizontal and/or Sync Vertical from the Window Arrange dialog box to make the two windows scroll together.

Examining the active cell

In addition to displaying formula information, you can display everything associated with the active cell. Select the Options ⇨ Workspace command and choose Info Window. The Info Window reveals the following characteristics about the active cell:

Attribute	Description
Cell	Cell address of active cell
Formula	Contents of cell as a formula
Value	Operand or result of formula
Format	Number, alignment, fonts, border, and shade formats
Protection	Protection status (locked or unlocked)
Names	Named ranges the active cell is part of
Precedents	Shows cells the active cell depends on for calculations
Dependents	Shows cells that depend on the active cell for calculations
Note	Displays any attached notes

By default, Excel shows you the active cell's cell address, formula, and note. To show additional attributes, make the Info Window the active window. Next, select Info from the menu bar and choose the cell characteristic you want (or don't want) to see from the pull-down menu. Now, make your worksheet the active window and select another cell to display its contents in the Info Window. You can use the technique just described to display your worksheet and the Info Window simultaneously on-screen, as shown in Figure 30-5.

Remember, you can view any existing range names and their corresponding cell addresses with the Formula ⇨ Define Name command and paste a similar list of information into your worksheet by choosing the Formula ⇨ Paste Name command.

Double-clicking a selected cell that has a note displays the Note dialog box.

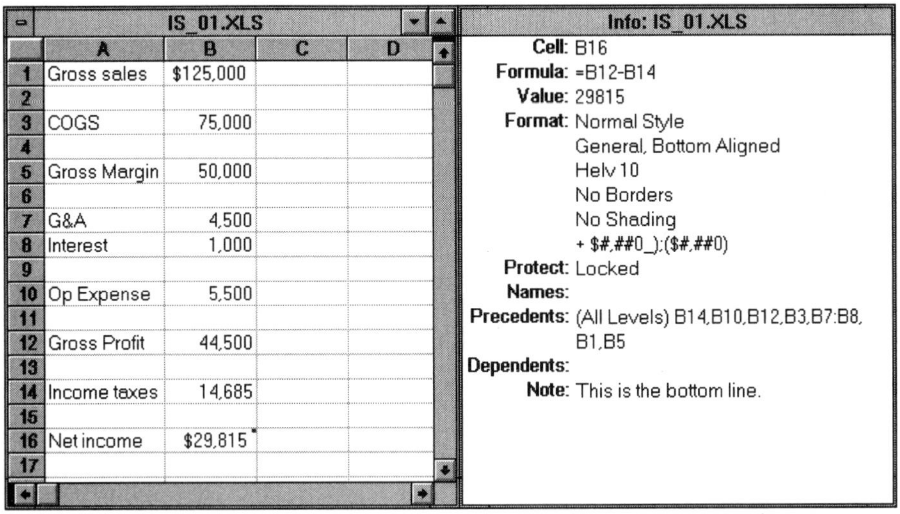

	A	B	C	D
1	Gross sales	$125,000		
2				
3	COGS	75,000		
4				
5	Gross Margin	50,000		
6				
7	G&A	4,500		
8	Interest	1,000		
9				
10	Op Expense	5,500		
11				
12	Gross Profit	44,500		
13				
14	Income taxes	14,685		
15				
16	Net income	$29,815		
17				

IS_01.XLS

Info: IS_01.XLS

Cell: B16
Formula: =B12-B14
Value: 29815
Format: Normal Style
General, Bottom Aligned
Helv 10
No Borders
No Shading
+ $#,##0_);($#,##0)
Protect: Locked
Names:
Precedents: (All Levels) B14,B10,B12,B3,B7:B8,
B1,B5
Dependents:
Note: This is the bottom line.

Figure 30-5:
You can
display both
the work-
sheet and
the Info
Window to
learn all
about the
contents of
a cell.

Understanding cell relationships

Worksheets can easily get out of hand, and you might have a complex network
of cell dependencies that are confusing and present a significant potential for
errors. Thus far, you've seen how to determine certain aspects about your
worksheet: its size and the contents of cells. In this section, we'll get down to
the nitty-gritty and learn how to uncover errors and understand your worksheet's logic.

Selecting cells the special way

There's a way you can have Excel select only the cells in your worksheet that
contain attributes you specify. To do this, you use the Formula ⇨ Select Special
command. You still need to select a range of cells (or a single cell for your
entire worksheet) to use Formula ⇨ Select Special, but the command has many
options that can tell you a great deal about the worksheet you're dealing with.

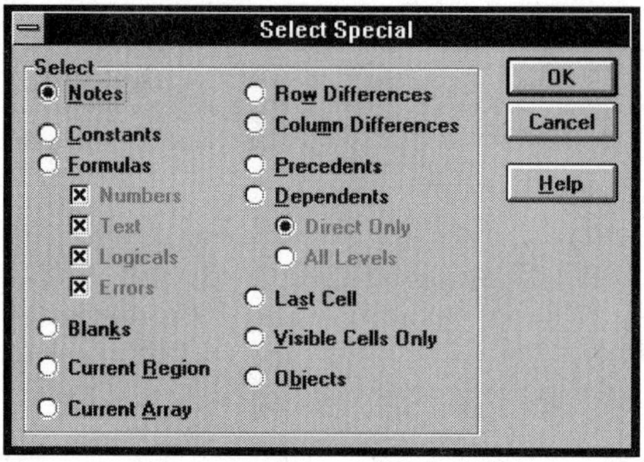

Figure 30-6: The
Select Special
dialog box, with a
plethora of selec-
tion type options.

The Select Special dialog box is shown in Figure 30-6. Excel can search your
worksheet for only one of these options at a time, as indicated by the use of
radio buttons. In the case of Constants and Formulas, however, you can look for
any combination of Numbers, Text, Logicals, or Errors. The following Select
Special choices are particularly useful in auditing your worksheet:

Notes	Selects cells that have a note attached to them.
Constants or **Formulas**	Selects cells that contain constants or formulas, respectively, based on the options (Numbers, Text, Logicals, Errors) you select.
Blanks	Selects cells that are blank.
Row Differences or **Column Differences**	Selects cells in rows or columns, respectively, that are different from other cells in the same row or column (as shown in Figure 30-7).
Precedents or **Dependents**	Selects cells that are referred to by formulas or cells that depend on other cells (as shown in Figure 30-8).
Last Cell	Selects the last cell (the cell whose address is the highest row number and column letter) containing data or formatting.

You can do a quick check for the existence of error values in your worksheet
using the Formula ⇨ Find command. Select the range you want to search, type #
and the error value you want to find in the Find What text box, and choose OK.

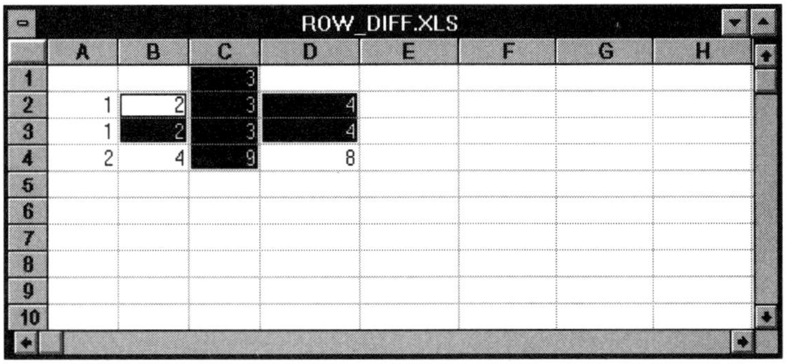

Figure 30-7: A cell whose formula is out of line with its respective cell counterparts.

The Precedent and Dependent options are particularly useful in understanding the relationships among cells. Precedent and Dependent enable you to mentally work through, or trace, the cells a formula depends on for its calculations. In this manner, you can identify the cells involved in a circular reference and take corrective action. These options also let you specify the level of precedence or dependence you want to see: Direct Only or All Levels. Direct Only displays cells that have a direct relationship with a cell containing a formula. All Levels displays cells that have a direct or indirect relationship with a cell containing a formula (an indirect relationship occurs when a direct cell refers to an indirect cell). Figure 30-9 illustrates some simple examples of these Precedent and Dependent options.

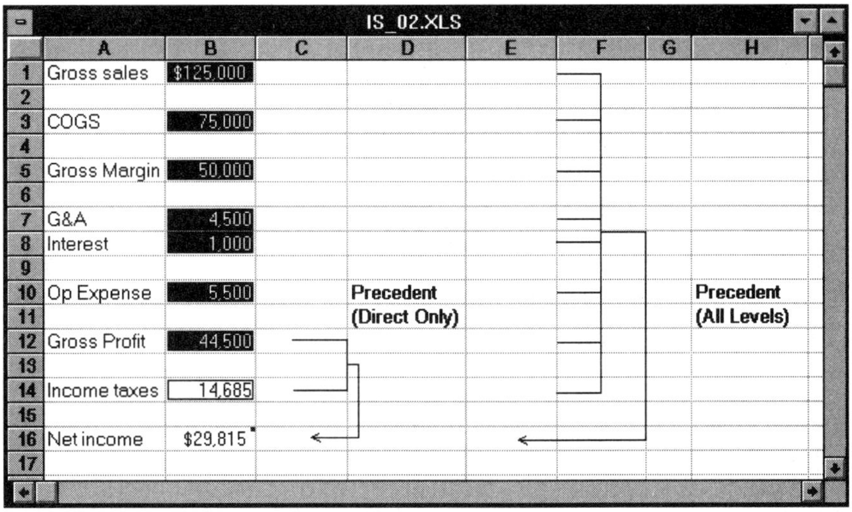

Figure 30-8: The formula in cell B16 is directly dependent on cells B12 and B14.

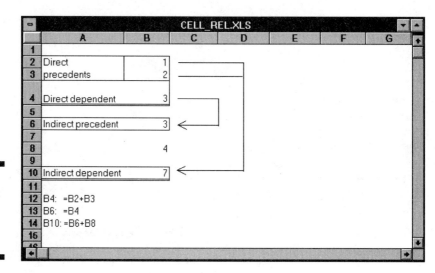

Figure 30-9:
Various incarnations of cell dependents and precedents.

Tracing interactively

The Formula ⇨ Select Special command's Precedent and Dependent options display their respective information nondynamically — that is, Excel highlights the appropriate cells if they meet the condition you specify in the dialog box. The Formula ⇨ Worksheet Auditor command's Interactive Trace option, however, lets you step through a cell's precedents or dependents one cell at a time. This feature helps you understand a cell's relationship with the other cells on your worksheet by viewing the actual cells that depend on or refer to the cell you're examining.

Once you've identified either dependent or precedent cells with Formula ⇨ Select Special, you can use Interactive Trace to perform a more detailed cell relationship analysis.

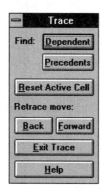

Figure 30-10: The Worksheet Auditor's interactive Trace dialog box — your gateway to uncovering the active cell's relationships to other cells.

To trace cell relationships interactively, select the cell you want to examine. Then choose Interactive Trace from the Worksheet Auditor dialog box. The Trace dialog box (see Figure 30-10) and the Info Window appear. Choose Find Dependents or Precedents to locate the first occurrence of the cells that rely and refer, respectively, on or to the active cell. Continue choosing one of these buttons until you've completed your trace. Each time you choose one of these buttons, the dependent or precedent cell becomes the active cell. Excel notifies you that the trace is complete by displaying the message box in Figure 30-11.

Figure 30-11: You've reached the end of the trace line when this dialog box displays

You can retrace your steps using the Back button or go forward using the Forward button. If you want to trace through another cell's dependencies or precedents, choose Reset Active Cell. Excel displays the Formula Goto dialog box. Select a range name from the Goto list box or type a cell address in the Reference box, then choose OK. When you're finished tracing, choose Exit Trace.

Creating an audit report

The Worksheet Auditor add-in can also generate a report about certain aspects of your worksheet. This report gives you an opportunity to analyze current or potential worksheet problem areas.

To create an audit report, choose Generate Audit Report from the Worksheet Auditor dialog box, clear the check boxes of the information you *don't* want included in an audit report, and then choose OK. Here are the available options:

Errors	Cells with error values.
References to Blanks	Formulas that refer to blank cells.
References to Text	Formulas that refer to text cells.
Circular references	All cells contributing to a circular reference.
Names	Unused or problem range names.

The audit report is placed on one new worksheet, regardless of the number of options you choose. The report includes the cell's address, formula, value, and description of the problem, as shown in Figure 30-12.

Depending on the size of the worksheet you're auditing, your audit report may be a bit unwieldy. To create a more manageable report, copy and paste each option's report section to its own new worksheet.

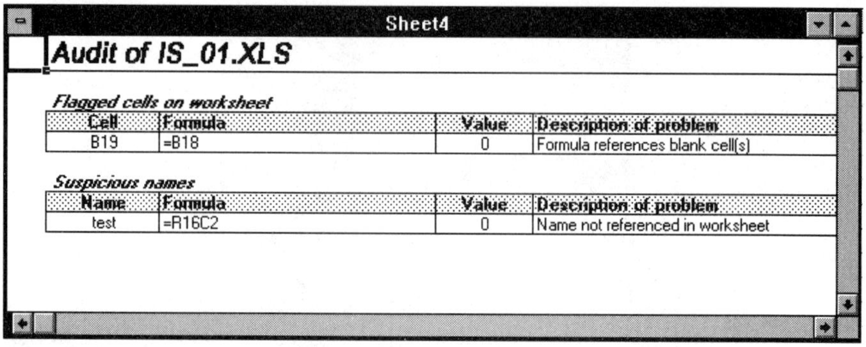

Figure 30-12:
Information
you can glean
from the
Worksheet
Auditor's
Audit Report.

More tools for you

Excel has two more add-ins you should keep in mind as you audit your worksheet. Both of these files are located in the \library subdirectory and can be accessed using the File ⇨ Open command.

The Summary add-in

This add-in macro (named summary.xla) provides a way to view and enter general information about a worksheet. After you open the add-in, Excel adds the Summary Info command to the Edit menu.

Choosing this command displays the dialog box shown in Figure 30-13, which Microsoft Word for Windows users might immediately recognize. You can view, add, or edit information as appropriate in the Title, Subject, Author, and Comments text boxes (but not in the Created text box). Choosing OK saves the information as hidden names with your worksheet, though be sure to use File ⇨ Save or Save As so you have the information available to you in your next Excel session.

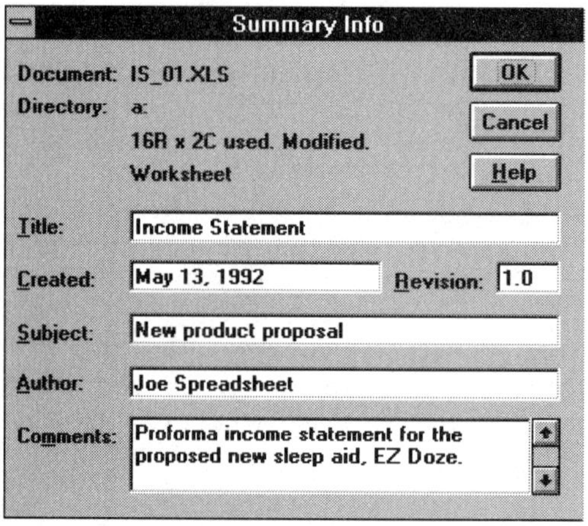

To get the most from the Summary add-in, load it before you begin working. You can then update the information contained in the Summary Info dialog box whenever you make an important

Figure 30-13:
Summary
information
available from
the Summary
add-in macro.

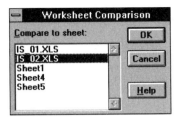

Figure 30-14: Use this dialog box to select the worksheet you want to compare with your active worksheet.

modification to your worksheets. The Summary add-in is especially useful if you use Excel or the worksheet on a network. Have the macro loaded automatically each time you start Excel by placing it in your x/start subdirectory.

The Compare add-in

The compare.xla macro creates a report that analyzes and then summarizes the differences between the active worksheet and another you specify. After you attach the add-in, Excel adds the Compare command to the Formula menu.

Choosing this command displays the Worksheet Comparison dialog box, shown in Figure 30-14, from which you select the name of the worksheet you want compared to the active worksheet. After you choose OK, Excel opens a new worksheet to create a report like that shown in Figure 30-15. The Compare report displays the number of rows and columns of each worksheet, as well as a cell-by-cell comparison of cell contents. The Compare add-in is especially useful if you have multiple versions of the same worksheet, which occurs during budgeting cycles and in multiuser computing environments, or when you want to compare old and updated versions of a custom application you developed.

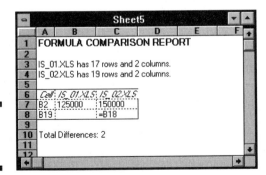

Figure 30-15: The results of comparing two worksheets.

Checking Your Spelling

You've checked your numbers, so what's left? Your spelling. Spell-checking was once the exclusive domain of word processing programs, but now Excel 4 has the capability to check your text. When you choose Spelling from the Options menu, Excel checks your entire worksheet, including words in headers and footers, embedded charts, text boxes, cell notes, and buttons, unless you want to check only a specified range.

If you begin a spelling check in any cell other than A1, Excel checks the balance of your worksheet and displays a dialog box asking whether you want to continue checking from the beginning of your document. The default is Yes.

You can also check the spelling of words in macro sheets, graphic objects, and Formula bars. To check the spelling of words in charts, chose Spelling from the Chart menu.

If Excel encounters a word that isn't in the open dictionary or is misspelled, the dialog box in Figure 30-16 appears. If you don't want Excel to take any action, choose Ignore or Ignore All, and Excel won't question any other occurrences of the word.

Choose Change if you want to accept the word Excel is suggesting in the Change To text box. You can also edit the word in the Change To text box or choose a word (if any) from the Suggestions list box, as long as you remember to choose Change after you've made your selection. Here's the complete set of options that are available in the Spelling dialog box:

Change To   Type or edit the suggested replacement word not found in the open dictionary.

Figure 30-16: Your chance to exchange words with your worksheet, when Excel encounters a word not in its standard dictionary.

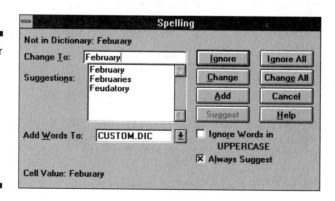

Suggestions	A list box that enables you to choose a word to replace the word not found in the open dictionary, or to edit in the Change To text box.
Add Words To	A pull-down list that lets you choose a custom dictionary you want to add correctly spelled words to.
Ignore	No changes to the selected word are made and Excel continues spell checking.
Ignore All	No changes to the selected word anywhere in the active document.
Change	The selected word is changed to the word in the Change To text box.
Change All	Changes all occurrences of the selected word in the active document to the word in the Change To text box.
Add	Adds the selected word to the chosen custom dictionary in the Add Words To box.
Cancel/Close	Stops spell checking. If you've changed a misspelled word or added a new word to the open custom dictionary, this selection closes the Options Spelling dialog box.
Suggest	Displays a list of replacement words. Not available if you've unchecked the Always Suggest box.
Ignore Words in UPPERCASE	Omits checking words in capital letters.
Always Suggest	Always displays a list of suggestions when a word is not found in the open dictionary.

When Excel comes across a word that's spelled correctly but that it doesn't recognize, it suggests changes. If you use such a word frequently, you can add it to a dictionary and Excel won't question the word again. If you want to include the word in the standard dictionary, choose Add. If you want to add it to a custom dictionary you create, choose or type the name of the dictionary from the Add Words To text box, then choose Add. If the dictionary is new, Excel displays the dialog box in Figure 30-17. Choose Yes (the default) to create the dictionary. Be sure to enter the word exactly as the way you intend to use it in your worksheets.

Figure 30-17: Excel requesting confirmation that you want to create a new custom dictionary.

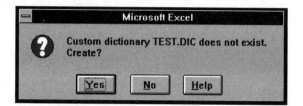

The Right Tool for the Job

There's more than one way to perform a task in Excel, and auditing is no exception. You can use the method or feature that most appeals to you and best fits your needs. The following table summarizes the auditing tools and recommends the most appropriate one for the task at hand.

Task	Command
Locate errors	Formula ⇨ Find Formula ⇨ Select Special ⇨ Formulas Errors Worksheet Auditor ⇨ Generate Audit Report ⇨ Errors
Determine cell precedents*	Formula ⇨ Select Special ⇨ Precedent Worksheet Auditor ⇨ Interactive Trace
Determine cell dependents*	Formula ⇨ Select Special ⇨ Dependent Worksheet Auditor ⇨ Interactive Trace
Find circular references	Status bar Worksheet Auditor ⇨ Generate Audit Report ⇨ Circular References
Determine if cells in rows or columns are similar	Formula ⇨ Select Special ⇨ Row Differences or Column Differences
Range names*	Formula ⇨ Define Name Formula ⇨ Paste Name ⇨ Paste List Worksheet Auditor ⇨ Generate Audit Report ⇨ Names
Cells with notes*	Formula ⇨ Note Formula ⇨ Select Special ⇨ Notes
View a miniature display of worksheet	Window ⇨ Zoom

Also shown in the (Options ⇨ Workspace) Info Window.   *(continued)*

Task	Command
Create a worksheet map	<u>W</u>orksheet Auditor ⇨ <u>M</u>ap Worksheet
Understand worksheet attributes	<u>W</u>orksheet Auditor ⇨ Worksheet <u>I</u>nformation <u>E</u>dit ⇨ Su<u>m</u>mary (Summary add-in) <u>W</u>orksheet Auditor ⇨ <u>M</u>ap Worksheet
Compare similar worksheets	Fo<u>r</u>mula ⇨ <u>C</u>ompare (Compare add-in)
Check spelling	<u>O</u>ptions ⇨ <u>S</u>pelling
Locate the furthest cell with data or formatting	Fo<u>r</u>mula ⇨ <u>S</u>elect Special ⇨ La<u>s</u>t Cell

* Also shown in the (<u>O</u>ptions ⇨ <u>W</u>orkspace) Info Window.

Summary

▶ Worksheet mistakes can occur without warning, making auditing a necessary component of your Excel routine. Fortunately, Excel has an impressive array of auditing tools at your disposal.

▶ Use <u>W</u>indow ⇨ <u>Z</u>oom to display a smaller version of your worksheet on-screen — get a bird's eye view.

▶ Display a map of your worksheet using <u>W</u>orksheet Auditor ⇨ <u>M</u>ap Worksheet.

▶ Display formulas and their results at the same time by opening a new window and displaying one window with <u>O</u>ptions ⇨ <u>W</u>orkspace ⇨ Fo<u>r</u>mulas.

▶ You can find out a lot about your worksheet with the <u>W</u>orksheet Auditor ⇨ Worksheet <u>I</u>nformation and <u>E</u>dit ⇨ Su<u>m</u>mary commands.

▶ Fo<u>r</u>mula ⇨ <u>S</u>elect Special enables you to find cells with certain characteristics..

▶ You can track down the cause of circular references by creating a report using <u>W</u>orksheet Auditor ⇨ Generate <u>A</u>udit Report ⇨ <u>C</u>ircular references and/or by stepping through the cells involved in the circular reference (using <u>W</u>orksheet Auditor ⇨ Interactive <u>T</u>race).

▶ You can check the spelling of the labels in a worksheet using <u>O</u>ptions ⇨ <u>S</u>pelling.

Chapter 31
Creating User-Oriented Applications

In this chapter . . .

▶ What you need to be aware of if the spreadsheets that you develop are used by others.

▶ A discussion of user interface issues — how a user will interact with the worksheet.

▶ How to use Excel's Dialog Editor to create custom dialog boxes for specialized spreadsheet applications.

▶ How to protect the integrity of your worksheet and keep your work from being inadvertently destroyed.

▶ Spreadsheet aesthetics — how your Excel application looks and feels is important.

▶ A useful example of a macro-driven application — a calendar generator for virtually any year and month you're likely to need.

Most of your spreadsheet work is done for yourself. Sure, you probably print reports and charts for others to see, but it's a safe bet that the majority of your worksheet files aren't shared with others. This chapter takes spreadsheet development to the next level and provides some pointers on how to create spreadsheet applications that others will use — people who haven't had the benefit of toiling for hours with formulas, inserting and/or deleting rows and columns, and getting the range names straight. Although we don't cover all the intricacies involved, this chapter should provide a good jumping-off place for your own explorations.

Why Create Worksheets for Others? _____

When you think about it, one of the most appealing aspects of computers and software is that they automate various tasks. For example, you don't have to understand your computer's boot-up process — it happens automatically. Similarly, there's no need to know how Excel calculates its PMT function; all you need to know is what the arguments are.

Excel is a highly programmable spreadsheet program — more so than any other product on the market. This means that you can almost approach Excel as you would a programming language such as Basic, Pascal, or C. This also means that you can create "applications" that others can use. As with any programming language there are certain rules and considerations that you must adhere to or your application will not work well. Here are a few examples why you might create worksheets that other people would use:

- You need to input a load of data — and your time is worth more than a clerk's (who couldn't tell a spreadsheet from a bed sheet). You can set the spreadsheet up so it's relatively foolproof and provide the clerk with some simple instructions.

- Your coworkers need to do some numerical analysis and what-if projections but they are only vaguely familiar with Excel. You can set up the worksheet with custom dialog boxes to make variable substitutions easy.

- Your secretary is in charge of tracking your budget expenditures but he's not very well trained in Excel. You can set up a menu-driven budget tracking sheet to enter the data and automatically generate reports.

- The field sales people need to generate price quotes on the spot. All of them carry laptops but they don't understand Excel. You can create a customized quote-generation worksheet that prompts the user for all of the relevant information and then displays or prints the results.

- Your boss wants to be able to see some important data that's accessible on the LAN. Since she's not so good with computers, you can set up a front-end that automatically loads the data she wants and display charts — all with push-button ease.

And this list goes on. You can probably think of a dozen more examples that are relevant to your situation. If you can't, perhaps this chapter isn't for you.

Worksheet Design and Layout Considerations

If you're like most users, you probably start a new worksheet in the upper-left corner and work your way down — and maybe across. You probably don't give a whole lot of thought as to how the final worksheet or group of worksheets will be laid out. After all, one of the great features of a spreadsheet is that you can always insert rows or columns and move things around as often as you like.

While there's certainly nothing terribly wrong with the relatively haphazard approach just described, you can probably see certain advantages to doing a little planning. The main advantage is that you can significantly reduce your development time if you know in advance what data is going to go where.

For complex applications some developers make diagrams for where various components will be located and how multiple documents interact with each other. This is a good practice for both development and documentation purposes. What you want to avoid is haphazard design. You might want to use multiple worksheets linked together if your application is modular and then you can combine these multiple files into a single workbook.

Excel's Window ⇨ Zoom command lets you zoom out to see the big picture. You can also use the Worksheet Auditor add-in (audit.xla) to generate a map of worksheets and macro sheets.

Range Names

By now you should realize the importance of using range names whenever possible. When you're developing large or complex applications you'll probably be moving ranges around and reorganizing your work — all the more reason to use range names. When you create worksheets that other users will be modifying or examining, range names are even more important. They provide an audit trail, of sorts, and you can easily paste a table of range names into a worksheet with the Formula ⇨ Paste Name command.

It's a good practice to delete any range names that are no longer valid. Again, the Worksheet Auditor can help you locate these.

User Interface Issues

A key consideration when you develop worksheets that others will use is the user interface. By user interface we mean the method by which the user interacts with the spreadsheet.

One way to approach the user interface issue is to rely on Excel's built-in features: its menus, toolbars, scroll bars, and so on. In other words, you can simply let the user work with the worksheet however he or she wants. In many cases, this is fine — assuming the worksheet is intended for a knowledgeable Excel user.

If the user is relatively inexperienced, you'll be better off by keeping things under control with macros. Excel provides four methods that let you design user interfaces:

■ Macro buttons

■ Custom dialog boxes

■ Custom menus

■ Custom toolbars

Macro buttons

A macro button is an object that's placed on the worksheet. The user clicks the button to execute the macro that's attached to it. Actually, you can attach a macro to any graphic object but using a button makes it fairly clear that some action will be carried out when the button is clicked.

You can add a button to a worksheet with the button tool. You'll need to customize a toolbar to have access to this, or you can display the Microsoft Excel 3 toolbar. If you customize a toolbar, you'll find the button tool grouped under the drawing tools category. See Chapter 19 for details on customizing toolbars.

When you click the button tool, the message in the status bar instructs you to "drag in document to create." Press and drag in the worksheet to create a button of any size. When you release the mouse button, Excel displays the Assign To Object dialog box (see Figure 31-1). If you have macros defined, this dialog box displays a list of them. Select the macro name that you want to assign or point to a cell reference on a macro sheet. Alternatively, you can choose Record to record a macro that will be attached to the button (you'll get the normal Record Macro dialog box).

The buttons in the Record Macro dialog box have default names: Button 1, Button 2, and so on. To change the name to something more meaningful, hold down Ctrl and click the button to select it (clicking on it without pressing Ctrl executes the macro that's attached to it). Select the text in the button and enter new text to replace it. You can also right-click on a button to get to the shortcut menu. This lets you change the macro assigned to that button or perform some other operations.

The main advantage to using buttons in a worksheet is that they eliminate the need to use the Macro ⇨ Run command or to press a key combination that executes a macro. Too many buttons, however, gets confusing. If you have many options to choose from, consider using custom menus or a custom dialog box. You can even combine them so clicking a button brings up a dialog box with more choices.

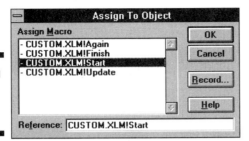

Figure 31-1: This dialog box is used to assign a macro to a worksheet object.

Creating custom dialog boxes

A complete discussion of custom dialog boxes is beyond the scope of this book — we're already ahead of our target page count. The following information should, however, provide enough for you to get started — or at least try out this feature.

The Dialog Editor is a stand-alone application (`excelde.exe`) that makes it easy to create custom dialog boxes. When you installed Excel, you had the choice of installing the Dialog Editor. If you didn't install it, run the Setup program again. You'll want to run the Dialog Editor at the same time you're working in an Excel macro sheet. You have two ways to run the Dialog Editor:

■ Move to Program Manager and double-click the Dialog Editor icon (normally located in the Excel 4 program group).

■ Open Excel's control menu (the box in the upper-left corner of the Excel window), select Run from the menu, and then choose Dialog Editor.

Figure 31-2 shows an example of the Dialog Editor in action.

You build a dialog box by adding items to it from the pull-down menus. For example, to add an OK button to your dialog box, select Item ⇨ Button and then select OK as the button option. This inserts the OK button into the dialog box. You can move it and resize the dialog box using normal click and drag techniques, and you can also change the size of the entire thing.

Double-click on a dialog box item to modify some of its properties. For example, double-clicking the OK item displays the dialog box shown in Figure 31-3. This shows the dimensions and location of the dialog box, as well as the text displayed in it (an OK button doesn't have to read "OK").

The Dialog Editor lets you insert group boxes with other items nested inside. For truly advanced applications, you can even create dynamic dialog boxes —

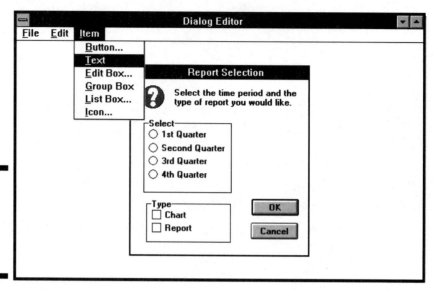

Figure 31-2: The Dialog Editor is a separate program that works in conjunction with Excel.

boxes that change depending on conditions. Excel's Formula Note dialog box is an example of this. The Record and Import buttons are grayed out if your system is not equipped to handle sound notes.

For most situations, using the Dialog Editor is simple and straightforward. When the dialog box looks right, you can copy it to a macro sheet so you can use it in a macro.

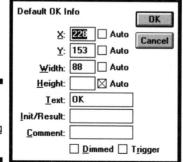

Figure 31-3: You can change the properties of dialog box items directly.

Steps: Attaching a dialog box to a macro sheet

Step 1. Make sure the Dialog Editor is active

Step 2. Choose Edit ➪ Select Dialog and then Edit ➪ Copy. This copies the entire dialog box to the Clipboard.

Step 3. Activate the macro sheet, find a blank range, and choose the Edit ➪ Paste command.

Excel converts the graphical dialog box into a range of data that's seven columns wide, with a row for each item in the dialog box — plus an extra row for the dialog box itself. This is the range that the `dialog.box` macro command should use for its argument. When the macro executes the `dialog.box` command, it displays the dialog box on-screen. The seven columns of dialog box data contain the following information for each item:

Item (column A)	A numeric code for the type of item.
X (column B)	The horizontal position of the item's upper-left corner (measured in pixels).
Y (column C)	The vertical position of the item's upper left-hand corner (measured in pixels).
Width (column D)	The width of the item, measured in pixels.
Height (column E)	The height of the item, measured in pixels.
Text (column F)	Text that is associated with the item.
Init/Result (column G)	The initial value or result for the item.

Figure 31-4 shows how the previous example looks when it's pasted into a macro sheet. The macro command to display this dialog box is `dialog.box(A1:G14)`.

When the user exits a dialog box, the values are returned in the seventh column of the dialog box range. The remainder of the macro (or other macros) can then use this information to control what happens.

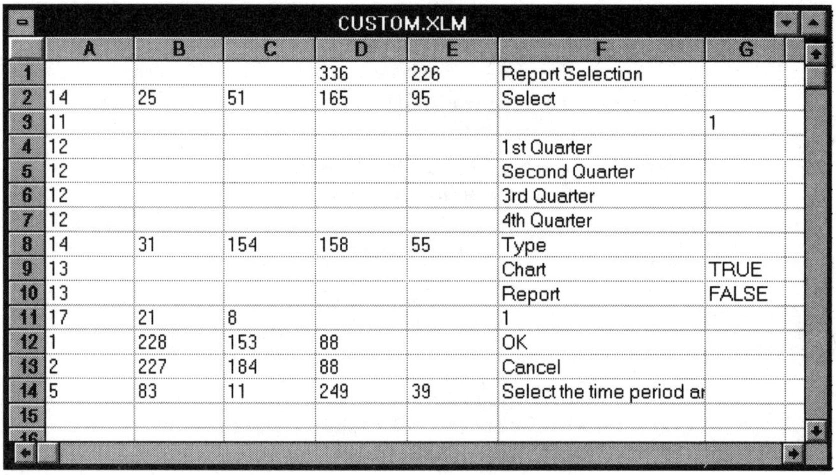

	A	B	C	D	E	F	G
1				336	226	Report Selection	
2	14	25	51	165	95	Select	
3	11						1
4	12					1st Quarter	
5	12					Second Quarter	
6	12					3rd Quarter	
7	12					4th Quarter	
8	14	31	154	158	55	Type	
9	13					Chart	TRUE
10	13					Report	FALSE
11	17	21	8			1	
12	1	228	153	88		OK	
13	2	227	184	88		Cancel	
14	5	83	11	249	39	Select the time period ar	
15							

CUSTOM.XLM

Figure 31-4:
Pasting a
graphical dialog
box into a macro
sheet results in a
seven-column
range of data.

You don't need to use the Dialog Editor to create custom dialog boxes — you can simply insert the data yourself. Nevertheless, the Dialog Editor is much easier since it lets you create the dialog boxes visually.

The Dialog Editor works both ways. You can copy a range of dialog box data from a macro sheet and paste it into the Dialog Box application. The data displays as a real dialog box.

Menu terminology

When you start modifying Excel's menus, it's easy to get confused. It's important to distinguish between menus, commands, and menu bars. Here's the difference:

Command
An option that appears on the pull-down list when you select a menu item. When you select File ⇨ Save, "File" is the menu item, and "Save" is the command.

Menu
A menu is the menu item that appears in the menu bar — plus the command that it pulls down.

Menu bar
A collection of menu items and their commands. You can create new menu bars with custom commands.

Customizing menus

Another way to control user interface in your spreadsheet applications is to modify the Excel menus or create your own menus. Rather than use buttons to execute macros, you can simply add one or more new menu commands that execute macros that you've created.

You have almost complete control over the menu system and can change the names of existing commands or reorder the commands. You can simply add a command or two to an existing menu, add a new menu item, or create an entirely new menu bar.

Commands that you add are based on a command table located in a macro sheet. A command table has five columns and uses one row for each command. The columns in a command table are:

Command name — The name that appears on the menu. Use a hyphen (-) to insert a separator line in the pull-down menu. Precede a character with an ampersand (&) to cause the character to be underlined so it can be used as a hotkey.

Macro name — The macro that executes when the command is selected. If the macro is in another sheet, precede the macro name with a filename reference and an exclamation point.

Status bar message — The text that appears in the status bar when the command name is selected. This is optional, so if you leave it blank no status bar message is displayed.

Custom Help topic — This is also optional. It lets you specify a custom Help topic that displays if the user requests help with this command.

Figure 31-5 shows an example of a new menu bar which might be used in a specialized custom application. In such a case, the user would not have access to the normal menu system and could only select the commands in the custom menu bar. These commands would each trigger a macro.

Again, though we have provided a brief, general overview, a complete discussion of this topic is not possible here. Suffice it to say that you need to know what you're doing before you start changing the menus. This type of interface design is best left to advanced Excel jockeys.

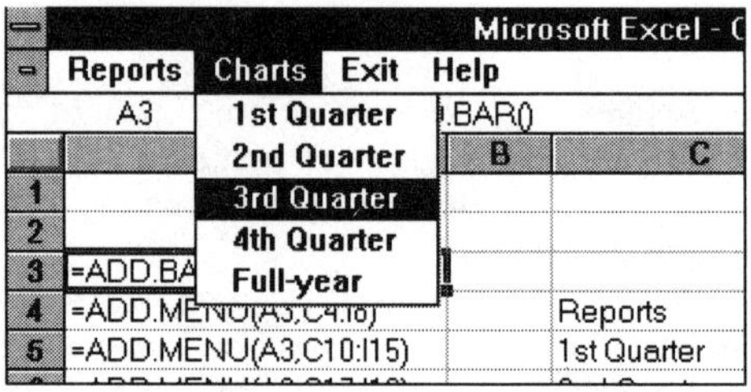

Figure 31-5: Excel lets you create entirely new menu bars with commands that execute macros.

Customizing toolbars

A final method of creating user interfaces is with the toolbars. You can create a custom toolbar which contains only those tools you want the user to have access to. In fact, if you attach macros to these tools, a custom toolbar becomes the equivalent of a group of macro buttons. A potential problem with macro buttons is that the tool icons are small and it might be difficult for some people to figure out what they mean. As a result, using a customized toolbar as your primary user interface is not recommended.

Protecting Files

When you think about it, it's fairly easy to destroy a worksheet. Often, erasing one critical formula or value can have a ripple effect and cause errors throughout the entire worksheet — and perhaps other dependent worksheets. Even worse, if the damaged worksheet is saved, it replaces the good copy on disk. Unless you have a backup you could be in trouble.

Obviously, it's easy to see why you need to add some protection when other users — especially novices — will be using your worksheets. Excel provides several techniques for protecting worksheets and parts of worksheets:

■ You can lock specific cells (with the Format ⇨ Cell Protection command) so they cannot be changed. This takes effect only when the document is protected with the Options ⇨ Protect Document command.

■ You can hide the formulas in specific cells (with the Format ⇨ Cell Protection command) so others can't see them. This takes effect only when the document is protected with the Options ⇨ Protect Document command.

■ You can lock objects on the worksheet (with the Format ⇨ Object Protection command). This takes effect only when the document is protected with the Options ⇨ Protect Document command.

- You can hide rows (Format ⇨ Row Height), columns (Format ⇨ Column Width), and documents (Window ⇨ Hide). This helps prevent the worksheet from looking cluttered and also provides some protection against prying eyes.

- You can designate Excel documents — including workbooks — as "read-only" to ensure that they cannot be overwritten with any changes.

- You can assign a password to prevent unauthorized users from opening your file.

The level of protection you choose to use, and how you implement it, will depend on the application and who will be using it.

Aesthetic Considerations

If you've used many different software packages, you've undoubtedly seen examples of poorly designed user interfaces, difficult-to-use programs, and ugly screens. If you're going to develop spreadsheets for others, you should try to avoid these problems.

Use color sparingly, since it's easy to make the screen look gaudy. Also pay attention to numeric formats, typefaces and sizes, and borders. Do whatever you can to make individual parts of the worksheet appear more cohesive.

Documentation

Putting a spreadsheet model together is one thing — making it understandable to other people is another. As with programming, it's important that you thoroughly document your work. Documentation can either be part of the spreadsheet model itself, or a separate document. For example, if you've been hired to develop an Excel model, you may not want to share all of your hard-earned secrets by thoroughly documenting everything. If this is the case, you should maintain two versions of documentation: one thorough, and the other partial.

How do you document a worksheet? For macros it's a good idea to store comments in a separate column next to the macro code. A clever use of a macro function may seem perfectly obvious today — but when you come back to it in a few months your reasoning may seem completely obscure.

Use the text tool to insert commentary — the nice thing about this feature is you can shrink the text box down without affecting the text and you can scroll through the box to read the text or enlarge the box temporarily.

Testing It Out

It goes without saying that any spreadsheet development you'll be doing for others should be thoroughly tested first. Depending on the eventual audience, you might want to make your spreadsheet bulletproof and anticipate all of the errors and screw-ups that could possibly occur.

Although it's impossible to test for all possibilities, your macros should be able to handle common types of errors. For example, what if the user enters a text string instead of a value? What if he or she cancels a dialog box without making any selections? What happens if the user presses Ctrl+F6 and jumps to the next window? Although you don't have complete control, Excel does let you control many aspects of the macro environment.

Building a Sample Application

Now it's time to translate all of this information into something useful. The goal is to create a perpetual calendar — an intuitive user-oriented application that displays and prints a full-page calendar for any month. Here's a list of the requirements for this application:

- The user need not know anything about Excel.
- The program will automatically display an accurate calendar month for any date between 1900 and 2078 (the limits of Excel's date system).
- The user can get a printout of the month currently displayed.

An overview

This project has two parts: a worksheet with formulas for calculating and displaying the calendar, and a macro sheet for holding the macros that control the application. We'll store the worksheet and the macro sheet as unbound files in a workbook. (See Chapter 21 for a discussion of workbooks.) We used the names `cal.xls`, `cal.xlm`, and `cal.xlw`.

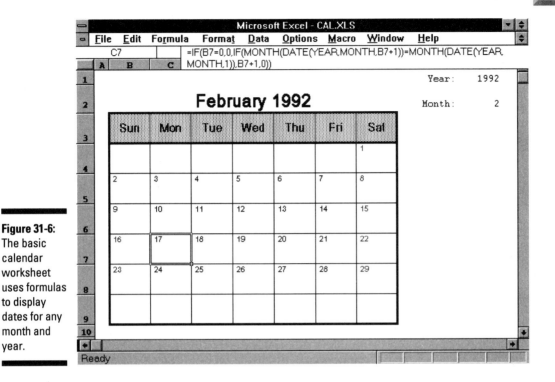

Figure 31-6:
The basic calendar worksheet uses formulas to display dates for any month and year.

If you store these as bound files you need to adjust any references to other sheets by adding the workbook name before the filename. For example, a reference to `cal.xlm!error` should be replaced with `[cal.xlw]cal.xlm!error`. (This assumes the workbook is named `cal.xlw`.)

The calendar worksheet

The first step is to set up the basic worksheet shown in Figure 31-6. The worksheet uses some rather complex formulas to determine the dates on the calendar for a specified month and year. The two variables that drive the application are named *month* and *year*. Changing either one of these displays a different calendar month.

We'll use this basic worksheet, along with a macro file, to create the application. If you would like to recreate this application, here are step-by-step instructions:

Steps: Setting up the worksheet

Step 1. Enter the following formulas into the indicated cells.

```
B2:    =DATE(YEAR,MONTH,1)
B4:    =IF(WEEKDAY(first)=1,1,0)
C4:    =IF(WEEKDAY(first)=2,1,IF(B4>0,B4+1,0))
D4:    =IF(WEEKDAY(first)=3,1,IF(C4>0,C4+1,0))
E4:    =IF(WEEKDAY(first)=4,1,IF(D4>0,D4+1,0))
F4:    =IF(WEEKDAY(first)=5,1,IF(E4>0,E4+1,0))
G4:    =IF(WEEKDAY(first)=6,1,IF(F4>0,F4+1,0))
H4:    =IF(WEEKDAY(first)=7,1,IF(G4>0,G4+1,0))
```

Step 2. Enter the following formula into cell B5 and then copy it to B6:B9.

```
B5:
=IF(H4=0,0,IF(MONTH(DATE(YEAR,MONTH,H4+1))=MONTH(DATE(YEAR,MONTH,1)),H4+1,0))
```

Step 3. Enter the following formula into cell C5 and then copy it to the range C6:H9.

```
C5:
=IF(B5=0,0,IF(MONTH(DATE(YEAR,MONTH,B5+1))=MONTH(DATE(YEAR,MONTH,1)),B5+1,0))
```

Step 4. Assign the following range names:

```
First       =$B$2
Calendar    =$B$2:$H$9
Year        =$K$1
Month       =$K$2
```

Step 5. Apply formatting to suit your tastes. You can select borders, colors, fonts, patterns, row heights, column widths, and so on.

If this worksheet is set up properly, you can enter a year into cell K1 (*year*) and a month number into cell K2 (*month*), and the appropriate calendar should display.

The goal of this exercise is to allow an inexperienced user to display and print different calendar months. To enable this, we use macros to prevent the user from interacting directly with the worksheet.

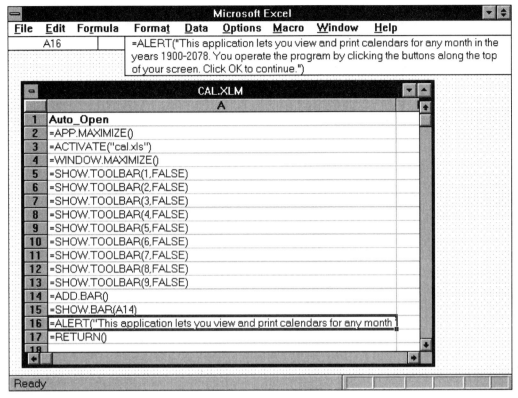

Figure 31-7: The Auto_Open macro in the calendar macro sheet.

The macro sheet

This application uses six macros:

- An Auto_Open macro that runs whenever the macro sheet is opened.

- Four macros that are executed by clicking buttons in the worksheet.

- A macro to display an error message if an invalid date is detected.

The Auto_Open macro

As you may know, any macro named Auto_Open is automatically executed when-ever the macro sheet is opened. We use this macro to perform some preliminary housekeeping. It maximizes the Excel window and the cal.xls window, removes any toolbars that may be displayed, removes the menu bar, and displays an opening comment to the user. This macro, combined with appropriate settings made with the Options ⇨ Display and Options ⇨ Workspace commands (these are saved with the workbook), creates a display that doesn't resemble a spreadsheet. The Auto_Open macro is shown in Figure 31-7 with the scroll bars, formula bar, and the status bar removed.

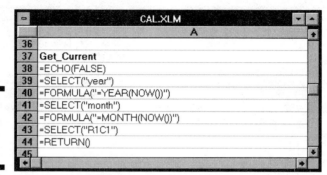

Figure 31-8: The Get_Current macro in the calendar macro sheet.

	CAL.XLM
	A
36	
37	Get_Current
38	=ECHO(FALSE)
39	=SELECT("year")
40	=FORMULA("=YEAR(NOW())")
41	=SELECT("month")
42	=FORMULA("=MONTH(NOW())")
43	=SELECT("R1C1")
44	=RETURN()
45	

Don't add the add.bar and show.bar commands to this macro until you're sure that everything else in the application is working properly. It's rather difficult to make changes to your macros without any menus!

The Get_Current macro

This macro displays a calendar for the current month. It works by entering formulas into the year and month cells. These formulas return the current year and the current month (assuming the system clock is set correctly). The formulas in the calendar itself rely on these values. The macro code is shown in Figure 31-8. This macro is executed when the user clicks the button labeled "Show Current Month."

The Get_Input macro

The Get_Input macro (see Figure 31-9) displays a custom dialog box that lets the user:

1. Select the month from an option box, and

2. Enter the year into a text box.

This macro is executed when the user clicks the worksheet button labeled "Change Year and Month."

The data used to create the dialog box is stored in the dialog1 range on the macro sheet. The first IF command checks to see if the user clicked Cancel in the dialog box; if so, the macro ends without doing anything. The other two IF commands are error checking commands to make sure the year entered is within the valid range. If not, the macro runs the Error macro (see later in this chapter). If the year is valid, the macro inserts formulas into the year and month cells on the worksheet. These formulas refer to the cells on the macro sheet that hold the results from the dialog box. Make sure cell I5 is named User_Month and cell I18 is named User_Year.

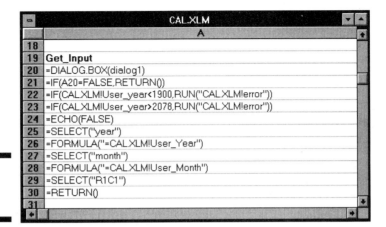

	A
18	
19	Get_Input
20	=DIALOG.BOX(dialog1)
21	=IF(A20=FALSE,RETURN())
22	=IF(CAL.XLM!User_year<1900,RUN("CAL.XLM!error"))
23	=IF(CAL.XLM!User_year>2078,RUN("CAL.XLM!error"))
24	=ECHO(FALSE)
25	=SELECT("year")
26	=FORMULA("=CAL.XLM!User_Year")
27	=SELECT("month")
28	=FORMULA("=CAL.XLM!User_Month")
29	=SELECT("R1C1")
30	=RETURN()
31	

Figure 31-9: The Get_Input macro in the calendar macro sheet.

The dialog1 code

We created a dialog box using Excel's Editor. The application produced the code shown in Figure 31-10. The range C1:I21 on the macro sheet is named `dialog1`. The year is returned in cell I18, and the month is in cell I11.

The Error macro

This macro (shown in Figure 31-11) is executed by the Get_Input macro only if the user enters an invalid year (Excel's dates are limited to years between 1900 and 2078). This macro uses the ALERT command to display a message which can be cleared by clicking OK. It then reruns the Get_Input macro so the user can try again.

	C	D	E	F	G	H	I
1				296	258	Select Month and Year	
2	1	10	43	88		OK	
3	2	11	76	88		Cancel	
4	14	133	7	136	216	Month	
5	11						12
6	12					January	
7	12					February	
8	12					March	
9	12					April	
10	12					May	
11	12					June	
12	12					July	
13	12					August	
14	12					September	
15	12					October	
16	12					November	
17	12					December	
18	7	177	230	55		User_year	1991
19	5	130	236			Year	
20	17	19	6			1	
21							

Figure 31-10: The dialog box code that's used by the Get_Input macro.

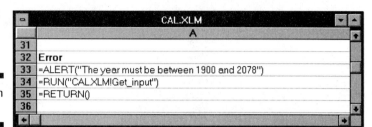

Figure 31-11: The Error macro in the calendar macro sheet.

	CAL.XLM
	A
31	
32	Error
33	=ALERT("The year must be between 1900 and 2078")
34	=RUN("CAL.XLM!Get_input")
35	=RETURN()
36	

The Print_Calendar macro

This macro, shown in Figure 31-12, selects the calendar range in the worksheet and defines it as the print area. The macro prints the calendar and then deletes the Print_Area range so the dotted lines do not appear on-screen. This macro executes when the user clicks the worksheet button labeled "Print."

This macro doesn't adjust the page settings so it's important that you get the page set up properly (with the File ➪ Page Setup command) and this information is stored along with the worksheet. For example, you might want to enlarge the printout so it fills an entire page, remove gridlines, provide a custom header or footer, and print in landscape mode.

The Exit_Excel macro

This macro makes a quick exit from Excel when the user clicks the button labeled "Quit." Any changes made in any open worksheets will be lost — which is fine, since the user isn't supposed to change anything. Before exiting, the WORKSPACE command restores the scroll bars, formula bar, and status bar for the next session. This macro is shown in Figure 31-13. Note the use of the error(false) command. This command prevents Excel from asking if you want to save any changes. This ensures a quick exit, with no questions asked.

Figure 31-12: The Print_Calendar macro in the calendar macro sheet.

	CAL.XLM
	A
45	
46	Print_Calendar
47	=ECHO(FALSE)
48	=SELECT("calendar")
49	=SET.PRINT.AREA()
50	=PRINT()
51	=DELETE.NAME("Print_Area")
52	=SELECT("R1C1")
53	=RETURN()
54	

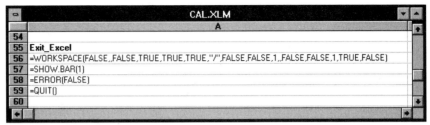

Figure 31-13: The Exit_Excel macro in the calendar macro sheet.

54	
55	Exit_Excel
56	=WORKSPACE(FALSE,,FALSE,TRUE,TRUE,TRUE,"/",FALSE,FALSE,1,,FALSE,FALSE,1,TRUE,FALSE)
57	=SHOW.BAR(1)
58	=ERROR(FALSE)
59	=QUIT()
60	

Don't use this macro while you're developing and testing the macros — you'll lose your changes.

Adding the buttons

After the macros have been entered, the next step is to attach them to buttons on the worksheet. You do this with the button tool. After you draw the button on the worksheet, attach the appropriate macro using the Assign To Object dialog box which Excel displays automatically.

Aesthetic considerations

Before you turn this application loose on a user, you might want to make a few other adjustments. For example:

■ Make sure the colors and patterns you've chosen look good on-screen and print clearly.

■ Turn off the display of gridlines, row and column borders, scroll bars, status line, and formula line. Use the Options ➪ Display and Options ➪ Workspace commands for this.

■ Make sure everything fits nicely on one screen by adjusting the column widths and row heights.

■ Hide or minimize the macro sheet.

Safety precautions

To prevent a user from accidentally erasing formulas or changing formats, you should lock all the cells using the Format ➪ Cell Protection command. In this example, where the year and month cells need to be updated by the macro, these should be left unlocked.

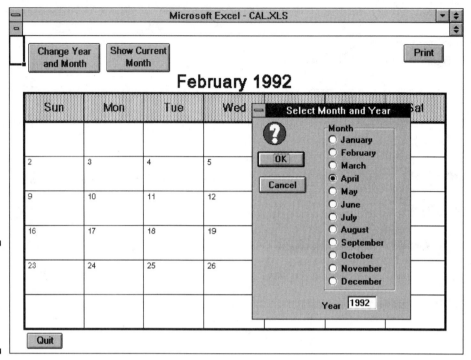

Figure 31-14:
The final
application
hardly resem-
bles a normal
spreadsheet.

To prevent the user from scrolling around the worksheet, you can freeze the
panes. Select a cell in the lower-right corner and select the Window ⇨ Freeze
Panes command.

Running the application

If you've done everything correctly, the finished application should look
polished and operate smoothly (see Figure 31-14). The user can select "Change
Month and Year" and complete the dialog box to select a calendar. If the date is
out of range, a message displays and the dialog box reappears. Choosing the
Current Month button displays the calendar for the current month. If you froze
the titles correctly, the user will not be able to scroll through the worksheet.

Undoubtedly, you can think of additional bells and whistles that could make
this application even more useful. You could add an option to print the entire
year, or add other buttons to display the next or previous months, for example.
In any case, this is a good simple application to work with as you build your
application development skills.

Summary

▶ There are many reasons why you might create spreadsheets for others. You need to consider the end user and adjust your work accordingly.

▶ The key to developing successful complex applications is planning. It doesn't hurt to sketch out diagrams.

▶ The user interacts with the application through the user interface. Excel provides some advanced tools for developing sophisticated user interfaces: macro buttons, custom dialog boxes, custom menus, and custom toolbars.

▶ Excel also provides several ways to protect the integrity of your application. You can protect cells from being changed and hide rows, columns, and documents.

▶ Remember the end user. Your application should be appealing to look at and intuitive to operate.

▶ You should get in the habit of documenting your work — especially macros.

▶ The final step in developing an application is to test it. Try to anticipate everything a user could do wrong and build error-handling into your macros.

Chapter 32
Improving Excel's Performance

In this chapter . . .

▶ What you can do if Excel is too slow for you. We offer solutions involving hardware, software, and the way you work in Excel.

▶ General tips on fine-tuning your Windows environment.

▶ What to look for when upgrading your computer system.

Many users who switch to Excel after using a character-based program such as Lotus 1-2-3 or Quattro Pro complain that Excel is slower. Well, some parts of Excel are slower — screen updating and scrolling, for example. This is to be expected, since your computer is doing a lot of background work to get those nice-looking graphic characters on your screen. On the other hand, carefully controlled benchmark tests that involve recalculation of complex worksheets typically find that Excel is faster at this task.

Speed, Speed, and More Speed

In reality, computers are never fast enough. Today's high-speed powerhouse is tomorrow's garage sale clunker. The key is to make the best of what you have. This chapter presents some tips on how to improve the overall performance of Excel. We've grouped the suggestions into three categories:

- **Hardware solutions:** These involve some capital outlay on your part.

- **Software solutions:** You can implement many of these tips using the software you already own.

- **Work-habit solutions:** No-cost tips that simply involve changing some of the things you may be doing inefficiently.

Hardware Solutions

Here's the part where we tell you how to spend more money. These speed-enhancing solutions all involve purchasing new hardware or new components to upgrade your system.

Get a new computer

If Excel is too slow, the most obvious — but least practical — solution is to purchase a new, faster computer system. If you're still using an 80286-based AT-class system, you're a prime candidate. Things aren't going to get any better; most of the software being developed today is designed for faster 80386 systems with more than the standard 1MB of RAM.

A recommended computer set-up

Here's what we're currently recommending to budget-conscious friends and associates who are looking to buy a new computer — one that will serve them well over the next few years:

- An 80386 clone system, running at 25, 33, or 40 MHz. Avoid IBM, unless you want to pay about 30 percent more than you should. Also, stay clear of systems with microchannel architecture (MCA), since add-in cards can cost you a bundle (if you can even find them). If you are buying a clone, make sure that it is fully compatible (most are, but a few clones can't run Windows in enhanced mode).

- At least 4MB of RAM (preferably 8MB).

- A hard drive that holds at least 100MB of data — but more if your budget allows.

- Both kinds of high-density floppy drives (3 ½-inch and 5 ¼-inch).

- A super-VGA video card — preferably one that is optimized to run Windows.

- A multisync monitor, capable of displaying graphics (specifically, Windows) at 800 × 600 resolution or even 1240 × 768, noninterlaced. The *noninterlaced* part is very important. Otherwise, the flicker will drive you crazy after about ten minutes.

- A PostScript or HP LaserJet III printer. Both of these printers have scalable fonts, so you can print your text in any size you want without having to purchase additional font cartridges.

- MS DOS 5, with Windows 3.1.

As we write this, a complete system as described above can be purchased for around $3,500 (and prices are dropping). If you can afford to be a bit more forward thinking, substitute an 80486/33. This processor is much faster and includes a built-in math coprocessor. The inescapable problem, however, is that sooner or later, even the latest and greatest computer becomes obsolete.

Table 32-1: The five main classes of personal computers			
Type	Processor	Status	Characteristics
PC	8088	Obsolete	No hard disk; 640K RAM; runs at 4.77 MHz; doesn't run Windows; introduced in 1981.
XT	8088	Obsolete	Basically, the same as a PC, but with a small (10MB) hard disk; doesn't run Windows.
AT	80286	Nearly Obsolete	Slow hard disk; memory beyond 640K; runs at speeds from 6 to 12 MHz; runs Windows poorly.
386	80386	Current Standard	Fast hard disk; runs at speeds from 16 to 40 MHz; runs Windows well (especially at 25+ MHz).
486	80486	Tomorrow's Standard	Fast and large hard disk; math coprocessor built-in; runs at speeds from 25 to 50 MHz; runs Windows great.

Table 32-1 describes the general classes of PCs in existence. For running Windows, the last two categories are your best bet.

Add more memory

If you already have a 386 system, you'll see significant performance increases in Windows if you add more memory. This RAM can often be added directly to your motherboard — or you may need to purchase an add-on memory card. Eight megabytes will give you plenty of room to run multiple applications at once — quickly.

Add a math coprocessor

If your Excel worksheets are calculation-intensive and you find yourself waiting for your worksheets to recalculate, you're a good candidate for a math coprocessor. This is a special-purpose chip, labeled 80287 or 80387, that's installed directly onto your motherboard in a slot designed for it. A math coprocessor won't increase display speed or scrolling — just recalculation. If you need a math coprocessor with Excel, then you probably needed it with your previous character-based spreadsheet program. If your computer uses an 80486 chip, the math coprocessor is already built-in.

Get a faster video card

Several models of video cards have appeared that are designed specifically to speed up the Windows display. Replacing your old VGA adapter with one of these new models can make a dramatic improvement in all applications that run under Windows. These cards cost a bit more than normal VGA cards, but if you're committed to Windows the cost is well worth it.

Get a faster hard drive

Windows does a lot of reading and writing to disk. Much of this is done behind the scenes and not as a direct result of your file save or retrieve commands. If you notice that the indicator light on your hard drive blinks more than you think it should, it's a sign that you could benefit by having more memory. In addition, you can also speed things up by getting a new, faster hard drive.

 Excel 4 provides a macro that can tell you a lot of details about your particular setup. To run the macro, select File ⇨ Open and then locate the macro file named `checkup.xlm`. It's probably located in the `\excel\library\checkup` directory. Opening the macro file runs the macro and displays a window of information. You can print this information by choosing Print or close the window by choosing Close. Closing the window removes the macro from memory.

Software Solutions

Following are some solutions that involve software — primarily fine-tuning Windows and its associated files. You might discover that the Windows manual is quite vague about some of these issues. If you really want to understand Windows, and get some excellent advice at the same time, pick up a copy of Brian Livingston's best-selling *Windows 3.1 Secrets,* available from — you guessed it — IDG Books.

Set up a permanent swap file

If you're running Windows in 386 enhanced mode, you should *definitely* set up a permanent swap area on your hard disk. This dramatically speeds up the disk swapping that Windows does in its normal activity. Before you set one up, you may need to defragment your drive using any of several disk utilities designed to do so (for example, Norton Utilities or PC Tools). This is because the permanent swap file must consist of consecutive clusters.

Setting up a permanent swap file is handled differently in Windows 3.0 and 3.1. Consult your Windows manual for details.

Use disk-caching software

Chances are, you're already using smartdrv.sys. This program stores information read from disk in memory. So if your application needs additional information, there's a good chance it's already in RAM and is avoiding the slow disk read and fetching the information from memory.

smartdrv.sys was installed in your config.sys file when you installed Windows. If you've added any memory since you installed Windows, you should consider increasing the size of the cache (see your Windows manual for details). You might also try substituting a third-party disk-caching program. Often, these are faster and more efficient than smartdrv.sys.

Set up a RAM disk

If you have enough memory, consider setting up a RAM disk — a simulated drive that's actually located in memory. Use the ramdisk.sys program that comes with Windows, and this will happen automatically whenever you boot your system. The speed increase comes when you tell Windows to use this RAM disk to hold its temporary files. Make sure there's a line in your autoexec.bat file that reads set temp=d:\ (this assumes your RAM disk is drive D:). You'll notice a dramatic reduction in the time required to spool a print job — so you can get back to work much faster.

Try running Windows in standard mode

If Windows normally starts in 386 enhanced mode, you may be able to get slightly improved performance by running Windows in standard mode. To force this mode, start Windows by typing win /s. It's been reported that some Windows applications run up to 50 percent faster in standard mode, compared to 386 enhanced mode (due to some additional overhead required in the latter mode).

 Standard mode, unlike 386 enhanced mode, does not support multitasking, and in standard mode the Clipboard won't work with DOS programs. Consequently, you'll have to forego these benefits if you run Windows in standard mode.

Work-Habit Solutions

Here are a few simple tips on how to use Excel and Windows most efficiently to speed things up and use less memory.

Close down unnecessary applications

Although much of the appeal of Windows stems from the capability to run multiple applications simultaneously, this practice does take up memory and results in disk swapping if you run short of memory. If you find that Excel is getting too sluggish, close any program that may be running — including screen savers, DOS windows, and anything else that you're not using.

Lose the Windows wallpaper

You can also claim a bit more memory by eliminating the cute "wallpaper" that you may have displayed as your background. Run the Control Panel, select the Desktop icon, and make sure the Pattern and Wallpaper boxes both display (None).

Work down, not across

Because of the way Excel allocates memory for worksheets, you'll use less memory if you create your worksheets vertically (in columns) rather than horizontally (across rows).

Format entire rows and columns

You can save memory by formatting entire rows or columns in Excel, rather than individual ranges. Select an entire row or column by clicking on the row or column header and then apply your desired formatting.

Don't use arrays

For maximum speed, avoid arrays. Although using array formulas can reduce the amount of memory used by a worksheet, it can also slow down recalculation considerably. If you use large arrays in a worksheet, consider using a different technique (see Chapter 22 for details on this unique feature).

Calculate only the active worksheet

If you have several worksheets loaded, and you've set recalculation to manual, you can save time by calculating only the current worksheet. Do this by pressing Shift+F9, rather than F9.

Don't use Adobe Type Manager or TrueType

Software-based fonts such as Adobe Type Manager and TrueType (included with Windows 3.1) give you nice-looking fonts on-screen and in your printed output. The cost, however, is that the accompanying background processing decreases your system's overall performance. If screen updating is slow to the point where it's intolerable, you might want to try living without ATM or TrueType.

Calculate a single cell

If you're using manual recalculation, you can get the results of a single formula by selecting the cell for editing and then pressing Enter.

Use entire rows or columns in formulas

If possible, use complete rows or columns in your formulas. For example, =SUM(A:A) will add up all values in column A. This uses less memory than a formula such as =SUM(A1:A1000).

Convert formulas to values

If you have some "dead" formulas in your worksheet — formulas that have calculated a result and will never change — you can convert such formulas to values. Copy them to the Clipboard with the Edit ⇨ Copy command and then use Edit ⇨ Paste Special (with Values turned on) to overwrite the formulas with their results.

Summary

▶ Excel's recalculation speed compares quite favorably with most other spreadsheet programs. But due to its Windows orientation, screen updating and scrolling may not be up to your expectations — especially if you're using a slower computer.

▶ The best way to see a significant improvement in Excel's performance is to buy a new, faster PC. Other hardware solutions include adding more memory, purchasing a math coprocessor, buying a faster hard disk, or getting a new video card optimized for Windows.

▶ You can optimize Windows in several general ways. These include setting up a permanent swap file, optimizing your disk cache (`smartdrv.sys` or a third-party alternative), and using a RAM disk.

▶ In addition, there are several tips and techniques that you can use within Excel to maximize the program's performance.

PART

IV

Appendixes

Appendix A
For Upgraders Only: What's New?

If you're an experienced spreadsheet user and want to get a quick overview of what Excel 4 has to offer compared to your *current* spreadsheet, you've come to the right place — assuming that your current spreadsheet is either Excel 3 or Lotus 1-2-3.

For Excel 3 Users

OK, Excel user. You've been happy with Excel 3, but you've read the rave reviews of Excel 4 and you want to know what all the hubbub's about. For example, you might have questions like these:

- Is Excel 4 really that much easier to use? You bet.
- Does it have new features for power users? Affirmative.
- Will my macros still work? Naturally.
- Will I have to learn things all over again? Not on your life.

The new features in Excel 4 fall into several categories, which we'll discuss separately. We don't go into great detail in this section, since that's the purpose of the rest of the book. But if you take a few minutes to read through this section, you'll know what to be on the lookout for.

File format

- Version 4 has a new file format. Unfortunately, it still uses the xls extension for worksheets (just like versions 2.1 and 3). Therefore, you can't tell which version a file was saved under until you try to read it.

■ Versions 2.1 and 3 cannot read the files generated by version 4, but you can use File ➪ Save As to save your file in either of these formats.

■ The product uses some new file types: xlw for workbook files and xlb for toolbar files.

Workbooks

■ The new workbook feature picks up where version 3's workspace left off. You can now save a group of related files (worksheets, charts, macros) in a single file.

■ Furthermore, it is easy to manage and manipulate related files when they are loaded into memory. For example, Excel presents a "table of contents" window of all the files in a workbook.

Scenario Manager

■ If you're the type who likes to use Excel for what-if analysis, the new version makes this task much simpler.

■ The Scenario Manager add-in lets you set up and manage different sets of assumptions and quickly see the effects of each. You can even provide names for your scenarios.

Wizards

■ Microsoft added some new interactive features that walk you through the steps necessary to perform certain procedures. For example, the Chart-Wizard uses five dialog boxes to ensure that the chart you produce is the chart you want.

■ Besides charting, Excel includes a nifty Crosstab Wizard that lets you set up sophisticated crosstabulations from a database.

Charts

■ Excel now offers several new chart types, including surface charts, wireframe charts, and radar charts.

■ You can now directly manipulate the rotation of 3-D charts by grabbing them with the mouse and spinning them before your very eyes.

Slide shows

■ Create compelling on-screen presentations to display charts, worksheet ranges, or images copied from other applications. Particularly impressive is the wide variety of transition effects to go from screen to screen.

■ If you have the Windows Multimedia Extensions (or Windows 3.1), you can even add sound to your presentations.

Printing

■ Printing is more flexible than ever. The redesigned Page Setup dialog box provides one-stop shopping for all of your print settings.

■ The new Report Manager lets you print a report that is a combination of several views of different spreadsheets or parts of spreadsheets.

■ You can also request that all colors and patterns used in cells be ignored when the worksheet is printed — avoiding the common problem of a great-looking screen, but unreadable printouts.

Spell checker

■ Reduce the possibility of looking like a fool when you hand in your budget report with a misspelled word. This new feature quickly checks the spelling of words in your worksheet — and your charts.

■ To conserve disk space, Excel uses the same dictionaries as other Microsoft applications (for example, Word for Windows).

Database

■ If you work with external databases, your options have been expanded to include dBASE, SQL Server, Oracle, and text files. Q+E is still available to gather the information from these sources.

General ease-of-use features

■ Select an object and click the *right* mouse button. Excel presents you with a shortcut menu of commands appropriate to the selection. About 99 percent of the time this menu will in fact have the command you need.

- Notice that the active cell or selected range has a tiny square in the lower-left corner. This is for the new Autofill feature. Use Autofill to "intelligently" copy text to adjacent cells. For example, copy a cell that contains "1st-Q" and you'll get "2nd-Q," 3rd-Q," and so on.

- You can also use Autofill to quickly copy formulas to adjacent cells simply by dragging the Autofill handle.

- The new Autoformat feature automatically applies any of several prede-signed formats to a table (unfortunately, you can't define your own formats — yet). This formatting includes type, numeric formats, color, shading, and column width.

- Drag and drop — grab a selection of cells by the bottom border and simply move it anywhere you'd like. Hold down Ctrl while you drag to make a copy.

- Most dialog boxes now have a Help button so you can quickly find out what their various options do.

Advanced analytical features

- A new add-in called the Analysis ToolPak includes a variety of sophisticated procedures for statistical analysis and other things people with Ph.D.s spend their time doing. But even mere mortals can benefit from some of these.

Toolbars

- The new toolbar is immediately apparent. Unlike the toolbar in Excel 3, the new version has several toolbars, appropriate for different tasks. In addition, you can create custom toolbars consisting of the tools you use most often.

- You can drag the toolbar anywhere you want — and even change its shape.

- You can attach your own macros to tools and place them on a toolbar.

For 1-2-3 Users

If you're upgrading from 1-2-3 (either Release 2.x, release 3.x, or 1-2-3 for Windows), you're in for a treat. Excel 4 is a much more powerful product. Once you learn the ropes, you'll also find it significantly easier to use.

One of the problems with 1-2-3 is that there are so many different versions available — and they all work differently. The information in this section is primarily for those who are upgrading from Release 2.*x* or 3.*x*.

A different approach to spreadsheets

Microsoft takes a much different approach to spreadsheets than Lotus. This is understandable when you look at the history. Lotus 1-2-3 was the first serious spreadsheet available for PCs, and when it was released it was a major break-through. 1-2-3 has always been the best-selling DOS spreadsheet, and Lotus has a huge user base to support. Consequently, the focus of Lotus has been more on *compatibility* with the past rather than innovation. The tremendous popular-ity of Windows seems to have taken Lotus by surprise. They rushed a version of 1-2-3 for Windows to market, but it was rather poorly designed, filled with bugs, and offered virtually no new features (except, perhaps, SmartIcons).

Excel is now in its third major version, and all versions have run under Win-dows. In fact, Excel virtually defined how spreadsheets work under Windows. Each subsequent version of Excel built upon the previous one. Lotus, on the other hand, has versions of 1-2-3 available for DOS (actually, two versions), Windows, OS/2, and Macintosh (plus several other non-PC platforms). Unfortu-nately, all of these products have different menu systems and approach spread-sheet issues in a different manner. It should be clear that there's much to be gained by having a consistent product — and Excel is an excellent example.

The remainder of this appendix discusses how Excel differs from 1-2-3. We have to be fairly general here because of the many different versions of 1-2-3 in use.

Menus

You'll immediately notice that the Excel menu has practically nothing in common with the 1-2-3 menu system you're accustomed to. While you may be able to whip off complex 1-2-3 commands in your sleep, you'll have to admit that Excel's menus are much better designed.

Movement

Although you can continue to use the Lotus cursor movement keys you're familiar with (see the sidebar "How Excel caters to 1-2-3 users"), you might eventually want to learn the Excel movement keys.

Selection

In 1-2-3, you normally make a menu selection and then specify the range on which the command will operate. Excel takes the opposite approach: you first make your selection and then issue the command that will affect it. You can make selections with the mouse by dragging or with the keyboard. The fastest way to make a selection with the keyboard is to hold down Shift and use the arrow keys. You can also do this in conjunction with the Ctrl key to move quickly to the end of a row or column.

Cell formatting

You might think that 1-2-3 offers a lot of cell formatting options (especially if you use one of the formatting add-ins such as Allways, Impress, or Wysiwyg). But you're in for a surprise when you discover what Excel can do — and how easy it is. 1-2-3 certainly has some limitations. For example, 1-2-3 can't center a number or align it to the left of a cell.

Excel 4 provides all the formatting you'll need, plus some features you might not need (but are nice to have, just in case). For example, you can display text within a cell vertically if you like, and even have it wrap around on multiple lines.

How Excel caters to 1-2-3 users

Excel includes many features designed to ease the transition from 1-2-3 to Excel. When you install Excel on your computer, it asks if you would like to activate these features. If you respond in the positive, Excel enables the following:

- Alternative navigation keys — lets you use the keys you're used to. For example, Ctrl+right arrow move to the right one screen.

- Function keys — some of the function keys will behave like you're used to.

- Text alignment prefix characters — you can use ", ', and ^ to specify the alignment of text in cells.

Note that you can deactivate any of these special features at any time through the Options ⇨ Workspace command.

In addition, the on-line help system includes special topics for 1-2-3 users that explain how to perform specific procedures in Excel. It also has a cross-reference for 1-2-3 functions and a list of common 1-2-3 slash commands and their Excel equivalents.

But the best feature of all is located in the Help menu. The Lotus 1-2-3 Help command brings up a dialog box in which you can enter the actual 1-2-3 command you would use in a particular situation, and Excel demonstrates how to perform that procedure in Excel. You can even set it up so this dialog box pops up whenever you press the slash key. Select Options ⇨ Workspace and then click on the box that reads Lotus 1-2-3 help.

We think you'll prefer the Excel menu system once you get used to it, but it's nice to have these features available to ease the transition.

Functions

1-2-3 has a good selection of built-in @functions, but Excel has many more to choose from. Most of the functions in Excel use the same names as their 1-2-3 counterparts. Syntax is slightly different (and sometimes the results they produce), so check your work carefully if you use any of the less-commonly used functions. By the way, if you start a formula with a function, use = in Excel instead of @. Also, range designations use a colon instead of two dots. For example, use =SUM(A1:D1) instead of @SUM(A1..D1).

Graphs

Excel's charting capabilities are much more extensive than 1-2-3's — and are a lot easier to work with. We devote three full chapters to charting.

Database

Excel's database features are similar to 1-2-3's and also offer easy-to-use database forms. Like 1-2-3 Release 3 and 1-2-3 for Windows, Excel lets you work with external database files. Microsoft provides a separate program, Q+E, that works in conjunction with Excel.

Macros

In 1-2-3, macros consist of recorded keystrokes and/or macro commands and the macros are stored in a normal worksheet. Excel's macros actually consist of functions that are evaluated one at a time. A macro function is available for every menu command, plus many others. Excel stores its macros in a special macro file (with an xlm extension), which must be loaded into memory before you can execute the macros. There's also a "global" macro sheet that's always available.

Recording simple macros is easy. Creating more complex macros is another story and can get confusing very quickly.

File linking

All versions of 1-2-3 now support file linking — the ability to use values from one worksheet in another worksheet. This is done by preceding the cell reference with a filename. Release 2 has a limited implementation of this feature, since you cannot use external references in formulas. Excel has extensive file linking capability.

Consolidating files

1-2-3 Release 3 users may have used the product's multisheet file feature, which allows you to "stack" worksheets in a single file — a 3-D effect. The advantage of such is feature is that you can easily work with groups of related files by storing each on a separate page and then developing formulas to manipulate and summarize the data.

Excel doesn't provide such 3-D worksheets, but it has a few other features that make up for it. First, Excel's new workbook capability simplifies the process of working with multiple files. You can request a "table of contents" window that shows all of your open windows, and you can move quickly among them.

Excel also lets you work with a group of worksheets in group edit mode. Formatting applied to one worksheet is automatically applied to the others in the group. The program also has a slick consolidation feature that can consolidate data across worksheets even if they aren't laid out identically.

Analytical tools

Excel offers the most analytical tools of any spreadsheet available. Engineers and statisticians will welcome all the new functions. In addition, the Analysis ToolPak automates many advanced statistical procedures — feats not available in any other spreadsheet product. Like Release 3 and 1-2-3 for Windows, Excel also provides a linear/nonlinear Solver.

Add-ins

Both Excel and 1-2-3 support add-ins — programs that add new functionality to the spreadsheet by providing new functions, macro commands, or procedures. Excel includes many add-ins that you can load or not, as you wish. In Excel, the add-ins are accessed via the File ⇨ Open command.

Information transfer

One of the advantages of Excel stems from the fact that it runs under Windows. Most Windows applications let you freely copy and paste information between applications. For example, you can easily copy a range of cells from Excel into a Windows word processor. Better yet, you can set up Dynamic Data Exchange links, so if your numbers in Excel change, the changes are reflected automatically in your word processing document. Excel supports Object Linking and Embedding — a handy tool that lets you embed objects from other programs (and edit them with the other program's tools).

In addition, Excel can read many common file formats. This includes all of the files produced by 1-2-3 — even the formatting files. Excel can even execute your 1-2-3 macros.

Ease-of-use features

As you get into Excel, you'll discover loads of minor features that make your day-to-day work much easier and faster. We think you'll be glad you made the switch.

Appendix B
Macro Function Reference

This appendix lists all of Excel's macro functions, along with their arguments. Note that these are the functions that can be used exclusively in macro sheets, and this list does not cover the worksheet functions (even though most worksheet functions can also be used in macro sheets). The worksheet functions are listed and described in the Quick Reference booklet that accompanies this book.

Limited space prohibits comprehensive coverage of each function. Rather, we refer you to the *Microsoft Excel Function Reference* — which is filled with useful examples — that's included with your copy of Excel.

We group the macro functions into the following categories:

- **Command equivalent functions:** Functions that simulate selecting a menu command. In some cases, the function simulates pressing a specific option button in a dialog box.

- **Information functions:** These functions return information about some aspect of Excel, the system, or a document. The information can then be used to determine how the macro will proceed.

- **Macro control functions:** These functions control how a macro flows.

- **ASCII file manipulation functions:** These functions allow a macro to manipulate (read from and write to) text files.

- **Functions for customizing Excel:** These functions are used primarily by those who develop custom applications with macros.

- **DDE/External functions:** These functions allow a macro to communicate with other applications via the Windows Dynamic Data Exchange feature.

- **Window manipulation functions:** These functions allow a macro to manipulate windows (document windows and the Excel window).

■ **Solver add-in macro functions:** These functions can automate some aspects of the Solver.

■ **Outlining macro functions:** These functions can manipulate an Excel outline.

■ **Movement macro functions:** Functions in this category simulate keyboard or mouse movement.

■ **Macro functions to manipulate workbooks:** These functions allow a macro to manipulate workbooks.

■ **Analysis ToolPak macro functions.** These execute procedures found in the Analysis ToolPak add-in.

■ **Other macro functions:** This group is made up of all the other macro functions that don't fit into any of the previous classifications.

Note: This classification system is somewhat arbitrary, since many functions can be put into several categories.

Command-Equivalent Functions

We've arranged these macro functions by the main menu selection that they are equivalent to: File, Edit, Formula, and so on. Commands that lead to a dialog box usually have another form that will display the dialog box so the user can make changes. To invoke the dialog box, add a question mark to the function.

You'll notice that the function names are by no means consistent. For example the function to change the active chart to a column chart is =GALLERY.COLUMN. But to change it to a combination chart, the function is =COMBINATION (not =GALLERY.COMBINATION, as you might expect). This inconsistency is a good reason to record macros or use the Formula ⇨ Paste Function command.

File menu

NEW(*type_num,xy_series,add_logical*)
Command equivalent: File ⇨ New

FILE.CLOSE(*save_logical*)
Command equivalent: File ⇨ Close

FILE.DELETE(*file_text*)
Command equivalent: File ⇨ Delete

CHANGE.LINK(*old_text,new_text,type_of_link*)
Command equivalent: File ⇨ Links (with the Change button)

OPEN(*file_text,update_links,read_only,format,prot_pwd,write_res_pwd,ignore_rorec, file_origin, custom_delimit,workbook*)
Command equivalent: File ⇨ Open

OPEN.LINKS(*document_text1,document_text2,[etc.],read_only,type_of_link*)
Command equivalent: File ⇨ Links

PAGE.SETUP(*head,foot,left,right,top,bot,hdng,grid,h_cntr,v_cntr,orient,paper_size, scale,pg_num ,pg_order,bw_cells*)
Command equivalent: File ⇨ Page Setup (This version is for worksheets and macro sheets.)

PAGE.SETUP(*head,foot,left,right,top,bot,size,h_cntr,v_cntr,orient,paper_size, scale,pg_num*)
Command equivalent: File ⇨ Page Setup (This version is for charts.)

PRINT(*range_num,from,to,copies,draft,preview,print_what,color,feed,quality,v_quality*)
Command equivalent: File ⇨ Print

PRINT.PREVIEW( )
Command equivalent: File ⇨ Print Preview

PRINTER.SETUP(*printer_text*)
Command equivalent: File ⇨ Page Setup (with Printer Setup button)

QUIT( )
Command equivalent: File ⇨ Exit

REPORT.DEFINE(*report_name,views_scenarios_array,pages_logical*)
Command equivalent: File ⇨ Print Report (with Add option). This function requires that the Report's add-in is loaded.

REPORT.DELETE(*report_name*)
Command equivalent: File ⇨ Print Report (with Delete option). This function requires that the Report's add-in is loaded.

REPORT.PRINT(*report_name,copies_num,show_print_dlg_logical*)
Command equivalent: File ⇨ Print Report (with Print button). This function requires that the Report's add-in is loaded.

SAVE( )
Command equivalent: File ⇨ Save

SAVE.AS(*document_text,type_num,prot_pwd,backup,write_res_pwd,read_only_rec*)
Command equivalent: File ⇨ Save As

SAVE.WORKBOOK(*document_text,type_num,prot_pwd,backup,write_res_pwd,
read_only_rec*)
Command equivalent: File ⇨ Save Workbook

SEND.MAIL(*recipients,subject,return_receipt*)
Command equivalent: File⇨Send Mail

UPDATE.LINK(*link_text,type_of_link*)
Command equivalent: File ⇨ Link (with Update button)

CLOSE.ALL ( )
Command equivalent: File ⇨ Close All

Edit menu

CLEAR(*type_num*)
Command equivalent: Edit ⇨ Clear

COPY(*from_reference,to_reference*)
Command equivalent: Edit ⇨ Copy

COPY.PICTURE(*appearance_num,size_num,type_num*)
Command equivalent: Edit ⇨ Copy Picture

COPY.TOOL(*bar_id,position*)
Command equivalent: Edit ⇨ Copy Tool Face (when a tool is selected)

CUT(*from_reference,to_reference*)
Command equivalent: Edit ⇨ Cut

EDIT.DELETE(*shift_num*)
Command equivalent: Edit ⇨ Delete

EDIT.REPEAT( )
Command equivalent: Edit ⇨ Repeat (last repeatable command)

FILL.DOWN( )
Command equivalent: Edit ⇨ Fill Down

FILL.GROUP(*type_num*)
Command equivalent: Edit ⇨ Fill Group

FILL.LEFT( )
Command equivalent: Edit ⇨ Fill Left (h)

FILL.RIGHT( )
Command eq uivalent: Edit ⇨ Fill Right

FILL.UP( )
Command equivalent: Edit ⇨ Fill Up (w)

INSERT(*shift_num*)
Command equivalent: Edit ⇨ Insert

INSERT.OBJECT(*object_class*)
Command equivalent: Edit ⇨ Insert Object

PASTE(*to_reference*)
Command equivalent: Edit ⇨ Paste

PASTE.LINK( )
Command equivalent: Edit ⇨ Paste Link

PASTE.PICTURE( )
Command equivalent: Edit ⇨ Paste Picture

PASTE.PICTURE.LINK( )
Command equivalent: Edit ⇨ Paste Picture Link

PASTE.SPECIAL(*paste_num*)
Command equivalent: Edit ⇨ Paste Special (This version is for copying from a chart to a chart.)

PASTE.SPECIAL(*format_text,pastelink_logical*)
Command equivalent: Edit ⇨ Paste Special (This version is for copying from another application.)

PASTE.SPECIAL(*paste_num,operation_num,skip_blanks,transpose*)
Command equivalent: Edit ⇨ Paste Special (This version is for copying from a worksheet to a worksheet.)

PASTE.SPECIAL(*rowcol,series,categories,replace*)
Command equivalent: Edit ⇨ Paste Special (This version is for copying from a worksheet to a chart.)

PASTE.TOOL(*bar_id,position*)
Command equivalent: Edit ⇨ Paste Tool Face (when a tool is selected)

UNDO( )
Command equivalent: Edit ⇨ Undo (last undoable command)

Formula menu

APPLY.NAMES(*name_array,ignore,use_rowcol,omit_col,omit_row,order_num, append_last*)
Command equivalent: Formula ⇨ Apply Names

CREATE.NAMES(*top,left,bottom,right*)
Command equivalent: Formula ⇨ Create Names

DEFINE.NAME(*name_text,refers_to,macro_type,shortcut_text,hidden,category*)
Command equivalent: Formula ⇨ Define Name

FORMULA.FIND(*text,in_num,at_num,by_num,dir_num,match_case*)
Command equivalent: Formula ⇨ Find

FORMULA.GOTO(*reference,corner*)
Command equivalent: Formula ⇨ Goto

FORMULA.REPLACE(*find_text,replace_text,look_at,look_by,active_cell,match_case*)
Command equivalent: Formula ⇨ Replace

GOAL.SEEK(*target_cell,target_value,variable_cell*)
Command equivalent: Formula ⇨ Goal Seek

LIST.NAMES( )
Command equivalent: Formula ⇨ Paste Name (with Paste List button)

NOTE(*add_text,cell_ref,start_char,num_chars*)
Command equivalent: Formula ⇨ Note

OUTLINE(*auto_styles,row_dir,col_dir,create_apply*)
Command equivalent: Formula ⇨ Outline

SCENARIO.ADD(*scen_name,value_array*)
Command equivalent: Formula ⇨ Scenario Manager (with the Add button). This command requires that the Scenario Manager add-in is loaded.

SCENARIO.CELLS(*changing_ref*)
Command equivalent: Formula ⇨ Scenario Manager (and editing the Changing Cells box). This command requires that the Scenario Manager add-in is loaded.

SCENARIO.DELETE(*scen_name*)
Command equivalent: Formula ⇨ Scenario Manager (with the Delete button). This command requires that the Scenario Manager add-in is loaded.

SCENARIO.SHOW(*scen_name*)
Command equivalent: Formula ⇨ Scenario Manager (with the Show button). This command requires that the Scenario Manager add-in is loaded.

SCENARIO.SHOW.NEXT( )
Command equivalent: Formula ⇨ Scenario Manager (and choose the next scenario in the list). This command requires that the Scenario Manager add-in is loaded.

SCENARIO.SUMMARY(*result_ref*)
Command equivalent: Formula ⇨ Scenario Manager (with the Summary button). This command requires that the Scenario Manager add-in is loaded.

SELECT.LAST.CELL( )
Command equivalent: Formula ⇨ Select Special (with Last Cell option)

SELECT.SPECIAL(*type_num,value_type,levels*)
Command equivalent: Formula ⇨ Select Special

SHOW.ACTIVE.CELL( )
Command equivalent: Formula ⇨ Show Active Cell

SOUND.PLAY(*cell_ref,file_text,resource*)
Command equivalent: Formula ⇨ Note (with the Play button)

Format menu

ALIGNMENT(*horiz_align,wrap,vert_align,orientation*)
Command equivalent: Format ⇨ Alignment

APPLY.STYLE(*style_text*)
Command equivalent: Format ⇨ Style

BORDER(*outline,left,right,top,bottom,shade,outline_color,left_color, right_color,top_color,bottom_color*)
Command equivalent: Format ⇨ Border

BRING.TO.FRONT( )
Command equivalent: Format ⇨ Bring to Front

CELL.PROTECTION(*locked,hidden*)
Command equivalent: Format ⇨ Cell Protection

COLUMN.WIDTH(*width_num,reference,standard,type_num,standard_num*)
Command equivalent: Format ⇨ Column Width

DEFINE.STYLE(*style_text,number,font,alignment,border,pattern,protection*)
Command equivalent: Format ⇨ Style (with the Define button). This version is used to define a style based on the format of the active cell.

DEFINE.STYLE(*style_text,attribute_num,format_text*)
Command equivalent: Format ⇨ Style (with the Define button). This version is used to define a style for numeric formatting.

DEFINE.STYLE(*style_text,attribute_num,name_text,size_num,bold,italic,underline,strike, color,outline,shadow*)
Command equivalent: Format ⇨ Style (with the Define button). This version is used to define a style for font formating.

DEFINE.STYLE(*style_text,attribute_num,horiz_align,wrap,vert_align,orientation*)
Command equivalent: Format ⇨ Style (with the Define button). This version is used to define a style for alignment formatting.

DEFINE.STYLE(*style_text,attribute_num,left,right,top,bottom,left_color, right_color,top_color,bottom_color*)
Command equivalent: Format ⇨ Style (with the Define button). This version is used to define a style for border formatting.

DEFINE.STYLE(*style_text,attribute_num,apattern,afore,aback*)
Command equivalent: Format ⇨ Style (with the Define button). This version is used to define a style for pattern formatting.

DEFINE.STYLE(*style_text,attribute_num,locked,hidden*)
Command equivalent: Format ⇨ Style (with the Define button). This version is used to define a style for cell protection.

FORMAT.AUTO(*format_num,number,font,alignment,border,pattern,width*)
Command equivalent: Format ⇨ AutoFormat

FORMAT.FONT(*name_text,size_num,bold,italic,underline,strike,color,outline,shadow*)
Command equivalent: Format ⇨ Font (This version is for cells.)

FORMAT.FONT(*name_text,size_num,bold,italic,underline,strike,color,outline, shadow,object_id_text,start_num,char_num*)
Command equivalent: Format ⇨ Font (This version is for text boxes and buttons.)

FORMAT.FONT(*color,backgd,apply,name_text,size_num,bold,italic,underline, strike,outline,shadow*)
Command equivalent: Format ⇨ Font (This version is for chart items that contain text.)

FORMAT.LEGEND(*position_num*)
Command equivalent: Format ⇨ Legend (in a Chart window)

FORMAT.MAIN(*type_num,view,overlap,gap_width,vary,drop,hilo,angle,gap_depth, chart_depth,up_down,series_line,labels*)
Command equivalent: Format ⇨ Main Chart (in a Chart window)

FORMAT.NUMBER(*format_text*)
Command equivalent: Format ➪ Number

FORMAT.OVERLAY(*type_num,view,overlap,width,vary,drop,hilo,angle,series_dist,
series_num,up_down, series_line,labels*)
Command equivalent: Format ➪ Overlay (in a Chart window)

FORMAT.TEXT(*x_align,y_align,orient_num,auto_text,auto_size,show_key,show_value*)
Command equivalent: Format ➪ Text

GROUP( )
Command equivalent: Format ➪ Group

JUSTIFY( )
Command equivalent: Format ➪ Justify

MERGE.STYLES(*document_text*)
Command equivalent: Format ➪ Style (with the Define button, and then the
Merge button)

OBJECT.PROPERTIES(*placement_type, print_object*)
Command equivalent: Format ➪ Object Properties

OBJECT.PROTECTION(*locked, lock_text*)
Command equivalent: Format ➪ Object Protection

PATTERNS(*apattern,afore,aback*)
Command equivalent: Format ➪ Patterns (This version for when cells are
selected.)

PATTERNS(*lauto,lstyle,lcolor,lwt,hwidth,hlength,htype*)
Command equivalent: Format ➪ Patterns (This version is applicable when a line
on a worksheet or chart is selected.)

PATTERNS(*bauto,bstyle,bcolor,bwt,shadow,aauto,apattern,afore,aback,rounded*)
Command equivalent: Format ➪ Patterns (This version is applicable when a
text box, rectangle, oval, arc, or picture is selected.)

PATTERNS(*bauto,bstyle,bcolor,bwt,shadow,aauto,apattern,afore,aback,invert,apply*)
Command equivalent: Format ➪ Patterns (This version is applicable when a
chart plot area, bar, column, pie slice, or text label is selected.)

PATTERNS(*lauto,lstyle,lcolor,lwt,tmajor,tminor,tlabel*)
Command equivalent: Format ➪ Patterns (This version is applicable when a
chart axis is selected.)

PATTERNS(*lauto,lstyle,lcolor,lwt,apply*)
Command equivalent: Format ➪ Patterns (This version is applicable when any
of the following is selected: chart gridline, hi-lo line, drop line, or a line on a
picture chart.)

PATTERNS(*lauto,lstyle,lcolor,lwt,mauto,mstyle,mfore,mback,apply*)
Command equivalent: Format ⇨ Patterns (This version is applicable when a chart data line is selected.)

PATTERNS(*type,picture_units,apply*)
Command equivalent: Format ⇨ Patterns (This version is applicable when a picture chart marker is selected.)

ROW.HEIGHT(*height_num,reference,standard_height,type_num*)
Command equivalent: Format ⇨ Row Height

SCALE(*cross,cat_labels,cat_marks,between,max,reverse*)
Command equivalent: Format ⇨ Scale (This version is for the category axis on a 2-D chart.)

SCALE(*min_num,max_num,major,minor,cross,logarithmic,reverse,max*)
Command equivalent: Format ⇨ Scale (This version is for the value axis on a 2-D chart or either axis on an xy chart.)

SCALE(*cat_labels,cat_marks,reverse,between*)
Command equivalent: Format ⇨ Scale (This version is for the category axis on a 3-D chart.)

SCALE(*series_labels,series_marks,reverse*)
Command equivalent: Format ⇨ Scale (This version is for the series axis on a 3-D chart.)

SCALE(*min_num,max_num,major,minor,cross,logarithmic,reverse,min*)
Command equivalent: Format ⇨ Scale (This version is for the value axis on a 3-D chart.)

SEND.TO.BACK( )
Command equivalent: Format ⇨ Send to Back

UNGROUP( )
Command equivalent: Format ⇨ Ungroup

VIEW.3D(*elevation,perspective,rotation,axes,height%,autoscale*)
Command equivalent: Format ⇨ 3-D View (in a Chart window)

Data menu

CONSOLIDATE(*source_refs,function_num,top_row,left_col,create_links*)
Command equivalent: Data ⇨ Consolidate

DATA.DELETE( )
Command equivalent: Data ⇨ Delete

DATA.FIND(*logical*)
Command equivalent: Data ⇨ Find

DATA.FORM( )
Command equivalent: Data ⇨ Form

DATA.SERIES(*rowcol,type_num,date_num,step_value,stop_value,trend*)
Command equivalent: Data ⇨ Series

EXTRACT(*unique*)
Command equivalent: Data ⇨ Extract

PARSE(*parse_text,destination_ref*)
Command equivalent: Data ⇨ Parse

SET.CRITERIA( )
Command equivalent: Data ⇨ Set Criteria

SET.DATABASE( )
Command equivalent: Data ⇨ Set Database

SET.EXTRACT( )
Command equivalent: Data ⇨ Set Extract

TABLE(*row_ref,column_ref*)
Command equivalent: Data ⇨ Table

Options menu

CALCULATE.DOCUMENT( )
Command equivalent: Options ⇨ Calculation (with the Calc Document button)

CALCULATE.NOW( )
Command equivalent: Options ⇨ Calculation (with the Calc Now button)

CALCULATION(*type_num,iter,max_num,max_change,update,precision,*
date_1904,calc_save,save_values, alt_exp,alt_form)
Command equivalent: Options ⇨ Calculation

CUSTOMIZE.TOOLBAR(*category*)
Command equivalent: Options ⇨ Toolbars

DISPLAY(*formulas,gridlines,headings,zeros,color_num,reserved,outline, page_breaks,object_num*)
Command equivalent: Options ⇨ Display (This version is for worksheet display.)

DISPLAY(*cell,formula,value,format,protection,names,precedents,dependents,note*)
Command equivalent: Options ⇨ Display (This version is for the Info window.)

EDIT.COLOR(*color_num,red_value,green_value,blue_value*)
Command equivalent: Options ⇨ Color Palette (with the Edit button)

PROTECT.DOCUMENT(*contents,windows,password,objects*)
Command equivalent: Options ⇨ Protect Document, or Options ⇨ Unprotect Document

REMOVE.PAGE.BREAK( )
Command equivalent: Options ⇨ Remove Page Break

SET.PAGE.BREAK( )
Command equivalent: Options ⇨ Set Page Break

SET.PRINT.AREA( )
Command equivalent: Options ⇨ Set Print Area

SET.PRINT.TITLES(*titles_for_columns_ref,titles_for_rows_ref*)
Command equivalent: Options ⇨ Set Print Titles

SHOW.INFO(*logical*)
Command equivalent: Options ⇨ Workspace (with the Info Window option checked)

SHOW.TOOLBAR(*bar_id,visible,dock,x_pos,y_pos,width*)
Command equivalent: Options ⇨ Toolbars (with the Show button or Hide button)

SPELLING(*custom_dic,ignore_uppercase,always_suggest*)
Command equivalent: Options ⇨ Spelling

WORKGROUP(*name_array*)
Command equivalent: Options ⇨ Group Edit

WORKSPACE(*fixed,decimals,r1c1,scroll,status,formula,menu_key,remote,entermove, underlines,tools, notes,nav_keys,menu_key_action,drag_drop,show_info*)
Command equivalent: Options ⇨ Workspace

Macro menu

ASSIGN.TO.OBJECT(*macro_ref*)
Command equivalent: <u>M</u>acro ➪ Assign to <u>O</u>bject

ASSIGN.TO.TOOL(*bar_id,position,macro_ref*)
Command equivalent: <u>M</u>acro ➪ <u>A</u>ssign to Tool

RESUME(*type_num*)
Command equivalent: <u>M</u>acro ➪ R<u>e</u>sume

RUN(*reference,step*)
Command equivalent: <u>M</u>acro ➪ <u>R</u>un

Window menu

ARRANGE.ALL(*arrange_num,active_doc,sync_horiz,sync_vert*)
Command equivalent: <u>W</u>indow ➪ <u>A</u>rrange

FREEZE.PANES(*logical,col_split,row_split*)
Command equivalent: <u>W</u>indow ➪ <u>F</u>reeze Panes or <u>W</u>indow ➪ Un<u>f</u>reeze Panes

HIDE( )
Command equivalent: <u>W</u>indow ➪ <u>H</u>ide

NEW.WINDOW( )
Command equivalent: <u>W</u>indow ➪ <u>N</u>ew Window

SPLIT(*col_split,row_split*)
Command equivalent: <u>W</u>indow ➪ <u>S</u>plit

UNHIDE(*window_text*)
Command equivalent: <u>W</u>indow ➪ <u>U</u>nhide

VIEW.DEFINE(*view_name,print_settings_log,row_col_log*)
Command equivalent: <u>W</u>indow ➪ <u>V</u>iew (with the Add button). The View
Manager add-in must be loaded to use this function.

VIEW.DELETE(*view_name*)
Command equivalent: <u>W</u>indow ➪ <u>V</u>iew (with the Delete button). The View
Manager add-in must be loaded to use this function.

VIEW.SHOW(*view_name*)
Command equivalent: Window ⇨ View (with the Show button). The View Manager add-in must be loaded to use this function.

ZOOM(*magnification*)
Command equivalent: Window ⇨ Zoom

Gallery menu

COMBINATION(*type_num*)
Command equivalent: Gallery ⇨ Combination

GALLERY.3D.AREA(*type_num*)
Command equivalent: Gallery ⇨ 3-D Area

GALLERY.3D.BAR(*type_num*)
Command equivalent: Gallery ⇨ 3-D Bar

GALLERY.3D.COLUMN(*type_num*)
Command equivalent: Gallery ⇨ 3-D Column

GALLERY.3D.LINE(*type_num*)
Command equivalent: Gallery ⇨ 3-D Line

GALLERY.3D.PIE(*type_num*)
Command equivalent: Gallery ⇨ 3-D Pie

GALLERY.3D.SURFACE(*type_num*)
Command equivalent: Gallery ⇨ 3-D Surface

GALLERY.AREA(*type_num,delete_overlay*)
Command equivalent: Gallery ⇨ Area

GALLERY.BAR(*type_num,delete_overlay*)
Command equivalent: Gallery ⇨ Bar

GALLERY.COLUMN(*type_num,delete_overlay*)
Command equivalent: Gallery ⇨ Column

GALLERY.LINE(*type_num,delete_overlay*)
Command equivalent: Gallery ⇨ Line

GALLERY.PIE(*type_num,delete_overlay*)
Command equivalent: Gallery ⇨ Pie

GALLERY.RADAR(*type_num,delete_overlay*)
Command equivalent: Gallery ⇨ Radar

GALLERY.SCATTER(*type_num,delete_overlay*)
Command equivalent: Gallery ⇨ XY (Scatter)

PREFERRED( )
Command equivalent: Gallery ⇨ Preferred

SET.PREFERRED( )
Command equivalent: Gallery ⇨ Set Preferred

Chart menu

ADD.ARROW( )
Command equivalent: Chart ⇨ Add Arrow

ADD.OVERLAY( )
Command equivalent: Chart ⇨ Add Overlay

ATTACH.TEXT(*attach_to_num,series_num,point_num*)
Command equivalent: Chart ⇨ Attach Text

AXES(*x_main,y_main,x_over,y_over*)
Command equivalent: Chart ⇨ Axes (this form is for 2-D charts)

AXES(*x_main,y_main,z_main*)
Command equivalent: Chart ⇨ Axes (this form is for 3-D charts)

DELETE.ARROW( )
Command equivalent: Chart ⇨ Delete Arrow

DELETE.OVERLAY( )
Command equivalent: Chart ⇨ Delete Overlay

EDIT.SERIES(*series_num,name_ref,x_ref,y_ref,z_ref,plot_order*)
Command equivalent: Chart ⇨ Edit Series

GRIDLINES(*x_major,x_minor,y_major,y_minor,z_major,z_minor*)
Command equivalent: Chart ⇨ Gridlines

LEGEND(*logical*)
Command equivalent: Chart ⇨ Add Legend, or Chart ⇨ Delete Legend

SELECT.CHART( )
Command equivalent: Chart ➪ Select Chart

SELECT.PLOT.AREA( )
Command equivalent: Chart ➪ Select Plot Area

Information Functions

These functions are typically used to obtain information about some aspect of Excel, the system, or a document. The information then determines how the macro will proceed.

ACTIVE.CELL( )
Returns the reference of the active cell in the selection as an external reference (in other words, the filename precedes the cell reference).

CALLER( )
Returns information about the cell, range, command, or object that called the current macro. This is used when a custom function needs to know some attributes of the caller.

DOCUMENTS(*type_num,match_text*)
Returns a horizontal array containing the specified open documents in alphabetical order.

ERROR.TYPE(*error_val*)
This is used to determine which type of error occurred so your macro can respond accordingly. The function returns a number that corresponds to one of Excel's error values.

GET.BAR( )
Returns the number of the active menu bar.

GET.BAR(*bar_num,menu,command*)
Returns the name or position number of a specified command on a menu, or a specified menu on a menu bar.

GET.CELL(*type_num,reference*)
This function is useful if a macro depends on an attribute of a particular cell. The function returns information about the formatting, location, or contents of a cell.

GET.CHART.ITEM(*x_y_index,point_index,item_text*)
Returns the vertical or horizontal position of a point on a chart item. This function might be used in conjunction with FORMAT.MOVE to change the position of a chart item.

GET.DEF(*def_text,document_text,type_num*)
Returns the name (as text) that corresponds to a definition.

GET.DOCUMENT(*type_num,name_text*)
Returns various information about a document.

GET.FORMULA(*reference*)
Returns the contents of a cell (as text), as it would appear in the formula bar.

GET.LINK.INFO(*link_text,type_num,type_of_link,reference*)
Returns information about a specific link.

GET.NAME(*name_text*)
Returns the definition of a specified name.

GET.NOTE(*cell_ref,start_char,num_chars*)
Use this if a macro needs to access the text in a cell note. The function returns the text from a note in a specified cell.

GET.OBJECT(*type_num,object_id_text,start_num,count_num*)
Returns information about the specified object.

GET.TOOL(*type_num,bar_id,position*)
Returns information about a tool on the toolbar.

GET.TOOLBAR(*type_num,bar_id*)
Returns information about a specific toolbar, or all toolbars.

GET.WINDOW(*type_num,window_text*)
Returns information about a window. Use this function if a macro needs to know specific information about the window (its name, size, and so on).

GET.WORKBOOK(*type_num,name_text*)
Returns information about a workbook document.

GET.WORKSPACE(*type_num*)
Returns information about the workspace.

LAST.ERROR( )
Returns the reference of the cell where the last macro sheet error occurred.

LINKS(*document_text,type_num*)
Returns a horizontal array of the names of all worksheets referred to by external references in the specified document.

SELECTION( )
Returns the reference or object identifier of the selection as an external reference. This is useful to determine what is selected.

WINDOWS(*type_num,match_text*)
Returns the names of the specified windows. This will give you a list of active windows for other macro functions to work with.

Macro Control Functions

These functions control how a macro flows.

ARGUMENT(*name_text,data_type_num*)
Used to define the arguments when you create a custom function or subroutine. Use this form if you want to store the arguments as a name.

ARGUMENT(*name_text,data_type_num,reference*)
Used to define the arguments when you create a custom function or subroutine. Use this form if you want to store the argument in a specific cell or range.

BREAK( )
Used to terminate a macro loop.

CANCEL.COPY( )
This is equivalent to pressing Esc after a copy command. This removes the dashed line "marquee" that normally remains after you copy a cell or range.

ELSE( )
Used with IF, ELSE.IF, and END.IF to control macro flow. This command signals the beginning of a series of macro commands that will execute if the results of all preceding ELSE.IF statements and the preceding IF statements are false.

ELSE.IF(*logical_test*)
Used with IF, ELSE.IF, and END.IF to control macro flow. This command signals the beginning of a series of macro commands that will execute if the preceding IF or ELSE.IF statements return false and if the argument is true.

END.IF( )
Ends a block of functions associated with the preceding IF function.

FOR(*counter_text,start_num,end_num,step_num*)
Begins a FOR-NEXT loop. The macro instructions between FOR and NEXT are repeated until the loop counter reaches a specified value.

FOR.CELL(*ref_name,area_ref,skip_blanks*)
Begins a FOR.CELL-NEXT loop. The instructions between FOR.CELL and NEXT are executed over a range of cells — one cell at a time.

GOTO(*reference*)
Redirects the flow of a macro by continuing macro execution at a specified location.

HALT(*cancel_close*)
This stops all macros. Unlike RETURN, HALT does not return to the macro that called it.

IF(*logical_test*)
This is used with ELSE, ELSE.IF, and END.IF to control which formulas in a macro are executed.

IF(*logical_test,value_if_true,value_if_false*)
Used to return one of two different values, depending on a logical test. This form can be used on either worksheets or macro sheets.

NEXT( )
Ends a FOR-NEXT, FOR.CELL-NEXT, or WHILE-NEXT loop and continues to carry out the current macro with the formula that follows the NEXT function.

PAUSE(*no_tool*)
This is used primarily as a debugging tool to pause a macro. It can also pause a macro to allow the user to interact directly with a worksheet.

RESTART(*level_num*)
If you have nested macros, this function removes a number of RETURN statements from the stack.

RESULT(*type_num*)
Specifies the type of data a macro or custom function returns. This function ensures that macros return values of the correct data type.

RETURN(*value*)
Ends the currently running macro.

SET.NAME(*name_text,value*)
Defines a name on a macro sheet to refer to a value.

SET.VALUE(*reference,values*)
Changes the value of a cell or cells on the macro sheet. This is most useful for initializing dialog boxes and for conditional tests in macro loops.

STEP( )
Stops the normal flow of a macro and executes it one cell at a time. This is useful for debugging a macro.

VOLATILE(*logical*)
Specifies that a custom function is volatile or nonvolatile. A volatile function is recalculated whenever the worksheet is calculated.

WAIT(*serial_number*)
Pauses the macro until the specified time.

WHILE(*logical_test*)
Executes macro statements between the WHILE function and the NEXT function until a specified condition is true.

ASCII File Manipulation Functions

This group of macro functions is used to manipulate text files and work with directories and files on disk. Some of these commands are more general in nature and apply to all types of files.

CREATE.DIRECTORY(*path_text*)
Creates a new directory on a disk.

DELETE.DIRECTORY(*path_text*)
Deletes a directory on a disk. The directory must be empty.

DIRECTORIES(*path_text*)
Returns a horizontal array of all the subdirectories in the specified path, or in the current directory.

DIRECTORY(*path_text*)
Sets the current drive and directory.

FILE.EXIST(*path_text*)
Checks to see if a specified file or directory exists.

FILES(*directory_text*)
Returns a horizontal array of the filenames in the specified directory.

FCLOSE(*file_num*)
Close a text file that was opened by FOPEN.

FOPEN(*file_text,access_num*)
Opens a text file, and specifies the type of read/write permission. This function does not load the file into memory.

FPOS(*file_num,position_num*)
Sets the character position in a text file for subsequent reads or writes.

FREAD(*file_num,num_chars*)
Reads characters from a text file, starting at the current position.

FREADLN(*file_num*)
Reads entire lines from a text file starting at the current position.

FSIZE(*file_num*)
Returns the number of bytes in a file.

FWRITE(*file_num,text*)
Writes characters to a text file at the current position.

FWRITELN(*file_num,text*)
Writes characters to a text file and then inserts a carriage return and line feed.

Functions for Customizing Excel _____

These functions are used primarily by macro writers who create custom user-oriented applications and who need to manipulate menus and toolbars or create dialog boxes.

ADD.BAR(*bar_num*)
Creates a custom menu bar or restores a built-in menu bar that has been deleted. It returns an ID number, which must be used in subsequent references to the menu bar.

ADD.COMMAND(*bar_num,menu,command_ref,position*)
Used to add a new command to a built-in or custom menu item. You can control where it is inserted in the pull-down list.

ADD.MENU(*bar_num,menu_ref,position*)
Used to add a menu item to a menu bar. You can control where it is inserted in the menu bar.

ADD.TOOL(*bar_id,position,tool_ref*)
Used to add one or more tools to an existing toolbar. You can control where the tool(s) will be inserted.

ADD.TOOLBAR(*bar_name,tool_ref*)
Creates a new toolbar with specified tools.

ALERT(*message_text,type_num,help_ref*)
Displays a simple dialog box with a message to the user. Optionally, you can provide access to a custom help topic.

APP.TITLE(*text*)
Changes the title displayed in Excel's application title bar. Normally, the title bar reads "Microsoft Excel."

BEEP(*tone_num*)
Used to sound a tone. This has no effect if sound is turned off via the Windows Control Panel.

CANCEL.KEY(*enable,macro_ref*)
Used to disable macro interruption by the user. Also used to specify a macro to run if the current macro is interrupted.

CHECK.COMMAND(*bar_num,menu,command,check*)
Adds or removes a check mark from a command name on a menu.

CUSTOM.REPEAT(*macro_text,repeat_text,record_text*)
Creates a Repeat command on the Edit menu, which can be selected to repeat a custom command.

CUSTOM.UNDO(*macro_text,undo_text*)
Creates an Undo command on the Edit menu. This is useful for custom commands and requires a separate macro to undo the effects of the original custom command.

DELETE.BAR(*bar_num*)
Deletes a custom menu bar created with the ADD.BAR function.

DELETE.COMMAND(*bar_num,menu,command*)
Removes a command from a custom menu or a built-in menu.

DELETE.MENU(*bar_num,menu*)
Deletes a menu item from either a standard or a custom menu bar.

DELETE.TOOL(*bar_id,position*)
Deletes a tool from a toolbar.

DELETE.TOOLBAR(*bar_name*)
Deletes a custom toolbar.

DIALOG.BOX(*dialog_ref*)
Displays a custom dialog box.

DISABLE.INPUT(*logical*)
Blocks all input from the keyboard and mouse, except input to a displayed
dialog box. This command also blocks input from other applications.

ECHO(*logical*)
Turns screen updating on or off while a macro is executing. Turning off screen
updating can often make the macro perform faster.

ENABLE.COMMAND(*bar_num,menu,command,enable*)
Enables or disables a custom command or menu. The disabled command will
be dimmed and cannot be selected.

ENABLE.TOOL(*bar_id,position,enable*)
Enables or disables a tool on a toolbar. Disabled tools are still visible, but won't
perform any action.

ENTER.DATA(*logical*)
Turns on data entry mode to allow the user to enter data into unlocked cells in
the current selection. This lets you use part of a worksheet as a data entry form.

ERROR(*enable_logical,macro_ref*)
This function lets you specify what action to take if an error is encountered
while a macro is running. This also lets you specify whether or not Excel's error
messages are displayed.

HELP(*helkp_ref*)
Use this command to start or switch to the Help application.

INPUT(*message_text,type_num,title_text,default,x_pos,y_pos,help_ref*)
Displays a simple dialog box to get user input.

MESSAGE(*logical,text*)
Displays and removes a message in the message area of the Status bar. This is
useful for displaying small amounts of text that don't require a response from
the user.

MOVE.TOOL(*from_bar_id,from_bar_position,to_bar_id,to_bar_position,copy,width*)
Moves or copies a tool from one toolbar to another.

ON.DATA(*document_text,macro_text*)
Runs a specified macro when another application sends data to a specified document via DDE.

ON.DOUBLECLICK(*sheet_text,macro_text*)
Runs a specified macro when the user double-clicks any cell, object, or chart item on the specified document.

ON.ENTRY(*sheet_text,macro_text*)
Runs a specified macro when the user enters data into any cell on a specified document.

ON.KEY(*key_text,macro_text*)
Runs a specified macro when the user presses a specified key or key combination.

ON.RECALC(*sheet_text,macro_text*)
Runs a specified macro when a specified document is recalculated.

ON.TIME(*time,macro_text,tolerance,insert_logical*)
Runs a specified macro at a specified time. The macro runs only if another macro is not running and Excel is in one of the following modes: Ready, Copy, Cut, or Find.

ON.WINDOW(*window_text,macro_text*)
Runs a specified macro when the user switches to a particular window.

PASTE.TOOL(*bar_id,position*)
Selects a tool and pastes the Clipboard contents as a tool face.

PRESS.TOOL(*bar_id,position,down*)
Formats a tool so it appears either normal or depressed into the screen.

RENAME.COMMAND(*bar_num,menu,command,name_text*)
Changes the name of a built-in or custom menu or command.

RESET.TOOL(*bar_id,position*)
Resets the specified tool to its original tool face.

RESET.TOOLBAR(*bar_id*)
Resets a specified built-in toolbar to its default tools.

SAVE.TOOLBAR(*bar_id,filename*)
Saves one or more toolbar definitions to a specified xlb file.

SHOW.BAR(*bar_num*)
Displays the specified custom or built-in menu bar.

SHOW.TOOLBAR(*bar_id,visib le,dock,x_pos,y_pos,width*)
Hides or displays a particular toolbar.

WINDOW.TITLE(*text*)
Changes the title of the active window to a specified title.

DDE/External Functions _____

These functions allow a macro to communicate with other applications through the Windows Dynamic Data Exchange (DDE) facility.

APP.ACTIVATE(*title_text,wait_logical*)
Activates a Windows application that is already open.

EDIT.OBJECT(*verb_num*)
Allows editing of an embedded object. This command starts the application and loads the object.

EXEC(*program_text,window_num*)
Starts another application (either Windows or non-Windows).

EXECUTE(*channel_num,execute_text*)
Use this to issue commands to other programs through DDE.

INITIATE(*app_text,topic_text*)
Opens a DDE channel to an application.

INSERT.OBJECT(*object_class*)
Inserts an OLE (embedded) object.

POKE(*channel_num,item_text,data_ref*)
Sends data to another application through DDE.

REGISTER(*module_text,procedure,type_text,function_text,argument_text, macro_type,category,shortcut_text*)
Used by advanced programmers to register a specific dynamic link library (DLL).

REGISTER.ID(*module_text,procedure,type_text*)
Used by advanced programmers to obtain the ID number of a specified DLL.

REQUEST(*channel_num,item_text*)
Requests an array of a specific type of information from an application via DDE.

SEND.KEYS(*key text, wait_logical*)
Sends keystrokes to another application via DDE.

SET.UPDATE.STATUS(*link_text,status,type_of_link*)
Sets or changes the update status (automatic or manual) of a link.

TERMINATE(*channel_num*)
Closes a DDE channel opened with the INITIATE function.

UNREGISTER(*register_id*)
Removes a DLL that was previously registered.

Window Manipulation Functions

These functions allow a macro to manipulate the Excel application window and its document windows.

ACTIVATE(*window_text,pane_num*)
Used to switch to another open window, or switch to a different pane in the same window.

ACTIVATE.NEXT(*workbook_text*)
Switches to the next window, or switches to the next document in a workbook.

ACTIVATE.PREV(*workbook_text*)
Switches to the previous window, or switches to the previous document in a workbook.

APP.MAXIMIZE( )
Used to maximize the Excel application window.

APP.MINIMIZE( )
Used to minimize the Excel application window.

APP.MOVE(*x_num,y_num*)
Used to move the Excel application window to a different screen location.

APP.RESTORE( )
Restores the Excel application window to its size and position before it was maximized or minimized.

APP.SIZE(*x_num,y_num*)
Changes the size of the Excel application window.

CLOSE(*save_logical*)
Closes the active window.

WINDOW.MAXIMIZE(*window_text*)
Expands the active window to fill the entire Excel workspace.

WINDOW.MINIMIZE(*window_text*)
Shrinks the active window to an icon.

WINDOW.MOVE(*x_pos,y_pos,window_text*)
Moves the active window to a specified location.

WINDOW.RESTORE(*window_text*)
Restores the active window from maximize or minimized to its previous intermediate size.

WINDOW.SIZE(*width,height,window_text*)
Makes the active window a specific size.

Solver Add-In Macro Functions_____

These functions allow a macro to operate the Solver add-in.

SOLVER.ADD(*cell_ref,relation,formula*)
Command equivalent: Formula ⇨ Solver (with the Add button)

SOLVER.CHANGE(*cell_ref,relation,formula*)
Command equivalent: Formula ⇨ Solver (with the Change button)

SOLVER.DELETE(*cell_ref,relation,formula*)
Command equivalent: Formula ⇨ Solver (with the Delete button)

SOLVER.LOAD(*load_area*)
Command equivalent: Formula ⇨ Solver (with the Options button, and then the Load Model button)

SOLVER.OK(*set_cell,max_min_val,value_of,by_changing*)
Command equivalent: Formula ⇨ Solver (with the Options button, setting options, and then the OK button)

SOLVER.RESET( )
Command equivalent: Formula ⇨ Solver (with the Reset All button)

SOLVER.SAVE(*save_area*)
Command equivalent: Formula ⇨ Solver (with the Options button, and then the Save Model button)

SOLVER.SOLVE(*user_finish,show_ref*)
Command equivalent: Formula ⇨ Solver (with the Solve button)

SOLVER.FINISH(*keep_final,report_array*)
Simulates pressing the Finish button when Solver finishes.

SOLVER.GET(*type_num,sheet_name*)
Returns information about the current settings for Solver.

SOLVER.OPTIONS(*max_time,iterations,precision,assume_linear,step_thru, estimates,derivatives,search,int_tolerance,scaling*)
Used to specify options for Solver.

Slide Show Macro Functions

These functions allow a macro to automate some aspects of creating a slide show.

SLIDE.COPY.ROW( )
Simulates choosing the Copy Row button on a slide show document. You must have the Slide Show add-in utility loaded to use this function.

SLIDE.CUT.ROW( )
Simulates choosing the Cut Row button on a slide show document. You must have the Slide Show add-in utility loaded to use this function.

SLIDE.DEFAULTS(*effect_num,speed_num,advance_rate_num,soundifle_text*)
Simulates choosing the Set Default button on a slide show document. You must have the Slide Show add-in utility loaded to use this function.

SLIDE.DELETE.ROW( )
Simulates choosing the Delete Row button on a slide show document. You must have the Slide Show add-in utility loaded to use this function.

SLIDE.EDIT(*effect_num,speed_num,advance_rate_num,soundfile_text*)
Simulates choosing the Edit button on a slide show document. You must have the Slide Show add-in utility loaded to use this function.

SLIDE.GET(*type_num,name_text,slide_num*)
Returns specified information about a slide show or a specific slide. You must have the Slide Show add-in utility loaded to use this function.

SLIDE.PASTE(*effect_num,speed_num,advance_rate_num,soundfile_text*)
Simulates choosing the Paste button on a slide show document. You must have the Slide Show add-in utility loaded to use this function.

SLIDE.PASTE.ROW( )
Simulates choosing the Paste Row button on a slide show document. You must have the Slide Show add-in utility loaded to use this function.

SLIDE.SHOW(*initialslide_num,repeat_logical,dialogtitle_text,allownav_logical, allowcontrol_logical*)
Simulates choosing the Start Show button on a slide show document. You must have the Slide Show add-in loaded to use this function.

Outlining Macro Functions

This group of functions allows a macro to manipulate an outline.

DEMOTE(*row_col*)
Demotes selected rows and columns in an outline.

PROMOTE(*rowcol*)
Promotes selected rows and columns in an outline.

SHOW.DETAIL(*rowcol, rowcol_num, expand*)
Expands or collapses the detail under the specified expand or collapse button in outline mode.

SHOW.LEVELS(*row_level,col_level*)
Displays the specified number of row and column levels of an outline.

Movement Macro Functions

These functions simulate movement and sizing of various Excel objects.

FORMAT.MOVE(*x_pos,y_pos*)
This simulates moving a chart object with the mouse.

FORMAT.MOVE(*x_offset,y_offset,reference*)
This simulates moving a worksheet object with the mouse.

FORMAT.SHAPE(*vertex_num, insert, reference, x_offset, y_offset*)
This simulates clicking the reshape tool and then inserting, moving, or deleting vertices of the selected polygon.

FORMAT.SIZE(*width, height*)
This simulates sizing a worksheet object or chart item in an absolute manner.

FORMAT.SIZE(*x_off, y_off, reference*)
This simulates sizing a worksheet object or chart item in a relative manner.

HLINE(*num_columns*)
This function scrolls through the active window horizontally by a specified number of columns.

HPAGE(*num_windows*)
This function scrolls through the active window horizontally, one window at a time for a specified number of windows.

HSCROLL(*position, col_logical*)
This function scrolls though the active window horizontally by percentage or by column number.

UNLOCKED.NEXT( )
Simulates pressing Tab to move to the next unlocked cell in a protected worksheet.

UNLOCKED.PREV( )
Simulates pressing Shift+Tab to move to the previous unlocked cell in a protected worksheet.

VLINE(*num_rows*)
Scrolls vertically through the active windows by the specified number of rows.

VPAGE(*num_windows*)
Scrolls vertically through the active window one window at a time, a specified number of times.

VSCROLL(*position, row_logical*)
Scrolls vertically through the active document by a percentage or by a specified number of rows.

Macro Functions to Manipulate Workbooks

These functions let a macro automate some aspects of dealing with workbooks.

WORKBOOK.ACTIVATE(*sheet_name,new_window_logical*)
Activates a specified document in a workbook.

WORKBOOK.ADD(*name_array,dest_book,position_num*)
Adds one or more documents to a workbook.

WORKBOOK.COPY(*name_array,dest_book,position_num*)
Copies one or more documents from one workbook to another.

WORKBOOK.MOVE(*name_array,dest_book,position_num*)
Moves a document from one workbook to another.

WORKBOOK.OPTIONS(*sheet_name,bound_logical,new_name*)
Lets you change some options in a workbook (document name, workbook name, and bound or unbound status).

WORKBOOK.SELECT(*name_array,active_name*)
Selects specified documents from a workbook.

Analysis ToolPak Macro Functions

This group of macro functions execute procedures found in the Analysis ToolPak add-in, which must be loaded for these functions to work.

ANOVA1(*inprng,outrng,grouped,labels,alpha*)
Performs a single-factor analysis of variance.

ANOVA2(*inprng,outrng,sample_rows,alpha*)
Performs a two-factor analysis of variance with replication.

ANOVA3(*inprng,outrng,labels,alpha*)
Performs a two-factor analysis of variance without replications.

CROSSTAB.CREATE(*rows_array,columns_array,values_array,create_outline,
create_names,mult_values,auto_drilldown,new_sh*)
Creates a crosstab table.

CROSSTAB.DRILLDOWN( )
Performs a database query to retrieve records that are summarized in the selected crosstab cell.

CROSSTAB.RECALC(*rebuild*)
Recalculates an existing crosstab table.

DESCR(*inprng,outrng,grouped,labels,summary,ds_large,ds_small,confid*)
Calculates a variety of descriptive statistics for a range of data.

EXPON(*inprng,outrng,damp,stderrs,chart*)
Performs an exponential forecast.

FOURIER(*inprng,outrng,inverse*)
Performs a Fourier transform on a range of data.

FTEST(*array1,array2*)
Conducts an F-test on a range of data.

HISTOGRAM(*inprng,outrng,binrng,pareto,chartc,chart*)
Generates a data distribution and (optionally) a histogram.

MCORREL(*inprng,outrng,grouped,labels*)
Calculates a correlation matrix.

MCOVAR(*inprng,outrng,grouped,labels*)
Calculates a covariance matrix.

MOVEAVG(*inprng,outrng,interval,stderrs,chart*)
Calculates a moving average of a range of data.

PTTESTM(*inprng1,inprng2,outrng,labels,alpha,difference*)
Conducts a paired two-sample *t*-Test.

PTTESTV(*inprng1,inprng2,outrng,labels,alpha*)
Conducts a two-sample *t*-Test.

RANDOM(*outrng,variables,points,distribution,seed,randarg1,
randarg2,randarg3,randarg4,randarg5*)
Fills a range with a specified type of random numbers.

RANKPERC(*inprng,outrng,grouped,labels*)
Calculates ordinal and percent rank of a range of data.

REGRESS(*inpyrng,inpxrng,constant,labels,confid,soutrng,residuals,
sresiduals,rplots,lplots,routrng,nplots,poutrng*)
Conducts a multilinear regression analysis.

SAMPLE(*inprng,outrng,method,rate*)
Returns a sample of data from a population.

TTESTM(*inprng1,inprng2,outrng,labels,alpha,difference*)
Conducts a two-sample *t*-Test for means.

ZTESTM(*inprng1,inprng2,outrng,labels,alpha,difference,var1,var2*)
Conducts a two-sample *z*-test for means.

Miscellaneous Macro Functions

This group of functions includes all the other macro functions that do not fit into any of the previous categories.

A1.R1C1(*logical*)
Displays row and column headings in either the normal letter-number style (such as A1) or RC style (such as R1C1).

ABSREF(*ref_text,reference*)
Returns the absolute reference of cells that are offset from a reference by a specific amount. The function argument is in the form of a relative reference (such as R[2]C[2]) and it returns an absolute reference in the form of $C$4.

CHART.WIZARD(*long,ref,gallery_num,type_num,plot_by,categories, ser_titles,legend,title,x_title,y_title,z_title*)
Tool equivalent: ChartWizard

COLOR.PALETTE(*file_text*)
This copies a color palette from an open document to the current document.

CONSTRAIN.NUMERIC(*numeric_only*)
Tool equivalent: Constrain Numeric (only available if you are using Windows for Pen Computing)

CREATE.OBJECT(*obj_type,ref1,x_offset1,y_offset1,ref2,x_offset2,y_offset2,text,fill*)
This draws an object on a worksheet or macro sheet. This version is for lines, rectangles, ovals, arcs, pictures, text boxes, and buttons.

DATA.FIND.NEXT( )
This is equivalent to pressing the down arrow key after the Data ⇨ Find command is executed.

DATA.FIND.PREV( )
This is equivalent to pressing the up arrow key after the Data ⇨ Find command is executed.

DELETE.FORMAT(*format_text*)
This deletes a specified numeric format (either built-in, or custom).

DELETE.NAME(*name_text*)
Deletes a specified name on the active document.

DEREF(*reference*)
Returns the value of the cells in a reference. This is useful for a few functions that do not automatically convert references to values.

DUPLICATE( )
Duplicates the selected object.

EVALUATE(*formula_text*)
Evaluates a formula that's in the form of a text string and returns the result.

EXTEND.POLYGON(*array*)
Adds vertices to a polygon created with CREATE.POLYGON. This function is best entered using the macro recorder.

FILL.AUTO(*destination_ref,copy_only*)
This simulates Excel's autofill feature.

FORMULA(*formula_text,reference*)
Enters a formula into the active cell or reference.

FORMULA(*formula_text*)
This enters a lable or a SERIES formula in a chart.

FORMULA.ARRAY(*formula_text,reference*)
Enters a formula as an array formula into the specified range or current selection.

FORMULA.CONVERT(*formula_text,from_a1,to_a1,to_ref_type,rel_to_ref*)
Converts the style of references (such as A1 to R1C1) and type of reference (such as A1 to $A$1). This is useful for changing input to a dialog box to an absolute reference.

FORMULA.FILL(*formula_text,reference*)
Enter a single formula into a specified range.

FORMULA.FIND.NEXT( )
This returns the cell that has the next occurrence of the contents of a Find dialog box.

FORMULA.FIND.PREV( )
This returns the cell that was previously found in a FORMULA.FIND or
FORMULA.FIND.NEXT.

HIDE.OBJECT(*object_id_text,hide*)
Use this command to hide or display a specified object.

LINE.PRINT(*command,file,append*)
Prints the active document, bypassing the Windows printer driver. The PRINT
function should normally be used for this.

NAMES(*document_text,type_num,match_text*)
Returns a horizontal array of all names (in alphabetical order) defined in a
specified document.

PRECISION(*logical*)
Sets or clears the Precision as Displayed check box in the Calculation dialog
box.

REFTEXT(*reference,A1*)
This function converts a reference to an absolute reference in the form of text.
This is useful if you need to manipulate references with text functions.

RELREF(*reference,rel_to_ref*)
Returns the reference of a cell relative to another cell.

REPORT.GET(*type_num,report_name*)
Returns information about the reports defined for the active document. This
function requires that the Reports add-in is loaded.

SCENARIO.GET(*type_num*)
Returns specified information about the scenarios defined in your worksheet.
This command requires that the Scenario Manager add-in is loaded.

SELECT(*item_text,single_point*)
Selects a specified chart item.

SELECT(*selection,active_cell*)
Selects a specified cell or range.

SELECT(*object_id_text,replace*)
Selects a specified worksheet object.

SELECT.END(*direction_num*)
Simulates pressing the Ctrl key along with an arrow key.

SHOW.CLIPBOARD( )
Activates the Windows Clipboard application (which must be running).

SOUND.NOTE(*cell_ref,erase_snd*)
Records or erases sound from a cell note, or imports a sound file. This function requires that the system has a sound card installed.

SPELLING.CHECK(*word_text,custom_dic,ignore_uppercase*)
Checks the spelling of a word.

TEXT.BOX(*add_text,object_id_text,start_num,num_chars*)
Replaces characters in a text box or button with specified text.

TEXTREF(*text,A1*)
Converts text to an absolute reference. This is useful to convert references stored as text so they can be used with other functions.

VIEW.GET(*type_num,view_name*)
Returns an array of views from the active document. The View Manager add-in must be loaded to use this function.

Index

— Z —

PC World DOS 5 Complete Handbook
by John Socha & Clint Hicks

Includes "detailed descriptions of virtually every command employed with DOS, from version 2 to version 5, that are much fuller and clearer than the ones in the official Microsoft manual."
— L.R. Shannon, *The New York Times*

Your complete guide to DOS 5, with a 250-page reference section on over 119 commands. Includes Special Edition of the Norton Commander software, your easy DOS 5 shell!

Highlights:

- Comprehensive review of basic and advanced DOS functions.
- Special coverage of the DOS Shell, memory, and system customization.
- Valuable software: BONUS Norton Commander Special Edition — best-selling DOS management program.

$34.95/$44.95 Canada, includes one 5 1/4" disk
ISBN: 1-878058-13-4
616 pages. Available now.

DOS for Dummies
by Dan Gookin

COMING SOON:
WordPerfect for Dummies
PCs for Dummies

"If all this talk of memory and megabytes has given you a headache, take two aspirin and, in the morning, buy a copy of DOS for Dummies." — L. R. Shannon, The New York Times

DOS
FOR
DUMMIES

BY DAN GOOKIN

A Reference
for the Rest
of Us!

Your First Aid Kit for
Dealing with DOS

Look Up the Problem—
Find the Answer

What to Do When Bad
Things Happen

Covers DOS 5

"If all this talk of memory and megabytes has given you a headache, take two aspirin and, in the morning, buy a copy of DOS for Dummies. . . . *It is a light-hearted survey of the operating system everyone loves to hate, with plenty of sugar coating on its information."*
— L.R. Shannon, *The New York Times*

Teaches even the most reluctant computer user DOS essentials with humor and style. This is a lighthearted book, but not lightweight — packed with useful information. A runaway best seller.

Highlights:
- Your first aid kit for dealing with DOS.
- Look up the problem and find the answer — no techno-jargon.
- Includes a special section on what to do when "bad things happen."
- Bonus Quick Reference Card . . . for when you're too lazy to read.

$16.95/$12.95 Canada
ISBN: 1-878058-25-8
312 pages. Available now.

**PC World You Can Do It
With DOS**
by Christopher Van Buren

This is the easy way to learn the basics of
DOS — with Step-by-Steps for solving DOS
problems. An overview, quick tips, and
troubleshooting ideas make learning easy.

Highlights:
- Get DOS productivity in a matter of
  hours with this simple guide.
- Learn to use the DOS shell.

- Easy explanations of DOS directories,
  path names, and file management tasks.
- FREE Cheat Sheet of DOS commands.
- Covers DOS 5.

$19.95/$26.95 Canada
ISBN: 1-878058-38-X
256 pages. Available now.

Official XTree MS-DOS and Hard Disk Companion, 2nd Edition
by Beth Woods

"Full of helpful information on running a hard disk with a minimum of hassle"
— L.R. Shannon, *The New York Times*

The only guide to all versions of XTree hard disk software and to hard disk management.

Highlights:
- Featuring all versions of XTree through 2.5 and includes XTree Gold Pro, and XTree Easy.
- Easy step-by-step instructions for simple hard disk tasks.
- Unique organization — speed bars and pop quizzes help reinforce learning.

Price: $15.95/$21.95 Canada
ISBN 1-878058-22-3
312 pages. Available now.

Official Spinrite II and Hard Disk Companion
by John Goodman, Ph.D.

The only guide to preventing hard disk disaster using Spinrite.

Highlights:
- Two-in-one book: How hard disks work and why they die — offers tips that prevent and cure hard disk nightmares.
- Advanced tips, undocumented features, and inside information on Spinrite.

Price: $14.95/ $19.95 Canada
ISBN: 1-878058-08-8
288 pages. Available now.

PC Systems Secrets
by Caroline M. Halliday

A comprehensive yet practical guide to optimizing your PC's performance, with two valuable disks of software utilities to help you configure, diagnose, analyze, and troubleshoot your system.

Highlights:

- An insider's guide to performance-tuning today's PCs — covers new microprocessors, peripherals, and systems hardware.

- Two disks of over 15 ready-to-use utilities, including Qualitas ASQ, VGATEST, Modem Doctor, and more!
- Clear explanations in the text show you how to optimize your system using these software utilities.

$39.95/$52.95 Canada, includes two 5 1/4" disks
ISBN: 1-878058-49-5
704 pages. Available July 1992.

PC World You Can Do It With Windows
by Christopher Van Buren

This is the easy way to learn the basics of Windows — with Step-by-Steps for solving Windows problems. An overview, quick tips, and troubleshooting ideas give you extra ammunition in the battle to learn easily.

Highlights:
- Get Windows productivity in a matter of hours with this simple guide.
- Use the new File Manager and Program Manager.
- FREE: Pull-Out Windows Cheat Sheet features command shortcuts.
- Covers Windows 3.1.

$19.95/$26.95 Canada
ISBN: 1-878058-37-1
328 pages. Available June 1992.

Windows 3.1 Secrets
by Brian Livingston

InfoWorld's Windows guru Brian Livingston reveals the secret power of Windows 3.0 and 3.1 and the Best in Windows Shareware — more than 40 useful programs.

Completely revised and expanded edition of the national bestseller.

Highlights:
- Loaded with new undocumented tips, workarounds, and tricks you won't get from Microsoft.
- Covers new TrueType fonts and Multiple Masters, networking, and application information new to version 3.1.
- Three disks loaded with over 40 Windows programs — including file editing and searching, Visual Basic programs, communications, power utilities, graphics, games and more — over 6MB of software.
- Special section on moving your company to Windows.

Price: $39.95/$52.95 Canada
ISBN: 1-878058-43-8
1024 pages. Available now.

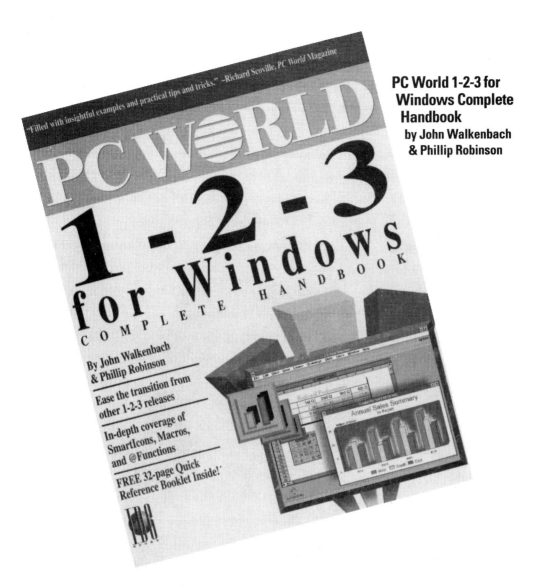

PC World 1-2-3 for Windows Complete Handbook
by John Walkenbach
& Phillip Robinson

The experts deliver all the basics, then add tips and insider techniques for mastering 1-2-3 for Windows.

Highlights:
- Eases the transition from other 1-2-3 releases.
- In-depth coverage of SmartIcons, Macros, and @Functions.

- FREE 32-page Quick Reference booklet inside for handy access and added value.
- BONUS Pull-Out Reference Card covers basic and advanced concepts.

$29.95/$39.95 Canada
ISBN: 1-878058-21-5
720 pages. Available now.

PC World WordPerfect for Windows: DOS to Windows Guide
by Greg Harvey

You'll make the move to WordPerfect easy with this guide for moving from 5.1 in the DOS world to 5.1 for Windows! With time-savings tips that make your job easier.

Highlights:

■ Every new WordPerfect for Windows command and feature is cross-referenced for a fast transition.

■ Loaded with time saving tips to make your job easier.
■ FREE Pull-Out Reference Card inside! Featuring DOS and Windows Commands.

$19.95/$26.95 Canada
ISBN: 1-878058-44-4
328 pages. Available now.

PC World Q&A Bible, Version 4
by Tom Marcellus

The only thorough guide to mastering Q&A, Version 4 with a valuable disk of applications. The disk includes over 500K of database and supplementary files.

Highlights:
- Get inside Q&A Version 4's powerful new features, then learn how to create customized business systems efficiently.

- Valuable disk includes a complete order entry and shipping system.
- Two FREE Pull-Out Command Reference cards inside!

$39.95/$54.95 Canada, includes one 5 1/4" disk
ISBN: 1-878058-03-7
928 pages. Available now.

Future Titles

Look in your favorite bookstore for these upcoming titles from IDG:

DOS Secrets
by Bob Ainsbury

The definitive guide to installing, optimizing, and customizing DOS — with two bonus disks loaded with valuable shareware. Filled with tips for getting maximum performance from DOS . . . including batch files, macros, and CONFIG.SYS.

$39.95/$52.95 Canada
ISBN: 1-878058-56-8
900 pages. Available: October 1992.

Quark XPress for Windows Handbook
by Barbara Assadi and Galen Gruman

Make the move to the new professional desktop publishing powerhouse, Quark XPress. Learn how to build effective, professional publications. Loaded with design templates and examples. Includes complete feature and task references: look up a problem and find a detailed answer and explanation.

$29.95/39.95 Canada
ISBN: 1-878058-45-2
568 pages.
Available: October 1992, subject to software availability.

PC World Word for Windows Handbook
by Brent D. Heslop and David F. Angell

Master Word for Windows 2.0's powerful features for your word processing and desktop publishing tasks with this complete tutorial and reference. Hundreds of hands-on examples, shortcuts, and tricks.

$29.95/$39.95 Canada
ISBN: 1-878058-55-X
752 pages. Available: October 1992.

PC World Paradox for Windows Handbook
by Gregory B. Salcedo and Martin W. Rudy

The definitive tutorial to the new Paradox for Windows. Building block approach moves new users from fundamentals to application development. Includes Bonus disk with ready-to-run applications, templates, report forms, tables, and examples. The authors are members of Borland's Advisory Council.

Price: $34.95/$44.95 Canada
ISBN: 1-878058-48-7
600 pages.
Available: September 1992, subject to software availability.

Order Form

Order Center: **(800) 762-2974** (7 a.m.–5 p.m., PST, weekdays)

or **(415) 312-0650**

Order Center FAX: **(415) 358-1260**

Quantity	Title & ISBN	Price	Total

Subtotal	_____
CA residents add applicable sales tax	_____
IN residents add 5% sales tax	_____
Canadian residents add 7% GST tax	_____
Shipping	_____
TOTAL	_____

Shipping & Handling Charges

Subtotal	U.S.	Canada & Int'l.	Int'l. Air Mail
Up to $20.00	Add $3.00	Add $4.00	Add $10.00
$20.01–40.00	$4.00	$5.00	$20.00
$40.01–60.00	$5.00	$6.00	$25.00
$60.01–80.00	$6.00	$8.00	$35.00
Over $80.00	$7.00	$10.00	$50.00

In U.S. and Canada, shipping is UPS ground or equivalent. For Rush shipping call (800) 762-2974.

Ship to:

Name _____

Company _____

Address _____

City/State/Zip _____

Daytime phone _____

Payment: ☐ Check to IDG Books   ☐ Visa   ☐ MasterCard   ☐ American Express

Card # _____   Expires _____

Please send this order form to: IDG Books, 155 Bovet Road, Ste. 610, San Mateo, CA 94402.
Allow up to 3 weeks for delivery. Thank you!

BK=BOBEXWIN

- -

Fold Here

Place
stamp
here

IDG Books Worldwide, Inc.
155 Bovet Road
Suite 610
San Mateo, CA 94402

Attn: Order Center / Excel 4 for Windows

IDG Books Worldwide Registration Card
PC World Excel 4 for Windows Handbook

Fill this out — and hear about updates to this book and other IDG Books Worldwide products!

Name _____

Company/Title _____

Address _____

City/State/Zip _____

What is the single most important reason you bought this book? _____

_____

Where did you buy this book?
- ❏ Bookstore (Name _____)
- ❏ Electronics/Software store (Name_____)
- ❏ Advertisement (If magazine, which? _____)
- ❏ Mail order (Name of catalog/mail order house _____)
- ❏ Other: _____

How did you hear about this book?
- ❏ Book review in: _____
- ❏ Advertisement in: _____
- ❏ Catalog
- ❏ Found in store
- ❏ Other: _____

How would you rate the overall content of this book?
- ❏ Very good   ❏ Satisfactory
- ❏ Good   ❏ Poor
- Why? _____

What chapters did you find most valuable? _____

What chapters did you find least valuable? _____

What kind of chapter or topic would you add to future editions of this book? _____

_____

Please give us any additional comments. _____

_____

How many computer books do you purchase a year?
❏ 1   ❏ 6-10
❏ 2-5   ❏ More than 10

What are your primary software applications?
_____
_____
_____

Thank you for your help!

❏ I liked this book! By checking this box, I give you permission to use my name and quote me in future IDG Books Worldwide promotional materials. Daytime phone number_____ .

❏ FREE! Send me a copy of your computer book and book/disk catalog.

IDG Books Worldwide, Inc.
155 Bovet Road
Suite 610
San Mateo, CA 94402

Attn: Reader Response / Excel 4 for Windows

SO WHERE DO YOU GO FROM HERE?

At the rate computer technology changes, you'll need more than a handbook to stay up-to-date. Now that you've made it through the trials and triumphs of putting PC's to work, and you've got the knowledge to prove it, you'll need one place you can turn to stay informed day after day, month after month—**PC WORLD**. In every issue, **PC WORLD** brings you hot news, useful tips, product previews, and authoritative reviews backed by our own testing laboratory. You'll learn new ways to use your system. New ways to use your software. New solutions to business problems. Plus...free programs and productivity tactics to further your PC knowledge and skills. We're dedicated to helping you succeed. That's why we're making you this special offer. **For just $19.97, you'll receive 12 monthly issues of PC WORLD—a savings of 58% off the annual newsstand rate.** But that's not all. As a special bonus for subscribing now, you'll receive **PC WORLD's** Power-Base*.* absolutely **FREE**. Discover a Word Perfect macro that jazzes up everyday checklists fast, move files with ease with our batch file utility, create a spreadsheet menu that retrieves 1-2-3 files with a single keystroke, plus 50 more time-saving techniques—all with our **FREE** PowerBase *.* disk. **Take advantage of this special offer and subscribe to PC WORLD today!**

FREE!
PowerBase *.* Disk
50 Tips, Macros
& Utilities!

PC WORLD.
LET US BE YOUR GUIDE. EVERYDAY.

PC WORLD brings you hot news, useful tips, product previews, and authoritative reviews backed by our own testing laboratory. You'll learn new ways to use your system. New ways to use your software. New solutions to your business problems. Plus—if you subscribe now—you'll receive PC WORLD's PowerBase *.* absolutely FREE! Take advantage of this special offer and subscribe to PC WORLD today! Complete and return the card below!

FREE!
PowerBase *.* Disk
50 Tips, Macros
& Utilities!